THE COMPANION GUIDE TO
MAINLAND GREECE

THE COMPANION GUIDES

GENERAL EDITOR: VINCENT CRONIN

*It is the aim of these guides to provide a companion,
in the person of the author, who knows intimately
the places and people of whom he writes, and is able to
communicate this knowledge and affection to his readers.
It is hoped that the text and pictures will aid them
in their preparations and in their travels, and will
help them to remember on their return.*

LONDON . NORTHUMBRIA
THE WEST HIGHLANDS OF SCOTLAND . IRELAND
THE SOUTH OF FRANCE . THE COUNTRY ROUND PARIS
NORMANDY . THE LOIRE . PARIS
FLORENCE . VENICE . ROME . NEW YORK
MAINLAND GREECE . THE GREEK ISLANDS
TURKEY . JUGOSLAVIA . MADRID AND CENTRAL SPAIN
EAST ANGLIA . KENT AND SUSSEX . THE LAKE DISTRICT

In preparation
THE SOVIET UNION . JAPAN . THE WELSH BORDERS
GASCONY AND THE DORDOGNE . UMBRIA . SICILY
PROVENCE . BRITTANY

THE COMPANION GUIDE TO

Mainland Greece

BRIAN DE JONGH

Revised and updated by
JOHN GANDON

COMPANION GUIDES

First published in two volumes as
Southern Greece (1972)
and *Mainland Greece* (1979).
Revised one-volume edition 1989

Reissued 1996
Companion Guides, Woodbridge

ISBN   1 900639 08 4

Companion Guides is an imprint of Boydell & Brewer Ltd
PO Box 9, Woodbridge, Suffolk IP12 3DF, UK
and of Boydell & Brewer Inc.
PO Box 41026, Rochester, NY 14604-4126, USA

British Library Cataloguing-in-Publication Data
De Jongh, Brian
The companion guide to mainland Greece. –
Rev. and updated, *by John Gandon*. – (The
companion guides).
1. Greece. Mainland. Visitors' guides
914.95'0476

Maps revised by RDL Artset, Cheam

Printed and bound in Great Britain by
Butler & Tanner Limited, Frome and London

Contents

List of Illustrations

List of Maps and Plans

GROUND PLANS

A Note on the Revised Edition

Brian de Jongh – my uncle – was originally commissioned to write the first edition of this book for publication in the early 1970s. In the event he found that he could not include all the material that he had written in one volume and two were produced. The first, *Southern Greece*, covering the Peloponnese, Attica and Boeotia, was published in 1972 and the second, *Mainland Greece*, covering the whole country apart from the Peloponnese, in 1979. Sadly, Brian died in 1977 when the second volume was in draft form and I took over and saw it through to publication.

When the time for a full revision arrived I felt that the advantages of having the whole Mainland covered in one volume outweighed the loss of some of Brian's original text – particularly as the original books had overlapped by several chapters covering the area from Athens to Delphi.

This revised edition is still essentially the book that Brian wrote; I have reduced its length by leaving out some of the mythological stories – which is a pity – and some of the more detailed descriptions of archaeological sites and artefacts in museums, information which is readily available in the excellent guides now available in Greece. However the benefits of having the whole of Greece in one book are considerable, not least the fact that Athens, being by far the most popular port of entry, is almost inevitably visited by travellers to the north and south of the country.

What I have tried to retain above all else is the evidence of Brian's love for Greece and the Greek people. There were some things he did not like – and of which he made no secret – but essentially he was a Hellenophile. He was born in Smyrna (now Izmir) to a family who, though originally of Dutch extraction, had lived in Greece and Turkey for several generations. His mother was in fact of Greek and Irish parentage. He was educated in Switzerland and at Oxford, became a British citizen and served in the Intelligence Corps in the Greek Islands during the War. Most of his adult life was spent in and

11

around Athens where he earned his living as a writer. This background made him a natural choice when Vincent Cronin was looking for an author for this Companion Guide. I hope that I have not betrayed his trust in this revision of the book that was the culmination of his writing career and the main pre-occupation of the last ten years of his life.

As I live and work in England and have only limited opportunity to travel in Greece, I have relied heavily on three stalwart friends of Brian, all of whom have been Greek residents for many years. First, Jane Rabnett who was for 25 years the Secretary of the British School of Archaeology in Athens; then Peter Sheldon who worked for the British Council in Athens for many years and is editor of the Fodor and American Express Guides to Greece; and thirdly Geoffrey Graham Bell, an inveterate traveller, who has been based in Athens, where he paints and teaches, since 1949. Without these three this edition would have been impossible. I also acknowledge the hard work of my wife, Liz, who has made the whole book more comprehensible by looking at it afresh – without the accumulated experience of the country of Brian, Jane, Peter, Geoffrey and myself – and sometimes rewording passages of obscure text. Finally, Sylvia Moore in Naxos has checked every sentence with the utmost care. On Brian's behalf I would like to thank these fellow collaborators for the patient, careful and thorough work that they have put into this book.

JOHN GANDON

Robert Liddell in his Foreword to the First Edition wrote:

In this Companion Guide Brian shows himself equally at home in prehistoric and in Classical Greece, in the Byzantine world (whose fantastic history had a special appeal to him), and among the Franks and Catalans of the later Middle Ages. More than most Hellenic travellers he shows an interest in the local civilization that survived the long years of the Turkish occupation; and, of course, modern Greece was his home.

He is therefore an ideal guide to the ruins of Philippi, or to the Byzantine churches of Thessaloniki and Boeotia, as well as the lesser known painted houses of Kastoria and Siatista.

Of contemporary life he writes kindly and amusingly, without condescension, but also without the gush of the romantic philhellene for whom the sourest retsina is nectar and the toughest lump of charred octopus ambrosia, who will talk of the frescoes of Mistra in the same breath as Giotto, or compare bouzouki songs to Bach. Nevertheless Brian appreciated these Greek things, and saw that they had no need to be 'belied by false compare'.

For he knew what it is about Greece that is beyond all comparison: the landscape. Travel writers from the time of Dodwell in the early nineteenth century have understood this, but too often guide books ignore it. Their authors will tell the visitor to go and see a heap of stones interesting only to the professional archaeologist without indicating that the trouble is indeed worthwhile because of the Greek genius for choosing superb sites.

Brian was a patient and brave traveller, an amusing and unselfish companion – and Greek travel even now makes a demand on such virtues. I have travelled over much of the Aegean with him and remember, first and foremost, his rueful but humorous reactions to sea-sickness on that very rough sea – and all the delays and hazards of the journey, and the dreadful food and comfortless lodgings that sometimes awaited the traveller. But he was aware that the very lack of amenities often protected lonely places from being swallowed up by tourism, and rejoiced in the fact that there are many hidden corners of Greece that can be discovered only at the expense of time and trouble.

ROBERT LIDDELL

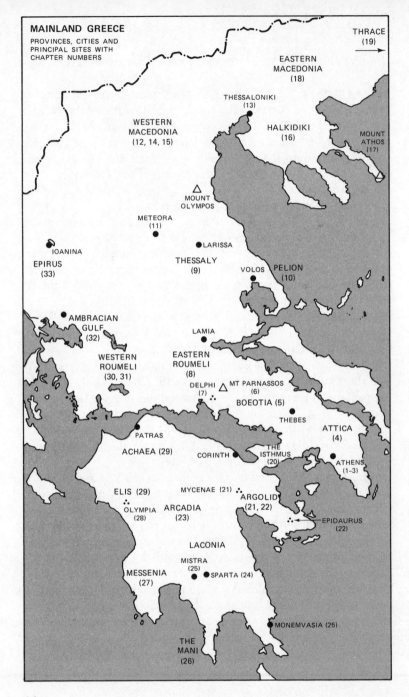

MAINLAND GREECE
PROVINCES, CITIES AND
PRINCIPAL SITES WITH
CHAPTER NUMBERS

THRACE (19) →

EASTERN
MACEDONIA
(18)

THESSALONIKI
(13)

HALKIDIKI
(16)

MOUNT
ATHOS
(17)

WESTERN
MACEDONIA
(12, 14, 15)

△
MOUNT
OLYMPOS

METEORA
(11)

IOANINA

EPIRUS
(33)

LARISSA

THESSALY
(9)

VOLOS

PELION
(10)

AMBRACIAN
GULF
(32)

LAMIA

WESTERN
ROUMELI
(30, 31)

EASTERN
ROUMELI
(8)

DELPHI
(7)

△ MT PARNASSOS
(6)

BOEOTIA (5)

THEBES

ATTICA
(4)

PATRAS

ACHAEA (29)

CORINTH

THE
ISTHMUS
(20)

ATHENS
(1–3)

ELIS (29)

MYCENAE (21)

OLYMPIA
(28)

ARCADIA
(23)

ARGOLID
(21, 22)

EPIDAURUS
(22)

LACONIA

MESSENIA
(27)

MISTRA
(25)

SPARTA (24)

MONEMVASIA (25)

THE
MANI
(26)

14

CHAPTER 1

Athens: The Acropolis

Syntagma Square – The Monument of Lysicrates –
The Theatre of Dionysus –
The Odeion of Herodes Atticus – The Propylaia –
The Temple of Wingless Victory – The Parthenon –
The Museum – The Erechtheion – The Areopagus –
The Pnyx.

The centre of Athens is **Syntagma Square**, midway between the hump of the Acropolis and the taller pinnacled crag of Lycabettus which overlooks the sprawling ellipse of the modern city. The square, lined with hotels, travel agencies and air terminals, has an up-to-date air. Historically it is without roots. The names that spring so easily to mind, as one approaches Athens and its Acropolis, ring rather hollow, for there is little here to recall the past. At night the skyline is bright with illuminated signs. The Grande Bretagne, overlooking the square, is the oldest and most individual of Greece's luxury hotels, with a pleasant restaurant, the GB Corner. From Syntagma Square streets branch out in all directions, their suburban tentacles encroaching on the foothills of limestone mountains that enclose the plain on three sides, with the sweep of the Saronic Gulf on the fourth.

Café tables spread across the pavements of the square. The kiosks, which are focal points in the life of the shopper in Greece, are festooned with foreign newspapers, magazines and paperbacks, with just enough room for the salesman to sit perched on a stool, smothered by stacks of airmail envelopes, films, soap, aspirin, after-shave lotion and other useful articles. Above the eastern end

15

of the square, beyond the orange trees and crowded benches, rises an austere war memorial. Behind it is a large bleak nineteenth-century edifice, once the royal palace, now the Parliament House. It is skirted to the south by the National Gardens, a pleasant refuge from the glare of the summer. Politics are the breath of life to large sections of the population. Personalities are rated higher than policies, and loyalty to the man of the moment is sometimes so fanatical that the only outlet lies in acts of violence. Interim periods of dictatorship (repressive or otherwise) are accepted as part of the pattern.

The Acropolis – an 'upper city' built on a natural bastion whose sides have been strengthened with massive walls – forms a ragged, somewhat elliptical, circle. This is the 'city of Theseus'. Around it extends the 'city of Hadrian', which merges into modern residential Athens. One can therefore walk, in little more than half an hour, from Syntagma Square to most of the main archaeological sites, strung out like an irregular garland round the Acropolis.

Even leaving aside its associations – mythological, historical, artistic – the Acropolis is physically omnipresent. Consciously or not, one is always looking up to see if the colonnades of the Parthenon or the porches of the Erechtheion are still there, outlined against a sky which, for weeks on end, can be an astonishingly vivid blue. The walls and bastions dominate the cream-coloured apartment blocks on the periphery of its slopes. A sense of intimacy with this gleaming hump of limestone is quickly acquired; and equally quickly taken for granted. Athens without the Acropolis would be unthinkable; not only would the skyline be different, but also the entire town plan, ancient and modern, would probably have developed otherwise – if at all.

There are several approaches. An obvious one begins at the south-west corner of Syntagma Square. There is much on the way that is historically irrelevant, though not without charm. If you follow Amalias Avenue, you will have the National Gardens on the left; to the right is the Church of *Agia Sotira* of Lycodemus, an attractive brick building, the first of several minor masterpieces of Byzantine architecture in Athens. Founded in the eleventh century, restored in the nineteenth, it is now the church of the Russian community. Opposite the Anglican Church of St Paul, grey, austere and incongruously Gothic in the urban Mediterranean setting, the narrow passage of Kydathenaion Street crosses two minute squares with wispy shrubbery: a crowded quarter, full of tavernas, snack-bars, churches and tourist shops.

At No. 17 Kydathenaion Street is the **Museum of Popular Arts**. The exhibits include elaborate and colourful national costumes and folk jewellery. Particularly striking is the work of the Epirot *terzidhes*, specialists in needlework with gold thread, who travelled across the country receiving orders for lavish embroideries whose designs were based on regional folklore patterns. At the southern end of the second little square, Pharmacis Street leads to the cruciform Byzantine Church of *Agia Aikaterini* in a sunken square. Two ancient columns stand in front of a little garden. The building has unfortunately suffered from tasteless restoration.

A few yards away is the **Choragic Monument of Lysicrates** in another square surrounded by a jumble of antique foundations. The monument is a fantasy: a cylindrical drum of marble on a square stone base, with six Corinthian columns engaged under the architrave. The mutilated frieze of the monument represents the episode of Dionysus's capture by Tyrrhenian pirates and the tricks he played in order to confound them. For the preservation of the monument much is owed to the French Government, which bought it in the seventeenth century. A Franciscan monastery was built around it, and this architectural extravaganza, restored in the nineteenth century, served as a monk's library. Byron lodged here in the winter of 1810–11; he read a great deal in the library, organized boxing matches between Catholic and Orthodox schoolboys and drank with the *Mufti* of Thebes and the *Kaimakam* of Athens.

From the Choragic Monument Byron Street leads into Dionysiou Areopaghitou Avenue, which ascends towards the Acropolis. On the right lie scattered marble slabs and truncated columns: fragments of the Sanctuary of Dionysus. A relative hush is perceptible. The tremendous weight of antiquity, which has done so much to fashion the mind and character of modern Greeks, begins to impinge. Two slender unfluted Corinthian columns, once surmounted by votive gifts, stand above a grotto in the south side of the Acropolis behind the ruined **Theatre of Dionysus**. Hollowed out of the hillside, the auditorium consisted of seventy-eight tiers, whose diameter increased as they ascended, divided into three sectors by *diazômas*. Originally the auditorium had an earth surface, but it was remodelled in the fourth century BC into a stone structure by Lycurgus, an able financier and patron of the arts.

The theatre is a good example of the Greek practice of utilizing a natural declivity for carving out an amphitheatre in some dominant yet central position. Situated at the foot of the citadel, it once commanded a view of the shrubby groves and undulations of the plain. Today nothing but an urban expanse meets the eye. Originally actors and chorus performed in the circular orchestra, surrounded in Roman times by a water conduit which enabled it to be flooded for the performance of mock naval battles. In the centre was the god's altar on a raised platform, marked by a large diamond-shaped paving stone, around which the chorus revolved in stately measures, chanting *dithyrambs* to the god. With the development of the art of the theatre, a proscenium, a narrow platform occupying a segment of the orchestra, was added as a stage for the main protagonists. The acoustics were improved by the placing of inverted bronze vessels on pedestals at various points in the auditorium where they received and redistributed the vibrations of sound. Painted scenic props were used and the actors wore large grotesque masks.

The stage area was partly restored in 1985; when the seating has been restored the theatre will be used for productions of classic plays. Here the tragedies of Aeschylus, Sophocles and Euripides were performed for the first time and European drama was born. The throne of the high priest of Dionysus, with its decorations of lions, griffins and, very appropriately, satyrs and a bunch of grapes, is easily identified in the centre of the front row. The concave seats, reserved for archons and priests and once shaded with awnings, are extraordinarily comfortable. The earliest theatrical compositions were accompanied by dancing, mimed scenes and impassioned dialogues. The annual performances, which formed part of the Great Dionysia, were held with much pomp in the spring sunshine, to the accompaniment of flute-playing and the banging of cymbals and drums. The audience did not only seek entertainment; they were genuinely moved by religious exaltation and the desire to honour the licentious young god. During the festival all work in the city ceased, a general moratorium was declared, law courts were shut and prisoners released from jail. Abstinence from wine was considered a mark of disrespect to the god, and bawdy, colourful processions wound through the streets.

From the highest tier of the theatre a row of cypress trees leads westward between the ruins of the Asclepeion – a sheltered sanctuary for the sick, dedicated to the god of healing – and the *Stoa* of Eumenes, the work of a philhellenic king of Pergamum in the second century BC, which consisted of a double colonnade and served as a foyer during the intervals between the trilogies of plays that lasted all day. From the *stoa* one regains Dionysiou Areopaghitou Avenue and mounts a broad marble stairway to the **Odeion of Herodes Atticus**, the gift of a wealthy public benefactor of the Antonine era to the people of Athens. The cedar-wood roof has vanished and the thirty-two tiers have been restored with modern facings. The stone façade of three stories is embellished with arches. When floodlit, it creates an effect of Roman splendour, the arched openings allowing for an interplay of light and shade, glowing and mysterious, which is absent from the classical simplicity of the monuments on the Acropolis. The contrast is striking – yet the two styles complement each other, as Greek and Roman architecture often do. In front of the semi-circular orchestra, a chequer-board of dark blue and white marble, rises the stage and behind it the *skene* (the stone or marble back-cloth to a stage) consisting of a colonnade with niches for statues, surmounted by a narrow ledge reserved for actors who impersonate the gods.

A festival, very different from the Dionysia, is now held every summer (June–September) in the restored theatre. Apart from a cycle of ancient drama, the festival includes performances by the world's leading orchestras, and operatic, ballet and theatrical companies. Acoustic imperfections are redeemed by the setting: especially the mellow glow of the arcaded *skene* and a glimpse of the Parthenon above the massive Cimonian wall. The impression made by the trumpet solo in the *Leonora No. 3* overture echoing across the ruins could not be more dramatic.

Beyond the Odeion, a paved road ascends to the **Acropolis**, which has the shape of an elongated lozenge with a flat top and is five hundred feet high. 'There is but one entry,' says Pausanius, 'it

19

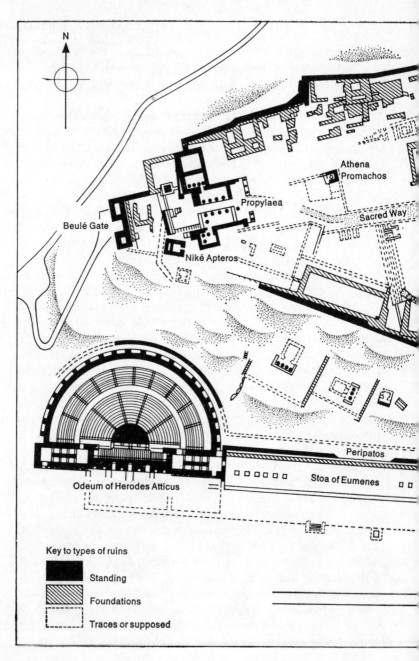

Key to types of ruins

Standing

Foundations

Traces or supposed

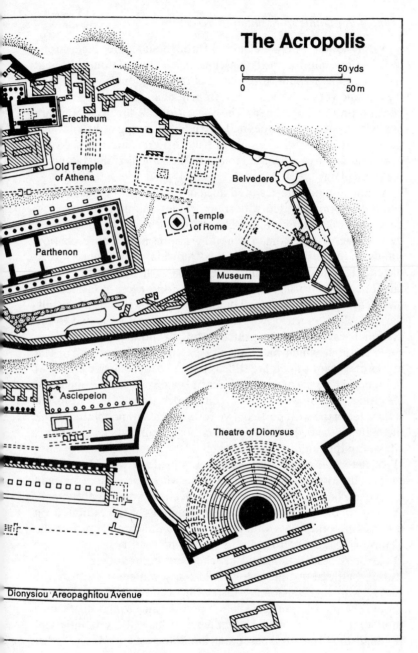

The Acropolis

0   50 yds
0   50 m

Erectheum

Old Temple
of Athena

Belvedere

Temple
of Rome

Parthenon

Museum

Asclepeion

Theatre of Dionysus

Dionysiou Areopaghitou Avenue

affords no other, being precipitous throughout and having a strong wall.' As one climbs, one is conscious of a feeling of isolation but at the same time of being at the heart of things; of one's proximity to the city and yet one's remoteness from it, of an atmosphere that has become unusually rarefied. The sheer sides of the Acropolis are honeycombed with grottoes and defended by strong walls, of which the earliest, below the Temple of Niké Apteros, are called Cyclopean, but are also attributed to the Pelasgi, the first inhabitants of the Attic plain.

As one ascends the restored ancient ramp past the ticket office and a platform crowded with touts, guides and motor coaches, a large pedestal of greyish-blue Hymettos marble, once surmounted by a statue of the Roman general Agrippa in a bronze chariot, stands on the left. In front rises the **Propylaia**, the entrance way to the citadel, one of the masterpieces of classical architecture. Commissioned by Pericles, it was built by Mnesicles, a fashionable fifth-century BC architect. Extending across the west side of the hill, the Propylaia, much of whose complexity of design is due to the asymmetrical slope of the ground, forms an entrance hall to the five gates through which men and horses entered the precinct. The marks of chariot wheels are still visible. A costly, massive edifice of Pentelic marble, it consisted of a central gateway with five openings, on either side of which Doric colonnades rise directly from the stylobate. In the west portico, two rows of three Ionic columns flank the main passage. The ceiling was coffered and embellished with a gilt star in the middle. The openings of the gateway, which are not all of the same height, had huge doors made of wood faced with bronze; the loud grating noise they made when opened is mentioned by Aristophanes. There are two projections: one to the north, leading to the Pinacotheke, where paintings were exhibited on boards; the other, less well preserved, to the south (towards the Temple of Niké Apteros). In the fourteenth century the Florentine Duke of Athens established his chancery here, adding a second storey, battlements and a tower; in the seventeenth century the Turks, with their customary disregard for historical monuments, turned the marble porticoes into a powder magazine. Struck by a thunderbolt, the gunpowder ignited and blew the establishment sky-high and the central part of the building caved in. Much of what we now see standing is the result of laborious restoration by modern archaeologists. A more majestic entrance to a holy precinct can hardly be imagined.

To the right, the **Temple of Wingless Victory** (Niké Apteros) seems minuscule in comparison. Only eighteen feet by twenty-seven, it is a memorial to the Greek victories over the Persians. Pericles entrusted the plan to Callicrates, who so constructed the temple, which rests on a stylobate of three steps, that its front pointed in the direction of the Parthenon: an effect probably designed to focus the eye on the more impressive building. This exquisitely proportioned little monument, with its eight Ionic columns composed of monolithic shafts instead of the usual series of superimposed drums, was demolished by the Turks and the materials were used for the construction of a defence wall. A century and a half later King Otho commissioned the reconstruction of the temple. The original materials fortunately lay at hand, but the greater part of the frieze is so mutilated that it is difficult to identify the headless figures. The east frieze represented the assembly of the gods; the other three are believed to have depicted scenes from the Persian Wars, which was contrary to the usual practice of portraying mythical feats on the friezes of temples.

Returning to the Propylaia, one passes out of the east portico into a vast esplanade littered with the debris of centuries. To the left is the Erechtheion, to the right the Parthenon, on a terrace crowning the entire precinct. There is no vegetation: nothing but rock and marble; and sky overhead. How often one has seen it all before – in paintings, drawings and photographs. However there is one thing not anticipated: the sheer physical dominance of the Parthenon over every other structure on the Acropolis. In the second century AD Pausanius described the Sacred Way, which led obliquely up the incline from the Propylaia to the east front of the Parthenon, as a jumble of statues, pedestals and votive offerings. Today nothing remains but the sun-baked bases, the ruts formed by ancient water-ducts, the sockets from which innumerable columns sprouted. At intervals faint incisions in the rock, intended to prevent horses and sacred animals from slipping on the hard, smooth surface, are noticeable. Here, as in the sanctuaries of Delphi and Olympia, buildings are seldom parallel to each other.

The Greeks sought symmetry, but not parallelism, which they considered monotonous.

The Temple of Athena Polias, tutelary goddess of Athens, or **Parthenon**, as it came to be known, stripped of its honey-coloured patina by acid rain to a white not seen since the original paint disappeared centuries ago, stands on the site of an earlier temple burned by the Persians on the eve of the battle of Salamis. The new temple was the brain-child of Pericles; Ictinus, assisted by Calli-crates, was the principal architect; and Phidias, the greatest sculptor of the age, was in charge of the decoration. The plans were the most ambitious and architecturally daring ever attempted. Little wonder that the great building, primarily a place of worship, soon came to be regarded as a national treasury, containing bullion, archives and votive gifts of immense value. It is constructed entirely of Pentelic marble, and not one of its forty-six Doric columns is exactly the same height as any other. The slight convexity in the middle of the columns prevents the eye from being carried upwards automatic-ally; the columns acquire volume and elasticity and thus monotony is relieved. This all-important *entasis*, as it is called, was intended to correct an optical illusion, for a perfectly straight column invariably appears thinner in the middle when seen against a background of bright light. The resultant effect of strength and harmony is particu-larly evident from either end of the north and south colonnades. Another architectural refinement was the gradual rise of the stylo-bate to a point which is highest in the centre. There is, in fact, hardly a straight line in the building. The ultimate effect of all this *entasis*, almost invisible to the untrained eye, is to create an impression of a perfectly proportioned edifice growing organically out of a natural eminence.

The sculptures, executed by Phidias and his pupils, and originally painted in bright hues of red, blue, yellow and green – the effect, it is thought, may have been rather gaudy – consisted of ninety-two *metopes*, a frieze five hundred and twenty-four feet long around the entire circumference of the exterior walls of the *cella*, and two gigantic pediments, at each corner of which lions' heads projected. The decoration is arranged in three tiers – on, as it were, three different religious levels – embracing the entire cosmos in which the Greeks of the fifth century BC had their being. First came the Phidias frieze, representing the procession of the Great Panathenaea: a masterpiece of animation, with men and animals depicted in motion. This frieze depicted every section of the population participating in the procession – on foot, on horseback, or in chariots. Parts of the frieze, though much damaged, may be seen on the west front. In the equestrian groups the prancing horses seem to be defying the attempts of the young riders to control them. Other plaques are in the Acropolis Museum and the remaining fifty-six in the British Museum. The angle of vision is very awkward, for the frieze is forty feet above the spectator, who has little room to manoeuvre in the narrow colonnade.

From the human bustle of the frieze we move on to the *metopes*, which represent the gods and mythological heroes engaged in epic contests with giants, Centaurs and Amazons, symbolic of the victory of mind over matter. These are of inferior quality to the frieze. Thirty-two remain in their original position, between *triglyphs*, but they are mutilated almost beyond recognition. Other surviving *metopes* are in the British Museum and the Louvre. There is also one in the Acropolis Museum. Finally, on the highest level, crowning the whole structure, we enter the realm of the divine, the sculptures of the pediments representing two of the most venerable scenes in Athenian mythology: the birth of Athena, when she sprang fully armed from the head of Zeus 'with a mighty shout, while Heaven and Earth trembled before her', and her contest with Poseidon for possession of the city. The most important fragments are in the British Museum. Except for a cement cast of Dionysus, the superb heads of three horses from the chariots of the Sun and Moon at either end of the east front, and two headless figures in the west, the Parthenon pediments are now no more than two gaping wounds in a scarred and mutilated structure.

The huge *cella* of the Parthenon is now open to the sky. The interior arrangement can easily be traced: first (east to west), the *pronaos* (an outer porch), then the *naos*, the inner shrine which housed Phidias' great chryselephantine statue of Athena, over forty feet high and adorned with precious stones – probably as garish as it was awesome in the sombre glow of the sacred chamber; then the Parthenon proper, the chamber of the goddess's virgin priestesses, where the treasure and bullion were kept (a nice

Companion Guide to Mainland Greece

juxtaposition of god and mammon); finally the *opisthodomos*, a back chamber corresponding to the *pronaos*.

In the fifth century the temple was converted into a Christian basilica consecrated to the Mother of God (there are traces of painting on the interior north-west wall) and Phidias' statue of the goddess was removed to Constantinople.

After the Frankish conquest of the Levant in 1204, the Parthenon became a Latin church. Two and a half centuries later, after the fall of Constantinople, Athens was visited by the conqueror, Sultan Mehmet II, who could not resist converting the Parthenon into a mosque, to which a minaret was added. As such it remained until 1687 when a direct hit, during a siege by the Venetian army commanded by Morosini, set off a massive explosion in the temple which was used as a Turkish powder magazine. Further damage was suffered during the War of Independence and it was not until 1930 that the restoration of the north colonnade, with the drums, capitals and fragments of architrave left lying about since the seventeenth century, was completed by Greek archaeologists. Thus, in spite of siege, pillage and desecration, the bare bones of Pericles's brainchild, with its brilliantly white columns and the matchless subtlety of its proportions, have survived the vicissitudes of centuries. Unfortunately the restoration caused unforeseen problems when the steel reinforcements corroded and started to expand, leading to splitting of the marble: work is now in hand to replace the steel and repair the damage.

The view from the Parthenon embraces the whole Attic plain. It is most spectacular at sunset, when the famous violet light spreads across the bare slopes of Hymettos and for one miraculous moment is reflected in the buildings of the entire city.

From the eastern front of the Parthenon you descend to the **Acropolis Museum**, a unique showcase of Archaic sculpture of the seventh, sixth and early fifth centuries BC. All the exhibits were found on the Acropolis. In Archaic sculpture the males, generally youths, are nude, whereas the females are fully clothed, for it is not until Hellenistic times that Eastern influences cause Greek modesty, with regard to the nude female figure, to be swept away in a wave of sensuous opulence. All Archaic statues, male and female, from the earliest to the latest, are, whether pleasing in a conventional sense or not, based on the Greek concept of perfection in shape. The *kouroi*, narrow-waisted youths exulting in their beauty and athletic prowess, stand rigid, left leg slightly forward, head and neck very erect. The oblique eyes protrude, and a faintly mocking smile, hinting at a quiet, sophisticated sense of humour, plays about the full sensual lips. In spite of the ritualistic stiffness of the figures, reminiscent of Egyptian statues, they are, in the words of Lord Clark, 'alert and confident members of a conquering race'. However, the best *kouroi* are in the National Museum and it is the reed-like maidens, the *korai*, presented as votive offerings to the goddess, that exercise the greatest fascination in the Acropolis Museum. In their main attributes they differ little from the *kouroi*, except that they are fully and stylishly dressed, and the arrangement of the hair is extremely elaborate. The *korai* represent fashionable young women of Athenian society in the aristocratic age of the Peisistratae. They are clad in a skin-tight tunic, the *chiton*, and a mantle, the *himation*, which is frequently jewelled, and which falls in symmetrically pleated folds in front of the breast. In spite of variations in size (most *korai* are about three-quarters life size), hair style and details of drapery, one is struck by the prevailing conformity.

In the entrance hall a large marble effigy of Athena's owl (No. 1347) establishes the goddess's symbolic authority. To the left, a charming fourth-century BC bas relief (No. 1338) depicts eight nude male figures preparing to perform a Pyrrhic dance. Room I contains part of a seventh-century BC pediment (the earliest one extant in Greece) from a small treasury, subsequently destroyed. Executed in painted tufa (traces of red, green and black), it represents the struggle of Heracles with the Hydra, whose innumerable coils are fashioned like octopus tentacles. In Room II fragments of a large, primitive pediment from the original temple of Athena (sixth-century BC) depict Heracles slaying Triton, while a friend of Triton's, a monster with three winged bodies (No. 35), looks on. The composition – what remains of it – is full of vitality, with expressions of grotesque whimsicality on the three faces of the monster. The **Moscophorus** or Calf-Bearer (No. 624), representing a man bearing a sacrificial calf to the goddess, is a far more evolved work of art. Of four exquisitely carved little Archaic horses (No. 575) the best-preserved are the two central ones, who turn their heads towards each other, as though engaged – somewhat shyly – in conversation.

Fragments from the early temple of Athena destroyed by the Persians are among the chief exhibits in Room III. But the greatest enchantments are reserved for Room IV. First comes the **Rider** (No. 590), which formed part of a small equestrian composition, believed to be the work of Phaidimos, greatest of Archaic sculptors. The head is a cast from the original in the Louvre, but nonetheless its charm and liveliness, with the almond-shaped eyes and firm, expressive lips set in the familiar teasing smile, make it one of the most attractive in the museum. Particularly decorative are the elaborate, bead-like curls across the forehead and the long locks, strung like corals, hanging behind the large ears. But it is the monolithic upward thrust of the torso from the wasp waist that is most impressive; a perfect achievement of grace and naturalness, in spite of the absence of movement. In the same room are the *korai*, ranged in a circle on pedestals: formal, architectonic in conception, often haughty, always amused. A world of aristocratic ease, poise and serenity, destined to perish forever in the holocaust of the Persian Wars. No. 679, the **Peplos Koré** (so called because she is wearing a heavy woollen *peplos* over her *chiton*), her bosom framed between parallel plaits of hair, is a masterpiece of sixth-century BC Attic sculpture, also probably the work of Phaidimos. The body, true, is block-like (the lower part flat at the front and round at the back), but the head is both authoritative and refined, the modelling miraculously rounded, the expression cynical, yet full of a kind of detached felicity.

Room V is dominated by a larger than life-size *koré* (No. 681), as formidable as her sisters in Room IV are diminutive. There are also fragments of a pediment from an older temple (No. 631), depicting gods and goddesses victorious over fallen giants in *gigantomachia*. Passing into Room VI one is suddenly conscious of a change, a break with the past. We are in the fifth century. The mocking smile has vanished, and emotion is reflected in pensive expressions and relaxed attitudes. The change of mood is most striking in the **Kritios Boy** (No. 698), a perfect reproduction of the human body, its weight evenly and naturally distributed. An effortless poise has replaced the taut formality of the strictly frontal position; but in the sweeping-away of rigid class distinctions, which followed the fall of the Peisistratae, the Kritios Boy seems to have lost his sense of humour.

A small plaque in low relief (No. 695) represents a **Mourning Athena**. Emotion has broken through, and the limbs have grown supple in the process. Again there is the new distribution of weight, the goddess's body being slightly tilted forward, leaning on her spear; only the toes and the ball of the left foot touch the ground.

In Room VII there is a well-preserved *metope* (No. 705) from the Parthenon, portraying a struggle between a centaur and a Lapith woman (remarkable for the modelling of her body in the round) and two fine heads of horses (No. 882) from the Chariot of Poseidon which formed part of the sculptural decoration of the west pediment of the Parthenon. Room VIII is dominated by **fragments from the Parthenon frieze**, stunning examples (notice how shallow the relief is) of crowds in motion, full of dash, energy and liveliness. No. 973, (relief from the balustrade of the Temple of Niké Apteros) depicts a maiden removing her sandal. Although her *chiton* is so thin that the contours of her body stand out firm and rounded, deep shadows lurk mysteriously in the folds of the loosely flowing drapery. Finally, in Room IX there is a fourth-century BC head of Alexander the Great (No. 1331), sensuous, full-lipped, conventionally handsome; also a fragment of a relief depicting a serene, authoritative Niké crowning Heracles, while Athena looks on.

From the museum one follows the line of the north-east rampart, past a belvedere overhanging a steep incline once cluttered with mean little medieval houses grouped round the blue-domed twelfth-century church of St Nicholas Rhangabes. Northward, below the walls of Themistocles, lies central Athens. Beside one rises the **Erechtheion**: for some, the supreme monument of the Acropolis, painstakingly restored after years of labour.

The temple, completed during the last years of the Peloponnesian War, occupied the site of the holiest place on the Acropolis. Its origins go back to the beginnings of the Attic religion. This is the spot where Athena brought forth the olive tree in her contest with Poseidon for the possession of the city.

The Erechtheion is situated on lower ground than the Parthenon, and its complexity is in sharp contrast to the monolithic grandeur of the larger temple. Built on different levels, on the foundations of the edifice destroyed by the Persians, it has no side colonnades but three porticoes different in size, style and execution. From every angle the spectator obtains a different view: startling, novel, sometimes confusing. The side opposite the Parthenon consists of a blank marble wall, broken at the west by the **Caryatid Portico**; it is the least attractive side, because the architect, probably Mnesicles, had to cope with a sloping site and the inclusion of three separate shrines in one building – those of Athena Polias, Poseidon and Erectheus – as well as the Pandroseion, which contained the ancient olive tree planted by the goddess, and altars of other semi-deities; the temple served several purposes, all of profound religious significance. Architecturally, the whole edifice was intended as a counterweight – more modest in dimensions and different in style – to the Parthenon. The heavy drapery of the Caryatids may have been meant to harmonize with the fluting of the columns of the Parthenon, but these six hefty maidens, in spite of their brave yet self-conscious simper, seem to be crushed by the weight of the ornamental roof they support on their cushioned heads. Replicas have replaced the originals; one of which was bought by Lord Elgin and is now carefully preserved in the British Museum. Her unfortunate sisters were reduced to leprous anonymity by acid rain and have been placed in a nitrogen-filled glass case in the Acropolis Museum to prevent further deterioration. The spacing of the figures resembles that of columns, so that the porch acquires the aspect of a lofty tribune. But nothing really compensates for the expanse of blank wall from which the portico projects with such aimlessness, dwarfed by the proximity of the Parthenon.

The **East Portico** consists of six narrow fluted Ionic columns of great elegance (one is in the British Museum), surmounted by elaborate capitals. Approaching the entrance, one gets side views of the Caryatid and North Porticoes which break up the symmetry but not the harmony of the edifice. It is not, however, until one has descended a flight of steps and reached the **North Portico**, through which the chamber of Erectheus was probably reached, that one receives the full impact of this unique and anomalous building perched above the sprawling city, with the long line of Mount Parnes forming a bluish-grey barrier in the north. The portico, although built on a lower level than the other two porches, gives a greater impression of thrust and delicacy, and, both in its proportions and adornment, may be considered one of the most perfect

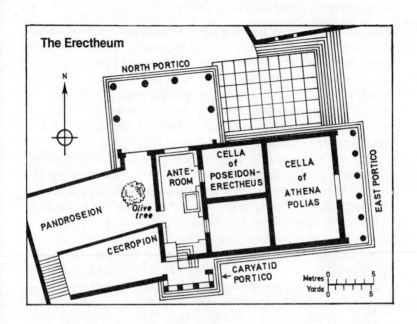

The Erectheum

NORTH PORTICO

N

PANDROSEION

Olive tree

ANTE-ROOM

CELLA of POSEIDON-ERECTHEUS

CELLA of ATHENA POLIAS

EAST PORTICO

CECROPION

CARYATID PORTICO

Metres 0 5
Yards 0 5

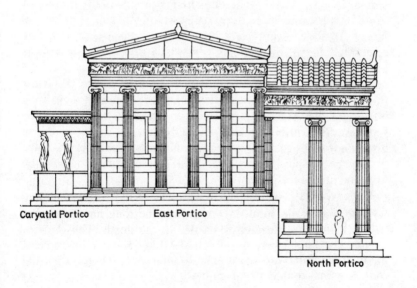

Caryatid Portico   East Portico

North Portico

examples of classical architecture. The six Ionic columns have a slight *entasis* and their bases are embellished with plaited decoration. The beautifully carved capitals, also extremely ornate, are no less elegant. The great doorway is narrower at the top and has a lavishly ornamented frame. An opening in the floor of the portico reveals a vault in which holes have been bored in the rock. The four half-columns in the west wall, between the North and the Caryatid porticoes, are a Roman restoration.

One now passes out through the Propylaia before walking down the paved way into the ancient part of the town round the Acropolis. In front rises the grey, flat-topped rock of the **Areopagus**. Here sat the oldest court of justice in the world, first summoned by the gods to judge Orestes for the crime of matricide. Here, too, Demosthenes was judged for bribery and St Paul addressed the people of Athens on the 'Unknown God'. They gave the apostle a polite but lukewarm reception. Only Dionysus the Areopagite, an erudite councillor, future patron saint of Athens, took up the Christian cause with sufficient fervour to suffer martyrdom.

To the south-west, across a busy road and beyond a stretch of ground covered with Aleppo pines, cedars and cypresses rises the eminence of the **Pnyx**. On a semi-circular terrace of the north-east slope, this rock-hewn platform, supported by a wall of polygonal blocks, is about twenty feet high; it has been identified as the celebrated *Bema*, the tribune from which generations of orators addressed the assembly of the people of Athens in the shadow of the temples of the Acropolis. Nightly performances of *son et lumière* (Greek, English and French versions), with splendid floodlighting effects on the Acropolis, are held on the Pnyx throughout the summer. The adjoining **Hill of the Nymphs** is crowned by an observatory, designed, like so much of nineteenth-century Athens, by Hansen and paid for by Baron Sina. It is scheduled to house the Museum of Old Instruments.

The paved way skirts the north-west bastion of the Acropolis and plunges into the maze of the Plaka – 'old Athens' – once gay and picturesque, now full of tourists and touts. But it is less confusing to explore the Plaka, the adjacent area of the Agora and the other monuments of the 'City of Theseus' by taking a completely different route starting from Syntagma Square.

CHAPTER 2

Athens: 'The City of Theseus'

The 'Little Cathedral' – The Plaka –
The Tower of the Winds – The Roman Agora –
Hadrian's Library – Monastiraki Square –
The Kerameikos – The Agora and Stoa of Attalus –
The Theseion – The Kapnikarea Church.

Skirting the northern slope of the Acropolis lies a district of small shops, offices and churches, dotted with little enclaves of classical ruins.

From Syntagma Square one descends Mitropolis Street. On the left is the tiny post-Byzantine chapel dedicated to *Agia Dynami* (the Holy Strength), now squeezed in, but intact, beneath a tall Ministry building. Straddling the crowded pavement, the chapel has an air of mild protest against the impersonality of the modern building towering above it; whiffs of burning incense, drifting through its miniature portals, mingle with the smell of petrol fumes and occasionally the chant of an officiating priest rises above the strident voices of pedestrians. The narrow canyon of Mitropolis Street debouches into a large square of the same name, where the official cathedral, constructed with materials plundered from seventy Byzantine chapels, raises its ugly, nineteenth-century façade. Beside it, somewhat dwarfed, rests the **Little Cathedral**, or *Panayia Gorgoepicöos* (The Virgin who grants requests quickly), a gem of Byzantine church architecture of the twelfth century, whose modest proportions (twenty-four feet by thirty-six feet) indicate the humble status held by Athens in the Byzantine world at a time when the Empire's fortunes were at their peak. In style it is cruciform and domed; the drum is slender and elegant and the exterior walls,

33

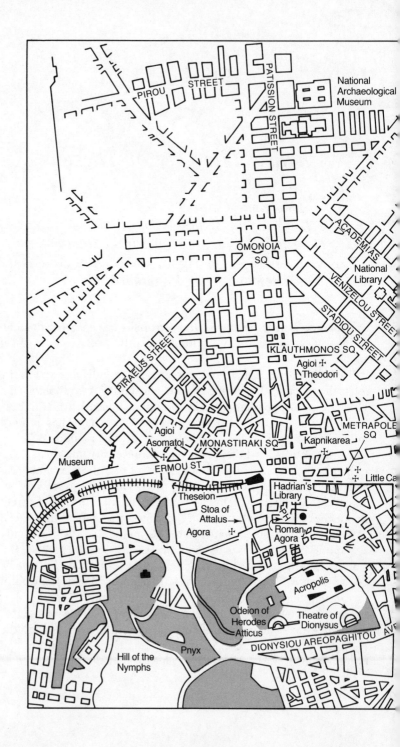

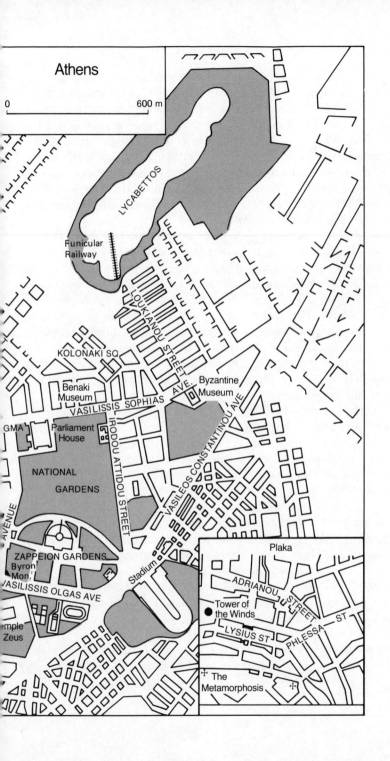

Athens

0   600 m

LYCABETTOS

Funicular
Railway

LOUKIANOU STREET

KOLONAKI SQ

Benaki
Museum

VASILISSIS SOPHIAS AVE.

Byzantine
Museum

GMA

Parliament
House

IRODOU ATTIDOU STREET

VASILEOS CONSTANTINOU AVE

NATIONAL
GARDENS

VASILEOS CONSTANTINOU AVE

AVENUE

ZAPPEION GARDENS

Byron
Mon.

VASILISSIS OLGAS AVE

Stadium

mple
Zeus

Plaka

ADRIANOU STREET

Tower of
the Winds

LYSIUS ST

PHLESSA—ST

✝ The
Metamorphosis

✝

which have a glowing, ivory-smooth patina, are studded with marble plaques. On the west front the quaint but charming fourth-century BC frieze, pilfered from some ancient monument, tells the story of the twelve months of the year. The decoration is a dotty historical jumble (something that one encounters again and again in Greece), with its ancient *stelae*, Corinthian capitals and Byzantine crosses, to which the coats of arms of the Villehardouin and the de la Roche families have been added – a reminder of that long-forgotten period of Frankish rule, when Athens was governed by the Crusaders and their Latin descendants.

Mitropolis Square is a good place to watch the *Epitaphios* (Good Friday Procession), when the bier of Christ, heaped with flowers, is borne through the street at night. The procession is led by the Archbishop of Athens and all Greece. He is followed by church dignitaries in tall cylindrical hats, flanked by acolytes in red and purple shifts. The acolytes totter under the weight of enormous banners. The procession is followed by a shuffling crowd of worshippers, hands cupped round lighted candles. Everywhere there is a smell of stock and incense. The *Epitaphios* has one point in common with the Panathenaic procession: the people are part of the procession, not just spectators.

At the southern end of the square, P. Benizelou Street leads into Adrianou Street, the 'aristocratic' quarter of Athens in the eighteenth and early nineteenth centuries; now a maze of shops, including many of the better tourist and handicraft stores.

At the Demotic School (neo-classical façade) one turns into Flessa Street. This is the beginning of the **Plaka** proper, its steep alleys criss-crossing the northern slope of the Acropolis. Parts of the quarter are for pedestrians only; the most garish and incongruous nightclubs have been removed, so that tavernas of all kinds and tourist shops hold sway. The genuine tavernas are a very good Greek institution and the ones in the Plaka are among the most popular, though by no means the best. Greeks do not go to tavernas only to eat and drink, but to indulge in *kephi*, which means to sing and shout and make a great deal of noise; and they expect other people to do so too. An orchestra of three guitarists is usual. The most popular drink is *retsina*. To some it is an acquired taste: dry and astringent, with a slight flavour of turpentine. A convivial party is quite likely to send a brimming carafe (or copper mug) over to a table of complete strangers; all the more reason to do so (this is very Greek) if they are foreigners. At all costs the foreigner must be fêted and, in return, the Greek flattered. The foreigner must be left in no doubt that Greeks are the finest people in the world and he is expected to say so – fulsomely.

The food consists of *taramasolata* (a purée of dried fish-roe), *souvlakia* (pieces of pork or beef grilled on a skewer), *kokoretsi* (chopped liver and sweetbreads encased in guts, strongly flavoured with garlic and roasted on the spit), the ubiquitous *feta* (a white, sometimes flaky, goat's milk cheese) and the inevitable tomato salad (in winter replaced by finely chopped raw cabbage). At the sophisticated tavernas the food is on more international lines. Among the bottled wines, Carras (red, white and rosé) is one of the best. Demestica (red and white) is much cheaper. At least half of the simpler tavernas are open at mid-day. Not so the pretentious tourist tavernas, which have many of the defects, but not the advantages, of the humbler ones. Some of them have floor-shows and dancing.

Flessa Street rises to the miniature houses of Erotocritos Street, which swerves right, past the Byzantine chapel of St John the Divine (eleventh- and twelfth-century), to a shady little terrace occupied by the tables of two tavernas at night, but peaceful in the daytime. Further right, between the indoor and outdoor tables of the popular '*O Yeros tou Mouria*' (The Old Man of Morea), the steps of Mnesicles Street lead into Prytaneion Street, at the end of which, on the left, appear the blue domes of the Church of *Agios Nikolaos Rhangabes*, twelfth-century, but so much restored as to retain little of its original antiquity. Above the church more tavernas command a superb view, with the pine-fringed and floodlit summit of Lycabettus crowning successive layers of apartment blocks.

From Prytaneion Street I like to descend into the sunken garden of the Church of *Agioi Anarghyroi*, St Cosmas and St Damian, the Arabian twins, patron saints of medicine and surgery, martyred by Diocletian. The saints are called the *anarghyroi*, 'the silverless ones', because they refused to accept a fee for their cures. The whitewashed church, to which a porch with four marble columns has been added, was built at the beginning of the Turkish occupation in the form of a single-aisle basilica.

One then enters Thrasyvoulou Street and, passing the tourist shops and nightclubs, ascends the first stairway on the left to reach the newly restored Old University, the modest mid-nineteenth-century seat of higher studies. A few steps above is the Church of the *Metamorphosis*, another charming Byzantine chapel of the fourteenth century, situated below the pines and cypresses skirting the 'Long Rocks' of the Acropolis. The tiny altar is made from the capital of an ancient column. To the right, at the corner of Panos Street, is the Kanellopoulos Museum, a remarkable collection of antique and Byzantine items. Outstanding are the Tanagra figurines dating from 330–200 BC and icons from the twelfth to the fourteenth century AD. From here the road, now wider, leads westward round the Acropolis to the rock of the Areopagus.

To the north, Panos Street descends to the spacious square of the Tower of the Winds, known as *Oi Aeridhes* (The Windy Ones). The pink and ochre-washed houses were once the balustraded mansions of the capital's embryo bourgeoisie. A railing runs round two sides of a complex of ancient ruins. At night, when moonlit, it is one of the most romantic places in Athens.

The **Tower of the Winds**, or *Horologium* of Andronicus Cyrrhestes, rises beside an umbrageous plane tree in a depression below the square. West of it extends the Roman Agora. The octagonal tower is an architectural fantasy, the creation of a philhellenic Syrian of the first century AD. In 1676 Dr Spon of Lyons, one of the earliest Western scholars to visit Greece, identified it as a hydraulic clock. A bas-relief, portraying the features of the different winds, runs round the eight sides. The roof, an octagonal pyramid, was surmounted by a weather-vane in the form of a Triton. A small round tower against the east front served as a reservoir for the clock, which was connected by an aqueduct to the spring of Clepsydra on the Acropolis.

Diogenes Street, more of a passage at the north-east of the square, leads to a decent unpretentious taverna, the Platanos, situated in a shady court.

In the rectangle of the **Roman Agora** are the ruins of an Ionic peristyle with a double gallery surrounding an interior marble-paved courtyard. Traces of a building with a loggia at the south-east corner have been identified as the *Agronomeion*, headquarters of

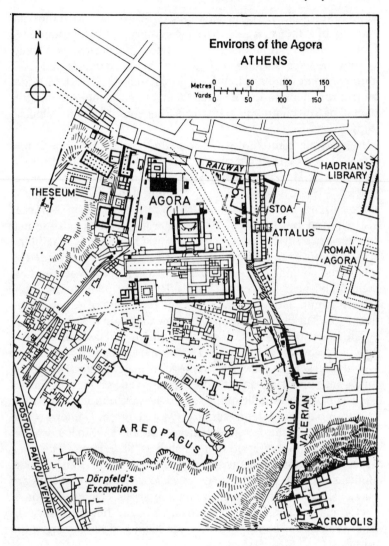

the market police. At the west end (Discouri Street) stands the gateway of Athena Archegates (first century AD), with four heavy Doric columns surmounted by an intact, unadorned pediment. Within the excavation area there is a square brick building with multiple domes and a colonnaded porch, once the Fetiye Mosque, built in commemoration of Sultan Mehmet's entry into Athens after the fall of Constantinople, later a clearing house for archaeological finds.

Beyond the Church of the *Taxiarchoi* (Archangels) one enters Areos Street; on the right rises the fire-blackened colonnade of the west side of **Hadrian's Library**. All that remains of the central portico, a single fluted Corinthian column, stands isolated from the smooth shafts of the colonnade. The façade of the main entrance, also charred by fire, is in Aiolou Street, where six Corinthian columns (two survive) supported consoles. Built by Hadrian in the second century AD, the library possessed a courtyard surrounded by a hundred columns, a pool and a garden. The library was in turn sacked, burned, converted into a Byzantine church and subsequently into a bazaar, which became the centre of Athenian life during the Turkish occupation. It is now the haunt of stray cats.

The most striking feature of the adjoining **Monastiraki Square**, hub of downtown Athens, is a Turkish mosque, the former *Pazar Djami* (Market Mosque), which consists of a square block faced by a loggia and supporting an octagon. It has served as both a prison and a museum. In the middle of the square rises the unusually tall drum of the modernized tenth-century Church of the *Panayia* (The Virgin), while at the eastern end there is the entrance to Pandrossou Street, commonly referred to in English as 'Shoe Lane'. This alley has several antique shops and is faintly redolent of a Turkish bazaar. Hellenistic coins, Attic figurines, rugs, icons and embroideries are on sale at the more expensive antique shops. There is a lot of Victoriana (opaline vases, egg-cups, etc.) and filigree silverware from Ioanina in the north. Prices are high, and bargaining is the norm.

At the right of Monastiraki railway station, Iphaistiou Street, a humble counterpart of Pandrossou, forms part of the blacksmiths' and coppersmiths' quarter. The shops are full of brass and leather objects. In an open market some way down the street there is a fine selection of old furniture and junk. On Sunday mornings a flea-market offers second-hand clothes and an amorphous assortment of rusty metal appliances. From Monastiraki Square one rejoins Ermou Street at its more squalid lower end and proceeds west, with a view of the gas-works which has long been scheduled for demolition.

Beyond the little Byzantine Church of *Agioi Asomatoi* (The Saintly Incorporeal Ones), its exterior brickwork decoration stylishly restored, is the entrance to a vast sunken field of ancient ruins in the form of an irregular rhomboid, dominated by a large coffee-coloured modern church. At the west end lies the **Kerameikos**, a necropolis of funerary altars.

Lying just outside the city walls, the cemetery of the Kerameikos, final resting place of countless public figures, was destroyed in the first century BC when Sulla breached the defences of beleaguered Athens. The level of the ground continued, nevertheless, to be raised by the superimposition of more sepulchres, and the excavation of graves continues, to this day, to yield funerary offerings. The place is now a jumble of shattered *stelae* (carved marble gravestones) on different levels, with fosses or ditches, corresponding to the ancient alleys, cleaving through the mounds and knolls, which look like abandoned earthworks.

The surviving *stelae* – the finest are now in the National Archaeological Museum – line the right bank of the Alley of the Tombs which begins at the Piraeus Street entrance (now closed) and whence it is best to start a tour (west to east) of the site. First, there is a relief depicting a Roman funeral banquet, attended by the dreaded Charon, conveyor of souls to the Underworld, followed by the representation of a huge Molossian dog, its paunch seamed with protruding veins; next comes the Monument of Dionysius of Cocytus, crowned by a lively, well-preserved bull about to charge, and then the Monument of Dexileos – with a cast of the original *stele* which is now in the adjoining museum. A large, well-preserved, though artistically inferior, *stele* depicting a girl seated beside her standing mother, rises above the bank of a lateral alley. Class distinctions are preserved, and the graves of slaves are marked by truncated columns. *Loutrophoroi*, slender pitchers with two handles, reserved for bachelors' graves, litter the banks of the fosse.

41

Slender marble *lecythoi*, which resemble the *loutrophoroi* except that they have only one handle, are scattered among the shrubs. A simple and beautiful relief of a maiden bearing a vase crowns the site of the shrine of Hecate above the Alley of the Tombs at the south-western end of the necropolis.

South-east of a large, unidentified circular building are vestiges of the city walls raised by Themistocles and restored by Conon. Next, to the east, are the ruins of the Pompeion, where all the props used in the Panathenaic procession were stored. Six small banqueting halls project from a court surrounded by a colonnade (column bases are preserved), once a favourite haunt of that somewhat bogus philosopher, Diogenes. To the north are the stylobates and fragments of walls of the Dipylon Gate, the main commercial entrance into Athens. The Gate was connected with the Agora by a *dromos* (public way) lined with statues of poets, philosophers and statesmen. The quantity of column bases, the water conduits and the ruts of chariot wheels in the paved ways give one an idea of the dimensions and the importance of this congested 'monumental' entrance way.

The little museum of the Kerameikos stands by the gate at 148 Ermou Street. In Room I are *stelae*; among the finest is the fifth-century BC **Monument of Dexileos**, depicting a warrior mounted on a frisky horse in the act of overwhelming his foe; in another, a young man – the departed soul – is represented draped in a flowing *chlamys*; a grandmother holds her dead grandchild on her lap, the folds of her *peplos* billowing over her head and following the contours of both her body and the baby's. In contrast, an earlier period is represented by a perky Archaic sphinx, its head turned at right angles to its body.

In Room II we go further back: to the funerary offerings of the late Mycenaean, Protogeometric and Geometric periods which include a ninth-century BC bronze bowl of Phoenician workmanship, a figurine of a beast of burden carrying a load of four jars, a round terracotta work-basket with a design of swastikas surmounted by four geometric horses, and a water-jug in the form of a ship's hull. In Room III, devoted to black-figured and red-figured vases from the Archaic to the Hellenistic periods, there is a fine sixth-century BC *amphora*, found in a child's grave. It is decorated with three black figures advancing across the painted band in a Dionysiac dance processional. Room IV is the repository of sherds of *amphorae* which received awards for their outstanding workmanship at the conclusion of the Panathenaic procession.

North-west of the Kerameikos a series of dreary streets leads to the site of Plato's Academy, the southern corner of which is marked by the Church of *Agios Triphon*. All that remains is an ancient boundary stone – amid the garages and workshops of suburban, working-class Athens. Nearby are the remains of a prehistoric settlement: sections of walls, the foundations of an elliptical building as well as other habitations, a necropolis which has yielded vases and tools in obsidian; proof, if it were needed, that the Attic plain was inhabited in the Heroic Age.

On the way back from the Kerameikos turn right at Monastiraki Square, after crossing the railway, you enter the **Agora**. It would be a mistake to expect any of the splendour, complexity or visible ruins of the Roman Forum. One's first impression is of a vast bomb-site: the ancient market place, once the social, commercial and administrative hub of Athens where business was transacted, legislation passed and gossip exchanged, lies in a hollow, littered with ruined fortifications, eroded plinths and truncated columns – a legacy of desolation left by the Heruli, a northern tribe associated with the earliest Gothic invasions.

The pathway follows the route of the Panathenaic procession. On the right, on plinths ornamented with olive branches, rise three giant statues of Tritons with elaborate fish-tails. This Stoa of the Giants – there were originally six – faces the odeion of the second century AD (the orchestra and proscenium are easily identified). The route followed by the Panathenaic procession then reached the vast **Stoa of Attalus**, now entirely rebuilt of Pentelic marble, Piraeus limestone and local clay tiles: the work of the American School of Classical Studies. The original *stoa* was commissioned in the second century BC by Attalus, a philhellenic king of Pergamum. Although destroyed in the Herulian sack, much of the original masonry and materials remained *in situ* and were used in the reconstruction, completed in 1956. The *stoa* consists of superimposed colonnades of 134 columns, the lower Doric, the upper Ionic (Pergamum style). The marbles have not yet acquired the patina of age, but it is a prodigious achievement and the cool, spacious colonnades are an authentic replica of a market hall at the end of the Hellenistic era. The sculptures discovered in the course of successive excavations are exhibited in chambers, corresponding to the ancient shops, adjoining the colonnade. They include a colossal headless Apollo of the fourth century BC (unnumbered; north end of colonnade, ground floor), a Hellenistic Aphrodite with a headless Eros perched on her shoulder (No. S473), a small but athletic Winged Victory (unnumbered; north end of colonnade, ground floor), a bronze shield (No. B262) captured by the Athenians from the Spartans during the Peloponnesian War, a statue base of the *Iliad* (No. I1628) with an inscription which begins: 'I am the Iliad, which lived before and after Homer . . .', a mechanical device called the Cleroterion (No. I3967) for the assignment of public duties by lot; as well as vases, inscriptions, figurines and sherds of different periods.

Proceeding clockwise from the *stoa*, one passes the foundations of public buildings: the Library of Pantainus (the restored eleventh-century Church of *Agioi Apostoli*, slightly to the south of the library, contains indifferent wall paintings); the Tholos, a circular fifth-century BC edifice, where dwelt fifty magistrates who constituted a permanent commission to the Senate; the fifth-century BC *Bouleuterion* (Senate); and the *Metroön*. At this point a path ascends to the **Theseion**, which dominates the Agora from a terrace laid out with flowerbeds. Myrtle and pomegranates grow in large clay pots: replicas of ancient vessels found in hollows cut out of the neighbouring rock, they were once watered by artificial streams whose source was on the Pnyx. The temple is not, of course, a temple of Theseus at all. The origin of the misnomer lies in the fact that the *metopes* depict the exploits of the Attic hero. It was, in all likelihood, a temple of Hephaestus, god of forges, and the whole vicinity was inhabited by blacksmiths.

The temple, of the Doric order, the first in Greece to be built entirely of marble, is dated to the mid-fifth century BC (just prior to the Parthenon) and was one of the earliest attempts to restore the monuments destroyed during the Persian invasion. Bronze statues of Hephaestus and Athena Hephaistia, patron deities of industrial workers, adorned the *cella*. It has thirty-eight columns (six instead of the usual eight on either front) with a pronounced convexity in the shaft. Of the remaining eighteen *metopes*, ten (east front) represent the exploits of Heracles and eight (north and south) those of Theseus. The *pronaos* frieze, which is very mutilated, depicts a battle (unidentified) watched by six Olympian deities. The vaulted roof of the interior dates from the fifth century AD, when the temple, like so many others, was converted into a Byzantine shrine. Although it is the best-preserved classical temple in Greece, the Theseion is not the most inspiring. The plain Doric style, so supremely effective in Ictinus's monumental plan of the Parthenon, loses much of its vitality in the smaller edifice. Its position, lying in a trough between the Acropolis and the western hills, may also account for its lack of authority. Nevertheless, when seen from the upper gallery of the Stoa of Attalus, framed within surrounding shrubberies, it appears startlingly alive in its exterior completeness.

The clockwise route leads down to the Agora again. On the left lie the foundations of a small temple of Apollo Patroös (fourth-century BC), followed by bases of columns and fragments of pediments marking the site of the Stoa of Zeus, in whose shade Socrates lectured to students. On the right is the site of the Altar of the Twelve Gods, the starting point for the measurement of all distances from Athens, and, beyond it, the main entrance to the Agora.

On the way back to Syntagma Square, you may turn left at the corner of Ermou and Aiolou Streets. A pretty flower-market extends across the little square of Agia Irene, beside a church of the same name. Pots of gardenias, oleanders and hibiscus, their scarlet trumpets turned towards the sun, are ranged beside orange trees in wooden tubs and boxes filled with basil; clematis and Bougainvillea trail from trellised bamboo sticks.

Halfway up Ermou Street there is a charming view of the little eleventh-century **Church of the Kapnikarea**. One of the best preserved Byzantine churches in the capital, the Kapnikarea is a typical example of the cruciform plan, which was established throughout the Greek mainland in the twelfth century. It is built of stone embellished with brick courses. The little cupola above the additional chapel on the north side is an example of the tendency to increase the number of domes. The outer porch with its two small columns has a very coquettish air, and it leads, in turn, to the

45

beautifully decorated door with its marble jambs and lintels. The frescoes in the interior are modern, but good.

Between the Kapnikarea and Syntagma Square, Ermou Street becomes a crowded shopping quarter. At the corner of Syntagma Square, two large pavement cafés, Papaspyrou and Dionysos, get all the morning sun. On summer nights they are the haunt of the demi-monde and the tourists.

CHAPTER 3

Athens: 'The City of Hadrian'

Hadrian's Gateway – The Temple of Olympian Zeus –
The Stadium – The Benaki Museum –
The Byzantine Museum – Mount Lycabettus –
The Church of the Holy Theodores –
The National Archaeological Museum – Colonus.

In summer the city might, with the help of an occasional strong north wind, resume its former impression of dazzling whiteness. But the enormous spread of undistinguished and undistinguishable blocks of flats now covering the plain from the sea to the foothills of the surrounding mountains, is often blanketed by the notorious *nephos* – the cloud – an obnoxious mixture of chemical fumes which has made Athens Europe's most polluted capital. The demolition of whole areas built during the nineteenth and early twentieth centuries was stopped too late to prevent an endless dreary, modern sameness. The one relieving feature, the lavish use of Pentelic marble, has been abandoned since the 1981 earthquake, for fear that the slabs might be dislodged. Here and there skyscrapers tower above the relentless sea of concrete.

However several worthwhile visits can be made, both in the ancient Roman city, an area of public gardens and residential streets lined with false-pepper trees, and in the modern city which surrounds it. One should begin at the entrance to the National Gardens and follow Amalias Avenue as far as the statue of Byron in the arms of Hellas, represented by a female figure. At this point, **Hadrian's Gateway** marks the boundary between the two ancient cities – Greek and Roman. Two inscriptions on the frieze give the directions: to the west, 'This is Athens, in times past the City of Theseus';

47

to the east, 'But this is Hadrian's and no longer the City of Theseus'.

The gateway, its Roman arch surmounted by a Greek portico probably intended to symbolize the marriage of the Greek and Roman worlds, was not one of the happiest architectural achievements of the Emperor's reign. Hadrian was himself something of an amateur architect: a fact which may account for the gateway's lack of professionalism. Originally, it may have looked more impressive framed between the two Corinthian columns on either side whose bases are still visible, but it could never have borne comparison with any of the great triumphal arches of Rome. The marble arch rests on two square Corinthian columns. The Greek portico on the upper level has three bays, the middle one crowned by a pediment. The effect is one of awkwardness, of something which has not quite come off. Nevertheless, it remains a landmark, marooned in traffic-choked central Athens.

The gateway leads to the esplanade of the **Temple of Olympian Zeus**, supported on both sides by strong buttresses, of which there were originally a hundred. The history of the temple, one of the most impressive ruins in Athens, is a chequered one. It was begun by the Peisistratae in the sixth century BC on the site of an older Archaic temple. Work was interrupted by the fall of the Peisistratae and the Persian wars, but was resumed in the second century BC by a Seleucid king of Syria who would employ none but the best Roman architects. It was finally completed in 132 AD by Hadrian, who placed a majestic effigy of himself and a jewelled snake beside the gold and ivory statue of Zeus in the *cella*. During the Middle Ages the temple served as a quarry.

Close by the partially restored Propylaia of the temple lie some gigantic column bases of the earlier edifice; to the west are vestiges of an ancient road and the ubiquitous walls of Themistocles. Further west are the foundations of a Roman thermal establishment with column bases at the west end and of two fourth-century BC houses among the juniper bushes.

The temple itself is approached from the Propylaia. With two rows of twenty columns at the sides, three of eight at each front, it was one of the largest in the Graeco-Roman world. The Roman architects' attempt to extend the columns to the greatest possible height, without giving them an air of exaggerated attenuation, is completely successful. No Greek architect of the classical age would have dreamed of going so far. Of the 124 columns only 15 remain – tall and fluted, their magnificent Corinthian capitals adorned with elaborate acanthus leaf mouldings. Impressive at all times, they seldom look more magical than when floodlit at night, emerging from the penumbra of the surrounding gardens.

To the left of the entrance to the temple enclosure an acacia-lined alley leads to another field of ruins below the retaining wall of the esplanade. It is a scene of considerable confusion, but archaeologists have recently identified the foundations of temples of the Archaic period and of the fifth and second centuries BC. To the south-east is a cliff-face: site of the Callirhoe Spring (the beautifully flowing), the only source of good drinking water in ancient Athens.

Beyond the Temple of Olympian Zeus, Vasilissis Olgas Avenue runs between the Zappeion Gardens on one side and a tennis club, swimming pool and playground on the other. A clearing between the shrubberies of the Zappeion Gardens reveals the neo-classical porch of a large horseshoe-shaped building, Athens' congress centre. Vasilissis Olgas Avenue ends in a curved junction. Turning to the left one almost immediately reaches the **Stadium**, built in a wide ravine of the pine-clad hill of Aedettos in the fourth century BC, and capable of accommodating more than sixty thousand spectators. Five centuries later its forty-four tiers were faced with marble at the expense of Herodes Atticus, a public-spirited millionaire. An idea of the magnitude of the work is obtained from the fact that as many as a thousand wild beasts took part in the gladiatorial shows and Roman circuses over which Hadrian presided. In the Middle Ages the stadium was reduced to a quarry. Later travellers described it as overgrown with corn, the crumbling *diazômas* as grazing grounds for goats. In 1895 a modern Herodes Atticus, George Averoff, a wealthy cotton merchant, financed the reconstruction and refacing of the tiers with Pentelic marble, and the first revived Olympic games were held there the following year.

From the highest tier of the Stadium there is a good view of Hadrian's Athens and its twentieth-century expansion. Irodou Atticou Street, a cool shaded way, mounts gradually from the Stadium to the new Palace on the right. Further up, at the junction with Vasilissis Sophias Avenue (corner of Koumbari Street) is the

Benaki Museum which acts as a curtain-raiser to the great religious art of Thessaloniki, Mistra and Mount Athos, where late Byzantine art flourished during the fourteenth and fifteenth centuries. Two generations of a family of cotton magnates from Alexandria have dedicated themselves to the assembly of this impressive collection of icons, jewellery, silverware, woodcarving, embroideries and relics of the War of Independence. Wandering through the spacious, high-ceilinged rooms of this former private residence, one is constantly being reminded, as one turns from bejewelled weapons to gorgeous chasubles, from religious paintings to lavish textiles, of the proximity of Italy in the west, of Islam in the east.

Room A contains relics of the War of Independence (No. 955 is Byron's portable writing-desk). Large canvasses of battle scenes by Greek nineteenth-century artists recall the swashbuckling manner of Delacroix's imitators. Ecclesiastical objects from various parts of Asia Minor fill Room B. No. 31 is a gorgeously embroidered banner from the Pontus. Room Γ is devoted to Byzantine and post-Byzantine works: an elaborate icon-stand in gilt carved wood; a large sixteenth-century icon of the Transfiguration (No. 123); a St Anne and the Virgin (in a scarlet mantle), painted by Emmanuel Tzanes, an important iconographer of the sixteenth-century Cretan School (No. 126); the Hospitality of Abraham (No. 64), a fourteenth-century symbolical representation of the Holy Trinity (the relaxed attitudes of the figures are unusual in a Byzantine icon, and the subtle shading of reds and blues is rendered with great sophistication).

Room E contains objects of Turkish provenance of the sixteenth and seventeenth centuries. The show-piece is a restored seventeenth-century reception room from Cairo, with a mosaic floor, a fountain and a cascade from which water trickles into a small basin. The tiles are Persian, the inscriptions Cufic, the atmosphere cool and redolent of a grand Moslem house. On the walls sixteenth-century velvet fabrics from Brusa are decorated with floral designs of brightly coloured tulips and carnations. Upstairs in Room Z there are two sixteenth-century icons of the Nativity (Nos 516 and 518) and the 'Miracles of the Holy Girdle' (No. 1150), all with a pronounced Venetian influence.

More relics of the War of Independence in Room H include an

unusual painting of the 'Battle of Karpenisi' (No. 646). The painter was an uneducated peasant and his aerial view of the set-piece battle is crude and childish, but the detail is full of charm and fantasy. Room K contains two early El Grecos. The first (No. 1542), a much-mutilated icon of St Luke painting the Virgin, is of purely historical interest, being the only extant work of El Greco in the style of the Cretan School of iconography; it was painted before he left his native Crete for Venice. The other (No. 1543) is an Adoration of the Magi, an early work, belonging to the period of the artist's apprenticeship in the studio of the aged Titian, whose guiding hand is discernible in the architectural background, the approach to foreshortening and the balanced grouping of the figures. In Room Λ there is a large seventeenth-century bed, its curtains and pillows embroidered with threads of light green, brick red and Prussian blue. The jewellery in Room N ranges from gold cups of the third millennium BC to French gold snuff-boxes. Case 106 contains a collection of rare Byzantine jewellery.

The Chinese ceramics in Room Ξ (Neolithic, T'ang, Sung, Ming) are displayed against a background of sumptuous carpets from Isfahan and Samarkand. In Room I there is a comprehensive selection of embroideries (mostly seventeenth- and eighteenth-century) from the islands of Greece and Epirus. The most elaborately worked pieces were usually reserved for household objects, such as pillow-cases, bedspreads and valances. In the basement there is a magnificent collection of national costumes and, in a small room beside the staircase leading to the upper storey, a collection of strange Graeco-Roman bone carvings – crude but fascinating depictions of Dionysus, Aphrodite and various marine deities and sea monsters gambolling in the waves, thought to have been used as ornamental adjuncts to pieces of furniture.

Koumbari Street leads into Kolonaki Square (more officially Filikis Etairias) on the slope of Lycabettus. The small garden, with orange trees round a fountain, is the haunt of the elderly in the mornings. The centre of a smart residential quarter containing the more sophisticated nightclubs, the square retains an atmosphere of old-fashioned intimacy, trying to come to terms with impersonal modernity. Two sides are lined with confectioners' shops, where Athenians, young and old, sit for hours in the spring and autumn sunshine, interlarding their conversation with Anglo-American slang. From Kolonaki Square you return to Vasilissis Sophias along Douka Street where the new Goulandris Museum is well worth visiting to see the beautiful Cycladic statuettes.

Vasilissis Sophias Avenue is lined with embassies and expensive blocks of flats which have replaced the nineteenth-century neo-classical houses of the old Athenian families. To the left, just beyond the isolated block of the Officers' Club, is the **Byzantine Museum**. Preceded by a rectangular court, with a marble fountain flanked by two cypress trees, the main building is a rectangular block with a double loggia, designed in 1840 (as the residence of the Duchesse de Plaisance). The Byzantine Museum might well be visited (or revisited) *after* the traveller has been initiated into the iconographic complexities of this thousand-year-old art at the more important sites of Daphni, Hosios Loukas and Mistra, for then the amorphous objects – many of a liturgical character – displayed in the museum fall into place more easily and their significance is more quickly grasped.

Room I (ground floor) contains early Byzantine sculpture: No. 92, a boy bearing a calf, reminiscent of the 'Moscophorus' in the Acropolis Museum; No. 93, Orpheus, his head crowned by an eagle, playing on a lyre to the animals which form an open-work frame round the figure; No. 95, a crude but charming nativity, with two Giottoesque papier-mâché trees on either side of the crib. More sculptures (plaques with crosses, Byzantine eagles and effigies of the Virgin) crowd Room II. Room III is in the form of a recon-structed but not altogether convincing Byzantine cruciform church with marble revetments. In Room IV there is an *iconostasis* with elaborate woodcarving, twelve panels representing scenes from the life of Christ and a canopy surmounted by a colourful model of a Byzantine church painted with floral designs and scenes from the life of the Virgin. The first room (right) on the upper floor contains illuminated manuscripts and icons. Among the latter: a Crucifixion (No. 157) with a star-studded background; a Virgin and Child framed within a sequence of the twelve feasts of the Orthodox calendar (No. 177); a beautiful fourteenth-century Crucifixion (No. 169), the elongated, columnar figures of an anguished Virgin and St John, wearing brown and dark blue, silhouetted against a background of the houses of Jerusalem depicted in a narrow band along the lowest section of the panel.

On the walls of the second room hang fragments of thirteenth-century church frescoes. In the third room are displayed censers, chalices, sprinklers and charming little diptychs and triptychs. The fourth room is full of church vestments, together with the celebrated *epitaphios* from Thessaloniki: an exquisite fourteenth-century embroidery depicting the Lamentation over the body of Christ. At once a technical *tour de force* and a masterpiece of one of the minor arts, it is composed in three panels, with the outstretched body dominating the middle one. The figures are woven with gold and silver threads, and stencilled with blues and greens against a gold background; the stitches are so varied that they create an impression of constantly changing colour-tones.

On the way out, it is worth entering the wing on the right which contains more icons of all periods, glittering with golds, reds and blues: a St Andrew (No. 1545); an austere seventeenth-century St John the Baptist (No. 1578), with chestnut-coloured wings outstretched against a background of gold and green; a seventeenth-century Descent into Hell (No. 1210), in which a scarlet-robed Christ is surrounded by prophets and kings; a fourteenth-century Virgin and Child (No. 1582), known as the *Panayia Glycophilousa* (The Sweetly Kissing Virgin), an outstanding relic brought to Greece by refugees from Asia Minor in 1922, which looks like the archetype of all Duccio's madonnas.

The adjoining block is the War Museum; weapons, uniforms, flags and martial miscellany. Opposite, Loukianou Street passes the British Ambassador's Residence. This was once the home of Eleutherios Venizelos, Greece's greatest twentieth-century statesman, liberator of Crete and architect of the victorious Balkan wars. Further along Vasilissis Sophias is the Hilton Hotel – a crescent-shaped palace of marble that might have aroused the envy of Hadrian. Beside the Hilton is the National Picture Gallery (*Ethnike Pinacotheke*), filled with Greek nineteenth-century paintings, some Flemish works and four El Grecos. One of these is of considerable distinction: 'The Angels' Concert', an unfinished work, depicting a complex group of swirling figures mantled in draperies that follow the contours of their contorted attitudes. At this point Ioannis

Gennadeiou Street leads up the slope of Lycabettus to the fine neo-classical building of the Gennadeion Library, which possesses a collection of books on Greece, Byronic relics and Edward Lear watercolours.

The streets leading from Vasilissis Sophias Avenue into Kolonaki ascend the lower slopes of **Mount Lycabettus**. At the top of Loukianou Street a path zigzags up to the summit of the pinnacled crag. The funicular railway starts from the corner of Aristippou and Cleomenous Streets. At Easter a Resurrection service is held in the whitewashed chapel of St George which crowns the peak, and soon after midnight a long candlelight procession winds down the hill like a trail of glow-worms. Immediately below the chapel there is an expensive restaurant. On the rare days of clear visibility the view embraces the whole of the plain and the Saronic Gulf, with the distant hump of Acro-Corinth in the west.

The streets leading down from Kolonaki to the centre of the city are lined with elegant boutiques. Two parallel one-way streets between Syntagma Square and Omonoia Square form the main axis of central Athens. Stadiou Street passes Kolokotronis Square, with its equestrian statue of Kolokotronis, hero of the War of Independence, and a more modest marble statue of Tricoupis, a nineteenth-century statesman, standing in front of the Old Parliament building which now houses the National Historical Museum. The Museum of the City of Athens, situated in a modest house built in 1833, King Otho's first residence in his new capital, is on Paparigopoulou Street at the side of Klafthmonos Square. Off the bottom corner of the square stands the eleventh-century Byzantine **Church of Agioi Theodoroi**, built of stone with brick courses and an exterior Cufic frieze. Cruciform in plan, with a tall drum (a feature of the small Byzantine churches in Athens), its proportions are exquisite.

From Klafthmonos Square, Korais Street (pedestrians only) leads up to E. Venizelou Avenue, more commonly known by its original name of Panepistimiou (University) Street. Immediately facing one rises an imposing group of neo-classical buildings. From left to right: the National Library, faced with a Doric portico; the University, with painted colonnade and, in front, two statues: of Korais, champion of linguistic reform, and of Gladstone, whose government ceded the Ionian islands to Greece in 1864; finally, the

Academy, with a portico and pediment, and statues of Plato and Socrates seated on either side of the entrance. All three edifices were built of Pentelic marble on plans drawn up by nineteenth-century Danish architects. The group of buildings is dominated by two tall, fluted columns crowned with statues of Apollo playing his lyre and Athena armed with lance and shield. The traffic jams, the creeping line of blue buses and yellow trolley-buses, the impatient pedestrians fulminating against the red lights – all the stridency of a modern Mediterranean street – seem to enhance the incongruity of this splendid display of neo-classical panache emphasized by Lycabettus in the distance, its fantastic peak rising out of a sea of apartment blocks.

Between the University and Syntagma Square there are several landmarks among the shops of Panepistimiou Street: the Bank of Greece; the Catholic cathedral of St Denis the Areopagite; the neo-classical mansion, scheduled to house the Numismatic Museum, in which Heinrich Schliemann, excavator of the sites of Troy and Mycenae, lived with his Greek wife. Parallel to Panepistimiou Street runs Academias Street, with more shops and offices and a little modern opera house, the *Lyriki Skene*, where in 1942 an as-yet unknown plump young girl called Maria Callas, with a hauntingly deep-throated voice, made her debut in *Tosca*. In the opposite direction from the University, Panepistimiou Street descends towards Omonoia Square, the centre of a network of crowded commercial streets, and a station on the railway which links Piraeus and the northern suburbs with the capital. The National Theatre, whose annual season (November–April) often begins with a play by Shakespeare, is round the corner in Constantinou Street.

From Omonoia Square, Patission Street, a long straight avenue, penetrates into another world: the residential area of Patissia, a dreary suburb dating from the inter-war years, once the mecca of the new bourgeoisie. The first large building on the right is the marble Polytechnic School and School of Fine Art. Beyond it a wispy public garden, with some tired-looking palm trees, forms a frontage to the **National Archaeological Museum**. Here are some, if not most, of the greatest ancient sculptures in the world: monumental and diminutive, Archaic, Classical and Hellenistic;

and a collection of painted vases ranging from huge *amphorae* to delicate *lecythoi*, so vast and varied in execution and detail that the imagination boggles at the ingenuity of the ancient potter's skill. Smaller objects, daggers, jewels, figurines, death-masks, shields, ornamental boxes, inscriptions, even toys, enable one to obtain a picture – hazy and confused perhaps, but still whole and in the round – of man's tastes and occupations, of his changing attitudes to religion, sex, death, recreation and athletics, from Mycenaean to Roman times. The existing arrangement of the exhibits is not ideal; the rooms are not always numbered (nor are some of the exhibits); and there is, as yet, no complete catalogue.

Immediately facing the entrance is the Mycenaean room, filled with gold objects excavated from the royal shaft tombs at Mycenae and other prehistoric sites. The quantity of gold objects is breathtaking; equally astonishing is the degree of sophistication achieved by the jewellers, potters and goldsmiths of this prehistoric age.

A pedestal, holding the gold death-mask of an Achaean king of the fifteenth century BC, faces the entrance to the Mycenaean room. No. 384 is a drinking cup in the form of a bull's head, with horns and muzzle of gold, and a golden sun, composed of strap-shaped petals on the brow. The bull-taming scenes on the 'Vaphio gold cups' (Nos. 1758, 1759) illustrate the perfection achieved by representational art in the Mycenaean age. In the large 'Warrior vase' (c. 1200 BC) heavily armed hoplites march in single file, while a woman standing at the end of the processional bids them farewell. All the robustness and militaristic vigour of the Mycenaean world, as opposed to the more effete charms of palace life in Minoan Crete, seem to be represented here. Two cases, on either side of the entrance, contain precious objects dating from 1500 to 1200 BC. In the right-hand annexe (where most of the exhibits are idols of Cycladic provenance), No. 3908, a crude but charming statuette, represents a male figure seated on a throne, playing an unidentified musical instrument, possibly a harp. In conception and execution, it might be an object from an exhibition of modern sculpture. Its date is c. 2400–2200 BC.

Back in the entrance hall, one proceeds clockwise into the first of six halls devoted to Archaic sculpture. An air of essential masculinity prevails. The powerfully-built *kouroi* (young men, often athletes, later soldiers), huge monoliths hewn out of the crystalline rock, represent a monumental image of man. The most striking of the earlier *kouroi* is No. 2720 (late-seventh-century BC), '**The Colossus of Sounion**'. The cast of his features, set and wooden, is distinctly Egyptian, but no Rameses possessed the muscular tension or freedom of pose enjoyed by this Greek youth. No. 3686, of a later date, is more evolved. The formal stylization is there, but the excessive stiffness is less evident; the hair is more elaborately arranged and there is a vestige of a smile on the lips which have grown more full and sensual. But it is No. 3851, the '**Anavissos Kouros**', (c. 520 BC) that dominates the scene: a strong-limbed youth, marvellously self-assured, a perfect embodiment of human – though not divine – dignity. Traces of red paint are visible on the coral-shaped locks that fall down his shoulders from the head-band, and the whole surface of Parian marble has a roseate glow. His smile is more radiant than that of any other *kouros*. The modelling is opulent, the tension less extreme.

In the next two halls we pass into the fifth century. The Archaic smile, and the iron self-control and taut muscular strain have gone. Realism has been substituted for symbolism. In the Eleusinian votive relief (No. 126), Demeter presents an ear of corn to her protégé, the youthful Triptolemus, who is commanded to instruct man in the cultivation of the earth, while Koré crowns him. The 'young athlete crowning himself' (No. 3344) is another work of Attic perfection. In spite of the low relief, the flesh has the resilient quality of youth; the boy's thoughtful expression reflects the solemnity with which victory on the race-track fills him.

The bronze **Poseidon** (No. 15161), a work of the mid-fifth century, drawn up from the sea-bed off Cape Artemision, represents the god as larger than life-size, his left arm outstretched, his right hand holding a trident (which is missing) about to be hurled. Nothing better expresses the Greek concept of a god as a physically perfect man than this springy, superbly healthy Poseidon.

The next six rooms (the first three separated from the others by a rectangular hall) contain the *stelae* (marble grave-stones carved in relief so high that the figures appear to be sculpted in the round) which lined the alleys of the Kerameikos and other ancient necropolises. The scenes represented are intimate family affairs. The departing soul, with a remote other-worldly expression, is often depicted in the act of shaking hands with its next-of-kin. Every visitor has, or will have, his own favourites. Among the ones I never like to miss are No. 717, an athlete, the so-called 'Salamis youth', who holds a bird in one hand and raises the other in a farewell gesture, his young escort leaning mournfully against a marble plinth; No. 3790, a servant girl holding up a baby in order that the departing mother may cast a last look at it; No. 869, the 'Illisus *stele*', a hooded old man taking leave of his son, a hunter, whose dog and little escort crouch at his feet. Every one of the *stelae* is a variation on the same disturbing theme of man's preoccupation with death, expressed in terms of the artist's sense of perfection of form. In none is the perfection so apparent as in No. 3472, in which a pensive husband, clad in a beautifully-draped *chlamys*, bids farewell to his seated wife.

At the end of the long, rectangular hall the famous '**Jockey Boy**' (No. 15177), a second-century BC bronze, rides a disproportionately large horse (recently and not wholly successfully restored). In the room on the left are terracotta and bronze figurines. No. 16546, Zeus about to hurl a thunderbolt, is almost a replica in miniature of the Poseidon of Artemioin, but perkier, more stocky.

Turning right, and right again, one enters a succession of halls filled with fourth-century BC and Hellenistic sculptures. The '**Ephebe of Anticythera**' (No. 13396) is a striking, if hefty, young man with somewhat effeminate features holding some round object, now missing, in his right hand; but there is a slickness, even an impersonality, about him, as in many fourth-century BC bronzes, which conjures up a vision of a highly efficient sculptor's workshop adept at mass production. The young man is entirely physical, but unlike the sixth-century *kouroi* or the fifth-century riders of the Parthenon frieze, he has no interior life.

Less spectacular, but more compelling, are two bronze heads: one of a 'bearded philosopher' (No. 13400), with piercing inlaid eyes and a face of remarkable intellectual power, and No. 14612, a man of the first century BC, known as the 'Man from Delos' – a meditative creature with a weak, undecided mouth and anguishing doubts. Then turn to the '**Tegean head**' (No. 3602), believed to be by Scopas, representing Hygeia, goddess of health. In the complete harmony of its form, this oval face, crowned by soft wavy hair, is the personification of serenity, a wholly-evolved expression of idealized feminine beauty in Parian marble.

Returning to the central rectangular hall, one passes into the hall of the bronzes (extreme south-east end). First there is a fully clothed and matronly Artemis of heroic stature of the third century BC. The fourth-century BC Athena, crowned by her familiar helmet, decorated with griffons and owls, possesses a more poised and relaxed air.

The second floor of the museum (staircase in the long rectangular hall) possesses the enormous collection of **painted vases**. The evolution of Greek painting from the earliest times can be traced in these products of the potter's workshop. The exhibits are displayed chronologically. But the absence of a catalogue is a handicap. First there are the vases of the Geometric period (twelfth to seventh century BC); then the Archaic period (seventh to mid-sixth centuries), characterized by Orientalizing features, such as lotus flowers, palmettes, sphinxes and other animals. These are followed by Attic vases of the sixth century. The bands have now disappeared and the decoration consists of mythological scenes, the figures painted in black. In the fifth and fourth centuries luminous figures in red appear. These acquire corporeality as they move from left to right in attitudes associated with Dionysiac processionals. By the fifth century the drawing has become exquisitely fine and pure: especially in the **white-ground lecythoi**, slender funerary vessels with black bases and necks. The figures are painted in very light shades with an extraordinary economy and sureness of touch. Originally placed on *stelae*, the *lecythoi* are one of the outstanding contributions made by the fifth-century BC Attic vase painters, with their melancholy depictions of sepulchral scenes in which the figures of the deceased seem to have lost all solid substance as they sit or stand wearily in a kind of occult silence; sometimes they are being ferried across one of the rivers of the Underworld.

At the time of writing, a selection of objects recently excavated on the volcanic island of Santorini, the ancient Thera, is displayed in an annexe to the vase rooms. If not from Plato's Atlantis, as some believe, the Thera finds cast another shaft of light onto the enigma of the prehistoric Mediterranean world. Geologists and archaeologists agree that, in c. 1500 BC, Thera was destroyed by an earthquake, followed by an eruption of such unprecedented violence that showers of pumice and ashes are thought to have buried the Minoan townships of the Cretan seaboard over a hundred miles to the south. A similar fate befell the island capital itself, where a relatively sophisticated civilization flourished contemporaneously with that of Minoan Crete. Patient archaeological research has brought to light a series of astonishing examples of this civilization. Among the **ceramics** are two vessels painted with swallows and ears of barley, nippled ewers used for fertility rights, spouted jars, and a strange utensil, its bottom perforated like a sieve and decorated with white lilies on a reddish-brown ground (Showcase 1); a wine jug painted with crocuses and another nippled ewer looking like a stork or a pelican with its long, upturned spout resembling a beak, are displayed in Showcase 2.

In the **frescoes** there is abundant evidence of the love of nature that inspired artists of the second millennium BC. The best-preserved is the 'Spring' fresco, which originally covered three walls of a room. On a white ground, red lilies sprout in bunches of three from inky-blue rocks, their yellow stems waving in the breeze, while pairs of mating swallows fly overhead. In the 'Boxing Match' fresco, two bejewelled boys with long Minoan-style locks, clad in loin-cloths, are depicted in the stylized attitudes of boxers about to engage in contest. The male head of a so-called 'African' with full, parted lips, wearing a large, round earring of the kind usually associated with Nubians, is thought to suggest the existence of commercial and cultural relations between the Minoan-Mycenaean states and the peoples of North Africa. The upper part of a fresco of a young priestess with pouting, vermilion lips and blue hair is remarkable for its state of preservation. But most astonishing of all is the large wall-painting depicting a naval expedition executed in the manner of a frieze, with scenes of warships, a coastline with three cities and a headland, groups of human figures and lions chasing deer.

Among the furnishings – mementos of a way of life obliterated in a cataclysm of more than Pompeiian proportions – are a three-legged table for keeping food warm, with charcoal placed on a lower shelf, and a wooden bed just large enough to accommodate a member of the undersized prehistoric Mediterranean race.

Before leaving the museum, the visitor should not miss the **Hélène Stathatos Collection**, displayed in a hall to the right of the Mycenaean. It consists of jewellery and gold decorative objects ranging from the Bronze Age to the Byzantine period. The refinement of execution of these objects of the Hellenistic period – probably used as household ornaments by wealthy Athenian families – provides a clear picture of the high standard of taste prevailing in ancient Athens in its days of political decline.

Finally, the Epigraphical Department has a large collection of historical inscriptions, including Themistocles's decree of 480 BC ordering the evacuation of Athens and proclaiming naval mobilization before the battle of Salamis. The Numismatic Department contains cameos as well as Greek, Roman and Byzantine coins. Both are situated on the ground floor of the main museum buildings (entrance in Tositsa Street).

From the Museum, one last pilgrimage leads to the birthplace of Sophocles. Epirou Street, then Neophitou Street, lead westward to Larissa Station, the terminal of all trains from Western Europe and the north. The station has an air of Balkan dereliction: trains are few and far between, as Greeks prefer travelling by plane or coach. A little to the south there is another station – the SPAP (Peloponnese railways) Station. From there Lenorman Street cuts across a sprawling working-class quarter, called Colonus, dominated by a flat rocky mound: the site of the ancient deme of **Colonus**, where Sophocles was born and which he immortalized in his *Oedipus at Colonus*. A marble slab and *loutrophorus* on the summit mark the graves of two philhellenic German archaeologists. There is no memorial to the greatest dramatist in antiquity.

It is a barren, stony place, with a few shrubby pines and dusty cactuses, the box-like houses of suburban Athens spreading for miles around, the Acropolis just visible in the south. The plangent twang of bouzouki records echoes from a little shack: the local taverna. Sophocles was a very old man when he wrote *Oedipus at Colonus*. It was his last play. A deeply religious work, it is full of nostalgia for his beloved birthplace. The story – probably apocryphal – is that he died at the age of ninety, choked by a grape pip, before he could see it performed.

CHAPTER 4

Attica

*The Piraeus – Faliro – Sounion – Thorikos –
The Mesogeia – The Sanctuary of Brauronian Artemis
– The Monastery of Daou-Pendeli – Marathon –
Rhamnous – Mount Pentelikon – The Amphiareion –
Acharnai – Fili – Mount Hymettos –
The Daphni Mosaics – Salamis –
The Eleusinian Mysteries – Eleutherai – Aegosthena.*

Attica is in the form of a triangular peninsula, washed on two sides
by the Aegean Sea. Its main features are its rockiness and the purity
of its light. The soil is poor, but the substratum is so solid and
imporous that it is less subject to earthquakes than most of the
country. Athens sprawls all over the central plain.

The coastline is broken by barren promontories and sandy
beaches fringed with aleppo pines. Ruined sanctuaries and
whitewashed chapels shelter in the folds of rocky valleys. Sheets of
pale grey asphodel, the immortal flower of Elysium, spread across
the hillsides and dusty paths are lined with aloe and wild fig trees,
from whose pliable wood theatre seats, garlands and other ornaments were made in antiquity. The streams are mere trickles, dry in
summer. Goats, for centuries the peasants' main source of wealth,
browse among parched shrubs. Everywhere there is the pungent
scent of thyme and wild marjoram. In spring the boulders are
speckled with round, apple-green tufts of spurge, and the hard
ground is covered by clusters of grape hyacinths and little mirror
orchids with yellow-bordered blue petals. In autumn there are deep
pink cyclamen and golden crocus-like Sternbergia, whose favourite

habitat seems to be around country graveyards. The landscape may not be the most beautiful in Greece, but it is seldom without interest.

An anti-clockwise route is the most practical. First comes **the Piraeus**: a headland five miles from Athens, to which it has long been connected by a flat, built-up area of factories, warehouses and suburban dwellings. It has three harbours which, in ancient times, possessed nearly four hundred ship-houses (sheds with sloping ramps situated on the water's edge). One of the greatest ports of the Eastern Mediterranean and the main industrial centre of Greece, its large residential area lacks distinction. In antiquity the open road-stead of Faliro, a mile and a half away, served as an anchorage. However, in the early fifth century BC, Themistocles realized the use to which the headland and its three sheltered ports could be put. Sea-minded and far-sighted, he built the harbour, encircling it with walls more formidable than those of the Acropolis, and created a fleet. The harbour was completed by Cimon, and Pericles built the Long Walls connecting the capital with its port.

At the end of the Peloponnesian War, when Athens submitted to the superior power of totalitarian Sparta, Lysander ordered the destruction of the Piraeus, as well as the demolition of the Long Walls. It was the end of the imperial dream. During the Middle Ages, the Piraeus was no more than a fishing village, known as Porto Leone.

South of the railway station is Karaiskaki Square and at the head of the port basin is the busy anchorage for the island ferries. Cruise ships dock in front of the huge customs house on the eastern side of the harbour.

From the main harbour it is about ten minutes' walk to the more attractive **Zea**, a crescent-shaped expanse of water, lined with modern blocks of flats. Once the battle station of four hundred triremes, it now shelters a much larger number of yachts and small craft behind the greatly extended breakwater. This is also the starting point for the hydrofoils to the Argo-Saronic islands. Parts of the corniche beyond the naval hospital to the south are buttressed by fragments of ancient walls restored in the fourth century BC by Conon, the distinguished Athenian admiral. To the north-west at Canaris Square is the site of the Skeuotheke, a great arsenal which,

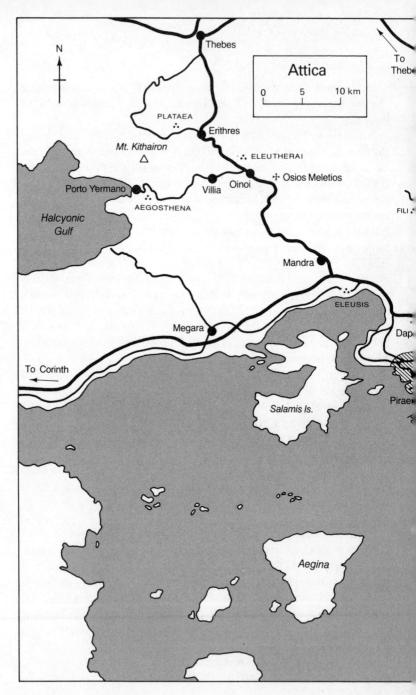

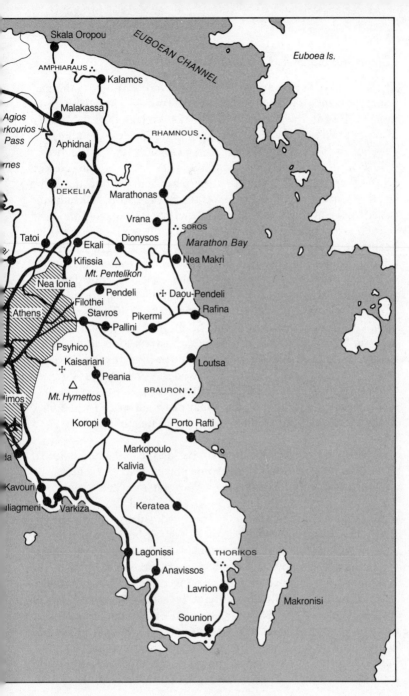

Skala Oropou

EUBOEAN CHANNEL

Euboea Is.

∴ AMPHIARAUS
Kalamos

Malakassa

*Agios
rkourios
Pass*

Aphidnai

RHAMNOUS ∴

rnes

∴ DEKELIA

Marathonas

Vrana

∴ SOROS

Tatoi

Ekali

Dionysos

Marathon Bay

i

Kifissia △

Nea Makri

Mt. Pentelikon

Nea Ionia

Pendeli

⊹ Daou-Pendeli

Filothei

Athens

Stavros

Pikermi

Rafina

Pallini

Psyhico

imos

⊹ Kaisariani

Loutsa

△ Peania

Mt. Hymettos

BRAURON ∴

Koropi

Porto Rafti

la

Markopoulo

Kavouri

Kalivia

liagmeni Varkiza

Keratea

Lagonissi

THORIKOS
∴

Anavissos

Lavrion

Sounion

Makronisi

says Pliny, contained arms for one thousand ships. Near the harbour, in Harilao Trikoupi Street, are the ruins of a little Hellenistic theatre. Beside the theatre the Piraeus Archaeological Museum displays a well-arranged collection of antique finds, including the very fine bronzes of Apollo and Athena found a few years ago.

A winding corniche, parts of whose sides are pock-marked with grottoes and niches for votive offerings, leads to the third and smallest harbour facing the sweep of the Bay of Faliro. **Mikrolimano** (The Small Harbour), the ancient Munychia, is composed of tiers of white houses clinging to two sides of a natural amphitheatre, with a headland, crowned by the Yacht Club, on the third. The waterfront is lined with open-air fish restaurants (indoors in winter) and yachts, caiques, *trechandiria* (fast-sailing fishing-smacks), motor launches and dinghies crowd the oily waters of the miniature harbour.

On the top of **Profitis Ilias**, the hill above the harbour, is a modern open-air theatre with fine views of the three harbours, and of Salamis and the Saronic Gulf. Traces of neo-classical architectural fantasy survive in the sea of concrete: peeling rosette-bordered casements and flaking spiral balustrades – sometimes a ruined Caryatid porch. The corniche winds down to the bay of Faliro where ambitious land reclamation has so far provided space for the huge Peace and Friendship Stadium, an open-air theatre and a fast, new road.

Several tavernas border the road beside the reclaimed land. At these tavernas orchestras of bouzouki players sometimes play to an audience of solemn-faced drinkers. The food is not always good and the uninitiated are inclined to be over-charged. Soon after midnight, which is the best time to go (having dined elsewhere, one can simply order wine and fruit), the local clientèle begins to turn up. As soon as they start to dance, the atmosphere undergoes a breathtaking change. All is now zest and enthusiasm, the music louder, the bouzouki soloists more dashing and inventive in their improvizations. The music, Anatolian in origin, brought to mainland Greece by refugees from Asia Minor, is invariably in the minor key. Of all the dances, the *zeibékiko*, a *pas seul* danced by a man, is the one nearest to the Greek heart. Its main features are complicated acrobatics, scything movements of the arms, repeated slappings of the ground and symbolic gestures connected with sex and Mother Earth.

Past the tavernas lies the Race Course. At right angles to it, Syngrou Avenue leads back to the centre of Athens. Beyond the Race Course the coastal road passes a marina for small cruise ships and yachts, and then the cemetery for British Commonwealth soldiers killed in the Greek campaigns of the Second World War and the 1944 revolution. In December of that year British troops, greeted a month before as liberators with ringing speeches and garlands of flowers, were reluctantly drawn into a murderous five weeks' battle with Greek Communist-led forces.

After Alimos – the ancient Halimus, birthplace of Thucydides – begin the beaches which are uncomfortably crowded at the height of summer. At Glifada there are numerous hotels, another yacht harbour, nightclubs, good (and expensive) fish tavernas; at Kavouri, green with pines, the Cape Zoster of antiquity, smart villas. The two pellucid bays at **Vouliagmeni**, although lined with cabins and hotels, are the most attractive and least polluted. The small harbour is reserved for the more luxurious yachts. The minute fresh-water lake is backed by a forbidding slate-grey cliff. On the isthmus between the two bays the foundations of a sixth-century BC temple of Apollo are surrounded by flowering shrubs. Varkiza comes next: a strand of fine white sand, with a hinterland of rolling vine country, followed by a fiord-like inlet approached through a tunnel of rock; then more and more seaside villas and Lagonissi, with its beaches, Xenias Hotel and expensive bungalows; and Anavissos, once the haunt of smugglers, on the edge of a salt marsh, where the great stocky-limbed *kouros* in the National Museum was discovered in 1936.

After Anavissos comes **Sounion**, the southernmost promontory of Attica, with its hotels and villas, and its temple. The hills behind the steep, pine-clad coastline are bare except for bushes of sage and juniper, with a new purity of contour that suggests the proximity of the Cyclades – Kea and Kithnos are clearly visible.

An isolated, rocky headland, surrounded by vestiges of an ancient semi-circular wall, is crowned by the fifth-century **Temple of Poseidon**, built on a massive substructure necessitated by the conical rise of the ground. The work of the architect of the Thesion, its columns – fourteen of the original thirty-eight still standing – are Doric but more slender than usual. They lack *entasis* and consequently look somewhat fragile, almost like stilts. The flutings, too, are fewer in number than usual and this also probably detracts from the stolidity associated with the Doric order. The dimensions are almost identical to those of the Thesion, except that here the architect has increased the height of the columns. As nothing remains above the architrave of the south colonnade it is difficult to judge what impression the building may have made when crowned with *metopes*, cornice and pediments. In view of the spectacular nature of the position, the increased height should have added something to the upward thrust so singularly lacking in the Thesion. The marble out of which the temple was built came from a local quarry: very white and without the mellow patina that the Pentelic crystalline limestone acquires. Column-bases are disfigured with the scratching of innumerable signatures, including Byron's. The sun-dappled sea is dotted with islands; on a clear day Milos, whence came the Venus in the Louvre, is visible.

The inland road back to Athens passes through Lavrion, the ancient Laurium, where zinc and manganese were until recently mined in place of the silver that contributed so much to the wealth of ancient Athens; by the second century AD the deposits had been exhausted. About one kilometre north of the dusty mining town, surrounded by slag-heaps and the melancholy silhouettes of abandoned chimneys, a branch road to the right leads to the extremely ancient site of **Thorikos**, a Cretan naval station during the Minoan age. Later it was fortified by the Athenians and served as an important military outpost guarding the maritime approaches to the silver mines. On the slope of a hill, overlooking the slag heaps and fields, are the remains of a fourth-century BC theatre, unique in shape and construction: following the declivity of the hillside, the cavea is elliptical instead of semi-circular; a typical example of Greek ingenuity in adapting architectural conventions to the requirements of nature. Originally it must have been little more than a place of entertainment for garrison troops.

Beyond the branch road to Thorikos, the road climbs a steep pass and descends slowly into the plains of **the Mesogeia**. This is the loveliest part of Attica, an undulating vine country streaked with olive groves and dotted with sugar-loaf hills, now in danger of being spoilt by suburban and industrial development. Far to the east the mountains of Euboea, a chain of peaks snow-capped in winter and infinite in their variety of forms, suggests the approach of another world. Byzantine shrines are scattered about the countryside. The most interesting are the eleventh-century Church of the *Taxiarchoi* (The Archangels) at Kalivia, believed to have been built on the foundations of an Early Christian basilica, and two churches at Markopoulo: the domeless *Agios Georgios* in an olive grove and *Agios Petros*, where fragments of Greek, Roman and Early Christian art have been discovered. All are within easy walking distance of the main road, although the keys may have to be obtained from the village as the churches are usually locked. Markopoulo has been proposed as the site of the Athens Wine Festival should it be moved from Daphni.

The red soil of the Mesogeia is the richest in Attica, the villages the most prosperous. Many inhabitants are of Albanian origin, and some still speak a native dialect. Descendants of seventeenth-century immigrants, imported to cultivate a countryside rapidly becoming depopulated under Ottoman maladministration, they continue to dwell in their original settlements, mostly in Attica and the Peloponnese.

The east coast has a succession of sandy beaches. One of the most attractive is Porto Rafti, an almost circular bay, its seaward entrance little more than a mile wide and guarded by a small island crowned with a Roman statue. A fork to the north from the Porto Rafti road leads past a Frankish tower of the thirteenth century into a shallow valley, where an orchard of fig trees winds towards a marshland and the sea. The swamp, bordered by low hills, is the site of **ancient Brauron**.

Excavations on the marshy site have revealed a large fifth-century BC *stoa* (parts of the colonnade have been restored) with a marble stylobate. Little now remains but the foundations of the Doric Temple of Artemis. A series of fifth-century BC reliefs of exquisite perfection, portraying sacrificial rites in honour of the goddess, is displayed in the large new museum; seldom have the billowing folds of women's garments been reproduced with such virtuosity. North-west of the sanctuary, on a hillside covered, in early spring, with sheets of pink and white anemones, are the ruins of an Early Christian basilica and a round building believed to have been a baptistry.

After rejoining the main road one reaches Paeania, most northerly of Mesogeian villages, where there is a modern church in the main square decorated with frescoes by Kontoglou, a painter of this century who turned to Byzantium of the Palaeologue epoch for his models. Every inch of space is covered with frescoes of saints, prophets, warrior angels, Fathers of the Church and all the familiar scenes from the lives of Christ and the Virgin. The great composition of the *Dodecaorton* (the Twelve Feasts), with which the traveller will soon become familiar, are as stylized as anything in the great Byzantine churches. The skill in imitation is so remarkable that one is inclined to ignore the technical virtuosity. In terms of pure pastiche, the Paeania church is a *tour de force*.

The Vorres Museum, an interesting folklore collection made by a Greek-Canadian, is housed in three restored village houses and a stable; the striking modern wing now accommodates a large and important collection of contemporary Greek art. A road zig-zags halfway up Hymettos to the Koutouki Cave, which is worth visiting; it is well lit, with multicoloured stalactites and stalagmites in several caverns. This side of Hymettos is steep, bare and desiccated, gashed with rocky ravines, and has none of the rounded smoothness of the western flanks which often make this extraordinary mountain look like a huge grey elephant sprawling across the plain.

At Stavros, north of Paeania, there is a fork and the west-bound road leads back to Athens, skirting the northern ridge of Hymettos, which is crowned by the little Byzantine church of St John the Hunter, rather stylishly restored. A whole circuit of south-east Attica has been completed: a long drive.

The eastbound road from Stavros cuts across the northern Mesogeia to the Euboean channel and the field of Marathon. At Pallini a branch road leads to the pine-fringed beach of Loutsa. Beyond Pikermi, where there are good tavernas, the road crosses the gully where a party of distinguished English and Italian travellers, driving back from a visit to the battlefield of Marathon in 1870, were kidnapped by brigands, and subsequently murdered.

At the next fork, one road leads east to Rafina, a little port lined with overcrowded fish restaurants, whence ferries sail for Southern Euboea, Andros and several of the Cyclades; another road climbs the foothills of Pentelikon in a north-westerly direction to the **Monastery of Daou-Pendeli**, concealed in a lonely pine forest. Osbert Lancaster called the church (twelfth-century, restored in the seventeenth), 'a dotty triumph of provincial art'. It is indeed a curiosity, with numerous arches and six domes, the tallest surmounting the narthex which is on a different level from the main hexagonal body of the church. Armenian and Georgian influences, seldom encountered on the Greek mainland, have been at work here.

The main road continues to dip down towards the sea: a wide bay, the **Bay of Marathon**, scimitar-shaped, the waves often flecked with white horses raised by the Etesian wind; opposite rise the mountains of Euboea, denuded of vegetation, without a village in sight. Pine-covered hills roll back from the narrow coastal belt, now dotted with bungalows, hotels and camping sites. Across these hills the runner, according to the apocryphal story, raced to Athens to announce the outcome of the battle, only to die of exhaustion on reaching the stadium.

Marathon (490 BC) was the first of the three great battles which the Athenians waged with such extraordinary success against the immensely superior power mobilized by Darius for what historians believe may have been an attempt at a great Asiatic invasion of Europe. The effect of the victory, though neither as important nor as decisive as Salamis (for the Persians came again, ten years later, in redoubled strength), was immense in terms of morale.

The site is now a reclaimed marshland. At the point where the foothills advance closest to the shore, a signposted road leads through groves of mimosa to the Soros, a mound raised over a floor on which archaeologists have found traces of charcoal and human bones: the bones of the Greek dead. Pieces of flint have been identified as arrowhead fragments, used by the Persian archers. Although Herodotus says the battle was fought close to a swamp, the Soros is surrounded now by arable land, with vineyards and lemon groves criss-crossed by ditches filled with Rose of Sharon lilies in early spring. On one side rise the woodland spurs of Pentelikon, on the other flow the blue waters of the Euboean Channel.

Beyond the fork to the Soros (with, to the north, the lovely

71

crescent-shaped beach of Schina, fringed with tall pines) another side road runs west to the hamlet of **Vrana**. Below a steep hill is another tumulus overgrown with asphodel, believed to be the tomb of the Plataeans, the only Greeks who came to the aid of the hard-pressed Athenians. In the Plataean memorial eight graves, each with a skeleton – one of an officer who is actually named – have been uncovered.

On the outskirts of Vrana is the museum whose chief interest lies in finds from the nearby estate of Herodes Atticus, banker and friend of the Emperor Hadrian. The large and ugly construction adjoining the museum, roofed with corrugated iron, covers two grave circles. They contain skeletons of the undersized men who inhabited Attica in the Middle Helladic period; there is also a skeleton of a horse, equally undersized. At various points on the Marathonian plain, vestiges of prehistoric foundations and masonry suggest the extreme antiquity of this part of Attica.

About a mile from the village of Marathonas, a turning to the right leads across a stretch of open country to the site of **Rhamnous**. The terrace was a sacred enclosure, supported on two sides by a retaining wall composed of blocks of dazzling white marble. The foundations of the larger of two edifices have been identified as those of a temple of Nemesis, Goddess of Retribution. Of the Doric order, probably the work of the architect of the Thesion, it contained a colossal statue in Parian marble of the goddess. The London Society of Dilettanti shipped parts of the head to the British Museum in the early nineteenth century, while the innumerable fragments of the body have recently been put together into the only surviving cult statue of the Golden Age: the work of Agoracritus, Phidias' pupil. The temple was never completely finished, for the three steps of the stylobate have not been smoothed and a number of drums of columns lying about the site have not been fluted. The small temple, almost contiguous to the larger, was a sixth-century BC shrine of Themis, Goddess of Justice, destroyed by the Persians.

From the sacred enclosure one descends along a steep path, lined by tombs, to the shore which is dominated by a knoll on which there are remnants of the ancient acropolis. A massive fourth-century BC stone wall, almost gold in colour, emerges from the evergreens: the remains of the ancient Temple of Rhamnous. Within the acropolis, thick with brushwood and tangled vines, there are vestiges of watch-towers, barrack-rooms, cisterns and the *cavea* of a theatre. Clearly a garrison was stationed at Rhamnous – presumably to guard the entrance to the Euboean Channel. The upland valley with its sacred enclosure, the lonely glen, and the crumbling fortifications on the deserted shore have an austere quality which few can fail to associate with the Goddess of Retribution.

Rhamnous is a dead-end, though there are vestiges of classical walls on the promontory of Cynosure (the Dog's Tail, so-called after its shape) which lies to the east and is best approached from the southern shore, beyond the Schina beach.

One may return to Athens by another road which forks right at Nea Makri, two kilometres south of the battlefield. This road skirts the northern slopes of Pentelikon, scarred by the modern marble quarries, as far as Dionysos and thence, through the pine-woods and villas of Ekali, to Kifissia and Athens.

Next comes northern Attica. The residential suburb of Psyhico, much favoured by foreign residents, is succeeded by Filothei, equally suburban, less fashionable and named after St Philothei, a well-born nun of the sixteenth century. She owned vast lands and founded a convent, a hospital and a workshop for weaving (from the profits of which she bought Greek girls out of Turkish harems). From Filothei one enters the working-class suburb of Nea Ionia, where it is worthwhile looking at the twelfth-century **Omorphi Ecclesia** (the Beautiful Church) which has a pretty octagonal drum. Much of the original structure has been spoilt by later, inelegant additions. The interior is decorated with frescoes (possibly fifteenth- or sixteenth-century) which are pleasant rather than remarkable. The windows are attractively adorned with Rhodian plates.

Back on the main road, one turns right at the eighth kilometre from Athens and cuts across the endless, undistinguished suburbs of the central Attic plain towards **Mount Pentelikon**, a bluish pyramid, scarred with the ravages of two and a half thousand years of marble quarrying. It is one of the loveliest of Attic landmarks, although crowned now with an all-too-conspicuous radar station. On the left the Pendeli Monastery is surrounded by plane trees. Streams trickle down the sides of the mountain. In summer the mountainside, an outpost of suburbia, is a vast holiday camp with tents and wooden shacks on the high ground above the maisonette belt.

The slopes above the monastery are seamed with disused, ancient quarries: a lunar landscape of white rubble. Mountain goats browse among tufts of heather and thyme which fail to conceal the centuries-old cicatrices. But one cannot approach Pentelikon without a feeling of veneration. The very stuff of the mountain has furnished the raw material for some of the greatest works of sculpture and architecture in the world. 'Of Pentelic marble' – the label is familiar enough from museum catalogues. Distinguished by its opaque quality, in contrast to the snowy whiteness of Parian, Pentelic marble contains traces of iron oxide which, when exposed to the weather, causes it to acquire a warm, honey-coloured patina.

Past the Monastery there is a large square from where a road climbs through the woods on the eastern slopes of Pentelikon to connect with the main road from Athens. However, only a track climbs to two thirteenth-century Byzantine chapels at the entrance to a cave, once the refuge of eremitical monks who chose to worship in this remote, wind-blown place high above the Attic plain. In the south chapel a fragmentary fresco of the Virgin and Child spreads across the little apse. The Annunciation is visible on the east wall. The painted decoration also includes a representation of Michael Choniates, an unusually enlightened Bishop of Athens of the late twelfth century. The decoration of crosses, eagles and inscriptions carved on the rock suggests that the chapel is of a much earlier date than the frescoes: in fact, of the pre-Iconoclastic period. The style of the best-preserved frescoes in the north chapel, which was used for burials, is of a cruder, more provincial character.

To the north-west lies Kifissia, where some old Athenian families still spend the summer, in villas set amid shady gardens where nightingales sing. There are also plenty of hotels and new blocks of flats. At No. 1 Metaxas Street, just off the main square, there is a famous confectioner's shop where an astonishing variety of exotic home-made jams can be bought.

North of Kifissia the National Road passes below a wooded spur of Mount Parnes, with terraced vineyards and olive trees on the slopes of the rolling hills, and cornfields and vegetable plots in the cup-shaped valleys, all rather hidden by the numerous factories beside the road. To the right there is a glimpse of an artificial lake, one of the main water supplies of the capital. The dam of Pentelic marble, completed by American engineers in 1926, prevents the streams that flow down the mountainside in winter from escaping through the numerous gullies into the Marathonian plain.

To the west of the National Road is the ancient village stronghold of Aphidnai. Beyond the village the pine-woods become thicker, more luxuriant. There are entrancing views of the Euboean channel which begins to contract as it nears the Euripos. Branching off the main road through Kapandriti and Kalamos one reaches the **Sanctuary of Amphiaraus**, the Argive seer. The sanctuary is situated in a secluded valley shaded by pine and plane trees. The wind rustling the pine branches is laden with the scent of resin; the only other sound is that of a stream, its banks overgrown with maidenhair fern, trickling down to the sea.

The ruins are easily identified: on the right, the substructure of a large altar; behind it, the foundations of a fourth-century BC Doric temple, with the base of the cult statue in the middle of the *cella*; next, the opening of a spring, sacred to Amphiaraus, from which he reappeared from the Underworld, and into which pilgrims threw coins as a thanksgiving. Numerous bases of statues litter the terrace above the altar; beyond them there is a marble bench, where consultants sat whilst waiting to be allocated sleeping quarters. The bench is at the side of a long and impressive fourth-century BC *stoa*, which had a façade of forty-one Doric columns and was separated into two galleries by a row of seventeen Ionic columns. Here the consultants slept and were visited with oracular dreams. In a pine-clad hollow behind the *stoa* is the most charming ruin of all: a miniature **theatre**, famous for its acoustics. The proscenium, judiciously restored, is embellished with eight Doric half-columns of grey Hymettos marble. Five seats for high priests, admirably preserved, are ranged in a semi-circle round the orchestra.

Another road from Athens to the north runs across the plain to the village of **Acharnai**, where ivy, the symbol of the god Dionysus, is reputed to have grown for the first time. Acharnai, once inhabited by descendants of seventeenth-century Albanian settlers, has now been engulfed by Greater Athens, spreading ever higher into the constraining ring of mountains. Beyond Acharnai the road ascends Mount Parnes, the highest though least beautiful of the mountains which enclose the Attic plain on three sides. About two-thirds of the way up, the firs begin. Just below the summit, where there are ski-runs, there is a cluster of buildings – roadhouses, sanatoria, chalets – among the dark conifers. It is all rather Swiss. There is a luxury hotel with a casino and a swimming pool, situated on a ledge with a spectacular view of central Attica.

A branch road from Acharnai follows a westerly course to the village of **Fili**. Beyond the well-tended Convent of the **Panayia ton Kleiston** (the Virgin of the Closed Defiles), probably of late Byzantine origin and perched above a ravine pock-marked with hermits' caves, the road climbs the lonely defile. In front extend contorted rock formations, escarpments and deep crevices; behind there are views of Athens and the plain, against the backcloth of Hymettos. The pass of Fili (over two thousand feet) is dominated by an impressive free-standing plateau surrounded by a ring of fourth-century BC fortifications, with the remains of ramparts and towers commanding the point of intersection of numerous gorges. These fortifications, which replaced an earlier fortress on a neighbouring peak, guarded the shortest route into Attica from Boeotia. In winter there are treacherous snowdrifts and many mountaineers and shepherds have lost their lives in the unexpected chasms. The final ascent to the fortress is precipitous. The quadrangular masonry of the walls, nearly ten feet thick, is well preserved, particularly on the east side. An interesting feature of the two entrances is that they were built in such a way as to expose the attackers' right shoulders, unprotected by shields, to the defenders within.

Another road turning northwards off the National Road leads to the thickly wooded area of **Tatoi** on the foothills of Mount Parnes. The taverna of Leonides is one of the coolest spots in Attica, crowded on August nights with Athenians escaping from the stifling air and burning pavements of the city. The Greek Royal Family, when not in exile, have a summer palace here, and a royal graveyard, amid the pines. Beyond the palace, on the spine of the mountain, there are vestiges of the famous Spartan stronghold of Dekelia (twenty minutes' hard climb from a little taverna surrounded by plane trees).

After the pass of Agios Merkourios the road descends in loops to Malakassa, where it rejoins the National Road and whence a branch road leads to Oropos on the Euboean channel. From Skala Oropou a ferry crosses to the opposite shore and the site of Eretria. Throughout one's travels in Attica the outline of Euboea, extending from the promontory of Sounion in the south to the Pagasitic Gulf in the north, has become increasingly familiar. There is a comfortable feeling of omnipresence about Euboea. Its peaks are nearly always visible behind the mainland ranges, and the blue streak of the channel is encountered again and again along the coasts of Attica, Boeotia and Phthiotis.

Before leaving Athens it would be a mistake, I think, not to take one last look at **Hymettos**, smooth and elephantine, most homely and familiar of Attic mountains. The road from the centre of Athens cuts across the working-class suburb of Kaisariani and enters a verdant little valley in a fold of the mountain: an oasis of cypress, olive and plane trees. At the head of the valley, under a large plane tree, a spring gushes forth: a fertility spring, according to superstition. Above the spring is the **Monastery of Kaisariani**, with its church, dedicated to the Presentation of the Virgin, built in alternating courses of brick and stone. An eleventh-century foundation, for many years inhabited by monks who kept bees, it has undergone considerable restoration. The wall paintings in the narthex, apse and pendentives are of the post-Byzantine period. Around the well-kept court are the monastic bakeries, a mill and a bath-house, which was also used as an olive-press. Kaisariani is not important in the history of Byzantine church architecture, but its elegant little drum and cupola, its warm red-brick roofs, even its somewhat incongruous seventeenth-century campanile, all shaded by pine trees, form a charming spectacle of rusticity on the fringe of the suburban belt.

Above Kaisariani the steep mountain-side is covered with stunted shrubs: cistus, juniper and terebinth; and aromatic sage, thyme and lavender, which, together with the grape hyacinth and the purple crocus of spring, feed the famous Hymettos bees. The Greeks believed that the first bees in the world came from here; now Hymettos honey is produced throughout Attica. Beyond the monastery the road climbs past the pretty little Byzantine church of Asteri to a bleak summit in the form of a plateau, which commands an immense panoramic view of the whole of Attica and the islands of the Saronic Gulf.

The road to the west, to Corinth and the Peloponnese, crosses a ridge of hills from which there is an incomparable view, best seen at sunset, of the city spreading round its rocky hills under the 'violet crown' of Hymettos. The road now joins the Sacred Way to Eleusis, once bordered with the tombs of illustrious citizens. Today there are petrol stations and suburban residences. On the left the red tiled dome of the church at **Daphni** and the tops of three cypress trees appear above the high walls within which the Crusaders established a Cistercian community in the thirteenth century. Dedicated to the Dormition of the Virgin, Daphni is one of the most important Byzantine monuments in the country. The church is of the eleventh century, a golden age of Byzantine art – the age of the Comnene dynasty, which held the stage for a century.

The interior is a classic example of eleventh-century church architecture: a wide, squat dome and drum, supported by four pendentives, the four arms of the Greek Cross plan meeting in the central square, with the sanctuary in the apse behind the *iconostasis*, the narthex in the west front. The mosaics have suffered from neglect and desecration; some have been restored; but enough survive to illustrate the perfection achieved by Byzantine mosaicists of this period.

On entering the church one's first impression is of a large expanse of whitewashed walls. There seems to be little of the Byzantine 'gorgeousness' that the Benaki and Byzantine Museums promised. But each of the extant compositions merits careful examination; each is a work of art. The iconographic disposition is not haphazard, but strictly liturgical and symbolical, for the church is a visual image of Heaven, and the iconographer the servant of the theologian. It therefore helps to have an idea of the iconographic arrangement (mosaics or frescoes) of a typical Byzantine church interior in one's mind. The dome is Heaven, where Christ reigns in glory. He is surrounded by guardian Archangels, fully armed. Below them are the apostles or prophets who announced His coming. In the central apse, behind the *iconostasis*, the Virgin holds the Child. She, too, is flanked by Archangels. We now descend from Heaven to Earth. The walls are covered with portraits of saints, monks, ascetics, and Fathers of the Church. Above them, on high panels, and in the squinches below the pendentives, unfold the great scenes from the lives of Christ and the Virgin, the *Dodecaorton* (The Twelve Feasts). Particular prominence is given to the Crucifixion and the Descent into Hell, which reveal the mystery of the Resurrection. Other scenes from the Gospels are often added, generally in the narthex.

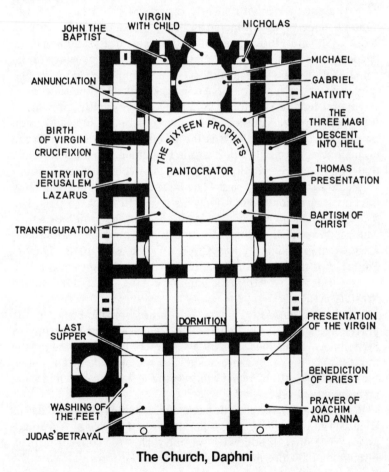

The Church, Daphni

At Daphni (as elsewhere) it is best to start in the narthex, where narrative tendencies are observed in the Betrayal, the Washing of the Feet and the Presentation, and then pass into the *naos*, the main body of the church, where the new 'humanism' is particularly evident in the **Transfiguration** in a squinch below the dome. The figure of Christ may be static, but it possesses an other-worldly majesty. The **Crucifixion** and the **Descent into Hell**, compositions of great poise and balance, are placed in lateral panels in the choirs. The Virgin in the Crucifixion is the personification of grief and bereavement, her mouth slightly turned down at the sides, her almond-shaped eyes contracted as though to hide a film of tears. She is one of the most moving figures in the whole of Byzantine mosaic decoration. The drapery of the angel with enormous wings in the **Annunciation** flows with an almost classical limpidity. Note the fine splendidly robed figure of the **Archangel Michael** in the sanctuary. A general lightness of tone, an almost pastel quality, prevails in these jigsaw puzzles of thousands of tesserae, pink, blue and green on gold backgrounds. But it is the formidable **Pantocrator** in the dome, one of the greatest portraits in Byzantine, or indeed any, art, that dominates the whole church – a terrifying Messianic vision. Depicted in bust, Christ raises one hand in blessing, the long bony fingers of the other clasping a jewel-studded Book of Gospels. The face, with the superbly arched eyebrows and the mouth of a man who is, beyond all things, decisive if not forgiving, is austere, Eastern, implacable. It is a Christ of Nemesis. In the Daphni Pantocrator the whole of Byzantine civilization comes into focus. He is worlds removed from the humanity of the Christ of Italian and Western art.

Beside the monastery there is a tourist pavilion and in the pine-wood above it an annual wine festival is held from July to September when wines from all over Greece may be tasted for the modest price of the entrance ticket. The red brick dome and roofs, the stone courses and arched windows of the floodlit church provide an impressive background.

Beyond Daphni the road descends towards the landlocked bay of Eleusis. On the right are the foundations of a temple of Aphrodite and a piece of rock hollowed out into niches for votive offerings. Fragments of white marble chiselled into the form of doves, the goddess's sacred birds, were found at the foot of the rocky hillside. The crescent-shaped bay, filled from shore to shore with laid-up, rusting ships, is sealed off from the open sea by the pine-clad island of Salamis. The battle of Salamis, the culmination of the second Persian invasion (480 BC), was fought in the narrow strait between the eastern tip of the island and the mainland, where Mount Aegaleos tapers off into the sea.

We continue on the **Sacred Way**, taken by Athenian pilgrims bound for the celebration of the Eleusinian Mysteries; once lined with statues, shrines and votive monuments, it is now a busy highway running across the Thriasian plain, bordered by factories and refineries. To the right, a few yards from the sea, is a narrow salt-water lake: the Rheiti, fringed with reeds, the haunt of wild fowl since time immemorial and incongruous in this agglomeration of industrial installations. Just before we enter the shabby little town of **Eleusis**, birthplace of Aeschylus, a road to the left leads to the ruins of the sanctuary: least inspiring of ancient Greek sites, yet second only to Delphi in religious significance. The ground is flat and featureless; Parnes in the background does not present its most impressive aspect and smoke trails from factory chimneys in the vicinity.

Below the rocky ledge, close to the sea, extend the ruins of the principal seat of worship of Demeter and Koré, in whose honour the Eleusinia, most sacred of Greek mysteries, was celebrated every September, attended by thousands of pilgrims from all over Greece. The holy edifices, whose jumbled foundations we now see, were built and rebuilt and yet again refashioned by the Peisistratae, by Cimon and Pericles (after the Persians had destroyed the sanctuary), by Lycurgus in the fourth century BC and by the Antonine emperors in the second century AD. Literally nothing remains standing, for Alaric and his Goths seem to have gone about their usual work of destruction with unprecedented thoroughness. Moreover, the successive reconstructions and restorations on different levels over a period of eight hundred years make it very difficult to identify the foundations of particular buildings.

The sanctuary, hemmed in by a nightmare complex of industrialization, lies between the low ridge of an acropolis and the sea. Left of the Great Propylaia, an Antonine reconstruction, is the

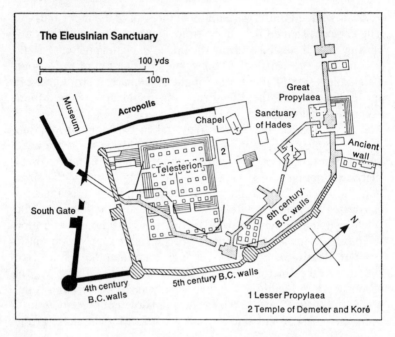

The Eleusinian Sanctuary

0 — 100 yds
0 — 100 m

Museum

Acropolis

Chapel

Great Propylaea

Sanctuary of Hades

Ancient wall

2

1

Telesterion

South Gate

6th century B.C. walls

N

4th century B.C. walls

5th century B.C. walls

1 Lesser Propylaea
2 Temple of Demeter and Koré

opening of a well, once the fountain around which the Eleusinian women performed ritual dances. Next comes the Lesser Propylaia, also a Roman construction, which had astonishingly opulent decoration. On the cliffs to the right two caves are preceded by a little walled-in terrace. This is part of the Sanctuary of Hades. The caves represent the entrance to the Underworld, and the exit, from which Koré emerged every spring to bring light and fertility into the world again. The outline of the god's temple is discernible in front of the larger cave.

Returning to the Sacred Way, one reaches the platform of the Telesterion, where the Mysteries were performed. Bases of columns are easily identified. The fifth-century BC interior consisted of six rows of seven columns, believed to have been Ionic, surrounded by tiers (those on the west side are well preserved), on which as many as three thousand people could stand. It had an upper storey, crowned by a wooden roof, where the *hiera*, the holy objects connected with the ceremony of initiation, were kept. The ruins of this extraordinary building are now no more than a mass of shattered blocks of masonry from successive restorations. Were the site less constricted by urban development and had the landscape one bit of the grandeur of Delphi or the serenity of Olympia, it might be easier to visualize the almost barbaric spectacle and to speculate on the religious exaltation experienced by the initiates, or *mystae*, as they proceeded in torchlight procession to the Hall of the Mysteries.

North of Eleusis the old road to Thebes winds across a rugged countryside. In March the *Anemone blanda*, with its sky-blue strap-shaped petals, grows profusely in the scrubland of the valleys below Mount Kithairon, an austere, even grim-looking mountain. Its contours are not elegant, but the steep slate-grey slopes, sprinkled with silver firs, and the lonely brushwood country at their foot, were reputed to be the haunt of Pan, god of shepherds. Here lions, bears and wild boar had their lairs, and stags roamed the forests. As one descends into a deep sunken valley, the remains of a stone tower rise immediately on the right. It was probably part of a system of ancient watch-towers along the frontier between Attica and Boeotia. At the village of Oinoi, a side road ascends to the **Monastery of Hosios Meletios**, a Byzantine foundation, considerably restored, situated on a little mountain ledge among plane and poplar trees.

Beyond Oinoi the entrance to a narrow pass is screened by a steep eminence crowned by ruined fourth-century BC ramparts: the fortress of **Eleutherai**, which guarded Attica and the Megaris from invasion from the north. It failed to do so in 1941, when British Commonwealth forces retreated through the defile after a vain attempt to hold up the German panzers. The fortifications are well preserved, particularly the north wall (eight feet thick and built in regular courses), and dotted with square towers provided with two gates in the lower storey and loopholes in the upper. The best view of the enceinte is the backward one, from the north, as one climbs the defile which ends in a bleak plateau, whence the road descends in hairpin bends into the Boeotian plain.

Just before Eleutherai a road to the left passes through the mountain village of Villia and descends in a series of wide loops between pine forests to the little harbour of Porto Yermano on an inlet of the Halcyonic Gulf. There are enchanting views of the calm expanse of water, with the Boeotian mountains forming a screen to the north, marred only by an ugly spread of modern buildings along the shore. At the end of the descent, the remains of the fortified **Acropolis of Aegosthena** are scattered among the pine-woods. To the left of the road rise admirably-preserved fourth-century BC ramparts in the form of a rectangle and the ruins of fifteen square towers, larger than those at Eleutherai, complete with gates, posterns and windows. The most impressive section, with four large, square towers crowning the east walls, is on the landward side, although the fortress must originally have been built as a defensive post against invaders from the sea. Many of the towers, especially those erected towards the end of the fifth century BC, were designed to carry wooden catapults, from which stones were hurled and arrows shot at attacking forces.

Two abandoned late Byzantine chapels add an incongruous note to the military site. On the lower ground are the foundations of an early Christian basilica. Along the placid, pebbly shore there are some modest tavernas. In summer the fields and olive groves, littered with blocks of ancient masonry, are crowded with campers, the beach infested with horseflies. The sun shimmers on the pellucid sea and a haze screens the spurs of Helikon that ascend abruptly from a barren deserted coastline.

CHAPTER 5

Boeotia

Thebes – Plataea – Leuktra –
The Sanctuary of the Cabeiroi – Thespiai – Askra –
Thisve – Aliartos –
The Sanctuary of Apollo at Ptoion –
The Monastery of Sagmata – Gla – Orchomenos –
Skripou: The Church of the Dormition – Livadia –
Chaironeia – Daulis.

Back in Athens, the traveller looks to the north-west: towards
Delphi. The approach, through Boeotia and the Parnassos Country, is very rewarding. The landscape, particularly the mountains, is
superb; there are fragmentary ancient sites, Byzantine churches and
a succession of famous battlefields.

A round trip is not practicable in Boeotia, which is virtually a
large hollow isthmus enclosed between coastal ranges. Most
travellers cross it in a day, with deviations to the more important
sites – Plataea, Orchomenos, Ptoion. Two, or even three, days
would allow time for a more roundabout and extensive itinerary. In
order to explore Boeotia thoroughly one can either stay at Delphi
where there is a wide variety of hotels, or at Thebes or Livadia,
though here there is only a limited choice of accommodation.

Beyond the watershed between Attica and Boeotia the landscape
becomes more continental, less Mediterranean. The vegetation is
no longer confined to olive, cypress and oleander. Maize, cotton
and tobacco take over. Flat agricultural plains succeed one another,
flanked by barren foothills – austerely grey on a cloudy day, a fierce
ochre at the height of summer – with hazy, fir-covered mountains in

the distance and Parnassos towering above them all. The marshes, now drained and forming large tracts of wheat fields, once abounded in wild fowl. Lying on the main invasion route from the north, Boeotia has witnessed the passage of many conquerors – Dorian, Persian, Macedonian, Roman, Frankish, Norman, Spanish, Turkish and German. Today the inhabitants are mainly devoted to agriculture.

From Athens, both road and rail follow a roughly parallel course towards the north-east. After making a wide loop round a wooded spur of Mount Parnes, they descend into the first and least interesting of the Boeotian plains and run north-westward across it. This plain is watered by the Asopos, the only local stream to flow straight into the sea without first forcing a way through an underground channel. There are tantalizing glimpses of the vivid blue streak of the Euboean Channel, now approaching its narrowest point. Between the road and the sea lies the field of Delium, where the Athenians, after committing the sacrilege of converting a Boeotian temple of Apollo into a fort, suffered their first major defeat of the Peloponnesian War in 424 BC.

Facing the channel is the Bay of Aulis, where Agamemnon's fleet was becalmed and Iphigenia sacrificed. The ruins of the Temple of Artemis are too negligible to justify a visit. Tanagra, once famous for its painted terracotta figurines, now has little to offer but a military airport. Beyond the airport there is a fork where the highway continues westward and another road turns north: towards Euboea. A few miles further on another road branches off to **Thebes**. 'No city in Greece,' we read in the *Dictionary of Greek and Roman Geography*, 'possessed such continued celebrity.' The celebrity is not always to its credit.

Theban mythology is among the richest in Greece, and Theban history, if less distinguished, is full of incident. Recalling its famous past, travellers are drawn to the City of the Seven Gates, only to find themselves, however, in a dreary provincial town with little to recommend it except good, lightly resinated rosé wine, scattered vestiges of ancient ruins, a fine museum and some dilapidated Turkish houses spreading across a chain of low hills overlooking the Cadmeian plain. But it is as difficult to avoid Thebes geographically as it is to ignore the fascination of its history and renown; indeed,

86

most of the main streets are evocatively named after the great figures of Theban mythology and history.

The centre of the town is on the highest hill, site of the ancient acropolis, the Cadmeia. Cadmus came from Phoenicia. He founded Thebes, colonized Boeotia and introduced writing into Greece (using the Phoenician alphabet which was the forerunner of modern Greek script). The record of Thebes during the Persian Wars, when its army joined with that of Mardonius in fighting the united Greeks, was beyond contempt. The slow-witted Thebans, obsessively jealous of the more lively Athenians, proved to be even more vindictive than the Spartans and after the Peloponnesian War, in which they sided with Sparta, they tried to persuade Lysander to raze Athens to the ground and sell the population into slavery. The Spartan leader, to his credit, refused.

In the second half of the fourth century BC, under the statesman-like leadership of Epaminondas, oligarchical Thebes appears in a more sympathetic light. However, after his death a decline set in and later, after the Macedonian conquest, a revolt instigated by the Athenian Demosthenes called down upon Thebes the fury of Alexander the Great. The future world-conqueror ordered his scarlet-coated soldiers not only to flatten the city, but also to slay 6000 Thebans and take 30,000 prisoners.

After this, the city sank into oblivion until the Middle Ages, when Benjamin of Tudela found it large and prosperous, and full of Jewish silk-workers whose lavish creations adorned Byzantine emperors and their consorts. The silk trade even survived a twelfth-century invasion by the Normans, who carried off many Theban workers to Palermo. The trade is dead now, but mulberry trees still grow around the town.

With the arrival of the Frankish barons, Estives, as it was then called, became the seat of the de la Roche family, who styled themselves 'Dukes of Athens and Thebes'. The plight of thirteenth-century Athens must indeed have been tragic for them to have chosen this dreary, humid place for their official residence instead of the Attic 'City of Light'.

Of the ancient walls there are only some rudimentary fragments. Alexander's sack was very thorough. The town was bounded to the east and west by the streams of Dirce and Ismene, as the centre of the modern one still is. Theban monuments have never been described as beautiful; they were built of dark grey Boeotian marble, giving the city a forbidding aspect, and few remnants have survived.

The archaeological enthusiast should start at the south-eastern end of Amphion Street (where it meets Polyneices Street), opposite a cypress-clad hill. Here a few courses of massive, primitively wrought limestone blocks form two round bases on either side of the street: foundations of the two flanking towers of the prehistoric Electran Gate, named after the sister of Cadmus. Crossing the centre of the town in a roughly northerly direction, one sees the foundations of what are believed to be a section of the palace archive building and a palace bathroom (corner of Epaminondas and Gheorghiou Streets). Turning right into Antigone Street, one encounters some impressive ancient masonry on superimposed levels. The rubble of a palace of the Mycenean period, in which Laius, Oedipus and Creon probably held court, lies nearby, on the left, in Pindar Street. Tablets found here are inscribed with Linear B dated to the thirteenth century BC.

At this point it is best to continue in a northerly direction along Pindar Street to the site of one of the seven gates, from which the ancient road led to the north. The site of the Homoloid Gate is now occupied by the **museum**, whose courtyard once formed part of the enceinte of the Frankish castle which overlooked the plain. This courtyard is now filled with Moslem tombstones and with the severed limbs of statues. The only surviving section of the thirteenth-century fortress is the fine, squat tower, called Santameri (a corruption of St Omer) which stands on the right of the courtyard. The castle was built by St Omer, an arrogant Flemish baron who spent a large part of his wife's generous dowry in raising fortifications throughout his scattered domains in the Peloponnese and on mainland Greece.

Even the most hurried traveller in Boeotia, though unlikely to be impressed by the prehistoric rubble of ancient Thebes, should not, in my opinion, fail to visit this museum, which is small and well-arranged. From the entrance hall you pass into the Tanagra room in which are displayed the *larnaces* – cinerary urns or coffins of baked clay – dated to c. 1400–1200 BC, excavated at nearby Tanagra.

Unique in Greece, these singular and beautiful urns, rectangular in shape and of varying sizes, stand on four squat legs. They contained, as some still do, the bones of distinguished Tanagran citizens who died over three thousand years ago. Stylized processionals of priests and animals with human faces are painted in black and orange – sometimes red – on the exterior surfaces. In a showcase on the left are prehistoric funerary gifts in the form of miniature pieces of furniture of exquisite workmanship. Once more we have an example of the veneration in which death was held by the Greeks of all periods. These enchanting little terracottas do not, admittedly, possess the lavish quality of the Mycenean grave gifts, wrought in gold and precious stones. However, the motive, the underlying idea, remains the same: the dead are immortalized in the minds of the living by the quality of the works of art beside which they rest in eternity.

The two halls to the left contain prehistoric pottery, fourteenth-century BC cylinder seals of lapis lazuli (whose Anatolian origin suggests the existence of trade relations between Thebes and Phoenicia), and ceramics of the highest quality from the Geometric, Archaic and Classical periods. The unusual **stelae of black stone**, carved with the finest of incisions, depicting Boeotian warriors in combat at the battle of Delium, are best seen from an oblique angle. Among the exhibits of the sixth and fifth centuries BC is a fine male torso displayed in the last hall. Though unfortunately limbless and headless, the statue is in the best fifth-century BC sculptural tradition. The showpiece of the museum is the sixth-century BC **Ptoion Kouros** which came from the Sanctuary of Apollo at Ptoion. The youth's smile is no less enigmatic, his posture no less heroic than those of the Attic *kouroi*; only the stylized, coral-shaped locks which fall down the back of the neck are much less finely modelled.

The normal axis of travel in Boeotia is east–west or vice-versa, with deviations into the foothills of the mountain ranges flanking the plains. The first such deviation is to the south, along the old Athens–Thebes road, through undulating fields, home of the *Tulipa boeotica*, a lovely bell-shaped flower with a black centre in the form of a star. The village of Tachi, where there is some classical masonry, may well be the site of Potniae, a shrine sacred to Dionysus.

At the village of Erithres, a third of the way up Mount Kithairon, a turning to the west leads to the ancient township and battlefield of **Plataea** where the third and decisive engagement of the Persian Wars was fought. Boeotia has always been the scene of violent armed clashes and none does more credit to Greek bravery than this battle. Plataea had a noble record of fidelity to the Athenian alliance, which dated from the sixth century BC. At Marathon it was the only state to send a contingent to assist the hard-pressed Athenians. During the Peloponnesian War the Plataeans never wavered and withstood a famous siege for two years. When the depleted garrison was forced to surrender, the Thebans did not leave a single Plataean alive and they destroyed all the buildings. Plataea thus paid heavily for her loyalty to Athens.

Philip of Macedon restored the city and Alexander the Great built the ramparts, which are now very ruined (best preserved on the west side); but one can walk for quite long stretches along a line of low walls overlooking the level meadows where so many Persian men, hopes and ambitions perished. These walls, about two and a half miles in circumference, can be traced round the cornfields which slope down towards the stream of the Asopos. There are no other vestiges of the ancient township except the foundations of a temple, possibly of Hera, on a terrace near the north-west wall. There is no sign of the sanctuary of Demeter around which there was fierce fighting, but on whose holy ground no Persian corpse was found. Herodotus suggests that the goddess, remembering the barbarians' desecration of her most sacred shrine at Eleusis, prevented them from setting foot in her Boeotian temple.

From Plataea a secondary road continues north-west, via Kapareli, to the hamlet of **Leuktra**, on a low hill overlooking the next battlefield on the westward route. This battle represented a historical milestone of a very different character. Of the victory of Thebes over Sparta in 371 BC at Leuktra, Pausanias says it was 'the most famous ever won by Greeks over Greeks'. It is the familiar story of Greek tearing Greek to pieces. The site is marked by a modern plinth adorned with some ancient marble slabs. The battle was fought north of a tumulus easily identified near the commemorative plinth. The tumulus we now see is probably the Spartan sepulchre. There is little else. I asked a peasant if there were any *archaia* (ancient things) nearby. He led me across a field, scrabbled among the corn and pointed to a stone slab, which might have formed part of a stele, inscribed with the name *MYPON*. The inscription could not have referred to the sculptor, who, although a native of neighbouring Eleutherai, died about a hundred years before the battle. The slab, the man said, was recently ploughed up by a tractor.

Five kilometres from Thebes a signposted track off the Livadia Road leads southward to the so-called **Sanctuary of the Cabeiroi** (reputedly the sons of Hephaestus) lying in a fold of rolling green hills, criss-crossed with hedgerow-bordered paths. The Cabeiria were mysteries or fertility rites, possibly orgies, celebrated chiefly in Samothrace and Lemnos, but also in Boeotia. The ruins are fairly extensive but infinitely perplexing, covering a considerable chrono-logical span. The eastern end of a temple now forms the *skene* of a theatre (parts of which are well preserved), remarkable for the shallow arc of the semi-circle, which focuses on an altar: the scene, no doubt, of some orgiastic rite. On the outskirts of the sanctuary an open square is formed by what were once three chambers. Masonry as late as that of the Roman period is evident. The confusion arising from the superimposition of successive levels of foundations, all of different periods, does not detract from the pastoral quality of the scene, with wild flowers growing in the shade of luxuriant shrubs and sheep browsing on the hillsides which enclose the curiously concave site.

Returning to the main road, one can make another southward deviation, longer and more rewarding, across an extension of the same hilly region, to **Thespiai** which, with Plataea, shares the distinction of being one of the two Boeotian cities that remained unrelentingly hostile to Thebes. (The traveller need not return to Thebes if he wishes to visit both Leuktra and Thespiai which are joined by a stretch of secondary road.)

Modern Thespiai, like its pretty twin village Leondari, from which it is separated by a shallow ravine, spreads across a shelf overlooking the plain to the south, where the barely identifiable ruins of the ancient site (notably the foundations of a Temple of the Muses) are scattered. The finds from the hitherto perfunctory excavations are at present stacked in a village house called *to museio* (the museum) to which it is not always easy to gain admission.

The god worshipped here was Eros, a primeval deity, symbolizing sexual vigour, armed with flaming torches which he aimed at gods and mortals alike. It is not until Hellenistic times that Eros is sentimentalized by poets and artists, becomes the son of Aphrodite and finally the plump little Cupid rendered so popular by Roman artists. The original Greek Eros was a more virile deity. A festival in his honour, known as the *Erotidia*, was held every four years, and the cult statue consisted of an erect monolith on which every bride offered a tress of her hair, representing her youth, and a girdle symbolizing her virginity.

Near here flowed the reed-fringed stream into which the youth Narcissus gazed so long and so intently that he fell in love with his own image. Pausanius finds the story 'absolutely stupid'; Sir George Wheler, travelling in Thespian territory in the seventeenth century was nevertheless pleased to find the narcissus growing everywhere in profusion.

From Thespiai a secondary road to the west climbs the rocky, cone-shaped foothills of Mount Helikon. You pass an eminence: possibly the natural stronghold to which the Thebans fled when their country was overrun by northern tribes at about the time of the Trojan War. On it stand the ruins of a medieval watch-tower like a skeleton in stone, commanding a view of a desolate pyramidal peak crowned by a ruined Hellenic tower: all that remains of **Askra**, birthplace of Hesiod, founder of the first school of poetry on the Greek mainland. Today it seems a remote and grandiose place, from which there is a wide prospect of the Valley of the Muses, now, alas, deforested. To visit the valley one must leave the car and walk for about an hour in order to scrabble amid the stony ground for traces of an altar and an unexcavated cavea of a third-century BC theatre. Of the supposedly idyllic beauty of the haunt of the Muses little remains but its evocative associations, some almond trees and the fir-covered heights of Helikon above.

Back at Thespiai, one can make an agreeable detour to **Thisvi** and the southern coast of Boeotia. The road runs west through a narrow plain, between the foothills of Helikon and Kithairon. It is pastoral country and in late spring the road is bordered by banks of pale bluish-mauve *Iris xiphium* (Spanish iris). To the south, on a clear day, one can see the peaks of the Peloponnesian mountains: a spectacular backcloth to the foreground of barren Boeotian coastal hills.

The red-roofed village of Thisvi lies at the foot of an outcrop of rock: a sleepy, undefiled place with a taverna, where I have had the best country bread in Greece. A plateau, east of the village, seemingly ringed round by vicious stinging-nettles, is littered with the remains of extensive walls and squat, square towers dated to the period of Alexander the Great, when the place must have served as a military outpost against invaders from the Corinthian Gulf. The circuit, which follows the crests of hills on different levels, is about a mile in circumference. The masonry is regular and polygonal and the joining of the blocks reveals fine workmanship. Foundations of walls shelve down in terraces to a fertile bowl-like valley, where flights of pigeons wheel overhead in the sky. At the foot of the plateau the rock is honeycombed with caves, thought to have served as ancient sepulchres.

Southward the road cuts across the hollow basin, following the course of an ancient causeway, built in order to prevent the whole plain being flooded when the autumn rains set in. It must have been a curious sight: one half a lake or at least a marsh; the other cultivated land. A bleak mountain stretch follows. One descends in hairpin bends to the rugged bay of Korini, broken by numerous coves and minute fiords. The road ends at the inlet of Agios Ioannis. Even on this remote shore, holiday shacks of doubtful taste have sprung up. Bare headlands stretch eastward. The great bay, with its islets and numerous anchorages, has always been noted for violent squalls, as the winds funnel down the stony valleys from the mountain-tops of Helikon and Kithairon.

At Tipha, which forms the eastern arm of the bay and is at present inaccessible by road (it can be approached by caique or yacht), there are substantial fifth-century BC walls, towers with polygonal masonry and doorways with pediments, as well as visible underwater masonry.

Whether a squall is blowing or whether the sea is blue and pellucid, the bay of Korini remains, in its remoteness and intricate configuration, one of the most impressive land and seascapes on the. southern mainland.

Beyond the southward fork to Thespiai and Thisvi the main

Thebes–Livadia road leaves the melancholy plain. The ground rises, then dips down into the basin of the former Lake Kopais: now a shimmering expanse of cotton fields, surrounded by cliffs and mountains which, in antiquity, rose sheer from the shallow water's edge. Once the haunt of cranes, now of migratory storks, the lake or swamp was reclaimed by French and British engineers at the end of the nineteenth century. Strabo's assertion that the whole basin had been drained by the inhabitants of ancient Orchomenos is borne out by the discovery of a primitive but intricate system of dykes encircling the entire Kopaic 'lake', whereby the various streams were diverted by a network of canals into *katavothra* which disgorged their waters into the sea. Archaeologists have located long, low mounds, the remains of ancient dykes, stretching across considerable tracts of the plain, either in unbroken lines or with gaps at intervals. Here, as indeed throughout most of Boeotia, one is constantly aware of geology: of water in subterranean channels coursing through limestone ranges; of curious hump-shaped mounds of slate-grey rock emerging out of a mirage of sun-drenched arable land; of lakes on different levels which descend like stepping stones towards the Euboean channel.

At the south-eastern end of the basin, beyond Mount Sphingion – a grim pyramidal rock – lies Homer's 'grassy Haliartos', still surrounded by 'well-watered meadows'.

At modern **Aliartos** the traveller has the choice of two routes. One leads directly to Livadia, skirting the base of Mount Helikon, whose constantly changing outlines dominate much of the Boeotian landscape. Neither as grand as Taigetos nor as beautiful as Parnassos – and not nearly as high as either – it is nevertheless well-wooded and rugged, but never forbidding.

If one opts for this route, it would be a mistake, I think, not to visit the site of yet another ancient battlefield and thus penetrate a more pastoral area of the Helikon country. West of Aliartos there is a wide arc of flat, cultivated land. A side road runs south through cornfields and olive groves between hedgerows of broom and wild pear. To the right a ruined Catalan tower crowns an isolated hill, site of ancient **Koroneia**, where the Panboeotia, a great religious festival 'common to all the Boeotians', was held at the temple of Athena Itonica. The temple stood in the plain in front of the hill.

It was on the level ground around the ancient town that the Boeotians inflicted a major defeat on the Athenians under the impetuous Tolmides in 447 BC. The victory had such a tonic effect on the morale of the Boeotians that they were able to throw the Athenians out of the whole of their country. The ruins of Koroneia are virtually obliterated. I have tried to identify the theatre, temple foundations and walls – all of considerably later periods than the fifth century BC – said to lie below and around the Catalan tower, but in vain.

Leaving the acropolis hill to the left, the road climbs the mountainside, which forms the eastern arm of a great bite into the Helikon range, making a perfectly shaped crescent around the olive groves and cotton fields. The road ends at the modern village of Koroneia, perched high above the fruitful plain. Hollyhocks grow in profusion in back gardens and the scarlet of geraniums is splashed across the whitewashed walls of village houses.

The second route, of greater interest, follows a rough arc round the plain, reaching Livadia via Ptoion and Orchomenos. From Aliartos a road cuts across the cotton fields to the north and reaches the main Athens–Thessaloniki highway below a line of hills, whose rocky sides rise abruptly from the reclaimed swamp.

A small canyon cuts through the cliff, opening out into a rugged little valley entirely enclosed by beige-coloured hills. Above the village of Akrefnio where the Thebans took refuge after their city was sacked by Alexander the Great, a track climbs the western slope of Mount Ptoion, which has a triple peak and was named after a son of Apollo. It is not easy to locate the ruins of the **Sanctuary of Apollo**. A whitewashed chapel, shaded by a large holm-oak, is the landmark to look for. Behind it rise the terraces of the Sanctuary which was an oracular seat. On the first terrace are the base of a *tholos* building and a rectangular cistern where consultants purified themselves before ascending to the second terrace, across which lie traces of *stoas* buttressed by a few courses of retaining wall, and finally to the third, marked by foundations of a Doric temple of Apollo. Above the temple a spring called *Perdiko Vrysi* (The Partridge Spring) has been identified as the site of the oracle. The waters of the spring, which gush out of the rock, connect with the cistern below. Climbing from one terrace to another, one sinks ankle-deep into soft moss through which water trickles. It is as though the whole mountain has a substratum of underground rivulets. From a ledge slightly south-east of the ruins there is a fine view of the winding inlets of Lake Iliki below.

The lake itself, part of the water supply of Athens, is skirted by the Athens–Thessaloniki highway. Obviously once a crater, its configuration is of fascinating complexity – a series of figures-of-eight of different dimensions. Barren, rocky banks rise from turquoise water. At times the conical summits and contorted volcanic shapes overlooking the winding shore give the impression of a lunar landscape; at others of Japanese prints. A *katavothra* connects Iliki with the smaller lake of Paralimni, which lies in an even deeper depression. This elliptical lake can be approached by a branch road from the highway which passes through the village of Mouriki and descends into a narrow, shut-in basin, where the shallow water lies motionless against a screen of slate-grey cliff. It is an astonishing sight: unexpected, desolate, bizarre.

On the way back from Paralimni one passes through the village of Ipato. From here a rough dirt road climbs the steep side of Mount Ipatos in a series of terrifying hairpin bends. On the higher slopes the track winds through tall *Arbutus andrachne* trees, amongst whose leathery grey-green leaves grow clusters of creamy-white flowers and whose wood was used in antiquity for making looms. The summit, a wind-blown plateau, carpeted in spring with grape hyacinth and yellow iris, is crowned by the buildings of the **Monastery of Sagmata** which, at the time of writing, was inhabited by a single monk. Ruined chapels below the summit suggest the monastery's one-time importance. The inhabitants of the plain, fleeing from the endless succession of invading armies, probably flocked to these chapels.

The Church of the Transfiguration, built on the site of the hermitage of a holy man, is a twelfth-century foundation of the 'golden age' of Byzantine architecture. Rising from an irregular courtyard bordered by cells (largely of the post-Byzantine period) and monastic outhouses, the church has an exo-narthex and a narthex added in the fifteenth or sixteenth century. The plan is cruciform and tri-apsidal, with a dome (which collapsed in 1914 and was replaced by an unimpressive wooden one) supported by four

The Temple of Athena, known as the Parthenon in 1754. An engraving by
Le Roy showing the damage caused by the explosion of 1687, when a direct
hit from the Venetian army commanded by Morosini ignited the Turkish
powder magazine inside the Temple.

The Acropolis – the Upper City – today; walls, temples and gateways,
crowned by the Parthenon.

The Ephebe of Anticythera may be the famous statue of Paris by
Euphranor. He holds some round object (the apple?), now missing, in his
right hand. *(National Archaeological Museum, Athens)*

slender columns of blue-veined white marble. The original marble screen of the sanctuary has been replaced by a marble *iconostasis*, but some of the original sculptural embellishment is embedded in the wall above the south door of the narthex. The **mosaic floor** (it covers 100 square metres) in the *naos* is a fine example of the floor mosaicist's art of the twelfth century, lavishly decorated with eight circular designs within a circle and a geometric border.

Rejoining the highway and proceeding north-west, one reaches the village of Kastro. A road to the right, less than a mile long, runs across the fields to the so-called **Island of Gla**, one of the strangest prehistoric sites in Greece. The 'isle' – it obviously was one once, washed by the shallow waters of Lake Kopais – is a natural curiosity: a low, triangular eminence with a ramp on the north side, flanked by two defensive buttresses and Cyclopean walls, two miles in circumference, which follow the contours of the cliff. Dominating the north-east basin below Mount Ptoion, it may have been a principality of the Minyans (a pre-Hellenic people who descended from Thessaly to Boeotia), forming part of a system of fortification guarding the shores of the lake. The cliffs, never higher than two hundred feet, are pitted with caves and *katavothra*. The ramp leads to a gate, on the inner side of which there was a small courtyard. Below the north-east redoubt is another double gate. Moving north-west you reach the central redoubt; to the north of this, on the highest point of the eminence, are the foundations of a palace with two L-shaped wings, built of sun-dried bricks (the base is of stone). All round, the countryside is dotted with rocky humps, like huge grey animals squatting on the cornfields of the drained marshland. There is not a house, not a tree, not a browsing goat. Only the bees, the sage and the fennel.

North-east of Gla lies the ugly mining village of Agios Ioannis. At the base of the hillside, immediately below a chapel of the same name, there is an enormous arc-shaped cave with a double entrance, which marks the site of the Great Katavothra where the Mavropotamos (Black River), one of the main Boeotian streams, is drained underground and, after flowing through the limestone barrier, pours into the Euboean channel.

The road continues across bleak mountain country; as it descends towards the coast, past the restored Byzantine Church of *Agios*

Nikolaos, wisps of foul-smelling smoke drift up from a straggling village at the head of a deep, narrow inlet ringed round with nickel mining installations. Site of ancient **Larymna**, whose name has been inherited by the modern village, it is believed to have been the chief port of the Minyans. In Hellenistic times Larymna, main emporium of Boeotia and a harbour of some strategic value, was defended on the landward side by a semi-circular enceinte of strong walls strengthened with towers, substantial remains of which are identifiable; the masonry is both rectangular and polygonal, the hewn stones being of a white and sometimes an unusual tawny colour. In the choking, polluted atmosphere one may search along the shore for fragments of fourth-century BC port installations – including piers used for closing the harbour in time of war, some of which are still visible, though submerged – and gaze through watering eyes at the grandiose scree-rent cliffs of Euboea rising sheer across the water.

West of Kastro, the road runs beside canals to the village of Orchomenos. The stream of the Mavropotamos issues out of a *katavothra* on the lower north side of Mount Akontion (The Javelin), part of a barren, forbidding chain of hills which guard the approaches to this region of fens through which streams course sluggishly between banks of waving canes. Between the road and Mount Akontion there are traces of one of the oldest prehistoric sites in Greece. Indeed, so great was the antiquity of **Orchomenos**, capital of the Minyans, that its golden age was little more than a memory in classical times.

The most impressive surviving edifice of the Minyan civilization is the **Treasury of Minyas**, claimed by Pausanias to be the first treasury ever built, and 'a wonder second to none either in Greece or elsewhere'. Situated just off the main road, this beehive tomb was excavated by Schliemann. It is approached by a *dromos* cut through the hillside, leading to a tapering doorway with a formidable lintel of blue schist. The diameter of the vaulted rotunda, now roofless, is about forty-five feet. Holes for bronze rosettes are discernible on the walls, of which eight courses survive. The fact that the circular chamber is open to the sky enables the spectator to get a good impression of the concavity of the structure. On the other hand, there is a total absence of that atmosphere of centuries-old putrefaction which contributes so greatly to the macabre quality of the

Treasury of Atreus at Mycenae. A corridor connects the rotunda with a small square funerary chamber, with palmettes and rosettes carved in low relief on the ceiling, where the original Minyans were supposed to have been buried.

From the Treasury the way up to the citadel is steep and stony. One passes traces of buildings of the Neolithic, third millennium BC and pre-Archaic periods. The upper terraces were reconstructed by Philip and Alexander. On the final jagged outgrowth of rock are the remains of a square tower. The ramparts, best preserved on the south side, are of the fourth century BC. Although by this time the greatness and wealth of Orchomenos were no more than a memory, Mount Akontion still possessed strategic value, dominating the bottleneck between the plains.

The end of Orchomenos came in 364 BC, as a result of the endemic feud with Thebes. Three hundred Orchomenian horsemen, aided by Theban traitors, prepared an attack on Thebes. The plot was betrayed and Orchomenos was totally destroyed, its male population slaughtered and the women and children sold into slavery. This barbarous attack aroused the revulsion of neighbouring states and confirmed the reputation for cruelty earned by the Thebans.

The Temple of the Charities is thought to have been situated east of the road, opposite the Treasury and a theatre of the Hellenistic period with well-preserved tiers and a ruined proscenium. The site is now surrounded by cotton fields, canals and mud-flats, and the temple replaced by the Byzantine **Church of the Koimesis** (Dormition of the Virgin) of Skripou, the oldest cross-inscribed church in Greece. An inscription dates it to 874. It is constructed from large stone blocks of unequal size, clearly of ancient origin (such as the drums of columns built into the interior west wall); and the general effect, though one of spaciousness and sturdiness, is heavy and awkward. The architect, whilst employing the Greek Cross plan, retained certain features of the basilica: the three aisles, for instance, and the triple windows of the narthex, each with two colonettes. More attractive are the courses of carved reliefs – a form of church decoration soon to disappear from Byzantine art – separating the three zones of the interior. Children play in the forecourt and old women sit in the sun, while hens peck desultorily around truncated pillars and among fragments of the cornice and closure panel of the original marble screen.

Close to Orchomenos lies **Livadia**, chief town of Boeotia, its houses with their red-tiled roofs spreading fanwise across the foothills of Helikon on either side of a narrow gorge. A clock tower, presented by Lord Elgin, is a conspicuous landmark. Behind the town rises a screen of pine-covered heights. Westward towers Parnassos, misty blue in colour, its summit snow-capped from November to May, and often wreathed in cloud. In the symmetry and harmony of its forms and in its dramatic upward surge from the plain, no other Greek mountain, except Taigetos in the Peloponnese, is more impressive. Livadia, with a local trade in blanket-making, has an animated air. Scarlet, green and magenta blankets hang out to dry from wooden balconies, ramshackle dwellings spread across the slope of a rocky eminence crowned by a medieval castle, and streams cascade down the hill.

At the foot of the castle hill the Erkina issues out of a sunless canyon. Plane trees form arbours over the ice-cold stream, which is spanned by a little arched Turkish bridge. The springs on the east bank flow into two pools: *Lethe* (Oblivion) and *Mnemosyne* (Remembrance). On the west bank niches for votive offerings have been carved out of the cliff-side. The largest of these forms a kind of stone chamber with rock-hewn seats, the favourite refuge of Turkish governors who came here to smoke their *narghiles* or doze through long, soporific summer afternoons. Everywhere there is water: oozing, trickling, gurgling. Below the rocky precipices, among the shady planes, there are open-air cafés and tavernas, and a modern swimming pool where divers plunge into water drained from the pool of Lethe.

Near to the pool was the oracle of Trophonius. The oracular chamber was in an underground chasm below a sacred grove. Above was the temple, with a statue of Trophonius, a Minyan semi-deity, by Praxiteles. Leake, most reliable of nineteenth-century topographers, suggests that the grove was on the eastern bank of the Erkina gorge, but not as far as the upland plateau associated with the hunting-grounds of Persephone, to which the gorge ultimately leads.

To the west of the gorge a high crag is crowned by the castle, the earliest Catalan monument in Greece. The ruined towers, walls and archways of the keep are reminders of a strange period of Spanish rule in Greece. In the winter of 1311 a band of Catalan soldiers of fortune, originally hired by the Frankish Duke of Athens to fight the Greeks and who were owed extensive arrears of pay by him, descended into Boeotia, accompanied by an immense train of women, children and baggage, resolved to settle accounts with their debtors by force of arms.

The Catalans, though outnumbered, had laid their plans with cunning and foresight. Flooding the fields between Skripou and Livadia by digging canals into which the waters of the Cephisus flowed, they were thus protected by a quagmire covered with a carpet of scum that looked like grass. The Duke of Athens, waving his banner of a golden lion on an azure field sown with stars, personally led the attack, followed by his golden-spurred knights in coats of mail. Plunging their horses into the morass, they were unable to move forward or back, and men and beasts became sitting targets for the bolts and arrows of the Spaniards who bore down on them yelling 'Aragon!' The massacre of the French was appalling. The battle was decisive. Frankish power in central Greece was broken in a few hours. Henceforth Attica and Boeotia became the domain of Spanish (and later Florentine) overlords.

West of the Cephisus battleground lie Chaironeia and Daulis. Both can be visited from Livadia in half a day. **Chaironeia**, where Plutarch was born and died (AD 46–120) and wrote most of his works, lies in the narrow plain between Mount Akontion and Mount Thurium. Astride the main invasion route from the north, it was a position of great strategic importance. In ancient times it was a flowery place, the Grasse of the Hellenic world, famous for the manufacture of therapeutic unguents distilled from lilies, roses and narcissus.

The antiquities are visible from the road. The *cavea* of a little theatre, without the usual supporting walls at the side, is well preserved (the *skene*, however, has gone). Behind it, fragments of the ruined towers and walls which enclosed the ancient city, ascend the hill. The marble Lion of Chaironeia stands in a cypress grove a few minutes' walk from the centre of the village. Its artistic merit, if any, is overshadowed by its historical associations, for it is believed

101

to surmount the collective grave of the Theban Sacred Band, wiped out in a murderous combat with the young Alexander's phalanx at the battle of Chaironeia in 338 BC. In the War of Independence, Odysseus Androutsos, most predatory of revolutionary leaders, hacked it to pieces in the hope of finding it full of treasure. Subsequent excavation of the tumulus on which it lay revealed over two hundred skeletons – presumably of the Sacred Band. The Lion, put together again at the beginning of the present century, now rests on its haunches, open-mouthed, staring fatuously from its marble plinth, against the imposing background of Parnassos. In the adjacent museum are displayed prehistoric armour, weapons and terracottas from the tumulus of the Macedonians who fell in the battle.

Chaironeia was a decisive battle. By the summer of 338 BC Philip of Macedon was ready to force the gateway into Boeotia and subjugate all continental Greece. On a blazing August day, the Macedonian army, well trained, admirably equipped and expertly commanded, faced an army of disunited Greeks, held together only by the exhortations of Demosthenes. Today road and rail follow their parallel course across the stretch of level ground between the Cephisus and the village where the battle was fought. After the engagement Philip is accused of indulging in unseemly mirth, of getting drunk on the field of battle and of jesting in the most ribald manner as he inspected the corpses of his foes piled up in the blood-soaked streams. However he is said to have wept at the sight of the Theban dead, privileged members of the Sacred Band. They had borne the brunt of Alexander's onslaught and fought with courage and self-sacrifice. They died to a man, all with chest wounds. In time the battle acquired a kind of romantic aura, its outcome being identified by succeeding generations as the end of the democratic Greek city state.

In 87 BC another decisive battle, equally disastrous to Greek pride, was fought on the field of Chaironeia. The Hellenistic world of Alexander the Great's successors was crumbling before the irresistible tide of Roman conquest. An army of Mithridates, King of Pontus, around whom Hellenism had rallied, put up a last stand in the Chaironeian bottleneck. The forces of Mithridates were so totally annihilated that Sulla himself claimed Boeotia to be impassable for the piles of corpses.

West of Chaironeia the foothills of Parnassos alternately advance and recede into the plain, forming a fascinating sequence of different perspectives. The first turning to the left leads to the village of Agios Vlasios and the acropolis of Panopeus, native city of Epeius, who built the Trojan Horse with the aid of Athena. There are the remains of two well-preserved gateways and six towers of the fourth century BC.

Another spur is crowned by **Daulis** (south-west of the main road) which is worth visiting, if only for its striking position. From the village of Davlia one climbs a cultivated slope, dotted with water mills, to the acropolis. There are the remains of a gate over ten feet wide between two towers – the one on the right is medieval. The square towers of the ramparts, covered in holly-oak, overhang a torrent-bed strewn with huge boulders. The whitewashed Convent of Jerusalem, surrounded by cypresses, is perched on a ledge of Parnassos above the acropolis, just below the belt of firs. To the south-west a road leads across desolate, contorted hills to the Cleft Way and thence to Delphi. The course of history has flowed past in the plain below, the never-ending armies from the north hardly ever pausing to desecrate this elegiac, fennel-covered place. Only Philip of Macedon halted long enough to destroy the town, where the men, though few in number, were renowned for their height and strength. The town was rebuilt; we know, because Livy refers to its impregnable position on its 'lofty hills'.

CHAPTER 6

The Parnassos Country

*Tithorea – Amfiklia – Lilea – The Gravia Pass –
Amfissa – The Sacred Plain – Galaxidi –
The Cleft Way – Antikira – Osios Loukas.*

Mount Parnassos dominates not only the country of the Boeotians,
but also that of the Phocians and Locrians: an amorphous geological
complex of spurs and foothills, narrow plains, sombre defiles and
cup-shaped valleys. In the centre of it all is Delphi, which can be
approached from several directions. I propose to describe two of
these approaches: (i) An arc running from Tithorea through the
Gravia Pass to Amfissa and Galaxidi on the Gulf of Corinth (easily
accomplished in one day), then back to Itea and up to Delphi. (ii)
The direct route from Livadia to Delphi with a southward deviation
to Antikira and the Monastery of Osios Loukas (also easily accomplished in one day).

The average traveller visits Osios Loukas, one of the most
important Byzantine monuments in the country, on the way to
Delphi. The journey Athens–Osios Loukas–Delphi can comfortably be completed in a day, allowing for leisurely stops and minor
deviations.

Tithorea is perched above the Kifissos valley at the end of a branch
road to the south-west, about halfway between Livadia and Lamia.
More spectacular than Daulis, Tithorea is protected to the south by
sheer cliffs which terminate in a huge ledge on the flank of Parnassos. To the east the precipice plummets into a desolate ravine. The
town's ancient fortifications were therefore strongest to the north
and west, where the approaches were undefended by nature.

Fragments of fourth- and third-century BC walls of regular ashlar masonry, with moss and ivy-covered towers, are scattered about the vegetable plots, forming an arc around the more exposed slopes.

Huddled at the base of the cliff, the village is picturesque and salubrious, its narrow streets interspersed with outcrops of ancient masonry. The eastern end overhangs the ravine through which flows the *Kakorevma* (The Evil Torrent). This ravine winds inland, into the heart of Parnassos. On the right, just beyond the last houses, is a cave where the Tithoreans took refuge during Xerxes' invasion.

At the Tithorea fork, a better road to the north-east crosses the Kifissos and leads to **Elatia**, once the most important place in Phocis after Delphi. Its capture by Philip in 339 BC, followed by the victory of Chaironeia, laid all central Greece at the mercy of the Macedonian king. The ruins are vestigial. Three kilometres to the northeast are the more impressive standing walls of the **Sanctuary of Athena Cranaea** on a hill now called Kastro Louzo.

The main Livadia–Lamia road continues to skirt the base of Parnassos. After passing the entrance to another great gorge, one reaches the undistinguished village of **Amfiklia**, the site of ancient Amphicleia, where orgies, which Pausanius found 'well worth seeing', were held in honour of Dionysus. West of the village, embedded in what must have been the retaining wall of the ancient acropolis, are the remains of Hellenic masonry. All is crowned by a ruined Venetian tower commanding a view of corn, tobacco and cotton fields, with formidable mountains closing in on all sides as the plains contract into a narrow enclave.

Leaving the shady village of Polidrossos behind, the road skirts the precipitous slopes of Parnassos, slashed by more gorges. About a kilometre before one reaches **Lilea**, vestiges of an ancient tower appear on the bleak ridge of a steep hill. Ancient Lilea was razed to the ground by Philip of Macedon during the Third Sacred War. It now marks the beginning of a mountain road which climbs to the beautiful village of Eptalofos. Amid streams and boscages of poplars and against a background of rugged cliffs remarkable for the perfection and symmetry of their forms, the village sprawls across seven hills on different levels.

After passing over the ridge, this road enters extensive fir forests, passes Greece's main ski centres and winds down to Arahova and

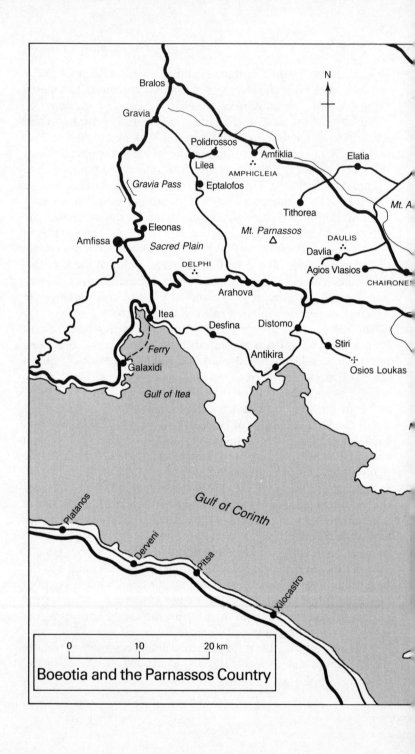

Boeotia and the Parnassos Country

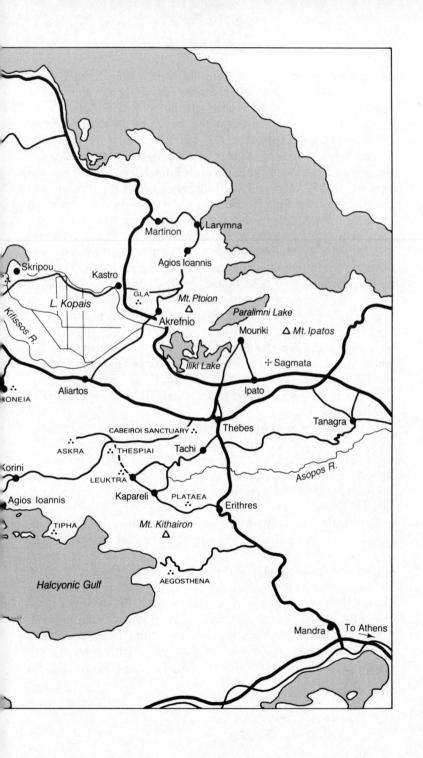

the navel-shaped valley of the Pleistos, with Delphi perched on its bastion in the west. In summer, driving or walking along one of the numerous tracks that wind through the cool, dark forests, one catches occasional glimpses of the scorching Phocian lowlands thousands of feet below.

Back in the plain, one can make a minor deviation from Lilea to a British military cemetery. Rows of well-tended graves contain the bones of British and Russian soldiers killed in the Macedonian campaigns of the First World War. It is as if they are set in an immense crater, the shadeless level ground surrounded by the razor-sharp crests of the mountain rim. To the south a slender nodular peak guards the entrance to the **Gravia Pass**, which we now enter in order to complete the circuitous route to Delphi. The road from here, originally built by the Anglo-French army in 1917 to shorten their lines of communication with the Macedonian front, runs between the torrent-rent buttresses of Parnassos and Giona. Forests of ilex and fir spread across the higher slopes. Beyond the watershed there are glimpses of a vast sea of olive groves curling round the bases of rocky foothills and flat-topped mountain ledges. No village could be more idyllically sited than Eleonas, amid a jungle of olive trees, with water cascading from one vine-covered terrace to another.

The descent ends at **Amfissa**. Built round a tapering crag planted with cypresses and littered with the ruins of a medieval castle, the town lies in the shadow of a crescent of jagged heights formed by Parnassos and Giona. By the nature of its commanding position at the head of the Crissaean plain, ancient Amfissa was the chief city of Ozolian Locris.

The castle was built in the thirteenth century by the d'Autremencourts of Picardy on the site of a classical fortress, whose impregnability was mentioned by Livy and of which there remain vestiges of quadrangular and polygonal walls. Originally called Salona, it was later renamed La Sol by Catalan conquerors who made it their most important fief in the country. The castle had three enceintes, whose ruined ramparts are now fringed with tall umbrella pines. The climb is steep, the medieval ruins exiguous. A fine monolithic lintel, probably of ancient origin, surmounts the entrance gate. A circular tower crowns the keep. There are also remnants of two churches – Byzantine and Frankish (or Catalan) and, at the foot of the hill to the south, a charming Turkish fountain.

The castle, which guarded the southern exit of the Gravia Pass, formed one of the bulwarks of central Greece. In 1821, when the War of Independence broke out, Amfissa was the first citadel on the mainland to be liberated by the Greeks. Turkish troops and inhabitants, rounded up on the castle slope, were massacred to a man on the orders of the Greek chieftain Panourias. No more than a brigand turned patriot, this unsavoury man devoted his period of rule in Amfissa to the sole cause of personal gain, and the long-suffering Amfissans, having exchanged a 'foreign tyrant' for a 'national hero', were compelled to maintain his retinue of robbers. The case of Panourias is an object-lesson.

From Amfissa a track winds up an escarpment, to a ledge on the mountainside overlooking the northern end of the plain. Here, where the olive groves contract between rocky foothills, stands the twelfth-century Byzantine **Church of Agiou Sotiros** (Holy Saviour), whose key must be obtained from the Church of *Agios Nikolaos* on the western slope of the town. The church is a classic example of twelfth-century architecture. The exterior apse, in front of which a plane tree provides shade, is interesting in that the central window, divided by a colonette, is placed within an arched frame, whereas the side windows are contained within square surrounds. The contrapuntal effect thus created is both harmonious and pleasing. Three parallel brick inlays decorate the window surrounds and there is considerable evidence of the tile decoration much favoured by twelfth-century architects who sought to embellish church exteriors with geometric designs. In the interior, the two columns supporting the dome are crowned by elaborately carved capitals. Some fine sculptured fragments from the original marble screen are ranged along the north wall of the *naos*.

South of Amfissa the road crosses the **Sacred Plain**, which is surrounded on all sides by lofty mountains. Peaks, ridges and slopes seem to have developed organically out of the primeval convulsion. The density of the olive trees is legendary, the gnarled trunks being among the most ancient in Greece.

This road leads to **Itea**, the port of Delphi, which lies at the head of a muddy gulf where cruise ships anchor. The place has a wasteland air, and its drab modernity, so close to the sacred land-scape, strikes one as a profanity. However there are adequate hotels at Itea which are useful when there is no accommodation at Delphi.

The spectacular coastal road to Nafpactos starts disappointingly along the barren western shore of the gulf, now rendered hideous by extensive mining installations. It leads to **Galaxidi**. This attractive village is built on a headland flanked on one side by a bay and on the other by a pine-fringed creek which provide excellent anchorages for yachts. There is a fine view across the inland sea towards Delphi and the escarpments of Parnassos. The houses, inhabited by caique-builders, are picturesque but without architectural distinction or historical associations. Skeletons of broad-beamed caiques litter the waterfront. The bathing is not good, for the rocks are spiky, the sea soupy, and at the height of summer there are swarms of flies.

Galaxidi, however, has a thirteenth-century Byzantine church. Above the town the road ascends into the olive belt, circling a bluff overlooking the sea. Across the Gulf of Corinth rise the Peloponne-sian ranges, slashed by great gorges, and here, nestling in a cypress grove surrounded by olive trees, is the **Church of Agiou Sotiros** (Holy Saviour). The church is usually locked but the keys can be obtained by asking at the police station. A transverse barrel vault at the southern end gives the impression, when seen from the interior, that a dome has been added to the basilica. The wall paintings are too poorly preserved to merit attention. Reliefs in the exterior apse, probably from the screen of an earlier church, are decorated with stylized pine cones and cypress branches in the angles of the crosses.

It is pleasant to take a boat from Galaxidi to Itea – a short but memorable journey. The oily waters of the gulf, dotted with barren islets like petrified porpoises, are ruffled only by the caique's wash. A silver haze hangs over the Sacred Plain, within an amphitheatre of tremendous mountains.

From Itea a road climbs one of the final seaward bulwarks of Parnassos. Providing an admirable view of the complexities of coastline, plain and mountain, it leads to a concave upland plateau on which lies the large village of Desfina. Thereafter the road descends through shadeless valleys to the deep, hidden bay of Antikira and thence to Osios Loukas.

*   *   *

There is only one way from Livadia to Osios Loukas – the road which ultimately leads to Delphi. It begins by winding round a series of rolling, eroded hills in a wide trough between Helikon and Parnassos. I know of no other point from which Mount Parnassos is seen to greater advantage: a well-ordered mass of soaring limestone, its buttresses and escarpments, square, regular or curvilinear, rent by deep ravines running in parallel vertical courses. It is lonely country. There is only a Vlach hamlet, some sheep-folds and a *khani*, or resting place, shaded by great plane trees. Goats scrabble among prickly shrubs on the precipitous slopes – a landscape, one feels, especially designed to guard the approaches to Delphi. On every side mountains soar above the **Cleft Way**, the ancient junction of the three roads from Delphi, Daulis and Thebes.

Soon there is a fork. The turning to the left (south) leads to Distomo, a centre of guerilla activity in the last war. Here there is another fork. The road to the south descends abruptly to the bay of **Antikira**, on the Gulf of Corinth. The rocky, barren coastline is dotted with mining installations. A corniche runs eastward, and the shell of a little Byzantine church lies at the mouth of a stony valley. Fragmentary remains of the ancient walls of Antikira are scattered across a bluff.

The other road from the fork at Distomo, going east, passes through Stiri, famous for the rich quality of its sheep's-milk yoghurt, and runs along a ridge of windswept hills to the **Monastery of Osios Loukas**. The church and its dependencies overlook a bowl-like valley with cultivated strips laid out in chequer-board fashion, enclosed on all sides by the steep, slate-grey spurs of Helikon.

The original chapel, dedicated to St Barbara, was built by the disciples of a holy man from neighbouring Stiri. He was called Luke ('Osios' being the Orthodox equivalent of a 'blessed man' in the Western Church) and his fame soon spread beyond his native mountains. He died in the middle of the tenth century. His humble shrine became a place of pilgrimage, and a monastery was founded. In Constantinople, Theophano, wife of three successive emperors, heard of it and arranged for its embellishment. Her son, the Emperor Basil II the Bulgar-Slayer, is believed to have given impetus to the enterprise during his triumphant tour of Greece at the beginning of the eleventh century. It was the beginning of the

111

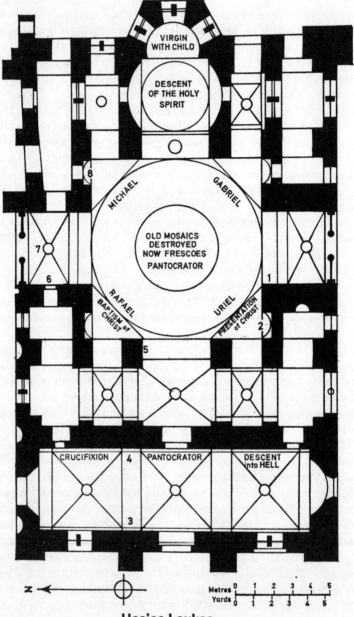

Hosios Loukas

Byzantine Golden Age and throughout the Empire there was a surge of creative activity. Osios Loukas remains a typical example of the Byzantine tradition of imperial patronage of remote monastic establishments.

The main church (eleventh-century) is a tall cross-inscribed edifice, with lavish exterior brickwork decoration, surrounded by monastic cells and a refectory. The windows, which possess sculptural embellishments, are divided into three sections by columns of different coloured marbles. The interior is one of the finest examples extant of the Byzantine desire to create a harmonious unity out of colours, cubes, bricks, paste, stone and marble. Bands of white carved marble divide the sumptuous multi-coloured revetments into two levels; the floor is of jasper and porphyry, the marble screen elaborately carved, and every inch of wall space in the narthex, the dome, the apses and the transepts glows with mosaics set against a golden background. There are also some less important frescoes of a later date.

The narthex comes first. The subtle and basic unity which underlies the arrangement of the figures of the apostles on the arches is achieved through their attitudes: they all ultimately point to the Pantocrator, whose image once filled the space above the door leading into the *naos*. Two of the most striking portraits are those of **St Peter** (east wall) and **St Andrew** (west wall), both with lively expressions and disproportionately large heads. Among the scenes from the life of Christ, the most impressive are the **Crucifixion** (left) and the **Descent into Hell** (right) in shallow lunettes. The bulky figure on the Cross, with its heavy tubular legs, is, in spite of its monolithic, columnar quality, contorted with physical pain.

In the main body of the church and in the side chapels, the iconographic arrangement adheres strictly to the established programme. In the first zone (vaults and chapels), saints intermingle with ascetics, prophets, bishops and provincial holy men in a gallery of portraits which, at first, tend to overshadow the narrative scenes on the upper register. There are few concessions to grace, none to sentimentality. Among the portraits, those of St Demetrius (south transept), St Basil (lunette in north-east transept), St Mercurios, the soldier-saint, with sheathed sword (north-west arch, left on entering) and a lively St Nicholas (lunette in south-west corner) are

113

worth noting. In the north transept there is a bust of the **Blessed Luke** himself, severe and monkish, his hands raised in worship. In numerous arches and vaults, the Archangels and military saints act as guards of honour. The busts within medallions, unlike those of the apostles in the narthex, are portrayed frontally.

High above the world of holy men extends the sphere of divine beings, at the summit of which Christ Pantocrator (in this instance, missing) dominates the Universe. In the apse, the Virgin and Child are represented seated on a cushioned throne decorated with elaborate inlay, against a concave golden background which creates an effect of immense spaciousness. In the dome of the sanctuary, the twelve apostles are seated round the symbol of the Trinity. Below the central cupola are the spandrels in which scenes from the *Dodecaorton* are depicted: a beautiful **Nativity**, in which the figure of Joseph, with enormous black eyes, and the animals leaning over the crib, lend an extraordinarily homely quality to the scene; and a **Baptism**, in which Christ stands shoulder-high in the waters of the Jordan as two angels advance towards him bearing elaborately decorated towels.

As there was little differentiation in colour tones, the austere, eleventh-century mosaicist at Osios Loukas tended to over-emphasize the modelling of his figures. The mosaics at Daphni are certainly more evolved and sophisticated in technique and execution, but Osios Loukas, in its completeness, in the power and intensity of the figures crowding its walls, in its elaborate decorative detail and majestic proportions, remains a more imposing and convincing example of the eleventh-century Byzantine church.

Below the church is the crypt of St Barbara, containing the tomb of the Blessed Luke, painted with crude frescoes of the peasant school of Cappadocia. Adjoining the main church is the Chapel of the Virgin, chronologically slightly earlier than the main church, and entered through a tenth-century exo-narthex with a triple portico crowned by a loggia. The dome above the cruciform *naos* is supported by four granite columns. The lavish Opus Alexandrinium pavement has a curious slant.

The almond orchards and patchwork fields in the cup-shaped valley are owned by the once-flourishing community of monks, now reduced to a few white-bearded old men relegated to cells in a far corner of the monastery. A small hostel, a restaurant and a tourist shop border the tree-shaded, rectangular terrace and the foothills of Helikon form a dark screen round the empty valley. In spring the air is heavy with the scents of broom, honeysuckle and lemon blossom.

CHAPTER 7

Delphi

Arahova – The Oracle –
The Sanctuary of Apollo: The Treasuries;
The Stoa of the Athenians; The Temple of Apollo;
The Theatre – The Stadium – Marmaria: The Tholos;
The Temple of Athena Pronaea – Sybaris –
The Corycian Cave – The Museum.

Isolated by a ring of mountains, Delphi has always been subject to violent climatic and geological pressures. Earthquakes and landslides are common. Clouds dissolve and re-form, casting their shadows across the olive groves. Torrential showers blot out the landscape and thunder echoes in the hollows of the valley. In summer the heat is trapped within the refractory limestone and the cliffs, pitted with primeval fissures, reflect a peculiar radiance which seems to derive its glow from the interior of the rock.

Several ways of approaching the sanctuary have been described in Chapter Six, but the direct route from Athens through Livadia is the one most travellers take. After the fork to Distomo the road climbs between jagged peaks. Fir trees spread across the higher slopes. Every outline acquires a razor-edge sharpness, the atmosphere a refined quality, the blue of the sky a new intensity and one senses one is approaching a place of immense significance in the affairs of men. At the top of the pass the curtain is raised with a tremendous flourish. The gorge lies below, the mountains crowding round to complete the famous umbilical effect. In the distance a buttress of cliffs, concealing the sanctuary, juts out to meet another wall of rock; beyond it is a tantalizing glimpse of the olive groves of the Sacred Plain.

In the immediate foreground a double-peaked bastion of Mount Parnassos, over three thousand feet high, is crowned by the grey stone houses of **Arahova**, its clocktower perched on the summit of a crag overhanging cultivated strips which descend in terraces to the bottom of the gorge.

Two modern hotels, in sharp contrast to the rustic atmosphere of this mountain eyrie, command a fine prospect of the gorge. Tourist shops display local handicrafts: woollen bags, carpets, blankets. The colours are crude and gaudy, but some of the bedspreads and tablecloths embroidered with old regional designs, and fleecy rugs called *flokates*, are attractive. The red wine of Arahova is good, if rather heady. The local cheese, made from goat's milk, its wax rind moulded in the design of a wickerwork basket, is more of a curiosity than a delicacy. Arahova is the starting-point for the ascent of Parnassos (a local guide being indispensable), for the visit to the Corycian Cave by car and for the drive across Parnassos to Gravia, via the ski centres.

Beyond Arahova the road descends, through terraces planted with almond trees, into the vine belt. The duct bringing water from the Mornos river to Athens makes an ugly concrete gash in the valley below. In the narrow gorge, the ruins of an ancient necropolis herald the approach to Delphi. The road loops round a huge projecting bluff and enters the inner amphitheatre of rock. Hawks and vultures hover over the wall of cliff which rises sheer from the highest ledge of the sanctuary. In the valley below, olive trees of immense antiquity mantle the precipitous banks of the Pleistos. The ruins of the sanctuary – broken columns, polygonal walls, grey stone tiers, red-brick Roman rubble – are spread out across the steep hillside though, sadly, the most prominent architectural feature is the modern building housing the museum, with its plate-glass windows and its shrubs and flowerbeds.

Hotels and tourist shops line the main street of the village of Delphi, which clings to another great projection of rock. The original hamlet, built over the sanctuary, was removed stone by stone to its present position when the excavations began at the end of the last century. Most of the hotels have magnificent views. One lunches and dines on terraces, shaded with awnings, overlooking the gorge. Shopping is better and more expensive than at Arahova.

117

The antiquities are confined to two areas: the Sanctuary of Apollo above the main road, and the Marmaria in an olive grove below the Castalian Spring. These (and the museum) can be rushed through in one day, but an overnight stay is strongly recommended.

It is only five minutes' walk to the **Sanctuary of Apollo**. The earliest references to it are purely mythical. They tell of roving shepherds, seized by uncontrollable frenzy owing to the potent vapours issuing from a fissure in the rock, pouring forth garbled prophecies in the name of Apollo. In time a temple to the god was raised above the fissure. Symbol of youth, light and beauty, Apollo was the most consistently Greek of the Olympian deities. Although vain, narcissistic and a philanderer, he had many attractive qualities: a love of music and poetry, an interest in medicine and astronomy; and traditionally he was the guardian of flocks and herds.

The Apolline cult developed rapidly and a priestess – the Pythia – was installed in the temple, where she chanted the ambiguous riddles that exercised such a powerful influence over men's actions for ten centuries. As a panhellenic sanctuary, Delphi possessed a far more profound religious influence than Olympia, and four Sacred Wars were fought for its preservation. From the beginning, the sanctuary's purpose was purely oracular, existing solely for communicating the counsels of the gods to mortals. Strabo believes 'the position of the place added something. For it is almost in the centre of Greece . . . and people called it the navel of the earth.'

The oracle was administered by five elected priests who claimed descent from Deucalion. They had complete control of administration, were responsible for the Pythia's political brief and were represented in Athens and elsewhere by agents. The fame of the prophecies was established as early as the eighth century BC; by the sixth, votive gifts were pouring in from every part of the civilized world. Croesus alone presented the shrine with a gold statue of a lion, a gold mixing-bowl that weighed a quarter of a ton and a silver wine vessel that held five thousand gallons. As an instrument of policy, the oracle's influence was by no means negligible. In the Persian Wars it tended to be defeatist, in the Peloponnesian Wars it showed a pro-Spartan bias. It was consulted among others by Oedipus, Agamemnon, Cleomenes, Philip of Macedon and Alex-

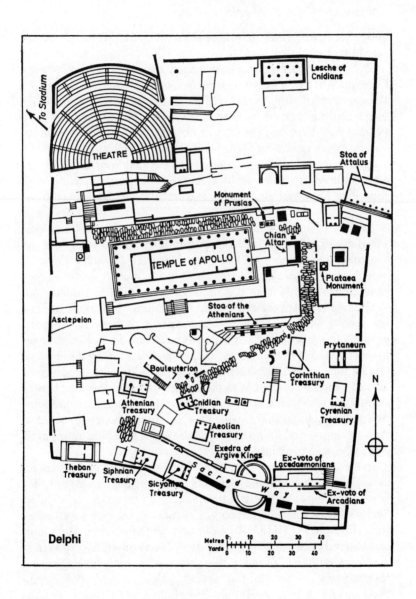

Delphi

ander the Great. To the latter the priestess cried: 'My son, none can resist thee!'

The oracles were generally extremely equivocal. Can one blame Croesus, when told he would destroy a mighty empire if he crossed the Halus, for failing to realize that the empire in question was his own? Little is known of the relations between priests and politicians, but there can be little doubt that string-pulling went on behind the scenes. Most of the problems upon which the consultants sought the god's arbitration related to the cultivation of crops or the sale of slaves, to loans or love affairs or intended marriages, to journeys. They had to pay a fee and sacrifice a goat, a sheep or an ox.

At an early stage Delphi was admitted into the Amphictyonic League, one of whose main responsibilities was to safeguard the sanctuary's interests and treasure. However the inhabitants of neighbouring Crissa grew increasingly envious and rapacious; they exacted heavy tolls from consultants approaching the oracle, and their assaults on female consultants scandalized the Delphians. The first Sacred War (c. 590 BC) broke out and Crissa was razed to the ground. In the second Sacred War Athens and Sparta fought over the ownership of the sanctuary. In the fourth century, the Phocians, out for loot, seized the sanctuary, thus provoking the third Sacred War. In the last Sacred War the aggressors were the Locrians of Amphissa, who wanted to cultivate their lands, until then undefiled by spade or ploughshare, which the League considered sacred to Apollo. In the end Philip of Macedon had to be called in to put an end to Locrian profanity.

In the third century BC bands of Gauls descended on the sanctuary. The invaders had the elements ranged against them: not only frost and snow, but also earthquakes, followed by landslides. Scrambling down the precipices of Parnassos, the Greeks attacked them in the rear. Panic broke out and, in their frenzy, the Gauls slaughtered each other by the hundred. It was thus left to Sulla, two centuries later, to plunder the shrine with his usual appalling thoroughness. After him the insatiable Nero carried off five hundred bronze statues to Rome. The philhellenic Hadrian and the Antonines did what they could to restore Delphi to its former splendour, but it was too late. The god's utterances no longer carried conviction. Acceptance of bribes by priests was rife and consultants became sceptical. In the fourth century Constantine the Great removed many works of art to Constantinople. The sanctuary was closed down by the Emperor Theodosius the Great in his famous edict of 393.

In time a hamlet grew up on the ancient deposits. In the seventeenth century Wheler observed traces of marble tiers on the terrace of the stadium and identified niches for statues beside the Castalian Spring. Between 1892 and 1903 the French School of Archaeology at Athens excavated the sanctuary and the Marmaria.

The sanctuary is screened by a semi-circle of cliffs, the rose-coloured Phaedriades, mottled with tufts of evergreens. Stunted pedestals and foundations of treasuries spread across a hillside covered with vetch, mullein and cistus. The bronze and marble statues have long since vanished: looted by Roman and Byzantine emperors or hacked to pieces by Goths and Visigoths. To the east the Castalian stream issues out of a rocky cleft and flows into the hollow valley, enclosed within the ring of mountains that no human hand could have fashioned with a more perfect sense of symmetry. Across the gorge, zigzag mule tracks climb the arid wall of Mount Kirfis like crude graffiti scratched by the hand of a giant. Hundreds of feet below, the Pleistos trickles sinuously between olive groves towards the Sacred Plain.

The **Sacred Way**, a steep, narrow ramp in the form of a double hairpin, begins at the lowest (east) end of the enclosure, beside the brickwork remains of a small, square Roman agora, identified by two unfluted Ionic columns. The paved ramp climbs between the foundations of buildings which once jostled against each other on the steep incline. It is all very congested and confusing and the fact that the sanctuary was built on a succession of narrow ledges further complicates the layout. In summer the sun is scorching and cicadas drone relentlessly among parched shrubs.

On the right lie the foundations of the rectangular **ex-voto of the Lacedaemonians**, with traces of a parapet, once adorned with statues of Spartan admirals. On the west side an imposing exedra, embellished with statues of Argive kings (the bases have been restored), was raised to commemorate the foundation of independent Messene. Next come the treasuries which contained the

121

archives and national treasures of the various states. On the left are the foundations of the **Treasury of Sicyon**, followed by the sub-structure of the **Treasury of Siphnos**. The visible remains are negligible, but there is a partial restoration in the museum. Other treasuries are scattered about the hillside. To the unprofessional eye they are no more than a mass of rubble, wholly incomprehensible.

At the apex of the first loop, the restored **Treasury of the Athenians** stands on a prominent ledge, one of the landmarks of the sanctuary. Only thirty-three by twenty feet, it was the first Doric edifice to be built entirely of marble. The walls grow thinner as they ascend in order to convey the illusion of height, and a feeling of squatness caused by the low roof was relieved by an acroterium of an Amazon on horseback surmounting the gable. But it is not one of the masterpieces of classical architecture.

The Sacred Way now slants obliquely up the hill between foundations of votive edifices. On the left are the remains of the **Bouleuterion**, or Senate House, where the Committee of Five transacted business and formulated policy. Beyond it is the rock, reinforced by modern masonry, from which the Sybil Herophile, who alternately called herself wife, daughter and sister of Apollo, chanted the first oracles. A natural fissure in the ground nearby is said to have been the entrance to the lair where the serpent Python dwelt. Three steps lead up to the **Stoa of the Athenians**, in which the spoils captured from the Spartans in the Peloponnesian Wars were displayed. Three of the original eight miniature Ionic columns which once supported a wooden roof are now ranged against the massive stones of a great polygonal wall. The interlocking and irregular stones have a smooth, honey-coloured surface and were designed to reinforce the god's temple in the event of earthquakes. Opposite is the open space of the *halos*, or threshing floor, where Apollo's victory over Python was celebrated every seven years.

At the apex of the second loop a sharp ascending turn to the left leads to the round pedestal for the votive offering, set up by all the states who fought at Plataea. Facing it is the **Altar of the Chians**, also commemorating the Greek victory over the Persians, composed of rectangular slabs of grey-blue marble; a conspicuous but uninspiring monument, twice restored during the present century at the expense of wealthy Chian shipowners. Beyond it is a rectangular plinth with a garlanded frieze, once crowned by an equestrian statue of Prusias II.

Sheer cliffs rise above the high-lying terrace. A modern ramp climbs to the eastern entrance of the stylobate of the **Temple of Apollo**, which commands a prospect not only of the whole precinct but also of the stupendous circular panorama. The perspective is enhanced by the restoration of three massive Doric limestone columns which reflect the changing light – grey, brown or gold, according to the time of day – their huge weathered drums conveying an impression of the scale of the building, which was almost as large as the Parthenon.

Of the historical origins little is known, except that the Archaic temple was gutted by fire. In the late sixth century BC it was replaced by a splendid edifice raised by the Amphictyons: a massive peripteral temple of the Doric order on a three-tiered stylobate of bluish marble, its front adorned with marble columns, several drums of which still survive. A panhellenic subscription was raised to obtain the necessary funds. This building was largely destroyed by an earthquake and the existing foundations and stylobate belong to the fourth-century re-construction. It was the sixth-century Amphictyonic temple that acquired the greatest fame.

Among the most famous of the sculptures in the temple was the golden effigy of Apollo, which was set behind an altar of eternal fire kept alive by piles of fir-wood. Little now remains of the sculptures – only some truncated limbs from the pediment, now in the museum. The seat of the oracle was in the *adytum*, a chamber penetrated only by priests. The fissure from which the vapours emanated has not been identified. The priestess was always a young virgin, until, on one occasion, she was raped by an impious lecher. After that only older and less attractive women were employed. She sat on a golden tripod above the narrow fissure, munching laurel leaves, and in a state of frenzied exaltation would recite the equivocal conundrums which, with the aid of qualified advisers, the bewildered consultants had to interpret. Sometimes the effect of the vapours on the priestess was so great that she would leap dementedly from her tripod, suffer from convulsions and die within a few days.

Above the temple a Roman stairway mounts to the **Theatre**, originally fourth-century BC and of white marble, but restored in grey limestone by the Romans. The *cavea*, divided by a paved *diazôma*, has only thirty-three tiers, but they are well preserved; so is the orchestra, which is composed of irregular slabs and is surrounded by the usual water-conduit. There is no more perfect example of a Greek theatre in harmonious relation to its setting: the sweeping forms of the stone tiers repeated in the rocky semi-circle of the Phaedriades. In the late afternoon the glow of the Phaedriades is reflected on the slopes of the encircling mountains which turn pink, mauve and finally a deep cobalt blue. The valley fills with obscure shadows. For all its grandeur, it is an intensely serene landscape.

To the right of the theatre is the dried-up stream of the Cassiotis, which used to water the sacred groves of laurel and myrtle and flowed through a secret channel into the *adytum* of the temple, where the Pythia drank from its waters before prophesying. Beyond this stream a path leads to the site of the **Lesche of the Cnidians**. Its walls were of unfired brick, and the interior was in the form of a rectangular atrium. Four stone sockets (*socles*) for the columns which supported the wooden roof are all that remain of this famous rest-house where pilgrims sought shade and shelter.

From the theatre, another path climbs to the left between bushes of arbutus and blackberry to the **Stadium**, the highest point of the ancient city. The best preserved of Greek stadia, it once seated seventeen thousand spectators. Built in the fifth century BC, it probably did not possess stone accommodation until the fourth and most of the existing tiers are of the Antonine period. Of the Roman triumphal arch four pillars remain. On the north bank, against the cliff, there are twelve well-preserved tiers divided into as many sections by stairways; on the west and south, where there is a sharp declivity buttressed by a polygonal wall supporting the mountain shelf, only six. A slight concavity in the centre was intended to prevent the spectator's view being obstructed by his neighbours.

Like the Olympic Games, the Pythian festival, also a panhellenic celebration, was held every four years. The athletic programme was the same as at Olympia, with the addition of a long race for boys and, last and most spectacular of all, a race in bronze armour. Victors were crowned with wreaths of laurel. There was no other reward except the adulation so dear to the Greek heart. The honour of a victory at the Pythian Games was second only to that of an Olympic award. Singing and music played on the flute and lyre formed an important part of the festivities.

From the stadium there is a short cut to the village. It is more rewarding, however, to zigzag down through the sanctuary, regain the main road and, walking east, reach the **Castalian Spring**. Even though coaches now park here, this remains an idyllic spot. Large plane trees shade the stream, which issues from a ravine that cleaves the Phaedriades in two. Above the spring, whose water is ice-cold and extraordinarily clear, is the niche of an old shrine. Consultants and athletes purified themselves by washing their hair in Castalia's lustral water before proceeding to the temple and the stadium. A path leads a short way into the gloomy ravine between the Phaedriades, strewn with huge boulders and pitted with unsuspected crevices. Rocks occasionally crash down from above.

Beyond the café below the road a path winds down past the ruins of the fourth-century BC **Gymnasium**. This was the practice-ground for the athletes entered for the Pythian games, with a covered race-track running parallel to an open-air one. Among the weeds and thistles lies a stone slab with a groove and socket, believed to have been equipped with a *husplex*, a mechanical device that made a loud noise as it fell, thus giving the signal for the start.

Beyond the gymnasium the path continues down the hill, under shady olive branches, to the **Marmaria**, the Sanctuary of Athena Pronaea – less spectacular than Apollo's, but no less beautiful. Carpeted in spring with grape hyacinths and bee orchids, it extends across a rectangular shelf below the eastern projection of the Phaedriades. First comes the stylobate of an austere fourth-century BC **Temple of Athena**, guardian of the precinct. Foundations of other temples and buildings, slabs of bluish limestone and fragments of broken drums litter the terraced olive grove. The pride of the sanctuary is the **Tholos**, a circular fourth-century BC edifice on a three-stepped platform. A work of extreme elegance which was originally crowned by a conical roof, it had an outer ring of twenty Doric columns surrounding an inner ring of ten Corinthian columns. The gutter of the entablature had a rich ornamentation, including lion-head spouts, one of which is preserved above a restored *metope*. Three stout, yet graceful, Doric columns, sur-mounted by a lintel and fragments of *metopes*, rise from the stylobate. What purpose the temple served is not known. The setting, with the valley contracting to its narrowest point, is peaceful and bucolic. Chameleons slither along ruts and cracks in the masonry; bees swarm in the sweet-smelling bay trees. There is none of the overcrowding that creates such a jigsaw-puzzle effect in the Sanctuary of Apollo.

Beyond the Tholos are the substructures of two **treasuries**: the first, that of Massalia, is thought to have been an elegant little building in the Ionic style, contemporary with the treasury of Siphnos. Next comes the debris of the early fifth-century BC **Temple of Athena Pronaea**, built of tufa on the site of a much earlier edifice. Three thick Doric columns still survive at the north-west corner and two enormous boulders, lying across the stylobate, provide evidence of repeated landslides. Beyond the Marmaria lies the necropolis of the ancient city.

Several paths descend through terraces of olive groves to the bed of the Pleistos. Vestiges of the polygonal masonry of supporting walls are visible. In autumn donkeys carrying huge panniers filled with olives clamber up the stony tracks. There are few dwellings: only an occasional chapel, ruined or abandoned. At the bottom of the gorge the feeling of isolation is complete. The stream of the Pappadia trickles down from the Castalian Spring, and there is a grotto, surrounded by contorted boulders, said to be the ancient Sybaris, where the Lamia, a sphinx-like monster which ravaged the countryside, dwelt in a subterranean lair. The walk takes about two hours.

A longer walk or ride (about six hours there and back) is to a more famous grotto, the **Corycian Cave**. The path climbs the southern wall of the Phaedriades behind the village to a highland plateau of stones and stunted pines, dominated by the summit of Parnassos. The cave, to which the track ultimately leads (it is essential to have a guide), is at the north-west end of the plateau below the fir belt. I confess I cannot share the enthusiasm of Pausanias, who found it, of all the caves he had seen, the finest. Euripides extols its 'mountain-chambers', of which there are said to be forty, their damp walls shining with pink and green reflections. The light of a candle reveals stalactites and stalagmites. The cave was named after the nymph Corycia, beloved of Apollo, and was sacred to the nymphs and to Pan. The final ascent to the cave (twenty minutes' hard climbing) can also be reached by car along a rough road from Arahova.

The **Museum** at Delphi is situated halfway between the Sanctuary of Apollo and the village, its barrack-like façade somewhat incongruous in this most classical of landscapes. Before entering, it is worth looking at two fourth-century **floor mosaics** at the right of the entrance. The decoration is chiefly composed of birds, though the larger one has a wider zoological range and the mosaicist has reproduced a number of stylized animals.

The interior of the Museum is spacious and well lit, but few of the precious fragments are numbered. At the top of the staircase stands an ovoid stone object: a copy of the original sacred stone, the *omphalos* or so-called navel of the earth, which was placed in the *adytum* of the Temple of Apollo, its interlocking marble fillets symbolizing the continuity of life. From here on the arrangement is more or less chronological.

Room 2 is full of interest. The **Naxian Sphinx**, a heraldic work of the sixth century BC, towers above the other exhibits on a marble plinth crowned by an Ionic capital. Seated on her hindquarters with her scythe-shaped wings and a bosom ornamented with feathers, she gazes imperiously into space.

Fascinating fragments of the **frieze of the Treasury of Siphnos** are ranged along the walls. Dated to the sixth century BC, the figures are without the least trace of crudity. The sculptures, though battered, quickly come to life. In the battle of the gods against the giants (north side) a tornado of agitation galvanizes the figures into action: Apollo and an exultant Artemis aim their arrows; a stocky-limbed Ares, smirking with self-confidence, takes on a couple of giants over the prostrate body of a third. The east side depicts seated gods debating the issue of the Trojan War. The detail of the frieze is fascinating. Both the pliability of the stylized drapery and the difference in texture between the naked flesh and the long ringlets of the head-dresses point to the chisel of a master sculptor. Particularly beautiful are the manes and tails of the horses in the south frieze. The reliefs originally ran around the entire building, framed between decorative fillets. In its entirety, with the crowd of agitated figures and prancing horses, the frieze must have been a master-piece.

Room 3 is dominated by two crude and impressive early sixth-century BC figures of **Cleobis and Biton**, the Argive boys who, in the absence of oxen, harnessed themselves to a chariot and bore their mother across the plain to the Temple of Hera, where she was chief priestess. For their pains, the goddess rewarded the youths with eternal sleep. Cleobis (right), who is better preserved than his brother, possesses all the 'inner mobility' associated with later, more polished Archaic *kouroi*. Tough, stocky, with short muscular arms, he is endowed with remarkable tension, ready to spring forward and harness himself to his mother's chariot.

Rooms 4–8 contain fragments of *metopes* from the Athenian treasury, figures (with uncompleted backs) from the Temple of Apollo, *metopes* and fragments of the coffered ceiling from the Tholos. In Room 7, beside two bronze *kalpis* (elegantly shaped ewers with three handles), there is a fine *stele* of an athlete extending his arms to the right, while a bereaved child, no doubt his servant, gazes up from the right-hand corner.

In Room 9 the **Column of the Dancing Girls**, an unusual monu-ment of the Hellenistic period, soars towards the ceiling. The shaft, about thirty feet high, was so carved as to resemble a gigantic acanthus stalk, the foot of each drum being surrounded by luxuriant foliage. Grouped round the highest tier of leaves are the three girls performing a hieratic dance. In spite of the fundamental awkward-ness of the composition, the girls' drapery is loose and flowing and they possess much of the life and grace lacked by the more solemn Caryatids of the Erectheion. The nude athlete, the **Thessalian Agas**, winner of fourteen awards at panhellenic festivals, is a good late fourth-century BC marble copy of a bronze work by Lysippus.

The bronze **Charioteer** stands alone in Room 10, against a pale grey background. He could not be more effectively exhibited. The life-sized figure, made up of seven separately cast parts, belonged to a *quadriga* which was placed on the terrace of the temple, the gift of a Sicilian tyrant in the first half of the fifth century BC. Only the shaft and the yoke of the chariot survive. The heavy tubular drapery of the tunic, perfect in its symmetry and rhythm, creates a columnar effect that distinguishes this work from all other Greek statues.

The Tower of the Winds or Horologium of Andronicos Cyrrhestus, Athens.
An architectural fantasy created by a philhellenic Syrian of the first century AD.

The Choragic Monument of Lysicrates, Athens. Engraving by Stuart and
Revett, 1751–53. This small, cylindrical monument is shown surrounded by
the Franciscan monastery built round it in the seventeenth century.

Marble stele from the Kerameikos: a mother bids farewell to her child.
(National Archaeological Museum, Athens)

Viewed from all sides the figure is stately, though somewhat dis-
proportionate, for the sculptor was endeavouring to correct the
distortion which is inevitable when life-sized figures are viewed
from below.

Room 11, although not without interest, is inevitably an anti-
climax, but passing out of this last hall one is suddenly confronted
with a staggering view of the Phaedriades through large plate-glass
windows. Russet-coloured, they tower up on either side of the
ravine that slashes them into two separate but complementary
volumes. On the periphery, the olive groves, watered by rivulets of
the Castalian Spring, shelve down into the valley and purple
shadows drift across the outer ring of mountains. The spirit of
harmony that existed between the creative genius of the Greeks and
the physical world in which they dwelt is not now beyond the bounds
of comprehension. What is more difficult to understand is how that
colossal hoax, the Delphic oracle, could have taken in so many
people for so long.

CHAPTER 8

Eastern Roumeli

Mount Oiti: Heracles's funeral pyre –
The Valley of the Sperhios – Lamia – Thermopylae –
The Castle of Bodonitsa – Ipati – Karpenissi –
The Monastery of Proussos.

Turning north from Delphi, one has to find a way across a confused
mountain region of Northern Greece known as Eastern Roumeli,
inhabited by a sturdy people, proud of their warrior traditions and
reputation for probity.

After passing through Amfissa and the Gravia Pass one reaches
the hamlet of Bralos overlooking the western apex of the Phocian
Plain. Just beyond the hamlet there is a fork. The road to the west
leads into a massif of great splendour. At all points of the compass
rise the peaks and escarpments of Mount Oiti, Giona and Parnassos. Winding up into the complex of ranges, the road passes through
the alpine villages of Oiti and Pavliani, ablaze with hollyhocks in
summer, often snowbound in winter. Then the chestnut forests
begin: dark tracts covered with bracken. The altitude increases and
one enters the conifer belt. At the signpost '*Pros Katafygion*' ('to
the refuge') a dirt road mounts the fir-covered slopes to a barren
upland. Another signpost marks the site of the **Funeral Pyre of
Heracles**, where an ancient shrine, among the loneliest in the
country, was raised to commemorate the hero's metamorphosis into
a fully-fledged deity.

According to tradition, Heracles, the symbol of incomparable
masculine strength, ended his career on this lonely seven thousand
foot high mountain-top. Sophocles wrote of his ascent, amid peals

of thunder and flashes of lightning, to the marble halls of Olympus, where his father granted him immortality and a charming wife.

The site, which includes the outlines of a *megaron* and *stoa*, is littered with limestone slabs, fluted drums and fragments of *triglyphs*. Unexcavated, these stones have weathered time and the elements for over two millennia. In this rarefied atmosphere, the contours of the central mainland massif assume the aspect of a map. Geography is omnipresent, the emphasis on symmetry pronounced. The vertical spine of the Pindos, dividing the country in two, meets the horizontal chain of Kalidromo, Oiti and Panetoliko. Parallel to it, the Giona–Parnassos–Helikon range shuts off all Central Greece from the south. It is like a reversed Cross of Lorraine, with the valleys and cultivated plains filling in the interstices between the lateral arms.

Back at the fork beyond Bralos, one follows the road that climbs a lower ridge of Oiti and descends through the dizziest hairpin bends in Greece into the shut-in **Valley of the Sperhios**. Eastward, hundreds of feet below, streams trickle through gorges, and *katavothras* force their way underground to pour their efflux of silt and sludge into the Sperhios and thence into the Malian Gulf. East of the road, the Athens–Thessaloniki railway line – a remarkable piece of French nineteenth-century engineering – winds through a silent wooded country. A long viaduct spans the Gorgopotamos torrent, scene of a much publicized exploit during the Second World War, when Greek guerillas, aided by British parachutists, blew up the bridge cutting one of the main supply routes to the Libyan front in 1942. The railway line passes through seventeen tunnels and, clinging to successive ledges, descends the rocky Trachinian precipices to the lowlands below.

At the base of the range the road runs across a flat cereal-and-tobacco-growing strip, watered by the streams of the Sperhios, to Lamia. Frogs croak on muddy banks. On moonless nights myriads of fireflies flit among the reeds bordering the streams. Achilles, who was born hereabouts, trained, from the age of six, to dispose of bears and lions in single combat and consequently developed such physical strength that when passionately embracing the objects of his affections he often broke their ribs.

Lamia sprawls across the foothills of the Orthris range. Although

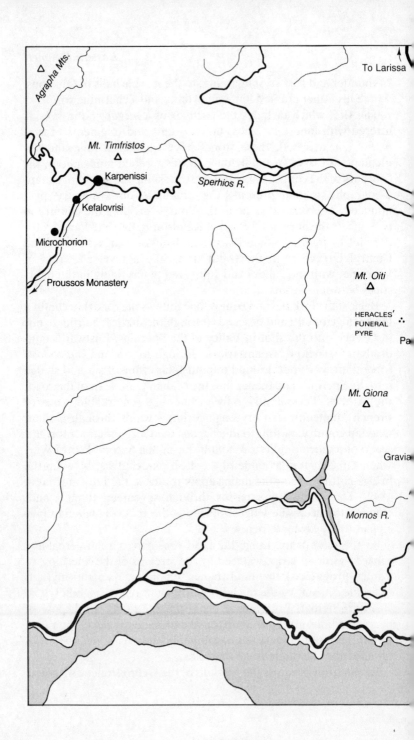

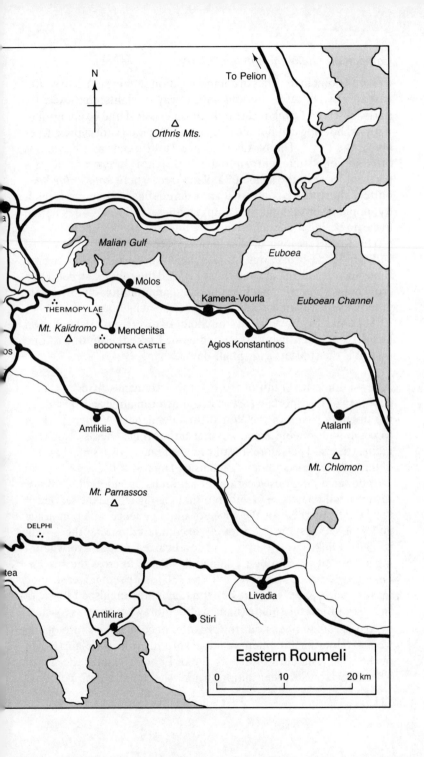

N

To Pelion

△
Orthris Mts.

Malian Gulf

Euboea

● Molos

Kamena-Vourla
●

Euboean Channel

∴
THERMOPYLAE

Mt. Kalidromo
△

● Mendenitsa

∴
BODONITSA CASTLE

Agios Konstantinos
●

OS

● Amfiklia

Atalanti
●

△
Mt. Chlomon

Mt. Parnassos
△

DELPHI
∴

tea

Antikira
●

● Stiri

Livadia
●

Eastern Roumeli

0   10   20 km

a pivotal point in the lines of communication running north to south, east to west, it offers nothing in the way of sightseeing except a partly restored Catalan castle, built on classical and Roman foundations, housing a minor museum on a hill spiked with cypress trees above the town. The battlements are Turkish but, as a brigade is often stationed here, entry into the castle is not always possible. It is pleasant to sit in the shade of a plane tree, where *kourambiédhes*, buttery shortbreads coated with powdered sugar (a Lamian speciality, popular throughout the country), are served with Greek coffee in a café beside the fountain in Laou Square.

The town has long been a military centre. When the War of Independence broke out in 1821, the Turks assembled twenty thousand men in and around the town, and the cobbled streets were crowded with horses, pack-animals and ammunition dumps, while greedy-eyed Albanian soldiers ravaged the neighbouring farms.

At Lamia, the traveller has the choice of diversions: east to Pelion (see Chapter Ten), south-east and west. I take the south-east one first. It is the shorter: a long half-day's driving.

A few kilometres south of the town the **Alamanas Bridge** spans a tributary of the Sperhios, scene of a much romanticized episode in the opening round of the War of Independence. A large Turkish force, moving out of Lamia, was met at the bridge – across which the main Athens–Thessaloniki traffic now streams – by a small band of determined Greeks under Athanasios Diakos, a deacon who had abandoned a religious vocation for a military career in the ranks of the local militia, whose members although officially in the service of the Sultan, worked for the cause of independence with a courage and sense of responsibility rarely encountered among the Greek patriots. Diakos was youthful and lion-hearted. But an overwhelming superiority in numbers enabled the Turks to cross the stream. Diakos was captured and roasted alive. His death remains enshrined in story book and folksong. In Lamia, an undistinguished statue of the hero adorns the square (named after him) where he was roasted.

As the valley opens out towards the once marshy shore of the Malian Gulf, the mountain wall rises abruptly from the plain. North of the road a modern bronze statue of Leonidas marks the site of **Thermopylae**. No other major ancient site is more disappointing.

The deposits thrown up by the 'Hot Springs' have created new alluvial soil and there is no sign of the pass where five thousand Greeks made their heroic stand in August 480 BC against Xerxes' army – according to Herodotus' doubtless vastly exaggerated estimate – of five million men. In the fifth century BC the swamp advanced so close to Mount Kalidromo that it left only the narrowest passage for men and chariots. Today the bog is replaced by cultivated fields.

A tumulus opposite the statue of Leonidas is supposed to cover the bones of the Spartan dead. Standing on this mound, one can try to work out the different moves in the battle. But it is all very baffling. Where was it that the Great King encamped, while he waited in rage and bewilderment at the temerity of this handful of Greeks? In the plain? But it was then an unbridgeable morass. Where was he stationed when, after launching the attack, he watched the battle? Throughout two whole days Xerxes beheld his best troops annihilated by the skilled archers of the little Greek force. Disheartened by such tenacity, he accepted the offer of a Malian traitor to lead part of the Persian army along a secret track into the heart of the mountain, whence it could wheel round and attack the Greeks in the rear. At dawn the Persians descended by the mountain path on the main body of the Greeks, whose soothsayer had already foretold their doom. Leonidas, the Spartan king, who claimed descent from Heracles, dismissed most of his allies, insisting that the honour of making the last-ditch stand should belong to Spartans only. In the morning Xerxes attacked 'the three hundred': all warriors of mature age, personally picked by Leonidas. Caught in the pincers, the Spartans performed prodigies of valour. After Leonidas was killed, they retreated into the narrowest part of the pass, where they fought with daggers, bare hands and even their mouths, until each one fell. After it was all over, Xerxes ordered the head of Leonidas to be cut off and fixed on a stake. Later, a column was raised where the Spartans fell – there is, alas, no vestige of it left.

For centuries the 'Hot Gates' remained the only pass through which an invading army could enter Southern Greece. In April 1941 officers and men of the Australian and New Zealand brigades of the British Expeditionary Force, encamped below the ridges of Kalidromo, watched German armoured forces, with the RAF driven

135

from the skies, assemble unmolested in the plain. Like the Persians, the German tanks suffered heavy casualties. But a repetition of the fatal turning movement – this time on an infinitely wider scale – caused the Expeditionary Force to abandon the position. It is curious how each time the defenders of Thermopylae have lost the battle.

From Thermopylae a side road climbs five kilometres south-east between hedgerows of arbutus and agnus castus, to the village of Anadra where the pine belt is reached. Eastward, where Kalidromo tapers off into a series of jagged peaks towards the Euboean channel, there is a sudden view of the **Castle of Bodonitsa** crowning a beige-coloured hill, around which the hamlet of Mendenitsa nestles among walnut trees and vegetable plots. Bodonitsa, site of ancient Tarphae, was one of the Crusaders' main bulwarks guarding Central Greece from invasion from the north. Any hostile force, attempting to round the Kalidromo range could not fail to be spotted by sentinels stationed on the battlements.

Most impressive is the north-west polygonal wall rising sheer from a sloping ledge. It is five minutes' climb from the modern war memorial to the keep, entered through a postern crowned by a massive lintel. Above it rises a squat tower. Ancient slabs, believed to have come from a temple of Hera who was worshipped here, are embedded in the masonry among huge thistles with purple flowers. Ruined ramparts overlook cornfields shelving down to the coast. Bodonitsa was an Italian, never a French, fief, and the fame and prestige of its Marquis was comparable to the strength of his castle and elegance of his court. It is not among the largest of medieval castles in Greece, but in the grandeur and beauty of its position it is comparable to any. In 1414 the last Italian Marquis, inspired perhaps by the proximity of Thermopylae, defended it against the Turks with a bravery and tenacity that would have done credit to Leonidas. With the fall of Bodonitsa, the whole of Central Greece passed into Ottoman hands. The Turkish conquerors destroyed the walls and sold the inhabitants, Italian and Greek, into slavery.

The enclosure is pitted with hollows: once vaulted chambers, now overgrown with wild fig trees which exude the sun-baked bitter-sweet fragrance of the milky sap secreted in their stalks. A Gothic arch surmounts one side of the pits, probably part of a chapel, beside the north rampart. The wall-walk is too ruined to serve as a promenade, but the village boys, who like to act as guides, scramble to the summit of the squat tower, where, silhouetted against a background of fir-covered peaks, they pass the time aiming stones at elusive grass snakes rustling among the thistles.

Shortly after Thermopylae the highway begins to skirt the coast, winding in and out of shingly coves. Across the water the western extremity of Euboea approaches. The entire maritime strip was once studded with ancient townships: for the most part unexcavated, unidentified or razed to the ground by earthquakes.

The hotels, restaurants and tavernas of **Kamena-Vourla**, a fashionable spa, are confined between the seashore and the foot of abrupt slopes sliced by wooded gullies filled with evergreens and coursed by rivulets bordered with maidenhair. Hotels, blocks of flats and villas line the coast south-east along the motorway – it is only two hours' drive from Athens – but most of the beaches are narrow, sometimes littered with sea-weed, and the water of the Euboean Channel lacks the sparkling quality of the Aegean. **Agios Konstantinos** is a fishing village turned summer resort; likewise **Arkitsa**, from which a ferry plies to Edipsos, a spa on Euboea. The highway then enters a triangular little plain of well-watered orchards, at the apex of which lies the village of **Atalanti** whence a road climbs over a shoulder of Mount Chlomon to join the old Athens–Thessaloniki road in the Boeotian plain. The islet in the bay of Atalanti was fortified by the Athenians during the Peloponnesian war as a deterrent to Opuntian privateers who harassed Athenian trade. After skirting the shallow bay, broken up by little spits of land, the highway climbs a saddle of Mount Chlomon and descends into the Boeotian plain at Kastro.

West of Lamia the spa of **Ipati** shelters under the wall of Mount Oiti. Over it all – café, restaurants and hotel lounges crowded with patients suffering from skin diseases – hangs the fetid smell of sulphur. More attractive is the village of **Ano-Ipati** on a high ledge above the spa. Here Apuleius lays the scene of *The Golden Ass*, in which the lusty Lucius, after rubbing himself with an ointment prepared by the witch Pamphile, is transformed into a dumb and docile donkey.

137

It is a painful climb from the village square to the site of the Catalan castle (it is essential to ask the way). During part of the near-vertical ascent, the path is shaded by plane trees and thick brambles which form an arbour over a trickle of water from a mountain stream. Winding round a rocky eminence, one perceives a lone crag crowned by a circular tower and fragments of ramparts. The Catalans could not have chosen a more inaccessible site on which to perch a castle whence they could detect hostile armies threading their way through the western and northern defiles of the mountain arena. But ruined watchtowers are not the sole legacy of the Catalan conquerors. The impact made by this strange Spanish interlude on the local inhabitants was considerable and lasting. Regarded as one of the perennial scourges the Greeks had learnt to accept as a law of nature, the rough soldiers of fortune of the Catalan Grand Company picked wives for themselves from among the Frankish aristocracy they had defeated at the battle of Cephisus and soon earned themselves a terrible reputation for cruelty.

Another more important road west of Lamia follows the course of the Sperhios until the tobacco and cotton fields peter out below the foothills of Mount Timfristos (7695 feet), linchpin of the Oiti and Orthris offshoots of the Pindos. Its elegant tapering peak is a landmark throughout much of Central Greece. The road ascends between silver firs, affording backward views of the ribbon-like valley, skirts a village named after the mountain, and enters a shut-in alpine valley through which flows the torrent of the Karpenisiotis. At the end of it is **Karpenissi**, a summer resort with some hotels and restaurants. Largely rebuilt after its destruction by both Germans and Communist rebels during and after the Second World War, Karpenissi has nothing to offer in the way of sightseeing. But the air is crystalline. It is also one of the two starting points (the other is Agrinio in Western Roumeli, a much more difficult climb across the Panetoliko) for a visit to a famous place of pilgrimage: the Monastery of Proussos. The road is easy and picturesque through narrow defiles and round overhanging precipices.

A short descent from Karpenissi ends in a well-watered valley of maize-fields, cherry and apple orchards. Here **Kefalovrisi** marks the site of a notable engagement during the War of Independence. A Turkish force of four thousand men was surprised one summer night in 1823 by Markos Botsaris, one of the ablest champions of Greek independence, and three hundred and fifty Suliots, a warrior tribe of Albanian descent. The Turkish commander's tent was pitched in a low-walled enclosure protecting the beehives which still spread across the hillside. Although the Turks were taken unawares, Botsaris was shot. The gloom cast over the Suliots by the death of their leader did not prevent them from indulging in an orgy of plunder.

The road passes through the tree-shaded village of Microchorion – site of the Suliot encampment – destroyed by a gigantic landslide in 1963 and re-built in neo-Greek style at the foot of Mount Helidona; another peak, that of Mount Kalliakhouda, towers immediately to the east of Gavros. One crosses the Karpenisiotis, bordered by ilex and plane, and enters a gorge rent with screes whose higher levels of rock reflect a bright purple light when just touched by the sun's rays. The gorge narrows to a point where it is no more than forty metres wide, with the road imprisoned between walls of granite, alternately brick-red, brown and purple. The chapel of *Agios Sostis* (St Saviour) clings to a ledge of cliff above.

Beside the torrent of ice-cold water there is a café, from which, in the gloomy shade, one can look up at the face of the cliff and see a hatchet-shaped aperture in the rock. Through this passage the venerable wonder-working icon of Proussos is said to have flown in its quest for a final resting place. The stratification of the winding gorge becomes more curious, the rock seamed with vertical zig-zags and squiggles like notes of music. Climbing above the bed of another ice-green torrent, the Krikelliotis, one sees the distant peak of Panetoliko, the ubiquitous 'Arab's Head', which dominates the Aetolian massif. As the road ascends one looks down on ranks of nodular outcrops of rock, overgrown with tufts of ilex, rising like ninepins out of the gorge. As the gorge opens out between fir-clad heights one catches a glimpse of the houses of Proussos scattered across a cultivated slope above an irregular bowl, out of which more rocky cones, sometimes with spherical or bulbous summits, rise in terrible disarray. Winding among these awesome precipitous bluffs, the road descends towards the bowl, making for a needle of rock crowned by a clock tower.

In the shade of plane trees, beside a chapel, lie the ruins of a

Companion Guide to Mainland Greece

Greek secret school, founded during the Turkish occupation by Cosmas the Aetolian who tried to instruct his uncouth fellow-mountaineers in the virtues of their Hellenic heritage. Nearby is the church of the **Monastery of Proussos**, thought to be the site of a sanctuary of Athena and later a Christian shrine which became the refuge of an anchorite. The monastery is an unattractive modern building raised on the charred foundations of several earlier monastic establishments. The church, an ordinary cruciform domed little edifice, is strikingly situated in a deep concavity of vertical rock; it has thus been protected for centuries from the boulders that hurtle down in the course of landslides. The painted decoration of the interior is undistinguished.

In the courtyard pilgrims, holding long tapers, drag themselves penitentially on hands and knees to a side chapel which contains the **icon of the Virgin Proussiotissa**, famous for its healing powers. Solemn-faced worshippers queue in single file to enter the dimly lit interior and kiss the holy image. Only the brown faces of the Virgin and a Semitic-looking Child are visible, the rest of the ancient icon being elaborately silver-plated. The icon is apocryphally attributed to the hand of St Luke and is, to this day, in spite of its inaccessibility, venerated by streams of pilgrims during a whole week in August. The library and museum of the monastery contain little of interest: post-Byzantine Books of Gospels, filigree work, reliquaries and crosses.

Returning to Karpenissi, a fine west-bound road winds through the highlands of the Southern Pindos, overhanging rugged gorges which run parallel in a north–south axis. To the north rise the Agrapha mountains. For pure form and structure there is little in Greece to compare with them. Hereabouts a British military mission had its nomadic headquarters during the Second World War, supplying Greek resistance forces with arms and gold pounds. Its efforts to prevent the rival Right- and Left-wing factions from fighting each other instead of the enemy were not always crowned with success. The road descends in loops through wooded country to two tremendous bridges spanning the narrowest branches of the huge artificial Kremasto Lake, formed by the damming up of the Afrifotis, Aheloos and Tavropos rivers. At the bottom lies a submerged Byzantine church of the ninth century. On two sides of

140

the lake, north and east, mountains rise sheer, ranged one behind the other like screens, escarpment upon escarpment, wooded on the higher levels, with the Aheloos flowing swiftly between scrub-covered hills towards the Acarnanian plains.

CHAPTER 9

Thessaly: The Plain

Domokos – Farsala – Larissa – Krannon – Tirnavos –
Elassona: The Church of the Olympiotissa –
Mount Olympos.

The northbound traveller on the National Road from Lamia who
may not wish, or does not have the time, to turn off and visit the
Volos area and the Pelion villages (see Chapter Ten) can drive
straight across the Thessalian plain to Larissa. There he can choose
between two northerly routes: across the foothills of Olympos,
described in this Chapter, or through the Vale of Tempe (see
Chapter Twelve). Both lead directly into Macedonia. The west-
bound road from Larissa leads to the Meteora monasteries (see
Chapter Eleven).

The Farsala road to the north of Lamia and the railway both climb
the Orthris mountains, a lateral offshoot of the Pindos range, once
associated with the legend of the flood of Deucalion, the Noah of
Greek mythology. When Zeus, incensed by the degeneracy of
mankind, caused a flood to wipe out the human race, Deucalion, the
Phthian king, hastily built a ship in which he placed his wife and
abundant provisions. When the swollen waters retreated, the vessel
is said to have landed on one of the summits of Mount Orthris. The
puce-coloured slopes, also associated with the seat of Hellen,
founder of the Hellenic race, are featureless and unwooded, but
there are fine backward views of the receding backcloth of Mount
Oiti. The monotony of the descent into the lowlands is relieved by
the ruined walls of a medieval castle on a rocky eminence above
Domokos, which commands an immense prospect of the flat
chequer-board plain of central Thessaly.

This plain of Thessaly, the most spacious in Greece – Herodotus, supported by modern geologists, says it was originally a lake – is sealed in by mountains: in the west by the serrated spine of the Pindos, in the north by Olympos and the desolate Kamvounians, in the north-east by Pelion and Ossa, with Orthris bolting the door in the south. When Xerxes entered the plain and the guides pointed out how thoroughly shut in by mountains it was, the Great King decided that, should the Thessalians not submit to him, he would block the only exit, the Vale of Tempe to the north-east, and flood the whole country. The climate is one of extremes, and in summer a metal-coloured haze hangs tantalizingly over the legendary mountains. So heavily blanketed in cloud is Olympos that even its foothills are seldom visible from the plain. The horses of Thessaly, which still graze in the cornlands, were famous throughout Greece, and the Thessalian cavalry was an important factor in every war. Philip of Macedon found the country hard to conquer; when he did, it was useful to him in grain, horses and manpower.

Why Strabo should call this featureless landscape, pock-marked with little oases of stunted trees, 'a country most blessed', remains a mystery. Deep cart-tracks furrow the corn-fields around dust-caked – in winter mud-encrusted – villages, and in spring storks perch with an air of impervious elegance on the domes of red-brick churches. Huge sows wallow beside filthy troughs, like the swine sacrificed to Aphrodite who was worshipped in the ancient cities of the plain. But most of the Thessalian lowlands defy description. How right Sterne was when he said there is 'nothing more terrible to travel-writers than a large rich plain if it is without great rivers or bridges, and presents nothing but one unvaried picture of plenty'.

The road passes through the villages of **Neon Monastiri** (the well-preserved walls of ancient Proerna, a minor Thessalian township, spread across the hillside to the right) and **Farsala** the ancient Pharsalia, scene of Caesar's masterly set-piece battle: the first of the three engagements fought on Greek soil or in Greek waters – Pharsalia, Philippi, Actium – that decided the fate of the Roman world. Low rocky hills overlook the fields through which the stream of the Enipeas flows, and where the 'flower and strength of Rome', says Plutarch, 'met in collision with itself'. The level ground was admirably suited to the advance of Caesar's brilliantly led battle-trained legions against the amorphous force assembled by Pompey whose morale was already shaken by a series of alarms and omens. 'In a few hours,' Plutarch continues, 'the plains of Pharsalia were covered with men, horses and armour,' and the great Pompey was fleeing towards the sea, his army routed, his tents and pavilions abandoned to Caesar's cohorts. Today Farsala is remarkable only for its earthquakes and *halva*, a popular sickly-sweet preparation made from sesame seeds.

Beyond the stream of the Enipeas a chain of barren hills crosses the plain in an east–west direction. The road continues across the plain. Occasionally there are settlements of Vlachs, descendants of the medieval Wallachians, who dwell in alpine villages in the Pindos, in winter descending into the lowlands with their sheep, women and prickly sense of personal pride. In the Middle Ages Thessaly was overrun by these nomads. After them came the Serbs, pouring over the Macedonian border. But by the end of the fourteenth century the rivalries of Serbs, Greeks and Wallachians were swept away in the Ottoman conquest. The Turks repopulated Thessaly with peasants from Asia Minor, and leisure-loving pashas carved large estates out of the lands abandoned by the frightened Greeks. Consequently Thessaly was one of the few provinces in the country in which villages grew up with mixed Greek and Turkish populations. This triple influx – Wallachian, Serb and Turkish – left a Balkan stamp on the province.

Larissa, the provincial capital, through which the vanquished Pompey fled to the sea, lies at the north-eastern end of the plain. A garrison town and important centre of communications with plenty of hotels, it is a useful halt for the traveller. More than one military plot has been hatched in the local barracks and officers' messes, and the success of any attempt at a military take-over of the country is said to depend largely on the role played by the army corps stationed here.

In antiquity the city was ruled by the Aleudae, and we know that Gorgias, the glamorous Sicilian Sophist, was greatly honoured as a teacher of rhetoric at the court. Pindar too was a much venerated guest, and Hippocrates died here at the age of over a hundred – a fitting life-span for the 'father of medicine'. The acropolis, which overlooks a loop of the Pinios, the chief river of Thessaly, is now crowned by a modern cathedral reached by a winding stairway with bizarre stone dressing. On the south side of the cathedral a fluted column, an Ionic capital and some broken marble plaques mark the site of a temple of Aphrodite. East of the cathedral rises a squat block of masonry, formerly a Turkish fort, with blind arches and a substructure which preserves features of the architectural style of the original market town to which all the produce of Thessaly was once carried by beasts of burden.

The new archaeological museum contains the fossilized remains of prehistoric monsters dated to the Inter-Glacial and Last Ice Ages discovered in the sandbanks of the Pinios, Neolithic tools and weapons from neighbouring sites – especially Sesklo, roughly carved fourth-century BC *stelae* excavated on the acropolis and reliefs with figures of mounted horsemen depicted riding towards a symbolic tree.

From the southern periphery of the town a dirt road runs south-west to the site of the ancient city of **Krannon**, seat of the Scopadae, a Thessalian royal family proverbial for their wealth and power. The custodian, without whom it is difficult to find the way, is generally in the café in the hamlet of the same name. The acropolis once spread across a low treeless eminence, nearly a mile in circumference. Now littered with sherds, it commands an immense prospect of corn and maize fields. In summer the site is best visited in the late afternoon, when the rolling fields of stubble turn pale yellow and the outlines of mountains – Pindos, Olympos, Ossa, ranged in a horseshoe round the northern end of the plain – emerge out of the heat haze.

The only extant remains of Scopadic power are three extremely well-preserved fifth-century BC *tholos* tombs: mausoleums with beehive conical roofs – a survival of the first Mycenaean-type royal sepulchre on a smaller scale. The first tomb I visited was circular, the second (further south) square with a square doorway supported by three half-engaged pieces of masonry resembling colonettes, the third (still further south), possibly the resting place of the Scopadic king, had traces of painting on the wall. The masonry of the three tombs is in the best fifth-century BC tradition. Numerous mounds of earth scattered about the acropolis are thought to be more tombs awaiting the attention of archaeologists. There is a spaciousness about the scene, untouched as yet by any visible human habitation;

the swallows' nests in the *tholos* tombs alone suggest the neglect to which this evocative site has been relegated.

To the east of the *tholos* tombs, walking eastward across humps and undulations, past the post-Byzantine Church of *Zoodochos Pighi* (The Source of Life) one comes to a large, well-preserved Roman kiln for firing pots. All this part of Thessaly was strongly contested by the armies of the Roman Republic in their wars with the Macedonian Empire, and after final Macedonian defeat, it became a flourishing Roman province.

North-west of Larissa, the first place of any importance is **Tirnavos**, a hot, dusty little town below a spur of Olympos. Allegedly the best ouzo in Greece is made here, and the cafés in the large public square are well stocked with it. On the first day of Lent an annual procession, originating in some primitive Orphic rite, winds through the streets. The participants, men only, carry large earthenware objects shaped like phalluses. They call themselves 'phallusbearers' and take the proceedings very seriously, turning a deaf ear to the ribald remarks of the youthful spectators.

After Tirnavos the main road to Elassona penetrates deep into the Kamvounian range, past the ruins of a second-century BC watch-tower perched on a conical hill at the entrance of a spacious valley streaked by the Titarissios, a fast-flowing tributary of the Pinios which curls round beige-coloured hills between thickets of poplars. A gradual ascent ends in a little plain, with **Elassona**, a market town, spreading on either side of a stream spanned by an old Byzantine bridge and surrounded by hills of white clay soil.

The ancient citadel stood on a hill above a ravine, now crowned by a somewhat over-restored Byzantine **Church of the Olympiotissa** (The Olympian Virgin). Commissioned by that indefatigable church-builder, the Emperor Andronicus Palaeologus II (1282–1328), the Olympiotissa is architecturally similar to many churches in Thessaloniki. The juxtaposition of a low narthex and tall *naos* is striking. Elegance is not lacking in the architect's conception. But the harmony of volumes and inter-relation of planes of the earlier cruciform church are markedly absent. The elongated drum, which we see again and again in Macedonia, at first excites, then palls. In the end, one realizes that it vitiates the sturdy structural unity for which earlier Byzantine church-builders were justly famous. The interior frescoes of the late Byzantine period are poor in artistic quality, narrative in style, conventional in execution. More striking are a fine marble column in the entrance door between the narthex and the nave and the carved wooden two-leafed door (west) dated c. 1300. Islamic influences are evident in the ivory inlay of the panels, each of which is carved with different designs of meshes forming circles, crosses and triangles.

Beyond Elassona the country becomes less domesticated. **Mount Olympos** draws nearer, the huge massif buttressed by chalky foothills. There are some formidable views of deep crevices, filled with snow all the year round, of the 'Needle' the highest peak in Greece (9750 feet), and of the dolomite of the Throne of Zeus soaring skywards. It was because of this physical dominance over all other structurally more beautiful mountains that the ancient Greeks presumably chose its summit, which represented heaven itself, as the residence of the gods.

After a bleak wind-swept saddle the road descends towards Servia in Western Macedonia and crosses the artificial Polifito Lake to Kozani.

An alternative route over the Olympos country into Macedonia begins at a fork beyond Elassona. The north-east-bound road climbs to a region of bare uplands at a very considerable altitude. In summer the cold can be penetrating. Crossing the watershed, the road, which has now completed a full semi-circle of Olympos, winds through forests of beech and oak. Immediately to the south the 'Needle', now seen from a new angle, projects above a mass of naked rock; chasms fall vertically to wooded foothills. The villages of Kallithea and Agios Demetrios afford a welcome sign of domesticity. The East Macedonian coastal strip comes into view and the road, after rounding bluffs and scarps, ends at the town of Katerini in the plain.

CHAPTER 10

Thessaly: The Pelion Villages

Phthiotic Thebes – Volos – Demetrias – Pagasae –
Mount Pelion – Milies – Tsangarada – Kissos –
Zagora – Macrinitsa – Ano-Volos – Pherae.

From Lamia to Volos, starting point for a visit to the Pelion villages, is an easy drive, mostly along the National Road. From Stilida, which lies on the Malian Gulf, the Kalidromo range is seen to peter out, not without some spectacular flourishes, into the Euboean Channel. The shallow waters of the gulf form one of those deep inroads which the Aegean is constantly making into the land mass.

Skirting the southern foothills of the Orthris range, one has some tantalizing glimpses of the Oreos Channel between Euboea and the mainland, with great cliffs alternately advancing and receding across the water. The road then enters the dreary seaward end of the Thessalian plain, with Almiros, a dusty shanty town, off the National Road to the left; to the right poplars fringe the pebbly shore of a mud-coloured inland sea. Beyond the coastal road to Volos, which branches off to the right of the National Road, rises a range of low hills, once crowned by the acropolis of ancient Pyrasus. To the left, between the ridge and the box-like houses of maritime Nea Anhialos extends a field of impressive ruins in a fenced-in enclosure. This is the Early Christian site of **Phthiotic Thebes** (not to be confused with the more illustrious Boeotian Thebes). In antiquity Pyrasus was the chief maritime centre of Thessaly, and in the Hellenistic era it endured a frightful siege by Philip V, a martial king of Macedonia and unbridled alcoholic, who ostentatiously renamed it Philippopolis.

The ruins are mostly of the Early Christian period; fragments of towers and ancient fortifications are discernible around a circuit of over two miles. The Early Christian site, not yet exhaustively excavated, is a muddle, and ground plans are jealously guarded by archaeologists still working on the site. It is best to make for **Basilica A**, which is easy to identify, for it is shaded by pine and cypress trees and lies directly west of the main road. The ground is strewn with colonettes and capitals, fragments of cornices decorated with acanthus leaf designs, plaques carved with rosettes, swastikas and roses. In the north aisle a Corinthian-type capital crowns an unfluted column standing amid the remains of a pebble mosaic floor with designs of lozenges, diamonds and circles. In the apse behind the sanctuary of the baptistry, where the fourth-century bishop officiated, are two large reversed capitals with finely carved acanthus leaf decorations: beyond it traces of an ancient road and, behind the museum, on what could have been the paved floor of a house, the most beautifully carved capital of all. The relief is shallow, the design a variant of the acanthus leaf, so delicately executed as to give the impression of filigree work. To the north is Basilica B, a mass of rubble. The vista of destruction is appalling: the work of invading Slav hordes which set fire to the city in the seventh century.

Basilica C (sixth-century), the largest of all three, is surrounded by hovels to the south of Basilica A. The architectural layout, deeply influenced by the feeling for inflated aggrandizement common in Late Antiquity – particularly in the East – is fairly clear even to the unprofessional eye: atrium, narthex, nave and sanctuary. Only bases of nave columns are preserved, but some unfluted ones stand in what may have been a subsidiary southern chamber. Leaning over the parapet of the side road from which the basilica is approached, one has a good view of another subsidiary edifice (south-west of the narthex) with a well-preserved floor mosaic. The stylistic history of the decoration of floor mosaics is a long one. The allegorical and mythological set-pieces of the Hellenistic era tend, in Roman times, to be replaced by landscapes and scenes from nature. Symbolism and idealism are replaced by more representational realism. By the Early Christian period the decoration has become more formal, more stylized. A rebirth of the Greek feeling for geometry is apparent. It is as though one were witnessing the

149

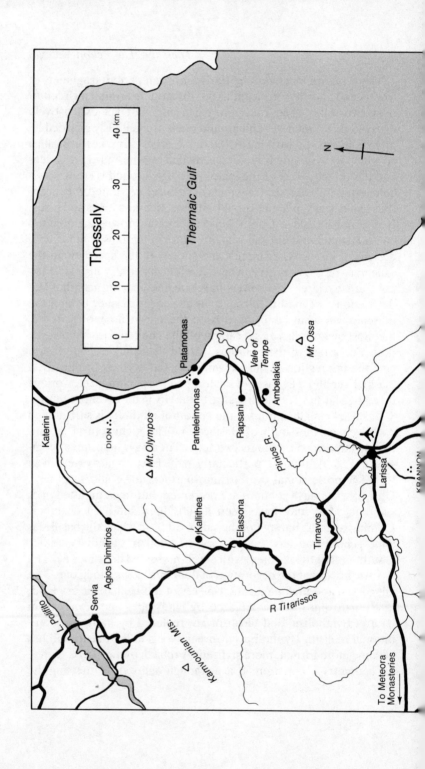

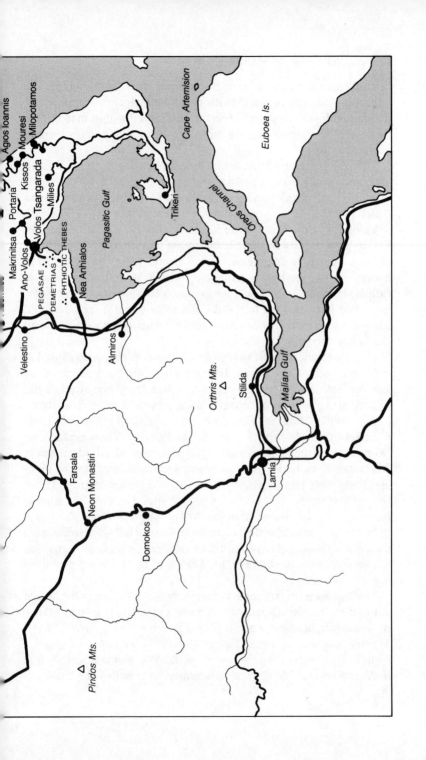

birth-throes of the static art of Byzantium. Here, as elsewhere, are admirable designs of ducks with green bellies, cornucopias over-flowing with fruit, a deer, a lobster, all framed within medallions. Some melon-shaped capitals with lace-like carving are scattered about the site.

The objects in the museum include Hellenistic pottery, Roman glass and ornate Early Christian *stelae*, among which is a crude but evocative one of a departing soul riding a horse towards an effigy of death.

Volos lies at the head of the Pagasitic Gulf, at the foot of Mount Pelion. In antiquity this fertile mountain bastion of Eastern Thessaly was known as Magnesia; it was always richer in legend than history. Destroyed by an earthquake in 1955, Volos has a somewhat raffish air, in spite of its prosperous bourgeois provincialism. But it has a fine port, and the holds of ships anchored in it are filled with some of the best fruit in Greece – apples, peaches, pears – grown on the Pelion foothills.

The site of ancient **Iolchos**, home of Jason, has been excavated at the west end of the town. Turning right, off the main road to Larissa, into Papapyriazi Street (and then left), one reaches the hillock of Agios Theodori overlooking a brick factory. The acropolis obviously commands the entrance to the head of the gulf. Only a cluster of hovels and remains of a medieval wall now replace the 'well made streets' described by Apollonius of Rhodes, where Jason dwelt in a house filled with 'many servants, men and women, and costly ornaments'. Strabo believes the town was destroyed from the earliest times. It is not an evocative site. The only identifiable feature is the dry river-bed of the Anaurus, which Jason happened to be fording on a rainy day when he saw an old lady in distress amid the swollen waters. He promptly carried her on his back across the stream, whereupon she revealed herself to be Hera and promised him her patronage.

The **Museum**, in Athanasaki Street, possesses a fine collection of painted *stelae* from Demetrias. Among the most striking are those of an austere headless warrior (No. 235), of Choirele (No. 55) and of three elegantly disposed figures (No. 355). The unpainted *stelae* include two fascinating examples of the late Roman period: one male and two female figures surmounted by bunches of grapes and the snake of Asclepius (No. 388); and a child flanked by two female figures (No. 422). Crude, rough, yet forceful, these reliefs have a distinct stylistic relation to works of the so-called 'expressionist' school of Early Christian sculpture, in which the Hellenic ideals of grace and charm are replaced by the desire to express a more profound inner emotion. There is also a lovely little torso of Aphrodite (No. 715). Among the prehistoric objects are Palaeolithic and Neolithic tools from neighbouring sites.

The coastal road due south of Volos leads to the site of **Demetrias**, which once enjoyed some fame as a flashy and ostentatious city founded by Demetrius Poliorcetes, one of the most brilliant person-alities of the Hellenistic world, whose military career was spent in far-flung campaigns against the Diadochi (successors of Alexander the Great). His private life was scandalous. In Athens he indulged in outrageous debaucheries, even polluting the sacred precincts of the Parthenon. On contemporary coins Demetrius is represented with horns, in emulation of Dionysus, his favourite deity.

To the right (west) of the road an ancient theatre is scooped out of a conch-like fold in the hill. The lower tiers are still faced with stone seats and the orchestra, more than a half-circle, is unusually large: probably designed to suit the tastes of its flamboyant founder. Towers rise from the lozenge-shaped enceinte of ruined walls that extend across the hillside.

Beyond the theatre the road bears east. The first turning to the right leads to the **Acropolis of Pagasae**, more ancient and venerated than upstart Demetrias, but with even less to offer in the way of visible ruins: only some fragments of ancient walls. The low hill, crowned with a whitewashed chapel, overlooks a salt pan. To the north, the spurs of Pelion rise abruptly from the inland sea which took its name, the Pagasitic Gulf, from this prehistoric site. On the beach below, now dotted with modest tavernas, was built the *Argo*, on which Jason and the Argonauts embarked.

Volos is the starting point for a circular tour of the **Pelion** villages, where a striking style of peasant architecture, showing distinct Macedonian influences, flourished during the Turkish occupation. Tall white houses, timber-framed, with projecting upper stories and rustic churches are scattered among the chestnut forests. I am accustomed to following an anti-clockwise route on which the 'star' villages can be visited in two days; a night can be spent at Tsangarada. There are daily buses to all the main villages.

The road to the east skirts the seashore. Coastal and inland hamlets spread across olive groves and gardens filled with roses from whose petals a fragrant oil is distilled, giant dahlias and Canna lilies; in early summer pink and blue hydrangeas, large as cabbages, speckle the silvery groves. A branch road ascends to **Milies**. During the Turkish occupation it possessed one of the most important libraries in Greece and a school where geography and natural sciences were taught in the early nineteenth century. Greek literary tradition was kept alive throughout the Ottoman period by patriot-scholars in the Pelion villages, whose inhabitants were never tamed by the conquerors. It was at Milies that the Thessalian standard of revolt against the Turks was raised in 1821.

The road winds along ridges of heather-covered hills, alternately overlooking the Pagasitic Gulf to the west, and the open sea to the east, where two of the loveliest Aegean islands, Skiathos and Skopelos, lie several miles offshore. The soil is of an unusual purplish-red hue.

Soon there is a fork. One road descends towards the scythe-shaped headland of Trikeri, inhabited by caique-builders, whose ancestors owned broad-beamed vessels which traded with all parts of the Levant. In the distance Euboea tapers away into Cape Artemision, off which Xerxes' cumbersome armada, strung out in eight parallel lines, fought the first major engagement of the war with the more nimble Greek triremes in 480 BC.

The other road, crossing the mountain ridge, affords a sudden breathtaking view of Mount Athos, a mirage-like peak thrusting skyward through a pale sea-haze. The heather is succeeded by evergreens. There are interminable windings around vertical clefts as far as **Tsangarada**, a straggling settlement of farmhouses in a forest of oak and chestnut trees, at an altitude of 1500 feet. The Xenia Hotel overlooks wooded gorges descending abruptly to the sea. The ferns and brambles are luxuriant; in autumn mushrooms carpet the undergrowth; in winter the rainfall is the highest on the Greek mainland. Everywhere there is the sound of running water – that wonderful crystalline water, served for drinking in thick-rimmed tumblers. Greeks do not drink water only because the body needs a certain amount of liquid. They savour it, like connoisseurs, and make comparisons between the waters of different springs – a civilized approach, Homeric in origin. Below Tsangarada, at a distance of less than eight kilometres, lies Milopotamos, the first of the tree-fringed sandy beaches along the north coast.

The road continues westward, at a considerable altitude, through Mouresi, where hollyhocks and hydrangeas blaze in shady arbours, to **Kissos**, its esplanade overlooking green hills with the sea beyond. The village is lively, less straggling than Tsangarada. The air is cool in summer, fragrant with sun-drenched grass and ripe fruit. The focal point is the **Church of Agia Marina**, dedicated to a Bithynian holy lady who dwelt in a monastery disguised as a boy and was maliciously accused of fathering a daughter by the local inn-keeper's wife. The church is a low three-aisled basilica, with a belfry pierced by arches on successive levels. The walls of the interior are covered with post-Byzantine frescoes by Paghonis, a local peasant artist, responsible for the painted decoration of many Pelion churches. His work is rustic in conception and rendering, the strict undeviating rules of Byzantine iconography are ignored. Superstition rides roughshod over the dogmas of religious painting. From the capitals demons rudely stick out deformed tongues. Although the bright gilding of the *iconostasis* creates a somewhat gaudy effect, the carving is inventive in detail; a meshwork of carved blooms, tendrils, pert little stags and stylized lions. At the right of the *iconostasis* is a strange fresco of a church perched on a tenuous rock pillar. One wonders if the iconographer had ever visited the rock monasteries of Meteora.

Beyond Kissos the road winds through chestnut forests and round an impressive gorge in the most precipitous part of the mountain. Occasional clearings in the forest provide fretwork frames for vistas of unbroken expanses of sea. A branch road to the north descends to Agios Ioannis, a sandy pine-bordered beach dotted with tavernas, the summer haunt of Voliot trippers, where there are caiques for hire. The main road continues towards Zagora. The deserted glades are carpeted with feathery fronds. Nothing stirs in the shade of the interlacing boughs.

The mountain figures in the earliest myths, from the time when the giants piled Ossa on Pelion in a bold attempt to besiege the gods on Olympos. It was on Pelion that Apollo, in one of his amorous escapades – he almost rivals his father, Zeus, in concupiscence – surprised the huntress Cyrene, while she wrestled single-handed with a lion, and carried her off to Africa.

Another mythological Pelion character is the wise old centaur, Cheiron, doctor, prophet, scholar, who dwelt below the summit, where medicinal plants grew in profusion, and who was the fashionable tutor of the period, entrusted with the education of such distinguished young men as Achilles and Jason. He paid great attention to physical fitness and character training, feeding Achilles on fawn marrow to make him run fast and lions' entrails to imbue him with courage.

Zagora is the showpiece of Pelion. Like Tsangarada, it is filled with the sound of streams running between banks of maidenhair. Its orchards produce peaches, pears and plums much prized in the Athenian market. Its wild strawberries unfortunately do not travel well. Like Milies, it was a centre of learning, enjoying local self-government under Turkish rule.

The older houses of Zagora present a blank wall of two stories to potential enemies, the projecting third storey being surmounted by a roof of irregular slates. Under the Turks, folk art, generally quaint, often charming, remained unaffected by the main currents of artistic fashion. Two eighteenth-century churches are typical. At Agia Kyriaki faience plates and moulded tulips (here the Turkish influence is clear) are embedded in the apsidal wall. The **Church of Agios Georgios**, another three-aisled basilica, situated in a paved square, has the added attraction of an exo-narthex in the form of a wooden colonnade roofed with slates running round the west front and part of the north and south sides (one more characteristic feature of Pelion church architecture). The exterior apses are embellished with three rows of half-columns with capitals crowned by trefoils alternating with marble plaques with geometric patterns and rosettes. The interior possesses an elaborate gilt *iconostasis*, also of the eighteenth century, which gives the impression of filigree work; the pulpit is one of the largest and most ornamental I have seen in a village church. On the south wall hangs an *epitaphios*, a fine piece of seventeenth-century embroidery depicting the body of Christ on the bier.

A narrow road descends from the village in hairpin bends to the beach, part sand, part shingle, of Horefto, famous for its shell-fish, fringed by olive groves and orchards of pear and apple. There are a few old abandoned houses and a taverna. Eastward the mountain rises sheer: a backcloth of shimmering woodland.

Above Zagora the road climbs through plantations of walnut trees. Streams cascade from successive ledges. Beyond the beech forests of the saddle, below the radar-crowned summit of Pelion and the winter ski-fields, the road begins a winding descent to the Pagasitic Gulf. Portaria is a summer resort with a Xenia hotel, an ugly rash of modern villas and a church with murky sixteenth-century frescoes. From here a branch road follows the contours of a precipitous ravine to **Macrinitsa**, a distance of two kilometres. Tall houses, with more slate roofs than elsewhere on Mount Pelion, are built on terraces so steep that the main entrance to the old timber-framed mansions, once the homes of a flourishing agricultural society, is often on the top storey. Unlike other Pelion villages, Macrinitsa is centred round a terrace, which forms a belvedere overlooking the ravine, shaded by plane trees and flanked by the Chapel of *Agios Ioannis*. The church bell hangs from the branch of a plane tree. From a marble fountain decorated with carved plaques water gushes out of a brass gargoyle.

The **Church of the Panayia**, restored after a recent earthquake, is situated on a higher level, its courtyard flanked by cypress and chestnut trees. Above the marble-framed south doorway an exterior eighteenth-century fresco depicts the Virgin, holding the Child, seated on an elaborate baroque throne. The three apses are decorated with sculptured plaques, the most striking of which depicts a lion hunt, with a chariot drawn by four horses. Within the church there is a fine thirteenth-century marble relief of the Virgin *Orans*. During the Turkish occupation secret classes in history and theology were held in two adjoining chapels. At Macrinitsa teachers and priests went about their clandestine activities, propagating Hellenic culture and the Orthodox faith, within sight of the Crescent flying from the fortress of Volos.

The descent continues. **Ano-Volos** spreads across the southern foothills. Mushroom-like roofs crown tower houses among orchards. The upper story of the **Condos House**, in a farmyard setting below Macrinitsa's great cliff, contains sixty square metres of frescoes by the eccentric peasant painter, Theophilos, a late nineteenth-century 'primitive', who peddled his way across eastern Greece, singing while he painted, asking for no payment other than the cost of his materials. Although his frescoes are devoid of scale and perspective, Theophilos often conveys an impression of verisimilitude to place and period, and his decorative detail has roots in a precise almost classical perception of objects. His subjects generally derive from episodes from the War of Independence (there are some splendidly bedecked military gentlemen, armed to the teeth, with frozen expressions and ferocious moustaches). Whimsical treatment and bold use of colour combine to make the stylized scenes come to life. Mythological subjects are not ignored. Hermes in a black mantle departs on one of his divine errands; Aphrodite holds a trident as she rises from the foam. One of the most attractive features of the frescoes is the decorative detail: a giraffe munching palm leaves, a blue peacock with emerald-green plumage.

From Volos one drives across the plain to Larissa. Just beyond the crossing with the northbound National Road a side road to the west leads to **Velestino**, a village among apple orchards: the site of ancient Pherae, ruled by a succession of bloodthirsty tyrants, who were the scourge of Central Greece in the fourth century BC and raised Thessaly to the status of a great power. The first of these was Jason (not to be confused with the mythical leader of the Argonauts) whom Xenophon describes as 'the greatest man of his times'. By nature he was violent and ostentatious. Like him, his successors were assassinated. Of these none surpassed in cruelty his lawless and foul-mouthed nephew, Alexander, whose sole religious exercise was the worship of the spear with which he slew his uncle. His own end was plotted by his wife and her three brothers. With his assassination, the power of the Thessalian despots declined, and the country was soon subjected by Philip of Macedon.

Next to the miniature public garden is a shallow pond with a tiled basin, its surface mantled with sedge: the scene painted by Edward Dodwell in one of his most charming 'Views of Greece'. In the nineteenth century the pond was fringed with minarets and trees, including a palm, with a broken column in the foreground. Assuming that Dodwell did not invent the column, one is justified in associating the site with the fountain of Hypereia, situated in the heart of the ancient city. Of antiquity all that remains today are some vestiges of a temple of Heracles and of the Larissa gate on the site of an acropolis, north of the town.

The remainder of the run to Larissa is without interest – across the flat Thessalian plain. It is wise to join the National Road at Rizomilos. To the north extends the former lake of Boeobeis, at the foot of Mount Ossa.

CHAPTER 11

Thessaly: The Meteora Monasteries

Trikala – The Church of Porta Panayia –
Kalambaka: The Church of the Koimesis –
The Broad Rock – The Great Meteoron – Varlaam –
Rousanou – The Monastery of Agia Triada –
The Monastery of Agios Stefanos.

The way from Larissa to the Meteora monasteries is across a flat, typically Thessalian, stretch of country, watered by rush-bordered streams. Geese waddle around stagnant pools; occasionally avenues of poplars shade the road, which runs parallel to the Pinios. The Palaeolithic fossils and tools excavated along this stretch of the river have been dated to a period between 100,000 and 40,000 BC. The barrier of the Pindos ridge, bluish in colour, gashed by chasms, draws nearer.

A sluggish tributary of the Pinios flows through **Trikala**, a lively market town with a ruined mosque, a castellated clock tower and a stone bridge spanning the poplar-lined stream. A furnace of heat in summer, it is dominated by the crumbling walls of a Byzantine fort, site of the ancient acropolis, from whose highest tower the Turkish governor used to hurl his enemies. Projecting hooks caught the bodies as they fell; there they were left, dangling in gruesome postures – a warning to all who passed below.

A road from Trikala to the south-west passes close by Gomfi, and beyond the village of Pili, which lies at the base of the Pindos range, a track crosses a bridge spanning the torrent of the Portaikos which issues out of a cleft in the mountain wall. In the middle of this natural gateway lies the **Church of Porta Panayia**. Lofty crags, their higher levels speckled with deciduous trees, frame the gorge. In the

Mount Parnes: the Monastery of Kleiston clings to the cliffside.

The eleventh century Byzantine church at Daphni.

The Pantocrator, one of the greatest portraits in Byzantine art, dominates the whole church at Daphni.

evening the dark mysterious tunnel is filled with shifting shadows. Mulberry, plane and cypress surround the monastic walls.

The church was founded in 1283 by John Ducas, the rebellious illegitimate son of an Epirot Despot, who ruled over Neopatras, allied himself with the Vlach nomads and fought both the Franks and the Byzantine Emperor. He married a Vlach, eventually became a monk and was buried in the church four years after its completion. Whether its foundation was a bid for salvation on his part must remain a matter of conjecture. Few Byzantines, however unprincipled in worldly affairs, were without a deep mystical faith in the Orthodox Church.

The brickwork decoration of the exterior walls of the church consists of rosettes, squares, overlapping arches and rows of elongated Z-shaped forms: a kind of embellishment repeated more lavishly in a number of churches at Thessaloniki and Arta. A spacious narthex, of a later date, is crowned by a broad drum pierced by narrow elliptical windows. The frescoes, of a late period, are very damaged. The *naos* – the walls are now whitewashed – is in the form of a three-aisled basilica, the height of which is increased at the east end by a transverse vault instead of a dome. In spite of this curious juxtaposition of vaulted nave and domed narthex, an air of uniformity prevails. At the west end of the south wall there is a portrait of the founder in the act of being introduced by an angel to the Virgin and Child. The Holy Door of the marble screen is flanked by two surviving mosaics of superior quality: late thirteenth-century figures, noble and austere, of the Virgin and Child (right) and Christ (left) – a deviation from the strict code of Byzantine iconography in which Christ is normally depicted on the right.

Beyond the church the defile contracts. The road north crosses the pass whence the Despots of Epirus rode from their capital at Arta to conquer the Thessalian Lowlands. A torrent is spanned by the elegant arch of a Turkish stone bridge, under a canopy of plane trees where nightingales sing. The bridge, like all those built by the Turks in remote parts of the country, is narrow, stepped and crescent-shaped, intended for the passage of a single man or beast. There is neither a parapet nor balustrade, and one needs to be immune to vertigo to cross the slender arch. There are simple hotels at Elati from which meadows stretch to the Pertouli fir forests below the Pindos range.

From Trikala the Ioanina–Lamia road cuts south–east across the plain to **Karditsa**, a market town of Turkish origin, served by a narrow-gauge railway running from Volos to Trikala. Storks' nests crown the roofs of ramshackle houses. General Plastiras, an ambitious cavalry officer with a fierce black moustache, who always rode a black charger and became one of the most controversial political personalities of the twentieth century, plotting military revolutions and brooding in exile when out of office, was born here. His name was given to a large artificial lake, one of the loveliest in Greece, created by damming up the Tavropos. The signposted road climbs past a twelfth-century monastery through oak forests into magnificent mountain scenery. A circular tour of the lake is easy and strongly recommended.

The traveller who chooses the north–west road from Trikala towards Ioanina is rewarded with one of the most extraordinary sights in Greece. The village of **Kalambaka** spreads fan-wise round a huge projection of dark grey contorted rock which thrusts forward into the plain. Behind it extends the labyrinth of rock pillars crowned by the Meteora monasteries, whose eremitical origins and subsequent prosperity form part of the history of Byzantine monasticism. One monastery alone, Agios Stefanos, is visible from the village: perched on the ridge of a lofty wall of rock with a smooth polished surface, slit and rutted at intervals by horizontal seams and honeycombed with caves and eyries. Over six hundred years ago a young monk named Athanasius, hearing of this wild place, crossed the mountain in search of the refuge it offered him. He had long sought a life of unremitting prayer for the salvation of men's souls, undisturbed by their physical presence. His quest was at an end; and although hermits had preceded him he was the founder of the first 'monastery in mid air'.

The screen of dolomites is omnipresent at Kalambaka; it seems to cast its reflection across the meadows and vineyards bordering the shingly bed of the Pinios like some sombre radiation from the interior of the rock itself. There are few amenities, other than hotels, petrol stations and a main square crowded with tourist coaches. Westbound travellers can take the fine mountain road which crosses the Pindos, via Metsovo, to Ioanina and thence descends to Igoumenitsa on the Epirot coast. Kalambaka possesses

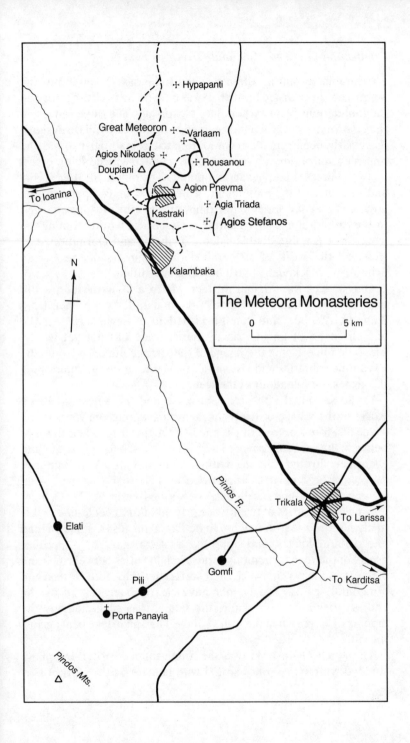

The Meteora Monasteries

0   5 km

a venerable Byzantine **Church of the Koimesis** (Dormition of the Virgin). A three-aisled basilica, it was built in the twelfth century on the foundations of an earlier place of worship. The stone canopy of the *ciborium* above the altar, carved with intricate foliate designs, has clearly been remade from more ancient materials; so has the imposing marble *ambo*, with its panels sculpted with double crosses, its two staircases and hexagonal pulpit. The quality of the carving and opulence of the monument, which has been compared to the great *ambo* at St Clemente in Rome, suggests the prestige attached to the cathedral in the Byzantine ecclesiastical world. Among the icons there is a fine double-sided Crucifixion and Dormition. The frescoes, the work of sixteenth-century painters of the Cretan School, are blackened almost beyond recognition.

Only five of the original thirteen **Meteora Monasteries** are still inhabited by a handful of monks (or nuns). They are open from 8 am to 12 noon and can be visited in a single day. All the paraphernalia of an increasing tourist trade has not yet wholly succeeded in effacing the image of the strange life once led by the Byzantine solitaries and visionaries of Meteora, nor in diminishing the grotesque splendour of the scene.

From Kalambaka the road curves round the so-called 'Black Rock' to the village of **Kastraki** sheltering among vineyards in the shade of a forest of towering pinnacles. On the lower levels the gaps between the rocks are covered with mulberries, oaks, cypresses and evergreen shrubs. Curzon, writing in the mid-nineteenth century, says '. . . the end of a range of rocky hills seems to have been broken off by some earthquake or washed away by the Deluge, leaving only a series of twenty or thirty tall, thin, needle-like rocks, many hundred feet in height; some like giant tusks, some shaped like pudding-loaves, and some like vast stalagmites.' A peculiar aspect of the rock formations, whose height varies between 600 and 900 feet, is the way in which their surface is slit by both vertical and horizontal seams. The former have clearly been caused by the endless trickle of rain water, the latter, it is suggested, by the lapping of waves when the waters of the Thessalian lake beat against the cliffs.

To the left of Kastraki rises the round-topped rock of **Doupiani**, studded with eyries, once scaled with ladders by the earliest hermits. Up there, far from the affairs of men, they communed with God and mortified their bodies. Deeming the flesh to be rank pollution, one monk left instructions that his mortal remains should be cast to birds of prey. Once a week the monks descended from their caves to worship communally in what is now a whitewashed chapel at the base of the cliff.

Above the village looms another huge pudding-shaped conglomerate mass, known as **Agion Pnevma** (The Holy Ghost), crowned by two iron crosses. It is suggested that this was probably the pinnacle on which the young Athanasius first settled, but when demons were seen circling round his cave, he was persuaded to move to another rock, so lofty that even the forces of evil hesitated to scale it. Bit by bit, Athanasius climbed the formidable **Broad Rock** with the aid of ladders clamped one above another. He chose a cave – halfway up the modern zigzag stairway – as his first abode. The remains of a ladder still dangle from a wooden doorway overhanging the abyss. The sanctity of his life attracted so many disciples that he was finally persuaded to establish a community on the Broad Rock. A monastery thus grew up and came to be known as the Great Meteoron. No woman was allowed near it. Once, when the widow of the Serb 'Caesar' of Thessaly asked for Athanasius' blessing, he not only refused to approach her, but abused her roundly for being a woman and prophesied her imminent death. Three months later she died. His successor Joasaph enlarged the church, and the monastery enjoyed a period of prosperity.

One enters the **Monastery of the Great Meteoron** by a steep rock-hewn stairway. A dilapidated wooden shed projects across the precipice. Here are the ropes, 124 feet long, by which men and provisions were originally hauled up. Describing his ascent, Curzon says:

the net was spread upon the floor and having sat down upon it cross-legged, the four corners were gathered over my head, and attached to a hook at the end of the rope. All being ready, the monks at the capstan took a few steps round, the effect of which was to lift me off the floor and launch me off the floor right into the sky, with an impetus which kept me swinging backwards and forwards at a fearful rate; when the oscillation had in some measure ceased, the abbot and another monk, leaning out of the door, steadied me with their hands, and I was let down slowly and gently to the ground.

The interior of the cruciform **Church of the Metamorphosis** is spacious and unusually high. The candelabra, pulpits and *iconostasis*, crowned by a large Crucifixion in an ornamental cross-shaped gilt frame, heighten the atmosphere of brilliance created by the recently restored frescoes, the work of late fifteenth-century Athonite artists. There is little subtlety in colour tones, and although the figures sometimes strike agile, even acrobatic, attitudes, they remain basically static. The large narthex, supported by four columns, is somewhat darker. The frescoes, fussy and full of stylistic mannerisms, are of a later date – the usual blood-curdling Last Judgement, and full-length portraits of Athanasius, founder of the monastery, and Joasaph, his successor, holding a model of the church: gaunt figures in long black beards.

The icons in the treasury are more interesting than the frescoes. After the fall of Constantinople, Byzantine fresco-painters seem to have been incapable of inspiration on the grand scale. No great churches were built during the post-Byzantine period; consequently the demand for the painting of large surfaces of wall virtually ceased to exist. But the icon-painter, working in a less expensive medium, preserved, developed and revitalized the best elements in the old tradition. Western influences crept in and enriched narrative iconography. At the Great Meteoron there are several outstanding examples, ranging from the fourteenth to the sixteenth centuries, including an Incredulity of Thomas, with a perky Maria Angelina, in royal robes, amongst the apostles; they are gazing at Thomas or chattering among themselves; a boyish St Demetrius thrusting his javelin into the leader of a Bulgar host investing Thessaloniki; a Baptism, with Christ immersed in the waters of the Jordan while St John baptises him and angels bear him towels. Equally attractive are the five Menologion icons, with calendars of saints' feasts painted on gold backgrounds: typical examples of sixteenth-century painting in miniature.

The refectory, separated from the church by a courtyard with cypress trees, has a vaulted roof supported by five elegant columns.

Below it were stored the enormous wine barrels drawn up by windlass. Water was supplied from cisterns hewn out of the rock.

The view from the Great Meteoron is astonishing. Twisted spectral forms, scarred and rutted, tapering into pinpoint cones, insulate the winding chasm, strewn with gigantic boulders, from the outside world. Occasional gaps between the rocks afford glimpses of the plain beyond and its welcome cultivated domesticity.

By the fifteenth century the number of monastic settlements had increased, and during the death agony of Byzantium the 'monasteries in mid-air' became asylums of Hellenism and Orthodoxy, where monks could commune with God and invoke his blessing on Greek arms, undisturbed by Ottoman armies advancing across the plain below. After the Turkish conquest there was a marked deterioration in monastic morals. At one monastery a cross-eyed monk had the effrontery to introduce two women, dressed as monks, to serve as his 'companions'. For a time the Great Meteoron was ruled by a contemptible abbot in the pay of the Turks, and for his sin of treachery to the Hellenic cause, always synonymous with that of Christian Orthodoxy, he was cursed and sent into exile. When he died, his body remained uncorrupted – a sign of God's displeasure. From the seventeenth century onwards, looting, sale and fraud robbed the churches of much treasure.

All that remain of the Monastery of *Hypselotera* (The Highest One), which crowns an offshoot of the Broad Rock, are an image of two saints painted on the rock and traces of a wooden ladder hanging from a narrow projection just below the summit. On another offshoot is the Monastery of *Agios Nikolaos*, with a basilica painted with sixteenth-century frescoes. The ruins of the little Monastery of *Agios Ioannis Prodromos*, uninhabited for over two hundred years, are scattered across the ridge of a vertically slit hump. More spectacular is a completely detached monolith soaring skyward, capped now by nothing but a debris of wood and stone, once the Monastery of *Agia Moni*.

North of the Broad Rock a path leads between mis-shapen tusks and perpendicular cliffs, seamed like organ pipes, to the rock of the *Hypapanti* (Presentation in the Temple). The monastery, long abandoned but recently restored, is situated in a cave halfway up the cliff, reached by a stone stairway. The tiny domeless church is decorated with frescoes of the late thirteenth to mid-fifteenth centuries. Icons adorn the elaborately carved *iconostasis* of gilded wood.

A terrible abyss separates the Broad Rock from a magnificent obelisk, on which the **Monastery of Varlaam** is perched, soaring out of a mass of bulbous rock. The retreat of a fourteenth-century anchorite, who gave his name to the monastery, it later housed such valuable relics as a finger of St John and the shoulder blade of St Andrew. The church was founded by two brothers, Theophanes and Nectarios. The monks of the Great Meteoron lent them mules to carry stones to the base of the rock; but records of how the materials for the original windlass were hauled up are tantalizingly withheld. The two brothers imposed a strict discipline on their disciples, partaking once a day of bread, beans and water, and praying half the night. Theophanes, avid of mortification, wore an iron chain tight round his waist, next to the skin. Shortly before he died – it was the hour of sunset and the day of the church's completion – he stretched himself on a couch, carefully arranging his limbs in the shape of a cross.

Varlaam is more animated than the other monasteries. An elderly monk, his long grey hair arranged in a plaited bun below his cylindrical hat, acts as guide, sells postcards, offers ouzo and accepts a gratuity. Other monks go about their devotions and chores. Although the monastery buildings are in utter disorder, the walls, eaves and roofs seem to grow organically out of the bluish-grey rock. They are capped by a church with two tiled domes resting on octagonal drums. A labyrinth of rotting floor-boards and worn paving-stones leads to deserted cells. One storeroom contains a barrel nearly twenty feet high with a diameter of over six feet, which must have sorely taxed the strength of the monks at the capstan when it was originally hauled up. The disused shed where the contraption was kept, buttressed by masonry, projects like some abandoned crumbling belvedere above the ravine.

In the **Church of Agion Panton** (All Saints) the sixteenth-century frescoes, restored in the eighteenth century and again recently, depict the familiar scenes from the Dodecaorton. Everywhere there are swirling draperies, huddled buildings, martyrs, hermits, soldiers; the gold of haloes, the flash of swords, the reds and purples of ecclesiastical vestments. In the narthex the mourners in the Dormition of Ephraim the Syrian are ranged round the saint's body like crude prototypes of El Greco's grandees at the funeral of Don Orgaz (painted a quarter of a century later). In the museum there is a small Book of Gospels, once the property of the Emperor Constantine VII (913–959), and a fine icon of the Virgin and Child surrounded by angels and apostles in robes of pale mauve, dark green and indigo, by Tzanes, the sixteenth-century iconographer.

Beyond Varlaam the road winds past **Rousanou**: a small monolith crowned by three stories of seemingly inaccessible masonry. Never one of the more flourishing monasteries, Rousanou, when visited by Curzon in 1834, was inhabited by two half-mad crones who refused to let the rope ladder down to the English traveller, preferring to jabber frenziedly at each other and shriek curses. The modern traveller is assured of a more courteous welcome from the few nuns who still inhabit the convent. Scenes of martyrdom of unparalleled cruelty decorate the walls of the narthex of the church, dedicated to St Barbara. More impressive than Rousanou is the **Monastery of Agia Triada**, its balconies and arcades projecting above a rock shaped like a rolling-pin. A cave, in the rock halfway up the stone stairway, contains a little chapel decorated with crude paintings of ascetic saints. The exterior of the church, spoilt by a large ill-proportioned narthex, is ornamented with brickwork designs. But the cypresses and shrubs growing around it create a pleasant rustic effect.

The road then emerges from the valley and runs along the ridge of an escarpment to the **Monastery of Agios Stefanos**, separated from the main rock formation by a narrow chasm spanned by a bridge. The change of scene is remarkable. Nothing towers overhead anymore. The horizon is clear. The monastic buildings are as usual crowned by the one rotund and two slender drums of the church which has little, architecturally, to recommend it. In relation to their commanding position on this great bastion overlooking the plain, the toy cupolas and untidy houses seem insignificant. The church still possesses two treasures: a silver reliquary containing the head of Charalambos, whose healing powers are said to have staved off many pestilences, and an *iconostasis* and bishop's throne of lavishly carved woodwork with designs of flowers, cranes pecking at vipers and little creatures swinging censers, all meticulously executed in the fussy high relief typical of Epirot carving of the late eighteenth century. A small chapel, hewn out of the rock, with an apse suspended on the brink, is reached through an abandoned refectory. Near the doorway is a portrait of a white-bearded monk holding a scroll: the fifteenth-century founder of the monastery, a certain Antonios, of the imperial family of Cantacuzenus. Today St Stephen's chief glory is the view from the terrace. The monastery is at the point where the arms of the angle formed by the Pindos and the Kamvounians are about to meet. Hundreds of feet below, the box-like houses of Kalambaka skirt the base of the cliff. Southward the plain extends in a soporific haze. There is only one way back to Kalambaka – the way one came.

In his account of the Meteora monasteries, Curzon says Greek monks seem to be obsessed by 'everything hideous and horrible'. His choice of adjectives is open to question. But one does see what he means. The violence of the geographical upheaval seems to be reflected in those 'hideous' mortifications of the flesh which Byzantine ascetics considered to be the necessary stepping-stones to salvation. It is also interesting to note that there is not a single reference to the valley of Meteora in classical literature. The ancient anthropomorphic Greeks were not impressed by wonders of nature – not unless they could relate them to some visible or symbolic association with a human entity or agency.

CHAPTER 12

The Approach to Macedonia

*Ambelakia – The Vale of Tempe – Platamonas –
Dion – Pidna*

No traveller in Northern Greece can – or should – avoid Macedonia, the largest and richest province in the country. Thessaloniki, the capital, is usually approached from Larissa along the northbound National Road. Notwithstanding stops, and two worthwhile deviations to Ambelakia and Dion, the distance is easily covered in less than a day.

The Pinios, now joined by the muddy Titarissios, meanders in S-shaped loops across the north-eastern apex of the plain, which is studded with brown cone-shaped hills. To the east rises Mount Ossa, whose quarries once supplied verd-antique and serpentine to the workshops of Roman architects and sculptors. At a point just before the tree-fringed river is about to force its way through the mountain barrier stands a derelict Turkish mosque named Baba, where, in spring, storks perch on the crumbling dome. Here the Ottoman Government's envoys, after passing through the Vale of Tempe, would pause to worship before entering the plain to impose new taxes on their Greek subjects.

At the toll-gate a branch road to the east climbs to the village of **Ambelakia**. On the last turn but one before entering the village there is a fine backward view of the pyramid-shaped hills vanishing into the haze. The immediate foreground is filled by an abrupt spur of Lower Olympos, across which extends the village of Rapsani, famous for its red wine.

In the late eighteenth century Ambelakia was the site of the first co-operative in Greece. It was founded by local weavers and dyers, who used the madder grown on Mount Ossa for dyeing their yarn a

171

particularly attractive shade of red. The chemical composition of the abundant waters of Ambelakia added a glossy hue to the finished product, which was exported to the markets of Europe. With the ascendancy of the Manchester cotton industry and the discovery of aniline dyes, the importance of Ambelakia and its co-operative declined. It is now rather a ramshackle place, open to the mountain breezes; so near, and yet off, the beaten track, and where one is seldom out of earshot of running water.

From the main square it is no distance to the eighteenth-century **Schwarz House**, once the property of a Hellenized Viennese family, now a folklore museum. The constant menace of brigandage and the fear of punitive forays by Turkish soldiers account for the heavy wrought-iron grilles protecting the few windows. The ground floor, formerly used for commercial transactions, with the accountant sitting in an enclosure shut off by a wooden balustrade, consists of a wide vaulted room with alcoves. The walls are painted with decorative designs which create an illusion of fluted columns. The wall paintings of the living quarters on the T-shaped first floor include an array of cornucopias filled with carnations and a fanciful evocation of the Bosphorus.

The high-ceilinged top floor, also T-shaped, is virtually one vast reception room with alcoves, in which the distinguished dyers and weavers of Ambelakia were entertained in style. Numerous wooden pillars crowned by carved capitals conjure up an image of colonnades receding into a succession of subsidiary chambers. On the walls are painted imaginary landscapes, flowers and foliate patterns of twigs and drooping branches. Everywhere the Turkish genius for creating a feeling of spaciousness by the judicious breaking up of space is reflected in this work of Greek architects schooled in Islamic lay architecture. The stained-glass windows are of Viennese provenance. The entire house, with its finely wrought woodwork of turned railings and corniced pillars, is a triumph of architectural and decorative folklore styles: an amalgam of the minor arts of post-Byzantium and Islam, with a touch of middle-class, early-nineteenth-century Vienna thrown in. To the uninitiated traveller, it serves as a curtain-raiser to the more impressive, if less well-preserved, eighteenth-century houses of Western Macedonia.

Back at the toll-gate one enters the **Vale of Tempe**. The narrow five-mile gorge, separating Olympos from Ossa, was believed by the ancient Greeks to have been cut by Poseidon's trident. Birthplace of the laurel, Tempe was associated with the worship of Apollo and visited every nine years by a delegation of aristocratic youths who marched through the vale in procession, accompanied by a flute-player, and plucked the sacred laurel destined for the god's oracular seat in Delphi. The mountain sides are steep, almost vertical, covered with dark evergreens; a mass of gnarled plane trees borders Homer's 'sylvan eddies', which have become rather muddy with the passage of time. Tempe does not compare with any of the great gorges of Greece, although its importance, linking the Balkans through Macedonia with the Thessalian enclave and thence the whole of Central and Southern Greece, was appreciated by the Romans, who built a military highway, roughly followed by the present rail and motor roads.

At the eastern outlet the change of scene is striking. Northward extends a cultivated strip, an unbroken coastline and the blue expanse of the Thermaic Gulf, into which two large rivers pour their mud and silt. This is Macedonia. A new climate. After Tempe the air is never so crystalline again, the outlines of the mountains never so sharp and dramatic, the sea and sky never so vivid a blue. There is no lack of historical sites and associations. But it is Philip and Alexander and their successors who dominate the scene.

On a bluff to the right, rise the ruins of the Crusader castle of **Platamonas**, which the Lombards lost to the Epirot Despot, Theo-dore Angelus, in 1218. After a brief but violent siege, the defenders fell from the castle walls 'like birds from their nests', in the words of a contemporary ecclesiastic. The well-preserved walls of the triangular enceinte, dominated by a fine octagonal tower, are outlined against the wooded hills sloping down to the village of Panteleimonas with its sandy beach. To the north there is a string of beach resorts, and on the main road there are several hotels suitable for breaking a journey. From now on the backward views of Mount Olympos are superb. For the first time one is able to associate the celebrated mountain with the home of the gods. Its contours are more awesome than beautiful. Forests of oak, chestnut and beech spread across the middle slopes. In the afternoon, shafts of sunlight fill the ravines, creating new perspectives, and great precipices fall from dizzy altitudes to the plain below. Through one towering glen there is a glimpse of the Throne of Zeus, thrusting its peak into the vault of heaven itself. But as often as not the traveller will see none of this. The gods still like to conceal their celestial abode in a blanket of cloud. Soon there is a signpost and a branch road to Litohoro, whence the ascent to the Throne of Zeus begins.

Hellenistic Macedonia, over which the figure of Alexander the Great looms so large, begins at a signpost pointing west, to **Dion**, where Philip of Macedon and his son trained their troops at the huge military camp. The wide road ends after a few miles at the ruins of Macedonia's sacred town, where an earth-goddess, identified with Demeter, originally held sway. Her two small archaic temples, c. 500 BC, were replaced by a larger Hellenistic building. Zeus dominated in classical times; at his sanctuary inscriptions were set up referring to important affairs of state for the information of the pilgrim crowds. Aphrodite was worshipped as Hypolimpidia, Goddess Below Olympos, whose cult-statue still stands in a graceful small temple. Dionysus was naturally honoured near the large theatre, built, like the stadium, by King Archelaos who brightened the religious festivals with athletic and theatrical performances. Livy and Pausanius refer to the number of statues that embellished the paved ways, including Lysippus' famous bronze group of twenty-five horsemen, commissioned by Alexander to commemorate his favourite companions who fell in the battle of the Granicus.

In the fourth century Philip was in the habit of celebrating his victories here with games and contests. And all the time the drilling went on, the camp echoing with the din created by the marching phalanx, each of whose members was armed with a long spear and short sword, a shield large enough to protect the whole body, a helmet, a coat of mail and greaves. No foreign army had as yet faced such a solid, impenetrable front. When going into action it was said to resemble a giant porcupine unfolding its erectile spines. Later the camp was the scene of Alexander's sacrifices before he crossed into Asia. In the course of the accompanying athletic and musical contests he entertained a hundred of the Companions in a magnificent marquee which accommodated a hundred couches. There is an elegant sanctuary of Isis: Hellenistic tolerance had superimposed Isis on Artemis when the Ptolemies had propagated Egyptian gods.

Due to a rise in the water-level after an earthquake, it was preserved from pillage in mud. Excavations were particularly difficult outside the south-east corner of the city wall but the reward consisted of a portrait and two cult-statues, still standing among the Ionic columns. In the Early Christian era Dion was a bishop's see, and the chants of pious choristers echoed through the basilicas raised on the ruins of the officers' messes which had once witnessed the drunken orgies of the young king and his friends. Then came Alaric's visitation, a final devastating earthquake, and Dion ceased to exist.

The remains are largely Roman, but follow (with additions) the original Hellenistic ground plan. So far, fourteen paved roads have been uncovered in the well planned, strongly fortified city. The eastern walls, with square towers and a marble gate, are clearly discernible. A unique group of statues, representing Asklepios' sons and daughters, was found in the north wing of the huge public baths, which took up a large area within the residential blocks. The foundations of an Early Christian basilica include a large mosaic pavement bordered by a red, black and white geometrical design. Excavations in 1987 revealed a very fine, second-century floor mosaic of Dionysus and four headless statues of seated philosophers. It is pleasant to rest here amid the shaded bracken, where the Macedonian cavalry, largely composed of upper-class Thessalian young men renowned for their horsemanship, also probably rested after training. It was somewhere near here too that Philip, while celebrating his presumptuously named 'Olympian' Games, bought a prize black stallion from a Thessalian horsebreeder. But the animal, with a lock of white hair across its forehead and branded with an ox-head, plunged and reared, proving totally intractable to the cajolings of even the most experienced horsemen. Plutarch tells the story of how Philip glanced, half-smiling, half-mocking, at the eight-year-old Alexander who was staring intently at the prancing steed. Approaching it unhesitatingly and realizing that it was only frightened by its own shadow, the boy turned it directly towards the sun and, after gently stroking the sleek black flanks, with 'one nimble leap securely mounted him . . . and let him go at full speed'. There was no mishap. Philip, squinting out of his one eye, cried: 'Oh my son, look thee out for a kingdom equal to and worthy of thyself, for Macedonia is too little to hold thee.' The boy named the horse

Bucephalus (Ox-Head), and it accompanied him throughout his campaigns. A city in the upper Indus valley was named after it and, when it died of old age, the horse was accorded a state funeral. Fidelity to his loved ones was one of Alexander's more attractive traits.

Spread over a large area outside the city walls are the sanctuaries, the stadium, the Greek theatre and Roman odeion, mainly intended for the pilgrims rather than the inhabitants, as in the principal Greek sacred towns. The large number of Macedonian coins found in the mound that covered the theatre are displayed in the **Museum**, together with the votive offerings and statuary.

From the Dion signpost the National Road runs along the flat coastline: site of numerous campsites. From Katerini it is preferable to take the inland road. It takes a little longer to reach Thessaloniki but it is less monotonous, rising and dipping between the hummocks of a rolling green countryside dotted with prosperous villages.

At Kitros a turning to the east leads to the site of ancient **Pidna**, where the passionate Olympias, Alexander's mother, was stabbed to death by order of Kassandros during the fratricidal wars between her son's successors. Here too the forces of Perseus, last king of Macedonia, were routed by Aemilius Paulus in a battle begun after an eclipse of the moon predicted by a Roman officer, expert in astronomy. The natural phenomenon struck such terror into the hearts of the black-frocked Thracians, mercenaries of the Macedonian king, that they ran dementedly, wailing loudly and beating their burnished shields. In this famous engagement, the scarlet-coated Macedonian phalanx collapsed under a formidable charge of Roman elephants, and the poltroon Perseus fled from the battleground on the pretext of sacrificing to Heracles – a deity, says Plutarch sarcastically, who was 'not wont to regard the faint offerings of cowards'. Livy has left an account of the way in which the Romans transported the terrified elephants down the precipices of Olympos, lowering them by means of a succession of broad planks, supported by wooden posts, used like drawbridges on different levels. Once they reached the low ground the great lumbering beasts felt more at home, and the thunder of their stampede across the plain, already alive, Plutarch says, 'with the flashing of steel and the glistening of brass', was decisive. The battle of Pidna (168 BC) turned the scales. In a matter of hours, Aemilius Paulus, the Roman patrician, was master of the moribund Macedonian kingdom, a Greek defeat that opened the way to the East for Roman arms.

After Kitros there is Methon, where Philip lost an eye while besieging the Athenians in their last colonial stronghold in Northern Greece (354–3 BC). He allowed the inhabitants to leave the city with no more than one garment on their backs and distributed their lands among his Macedonian henchmen.

From the village of Methoni the National Road sweeps round the head of the Thermaic Gulf. The Aliakmon River is crossed near its mouth – higher up, at the old bridge, the British Commonwealth Expeditionary Force made an unsuccessful attempt to stem the Nazi onrush in 1941. Real rivers, rising in the Balkan highlands, now replace the oleander-bordered streams of Thessaly. The traffic increases and the flat monotony of corn, rice, tobacco and beet fields gives way to the factories on the outskirts of Thessaloniki.

CHAPTER 13

Thessaloniki: The Second City

Via Egnatia – The White Tower –
The Archaeological Museum – The Arch of Galerius –
The Rotunda of Agios Georgios –
The Basilicas: 'Acheiropoietos'; Agios Demetrios;
Agia Sofia – The Panayia Chalkeon –
The Roman Agora – The Ramparts –
The Chapel of Hosios David –
The Latin Churches: Profitis Elias; Agia Aikaterini;
Agioi Apostoli;
The Church of Agios Nikolaos Orfanos.

In Roman times travellers passed through the Golden Gate into what is now **Platia Vardari** (Dimokratias). From here **Egnatia Street** crosses the city from west to east, roughly following the ancient Via Egnatia, which began on the Adriatic and ended on the Hellespont, marked throughout with milestones commemorating the names of deified emperors. Triumphal arches spanned the highway; under them marched the legions, bearers of Roman law and order in exchange for oriental riches. Here in Turkish times Edward Lear watched peasants bringing goods for sale 'in carts drawn by white-eyed buffali'. Trucks loaded with fruit and vegetables have replaced the wild oxen of the Macedonian plains, and instead of a mob of 'blackamoors and Jewesses', office and factory workers now thread their way through the congested traffic.

For over thirteen centuries Thessaloniki has held the rank of second city of the Greek world: second after Constantinople in the Byzantine period and after Athens in modern times. Founded by

Kassandros in 315 BC on the site of ancient Therma, where Xerxes stayed in the summer of 480 BC while his fleet cruised in the gulf, it later served as a refuge for the exiled Cicero, and St Paul had an affection for the inhabitants. For a time it was to Thessaloniki, strategically situated at the outlet of the Balkan trade routes, that Constantine the Great contemplated transferring the capital of the Empire, and when his choice fell on Byzantium, the chagrin of the inhabitants was equal only to their indignation that such a prize should go to an upstart colony on the Bosphorus. However by the end of the fourth century, with the triumph of Christianity assured, the city's course was fixed. Scene of countless sieges and hair-splitting theological disputes, it was destined, under the protection of its patron saint, Demetrius, to play a role in Byzantine affairs – eventful and often heroic – second only to Constantinople.

The modern city, not liberated from the Turks until the conclusion of the First Balkan War in 1913, is strung out along a grid of parallel and intersecting streets between the hills and the sea. Uniquely well-preserved basilicas and domed Byzantine churches, among the most important in the country, provide an air of mellowness to an otherwise wholly urban prospect. Parallel to Egnatia St runs **Tsimiski Street**, the main shopping quarter, its pavements bordered with horse-chestnut trees. The food is better than elsewhere in the country, and the confectioners are crowded with Thessalonikian ladies devouring cream cakes and oriental pastries. There are hotels for every purse, with the Makedonia Palace, on Megalou Alexandrou Avenue overlooking the eastern waterfront, being one of the best. The climate is one of extremes. In winter icy winds funnel through the Balkan valleys; fog is not unknown. In summer a pall of torrid humidity hangs over the tall new blocks stretching round the bay towards the eastern suburbs where there are good fish tavernas.

For the sightseer Thessaloniki is, above all, a Byzantine pilgrimage. There are two obvious alternatives: the traveller in a hurry can look briefly at the mosaics of the Rotunda and St Demetrius; the Byzantine enthusiast should book a hotel room for three nights and visit the twelve most important churches. The evolution of styles, architectural and decorative, covers the whole span of Byzantine history and the itinerary is roughly chronological. Roman ruins,

Byzantine monuments and old Turkish houses are all enclosed within a horseshoe-shaped enceinte of Byzantine ramparts with Turkish additions.

It is best to begin at the end of the waterfront, at the cafés among the shrubberies below the **White Tower**, the only surviving fort of the maritime defences. Within the circular walls of the tower a body of mutinous Janissaries, grown from a praetorian guard into a power-hungry rabble, were put to the sword in 1826, when Sultan Mahmud II the Reformer carried out a wholesale liquidation of this increasingly reactionary corps. On the landward side of the 'Bloody Tower', as it came to be known, extends a public garden speckled with the peony-like flowers of Syrian hibiscus, their large curled petals creating a spangled effect against the dark green bushes on moonlit nights.

To the east of the gardens lie the grounds of the International Trade Fair (held every September), whose origins go back to a medieval market organized on St Demetrius's day to promote the city's handicrafts. Facing the gardens is the **Archaeological Museum**, housed in a well-designed modern building. The wide range of exhibits, both as regards style and provenance, reflects the proximity of those northern lands which have done so much to shape the history and character of Thessaloniki. There are the usual ancient vases, greaves, weapons, terracottas, animal figurines, bronze kraters with mouldings of sphinxes and grotesque theatrical masks; all, or mostly all, of Macedonian provenance. They make nonsense of the once popular belief that the 'barbarous north' was incapable of producing first-class craftsmen.

Among the more interesting objects in the museum are the small **stelae of the Thracian Horseman**, a primitive cult figure who exercised a profound influence on the national consciousness. The horse was the emblem of the Scythians whose territory bordered on Thrace. Consequently, the religious cults of both peoples possessed many points in common. In the early carvings (they were funerary or votive offerings), roughly modelled in shallow relief, the enigmatic Horseman is represented as a hunter, holding a spear and galloping towards a tree, around which a snake is coiled. Later the heroic hunter assumes a semi-divine character and is depicted crowned with a wreath. In Roman times he wears military dress. In the Early-

Christian period his memory helped to mould the popular image of St Demetrius. He is still mounted, but now proceeds in stately fashion towards an altar crowned by a pine-cone in front of the serpent-entwined tree. A composite figure, probably some father-figure of the Thracian race, he is also part Asclepius, god of healing, whose emblem was the snake that possessed curative properties, part Rhesus, leader of the Thracian contingent in the Trojan War.

The museum is, above all, a treasure house of Hellenistic objects of intricate workmanship found in Macedonian tombs. Gold and silver trinkets studded with pearls and enamelled brooches alternate with bronze kraters, drinking bowls and skilfully wrought jewellery from the fifth to the second century BC. The sensational finds from the royal tombs at Vergina have given the museum world renown but, even so, do not eclipse earlier great finds such as the gold objects from the cemetery at Sindos, now an industrial suburb of Thessaloniki, and, above all, the **Derveni krater**. The bronze surface of this huge urn is covered with appliqué silver gilt figures in a crowded bacchanalian procession. Prowling animals intermingle with human forms striking ecstatic attitudes, vine tendrils terminate in ornate leaves and maidens and youths recline gracefully below the lip. One moves round the glittering object with increasing fascination. Attributed to Lysippus, one of the great Peloponnesian sculptors and a contemporary of Alexander the Great, the Derveni krater possesses all the natural ebullience of Hellenistic art before the elegance and discipline inherited from the Classical age was tarnished by over-sumptuousness and florid ostentation.

From the museum it is five minutes' walk to the junction of Panepistimiou and Egnatia Streets, with the Aristotelian University on the right. All this area, which once formed part of a vast imperial compound – palace, circus and mausoleum – is now a commercial and residential quarter, dominated by the triple **Arch of Galerius**, the Dacian shepherd who became a Roman Emperor – and not a very attractive one. The south arch has gone, but the middle piers are carved with stone reliefs of puny figures devoid of grace and individuality. An unimpressive replica of the great triumphal arches of Rome, it was probably considered good enough for a provincial capital. The sculptures tell the story of the success of Roman arms against the Parthians in the early fourth century.

South-east of the arch extended the circus, scene of a horrible massacre in the year 390. The most popular charioteer of the day courted the favours of a boy slave of Botheric, the hated Gothic commander of the local garrison. Shocked by the laxity of Mediterranean morals, Botheric imprisoned the charioteer, whose outraged followers promptly murdered the commander and his officers. Their bodies were dragged through the streets amid scenes of great acclamation. The prudish but choleric Emperor Theodosius I the Great, who relied on his Gothic commanders for discipline in the army, ordered a swift and savage retaliation. The people of Thessaloniki were summoned to the circus to applaud their released idol. The exits were barred and Theodosius's troops fell on the unsuspecting crowd with drawn swords. According to Gibbon, the carnage lasted three hours; at a conservative estimate seven thousand Thessalonikians were slaughtered.

A colonnaded avenue connected the Arch of Galerius with a circular edifice, raised as a mausoleum for this 'notorious and faithful servant of the demons', as a medieval monk described the bull-necked, pale-faced Caesar, arch-persecutor of the Christians. However destiny played a trick on Galerius. In the mid-fifth century his mausoleum was converted into a Christian place of worship, later dedicated to St George, most popular of Eastern warrior-martyrs; now a museum of Early Christian art, it is known as the **Rotunda of Agios Georgios**.

Architecturally the Rotunda owes much to the circular buildings which Galerius probably saw when campaigning in the East. The basic plan is simple and grand: a towering cylinder with eight bays supporting a wide dome. Its Eastern character remains unaffected by the transformation of the arched recess opposite the entrance into an apsidal altar-space. Fragments of sculpture, Roman, Early-Christian and Byzantine, ranged along the walls of the other bays, include a fine tenth-century **plaque of a Virgin Orans** (the Virgin with arms outstretched in an attitude of prayer). The symmetrical yet gentle pliability of the folds of the mantle recall the drapery of classical Greek sculpture. Equally impressive is another tenth-century **plaque representing the Hosios David**, a holy man in the act of prayer.

Mosaics surviving from the original Christian decoration include

Alexandrian motifs of birds and fruit within the octagonal medallions which decorate the soffits of several bays. However, it is the huge **mosaic panels**, originally made up of some thirty-six million *tesserae*, in the circular band around the shallow dome that provide the mystical quality peculiar to this extraordinary building. Only seven panels survive. In each, two martyr saints, ritualistic figures with arms outstretched in the *orans* gesture, stand against crowded architectural backgrounds of immense fantasy. Examination of detail is unfortunately ruled out by the height of the dome; photographs however reveal the refined modelling of the martyrs' heads, the vivacity of their expressions and the classical folds of their *chitons*. These fantasies, which were to exercise a powerful influence on later book illumination, are full of Eastern motifs: knotted columns crowned with Corinthian capitals, arches, friezes and cupolas. In each panel, pavilions frame the centre-piece, generally an apse or *exedra*. The mood is elegiac. Peacocks strut across parapets and swans float above the ornamental cornices; candelabra hang from bejewelled canopies and turquoise curtains are drawn back to disclose pendant lamps or lighted candlesticks. There is little hint of Byzantine austerity. All the ecstasy of Eastern Christendom is symbolized in this opulent image of the Church Eternal.

During the Turkish occupation the church was converted into a mosque and a minaret raised beside it. Today the vast echoing interior is empty, except for the sculptural fragments in the bays and the celestial fantasies of masterly mosaicists. However it provides a unique setting for occasional concerts of Byzantine and classical music.

To the west of the Rotunda, out of a secluded court, where the local inhabitants assemble on hot summer evenings to gossip, rises a shapely brick-domed drum crowning the twelfth-century **Church of Agios Panteleimon**, once a dependency of an Athonite monastery. Regaining Egnatia Street and turning right up Agia Sofia Street, one reaches the fifth-century Basilica of the Mother of God, restored in 1910, squatting in a sunken square. Its exterior architectural severity reflects the dignity implicit in its polysyllabic name – the **Acheiropoietos** (Not made by human hands) – so-called because in it once hung a miraculous icon of the Virgin that no human hand had fashioned.

The interior of the church has, in spite of a certain bleakness, an imposing overall architectural unity. The windows, divided by short columns, are disposed symmetrically in two rows, thus relieving the general design of both monotony and clumsiness. Columns of greyish-white marble are crowned by magnificent **Theodosian capitals**, an elaborate version of the Corinthian, with spiky acanthus leaves turned back on themselves as though by the wind, which was evolved in the fifth century and has been named after the Emperor Theodosius II. The fashion spread, but it was in Thessaloniki and Constantinople that this sumptuous marble embellishment achieved its most sophisticated form.

Many images were probably removed during the Iconoclast periods of the eighth and ninth centuries, when the reproduction of the human form in religious art was proscribed by the puritanical emperors of the Isaurian dynasty; consequently only a few **mosaics** – decorative work of a high order – survive in the soffits of the arches. The colours are unusually lavish with lilies, poppies, sunflowers, nasturtiums and fruit-bearing branches sprouting from ornate vases; foliate wreaths wind round crosses and sacred books; gold backgrounds swarm with fish and plump blue pheasants.

Agia Sofia Street mounts directly from the *Acheiropoietos* to Agiou Demetriou Street along which, to the left, is the holiest spot in Thessaloniki: the site of St Demetrius's martyrdom. A spacious church with sloping roofs and rows of arched windows spreads across a narrow esplanade. The unweathered brick indicates a modern construction, but the amplitude of the proportions suggests an ancient design. It is, in fact, a faithful reconstruction – the result of years of patient archaeological research – of the **Basilica of Agios Demetrios**, twice destroyed by fire. On feast days the ringing of the bells of the Basilica echoes across the roofs of hotels and office blocks shelving down a slope once crowded with medieval mansions, hospices and public baths. The whole history of Thessaloniki is bound up with this church. It is the spiritual centre and common meeting-ground of the inhabitants in a way that no other Christian place of worship in Greece has ever been.

Of Demetrius himself we know little, except that he was an upper-class young man whose military prowess won for him the patronage of Galerius. However his conversion to Christianity infuriated the Caesar, who promptly imprisoned him in a bathing establishment. To make matters worse, Nestor, an athlete friend of Demetrius's, also a Christian, challenged and killed the champion gladiator, the imperial favourite of the moment. This was too much for the irascible Galerius. Nestor was summarily executed and Demetrius speared to death in the public baths (now the crypt of the church), where he was afterwards buried by Christian friends. From this contemptible exhibition of human vindictiveness an obscure martyrdom derived its venerable character and a great cult centre acquired its popularity.

The church has been rebuilt on the fifth-century plan. Original materials, such as chancel portico arches, Theodosian capitals and column shafts of green and dark red marble, were re-used in the modern construction. However the frescoes, porphyry revetments and the mosaics which adorned the north aisle were lost forever in the 1917 conflagration.

It is curious that the Iconoclasts removed neither these north aisle mosaics nor the few panels which are preserved elsewhere in their original positions. They may have feared a public outcry. Healer of the sick, protector of children, Demetrius was also guardian of the city. He *is* the city. When Thessaloniki fell to the Turks in 1430 only the shrine of St Demetrius was spared from desecration; all other churches were converted into mosques and the inhabitants put to the sword. The fall of Thessaloniki, which preceded that of Constantinople by twenty-three years, was the penultimate warning to the pusillanimous leaders of the West, who stood by, as though bemused, watching the downfall of an empire which, for all its cruelty and corruption, was still the heir of Athens and Rome and the repository of every human value they cherished. Within a century the Ottoman armies had entered Budapest and were besieging Vienna.

The layout of the reconstructed basilica is simple: narthex, nave and two aisles separated by colonnades, transept and tribunes on three sides. At the west end of the south aisle colonnade, a Theodosian capital of great fantasy surmounts an ancient pilaster. Stone images of birds nestle among bunches of grapes, and fat peacocks with rippling feathers drink out of a *cantharus*. Other fifth- and sixth-century capitals crown dark green columns with strange effigies and serrated lace-like leaves, carved in deep relief and curled backwards, which create astonishing effects of light and shade.

The surviving **mosaics**, probably of the early seventh century, are half-hidden among the aisles and piers. The technique of mosaic work was even more highly developed in Thessaloniki than in Italy. In the grading and setting of *tesserae* (the average measurement in the St Demetrius panels is four millimetres), in the blending of colours and the creation of shading effects, Thessaloniki was in advance of Rome. Even at times of acute military crisis the mosaic workshops hummed with activity. The panels, which are not disposed in any apparent order, were votive offerings to the saint. The holy persons are represented frontally; great attention is paid to symmetry, and, in spite of their wooden attitudes, they emerge as figures of great nobility.

The two panels on the north-east pier of the nave, placed like icons in front of the sanctuary, are impressive. The first is of **St Demetrius and the children**. The young saint has thick, wavy hair and the expression of his large black eyes is compassionate yet penetrating. The round-eyed faces of the two children, over whom the slender saint towers protectively, are so life-like that little seems to distinguish them from the small boys playing hide-and-seek among the marble columns, to the accompaniment of their mothers' unabashed chatter in the side aisles. In the other panel, the Virgin and St Theodore, the colouring is more sober. The slim, elegant figure of the Virgin is represented in the act of intercession on behalf of mankind. St Theodore, a military gentleman, black-haired and black-bearded, hands outstretched, possesses all the weight and volume that the ethereal Virgin lacks. There seems to be no relation between the two figures, as though their juxtaposition were a matter of pure accident.

The three panels on the south-east pier are probably the best known. The faces are clearly portraits, the style monumental and there is no attempt at symbolism. In the central panel we see **St Sergius**, a young Roman officer martyred in Syria, where the desert nomads revered him as their patron saint. There is an unmistakable similarity between the modelling of the saint's face and that of St Demetrius in the panel with the children. Perhaps both mosaics were the work of the same artist. Both are equally moving. The flanking panel depicts **St Demetrius between the founders**. The figure of the young martyr, just perceptibly levitated so as to suggest his saintly status, is grand and noble. The ascetic face is unusually small and somewhat pinched, and although it lacks the spiritual quality of the beautiful head towering above the children, the eyes retain the same penetrating expression. The founders, by contrast, are robust, stocky officials with slab-like beards, their feet planted firmly on the ground. The third panel represents **St Demetrius and a deacon** who was so distressed by the church's destruction by fire that the saint took pity on him, visited him in a dream and prophesied its imminent restoration. A report of the dream reached the ears of a senior cleric, and shortly afterwards some wealthy patrons were persuaded to commission the rebuilding of the church (the seventh-century edifice). The saint's right hand is placed affectionately on the shoulder of the deacon, a stolid wooden figure, who reverently touches his protector's *chlamys*.

A stairway to the right descends through brickwork chambers to the **crypt**. Adjoining a marble-paved cloister, lighted by windows on the street level, is an apsidal chamber, the centre of the cult, connected with the sanctuary by two stairways, which incorporates part of the original structure of the Roman baths where Demetrius was murdered. A shrine built above the martyr's grave possessed healing powers and thousands of pilgrims flocked to it to be cured. In the fifth century Leontius, a prefect of Illyricum, was so impressed by the relief that he obtained from a paralytic condition, diagnosed as incurable by his physicians, that he commissioned the construction of a magnificent church (the original building destroyed in the seventh century) in honour of this new Asclepius.

Proceeding down the south aisle, past remains of wall paintings of a later period, one reaches the last major mosaic, depicting **St Demetrius and a woman and child**, on the west wall. It is fragmentary but beautiful. The saint, wearing a gold *chlamys*, stands in front of a *ciborium*. His pale face, lit by almond-shaped eyes, is more mature than in the other panels. On the right a mother and child, bending forward in attitudes of humility, approach through a garden in which a stylized tree grows behind a pilaster surmounted by a vase. The contrast between the Eastern-style background and

189

the Hellenic symmetry of the draperies is characteristic of Thessalonikian ambivalence towards artistic influences during the Early-
Byzantine period.

One returns to the nave, where at the end of the south aisle is the
Chapel of St Euthymius, a miniature three-aisled basilica, donated
by an official in the Byzantine administration. The work of a single
painter, its early fourteenth-century frescoes provide evidence of
the more attractive characteristics of Late-Byzantine painting:
light, fresh colours, a predilection for free brushwork and statu-
esque figures given to dramatic attitudes. The episode from the
Communion of the Apostles in the sanctuary is an outstanding
example.

Descending from *Agios Demetrios* down Agia Sofia Street, past the
Acheiropoietos, one crosses Egnatia Street into a small square with
palm trees. At its east end lies the domed **Basilica of Agia Sofia** of the
eighth century. The exterior is plain with an ugly ochre wash above
the brick course of the façade; but the interior, in spite of architectural imperfections, is impressive. The aisle columns are crowned with
massive capitals and the whole of the square *naos* is filled with a pale
gold light spreading downwards from the shallow dome, decorated
with well-preserved mosaics depicting the Ascension, probably of
the tenth century. Only the Christ Pantocrator, in a medallion
supported by two angels, is an earlier work, possibly of the late
eighth century. A great deal of the disproportion evident in the
mosaic decoration of the church stems from the Byzantine artist's
attempt to present a seated figure within a curved surface to the
onlooker below. As yet he knew little about perspective correction.

Chronologically (and topographically) the next church is the
Panayia Chalkeon in Egnatia Street: so-called 'The Virgin of the
Coppersmiths', because it served as the mosque of the Turkish
coppersmiths in whose noisy quarter it lay. The din of hammers
crashing on anvils has been replaced by the cries of fruit-sellers from
the neighbouring market. Founded in 1028 and heavily restored in
1934, the church is small in comparison with the spacious basilicas.
The transitional style of the domed basilica, as represented by *Agia
Sofia*, is now succeeded by that of the cruciform church. The
triangular pediments and the vaulting of the arms of the Greek
Cross of the *Panayia Chalkeon*, as well as the exterior brickwork

decoration (a faithful reproduction of the original), are forerunners of the inventiveness of later architects. The interior of the church is noteworthy for the faded remains of its original fresco decoration.

On either side of the church are two charming relics of Turkish times: on the east, a little brickwork *hammam* with multiple shallow domes called **Loutra Paradeisos** (The Baths of Paradise) resting on the foundations of the Roman *Agora*, a section of which is discernible from the street; and to the west, an octagonal mosque converted into an amusement hall called the Alcazar, where boys play billiards and older men drink ouzo. Thessaloniki is full of these little Turkish 'islands', but it is a pity that the minarets have gone – for the most part demolished in an orgy of nationalism unleashed by the assassination of George I, founder of an ill-fated Glucksberg dynasty, shot, while taking a walk in Thessaloniki one spring afternoon in 1913, by a lunatic whose only grudge against the sovereign was that he had once begged money of him and allegedly been refused.

Behind the *Panayia Chalkeon* and the *Loutra Paradeisos* extends the wasteland of Dikastiriou Square, where the **Roman Agora**, once the commercial hub of the ancient city, has been excavated. Undistinguished modern blocks border three sides of a large quadrilateral of confusing ruins. At the north-east corner to the left of the entrance, are the remains of a marble *stoa* running on a north–south axis. An unfluted column crowned by a Corinthian capital provides perspective. Close by is the Odeion, its entrance way paved with fragments of mosaic and its proscenium embellished with six arched recesses in which musicians played in the instrumental contests popular with the Romans. At the south-east end of the *stoa*, rubble conceals what may have been an Early-Christian chapel – catacomb-like, safe from the prying eyes of Galerius' spies – with a fragment of wall painting, Roman in style, in which two saints are represented against a background of pale blue sea. Fragments of ancient wells and an intricate system of waterworks, including stone bath-tubs, have been identified along the east–west axis of the quadrilateral. Below ground extend vaulted galleries roofed with shallow domes. A flight of steps leads down to a chamber, penetrated by opaque shafts of light from arched windows, in which a stone pedestal is preserved. On it stood the auctioneer, ringing his bell, amid the swarm of Jews, to whom St Paul addressed his letters.

*   *   *

Eleftheria Square on the harbour is a convenient starting-point for a tour of the ramparts and churches of the Late Byzantine period. In the tenth century the arms of a mole, originally constructed by Constantine the Great, enclosed the inner port in which the largest vessels sought protection from Saracen pirates. One day in 904 sentinels observed the Arab fleet, consisting of fifty-four galleys, nosing its way around Cape Agia Triada. As the high-pitched yells of Arabs and Ethiopian mercenaries drew nearer, the Thessalonikians gave themselves up to loud lamentations. Fire belched forth from the enemy's long copper guns and cages, filled with half-naked negroes waving scimitars, were swung over the seawall. Arrows, stones and fiery missiles rained down on the dazed defenders, who were rapidly overwhelmed. The massacre that followed was total and indiscriminate. However in spite of their success, the conquerors, glutted with loot, slaughter and slaves, sailed away after two days. The pattern of Arab aggression was set for years to come.

From Eleftheria Square one may take a bus or climb to the **Monastery of Vlattadon**, last surviving monastic establishment of the twenty that once flourished in this most Orthodox of Greek cities. Situated on a ledge below the ramparts, overlooking the city and the gulf, the fifteenth-century church, largely rebuilt in the nineteenth, is of little interest, but the garden is pretty. Behind the monastery rises the huge neo-Byzantine Institute of Patriarchical Studies, next to a line of **watch-towers**, forming part of the defensive circuit of the medieval city. The ruined ramparts descend on both sides of the steep escarpments.

Behind the monastery the line of towers runs eastward. The fourteenth-century **Gate of Anna Palaeologaena** (named after the wife of the Emperor Andronicus III) leads through a working-class area to the ruins of the **Heptapyrgion**, which consisted of seven strong towers, whence the Sultan's troops poured into the city in 1430, killing every Christian they encountered. The central tower, the most formidable, now restored, was raised by the Turks a year after they captured the city. At the apex of the angle formed by the arms of the north and east walls rises the **Chain Tower** with a fine circular keep. From here the ramparts descend to the sea. The surviving section of the east walls includes the well-preserved Tower of Hormidas built, at the time of the Emperor Theodosius the

Delphi: the Theatre and Temple of Apollo.

Trikeri, one of the Pelion Villages.

Great, by a Sassanian prince who, according to an inscription on the upper part of the bastion, 'completely fortified the city by indestructible walls'.

The descent from the Monastery of Vlattadon leads through the heart of the former **Turkish Quarter**, a rapidly vanishing area of winding, precipitous alleys, bordered by vine-trellised yards littered with the refuse of decades. If you are fortunate enough to come across one of these little oases, you may see priests in pill-box hats panting up stepped paths and hear doves cooing in walled gardens, while children with huge black eyes stare at you from under stunted acacias and flea-ridden donkeys loaded with panniers of fruit stumble across the cobblestones. The smell of dust, dung and over-ripe vegetables is mixed with that of syringa and jasmine.

At this point the clock has to be turned back – over a thousand years. An intricate system of alleys leads to the fifth-century **Chapel of Hosios David**, once part of a large monastery, in a little garden filled with pots of basil and fuchsias. Originally a square edifice, subsequently truncated, it contains, within its apse, a damaged but very beautiful mosaic, primitive but profound in religious feeling, untarnished by the more sophisticated techniques of later centuries. The crowded composition depicts the **Vision of Ezekiel**, who raises his hands in fear with an almost elfin expression on his face. Opposite him Habbakuk, more meditative, records the miracle in an open book. Above the prophets a young and beardless Christ sits on a rainbow with shafts of light radiating from him like spokes from the hub of a wheel. His face, more Early-Christian than Byzantine in feeling, emanates sanctity, compassion, authority. At his feet flow the four rivers of paradise, in whose waters two fish and a frightened river god, symbolizing paganism, take flight.

From *Hosios David* you descend to the **Church of Profitis Elias**. Probably of eleventh-century origin, built on the site of a Byzantine palace overlooking the city, this bulky edifice, frequently reconstructed, is architecturally very complex, with additional north and south apses creating a trefoil effect, and an elongated apse projecting clumsily from a box-like cruciform structure crowned by a high polygonal drum decorated with blind arches.

To the west, nestling among painfully modern houses, is the more attractive **Church of Agia Aikaterini**, in the purest architectural style of the fourteenth century. Airy little cupolas crown tall polygonal drums and a portico surrounds three sides. The exterior brickwork decoration is elaborate. The fragmentary frescoes, depicting Christ's miracles, were badly damaged when the church was converted into a mosque, but the artist's endeavour to create an illusion of architectural depth by means of successive planes and to model the rounder somewhat fleshy faces in a freer, more painterly manner is evident. Although lacking the sturdiness of Early-Byzantine architecture, *Agia Aikaterini* possesses all the elements that make up the typical small church of the Palaeologue period: warm-coloured brickwork decoration, multiple domes, arched windows, arcades with glass frontages and a clearly defined Greek Cross plan.

The westerly route continues downhill past traces of the west rampart. It is best to head for Agiou Demetriou Street, cross it and enter a little square, undisturbed by motor traffic, where the walls, apses and domes of the early fourteenth-century **Church of Agioi Apostoli**, girdled with multiple bands of brick inlay, rise out of a sunken enclosure. On summer evenings, when the sun goes down, women drop in for vespers and a priest waters the orange trees and flower-beds in the court.

One of the most attractive churches in Thessaloniki, architecturally it differs little from *Agia Aikaterini* (except that it is larger), with a lofty central drum and four subsidiary ones at the corners of the square. The narthex façade is embellished by four pilasters with Theodosian capitals supporting arches filled with brick inlay. The whole exterior is a masterpiece of lavish and ingenious interplay of stone, mortar and brick. The fashion certainly had earlier origins, but it is not until the fourteenth century that Byzantine architects achieve an extraordinary virtuosity in the creation of unlimited geometrical permutations with bricks of different colour, size and shape which they handle with the skill of a mosaicist. This art, a minor yet characteristically Byzantine one, is nowhere better illustrated than at the *Agioi Apostoli* (there are other outstanding examples at Arta and Kastoria). The zigzag cornices, rosettes, crosses and colonettes, the string courses and step-patterns, especially those of the three apses, are integrated with the harmony and brilliance of design of a Persian carpet, and with as much feeling for

Church of the Holy Apostles, Salonica

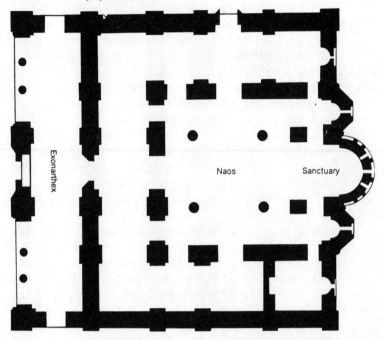

Exonarthex

Naos

Sanctuary

poetry as for geometry. An element of frivolity, almost of skittishness, is sometimes apparent in the garlands of hieroglyphics.

This last phase of artistic creation at Thessaloniki, of which the *Agioi Apostoli* is the highlight, corresponds with the development of the Hesychast movement which set priest against priest and split their flocks into hostile factions. Bricklayers and mosaicists were adding their final touches to the *Agioi Apostoli* when the storm of the Hesychast dispute swept Thessaloniki. The word is derived from *hesychia*, the Greek for quiet, and the Hesychasts, like Hindu exponents of Yoga, with eyes staring at their hearts, their limbs arranged in specially prescribed postures, devoted themselves to prayer and meditation by means of physical aids to spiritual concentration. The battle raged throughout the fourteenth century. At the *Agioi Apostoli*, gorgeously robed prelates hurled anathemas at each other. The unity of the Church was threatened and families were split in two in the best traditions of Greek party politics. In the sphere of art, the static liturgical canons of Byzantine iconography, so tenaciously preserved for nearly ten centuries, were not unaffected. The greater stress on physical movement, strictly denied to the monumental figures of an earlier age, may owe something to the Hesychast contention that the body in itself is not evil, as well as to the fact that Byzantine artists, now visiting Italy in increasing numbers, were unlikely, on returning home, to have forgotten wholly the lessons they learnt in the West.

The *naos* of the *Agioi Apostoli* is a perfect Greek Cross, with four marble columns, crowned by Theodosian capitals supporting the central drum; behind the sanctuary are three elliptical apses. The smell of incense is strong. The greater part of the walls is washed a dirty pink. Turkish graffiti pock-mark the damaged frescoes of the first zone.

The surviving mosaics, stylistically typical of the so-called Palaeologue 'renaissance' in religious art, are clearly the work of first-class Constantinopolitan artists. The emphasis is on movement and tension. In the **Entry into Jerusalem** (west vault of north side) the elders rush forward to meet the procession against a background of towers, roofs and domes. The **Descent into Hell** in the north vault (east side) is treated in a very dramatic fashion. A dour, purposeful Christ with heavy-lidded eyes, the corners of his mouth turned down, his mantle blown back by the wind, raises the aged Adam from Limbo, while Eve, her hands outstretched, awaits her turn in front of a crowd led by Abel and a prophet. The balance and symmetry of the central interlocking figures of Christ and Adam are apparent in every line, whether of limbs or drapery.

In the **Nativity** (south vault of the east side) the crouching Joseph and the shepherds who bear the tidings are simple rustic creatures. The faces of the mourning apostles in the **Dormition of the Virgin** above the main doorway are treated as portraits with individual expressions. The cruel bony hand of the Pantocrator in the dome hints at the familiar representation of a militant uncompromising Christ, a saviour of souls on his own terms. Of the four Evangelists in the pendentives, the contemplative **Matthew** is the best preserved. Occasionally, a hint of preciousness is evident in the facial expressions. In his desire to dramatize, to stress human individuality, the fourteenth-century artist no longer appears to be filled with the same deep religious fervour that inspired the great static monumental figures of the St Demetrius panels. Only in the frescoes, which are in a much poorer state of preservation, one observes a more monumental character reminiscent of slightly earlier models.

There remains one last Byzantine pilgrimage. On the way, however, the sightseer must project himself for a moment into the closing years of the Ottoman Empire. From the *Agioi Apostoli*, Agiou Demetriou Street goes eastward and, near its end, Agiou Pavlou Street winds to the left up the hill through the fringe of the former Turkish quarter. A plaque on a crimson-painted house, beside the Turkish Consulate, identifies it as the **birthplace of Mustafa Kemal**. The son of a local customs official and a fair-skinned Macedonian lady of Moslem faith, the future Ataturk, 'father of the Turks', grew up here in the late nineteenth-century squalor of the decaying Levantine port, where shadows of minarets lay across potholed streets littered with dung and dimly lit cafès echoed with the screeches of pig-tailed schoolgirls weaving through groups of soldiers bristling with sabres, daggers and pistols, their close-cropped Tartar-shaped heads crowned with furry black fezes. At the army cadet school, Kemal galvanized the Thessaloniki branch of the 'Young Turk' movement and plotted the overthrow of the corrupt regime of Sultan Abdul Hamid II: the first step in a programme of national regeneration which was to culminate in the expulsion of Greeks from Asia Minor, the foundation of the Turkish republic and the doom of the *Megali Idhea* (the Great Idea) of a revived Byzantine Empire romantically fostered by Greek nineteenth- and twentieth-century politicians.

Beyond Ataturk's house a labyrinth of narrow streets leads to Kallithea Square and the small but important **Church of Agios Nikolaos Orfanos** (St Nicholas the Orphan), which once formed part of a fourteenth-century convent and became, in the seventeenth century, a dependency of the Vlattadon Monastery. Built in the form of a Greek letter π, it is chronologically the last of the surviving Byzantine churches in Thessaloniki. Good lighting and the church's diminutive proportions enable one to devote attention to the details of the paintings which the lofty ill-lit interiors of earlier churches preclude.

197

The **frescoes** are not among the masterpieces of late Byzantine art. Illustrative, picturesque, even fussy, they nevertheless possess a quality of ingenuousness which is wholly disarming. Take the narthex first. Across the east wall extend two bands of small compositions depicting the miracles of St Nicholas, the Lycian bishop who was patron of sailors, merchants and pawnbrokers. The cycle is full of story-book detail. In one episode the saint, standing in a boat propelled by five rowers, gazes up at a billowing crescent-shaped sail as he prepares to cast a phial of soothing magic oil on the troubled waters. The south wall is devoted to **scenes from the miracles of Christ**. In the Wedding at Cana the bridal couple, crowned and wearing jewel-studded robes, are seated at an ornate table loaded with food, while the Virgin whispers in Christ's ear: 'They have no wine.' On the north wall a beautiful Christ, depicted as a beardless boy with haunting eyes, is seated on a throne surrounded by priests and choristers.

In the apse the **Virgin Orans** stands on a golden dais, flanked by two adoring angels: a figure of authority, her eyes fixed in an oblique glance to the left, her gold-fringed robe draped in symmetrical folds. The cycle of Twelve Feasts spreads across the nave, with the Transfiguration flanked by the Entry into Jerusalem and the Crucifixion, crowned by the Ascension. In the **Nativity**, subsidiary episodes full of homely detail are grouped round the conch-shaped manger: Joseph meditating; the rustic shepherds hear the news; the bathing of the Child in an ornamental basin into which an attendant pours water from a gold ewer while another dips her hand in to test the temperature. At the east end of the south aisle Christ holds an open Book of Gospels. The austerity of previous centuries has been tempered. His beneficent expression is identical throughout the church – an indication that a single artist employed the same model for all the portraits of Christ.

Everything is in the minutest scale; but colour, opulent as a peacock's plumage, is used unsparingly to match, blend and contrast. Lime greens vie with sealing-wax reds, sombre purples fade into amethyst shades, and the brown, maroon, puce or copper tones of gold-fringed robes glow against inky-blue backgrounds. No longer are the heavenly beings the austere symbols of a mystic revelation. Beautiful, pert, playful, contemplative – they are all somehow identifiable: the plump, lavishly bedecked page attending the horses in the Adoration, the aquiline-faced apostles in the Washing of the Feet, the forbidding Caiphas giving counsel to the Jews, the bored, indifferent Pilate washing his hands, the compassionate Christ who appears above the myrrh-bearers in the garden, the prophets and saints in the lower register. One sees their faces in Thessaloniki every day.

CHAPTER 14

Western Macedonia: The Lowlands

Pella – Edessa – The Macedonian Tombs – Mieza –
Veria – Vergina.

West of Thessaloniki extend the lowlands of the large province of
Macedonia. The Hellenistic sites, including Pella, birthplace of
Alexander the Great, and three beautifully situated towns on the
mountain periphery, overlooking the Imathian Plain – Edessa.
Naoussa and Veria – can be visited in one long day.

Twenty kilometres west of Thessaloniki the road to Edessa
crosses the highway from Athens to the Jugoslav border (near
which, at Polikastro, there is a British military cemetery – reminder
of the long, frustrating campaigns of the 'forgotten front' of the First
World War). The Edessa road continues westward and, shortly
after the bridge over the Axios, passes a south-westerly fork (to
Veria) and enters the reclaimed marshland of Imathia. In the
middle of it lies **Pella**, founded by King Archelaos (413–399 BC),
where the conquest of Asia was conceived in the royal residence of
Philip of Macedon. In the south Olympos looms in the haze. In the
west the Vermion range forms a barrier, thickly wooded, skirted by
orchards. Foundations of Hellenistic houses paved with floor
mosaics spread across the fields. The recent discovery of the vast
Agora has added new dimensions, but the acropolis to the north has
still to be excavated; also the palace where Alexander was born – at
the very hour, according to Plutarch, when the temple of Diana at
Ephesus was destroyed by fire and panic-stricken soothsayers ran
through the city, prophesying that: 'this day has brought forth
something that will prove fatal and destructive to all Asia.'

In antiquity Pella was surrounded by navigable marshes extending from the acropolis to the Thermaic Gulf. It is, for most of the

year. a damp. torrid place. Livy says the citadel rose 'like an island from the part of the marsh nearest to the city. being built upon an immense embankment which defies all injury from the waters'. He also mentions 'a wet ditch' spanned by a single bridge 'so that no access whatever is afforded to an enemy . . .'.

At the right of the road are foundations of what must have been a complex of spacious habitations. not far from Philip's palace. Here he discovered his wife Olympias lying in such a compromising position with a serpent that he presumed her to be having intercourse with a god in disguise. God or serpent – it was exactly nine months later that this extraordinary woman gave birth to Alexander.

Entering the site (north of the road). the visitor faces a temporary storehouse; here are displayed two of the great **floor mosaics** composed of large pebbles of different colours. In Hellenistic times the subjects of this lavish form of house decoration were generally confined to historical and mythological events. Later. throughout the Roman world. the mosaicist's art became a flourishing trade. the artist himself an interior decorator with wealthy patrons. The Pella mosaics are among the earliest and grandest examples extant. The first is the **Lion Hunt**. in which two male figures. brandishing swords. attack a lion with dark mane and erect tail. The attitudes of both men and beast. with the agitated backward sweep of the hunters' mantles. form a perfectly balanced composition. Clearly outlined shading. achieved by the use of grey pebbles. marks the sinews of naked limbs and folds of drapery. The second mosaic represents **Dionysus riding a panther**. The god is depicted as a flabby young man holding a *thyrsus*. his soft effeminate body providing a striking contrast to the lithe and powerful panther.

In the **Museum** there is an outstanding small bronze Poseidon. attributed to Lysippos. as well as a large assortment of architectural fragments. jewellery and Hellenistic paintings. Among the sculptures are a fifth-century BC life-size dog couchant. relaxed yet alert. and a small male torso crowned by a Hellenistic head with a voluptuous expression. thought to resemble Alexander. The bronze figurines include a supple little panther devouring a stag: a masterpiece of anatomical observation.

North of the museum are foundations of four palatial houses with pebble mosaic floors; to the east lies the clearly outlined structure of the late fourth-century BC **House of the Lion Hunt** (so-called after the mosaic pavement found there), which consists of a succession of chambers with a peristyle court surrounded by broken fluted Ionic columns (six have been restored), bordered on the east by an ancient street. The ruined house lends scale and perspective to the whole site. Fragments of plaster-work, bronze doorways and ornamental blocks suggest that it was an important official residence. In some such colonnaded court it is possible to imagine Philip, one-eyed and lecherous, surrounded by his under-age concubines, indulging in nightly debauches. On one of these occasions, relates Plutarch, he so infuriated Alexander that the young prince seized a wine-cup and hurled it at his father. There was little family unity at Pella, and soon after this incident Alexander fled with his morbidly possessive mother to the court of her brother, Alexander, King of Epirus.

West of the House of the Lion Hunt, across more foundations, is the magnificent mosaic of the **Stag Hunt**, which adorned a floor of another residence. Two stags are hunted by two naked youths armed respectively with a sword and a double axe. Anatomical details – muscles and joints – are subtly emphasized by shading effects, fingernails and toenails outlined in black pebbles, and the hunters' wavy hair is reproduced by the juxtaposition of alternately light and dark coloured stones. In spite of the formal framework the figures remain intensely alive, and their predatory expressions reflect the excitement of the kill. In contrast, the border, a formal flower pattern, is pastoral and tranquil in tone: crocuses, lilies and honeysuckle are drawn by an artist with a professional knowledge of beauty.

South of the main road a modern building is filled with fragments of pebble pavements from the House of the Stag Hunt. Huge pieces of a series representing the Rape of Helen (a charioteer, horses and the flowing garments of a handmaiden are the best preserved) indicate the extent of floor space originally covered. The remains of a theatre and small temple are less impressive than the *Agora*, an immense square surrounded by a Doric colonnade, behind which sheltered market stalls and workshops. The town was bisected by a wide avenue. The water supply and drainage would do credit to any modern urbanization.

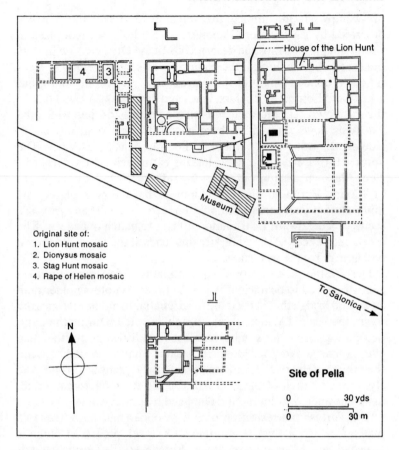

House of the Lion Hunt

Original site of:
1. Lion Hunt mosaic
2. Dionysus mosaic
3. Stag Hunt mosaic
4. Rape of Helen mosaic

Museum

To Salonica →

N

Site of Pella

| 0 | 30 yds |
| 0 | 30 m |

Much excavation remains to be done at Pella before we know more about the actual physical surroundings in which Alexander spent his childhood. After he had embarked on the conquest of Asia, Antipater became Governor of Macedonia and kept his official residence at Pella. In the late fourth century Kassandros, after assuming Alexander's mantle in Europe, established a new capital, named after his wife Thessaloniki, Alexander's sister. Pella declined in importance, though in Roman times it was crossed by the Via Egnatia.

Beyond Pella the plain is dotted with pine-clad mounds. Patches of swampy ground among the wheat fields recall the marshes described by Livy. After Giannitsa, once a holy Moslem place in whose dilapidated mosque descendants of the Ottoman conquerors of Macedonia are buried, the plain contracts, and avenues of trees relieve the monotony: not the cypress and olive of the south, but aspens and Lombardy poplars, limes and dwarf oaks. Cows graze in the meadows. At Skidra, a fruit-canning centre through which the Edesseos flows sluggishly, there is a fork. One road mounts to Edessa, the other runs parallel to the railway as far as Veria. The approach to **Edessa** and its waterfalls is through cherry orchards. The little town is strung out across the ridge of a wooded escarpment of Mount Vermion. Factory chimneys have now replaced the minarets that once thrust their pointed turrets out of shady groves: a scene which Edward Lear found 'difficult to match in beauty'. The ascent, streaked by cascading streams, ends at the hotel and tourist pavilion above the waterfalls.

Despite the lack of any antique remains, Edessa was until recently believed to be ancient Aigai. Yet there is nothing older than an arched bridge that carried the Via Egnatia. In medieval times the town, then called Vodena, was strongly fortified. During the Latin occupation, after the knights had lost what little control they had ever exercised over Macedonia, it became a battle-ground between the armies of the rival exiled aspirants to the Byzantine throne. The Byzantine Church of the *Koimesis*, beside the modern cathedral, has some ancient columns and damaged frescoes. Alleys, bordered by old Turkish houses with projecting wooden balconies, lead to a plateau, where a Turkish mosque with a well-preserved porch is crowned by a large tea-cosy dome. Remains of Byzantine capitals and inscriptions are displayed within. A minaret with a crumbling circular balcony casts an oblique shadow. Under the Turks, Edessa was a flourishing commercial and industrial centre; carpets are still produced.

But Edessa is mainly visited for the waterfalls. On the plateau behind the escarpment the Edesseos divides into two streams which flow between weeping willows before cascading into the plain. This plain stretches eastward in a haze of fruit orchards and poplar groves. A cool shadowy public garden, neatly laid out with flower beds and filled with rustic belvederes and kiosks at which hideous souvenirs are sold, overhangs a vertical bluff. Down its sides roar the waters of the Edesseos, spray drenching the leaves of walnut, pomegranate and wild fig: trees which sprout from mossy ledges thick with maidenhair ferns.

Returning to the fork at Skidra, one follows the road south skirting the foothills of Mount Vermion. In spring a haze of pink peach blossom stretches for miles across the orchards. At the end of a side-road to the right lies the hamlet of **Lefkadia**, close to the signposted temple tombs which are concealed among plantations of peach trees. This pastoral fringe of the Imathian plain is littered with sepulchres containing the ashes of princes and generals who fought fratricidal wars for the mastery of the East, whence they brought back the orientalizing influences that characterize so much of the art and architecture of the Hellenistic period.

The first tomb, of ashlar masonry, was built in the middle of the third century BC and is visible from the road. The façade, covered with a thin layer of marble, is crowned by a frieze: six yellow *metopes* and a cornice with painted moulding. An antechamber, around which runs a narrow bank with traces of floral decoration, leads into a vaulted sepulchre, also once painted.

More impressive is the so-called **Great Tomb**, which is dated to the period of Alexander the Great. Although protected by a modern concrete roof, this quasi-oriental monument makes an astonishing impact. After plodding through well-tended orchards, one is suddenly confronted with a two-storied structure, composed of large stone slabs set in regular courses, emerging, like some Babylonian temple in miniature, out of an excavated pit. On the first story six columns frame panels painted with life-size representations unique in their layout both in monumental painting and sculpture: (left to right) (i) the deceased, holding a spear and the sheath of his sword; (ii) Hermes in his role of conductor of the dead to the Underworld; (iii–iv) Aicus and Rhadamantus, Lords of the Elysian Fields. On the second zone of the first storey sculptured *metopes* depict the battle of the Centaurs and Lapiths. The third is decorated with a sculptured frieze, also painted, of skirmishes between Persians and Macedonians. The second storey consists of six Ionic half-columns alternating with painted doors within frames. Little remains of the architrave and pediment. Beyond the façade

205

an antechamber leads into the vault, on the walls of which columns alternate with painted panels. As an example both of architectural complexity and of the Hellenistic attachment to the symbols of human mortality, nothing could be more arresting than this grotesque monument.

The entry into the **Tomb of Lyson and Callicles** (second-century BC), so-called after an extant inscription on the doorway, is less imposing but more curious. It is entered through what looks like a well-head flush with the ground. An iron stairway descends a narrow shaft into a man-made subterranean cavern, once the sepulchre of a princely Macedonian family. The walls are painted with garlands, effigies of arms and an altar on which writhes a snake, symbol of the underworld. Twigs and pomegranates painted on either side of the columns *in antis*, just below the capitals, give the impression of being suspended on hooks. Outlines of towers and ramparts decorate the ceiling of the vault. Twenty-four ossuaries can be counted in niches on the walls. Of the gold objects offered to the dead none remain – the result of looting – but some arms still hang from nails, one of which is decorated with a star within a border of laurel leaves. There is little oxygen in this macabre folly of a charnel-house, and it is a relief to return to the orchards and the light of day.

About five kilometres west of the tombs a track climbs the foothills between banks of campion and golden drop, skirted by sheets of butterfly orchids, to Eisvoria, site of **ancient Mieza**. It is best to leave the car at a confluence of little streams and walk up a path bordered by moss-covered boulders and clusters of giant mullein whose blooms are still used as fish poison. Opposite rises a wall of cliff divided into just perceptible ledges, believed to be the site of Aristotle's Academy, founded by Philip of Macedon within the precinct of a sanctuary of the Nymphs. Here the thirteen-year-old Alexander, far from the palace intrigues of Pella and the overpowering influence of his mother, could be instructed in a more tranquil atmosphere in the art of government and kingship. He was taught ethics, physics, politics and geography. It is said that, in later years, he never went to bed without a well-thumbed copy of the *Iliad*, annotated by Aristotle and kept in Darius' jewelled casket beside his unsheathed dagger. In practice, he paid little attention to the application of his tutor's principles on the art of government, but the seed of the love of learning, implanted at Mieza, prevailed throughout his brief meteoric career. Bas-reliefs of gorgons, lions' heads and floral decorations, as well as Roman coins have been found, and in the small caves in the escarpment there is evidence of the grotto with stalactites mentioned by Pliny. There are also the remains of a Hellenistic stairway and of structures, including an Ionic portico, at the top of the ledge from which water cascades into copses of oak, walnut and Judas trees.

A branch road ascends the foothills to **Naoussa** where vineyards alternate with apple orchards. An esplanade with flower-beds and a belvedere and cafés, shaded by great pines, overlooks the cultivated plain that was formed centuries ago by the silt of numerous streams pouring down from the sides of the Vermion range. In the mountains the village of Seli has become an important ski resort.

Regaining the main road, one ascends the escarpment again: this time to **Veria**, spreading across a ledge of the foothills. As in many Macedonian towns, a somewhat muted air prevails. Instead of the usual Greek dust there is running water; instead of brilliant light, an opalescent haze. Outlines are blurred and rounded. It is a painter's scene, not a sculptor's. Some old Turkish timber-framed houses put up a brave show among the cheap modern buildings.

The Museum, situated on a ledge overlooking the orchard country, houses a collection of Roman sarcophagi, column bases, Roman and Early Christian carved plaques from neighbouring sites and fragments of idols and axes (which are ascribed to the impressive date of 6200 BC) from Nicomedia, the oldest Neolithic site in Greece, situated in the plain below.

Vestiges of Roman fortifications – a ruined tower of the third century AD is conspicuous – crown the hill at the entrance to the town where Pompey spent the winter assembling his legions before the battle of Pharsalia. St Paul also stayed here for three months, converting large numbers of the inhabitants. In Byzantine times the town was a bulwark guarding the western approaches to Thessaloniki, and consequently one of the first objectives in the lightning campaign waged by Theodore Angelus II, Despot of Epirus, in the thirteenth century, when this fiery claimant to the Byzantine throne freed all Northern Greece of Franks, Bulgars and other foreigners.

Post-Byzantine churches and timber-framed chapels are tucked away in secluded courtyards, where Christian devotions could be performed in the privacy of the family circle without drawing undue attention from hostile pashas and fanatical imams. Most important is the fourteenth-century **Church of Christou** in a sunken garden in Kotoyiorghaki Street, a single-aisle basilica with frescoes by Callerghis, who is described in an inscription as 'the best painter in Thessaly'. His style is elegant and fluent, probably influenced by that of icon painting, and his faces are remarkable for their liveliness of expression. In the Descent into Hell, Christ, wearing luminous yellow garments instead of the usual scarlet mantle, is more the gentle saviour of mankind than the formidable judge of the souls of the dead so dear to earlier Byzantine iconographers. The same limpidity of outline prevails in the Crucifixion. The Dormition of the Virgin is rendered with little originality but with an impressive blend of colours. In the Annunciation, the Angel, seemingly propelled by some inner force, advances eagerly towards the Virgin under a triumphal arch.

The maze of the ramshackle upper town is dominated by the curious basilica of the recently restored **Old Metropolis** in the main street. The original structure goes back to the fifth century. On the north side of the spacious *naos*, entered from the narthex between chocolate-coloured pillars, a colonnade is laid out in three groups of ninth-century columns. Brick inlay of a later period surrounds the exterior of the apse. The last transformation was made in the fifteenth century when the frescoed walls were whitewashed, Christian symbols ripped off the desecrated sanctuary and a Moslem congregation appropriated the *naos*.

At the south-western apex of the plain, ten kilometres east of Veria, the road crosses the reed-fringed Aliakmon, flowing between banks bordered by copses of poplars, out of a chasm between the Vermion and Pieria ranges. East of the village of **Vergina**, named after a legendary queen of Veria, one square kilometre of the plain is studded with more than three hundred small tumuli, many little more than one metre high. This Cemetery of the Tumuli was used for some eight hundred years by the tribesmen who dwelt on the wooded Pierian Mountains, the oldest graves, often in distinct groups indicating clans, dating from the Early Iron Age

(1000–700 BC). These burial places attracted much greater interest with the discovery of the first Macedonian tomb here by Leon Heuzey in 1861 (he had already discovered another at Pidna earlier in the same year). Six years earlier the young French archaeologist had been shown the imposing but forgotten ruins of a palace. He interested the Emperor Napoleon III in his find and returned with a research expedition. A subterranean vaulted building, flooded during his first visit, could at last be explored. The unusual features and originality of style were duly noted and the marble doors, the first example of their kind, were removed to the Louvre; but still the full significance of the discovery was not recognized. It was only in 1938 that the second **Macedonian tomb** in the area was found, on the terrace north-west of the palace. The façade resembles that of a little Ionic temple, with four half-columns, a frieze of painted flowers and a pediment. Marble slabs, which formed part of the doorway, lie across the floor of the antechamber. In the barrel-vaulted burial chamber are a grave, a ledge on which the urn containing the deceased's ashes was placed and the damaged but imposing throne of a Macedonian king. The arm-rests are supported by carved sphinxes. Traces of painted griffins devouring a yellow stag against a red ground are visible on the sides and footstool. Though robbed like most tombs, the marble throne left no doubt that this was indeed a royal burial chamber, most likely of the third century BC.

The huge mound on the western edge of the Cemetery of the Tumuli, 12 metres high with a diameter of 110 metres, unique in the Greek world, had been observed by Heuzey but excavations, begun in earnest in 1976, yielded within three years discoveries that have completely changed our idea of Macedonia before Alexander. The Great Tumulus had been raised to cover **three royal tombs**, including the untouched resting place of Philip II. Beneath superb frescoes were arrayed the treasures buried with the king: two gold caskets of splendid workmanship that contained his and, perhaps, the queen's bones; the royal diadem and gold jewellery; his armour and shield; five ivory statuettes of the royal family, with the unmistakable likenesses of Philip and Alexander, to name only the historically most important finds, which are now on display in the Thessaloniki Archaeological Museum.

These remains, together with the excavations of the acropolis wall, a temple with votive offerings from Philip's mother Eurydice, and above all, next to the palace, the theatre in which Philip was assassinated, leave little doubt that this – and not Edessa – is ancient Aigai. First capital of the Macedonian kings, Aigai remained their burial place until the time of Alexander. In 336 BC it was the scene of a splendid ceremony in honour of the marriage of Philip's daughter to an Epirot prince, but the festivities ended in disaster when an assassin's knife was thrust into the king's back as he entered the crowded theatre.

Glory returned in the last years of the fourth century BC with the construction of a new **Palace**, the outstanding Macedonian building, not merely because of its size, but even more because of its architecture and execution. South-east of Vergina, on a terrace in the northern slope of the Pierian Mountains, the ruins of buff-coloured limestone round a colonnaded court, cover an area of 105 metres by 90 metres. The dimensions alone suggest royal pomp of the first magnitude, certainly the residence of Antigonus Gonatas. The ruins are scarcely more than shoulder-high, but the architectural layout is clear. The only shade is provided by a large oak tree at the north-east end. You enter from the east, like the courtiers and palace attendants, through what was a pedimented portico flanked north and south by four large rectangular chambers, thence into the *propylaia* – the small Ionic columns previously decorating the upper story are now strewn about the ground – and finally into the court, once bordered by sixty massive Doric columns but now littered with pieces of cornice and architrave, drums and capitals, all eroded by time and weather. South of the *propylaia* are the foundations of a circular chamber believed to be the ceremonial room in which the king received ambassadors and generals. One of the chambers of a succession of five, which constituted the south wing running along the base of the scrub-covered hillside, is covered with a beautiful, well-preserved **floor mosaic** with foliate designs radiating outwards from the central star and enclosed within a medallion with decorative borders and female figures in each corner. Judging from traces of Erotes and Tritons riding dolphins in the floor decoration of the side chambers, archaeologists believe that representations of erotic scenes were removed later by more prudish inhabitants. The west side consists of three small and three larger chambers paved with small marble plaques joined by red mortar, with a drainage hole in the centre. Excavations at the south-west end of the palace have revealed a colonnaded open court, beyond which were porticoes and chambers forming an annexe to the tetragon of the palace proper. The north side, now completely destroyed, overlooked steep sloping ground and is thought to have been a covered terrace overlooking the Aliakmon as it flowed through the mountain cleft and the strange necropolis of burial mounds extending across the plain.

In its dimensions alone, thrusting aggressively from the ledge above the plain, the palace, in its now somewhat naked geometric state, still remains a very impressive ruin. Vergina was partly destroyed by the Romans; some sections of the palace survived, however, to serve different – probably religious – purposes during later periods.

CHAPTER 15

Western Macedonia: The Highlands

The Aliakmon Valley – Kozani – Servia – Siatista –
Grevena – Kastoria – The Edesseos – Lake Vegoritida
– Florina – Lake Prespa.

North to south, the mountain mass is seamed with tracts of agricultural land – rice paddies, fruit orchards, fields of corn, sugar-beet
and poppy-seed – through which the Aliakmon flows in a great
horseshoe loop. The forests, lakes, snow-capped ranges and passes
are not yet the haunt of tourists. The goal of most travellers is
Kastoria, one of the most important Byzantine sites in Greece. The
landscape is varied, often magnificent, but never classical; at no
point is the Mediterranean visible. It is a journey into the periphery
of the Balkans, whose remoteness ensured the survival of folklore
traditions during four centuries of Turkish occupation.

Kastoria, where it is worthwhile spending two nights, can be
approached either from Veria across the Vermion range and along
the course of the Aliakmon or from Edessa whence the road runs
parallel to the Jugoslav border and then turns south. The former
route, which I describe first, is the shorter one.

West of Veria the road climbs Mount Vermion between beech
forests where primroses grow. At the top of the pass there is a
tremendous aerial view of the **Aliakmon Valley**, with the river
winding between green banks against a prodigious background of
the wooded Pieria ranges rising to 7000 feet. The scale is immense.
A long dizzy descent in hairpin bends terminates at the unattractive
town of **Kozani**, a road junction in the plain of Ptolemais, where
lignite mines have brought heavy industry and prosperity to the
region.

212

South of Kozani the Pieria range forms an unbroken backcloth to undulating countryside. The southbound road crosses the elongated Polifito lake, formed by the damming-up of the Aliakmon. A gap suddenly appears in the mountain barrier, with a group of twisted outcrops of rock guarding the entrance to a profound defile. At their foot lies the sleepy little town of **Servia**, originally founded by Serbs settled here by the Emperor Heraclius in the seventh century to defend the strategic pass into Central Greece. Opposite the needle-shaped rocks a hill is crowned by the ruined towers of a Byzantine fortress overlooking a loop of the Aliakmon. Little else survives of the military fortifications of this former key-town, where Michael II, the violent hot-blooded Despot of Epirus, met his pious consort, Theodora, and carried her in state across the mountains to his capital at Arta. South of Servia, a number of narrow passes are succeeded by tracts of inhospitable moorland whence the road descends into Thessaly at Elassona.

To visit **Siatista**, seat of a remote feudal society that flourished in the twilight era after the fall of Constantinople, one turns right at the twenty-fourth kilometre west of Kozani, just before the junction of roads from Kastoria and Grevena. The branch road climbs into limestone mountains with fine structural forms uncommon in these parts. The multi-coloured houses of Siatista spread across a line of broken hills. Once inhabited by rich furriers, Siatista seems to have been left unmolested by the Turks. Straddling no centre of communications, it was a retreat to which wealthy merchants retired, untroubled by Turkish tax-collectors, and dwelt in lofty houses with projecting third stories supported by wooden brackets and painted with stylized flowers and foliate patterns below the cornices. The chief interest of the timber-framed houses, some recently restored, lies in their oriental-style interiors and frescoed walls, evocative of a rural seignorial way of life swept away in the holocaust of the War of Independence. There is no feeling of continuity here. Unlike Edessa, Veria or Kastoria, Siatista has no roots in Macedonian history. A phenomenon of the post-Byzantine age, it was the product of its own inaccessibility.

Two eighteenth-century houses are easily accessible. First the **Nerantzopoulos House**, which is still inhabited. As in most large residences of the Turkish period, storerooms and wine-cellars are

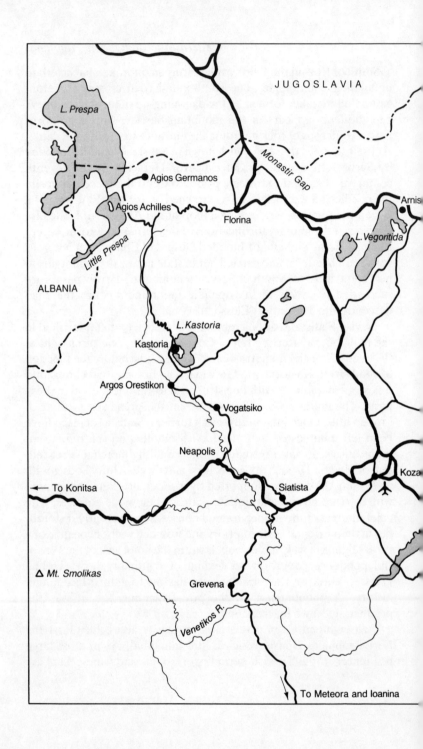

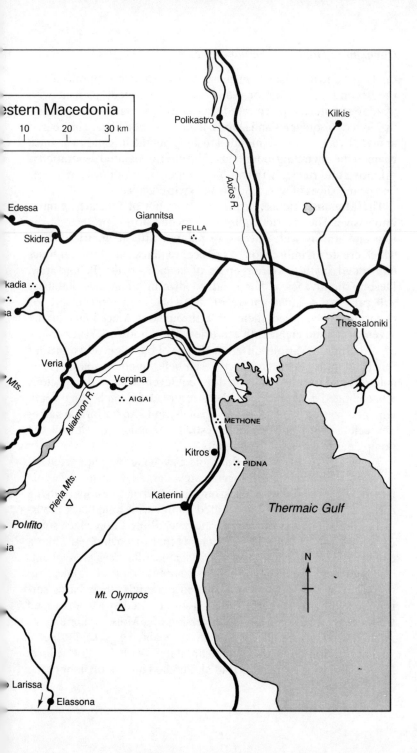

on the ground floor, sleeping quarters on the first, reception halls on the second. The exterior walls are whitewashed, pierced with windows protected by coffered shutters and wrought-iron gratings fashioned in squiggles and spirals. The nail-studded gate is secured at night by a heavy bar, intended to keep out the brigands who once roamed the encircling mountains. The interior painted decoration is primitive and rustic, with still-life compositions of bowls of apples and pears, slices of water melon and stylized flowers.

The **Manoussi House**, virtually a museum of folk art, is more impressive. The exterior walls of the second storey, protected from rain and sun by wide eaves, are painted with geometric designs which create an impression of faience, reminiscent of the ceramics embedded in the exterior apses of chapels in the Pelion area. Despite the ravages of damp and woodworm, numerous chambers still preserve a faded image of the work of the rustic interior decorators who plied their craft throughout Macedonia in the seventeenth and eighteenth centuries. The woodwork is admirably carved, and the various different shapes of banisters add a further touch of fantasy to the architectural embellishment. A maze of little galleries and panelled halls on different levels leads to the spacious low-ceilinged reception chamber, reserved for night-long death laments chanted by black-draped crones; and also for formal name-day celebrations and wedding festivities conducted with all the pomp dear to a peasant community.

The walls of the sun-parlour, its bay windows supported by columns like a miniature loggia, are adorned with mock-heroic frescoes: a stag-hunt with black-birds perched on tree-tops or flying across a lemon-yellow sky; a kilted hunter with long black moustaches drawing his sword, preparatory to killing a lion which sticks its tongue out at him. The drawing is that of a child and, like a child's, it has a dream-like quality; Islamic influences are evident. The bedrooms are distinguished by a curious architectural feature: fireplaces in the form of apse-shaped pyramids, their bases surrounded with marble kerbs and each surmounted by a cone capped with a cross, like some Christian version of a Moslem monument. Arched windows are filled with panels of stained glass set in stucco: an importation from the Danubian states, with which the local furriers and wine merchants traded. Perched on the top floor of the house is the minute and only lavatory – Turkish style, a hole in the floor – projecting above the neglected garden. The whole affair is a gigantic doll's house – it must have been a place of fantasy to live in – set against a background of desolate mountains from which jackals descend at night to shriek in the stony wastes around the village.

A descent between slate-grey hills brings us to the main north–south road: to Kastoria and Grevena respectively. As an alternative route into Thessaly and the south, the way through **Grevena** has little to offer but its spectacular climax. In summer heaps of melons are piled up in gigantic pyramids in the main square of Grevena – I know of little else to recommend this dreary provincial town. The road crosses the ravine of the Venetikos, its rocky banks eroded into strange forms above pools of ice-green water. This is the ancient country of Elimeiotis, across which the nineteen-year-old Alexander, just crowned king and flushed with a resounding victory over the Illyrians, force-marched his army at a pace then unknown in military history in order to reach Southern Greece and chastise the rebellious Thebans. Descending gradually across a barren, melancholy mountain tract, one is rewarded by a novel and superbly theatrical view of the Meteora rock-pillars barring the way into the Thessalian plain. To the west the Pindos mountains rise sheer, with dark chasms biting deep into the range. Between awesome heights, the road, by contrast, follows a lovely fertile strip traversed by a stream which feeds the Pinios. Plane trees shade a jungle of brambles, wild fig and mulberry orchards; the long grass sizzles with the chirping of cicadas; hornets and dragon-flies whirr crazedly in the sun-drenched foliage. The road enters the plain at the base of a cluster of obelisks and pinnacles of stratified conglomerate, rent by gloomy caverns leading into the heart of the valley of the Meteora, and joins the main road from Lamia to the west which scales the Pindos to Metsovo and thence to Ioanina, capital of Epirus.

Back at the junction of the main northbound road to Kastoria and the Siatista branch, one continues along the upper valley of the Aliakmon. Westward runs the spine of the northern Pindos, capped by the formidable snow-capped peak of Smolikas (8640 feet). Groves of poplars spread across shallow gullies through which mountain streams feed the Aliakmon. The village of Vogatsiko, built on seven hills, surrounded by oak and beech woods, overlooks the river valley. Barns with thatched roofs suggest the increasingly northern character of the country. The road by-passes the village of Argos Orestikon, which is now the centre of a trade in sheepskin rugs. Soon the road is winding along the shore of a mountain lake. Mist clings to the banks in the early morning, and wild fowl skim the placid waters.

The houses of **Kastoria** rise from the twin shores of an isthmus onto a rocky headland. Among the highest of them, the Hotel du Lac commands a prospect of the ice-blue lake with its fringe of poplars; behind, a screen of wild mountains piles up towards Albania in the west and Jugoslavia in the north, the whole dominated by the cone-shaped peak of Vitsa. Byzantine churches and chapels spread fan-wise round the hotel, which is a good starting-point for sightseeing. A full day is required to visit the main churches scattered among abandoned tower-like eighteenth-century houses overlooking derelict courtyards. The climate is harsh and northern. In winter the lake freezes; in spring adders glide in the undergrowth; summer does not come till June. A thriving fishing industry (perch, pike, eels) is undergoing rapid development. But it is the fur trade which has brought prosperity to Kastoria – for centuries a recognized dumping-ground for scraps of mink and other pelts discarded by the more fastidious furriers of Europe and America.

The history of the town, the ancient Celetrium, is uneventful until the Middle Ages when a succession of invaders made it an important staging-post on the way to the East. Among the first was Robert Guiscard, Norman Duke of Apulia and Calabria, who opened the eyes of western princes to the glittering prospect of dismemberment of the Byzantine Empire. Later, during the Frankish occupation, Michael II conducted a guerilla war in the neighbouring hills against the Eastern aspirant to the Byzantine throne. Then came the Albanians, and finally the Turks who stayed for over six centuries, and the Jews who developed the fur industry. In 1947–49 insurgent Communists waged a two-year struggle against the Greek army from hideouts among the surrounding villages.

The monuments are wholly Byzantine, but there is no evidence of the multiple domes that crown the Palaeologue epoch; here the more austere basilica form endures almost unchallenged, the

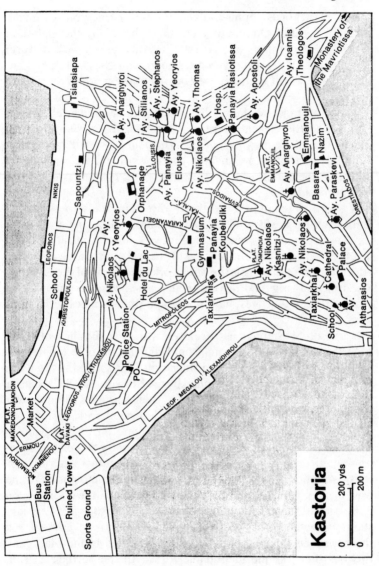

Kastoria

angular planes of its sloping roofs conforming harmoniously with the northern setting. On summer evenings, however, the elaborate brickwork decoration of the exterior walls glows with a warm roseate hue. Of the seventy-two Orthodox churches and chapels, at least six are worth visiting. They belong to the tenth to fourteenth centuries.

At the entrance to the public garden, beside the Hotel du Lac, stands the little eleventh-century **Church of Agios Nikolaos**, with some sixteenth-century frescoes, of which the most striking (left, on entering) presents a melancholy youth wearing a fez, probably a relative of the donor, who died at an early age. His bereaved mother laments beside him.

A sharp descent in a northerly direction leads to the small tenth-century **Basilica of Agios Stefanos**, with single columns separating the naves from the diminutive aisles. Its unusual height, together with the charred surface of the walls, produces a sombre effect. More interesting is the brickwork decoration of the exterior, a conspicuous regional feature, which has a complex interplay of cubes, crosses, lozenges, half-moons and wheel-spokes within sun-discs.

North of St Stephen is the more attractive **Basilica of Agioi Anarghyroi** (Saint Cosmas and Saint Damian), the oldest in Kastoria. Destroyed, it is said, by the Bulgarian Tsar Samuel in the tenth century, the church was refounded by the Emperor Basil II when he spent the autumn of 1018 in Kastoria, celebrating his triumph over the Bulgars. The exterior walls are decorated with an intricate pattern of brick inlay. Two sun-discs frame an arched window divided by a colonette above the apse. Symmetry and picturesqueness are nicely blended. Eleventh- to twelfth-century exterior frescoes – another provincial feature – break up the monotony of the west façade. Figures of St Peter and St Paul flank the doorway; on either side of them the two patron physicians, Cosmas and Damian, stand protectively. The interior is so dark that it is advisable to ask the custodian to open both doors. The figures in the blackened frescoes then assume identifiable forms. In the narthex a grim, bearded St Basil with a nasty turned-down mouth reflects an unusual aspect of the beneficent bishop who devoted his life to relieving the miseries of the poor. In the later frescoes of the *naos* the faces are softer and the garments less rigid. In a haunting vision of the Pentecost, rays of light fall on the heads of the apostles grouped on either side of a double arched window.

Several tower-like houses of the seventeenth to eighteenth centuries, built for prosperous furriers and once the grandest in Macedonia, extend along the north shore of the lake. Some had been left to decay beyond repair and were finally pulled down. In about half a dozen the frescoed sun-parlours and panelled halls, painted ceilings and ornamental doorways have been restored. The **Nerandzis Mansion** has been transformed into a folklore museum. The **Tsiatsapas House**, in a lane behind the waterfront (Nikis Avenue), is distinguished by latticed windows, recessed balconies and wooden brackets. Cobbled alleys lead west to the **Sapoundzis House**, architecturally very formal and symmetrical, approached through a court. The first two stories are of stone, the third timber-framed, shaded by eaves that protect the walls from the drip of melting snow in spring. Other mansions are those of the Emmanuel and Nantzis.

Fragments of Byzantine ramparts, which protected the isthmus from the west, are visible from Davaki Square. From here Agiou Athanasiou Avenue climbs to the Hotel du Lac, and thence to another group of churches on the steep southern slope of the headland. Below the *Gymnasium* (Secondary School), conspicuous for its neo-classical façade, stands the picturesque little **Church of the Panayia Koubelidiki**. Another early foundation, the usual exterior brickwork decoration is tidier though less inventive than elsewhere. The fifteenth-century frescoes of the exterior walls of the narthex give a coquettish air to this little architectural folly.

To the west, the eleventh-century **Basilica of the Taxiarchoi** (Archangels) produces an almost barn-like effect, in spite of the jigsaw puzzle of brick inlay, after the extravagance of the Koubelidiki. Frescoes, with the Archangels flanking the entrance and the two pygmy-like figures of the donors, a Bulgarian prince and his half-Greek mother, cowering at St Michael's feet, spread across the façade. The fourteenth-century frescoes in the interior possess unmistakable affinities with the Southern Serbian school of Byzantine painting. There is a realism and fluidity of movement, a suggestion of three-dimensional style foreign to the classical, more static, iconography of Constantinople.

South of the Archangels, Metropoleos Street enters Omonoia Square, a confined space, lively at night with open-air tavernas on different levels, crowned by the little single-chamber Basilica of *Agios Ioannis Prodromos*. More important is the twelfth-century **Church of Agios Nikolaos Kasnitzi**, which repeats the familiar architectural and decorative pattern of the Kastorian basilica. In the thirteenth-century frescoes the well-known figures play their accustomed liturgical roles. In the apse the Virgin *Orans* is flanked by two angels bearing kerchiefs. Their movements are free and articulate. Above the apse presides another effigy of the Virgin, this time of greater dignity, approached by the Angel Gabriel with an alert expressive face. Above the west door the Dormition of the Virgin is crowned with mourning figures in pastel-shaded garments. Above the Dormition, the Transfiguration depicts Christ as an emaciated figure with matchstick legs, his white garments fluttering in the breeze. The frescoes of St Nicholas Kasnitzi are not among the great masterpieces of Byzantine painting, but they possess freshness and vigour, tempered by an engaging rustic simplicity.

The way down to the waterfront leads past another group of large houses, their roofs crowned with storks' nests. The **Nazim House**, preceded by a little loggia, is one of the finest in Kastoria. A musicians' gallery, its walls painted with garlands of flowers, over-looks a reception room, where engagements and marriages were celebrated. The *saloni*, or drawing room, and halls are elaborately frescoed, and the decoration has all the story-book whimsicality of Siatista.

The south shore is bordered by plane trees. Flat-bottomed fishing boats with blunt bows glide across the slime-covered waters of the southern bight of the lake. In the evening, loaded with perch and carp, they emerge ghost-like out of the mist, nosing their way towards wooden jetties. After skirting a sandy beach littered with hulks of half-constructed boats, the narrow road, bordered by weeping willows, becomes a favourite strolling ground, with cyclists and holiday-makers bound for the lakeside tavernas. Between the shore and a rocky hillside the **Monastery of the Mavriotissa** nestles in the shade of plane trees. A landing was effected here by a Byzantine army led by Alexius I, most astute of Comnene emperors, who laid siege to the Normans occupying Kastoria. The

Emperor probably founded the monastery later. It was considerably rebuilt during the fourteenth-century Serb occupation.

The church, chapel, some cells and a belfry spread along the lakeside. It is a secluded place, once the haunt of Byzantine and Slav princes who came here to worship. The exterior side wall of the chapel of St John the Divine is painted with crude post-Byzantine frescoes of saintly figures. But in the Last Supper (interior north wall) there is a charming arrangement, totally devoid of perspective, of glass and cutlery, plates, goblets and bowls laid out on a half-moon table.

In the main church, a single-aisle basilica with narthex, the frescoes of the late twelfth century are, in spite of clumsy execution, vigorous in conception, with detached groups of figures depicted in a state of arrested movement. Within the narthex there is a crude but animated Last Judgement, crowned with militant angels and deformed, cringing creatures representing the various categories of sinners: slanderers, moneylenders (hanging upside down), and harlots with long black ringlets. A wooden door carved with crosses and diamond-shaped lozenges leads into the *naos*. The dominating fresco is the **Dormition of the Virgin** (west wall) which is grand and tragic, the figures stilted but expressive, the mourners' faces turned towards the bier so that the focus is on the centre of the picture, where lies the formidable, almost masculine, corpse. There is a grand **Ascension**: first a frieze of apostles between stylized trees, with the Virgin *Orans* in the middle; then Christ, with a terrible Messianic expression, a protruding stomach and short legs. Neither faulty drawing nor clumsy execution deprive the composition of power or intensity of feeling.

The numerous post-Byzantine chapels scattered about the headland are destinations for walks. The walls of many, both interior and exterior, are frescoed. In the Apazari quarter (north shore), the Church of *Agios Ioannis Prodromos* is worth visiting, if only to look at the frescoes in the women's gallery. Demons are seen torturing the malicious gossiper, the cheating miller and the female usurer; an adultress suffers ignoble torments inflicted by a demon in the form of a snake, while the most shocking treatment of all is reserved for the harlot.

*   *   *

The beginning of the longer northern route from Edessa to Kastoria follows the upper reaches of **the Edesseos**. The configuration of the land, with its wooded ledges ascending the Vermion range, has none of the dramatic quality of the Central Greek mountain formations. Everything is tamer, somewhat lacking in definition. It possesses all the fertility of the Emathian plain but without any of its domesticity. There are no towns, few villages. The route must be the one followed by Alexander when, weary of the rumbustious brawling of family life at Pella, he retired to sulk in Illyria.

After leaving the Edesseos valley, the road crosses a plateau of rushes surrounded by ilex-covered hills. Below, to the west, beyond the maize fields, appear the sparsely inhabited shores of **Lake Vegoritida**, its pale blue waters making deep inroads into the arid mountain sides. At the north-east end of the lake a huddle of habitations is all that remains of ancient **Arnissa**, once a station on the Via Egnatia, better known as medieval Ostrovo, which was fiercely disputed by the armies of rival claimants to the Byzantine throne when Frankish Greece was beginning to fall apart. In the general confusion of civil war the shores of Vegoritida were often littered with the abandoned impedimenta of defeated armies. There are ruins of a Turkish mosque on an islet off Arnissa: once the centre of a village said to have been submerged in the lake.

Sparsely inhabited valleys follow, their highlands covered with scrub, where the armies of the Emperor Basil II and the Bulgar Tsar Samuel contended for the strategic prize of Ostrovo in the early eleventh century. It is a melancholy scene, with several abandoned stone-built villages, but the descent leads into a warmer climate, with a fertile plain running north to south between hazy mountain ranges. To the north, at the head of the broad strip of cultivation lies Pelagonia, where the Byzantine emperor in exile decisively defeated the Frankish armies in a battle which preceded the expulsion of the Crusaders' descendants from Constantinople by only two years. More recently, in the twentieth century, Balkan and German invading armies poured through the Monastir Gap in the mountains.

Across the gap the garrison town of **Florina**, fought over during the First World War and destroyed during the Communist rebellion of 1947–49, stands in a commanding position at the mouth of a

Meteora: the Rousanou Monastery at sunset.

Pella: Lion Hunt floor mosaic. The attitudes of both men and beast form a perfectly balanced composition.

Philip II of Macedon. A small ivory head from Vergina, fourth century BC. *(Archaeological Museum of Thessaloniki)*

mountain valley. This is the ancient land of Lyncestis, famous for its waters which were said to possess intoxicating qualities and whose royal house married into that of the Macedonian kings, only to find the connection used as a pretext for the annexation of the country. There is little to say about Florina; a museum and an art gallery fail to compensate for extremes of climate and a surfeit of concrete. Unsmiling square-faced peasants bring their produce to market, and bored-looking soldiers stroll along the unattractive streets. Both seem as remote from Mediterranean Greece as the Balkan landscape itself. But there is one last lap: to the Prespa lakes.

The road climbs a flank of the mountains west of Florina above a fertile valley; otherwise the country seems uninhabited, muted. One senses the proximity of frontiers, of an end to all things Greek. After winding between puce-coloured hills, one is suddenly peering over the rim of a great bowl surrounded by the mountains. The configuration is confusing. North to south runs the lake of **Little Prespa**, appendix-shaped: a Greek-Albanian lake, its surface is a cold, hard blue. Beyond an isthmus extends **Big Prespa**, whose waters are shared by Greece, Albania and Jugoslavia, heart-shaped in the north, tapering at the southern end into an inlet which runs parallel to Little Prespa, biting deep into Albanian territory. To the west rise the stark Albanian mountains, at the foot of which once wound the Via Egnatia. The descent is through domesticated but deserted country, the red soil contrasting sharply with the naked grey mountains on whose ridges snowdrifts lie in crevices. The scale and range is immense, the desolation grandiose. I know of no more inhospitable place than this meeting-point of three countries, where Alexander defeated the Lyncestrian tribes, whose subjection ensured the safety of his rear, at a time when he was concentrating the bulk of his forces in the east for the passage into Asia. In the late tenth century Tsar Samuel established his military headquarters and a court, noted for its savagery, in this inaccessible area, from which he waged a long, defiant and ultimately hopeless struggle for possession of Northern Greece.

Along a level stretch of shore washed by Little Prespa extends a **bird sanctuary**, to which birds from all over south-eastern Europe migrate – 177 species have been recorded – one of the few sites in Europe where pelicans are known to nest. A watch-tower has been built for the benefit of birdwatchers. On the islet to the south of the isthmus, somewhat quaintly named St Achilles, there is a Byzantine church, founded in the tenth century by Tsar Samuel, with remains of contemporary frescoes. The road continues along the north-east shore of Big Prespa as far as Agios Germanos, which lies at the foot of beige-coloured hills, the last village this side of the Jugoslav border: a bucolic place with houses scattered among poplars in which myriads of birds twitter. One hears villagers talking Serbo-Croat as well as Greek. This is the end of the road, as there is no border crossing into Jugoslavia.

After re-crossing the line of hills above the Prespa basin there is a fork. The road to the south runs through a shut-in, wooded country. Donkeys are tethered to tree-trunks in groves of silver planes and goats browse in terraced glades where the parched grass of summer replaces the narcissi of early spring. Streams unite and separate, forming shady pools where the water freezes hard in winter; the whole place is alive with bird-song. In antiquity the Orestae, a barbarian tribe, dwelt here, more happily blessed by nature than many of their neighbours, until they were subjugated by Philip II and their well-watered valleys annexed to 'Greater' Macedonia. The road climbs through beech woods and then winds down in successive loops, each of which affords a more entrancing view of the northern shores of Lake Kastoria, the tall houses of the town strung out along the isthmus and the mallet-shaped headland projecting into the shallow waters.

CHAPTER 16

The Halkidiki

*Potidea – Kassandra – Olynthos – Sithonia – Toroni –
Poligiros – Stageira – Ierissos – Xerxes' Canal –
Ouranoupoli – Stavros – Langadas.*

The traveller in Macedonia has a choice of routes into the central
and western parts of the country. But much that merits attention
still lies east of Thessaloniki. From the Macedonian capital, one has
the option of two itineraries: (i) the highway running eastward
across the rest of Macedonia and Thrace to the Turkish border; (ii) a
somewhat circuitous route, including several deviations, round the
Halkidiki peninsula – which I have described in the form of a round
trip based on Thessaloniki. The long, two-day drive can be broken
at any one of the numerous huge hotels situated on, or overlooking,
beaches of the finest sand. The two westerly prongs of the peninsula
have been developed into what the brochures describe as a 'tourist's
paradise', with all the amenities of good roads, anchorages for
yachts, camping sites, swimming pools and even conference
centres.

South-east of Thessaloniki the Halkidiki juts out into the Aegean
like a huge deformed lobster with three claws. The poor state of
preservation of the antiquities sometimes belies their historical
importance, and much of the woodland country (as opposed to the
bungalow-pocked beaches) across which Xerxes' army marched in
the summer of 480 BC, is still sufficiently off the beaten track to
recall a virgin land. Washed by the Thermaic and Strimonic Gulfs,
the peninsula has, by the nature of its strange contours and sparsely
populated forest, remained a self-contained geographical unit, with
a character different from the rest of Macedonia. The original

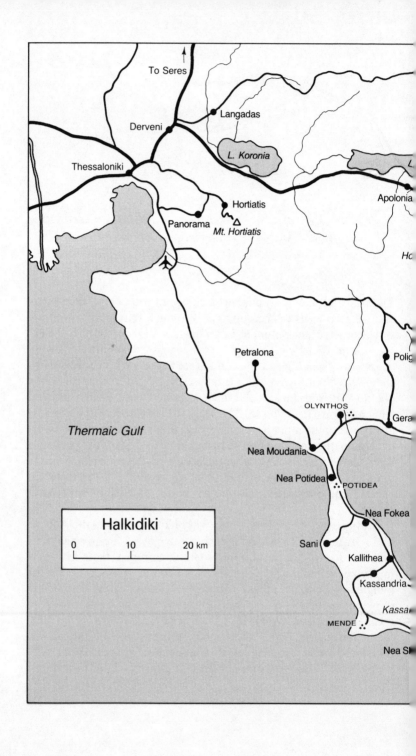

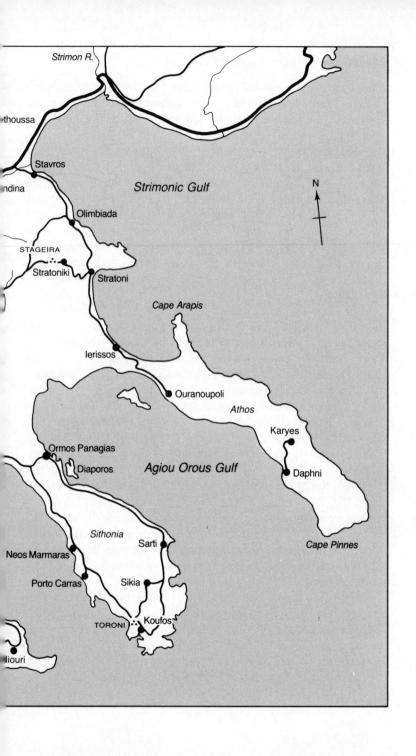

inhabitants, the Paeonians, a rustic people cut off from the two-way traffic of trade and ideas that crossed the neck of the peninsula, developed independently of the Thracians; but in the eighth and seventh centuries BC the coast was colonized by Euboean settlers who intermarried with the natives. For centuries the forest tracts remained wild and uninhabited, the thirty cities founded by the colonizers being strung out along the shores of the three prongs. Athens too founded colonies here. Corinth and Sparta objected and the Peloponnesian War followed. Finally Philip II of Macedon reduced the country to subjection. The present inhabitants, mostly woodcutters and fishermen, are a dark, taciturn people; unlike most Greeks, they seem, except in the tourist centres, to be impervious to the presence of strangers, indifferent to their provenance or destination.

From Thessaloniki the road runs through dreary suburbs to the nineteenth-century Villa Alatini, a landmark situated on a bluff above the sea, where Sultan Abdul Hamid II, 'The Damned', was interned after his deposition in 1909. Just before the villa, a branch road to the north climbs Mount Hortiatis to Panorama, a summer resort of red-roofed houses amid dark green conifers. There are hotels, restaurants and a panoramic view of the city, the Thermaic Gulf and Western Halkidiki. On torrid summer evenings the air is wonderfully bracing. A five-kilometre stretch of ribbon develop-ment ends at the village of **Hortiatis**. Here, beside an ochre-coloured church, there is an unassuming little twelfth-century Church of the Metamorphosis, with four niches in the angles which create the illusion that the building is octagonal. It is crowned by a shallow windowless dome, probably a later addition of the Turkish period. The narthex has disappeared to make room for an adjacent hovel. The original Comnene frescoes are unfortunately covered with plaster, but vestiges of the fine head of a young saint within a sombre-coloured halo suggest their quality.

Down below in the plain, the southbound highway skirts crowded beaches linked by a ferry service with Thessaloniki. At the fifty-first kilometre a branch road runs east to the locality of Petralona, where the cave of *Kokkines Petres* (The Red Stones), famous for its refulgent stalactites, is situated at the base of a foothill of the Holomon range. One day in 1960, a party of visitors entering the cave stumbled on a fossilized skull, later identified as that of a Neanderthal woman who probably lived some seventy-five thousand years ago. Greece, it was thus established, was inhabited by primitive man in the Pleistocene age.

The road continues across open country – a golf-course landscape with views of distant, cone-shaped hills – which soon contracts into a narrow isthmus. Here begins the geographical area associated with the 'Thracian tribute': the detested levy exacted from the colonies allied under duress to Athens in the fifth century BC. At **Nea Moudania**, a fishing village and summer resort which can make an inexpensive base for an extended tour of the Halkidiki, there are tavernas and an hotel.

At the hinge of the westernmost prong or claw, the site of ancient **Potidea** extends beyond a narrow canal. Xerxes' fleet anchored here and took on provisions. Half a century later, the Corinthian-inspired revolt of Potidea against Athens was one of the incidents that triggered off the Peloponnesian War. Athenian pride, stung by the insolence of Potidean defection, demanded instant retribution. However, neither battering ram nor other aggressive weapon could help the assault troops, led by the brilliant Phormio, to break Potidean resistance. Blockaded by the Athenian fleet, and deci-mated within the walls by the plague, it nevertheless took the besiegers two years to reduce the city. It was here also, in the Halkidiki, geographically so remote from Athens and Sparta, that some of the decisive campaigns of a war in which the whole Hellenic world was involved, were fought. In the Hellenistic period, Cassan-der, who had assumed Alexander the Great's mantle in mainland Greece, founded a new city on the site and called it Cassandreia.

Nea Potidea is a fishing village beside a muddy canal crossing the isthmus. Brightly-painted caiques anchor in the creeks where the Macedonian triremes were once built – Livy talks of a hundred vessels at a time being constructed in the docks. Blocks of masonry near the sea mark the point where the line of forts guarding the entire headland once began. I have counted eight ruined towers extending across the isthmus – all medieval – in which classical masonry has been re-used, and archaeologists have identified ancient slabs among the village refuse. Fishermen talk of ancient under-water stairways: visible only when the sea is calm and translucent.

231

From Potidea the **Kassandra** headland (the western prong of the Halkidiki peninsula) runs southward in a series of low, neatly sliced cliffs. The road follows the east coast of the prong. Above the beaches, reddish-brown cliffs are studded with tall pines, whose wood was used for the construction of triremes in antiquity. At **Nea Fokea**, a medieval tower crowns a bluff overlooking the little harbour. Until recently inhabited exclusively by sheep-farmers, the countryside has been developed into a complex of camping sites and tourist hotels; though among the shady, still undesecrated woods the copses are pock-marked with beehives. At Kallithea, cliffs screen a number of large hotels situated on a beach of fine sand. Beside them is an ancient ruin: the foundations of a fourth-century BC temple of Zeus Ammon, with a north–south axis (instead of the usual east–west), strewn with Doric, Ionic and Corinthian capitals. A nearby spring, which provides water for the hotels, is popularly associated with the stream diverted by Zeus to flow underground from Mount Olympos in order to irrigate his maritime sanctuary.

Southward, the bungalow compounds continue. Monster hotels, such as the Athos Palace, succeed each other as far as the Xenia, where the coastline, more broken, offers greater variety. The road turns inland across the saddle of the prong and passes through the village of **Agia Paraskevi**, where there are traces of the architecture of the Turkish period. Children playing in pot-holed lanes glance at one and go on with their games; in the café, men briefly look up from their backgammon boards and continue to rattle dice. But no Halkidian, for all his lack of inquisitiveness (so rare in Greece), is likely to be unfriendly when asked for help.

At **Nea Skioni** on the west coast of the prong, below the pine-clad hills, carpeted in spring with shrubs of bright-coloured cistus, is the as yet unexcavated site of ill-fated Skioni, where the Athenians took revenge on the inhabitants for welcoming Brasidas, the Spartan leader. Retribution took the form of the massacre of the entire male population of the city which had held out against the Athenian siege for so long and so courageously in 423 BC.

The road skirts another fine beach as far as a wooded bluff crowned by a modern hotel, the Mendi: site of ancient Mende, once famous for its delicious wine. Here too there was fierce fighting during the Peloponnesian War, with triremes manoeuvring along the coast. The north-bound road back to Potidea and the isthmus continues across low, flat-topped promontories. North-east of Potidea, the village of **Olynthos** lies at the head of the deep Gulf of Kassandra. A road runs through fields dotted with clumps of chestnut trees. The air is heavy with humidity, the drone of cicadas deafening. The ancient city, laid out by Hippodamus, the greatest town-planner of antiquity, extended across a squat eminence, like a table mountain rising sheer on all sides out of the pasture lands, crowned by towers and walls. Lilac-coloured, nutty-scented heliotrope spreads around the base. There is no custodian, no visible habitation: only horses grazing in the groves.

By the early fourth century BC, the political prestige and economic prosperity of the Olynthian Confederacy had become a byword. Narrow nationalist motives, however, induced neighbouring Acanthus and Apollonia to solicit the intervention of Sparta, whose gimlet-eye had long been fixed on this progressive and potentially powerful state. At first the Lacedaemonian attackers made little progress and even suffered humiliating defeats. But sustained blockade (382–379 BC) ended in surrender, and the Olynthians had to accept subjection to Sparta. The destruction of the confederacy was a blow to Greece and the nascent democratic ideal. Some thirty years later Philip of Macedon unleashed an avalanche of conquest on Eastern Macedonia. Sparta sullenly refused to raise a finger in aid, and Athenian assistance – fourteen thousand men and fifty triremes – came too late to be of use. Shorn of all power by their Spartan 'protectors' and undermined by treachery, the Olynthians surrendered to the Macedonian phalanx. On the site of the battle Philip staged a festival, with athletic and (for the Macedonian king had his softer side) poetical contests.

The climb to the summit of the rocky mound is steep but short. From here the besieged Olynthians had a grandstand view of their cavalry charging down the hill against the Spartan helots massed before the walls. The American School of Classical Studies has carried out some excavations, but little of importance has been uncovered. Cisterns and substructures seem inadequate legacies of a city once so politically mature for its times. The area covered by the fragmentary ruins, however, gives an idea of the extent of the town-plan. Vestiges of neolithic dwellings reveal that the hill was inhabited as far back as the third millennium BC. To the west rises an escarpment, brick-red in colour, with a flat top from which the Spartans watched the assembly and disposition of Olynthian units within the citadel.

Beyond the Olynthos branch, the road continues eastward past the tourist beach of Gerakini. At the top of the rise there is a fork in the road. One way leads across the isthmus to the Agiou Orous Gulf, the other penetrates the middle prong of the Halkidiki: hilly, wooded **Sithonia**, once scattered with the cities of the earliest colonizers. Range upon range of mountains of ever-increasing height, sliced with gullies filled with plane and olive trees, rise from the sandy coves of the west coast. An abandoned dependency of an Athonite monastery – windowless buildings with slate roofs and tall chimneys amid poplars and cypresses – spreads across the mouth of a valley. The beaches continue, pine-fringed. Beyond the harbour of Neos Marmaras and its cone-shaped islet, the resort of Porto Carras is the largest and most luxurious tourist complex on the whole coast. From here the road I prefer climbs into the hills, past a huge agricultural estate; its terraced vineyards, olive groves and citrus orchards affording sudden glimpses of the sea, wooded spits of land and rocky islets. From a considerable altitude one looks down on an inland bowl which conceals another ruined dependency of an Athonite monastery. The descent to the coast leads through alleys of mulberries and beside pine-fringed lagoons. To the south rises the hatchet-shaped bluff of Vigla. At the southern end of the crescent-shaped bay another bluff, which repeats in miniature the forms of Vigla, marks the site of the acropolis of ancient **Toroni**. There is not much to see, but it is one of the most evocative places in Northern Greece. Toroni was the chief settlement of the early colonizers. During the Peloponnesian War, although allied to Athens, the city welcomed the Spartans as liberators. However when Cleon, the Athenian demagogue-general, recaptured it, the Toronians paid for their fickle behaviour. The male population was deported to Athens and the women and children sold into slavery.

Vestiges of Byzantine fortifications can be identified along the line where the ancient ramparts extended, and Hellenic masonry is embedded in the soil of the strip of land connecting the acropolis with what must have been the ancient town. The visible blocks of granite probably formed part of Hellenic edifices. As yet, it is a remote and undeveloped place.

Immediately to the south, the deep inlet of Koufos is cunningly concealed by the northern arm of the Vigla promontory which scythes around to create a lovely landlocked bay with a sandy beach and perfect anchorage. The road now climbs into hills covered with heather and arbutus. Vultures perch on rocky ledges and suddenly flap their wings, wheel, hover and swoop down to peck at a carcase. The east coast is very rugged, less wooded, more sparsely inhabited than the western shores. From above the bay of Sikia there is a spectacular view of the Athos peninsula running north to south, with the tip, Cape Pinnes, crowned by a conical peak which is repeated, at a much greater altitude, by the dramatic summit of the Holy Mountain itself. Monasteries, hermitages and maritime arsenals are discernible along the length of this tremendous backcloth.

North of the bay and beach of Sarti, the coast becomes grander, its broken forms more intricate. Pine-clad spits project into the still waters of the Agiou Orous Gulf. Poplar-lined lagoons girdle the low, sand-fringed islet of Diaporos. At the cove of Ormos Panagias one turns westward, back to the point where the road penetrates the Sithonian headland.

At the head of the Gulf of Kassandra, not far from the Gerakini beach, a road climbs the Holomon range, the central massif of the peninsula, winding between hills of increasing height covered with arbutus, whose wood was used for making flutes, and whose large berries are supposed to taste like strawberries. **Poligiros**, a pretty village with red-tiled roofs, spreads among poplars in the folds of hills where myriads of birds sing. Hereabouts, according to Xenophon, was the site of Apollonia, one of the cities which undermined the Olynthian Confederacy by inviting Spartan intervention. Beautiful silver coins, minted in Apollonia and showing the head of Apollo, can be seen in the Numismatic Museum in Athens. Further north a road to the east climbs, dips and winds around oak-covered ridges to the summit. The landscape is unlike any other in Greece. The massif is cut by no deep valleys, conceals no high-lying plains; there are no bold dramatic contours, no vast perspectives. Foreground and background melt into each other in gentle undulating folds; a faint opacity tinges the light; wisps of smoke spiral up from woodcutters' fires. The descent in hairpin bends through silent chestnut forests has an elegiac quality. A muted feeling seems to hang over the village of Arnea, its large square bordered by lime-washed houses, their balconies ablaze with morning glory and climbing roses. Around here once stretched a tract of virgin forest where lions roamed in packs and which, in 480 BC, attacked the caravans of camels loaded with Persian stores.

The road descends towards the village of **Stratoniki**. On the right, a statue of an ancient Greek figure holding a scroll stands commandingly on a ledge. The effigy, which is modern, glossy and without artistic merit, represents Aristotle, and the terraced ground is the site of **Stageira**, the philosopher's birthplace. The son of a local physician, he spent his childhood roaming the woods, absorbed in the study of natural history. After the peninsula had been laid waste by Philip, Aristotle persuaded his pupil, Alexander the Great, to rebuild Stageira, of which he always remained a citizen; but by the first century AD Strabo found the city totally abandoned. Substructures of Hellenic masonry can be identified around the terraced ground. There are also ruins of a tower and an edifice with built-in arches of a later period.

The road reaches the coastline of the Strymonic Gulf at Stratoni, below a forbidding cliff where the mines, now producing magnesite, once provided silver for coins. Sandy beaches littered with grotesque outcrops of rock stretch southward as far as **Ierissos**, once Acanthus, the jealous rival of Olynthos. Beyond the town, the last prong of the trident culminates in the peak of Athos, hidden by the headland of Cape Arapis. The mole, which affords shelter to small craft from the winter gales that lash the Thracian sea, is built on Hellenic foundations. A caique sails daily to the monasteries on the east coast of the Athos peninsula. Ancient marble slabs and square granite blocks are scattered across the hill above Ierissos, where the acropolis once stood. Vestiges of tombs of a classical necropolis have been excavated on the sands. But the modern small town has little to offer, other than its fine beach and some small hotels, useful to travellers bound for the monasteries. A prevailing air of melancholy is only relieved on summer nights when the seashore tavernas are visited by an itinerant bouzouki orchestra.

The road across the mile and a half wide isthmus roughly follows the course of **Xerxes' Canal**, dug by his engineers to allow the passage of the Persian fleet, two triremes abreast. There is evidence of wall substructures and some man-made mounds but the ditch itself is now filled with soil. Men of all nations were employed in shifts 'and put to the work of cutting a canal under the lash', for, according to Herodotus, the Great King 'wanted to show his power and to leave something to be remembered by'.

On the west side of the isthmus the little port of **Ouranoupoli** shelters in a wide, tranquil bay skirted by sandy beaches and dotted with wooded islets. A luxury hotel, the Eagles' Palace, and the more modest Xenia, both with bar, restaurant and private beach, offer a pleasant refuge for weary travellers. A daily caique carrying a passenger-load of shaggy monks and unshaven pilgrims chugs into the port from the monasteries of the west coast of Mount Athos. The village, built in 1923 by refugees from Cappadocia on the site of a Hellenistic city, is tidier and more attractive than Ierissos. The five-storied **Tower of Prosphori**, with gun-slits and wooden balconies, dominates the landscape from a cliff above the mole between two coves. Once a lay dependency of the Athonite Monastery of *Vatopedi*, the abandoned tower was bought in the 1920s by an Anglo-Australian couple who converted the ground floor into a workshop, where peasant girls learnt to weave knotted rugs decorated with traditional Byzantine patterns.

From Ouranoupoli one can return through Stratoni and continue north and then west to complete the circular tour of the Halkidiki. Leaving the road to Stageira to the left, one climbs a seaward spur of Holomon and descends in hairpin bends to the northern shore of the Strimonic Gulf. Beaches of white sand are broken up by rocky inlets. Chestnut forests spread across the flanks of the valleys, and ice-cold streams trickle through shallow gullies to the sea. The smell of iodine and wet sand is mixed with that of pungent evergreens. To the east rises the outline of mountainous Thassos. There is probably no finer series of beaches in Greece – though development with villas, hotels and camping grounds has started. At **Olimbiada**, the ancient Caprus, port of Stageira, a wooden jetty extends into the poplar-fringed bay, where rowing boats, moored to an island mentioned by Strabo, rock in the oily swell. At night, flotillas of brightly painted fishing-caiques put out to sea, their carbide flares, which attract the fish, strung out across the dark in phosphorescent formations. To the north-west, where the Strimon flows into the sea through a wide estuary, looms Pangeo, the mountain of gold. At **Stavros**, plane trees skirt the shore and a broad walk is lined with cafés. The little port was discovered by the British army, based in the Strimon valley during the First World War, when it became a rest camp provided with swimming facilities and tennis courts in summer, woodcock shooting in winter. There is always the song of nightingales in the cool, dark arbours formed by the giant planes.

The road veers westward through a lush ravine to the village of Rendina. A road to the north leads to Arethoussa, where the aged Euripides, driven out of Athens by a campaign of calumny provoked by his cynical questioning of the gods' infallibility, was torn to pieces by the dogs of the Macedonian king, set upon him by rival poets. Later, Arethoussa became a staging-post on the Via Egnatia. There is nothing to see there now. Beyond Rendina the main road follows the course of the Via Egnatia across a featureless plain. To the north stretch the shallow waters of Lake Volvi, on whose southern shore lies the village of Apolonia (not to be confused with ancient Apollonia) through which St Paul and Silas passed when they left Philippi after the earthquake. Another lake, Koronia, is equally without scenic distinction.

At the end of the lake a fork to the left leads to **Derveni**, where some of the treasure exhibited at the Archaeological Museum at Thessaloniki was discovered in fourth-century BC burial chambers. From Derveni the road to Seres leads to another fork. The branch to the right crosses the plain through alleys of poplars to **Langadas**, where a macabre religious rite is performed by a sect of Thracian firewalkers on the feast of St Constantine and St Helena (21 May). The firewalking rite, manifestly pagan in origin, translated into thinly veiled Christian terms, has recently received the blessing of the Church. So the slaughter of animals, the burning coals and the primitive music are now invested with all the trappings of officialdom, and the ceremony, held on waste-ground near the cemetery, draws increasingly large numbers of visitors.

The ceremony begins in the morning. A garlanded calf with candles stuck in its ears is led out, to the accompaniment of ritual dances and the thud of drums. Clarinets wail. Occasionally there is a fanfare of trumpets. The moment the knife is plunged into the squealing animal a great moan escapes from the crowd. Women's shrieks pierce the air. In the afternoon the bonfire is lit, and the firewalkers, bearing the holy icons, caper shoeless on the red-hot coals, accompanied by banging tambourines. Sometimes they interrupt their tripping measures to shout and leap in the air. In the tavernas wine and ouzo flow. Doctors are said to have testified that the soles of the firewalkers' feet are neither blistered nor discoloured. After 21 May Langadas lapses for another year into the routine of agricultural domesticity. Only cinders remain, scattered over the waste-ground until the autumn rains turn them into squelching mud.

CHAPTER 17

Mount Athos: A Traveller's Journal

*Karyes: The Protaton – Chilandari – Vatopedi –
Iviron – The Grand Lavra – The Sketes – Dionysiou –
St Paul – Gregoriou – Simonopetra – St Panteleimon
– Xenophontos – Docheiariou.*

The thousand-year-old monastic republic of Athos, nominally independent of the Greek state although policed by its officers, extends
along the eastern prong of the Halkidiki peninsula. Fortified
medieval monasteries fringe the wooded coast; hermitages and
eyries cling to the sides of vertical cliffs. Some settlements are
abandoned; others are still inhabited by a handful of monks who
celebrate daily services in frescoed churches filled with icons,
golden candelabra and carved, gilded *iconostases*. Outwardly it
remains the truest extant image of Byzantine monasticism. In
reality it is a twilight place, nostalgic, muted, dying of apathy
and dereliction, though there has been some revival over the past
fifteen years, to the extent that there is a shortage of accommodation for new recruits – a result of the earlier neglect of vacant
buildings.

The fertility of the promontory is legendary and the landscape,
with the Holy Mountain soaring to a tapering peak at the south-
eastern extremity, could not be more splendid. The Virgin herself
found the prospect so bewitching that she fell in love with it when
she was forced to land in the Bay of Iviron, after her ship, bound for
Cyprus, where she and St John were about to pay a visit to Lazarus,
had been blown off-course. Enchanted by the shady forests and
flowery meadows, she annexed the peninsula, declared it her

private garden and forbade any member of her sex to enter it. The whole spiritual development of the community stems from the worship of the Mother of God, and her mantled form, the monks say, still haunts the groves and coppices below the woodland monasteries.

The earliest hermits came in the eighth century, seeking refuge from the persecutions of Iconoclast emperors. The first recorded solitary was Peter the Anchorite in the ninth century. Beset by demons and wild beasts, he dwelt for fifty years in a cave on the marble mountain. The influx of anchorites increased and in 872 the Emperor Basil I granted them a special charter of protection. The future pattern of the republic was established by St Athanasius, a Bythinian monk, who founded the first monastery, the Grand Lavra, and reaffirmed the Virgin's injunction that no woman or female animal should enter the holy territory (an edict that still holds good today).

Pious men, anxious to escape from the world of temptation, flocked from the Orthodox countries and founded monasteries which were financed by princes and statesmen and which, while preserving their independence, acknowledged the suzerainty of the Byzantine emperor. Artists from Constantinople, Thessaloniki and Crete were commissioned to fresco the walls of churches and instruct the monks in the art of iconography. Religious learning and scholarship flourished, with the best brains in the ecclesiastical world gravitating to the Holy Mountain, which gradually became the symbol of the Church's undisputed influence over every sphere of national consciousness. In the fifteenth century the idiorrhythmic system, which meant that each monk fed and clothed himself from his own resources, was introduced in several monasteries where the rule was milder than in the cenobitic or communal (and more austere) establishments.

During the centuries of Latin, Slav and Ottoman occupation the monasteries preserved the prestige of Byzantine religion undiminished and, when the War of Independence came in 1821, Finlay was justified in saying that Mount Athos 'held a more revered place than the memories of Marathon and Salamis' in the minds of ordinary Greeks.

In the nineteenth century wealth poured in from Tsarist sources and the number of novices from Slav countries threatened to exceed those from Greece and Asia Minor; but the Russian Revolution put an end to that. After the Second World War the flow of recruits from the other Slav countries was also cut off at source. Thus, where there were once forty thousand monks, there are now about fifteen hundred, and narrow Greek nationalism paralyses any form of twentieth-century theological stimulus.

Most of the monasteries, which are filled with treasures of religious art, provide little more than a refuge for aged monks of peasant origin and limited education. Almost all artistic activity has ceased; the fields and vineyards owned by the idiorrhythmic orders are largely abandoned; parasitic plants wind murderous shoots round the trunks of fruit and nut trees; deforestation is rife and the bracken grows so high that it is difficult to locate the shady mule-tracks that once linked one monastery with another.

What remains to be seen? Just some decaying monasteries inhabited by a few aged, illiterate monks? No. Each monastery is a castellated stronghold. The architecture, if not always good, is either striking, picturesque or spectacular. In every instance the monastic buildings gravitate round the main church, which is cruciform (Greek Cross plan) with varying numbers of side chapels. All contain frescoes; mostly of the late Byzantine and post-Byzantine periods – some very good, others indifferent. Many of the libraries and treasuries possess priceless works of silverware, icons and illuminated manuscripts, as well as a variety of other religious works of art wrought in gold, bronze, jasper and marble, including holy relics so dear to the Orthodox faithful. There are also some mosaics.

It is helpful to bear in mind the uniform iconographical arrangement of an Athonite church, which, generally speaking, applies to every Byzantine church in the country: in the dome of heaven reigns Christ Pantocrator, surrounded by worshipping angels, while the Virgin and St John the Baptist intercede on behalf of mankind; in the central apse (there are three) the Virgin and Child sit enthroned within a golden aureole above the altar. Around this focus of divinity, in the pendentives and vaults, unfold the scenes of the Twelve Feasts and the Passion (these sometimes overflow into the narthex). On the lower register – the terrestrial one – prophets, saints and holy men are ranged in strict order of precedence.

Finally, monks and lay worshippers assemble on the historiated pavements. The church thus represents the universe in miniature.

The traveller will encounter hardship and frustration, an unappetizing diet and (sometimes) dirty sheets. He may even encounter something unusual in Greece – unfriendliness. However, the loneliness and the tranquillity, the emphasis on superstition and demonology, the obsession with the past and the indifference to the future, the sheer anachronism of it all, combine to produce in one a state of almost traumatic fascination. The journey may be the most arduous in Greece; it is also probably the most exciting. The lover of landscape will find little in the whole country to match some of the prospects encountered.

A three-day tour enables the visitor to visit two of the three senior monasteries – Iviron, Vatopedi and the Grand Lavra – and cast a quick glance at the frescoes of the Protaton at Karyes en route. Yachtsmen, after going through the usual formalities at Karyes, can sail round the peninsula, visiting any monastery (or indeed all) at will.

On my last visit I worked out a practicable eight-day tour by caique (*see Appendix*), starting at Ouranoupoli. This is the minimum time required to visit the ten most important monasteries. I have described the journey in the form of a personal journal, hoping that it will give the traveller some useful hints as to what to expect from Athonite habits and monkish idiosyncrasies. Mount Athos is not the mere sum total of its monasteries and hermitages. It is a way of life; to understand it requires a little insight into the character of its strange inhabitants.

Some practical details on travel, formalities and accommodation, together with details of the remaining ten monasteries are given in the Appendix.

21 August

We left Ouranoupoli at ten o'clock by the public caique. Among the passengers were three elderly monks who had been visiting relations in what they call 'the world'. A profound, almost reverential, silence descended as we sailed into holy waters below pine-clad cliffs fringed by sandy beaches. Occasionally an abandoned hermitage appeared in a clearing in the woods. Somewhere along here was

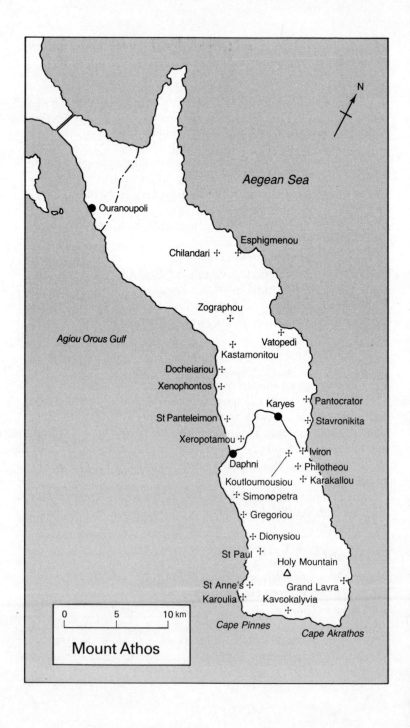

Mount Athos

the site of ancient Dium, one of the few Chalcidian colonies which refused to fall for Brasidas' blandishments and join the Spartans in the great war against Athens. In the south-east the peak of the Holy Mountain, a pyramid of white limestone, was wreathed in wispy clouds, its tapering form repeated in a similar cone at the tip of the promontory. Strabo calls it 'breast-shaped'.

Arsenals – fortified tower-like structures, surrounded by disused port installations which serve as landing-stages for the monasteries – began to skirt the shore. The first was that of Zographou, where logs of wood were laid out in rows along the beach, awaiting export, and from which the *arsenaris* (arsenal-keeper) waved to us from a projecting balcony; then that of Docheiariou, crowned by a crenellated tower flanked by cypress trees; Xenophontos, its wooden galleries overlooking the placid bay; St Panteleimon, with its lime-green onion domes and derelict warehouses, and Xeropotamou, an inland monastery. We were soon entering the port of Daphni, a huddle of hovels at the foot of a steep hill.

After showing our passports and having lunch (an oily stew served stone-cold) in a taverna under a vine trellis, we took the afternoon bus to **Karyes**. The passengers included two men wearing caps with the badge of the double-headed eagle – emblem of the ecclesiastical police force. Climbing potholed hairpin bends, we passed the Monastery of Xerapotamou which spreads across a shady ledge with deep ravines on either side, and ascended through a jungle of shrubs. The smell of sun-baked myrtle was pungent. The forest now closed round on all sides, and we drove through a tunnel of trees, whose trunks, entwined in creepers speckled with purple berries, grew out of a bed of ferns so dense that no path has ever been cut through it. After crossing the watershed the road descends into a bowl-like valley, seamed with verdant gullies and scattered with nut-groves and farm-houses. 'Karyes!' called the driver with a flourish, and we observed the domes of churches and ecclesiastical colleges crowned with crosses glistening in the afternoon sun.

In Agiou Pnevma (Holy Ghost) Street, where the bus stops, there are grocers, cobblers, the only post office on the peninsula and a shop filled with postcards, rosaries, wooden wine-jugs and eucharistic bread-stamps carved by monks in outlying sketes. Respect for the Holy Ghost precludes smoking, wearing a hat or short-sleeved

245

shirt in the street. We climbed a cobbled lane between well-watered gardens to the house of the Archimandrite, to whom we had a letter of introduction. Pigeons piped in the surrounding orchards. A white-bearded *yerondas* (servant of a senior cleric) brought us coffee and ouzo in a courtyard filled with roses, oleanders and hydrangeas. He told us he had not been outside Karyes for forty years. The Archimandrite, who was more worldly (an iconographer and landscape-painter), conducted us to the authorities who issued us with residence permits. We looked at the Assembly House of the Holy Community, where novices hurried across the marble halls carrying cups of coffee to high-ranking prelates, while the Archimandrite fetched the key of the church which is the chief glory of Karyes.

The **Protaton** or Church of the Holy Community, joint property of all the monasteries, is a basilica of the tenth century, restored in the thirteenth and sixteenth. The belfry, with striped bands, is a later addition. The exterior is plain enough, but the walls of the *naos* are covered with early fourteenth-century frescoes of the Macedonian School. The best of them are probably by Manuel Panselinos, an enigmatic figure of Thessalonikian origin, whose work is characterized by sturdy modelling, depth of expression and a realism apparent in both portraiture and detail.

Unhampered by the architectural complexities of the Greek Cross plan, the master painter was able to achieve an unusual unity of composition across large surfaces. The painted decoration is divided into four distinct zones, with the topmost reserved for standing figures of, for the most part, Christ's ancestors. Across the third zone (from the bottom) spread the noble groupings from the life of Christ and the Virgin in a flowing, frieze-like continuity. In the **Birth of the Virgin** St Anne's exhaustion from the pangs of labour is suggested in the support she seeks from her attendants while trying to take some food. In the **Presentation of the Virgin in the Temple** a timid little Virgin appears before the hoary old priest, followed by maidens carrying lighted candles. Puckish figures, in the form of Hellenic river gods personifying the Jordan and the sea, retreat before the Lord's displeasure in the **Baptism**, while three children dance across the bridge spanning the river. Architectural backgrounds are used to stress the unity of the compositions, as in the **Incredulity of Thomas**, in which Christ stands in the central arch, the apostles in the other two. A similar symmetry of arrangement, both of figures and architectural features, is apparent in **The Last Supper**. Harmony becomes the keynote.

Representations of evangelists, prophets, military saints, bishops and martyrs extend across the two lower zones. An austere spirituality haunts the faces of the ascetic saints, each of whom is depicted with a distinct individuality rare in Byzantine iconography: particularly the white-bearded **Euthymius**, who lived to be ninety-six, his sunken eyes reflecting the disillusioned wisdom of his years; **Hosios David of Thessaloniki**, whose gnarled, knobbly features recall those of generations of Greek monks; **St John the Baptist**, tragic in the force and intensity of his expression. In the prothesis, within the sanctuary, there is an unusual portrait of a **youthful Christ**, full of vigour and freshness. Throughout the church the colour scheme is remarkable for its glow of different shades of pink and red (coral, flame and claret, pale and ruddy flesh tints) set off by sea blues, ambers and silvery greens. Shading is effected by black or indigo and green brush-strokes. The use of yellow against white produces a bold effect. Everywhere luminosity and chromatic harmony prevail.

In the Protaton we saw the holy icon of *Axion Esti* ('It is meet and right'), which was found in a cell near Karyes, where a tenth-century monk was visited by the Archangel Gabriel and instructed how it was 'meet and right' to glorify the Virgin. On Easter Monday the image, shaded by an umbrella, is borne in procession to the homes of the local representatives of each monastery, who sprinkle rose water and incense over it while church bells ring and spectators shout: 'Long live the Virgin!'

It was too late to visit the nineteenth-century Russian skete of St Andrew, a fantasy of onion domes and coloured roofs, crosses and towers, set among groves of hazelnut trees to the north of the village. Its most important possession is a relic of St Andrew – part of his forehead. We went instead to the inn for supper. I do not remember what we had to eat (perhaps it is just as well), but we drank resinated wine. We slept in a room with six beds, after asking for clean sheets. Washing arrangements were confined to a cold water tap in the court where we dined. But the view from the rickety

247

wooden balcony outside our room was unforgettable. The steep side of the Holy Mountain rose sheer above woods and vineyards, haunted, it is said, by seductive Nereids who have trespassed into the Virgin's garden. The whole countryside was mantled in a velvet sheen of moonlight. Occasionally the shriek of a jackal broke the spectral silence.

22 August

We got up at 6 am to catch the bus to the Bay of Iviron. The cobbled alleys of Karyes were deserted. The absence of women's and children's voices had begun to make an impact. Some travellers find that this feeling of absence grows stronger the longer they stay on the Holy Mountain, until they finally become aware of a great void at the heart of things. It is hard to get used to the idea that nobody has been born here for over a thousand years.

The road wound down to the coast, past the Monastery of Koutloumousiou, its crimson church surrounded by high walls. The gullies were a paradise of vegetation: oleanders, mulberries, olives, walnuts and hazels; ferns, ramblers, spiky shrubs and thick coverts where jackals hide. The smell of aromatic herbs drifted across the hillside. To the south a wisp of cloud formed a perfect halo round the peak of Athos. At the landing stage of Iviron the caique had just put in. A high sea was running, the *meltemi* – the etesian wind that funnels through the Hellespont and hits the Aegean with redoubled force – breaking the waves in sprays of foam against a primitive sea wall. We hurled ourselves and our luggage into the pitching caique. One of the passengers, a policeman, his complexion the colour of his uniform – pea-green – groaned and leant, gurgling, over the rail.

The coast is wild, grand and rocky, fringed with bluffs and crags from which a succession of monasteries overhang the sea: the medieval tower of Stavronikita crowning a huddle of monks' cells, 'like a Gothic castle perched on a beetling crag' said Robert Curzon, who travelled to Mount Athos in 1837; Pantocrator, astride a cliff lashed by waves so high that our caique could not enter the minute harbour; Vatopedi, largest of all the monasteries, a fortress sprawling across a sea-washed woodland; Esphigmenou, compressed, as its name – the Squeezed-together One – implies, within a narrow, green valley.

About mid-morning we reached the arsenal of **Chilandari**, the first monastery on our itinerary. The way inland is up a gentle incline. It took us almost an hour to walk – carrying our bags. On the left a fine thirteenth-century watch-tower commands the maritime approach. The country is green and open. We did not pass a single human being, not an animal. At last we saw kitchen-gardens, then the encircling walls of the great Serb monastery within a ring of hills covered with pine and chestnut trees and dark cypresses thrusting their tips through latticed olive branches. The only sound was the low piping of wood pigeons which nest in the arbours of ash and pine.

The monastery was founded in the twelfth century by Stephen Nemanja, unifier of the Serbs, who donned a monk's habit and died here. A century later, when it was the fashion for Slav princes to marry into Byzantine ruling families and found churches, hospitals and charitable institutions on Greek territory, the monastery was enlarged by Stephen, son-in-law of the Emperor Andronicus II Palaeologus. Chilandari soon became a cradle of Slav culture, visited by Serbian kings and national heroes. It is now inhabited by some twenty monks, mostly anti-Communist refugees from Jugoslavia. Relations with Belgrade, however, are not severed, and Marshal Tito presented the house with a tractor.

We passed through a frescoed gateway into the court, the loveliest on Mount Athos. The layout of the monastic precincts is more or less identical throughout the peninsula: a central court, varying in size, with the church in the middle and the refectory, cells, chapels, oratories and sometimes cloisters grouped around it, the whole encircled with high walls. Fan-shaped, the court at Chilandari is a perfectly composed complex of tall brick buildings – rebuilt after a fire in 1722 – with whitewashed upper stories supported by wooden brackets. A fourteenth-century tower, its windows set within arched frames, overlooks slate roofs of a dull pink colour and domes crowned with crosses. In the late afternoon a roseate glow is reflected from walls striped with tiles of different brick-red shades. In the centre of the court stands a seventeenth-century octagonal *phiale*, a holy water basin, roofed with a domed canopy. Beside it

249

rise two tall, ancient cypresses, in whose foliage the monks once hid their treasure of relics, icons and manuscripts when Latin pirates attacked the monastery. Nature came to their rescue. A clammy fog rose suddenly from the valley, enveloped the pirates as they scaled the walls and completely confounded them. Losing their bearings in eddies of white mist, and panicking, they slaughtered each other. Only three survived; they were succoured by the monks and converted to the Orthodox faith. Their portraits adorn the walls of the refectory.

The guest-master led us to a cool, spacious gallery with settees ranged along the walls. We were offered *ouzo*, coffee and *loucoumi*, and shown our sleeping quarters – an enormous dormitory, all to ourselves. The primitive lavatory overlooked a sundazzled glade surrounded by cypress and olive trees thrumming with cicadas. We had lunch – boiled marrows, tomato and onion salad, gherkins, bread and wine – with the abbot (who was fond of his glass of wine) and a theology student from Athens University who gave Greek lessons to the Serb monks during the summer vacation. After a siesta we started sightseeing, conducted by the librarian.

The **Church of the Presentation of the Virgin** is of the twelfth century, enlarged in the fourteenth, with later additions and transformations. The exterior brick decoration, largely composed of striped bands and arched surrounds, tends to obscure the purity of the architectural ensemble, with its five domes, apses, arches and barrel-vaults. You enter through the rectangular *liti*, which is a virtual exo-narthex and is a feature of all Athonite churches, whose layout is uniform: first the *liti*, followed by a large square narthex, then a cruciform *naos* with a gilded *iconostasis* pierced by three doors, and a tri-apsidal sanctuary. At Chilandari the *naos* is distinguished by a beautiful twelfth-century **pavement of Opus Alexandrinum**: slabs of verd-antique within a border of petals and concentric circles of different marbles – grey, blue, green and off-white – with cubes and rectangles superimposed. Most of the frescoes (c. 1300) have been ruined by tasteless nineteenth-century repainting. Noteworthy exceptions are the untouched portraits of Stephen Nemanja, the founder, and King Stephen Milutin, the thirteenth-century benefactor, on the south-west pilaster above the tomb of the former.

Beside the Bishop's throne hangs the miraculous icon of the Virgin Tricherousa. The face, brown with age, is surrounded with votive gifts – jewelled crosses, gold, strings of coins. Next to the icon is a bejewelled staff belonging to the Emperor Andronicus I Comnenus, who paid for his crimes by being paraded, strapped to a camel's back, through the hippodrome where he was torn to pieces by an angry mob in 1185. Above the Bishop's throne is a set of charming thirteenth-century miniatures.

In the **Library** we saw an eleventh-century edition of the homilies of St John Chrysostom and a fourteenth-century illuminated **Book of Gospels** of Serbian origin with letters of gold and silver on white parchment. This was much admired by Robert Curzon, who seems to have had no scruples about exacting precious manuscripts from ignorant monks in exchange for a few drachmae, and it is to the credit of the monks of Chilandari that they did not fall to his usual blandishments. We looked at a small **mosaic panel of the Virgin and Child** in the grand, austere manner of the twelfth century. However, our unstinted admiration was reserved for a set of superbly painted **icons of the fourteenth century** which are probably the finest on Mount Athos: four contemplative Evangelists holding bejewelled Gospels, clothed in mantles of subtly matched purple, olive green and smoky blue shades; a *Deisis* – Christ, authoritative and compassionate, between the Virgin and St John; the Archangels with Gabriel in blue and green robes. A softness of texture and limpidity of outline, suggestive of Slav influences, distinguishes these beautiful panels.

The refectory, largely disused, is less interesting. Apsidal and T-shaped, its walls are covered with seventeenth-century frescoes representing, *inter alia*, the life of St Sabbas, the pious son of Stephen Nemanja. The figures are loutish and lifeless. The Last Judgement, which always figures prominently in the apses of refectories, is more attractive, with its semi-circular architectural background of arches and towers.

Descending into the court, we saw an old monk with a flowing white beard bearing the *simandron*, an oblong wooden board which is tapped with a wooden mallet to summon the community to prayer. The whole place – the weed-grown court, the flimsy wooden stairways, the maze of cells and chapels – echoed with the repetitive beats which obviously derive from a set score, the introductory *lento* passage working up to a lively *vivace* climax, only to die down and begin all over again. Soon we heard the rise and fall of a feeble voice chanting the litanies in Slavonic. As it grew dark the cypress trees flanking the *phiale* stood out like sentinels, guarding the isolation.

We dined with the friendly abbot and the theology student. By the time we went to bed – about nine o'clock – the galleries overlooking the court were empty. No light showed anywhere, except a kerosene lamp fixed in a bracket pointing the way to the lavatory. A bat was making frenzied gyrations around it.

23 August

The abbot placed Marshal Tito's tractor at our disposal to carry our bags to the arsenal. We bathed and had a picnic lunch on a sandy beach. Later the abbot, who was on a visit to the *arsenaris* and had exchanged his cylindrical hat for a floppy straw one, trailed across the sands and presented each of us with a little bunch of sea-daffodils. Except at Dionysiou we were not to meet with such friendliness again.

The caique left at two o'clock. The theology student, on his way to post letters at Karyes, was seated next to me. As we pitched and rolled between huge waves, he inveighed against the iniquities of British foreign policy in Cyprus and British ingratitude (it would have been American ingratitude had I been an American) to Greece, which had saved the Western world from Communism, etc. etc. Illogical, rhetorical, cliché-ridden, the discourse continued relentlessly, though, politics and heroics apart, the young man was both charming and intelligent. Typically, we parted the best of friends.

The climb from the landing-stage to the **Monastery of Vatopedi**, screened by wooded hills watered by streams, is steep but short. A squat watch-tower overlooks the arsenal and a huddle of wood-cutters' huts. A crescent-shaped bay sweeps northward at the foot of hills seamed with valleys where pomegranates and Japanese medlars grow between hedgerows of blackberry bushes festooned with clematis and wild vine. On late summer evenings caravans of mules wind down the paths to the monastery gates where logs of wood (the monks' sole supply of fuel in winter) are unloaded. You enter the monastery through a porch in the shape of a canopy guarded by an icon of the Virgin. A Turkish soldier once had the temerity to shoot at her hand. The Virgin retaliated swiftly. She drove the Turk so mad that he hanged himself from a tree, whose branches subsequently withered and died.

After a long wait in the guest-house, a sulky guest-master offered us coffee (no *ouzo* or *loucoumi* here). We wandered round the polygonal **court** – larger than that of Chilandari, less well composed, but suffused with an even brighter glow from crimson stuccoed walls and brick courses with fantastic geometric designs. A warren of cells, chapels and storerooms extends across a slope within fortified walls. Here patriarchs, bishops and archimandrites once strolled, and aristocratic novices mingled with the suites of princes and statesmen from every quarter of the Orthodox world. Vatopedi was always the 'smartest' of Athonite monasteries, its wealth exceeding even that of the Grand Lavra. Here stayed John Cantacuzenus, a statesman who fomented a civil war in Constantinople, usurped the throne, became one of the outstanding emperors of the late Byzantine period and finally a nomadic monk. Now there are about thirty monks, as bigoted as any on the mountain, who stare suspiciously from wooden balconies at modern pilgrims, loaded with rucksacks and thermos flasks, desecrating the place with their unseemly garments and clicking cameras. The skyline is broken by turrets, domes and belfries of different periods. The octagonal *phiale* has a circular colonnade and a frescoed *baldacchino*. A painting of the Eye of God and a chocolate-coloured puppet figure of a Saracen, who strikes the hours on a church bell, add the final touch of fantasy.

In Athonite legend, the origins of the monastery go back to the fourth century, when Arcadius, son of the Emperor Theodosius the Great, was shipwrecked off the coast. The Virgin took pity on the boy and permitted him to land in her garden, where he was found resting in a blackberry bush. So the place was called Vatopaidi – 'blackberry bush boy' (the spelling is now Vatopedi, which means 'blackberry field'). The Emperor was so grateful to the Virgin that he built a monastery on the spot and dedicated it to the Annunciation. According to the historical record, the house is a tenth-century foundation.

I had time before vespers to look at the **Church of the Annuncia-tion** (commonly known as the Catholicon), the most important on Mount Athos. The exterior, whose walls are painted bright crimson, is a jumble of domes, arches and apses. The interior of the colonnaded *liti* is covered with eighteenth-century frescoes, whose whimsical folklore character is epitomized in the coy expression on the faces of the damned souls floundering in the river of Hell. Above the doorway into the narthex are three mosaic panels: a severe, unsmiling Deisis of the eleventh century, flanked by the Virgin and the Angel of the Annunciation (fourteenth-century). The figures are heavy and forceful, in the monumental style. Magnificent fourteenth-century **bronze doors**, decorated with designs of leaves and birds and figures of the Virgin and the Angel Gabriel, lead into the narthex, where the early fourteenth-century frescoes are distinguished by a pink glow reminiscent of the Protaton.

From the narthex I passed through sixteenth-century ivory-inlaid doors into the **naos**, which is paved with lavish polychrome marbles laid out in geometric designs. The dome is supported by granite columns with brass rings. The **frescoes**, despite restoration in the eighteenth and nineteenth centuries, are among the supreme achievements of the Macedonian School of painting in the early fourteenth century. An important new trend, later developed in other Athonite frescoes, is observed for the first time. A series of individual pictures seems to replace the strictly liturgical sequence of symbolical scenes. Overall uniformity is sacrificed to narrative. The colours are colder than usual: perhaps owing to restoration. An austere blue predominates and the familiar figures of the Dodecaorton pursue their tragic destinies in an inky haze, through which it is not always possible to distinguish the detail.

The grandest compositions are the **Entry into Jerusalem** and the **Crucifixion**, both larger than life-size. The atmosphere of expectancy prevails in the Entry. Christ in luminous dark blue robes rides on the donkey as he listens to the arguments of the Apostles, while the people of Jerusalem pour out of the ornamental city gate. The branches of the palm tree wave in the breeze. The background is a tortuous complex of domes, roofs, cornices and pediments, red against an inky, star-studded sky. In the Crucifixion the use of rigid straight lines – in the draperies of the stricken Virgin and the

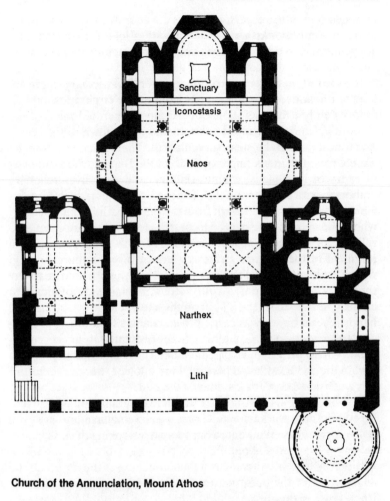

Church of the Annunciation, Mount Athos

anatomical details of the figure of Christ – heighten the sense of anguish. Only the figure of St John is conventional and unconvincing.

Two thirteenth-century icons flank the sanctuary: a Holy Trinity, disfigured by flashy haloes in gold filigree, and a Virgin and Child distinguished by the poignancy of the Virgin's expression. Above are dark mosaics of the Virgin and the Angel of the Annunciation, protectors of the church, guarding the entry into the sanctuary. The eighteenth-century *iconostasis* is very elaborate, the work, probably, of some monkish woodcarver with a love for pastoral life: stags, hunters and boys picking grapes frolic among flowers, pinecones and vines.

It is important to get permission to enter the sanctuary. Here are kept tenth- and fourteenth-century icons of the Virgin and Child, St George and St Michael. Some of the most venerated **relics** of the Orthodox Church are also kept here and only shown to the visitor on request (and under strict surveillance). They include parts of the True Cross, the index finger of St John the Baptist, the skull of St Gregory of Nazianzus, a ninth-century gold and silver reliquary embossed with scenes from the life of St Demetrius, which contains a piece of blood-soaked earth from the public baths at Thessaloniki where the martyr was speared to death. However the most revered relic of all is an enamelled box studded with gems containing a fragment of the Virgin's girdle: a piece of russet-coloured ribbon woven with gold thread and subsequently sewn with seed pearls by the Empress Pulcheria, a cultivated Athenian lady of the fifth century. Dropped by the Virgin on the site of Golgotha, it changed hands several times, was carried from country to country, allaying epidemics of the plague, and was finally presented by a fourteenth-century Serb prince to Vatopedi. When Curzon visited the monastery in the 1830s, afflicted persons were allowed, he says, in return 'for a consideration', to kiss it and be cured.

We dined in the guest-house with some itinerant monks. The fare was vegetarian, without wine. There was no conversation, not even polite formalities. We went to our room overlooking the mysterious velvety hills. It was about eight o'clock. We talked for a while in whispers. Suddenly there was a loud knocking at the door and the angry voice of the guest-master was heard inveighing against our irreverence in this house of God.

24 August

We got up at six and breakfasted on biscuits and Nescafé (our own). We visited the beautiful church again and persuaded a relatively amiable monk to let us see the library and the refectory. Visitors need waste no time on the latter. It is cross-shaped with marble-

A silver wine jug from Vergina, 350–325 BC. (*Archaeological Museum of Thessaloniki*)

Church of the Holy Apostles, Thessaloniki: Mosaic of the Transfiguration.

topped tables and ugly frescoes of the eighteenth century. The most striking object in the library is an extremely elegant specimen of Byzantine silverware: a **jasper cup** of the mid-fourteenth century on an octagonal stem with the monogram of the donor, Manuel Cantacuzenus, Despot of Mistra, inscribed on the base. Among the six hundred manuscripts – over half on parchment – are an eleventh-century psalter with the monogram of Emperor Constantine IX Monomachos and one of the few illustrated copies of Strabo's *Geography* in existence, with a crudely drawn but extraordinarily accurate map of the course of the Nile.

We looked at the ruins of the Theological School above the monastery, then descended along lanes between ilex, arbutus and Judas trees to the crescent-shaped shingly beach, where we ate our picnic lunch. Horseflies and wasps plagued us, while striped butterflies fluttered among the blackberry bushes. We then took the south-bound caique and sailed back to the Bay of Iviron.

The ascent from the arsenal to the **Monastery of Iviron**, which spreads across a densely wooded ledge, is easy by Athonite standards. The monastery was founded in the tenth century by three Georgian monks. Its maritime situation invited pirate raids and the monastery suffered much from Saracen attacks. In the fifteenth century the King of Georgia financed its reconstruction. However fire and earthquake took their toll, and most of the surviving buildings around the large irregular court, including belfry and *phiale*, are of the seventeenth century and are not very distinguished: some of the chapels are painted red and one bright mauve. The south buttress wall, cracked from top to bottom by an earthquake, supports a ruined tower, one of the five that formerly crowned the walls.

Before the sun went down we looked at two of the smaller churches. First the **Chapel of the Portaitissa**, situated where the Virgin addressed the pagan inhabitants and forbade any woman or female animal ever to enter her private garden. Ivory-inlaid doors lead from a hideously frescoed narthex into a small *naos* where the miraculous gold-sheathed icon of the Portaitissa (The Virgin of the Gate) is kept. The dark brown face is discernible through an overlay of gold decoration, surrounded by votive gifts. The monks claim it to be the work of St Luke. According to a popular Athonite legend the icon, cast into the sea by its owner during the Iconoclast persecution, appeared seventy years later in the Bay of Iviron, standing upright on the waves. Above it, a column of fire rose to heaven. The monks set out in rowing-boats to rescue it, but each time they approached the image it retreated and a celestial voice was heard saying that only Gabriel, a Georgian anchorite who dwelt in a cave above the monastery, was worthy of recovering it. So Gabriel was summoned from his eyrie; after walking on the waves, he grasped the image and carried it lovingly to the church. But every night the image moved of its own accord to the monastery gates, until the Virgin told the perplexed monks in a vision that she had not come to Mount Athos to be protected, but to protect them, and not until they were all gone would she leave her beloved garden. So a chapel was built near the gate and the icon has stayed there ever since.

The second chapel, that of St John the Baptist, is built, superstition has it, on the site of a pagan temple, where the idols fell down when the Virgin landed here. Disappointment awaited us in the Library, where all the illuminated manuscripts (several hundred) were packed and ready for removal to a new museum.

Our sleeping quarters overlooked a steep slope of woodland – the drone of insects and cicadas in the hot, airless valley was deafening – with just a glimpse of the Holy Sea beyond. The room was primitive, but there was no sign of the 'numberless tribes of vermin' which tenanted Curzon's chamber in the mid-nineteenth century. A tap at the end of the gallery provided us with washing facilities. For dinner (served in an annex of the kitchen) we had boiled beans and bread soaked in rancid olive oil, supplemented by our own processed cheese and *loucoumi*. There was as much wine as we wanted. We sat up late talking to the guest-master, who was an authority on Athonite legends. It was very pleasant after the regimentation of Vatopedi.

25 August

In the morning we visited the **Church of the Koimesis** (Dormition of the Virgin). The frescoes in the *liti* and narthex are over-restored and unattractive, but a set of beautiful Iznik tiles set into the interior wall of the *liti* serve as a curtain-raiser to the quasi-Oriental lavishness of the *naos*: a scene of exceptional opulence, with pendant silver censers, bronze candelabra from which lighted tapers flicker in front of a gilded *iconostasis*, a huge chandelier, frescoes on the upper register and icons with gold backgrounds hanging on walls and pillars. The tenth-century **pavement of Opus Alexandrinum** – marbles of orange, pink and mauve blending with ophite, porphyry and verd-antique – is contemporary with the original foundation. The great chandelier, a trophy captured by a Byzantine emperor in a campaign in the East, is carved with pygmy-like effigies including an allegory of Love, a Buddha-like deity and Persian soldiers; the immense enamelled corona which surrounds it is decorated with crosses, double-headed eagles and arched frames for icons, and came from Moscow in 1902. Behind the *iconostasis* there are chalices, crucifixes and a beautiful **silver gilt cross**, a masterpiece of Byzantine silverware. The whole church is lambent with copper, brass, gold and silver; the effect is almost barbaric in its splendour. It is not easy to forget its Georgian origins.

Frescoes cover every inch of wall space in the upper register. The finest is the **Pantocrator** in the dome (probably twelfth-century) set against a gold fan-shaped background ribbed with lines like the spokes of a wheel, the hub of which is Christ's head. His expression is haggard but serene. Below him are the Virgin *Orans* and the Archangels (fifteenth-century).

The church is rich in icons which include an early image of the Virgin, set in a rococo frame, holding the Child and surrounded by angels (north transept) and a magnificent **Deisis** (south-west transept) overlaid with gold plate so finely embossed that the draperies recall the work of some ancient sculptor. More icons, some of which are ancient and a few beautiful, adorn the walls of the restored refectory.

After lunch I walked over a shoulder of steep woodland north of the monastery and looked down at the coastline: at the castellated pile of Stavronikita and the waves breaking on the cliff of Pantocrator. Higher up the valley, abandoned hermitages were scattered among copses of poplars, and the domes of Karyes glistened in the sun.

The caique for the Grand Lavra arrived at about four o'clock; the

259

wind had dropped and the Holy Sea was smooth, with just a faint swell. As we chugged to the south-east the coast became more abrupt; forest smells drifted across the water, which turned from indigo to aquamarine and pearl grey. The peak of Athos, divested of its nebulous corona, tapered into the clear air. A waste of sea stretched east and south. Beyond the arsenal of the inland monastery of Philotheou we caught a glimpse of Karakallou and its handsome tower surrounded by cypress trees and nut groves. The coast, almost unbroken, became more wild and desolate. Suddenly we were sailing into a hidden creek, like a pirate's lair, in the shadow of a concrete tower – the arsenal of the **Grand Lavra**. We climbed for over half an hour up a steep hill pock-marked with bushes of holly-oak and arbutus, along the path that St Athanasius climbed when he first landed here, fighting prowling demons all the way, to found the first monastery.

In the failing light we discerned grey stone shapes ahead: a tower and rampart; then the wall-girt buildings of the monastery stretching across a ledge surrounded by vineyards and dominated by a rocky spur of the Holy Mountain. The sun had just set and we heard the creak of wood on ancient hinges as the gates were slammed behind us. We passed through a domed porch and entered what seemed to be a small medieval town: a maze of cobbled alleys, vaulted passages and small courts surrounded by low buildings with cupolas and slate roofs. Monks were chatting with lay labourers. A German student, who had left Dionysiou early in the morning and walked all day across the wildest and stoniest part of the peninsula, told us of views of 'unparallelled splendour'; his shoes were in a terrible state. We ate dinner in the guest-house – over twenty of us, all lay visitors. By nine o'clock everybody had gone to bed. From the gallery above the court, speckled with shadows of lemon trees, I could hear jackals shrieking in the vineyards. Gradually the unearthly whine drew nearer until I had the impression that entire packs of these scavenging beasts were prowling below the walls, hunting for carrion.

26 August

Early in the morning the court was full of animation. Monks were unloading baskets of marrows from the backs of braying donkeys, gardeners carrying picks and shovels, accompanied by shouting boys, set out for the fields and vineyards. Fruit trees and vine trellises, beds of straggling zinnias and pots of flaming salvias give the Lavra a rustic village-like air. There is little order in the layout of chapels, cells, arched troughs, wooden stairways and turrets, covering an area of several acres and all surrounded by grey walls. The court preserves something of the original *lavra*, a community of hermitages which existed before the monastery was built in 963. The foundation arose out of the friendship between Athanasius, a Bythinian ascetic, and a dour, puritanical General, Nicephorus Phocas. At the outset of the Cretan campaign (961) the General persuaded his pious friend to bless Byzantine arms. As soon as victory was won, he vowed, he would himself become a monk. However, after inflicting a decisive victory on the Saracens, Phocas found the prospect of usurping the throne more attractive than fulfilling his promise. So he placated Athanasius by founding the monastery which was to take precedence over all others on Mount Athos. Unlike most Athonite monasteries, the Grand Lavra has never been destroyed by fire and the main tower is part of the original tenth-century foundation.

The librarian guided us round the sights. The *phiale*, a seventeenth-century restoration of an earlier construction, shaded by two ancient cypresses, is the most beautiful on Mount Athos: a tea-cosy dome resting on arches filled with brick inlay and supported by little columns crowned with block capitals. The balustrade is composed of marble panels carved with designs of rosettes, birds, leaves and pine-cones. At Epiphany the holy water is consecrated in the huge porphyry basin before the whole community of monks. The **Church of the Koimesis**, whose architectural pattern – Greek Cross flanked by two cruciform chapels – became the model for all Athonite churches, is not without blemish. There is a squatness about the proportions, with weighty vaults and massive apses; the cupola is the largest on Mount Athos; the exterior walls are painted bright puce. The frescoes of the *liti* and narthex are tasteless examples of early nineteenth-century work. Impressive metal-faced oak doors of the Middle Byzantine period, elaborately decorated in *repoussé* technique with rosettes, petals, scrolls, vine leaves and crosses studded with gems, open into the *naos*, which is less splendid than that at Iviron. The two columns at the west end are part of the original tenth-century structure. On the screen – a nineteenth-century castellated stone monstrosity – hang two splendid **icons**, gifts of the Emperor Michael IX Palaeologus (1293–1320): the Virgin with doe-like eyes; and Christ, with aquiline features and a deep, penetrating expression, holding a Book of Gospels. Part of the main apse is hallowed ground and no human foot is allowed to tread on the spot where St Athanasius fell, broke his back and died, while helping to raise the dome. The Chapel of the Forty Martyrs on the left contains his tomb, encased in silver and draped in a mauve cloth decorated with crosses.

More important, though restored, are the **frescoes** of the *naos*, the work of Theophanes, a master of the Cretan School of painting, who died at the Grand Lavra in the early sixteenth century. His work seems more monkish and mystical than human and emotional; but his draughtsmanship and feeling for clarity are apparent in the grandiose Dormition of the Virgin, dominated by the noble figure of Christ holding the Virgin's soul. For an agreeable blend of colours one should turn to the Transfiguration, with its ochre rocks and mauve-tinted draperies and to the procession of saints and fathers of the church on the lower zone. Every known trick of the brush is used to make the figures identifiable and to heighten the dramatic allegory.

The walls of the disused **refectory**, the largest on Mount Athos, built in the shape of a cross, are also covered with frescoes by Theophanes and his Cretan disciples. The Last Supper spreads across the west apse, where the abbot once sat. Other scenes have to do with eating: the miracle of the loaves of bread, the supper at Emmaus, Elijah fed by the raven. More moving is the **Dormition of St Athanasius** in the north apse, a lyrical scene filled with mourning figures, a pink church symbolizing the dome that caused the saint's death. The south transept is filled with a panoramic vision of the **Last Judgement**, a confused assemblage of figures, incidents and allegories.

To the right of the refectory, a huge *simandron*, twelve feet long, beaten only on the most solemn of occasions, hangs from metal chains beside a bell-tower. We passed the goldfish basin, dragged up the hill in the form of a block of unhewn stone by St Athanasius, as he warded off the assaults of demons who were finally driven off by blows from his metal-tipped staff. The spot where the saintly foot was imprinted on the rim of the basin in the course of the skirmish is marked with a cross.

The librarian, anxious to hurry us on, and inclined to gabble his information, led us to the **treasury**, which houses the gifts of two Emperor-benefactors of the tenth century: the chasuble of Nicephorus Phocas, which he wore over a hair shirt; his imperial crown, studded with pearls and precious stones and surmounted by a jewelled cross, and his **Book of Gospels**, a superb piece of Byzantine gold and silver work; an early **mosaic icon of St John the Divine**, presented by John I Tsimisces, set within a frame of mosaic medallions in each of which a saint is portrayed, and an exquisitely wrought jewel-studded **gold cross**, in whose arms splinters of the True Cross are concealed.

The **library** contains eight hundred manuscripts on parchment. We looked at some leaves of St Paul's Letters to the Corinthians and Galatians from a sixth-century codex, a tenth-century illuminated manuscript of Dioscorides's *Manual of Botany* and a fifteenth-century edition of Homer – its first printing.

After an early lunch of bean soup and tomatoes, we descended to the arsenal to catch the two o'clock caique. The wind had dropped and the sea was smooth, metallic. The caique hugged the coast, which became increasingly abrupt and desolate beyond the arsenal of the Romanian *skete* of Prodromou. Nothing could be more spectacular, or in a sense more forbidding, than the journey round **Cape Akrathos**: we passed the mouth of the **Cave of the Wicked Dead** high up on the cliff-side. Its fetid chambers, the exile of excommunicated monks, were said to have been littered with bloated corpses, their nails turned to horny talons and their hair growing to their ankles, for the bodies of renegade monks, contrary to the laws of nature, did not undergo decomposition.

We rounded the cape. Towering screes are fringed with gigantic boulders that hurtled down in primeval landslides, forming ramparts of contorted stone. Grottoes are made up of a succession of arched tunnels in which the water swishes and gurgles. Around here, Mardonius's fleet was smashed to pieces in a storm in 492 BC

and the Persian soldiers were 'seized and devoured', says Herodotus, by the 'man-eating monsters' that infested the waters.

The Eastern mystical tradition of attaining the good life through
the purest asceticism is easily comprehended in this savage setting:
sailing between razor-edged reefs, we saw two seemingly inaccessible *kellia* (solitaries' eyries), perched hundreds of feet above the
sea, and the formidable ravine up which Peter the Anchorite, the
first hermit, climbed single-handed. Another cave, until recently
inhabited by a solitary, overhangs a dizzy ledge, forming part of the
eyrie of St Neilos, from whose corpse myrrh was said to have
trickled down the side of the scree and floated on the waves in
patches of luminous gold so that sailors came to collect it and
afterwards sold it to pious worshippers.

Six thousand feet above towers the limestone crest of Athos,
crowned by a white chapel. Strabo said that people who scaled the
final peak could 'see the sun rise three hours before it rises on the
seaboard', and its shadow is supposed to be cast across the Aegean
as far as the island of Skiathos, which means 'in the shade of Athos'.

Suddenly the desolation is relieved by a glimpse of human
habitation. The *skete* of **Kavsokalyvia**, a dependency of the Grand
Lavra, winds vertically up the side of a fertile valley. Chapels with
domes and slate roofs, and whitewashed cottages inhabited by
monkish wood-carvers are surrounded by clusters of bay trees from
whose leaves laurel oil is pressed. Here dwelt St Akakios, who took
flight one day in a religious transport and floated up to the summit of
Athos where he met the Virgin.

We passed two rowing-boats propelled by black-robed hermits
with white beards. They waved and went on fishing. As we rounded
Cape Pinnes, where the screes acquire a deep pink, almost fiery,
hue, the skete of **Karoulia** burst into view: a chain of eyries
straggling up a perpendicular streak of vegetation. They are connected to each other by a cobbled track, just wide enough to allow
the passage of a single mule, which has replaced an ancient system
of communication whereby the hermits, on visits to each other,
clung to ropes or chains passing over makeshift pulleys. Little
shelves of soil are terraced one above another, planted with vegetables and a few vines, surrounded by cacti. It is like the Ladder of
Heaven in the Last Judgement. A blue dome was visible and some

huts where more worldly hermits carve religious souvenirs and crosses from deer-horn, which are sold in Karyes.

The next *skete* was **St Anne's**. Each shelf of the vertical succession of eyries is connected with the next by primitive aqueducts made of hollowed-out trunks of pine and cypress, through which streams cascade from one vegetable plot to another. Modern icons are painted by the inhabitants of these vertiginous abodes. In the Church of St Anne there is a venerable relic: St Anne's left foot.

We had now rounded the promontory and put in at Nea Skete, an eighteenth-century dependency of the Monastery of St Paul, where the woollen socks worn by Athonite monks are knitted by hermits. The slope of the mountain is less abrupt here and there is a green foreshore, with some modern houses scattered among orchards.

We sailed into the Singitic Gulf. To starboard, high up on the mountainside, rises the fortress of the Monastery of St Paul. The coast was still steep, but wooded and more broken; one could imagine men dwelling in this country. We were chugging towards the **Monastery of Dionysiou**: four stories of whitewashed cells with projecting balconies, roofed with slate tiles and crowned with a medieval tower, soaring above an immense foundation wall that rises like a stone pier from an isolated bluff above the shore.

From the arsenal we climbed a cobbled path between plane and walnut trees overhanging the torrent-bed of the Aeropotamos (The Windy River), so-called because sudden currents of cold air whistle down it from the mountain. Terraced kitchen-gardens were bordered with oleanders and we noticed peach trees heavy with golden fruit. By the entrance gate there is a fountain of cold water and a belvedere overlooking the peaceful gulf. The rock on which the monastery is perched allows no room for outward expansion. Cells, storerooms and galleries pile up, supported on struts, one above the other; at the summit of the pinnacle is the crimson-painted church within its cramped court.

The origins of the monastery's foundation go back to an eremetical vision. In the fourteenth century a hermit called Dionysius dwelt in a neighbouring eyrie. One night he noticed flames leaping heavenward from the bluff above the sea. Every night the supernatural blaze grew brighter. Interpreting the message correctly, he begged his brother, a Trapezuntine bishop, to persuade the

Emperor Alexius III of Trebizond to build a monastery on the holy spot. It was called after him – Dionysiou.

It was five o'clock and we were hustled off to dinner in the refectory. The rhythm of life would be different here. We were in a cenobitic house – one of the friendliest and most beautiful on the peninsula. The monks here are not just refugees or vagabonds from the world, anxious to secure free board and lodging in return for the gabbling of praises to the Lord, parrot-fashion, in a haze of incense; here the spirit of contemplation and communion still exists, and frugality has some relation to godliness.

The beautifully proportioned **refectory**, entirely frescoed, is T-shaped, with arches at the point where the arms join the stem. As we ate – a Lucullan feast by Athonite standards: pilaff with fried squid, tomatoes stuffed with rice and garlic, peaches, bread and rough red wine – a deacon mounted the brightly painted pulpit and read from the menology, while we gazed round the frescoed walls. Shafts of light, slanting through the windows, fell on gruesome scenes of martyrdom: severed heads, surrounded by golden nimbuses, rolling on marble floors, ferocious Roman legionaries brandishing blood-stained swords. The principal frescoes are of the sixteenth to seventeenth centuries: the Last Supper in the east apse above the abbatial table, and a vast **Last Judgement**, in which the Ladder of Heaven is full of animation, with figures scaling the celestial rungs, urged on by officious angels. At the top they are received by Christ standing against a star-studded sky. The cool, pleasant cloister of the refectory is frescoed with lively apocalyptic scenes: the Four Horsemen, martial and purposeful, and the Earthquake, with the roofs of buildings collapsing in a strangely geometrical fashion.

We attended vespers in the dark, frescoed church, spellbound by the voice of a young, beardless monk chanting the litanies in a soaring tenor, while hoary old men, bent double with fatigue and infirmity, muttered '*Kyrie Eleison! Kyrie Eleison!*'. They then kissed the holy images and shuffled out, removing the veils they attach to their hats during the liturgy. There was little to do but retire to our bedroom on the top floor of this complex eyrie of corridors and projecting balconies. From the windows there was a drop, absolutely sheer, of hundreds of feet, to the base of the bluff fringed by a rocky shore.

28 August

In the morning an amiable librarian took us sightseeing. The **Church of Agios Ioannis Prodromos** follows the usual Athonite plan. The sixteenth-century **frescoes** possess a harmony, a fluidity of design and a freshness of colour rare in the grandiose wall-paintings of the ancient and more venerable churches of Vatopedi and Iviron. Less opulence, in the way of gold and marble decoration, creates an atmosphere of greater restraint and concentration. The artist was Zorsi, a native of Crete, possibly of Venetian origin. His work is more Italianate, less monkish, than that of his compatriot Theophanes. His draperies billow and swirl and his architectural backgrounds are more integrated. From the dome the Pantocrator blesses mankind, with angels, standing on a green lawn, surrounding him. Opposite the Nativity, on the barrel vault of the south apse, St John baptizes Christ, who is immersed in the waters of the Jordan, against a star-studded sky.

In the library we saw the famous **chrysobull of Alexius III of Trebizond**, the imperial charter confirming the foundation of the monastery, which Finlay calls 'one of the most valuable monuments of the pictorial and calligraphic arts of the Greeks in the Middle Ages'. On the piece of parchment, more than twelve feet long and eight inches wide, a majestic Christ is depicted in the act of blessing Alexius and his Empress, the scarlet of the imperial ink vying with the golds and bluish-greens of uncials entwined with tendrils. Among the manuscripts are a twelfth-century Book of Gospels, its cover decorated with a figure of Christ on the Cross between the Virgin and St John, and another of the thirteenth century with an earlier cover minutely carved in wood with scenes from the *Dodecaorton*.

After nine o'clock lunch in the refectory we chartered a caique to take us to the Monastery of St Paul. From the jetty we saw baskets of peaches, dangling at the ends of long ropes, being hauled up by monks to a balcony that projected above the great supporting wall. We struck a bargain with the caique-master and chartered his boat for the next two days. This would enable us to visit the last group of monasteries on the west coast without having to spend a night in each of them.

From the arsenal of the **Monastery of St Paul** we walked for over an hour up a stony path in a wild and rocky landscape. The monastery straddles the mouth of a savage ravine against a background of terrific precipices, its walls rising like a vast medieval stronghold out of the scrubland. To the east, a lofty crenellated wall protects the monks' cells from the icy blasts that funnel out of the ravine in winter. The approach is strewn with boulders washed down by torrents or thrown across the thyme-scented mountainside by landslides. The last lap of the painful ascent is along a cobbled path, trellised with vines. Beside the gate there is a pergola where we rested, listening to the gibberish of a lay vagrant – one of the many who roam the peninsula in search of a bed and a free meal – whose limbs shook as though he was stricken with the palsy. Fumbling in the pockets of his verminous clothes for a Book of Gospels, he then read several passages aloud, looking up occasionally to leer obscenely at us. Wandering through empty courts and galleries, we finally tracked down the guest-master who led us to a spacious guest-house overlooking the stony waste and offered us plum jam, coffee and *ouzo*.

The original establishment was founded in the tenth century by a hermit named Paul, a contemporary of St Athanasius, who heard an unearthly voice instructing him to build a house of God on the site of his cave. The monastery was largely destroyed by fire in 1902. Monkish carelessness, the lavish use of woodwork for constructional purposes and candles burning beside holy images, have all contributed to the outbreak of these devastating conflagrations in which much of the original structure of numerous Athonite houses has perished. At St Paul, only the Chapel of St George, the great east wall and the sixteenth-century tower (which is the tallest on Mount Athos) survive. The other buildings are modern and of little interest.

We climbed a series of wooden stairways to the **Chapel of St George**, built into the fortified wall which forms the backcloth of the monastery against a screen of stupendous cliffs. The chapel, overlooking the domes of the Church of the Presentation of the Virgin, is small: a barrel-vaulted basilica with a narthex. An inscription, possibly spurious, dates it to 1423, but the frescoes are more closely related to the Cretan School of the sixteenth century. Whatever their date they have the distinction, rare among frescoes of Mount Athos, of being wholly unrestored. In their freshness and luminosity, in the subtlety, delicacy and transparency of their colour tints they compare favourably with the best work of the late Byzantine period. The tone is set immediately by the saints and ascetics ranged around the walls of the narthex; each figure stands out as an individual. The frescoes of the *naos*, battered though untarnished, still glow with much of their original variety of colour. The faces are expressive and the garments lavish. The mood of the **Nativity** is serene and pastoral, with a relaxed Virgin reclining on a faded pink couch while the Child lies swaddled in the crib. In the **Raising of Lazarus**, white-bearded figures in robes of dove grey and pink, framed between yellow rocks, watch the unwinding of the shroud against a snow-white, castellated background beneath a sombre sky. Across the vault are medallions of the Virgin and Child and six prophets, each a compelling portrait.

We walked down to the arsenal in the sizzling heat. Lizards scuttled among scorched shrubs. We swam off a pebbly shore in what are said to be shark-infested waters. Centuries ago, the inmates of Dionysiou, perched on their highest balcony, watched a shark frustrated in the act of swallowing a monk bathing in the cove below. Stretching his arms outwards, the holy man arranged his body into the shape of a cross so that the shark was unable to devour him; but no sea monsters disturbed the translucent waters on this occasion. The boulders and cliffs, rising sheer above, are horizontally seamed with brightly coloured stratifications: puce, brown, amber, olive green and pink.

We got back to Dionysiou to find the monks in a state of unusual animation. It was the eve of the feast of the Assumption of the Virgin, and the beardless chorister whose voice had so impressed us the night before wandered round the monastery, beating the *simandron* with his little mallet. The tinkling tune echoed across the galleries girdling the crimson church, and there was a strong smell of incense.

The service lasted all night, without a break. We went into the church several times. Some of the weary, hungry monks, who had not touched meat or fish for a fortnight, slept as they leant on their staffs; others sneezed when a deacon swung a censer under their noses. There was no formality – the absence of pews in an Orthodox church tends to make clergy and congregation wholly unselfconscious. Priests came and went. Hour after hour the Divine Office went on, to the accompaniment of the plaintive eight-tone chant. In the cloisters and passages veiled, black-robed figures lingered, whispered for a moment and disappeared into church, crossing themselves.

29 August

Early in the morning we sailed in our chartered caique to the **Monastery of Gregoriou**. Like Dionysiou, though less beautiful and interesting, it is perched on a bluff above a creek. A ruined tower and a wilted palm tree crown the pile of buildings, whose wooden balconies of different colours overhang the sea.

We were received by the abbot, who led us to an ugly refectory where with all the monks we lunched on pieces of dried cod fried in the most rancid oil I have ever tasted, followed by custard, washed down with vinegary wine. We soon recovered our spirits, however, in an airy gallery with walls painted sky blue, from which there was a prodigious view of the wild, steep coastline stretching southwards. A heavy bank of cloud was settling on the peak of Athos.

The monastery was founded by Gregory, a hermit of Mount Sinai, in the thirteenth century. Fire destroyed it in the eighteenth and all the buildings are relatively modern. The exterior walls of the **Church of Agios Nikolaos** are painted blue, and dark magenta drums support grey domes. The eighteenth-century frescoes of the interior are without distinction. At the north end of the *naos* there is a venerated but not very ancient icon of the Galaktotrophousa (The Virgin Giving Suck), in which the Virgin is depicted with a peevish expression, offering her breast to the Child.

By mid-morning we were sailing north-westward below the fourteenth-century **Monastery of Simonopetra**, seven stories of strut-supported wooden galleries crowning a foundation wall twice as formidable as that of Dionysiou, soaring into the air out of the dark green woods a thousand feet above sea level, and joined to the mountainside by an imposing aqueduct with a double tier of arches. During a great fire in the sixteenth century, panic-stricken monks hurled themselves over the balconies and were dashed to pieces on the boulder-strewn vegetable plots below. From the arsenal it is about an hour's steep climb to the monastery. Simonopetra's façade may be the most theatrical on the Holy Mountain, but otherwise it has little to offer except an aerial view of the peninsula and gulf.

Beyond the arsenal of Simonopetra the scenery becomes tamer. We put in at Daphni, our original starting point, in time for a second, late, lunch, then continued by boat, hugging the coast, the most domesticated on Mount Athos. The sky had become overcast and by the time we reached the Arsenal of St Panteleimon drops of rain were falling on an oily grey sea. A gentle ramp leads from a waterfront of tall, gutted warehouses and woodcutters' shacks into a fantasy: a miniature 'Russian' town.

The **Monastery of St Panteleimon**, commonly called Roussiko (The Russian One), is one of the most extraordinary sights on Mount Athos; not because of its antiquarian interest – it has none – but because of its decayed splendour: a vast nineteenth-century Russian enclave of spires, bell-towers and paved courts on different levels, with thirty churches and chapels, their red roofs crowned with onion domes and gold crosses, all in an Aegean setting of pine-woods, cypress thickets and olive groves.

The early twelfth-century foundation was dedicated to St Panteleimon, a court physician and convert to Christianity, whose martyrdom in the reign of Diocletian was distinguished by the extraordinary resistance shown by his head to every attempt at severance by the most stalwart executioners. It finally succumbed, wreathed in a resplendent halo, to the blows of the mightiest axe in the Roman Empire; St Panteleimon remains a popular patron of doctors and medical institutions.

After the Byzantine era the monastery fell on bad days and it was not until the early nineteenth century that the influence of Mother Russia, head of Christian Orthodoxy since the fall of Constantinople, reached the Aegean and led to a rapid influx of Russian monks. The Russian Government, always eager to secure support in Greece against their traditional common enemy, Turkey, exploited the link between the sister churches and showered wealth on the Holy Mountain and on St Panteleimon in particular. At the turn of the century it was the largest and most active monastery in the whole Athonite community, the number of Slav monks on the peninsula amounting to two thousand, as against three thousand Greeks. This was the culmination of a connection between the Byzantine and Slavonic worlds first made a thousand years before, when St Cyril and St Methodious left Constantinople to convert the first Slavs to Christianity. However after 1917 few novices found their way to St Panteleimon. Less than a dozen monks, flat-faced Russian peasants, have survived to drag out their last senile years in this decaying nineteenth-century stage-set.

We carried our bags along tiled paths, past deserted chapels covered with lichen, until we reached a large, unkempt court. An old monk with a matted red beard, prominent cheek-bones and light-coloured, rheumy eyes was crouching on the ground. As we drew nearer we observed that he was feeding armies of ants with bread-crumbs. We addressed the monk in Greek. He replied in Russian, but seemed to understand what we wanted. Arranging his breadcrumbs in a little pile on the ground, he shuffled off, returning after a few minutes with a lay guest-master, who led us through a gloomy gallery to a shuttered drawing-room filled with peeling leather armchairs and sofas covered with antimacassars. Photographs of the Tsar, Tsarina and Tsarevich and related royalty (Edward VII, the Kaiser) hung on the walls. The ritual coffee and *ouzo* were produced.

Later, shafts of sunlight, penetrating the cloud bank, shone on gold crosses and green domes as we wandered among trellised passages, across tiled courts, up and down stairways with ornamental balustrades and past neglected flowerbeds shaded by limp palms. We saw a chapel, its columns crowned with Corinthian capitals, a fountain and pedestals with cornucopias from which dusty ferns drooped languidly.

The exterior of the Church of Agios Panteleimon is pleasing, its walls painted coral pink, its domes sheeted with grey metal. The interior is a mass of gold and gilt, with an outsize chandelier and corona. The frescoes would have done credit to the illustrator of a children's book of Bible stories published in about 1910. Across the inner court, opposite the church, is a huge refectory in the shape of a basilica with barrel-vault aisles and an apse at the west end; 1500 monks used to dine here. A belfry on three stepped levels, topped by a lime-green spire, surmounts the edifice.

On the highest level of the monastery, crowning the whole fantastic pile, are the two enormous **Chapels of the Protection of the Virgin and Saints Alexander Nevsky, Vladimir and Olga**, which together virtually form a single large cathedral, all gilt and ormolu with gold crosses and rococo columns, capable of accommodating a congregation of two thousand. The walls are hung with hideous icons and marble pillars with Ionic capitals support the gallery. After this we visited the official reception hall of the guest-house, filled with more gilt-framed photographs of Tsars and other royalty, of Rasputin and famous abbots. All that was lacking, one felt, was an empty ballroom, ghost-like, echoing with familiar tunes from *Swan Lake*. (Since this visit to the monastery, fire has once more ravaged several buildings described here. Restoration work is in progress.)

Meals are no longer served in the refectory so we dined by candlelight in the kitchen of the guest-house. Afterwards there was nothing to do but wander across the empty courts and watch sheet-lightning flash across the southern sky above the Holy Mountain. Stumbling along a dark gallery I heard mice scuttling about and thought I saw a gigantic spider hanging from a beam in the ceiling. No other monastery on Mount Athos has such a haunted air.

30 August

Early in the morning we walked to the **Monastery of Xenophontos**: two stories of projecting balconies crowned by domes and broken towers, supported by strong walls and overlooking a sandy beach. It is a peaceful place surrounded by green hills. A convoy of donkeys, carrying loads of wood, wound through the groves. The monastery owes much to Balkan benefactors. Founded in the eleventh century by a pious Byzantine nobleman called Xenophon, it was restored in the sixteenth century by Moldo-Wallachian princes and in the eighteenth by Romanian hospodars.

Steps lead up from an irregular sloping court to the **Church of Agios Georgios**, frescoed by two sixteenth-century artists of the Cretan School, Antonios and Theophanes (not to be confused with the more important Theophanes who worked at the Grand Lavra). Though their work is somewhat cold and hard, that of Antonios is none the less bold and original and the large scenes in the upper

273

zone merit attention. The tragedy of the **Crucifixion** is stressed by sharp angularities, by hooded effigies of the sun and moon illustrating the darkness that fell over the earth between the sixth and ninth hours. The **Entry into Jerusalem** has a quality of starkness, an absence of architectural and incidental detail rare in this composition. Antonios's skill as a draughtsman may be halting, but he possesses remarkable virtuosity in the manipulation of colour; in the violence of his contrasts he is often extremely original, using pitch-black skies as a background for his favourite Sienna reds, corals and clarets. Here, more than anywhere else on Mount Athos, it is possible to discern the origins of that explosion of luminosity and dramatic impressionism which was to distinguish the masterpieces of El Greco less than half a century later. In comparison, the work of Theophanes in the same church seems trivial and insipid.

As the monastery grew in size and importance, the church became too small and a larger edifice, also dedicated to St George, was raised in the early nineteenth century further up the slope. It is unfrescoed but possesses a fine collection of icons, a reliquary containing a drop of St John the Baptist's blood and two magnificent **mosaic panels** of the thirteenth century, representing St George and St Demetrius. They are executed in the minutest *tesserae*. Both faces emerge as portraits: young men of nobility, virile, sensitive and chivalrous.

Later, descending the ramp to the beach, we noticed a little stream of fresh water trickling through the pebbles on the spot where an icon of St George was found by monks centuries ago. Roughly handled by Iconoclasts, the icon is said to have oozed blood from a crack in the panel and was thrown into the sea. Months later it was tossed up on the shore of Xenophontas, whereupon the holy spring, whose waters are said to be purgative, gushed forth for the first time.

We began the last lap of our journey and were soon dropping anchor off the landing-stage of the **Monastery of Docheiariou**. From the sea the monastery can be seen to be one of the finest architectural ensembles on the peninsula, its buildings and dependencies spreading fan-wise against a background of hills speckled with pines and cypresses. Balconies overhang stout walls with elliptical blind arches, and a geometrical pattern of belfries, chimneys and slate roofs is dominated by a tower flanked by cypresses. A frescoed porch leads through a labyrinth of cool, shady passages painted with murals, into a small court. Pomegranate trees grow in the shade of walls covered with flowering creepers.

The monks say the monastery was founded by Euthymius, super-intendent of stores (*docheiarios*) at the Grand Lavra and a personal friend of St Athanasius. According to the historical record, the site was purchased from the monks of Xenophontas in the eleventh century and the church dedicated to the Archangel Michael, a staunch champion of Athonite holy men against Saracen pirates. The monastery enjoyed imperial benefaction and later that of the Voivodes, the Moldo-Wallachians who restored the church after its destruction by corsairs in the sixteenth century.

In the shadow of the great tower, dated to the early sixteenth century, the wooden loggia of the charming guest-house overlooks roofs and domes on different levels. After the usual refreshment, we visited the **Church of the Archangels**, the largest and one of the most beautiful on the Holy Mountain. The exterior is of brick – a welcome change from the usual crimson stucco – and the blind arches are inlaid with dark, wedge-shaped tiles. The interior is covered with sixteenth-century **frescoes** of the Cretan School, poss-ibly by Zorsi, who worked at Dionysiou; mid-nineteenth-century restoration has not deprived the paintings of their original liveli-ness. Across the north wall of the exo-narthex there is an enchanting representation of the **Dormition of St Ephraim**, the Mesopotamian bath-keeper who became one of the most popular hymnographers of the fourth century. The mourners fan out around the bier, long white beards, draperies and striped vestments forming a symmetri-cal pattern of vertical lines. The conch-shaped centre-piece is framed within bucolic scenes of eremitical life: hermits praying, reading holy books, riding donkeys and tending fields. A stylite perched on a column casts a rope to haul up a basket of provisions. An air of muted serenity pervades the composition and the lyrical mood recalls the Dormition of St Athanasius at the Grand Lavra.

The *naos* is lofty and beautifully proportioned, the tall central drum supported by four granite columns. As in the two narthexes, every available inch of wall space is frescoed. On the gilded *iconostasis*, a typically fussy example of eighteenth-century woodcarving, biblical episodes intermingle with bucolic scenes and hunters stalk their prey among stylized bushes. A slab of green marble on the pavement commemorates one of the Archangel's miracles: a shepherd boy of Sithonia, who had found hidden treasure, was assaulted by monks possessed by demons. They tied a marble slab to his neck, dropped him into the sea and made off with the treasure. Floundering in the waves, the boy called on the Archangel for help. St Michael promptly came to the rescue, carried him tenderly to the shore and laid his body, dripping wet, on the floor of the church at Docheiariou, where he was found by a monk beating the *simandron* just before matins.

Outside the church we admired the charming *phiale*, the interior of whose dome is frescoed with scenes of monastic vessels pursued by Saracen fleets and defenceless monks being rescued from corsairs by the Archangels – the monastery, rising directly from the water's edge, was always an easy target for maritime marauders. A cool, frescoed colonnade leads to the sombre little shrine of the *Panayia Gorgoepeiköos* (The Virgin who grants requests quickly), which possesses a wonder-working tenth-century icon of the Virgin, strung with votive offerings. A careless monk once allowed the smoke from his candle to blacken and disfigure her face. The Virgin commanded the monk to be more careful; but, forgetful by nature, he repeated the offence. This time the Virgin, acting like an outraged Athena or Artemis, instantly blinded him. The stricken man pleaded for mercy, whereupon the Virgin appeared to him in a vision and declared: 'Monk, your prayer has been heard and you shall see again as you used to, for I am the Ready-Listener.'

The refectory is frescoed with apocalyptic scenes, slightly earlier in date than those in the church. The most remarkable of these is a strange representation of **God Enthroned** against a background of lighted arches: an elderly, haloed figure with a homely expression, holding the bejewelled book 'sealed with seven seals' which could only be opened by the Lamb with seven horns (Revelation, V: 1). The white lamb is depicted here with green horns; it stands on its hind legs, about to receive the book from God.

We left Docheiariou and its atmosphere of tranquillity with regret. The sea was calm, the sun hot, as the caique chugged westward – back to the world. We bathed off a sandy beach at the foot of a pine-clad cliff crowned by the ruined buildings of a deserted *skete*. The shore was littered with beautiful pebbles of different colours, smoothed into oval shapes by the endless friction of the waves.

In the late afternoon we saw the Tower of Prosphori rising above the port of Ouranoupoli. On landing, we found the car, parked under the shadow of the tower, caked in dust. We sat at a waterfront café. A few tables away, two boys in jeans and striped shirts fiddled with a transistor radio which emitted snatches of the duet from the first act of *Traviata*. A girl in a multi-coloured cotton dress brought us iced lemonade and the sudden realization of where we now were, of where we had been, was breathtaking. A child was cuffed by another and began to howl. Its cries drowned the last echoes of wood pigeons piping in the copses of the Virgin's empty garden.

CHAPTER 18

Eastern Macedonia

The Strimonas – Seres – Amphipolis –
Mount Pangeo – Kavala – Philippi – the Nestos.

North and east of the Halkidiki lies Eastern Macedonia, originally
the country of the Thracians but annexed by Philip II to the
Macedonian Empire after a series of lightning campaigns in the
fourth century BC. Fertile, but less beautiful than the Halkidiki, it is
full of military associations. Rivers flow north to south through
marshy estuaries into the Aegean. The climate is one of extremes,
and the winters are of unparalleled coldness by Mediterranean
standards. Xenophon refers to the soldiers wearing fox-skin caps
and to wine being frozen. Oxen and cattle, now as then, are
plentiful; so are the eels in the river mouths. In antiquity the natives
were noted for their barbarous character. Disloyal and faithless,
they did not hesitate to sell their children; they spoke an uncouth
non-Hellenic tongue, were idle by nature and drunken by predilection. Today, by contrast, the inhabitants are thrifty small farmers
and tobacco merchants.

The return journey from Thessaloniki to the River Nestos on the
border of the province of Thrace can be accomplished in one day;
but this allows for few deviations, one of which at least, to Philippi,
is of outstanding interest. Spending the night at the attractive port of
Kavala, one can also visit Seres and Amphipolis and then either
return to Thessaloniki or penetrate deeper into the Thracian plains.

The road from Thessaloniki to Seres, after crossing a rolling,
featureless landscape, descends to the west bank of the **River
Strimon**. Throughout Greek literature great emphasis is placed on
the omnipotent character of the river and the winds that blow across

278

its spacious valley, affecting the weather of the whole country. In 1916–18 the river constituted the demarcation line between the armies of the Allies and those of the Central Powers. In 1941 German tanks streamed down the valley from the Bulgarian frontier to reach Thessaloniki within three days. East of the bridge, at the foot of Mount Vrondou (Thunder) lies **Seres**, the ancient Sirris, where Xerxes left large numbers of sick and wounded during the retreat after the battle of Salamis.

The modern town, seat of a bishopric and a centre of tobacco-growing, is distinguished only by its pleasant rectangular square (*Plateia Eleftherias*), bordered by poplars and weeping willows, and with a basin in the centre around which peacocks strut. At the west end stands a large abandoned mosque crowned by six domes. Seres was an important place in medieval times. At the foot of the castle hill the **Metropolis**, dedicated to the Holy Theodores, rises out of a depression surrounded by small houses. It is a large brick basilica, somewhat cumbersome in outline, its date uncertain, but the mosaics of the interior apse, largely destroyed by the retreating Bulgarians at the end of the Second Balkan War in 1913, have been assigned to the eleventh century. The little domed chapel of a later date at the north-west end was connected with the medieval keep by an underground passage used by Stephen Dusan, the Serbian national hero, who conquered large tracts of Northern Greece in the fourteenth century. The interior can only be visited by permission of the bishop (secretariat in Kyprou Street), who deputes a deacon to show visitors round. The walls are bare, and only two of the original six grey marble columns of the aisles are preserved, but the proportions are lofty and harmonious. There are some finely carved bas-reliefs lying about: a Pantocrator in low relief, griffins and horses, elaborate crosses. Fragments of an eleventh-century mosaic of the Last Supper, said to have been of outstanding quality, can be discerned in the apse.

A single bastion crowns the remains of the Byzantine castle at the summit of a pine-clad hill overlooking the city. The castle was occupied in turn by invading Franks, Serbs and Turks as the tides of war swept back and forth across the Byzantine empire. Southward, beyond the ugly urban agglomeration, extends the cultivated plain in a pale yellowish-green haze. To the north, chalky cliffs and

279

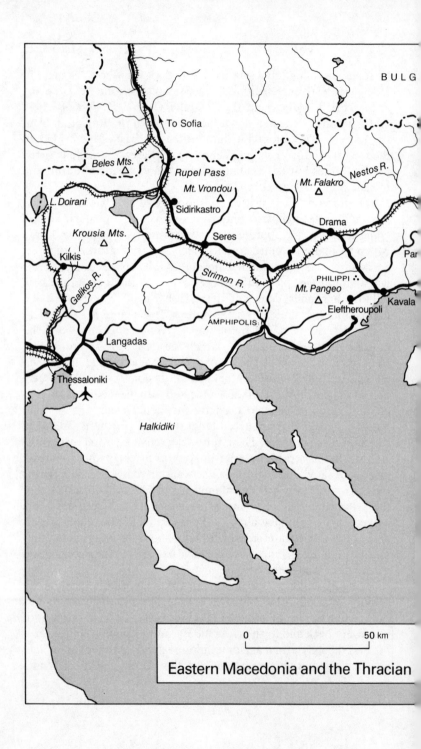

Eastern Macedonia and the Thracian

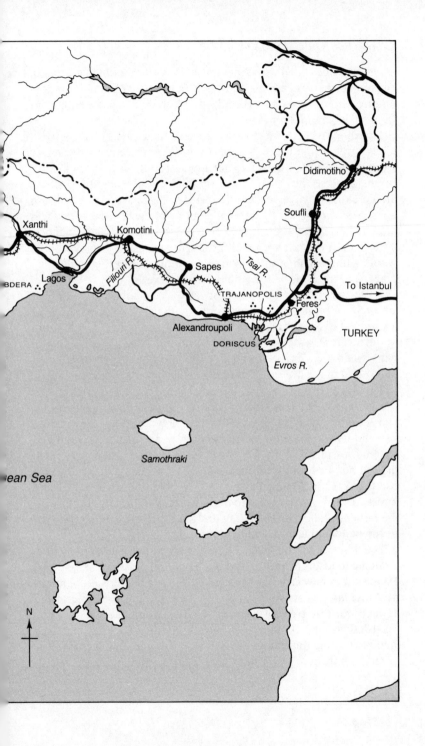

shallow ravines filled with pines and evergreens mount in a series of rugged forms towards the desolate heights of Mount Vrondou, among whose snow-capped peaks the thunder is said to roll louder than anywhere in the world.

About halfway down the east slope of the castle hill a side-road leads through the trees to the little fourteenth-century Byzantine **Church of Agios Nikolaos**. Recently restored, its red-brick walls bright against the dark green of pines, it is something of an architectural extravaganza, crowned at each end by domes and with an exo-narthex wider than the main body of the church. A belfry is attached at the southern end. There are three absurd little cupolas above the narthex and a well-proportioned drum surmounts the whole edifice. The interior is without interest. But it is a secluded place, and the air is balmy with the scent of resin.

From Seres the road runs eastward across tobacco and wheat country, its monotony relieved only by the snow-capped shape of Mount Pangeo to the east. After branching south towards the mouth of the Strimon, a sign-posted road winds up to the village of **Amphipolis**, where the services of a local guide should be engaged to conduct one round the scattered ruins of this once important ancient city.

The flying ants are a pest, the brushwood thick and prickly, and the distances between the groups of unidentifiable foundations considerable. One is impressed by the sprawling dimensions of the site and its commanding position between the Strimonic Gulf and the interior plains, with the river winding in two wide loops round the hill before flowing through a lagoon into the gulf. To the east rise the spurs of **Mount Pangeo**, whose gold and silver mines and forests contributed so much to the prosperity of the city. In the west the wooded Halkidiki massif dips down towards the isthmus; beyond it, the headland is crowned by the magical peak of Athos.

The history of the place, which was at the junction of nine strategic roads, is eventful. During the period of Athenian imperial expansion, a new city was founded on the site and it was colonized by Athenian settlers who lost no time in exploiting the mineral and agricultural resources of the region. Thus Amphipolis came to be regarded as one of the chief jewels of the Periclean maritime empire. During the Peloponnesian war, this commercial prize was bitterly contested by Athens and Sparta, and it finally fell to

Brasidas in 422 BC at the battle of Amphipolis; a Spartan victory of the first magnitude, though Brasidas himself, the architect of the triumph, was killed. The Athenian defeat became an undignified rout and Thucydides, in command of the Athenian triremes, failed to recapture the city. After the battle Athenian prestige was never to stand so high again; and moreover, the double event of the Athenian defeat and the death of Brasidas made such an impact on Hellenic consciousness that it increased the influence of the pacifist parties, enabling them, a year later, to negotiate the abortive Peace of Nicias. Over half a century later Amphipolis fell to Philip of Macedon.

So much history, and how little to show for it! Of scientific excavation there has been hardly any – a mere scratching of the ground. At intervals across the cornfields of the rolling eminence you see truncated pedestals of grey marble, white unfluted columns lying in hollows, a trench in which broken pillars stand in a row, fragmentary remains of walls, some Corinthian capitals and, far removed from any other vestige of antiquity, the legs and buttocks of a large marble horse. Some of the foundations of the buildings possess apse-shaped east ends: remains of the Early-Christian township that rose on the debris of the pagan city.

Shortly before reaching the east–west highway a path to the left climbs a mound: a natural tumulus, out of which the sepulchre of a Macedonian prince has been carved. Steps descend into a barrel-vaulted chamber with an L-shaped stone couch (or tomb), sufficiently large and imposing to have been the last resting-place of a person of considerable distinction.

Reaching the highway, make a detour west. The road soon crosses the wide bed of the Strimon, where Xerxes built a bridge for his prodigious army. On the west bank of the river, on a stepped pedestal in a wispy pine grove, stands the **Lion of Amphipolis**, a colossal lion, with magnificent mane and gaping, predatory mouth, re-assembled from fourth-century BC fragments. His eyes fixed across the estuary at the flat-topped acropolis of Amphipolis, he is a superb animal, guarding the mouth of the river. In Hellenistic times these monumental lions, symbols of virility, were generally raised as war memorials. At Amphipolis this one is thought to crown the tomb of some distinguished Macedonian prince.

East of the estuary there is a choice between the coastal road along the shore into Kavala's waterfront and the mountainous inland road which follows the base of Mount Pangeo, whose ancient gold mines were the goal of every invader and would-be conqueror. From earliest times the mountain, with its bulbous spurs and knobbly summits, has exercised a powerful hold over Greek imagination, both as a haunt of the deities and as a source of economic wealth. The gold mines figure in mythology, for the wealth of Cadmus, founder of Thebes, is supposed to have come from the precious ore of Mount Pangeo. The deposits – gold, silver and other metals – were situated on the lower slopes which rise directly above the road. At (or near) Eleftheroupoli, now a tobacco-growing centre, Thucydides had an estate, whose soil was seamed with veins of gold and to which he retired after the debacle at Amphipolis. It was here, according to Plutarch, that under the shade of a plane tree he began to write his history of the war. When the mines were exhausted is not established, but as late as the first century AD Strabo refers to inhabitants finding nuggets of gold throughout the country between the Strimon and the plains of Philippi.

Round Eleftheroupoli the road skirts the southern end of the plain of Philippi and zigzags down a wooded hillside, offering an enchanting view of the port of **Kavala**, protected by a headland crowned with crenellated Byzantine walls. Colour-washed houses rise steeply up the pine-clad slopes; ferries ply between the port and the offshore island of Thassos. During the campaign of Philippi the galleys of Brutus and Cassius were anchored in the harbour, which was called Neapolis in antiquity. An emporium for the tobacco-growing plains of the hinterland, the port was a bone of contention between Greece and Bulgaria for many years. In both World Wars the Bulgarians seized and occupied it, but have left no trace of a Slav minority behind them. Today it is the second largest town in Northern Greece and, although the central area is dominated by large, modern buildings, it is still one of the most attractive, with its gaily painted houses (interspersed with a few crumbling neo-classical nineteenth-century mansions) mounting in terraces up a crescent-shaped screen of wooded hills, its animated waterfront and the picturesqueness of its old Turkish quarters.

It is worth spending a day in Kavala. The **Museum** lies near the

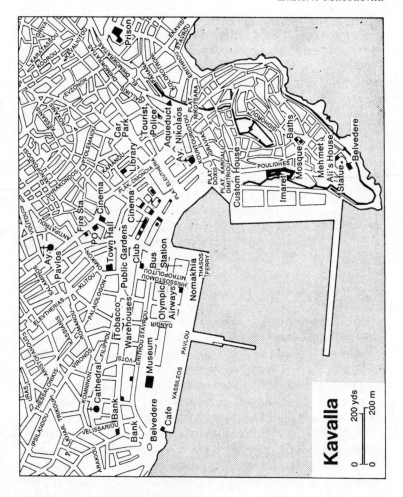

285

tobacco warehouses, west of the waterfront. In the Neapolis hall (first on the left) are fragments of seventh-, sixth- and fifth-century BC pottery, terracotta figurines and two squat fifth-century BC fluted columns with elaborate Ionic capitals from the Temple of Parthenos, the virgin goddess of Neapolis. However the Amphipolis hall (second on the left) is more rewarding. There is a delicate mid-fourth-century BC ewer with two gilded wreaths, a fourth-century BC statuette of a siren in a state of exaltation and a fourth-century BC *stele* of a funeral banquet in which a reclining male figure (the departed soul) is surrounded by his mourning wife, children and attendants. But the most impressive object is a restoration of a Macedonian tomb from Amphipolis faced with fragments of original frescoes. A gold wreath and a beautifully shaped silver hand-mirror, found in the tomb, are displayed in a special showcase. Like the exhibits in the museum at Thessaloniki, they tell the same story: the sculptor's art in Northern Greece never achieved the perfection reached in Southern Greece; but in the Hellenistic age the Macedonian artist's observation of nature, his sense of fantasy and delight in variety seldom fails to charm.

'Old' Kavala is worth visiting, and it can be seen in a leisurely two-hour walk. It is best to start from Eleftheria Square and bear east along Omonoia Street to the conspicuous landmark of the sixteenth-century Turkish aqueduct, known as the *Kamares*, straddling an isthmus which joins a fortified bluff to the mainland.

From the aqueduct one returns to the old port and follows Poulides Street, climbing the west side of the headland, along the ridge of which run well-preserved Byzantine walls. This is the heart of the old Turkish quarter: a maze of steep alleys and sudden unexpected declivities. On the right extend low, shallow-domed buildings which compose into Mehmet Ali's *Imaret*, an almshouse for the aged and needy, which is wretchedly dilapidated. Unfortunately Greek nationalism precludes the conservation, let alone restoration, of monuments built during the centuries of subjugation. But in spite of the delay and neglect, the *Imaret* still reflects a forgotten aspect of a vanished Moslem world. A colonnade surmounted by eighteen metal-sheeted tea-cosy domes surrounds a sunken, irregular-shaped courtyard. Here the aged turbaned figures would wander, when they were not snoozing in the cells which contained three hundred divans. At the southern end of the court a convex projection like a bastion, surrounded by a water conduit where the old men performed their ablutions, supports a domed mosque with a portico overlooking the court. A second colonnaded court, square this time and full of the sound of cooing doves, has the remains of fretwork screens between square columns. The sunken courts are now deserted. A place of oblivion – little more than a hundred years old.

Beyond the *Imaret*, Poulides Street mounts to a belvedere overlooking the island-studded Thracian sea. A pedestal is crowned by a bronze equestrian statue of Mehmet Ali, his scimitar drawn, mounted on a splendidly caparisoned horse impatiently pawing the ground. A prosperous Albanian farmer, born in Kavala in 1769, Mehmet Ali was to become Pasha of Egypt and founder of the Egyptian royal dynasty which ended with Farouk. Beside the statue is his birthplace, a rambling Turkish house in an excellent state of preservation, thanks to the care and money expended on it by the Egyptian Government. From the kitchens and storerooms of the ground floor one ascends to a harem with latticed shutters. Here are arranged the broad divans where the little ladies, showing nothing but their dark, doe-like eyes above their yashmaks, reclined, eating syrupy sweetmeats. The primitive bathroom, in which the ladies stood while attendants poured water all over them, is only surpassed in stark simplicity by the lavatory – a triangular hole in the ground. In Mehmet Ali's study, which communicates with smaller chambers where his scimitar-armed bodyguards kept watch, one relic remains: his writing-desk, adorned with framed photographs of all the members of the dynasty. An elaborate tomb, in which Mehmet's mother is buried, embellishes a shady garden full of birds and well-tended flower-beds.

Fifteen kilometres inland, the ruins of **Philippi** extend across a fertile plain at the foot of a pyramid-shaped hill. From no other point is Mount Pangeo – a huge isolated cone rising out of the aspen-studded fields – seen to better advantage. Originally Crenides, the place was renamed Philippi and fortified by Philip of Macedon, who needed the gold of Mount Pangeo to wage the wars that would make him master of Greece. In 42 BC Philippi became famous as a battleground when the two largest Roman armies ever

287

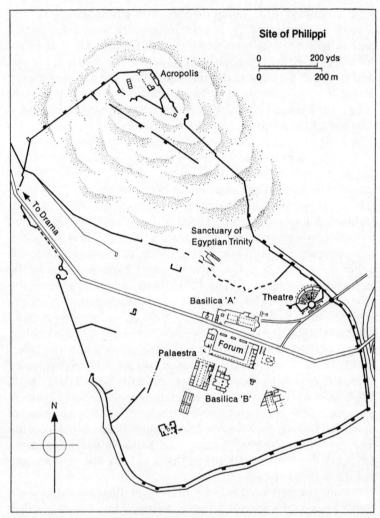

Site of Philippi

engaged in hostilities against each other manoeuvred across the plain, much of which was then a marsh. The strategic importance of the site of this decisive battle is self-evident, for it guarded that part of the Via Egnatia which passes through a narrow defile and ensured the security of Neapolis and the maintenance of maritime communications with Asia Minor.

288

The Battle of Philippi, inevitable result of the struggle for power following Julius Caesar's murder, consisted of two separate engagements, both fought west of the town between the marsh and the eastern ring of hills, both initiated by the Republican leaders – Brutus and Cassius – who seem to have repeated Pompey's mistake at Pharsalia, that is, provoking an untimely head-on clash instead of trying to wear the enemy down. In the first engagement, Octavian, feeling wretchedly ill, was completely routed by Brutus' legions. The sickly future master of the world escaped capture by fleeing to Antony's camp. Also in this engagement Cassius, warned by unfavourable omens, was worsted by Antony and, in his despair, committed suicide. Deeply distressed by the death of his friend, Brutus decided to 'try fortune in a second fight'. However, this time Antony's legions infiltrated the Republicans' position and Brutus was trapped and overwhelmed. Thus perished the Roman Republic on the marshy fields of Thrace. The way now lay open for a final struggle, eleven years later at Actium, between the two victors of Philippi. After that battle Octavian, now Augustus Caesar, remembered the strategic value and agricultural wealth of the plain and sent colonists to Philippi, so that by the time of St Paul's visit it was a completely Roman city, its wide and beautiful streets crowded with strutting praetors, lictors and magistrates.

The religion of the people was still that of the indigenous Thracians, who worshipped the goddess Bendis, an Underworld deity, and the heroic Thracian Horseman. The official faith of the governing class, of course, was that of Pagan Rome. Such was the religious background which St Paul found when he reached Philippi; beside a stream outside the city he met and baptized Lydia and her household. However neither the Thracian multitude nor the Roman magistrates took kindly to the Apostle's exorcism of a soothsaying damsel's evil spirit; so they rent his and Silas' clothes in the market place and cast them into prison.

The ruins, Early-Christian rather than Roman, are extensive, impressive and easy to identify. From the entrance gate (immediately right of the road from Kavala), you climb a stairway and turn north (left) to reach a confusing mass of rubble which has been labelled **Basilica A**, probably destroyed in an earthquake. Dated to the fifth century, it is an aisled basilica with transepts and a semi-circular apse. Among the debris are several fragments of the sculptural decoration that once adorned the interior: Corinthian capitals, pieces of cornice, carved plaques and column bases. The marbles, grey and Thessalian, must have added splendour to the scene as the sun's rays, piercing the clerestory below the timber roof, fell obliquely across the colonnades separating the aisles. With the eclipse of the Roman Empire in the West, the Via Egnatia had declined in importance, and Philippi may no longer have been an important commercial centre; but the size of its churches and their surviving decoration provide evidence of the city's prominence as a place of pilgrimage, the first in Europe at which the Gospel was preached.

Immediately below Basilica A, a barrel-vaulted chamber is said to have been the **prison of St Paul**. But nothing remains of the doors that the earthquake caused to open, rocking the foundation of the cell and loosening the prisoners' bonds, whereupon the panic-stricken guards were promptly converted and the Romans, both frightened by the earthquake and tired of the Apostle's nuisance value, let him and Silas go unmolested on their way to Amphipolis.

From here a path climbs to the terrace of the **Sanctuary of the Egyptian Trinity**, where more than one *cella* and the remains of stuccoed walls are discernible. The incongruity is bewildering. It is difficult to avoid a feeling of historical and geographical disorientation. Flying insects sting one and lizards slither across the path as the ascent grows steeper until one reaches the summit of the conical hill which dominates the ruined city. Traceable fragments of the medieval enceinte are superimposed on the fourth-century BC walls, with three towers silhouetted against the skyline.

Starting from Basilica A again and following a southerly course, one passes first a series of curious rock-hewn chambers: tall vertical niches, possibly connected with the worship of Bendis; then a railed-in enclosure with a well-preserved chequered marble pavement and two tall columns crowned with impost capitals. Finally one reaches the **Theatre**. Originally a Hellenistic edifice, it was remodelled in the second century to suit Roman tastes, with an unusually large orchestra to allow sufficient room for gladiatorial shows. The original Greek proscenium was removed to make way for more showy imperial embellishments. There are about half-a-dozen Roman tiers built of limestone, the rest of the *cavea* being somewhat tastelessly restored in the late 1950s. From the topmost tier, alongside which ran a vaulted gallery, there is a fine view across the agricultural plain to a ridge of wooded hills separating the hinterland from the sea.

But the more impressive ruins lie east of the road, opposite Basilica A, on flat ground. First there is the rectangle of the **Forum**, on a truly Roman scale, much of it dated to the reign of Marcus Aurelius. Little remains standing above waist-level, but many of the stone and marble slabs, carved with Latin inscriptions, are of great size. With a little patience and imagination, one can identify the main features: the foundations of two temples at the north-east and north-west angles and a library on the east side; to the north a stepped tribune, whence St Paul probably preached the Word. Around it lie fragments of Roman statues. At the south-east end fluted columns stand on huge plinths; at the west end is a well-preserved stretch of paved road, flanked by a parapet with a row of slender unfluted columns. The havoc and destruction is nightmarish and the sheets of forget-me-not that carpet the ground and the clusters of asphodel that sprout from crannies in the shattered masonry in spring only seem to emphasize the totality of the city's ruin. Recent excavations have revealed the foundations of an Early-Christian octagonal church, which had an altar on one side and colonnades on the other seven.

Immediately west of the forum extend the ruins of Philippi's chief glory, **Basilica B**, the warm, cream-coloured stone of its surviving piers dominating the ruins. Dated to the reign of Justinian, the plan in itself must have been exciting: a domed basilica, with an additional cupola above the sanctuary taller and higher than the shallow one covering the nave. These were lighted by a clerestory and preceded by a vaulted narthex with three entrances. But disaster intervened before the intriguing architectural experiment, which represented a step in the transition between the Hellenistic-style basilica and the Byzantine domed church, could be completed. The great dome above the sanctuary collapsed and the architects lost heart; the would-be great church remained unfinished and was never consecrated.

The sanctuary arch, a perfect ellipse of brick, is flanked by piers composed of rectangular slabs of re-used ancient masonry. At the north-east end rises another pier with courses of carved decoration. On the east side stand two truncated columns of tessellated marble. The sculptured decoration is of the highest order and all the Early-Christian love of zoological and botanical detail, inherited from Hellenistic Asia and pagan Rome, is exploited. Most beautiful of all are the two nave capitals and imposts which crown pieces of a pillar and a base. The acanthus leaves, which appear to grow organically from roots embedded in the impost, are so beautifully and so deeply carved that, with sunlight playing on them, they appear to be real.

Passing through the horseshoe-shaped sanctuary arch of the basilica, one enters the pagan *palaestra*. Apart from a fine acanthus-leaf capital, the debris of this ancient exercise-ground for Macedonian and Roman youth conveys little to the unprofessional eye. To the south-west there is a remarkable, if unbeautiful, monument of Roman times: seven steps descend to a doorway, crowned by a well-preserved lintel, leading into a rectangular sunken court which served as a latrine. The marble seats are ranged in rows along the sides of three walls. I counted more than twenty in a tolerable state of preservation.

East of the ancient enceinte extend the foundations of the **Basilica 'Extra Muros'**, littered with slabs, which may have been a fourth-century edifice, subsequently restored and modified. Its main interest lies in the sixteen crypts below what was once the nave which, according to epitaphs discovered *in situ*, were the sepulchres of distinguished Philippian prelates. Fragments of floor mosaic are also preserved.

East of Kavala the road crosses open country as far as the village of Paradeisos, where there are some attractive Turkish-style whitewashed houses with wide eaves, overlooking the **Nestos** as it flows between poplar-lined sandbanks out of a narrow gorge, against a background of wooded hills. The road only partly penetrates the intricacies of the Nestos Gorge, following the railway designed (in the nineteenth century by the Turkish rulers of Macedonia) to follow a course that would not lie within the range of the guns of the Greek fleet. This railway follows an extraordinarily roundabout route from Xanthi to Drama – obviously conceived in purely military terms – but it gives the traveller the opportunity to see a part of Greece that is not covered in the normal itinerary by car. At first the defile is sombre and constricted, with the river flowing swiftly between precipitous cliffs eroded into strange forms studded with evergreens; but the gorge opens out, the aspect becomes grander; the banks are lined with poplars and the higher levels with ilex, pines and Judas trees.

Drama, the ancient Drabescus, where the Athenian colonizers of Amphipolis, venturing too far inland, were cut off from their base and slaughtered by Thracian tribesmen, lies at the foot of Mount Falakro, but the town has little to offer. Southward extends the tobacco-growing country, the so-called 'golden plain'. The road runs south–west, under the shadow of Mount Pangeo, buttressed by subsidiary ranges. After Seres the road to Bulgaria turns sharply to the north, towards **Sidirokastro**, picturesquely situated at the foot of rocky hills, one of which is crowned, as the town's name implies, by an 'iron castle'. To the north rise the gloomy ranges of Bulgaria, the Beles mountains, at the base of which the road joins the upper reaches of the Strimon where it emerges from the Rupel Pass: a strategic point for every invader, commanding the wedge-shaped Strimonic basin, key to all Eastern Macedonia. Turning west after Sidirokastro the road and railway fringe the east shore of Lake Doirani, where scattered hamlets spread across the border of Greece and Jugoslavia. They then turn sharply to the south and, beyond Kilkis, a garrison town at the foot of the Krousia mountains, descend towards Thessaloniki along the banks of the Galikos river.

CHAPTER 19

The Thracian Plains

Xanthi – Abdera – Komotini – Alexandroupoli –
Trajanopolis – Feres: Church of the Dormition –
The Evros – Didimotiho: The Turkish Border.

East of the Nestos extends the modern province of Thrace, which
remained under Turkish rule until 1913. Flat fields of corn and
tobacco-growing plains, unrelieved by groves, woods or vineyards –
only the occasional poplar or aspen – are enclosed between the sea
and the Rodopi mountains. Painted carts rattle along side-roads
and groups of dark-skinned Sarakatsans, members of nomadic and
self-contained ethnic communities found all over Northern and
Western Greece, stare sullenly at strangers from their fields. Some
villages are still largely inhabited by Turks who, though Greek
subjects, still speak their own tongue, attend their own schools and
worship at their own mosques.

It can all be seen in a day. If the traveller, motoring to or from
Turkey, wishes to spend a night in a Thracian town, Alexandroupoli
seems the obvious halt: it has the best hotels and an airport. It is a
journey into an incongruously un-Greek world. The prairies,
traversed by muddy streams, and the barrier of the Balkan ranges
shrouded in haze or cloud, have little in common with the shimmering plains of Greece encircled by their grandiose mountains. The
light, landscape, architecture, even the people, herald a new climate. It is, in fact a prolonged frontier region, with the Turkish
border as the goal.

Xanthi is the first stop. Vasileous Constantinou Square, with its
little *hamman* and clock-tower, is the town's main hub. Even the
kiosks have Turkish-style pointed roofs, once crowned with cres-

cents. North of the square there is a fruit-market bordered by rows of red *kilims* – brightly coloured, handwoven rugs – hanging out to dry on wires. Pigeons murmur in acacia trees, and rivulets flow under miniature arched Turkish bridges. North-east of the market, cypresses surround a fine minaret against a background of steep pine-clad hills, across the higher slopes of which spread the whitewashed buildings of a monastery. Another hill to the west is crowned by the ruins of a medieval castle which once guarded the opening of the defile from Bulgar invasions.

From Xanthi you cross the flat cultivated plain in a south-easterly direction and then turn south. To the north extends the chain of the Rodopi mountains: stony, inhospitable, matt-grey in colour. At the end of the road, remote and deserted on the shore of a lagoon-like inlet, lies the site of **Abdera**, founded, according to legend, by Heracles, in honour of his favourite, the youth Abderus, who was devoured by the man-eating mares of Diomedes, King of Thrace. This ancient city was famous throughout Greece for its beautiful coinage and also, incongruously, for the dullness of its inhabitants; but today the ruins are insignificant. Xerxes was entertained here with such pomp in the summer of 480 BC that the inhabitants were crippled financially. However on his less triumphal return journey, he remembered their hospitality and had the grace to present them with 'a tiara and scimitar of gold'.

The rocky coastline sweeps westward in a large crescent, the southern end of which gives the impression of being joined to the island of Thassos. There is no lonelier maritime site in Greece. At the end of the road, beside the sea, are the foundations of a large Hellenistic edifice consisting of two courts and twenty-six chambers, all filled with slimy water. Frogs keep up an interminable croaking and mosquitoes whine overhead. There are some slabs of masonry, some foundation stones and a single broken column – little else.

One rejoins the main road which makes for the coast again further to the east. On one side extend salt-pans, on the other a huge muddy lagoon, pear-shaped, famous for duck-shooting. The fishing village of Lagos is remarkable for the intricacy of the channels joining the lagoon with the sea and for its Church of *Agios Nikolaos* squatting on an island in a shallow inlet. Waterfowl fly overhead, and innumerable causeways cross the lagoon, giving one a strange feeling of disorientation. The road veers inland across the cattle-grazing ground to **Komotini**, capital of Thrace.

A market centre for tobacco and agricultural produce, it possesses the largest Turkish minority in Thrace; in streets and cafés the strident, peacock-like screech of Greek women contrasts strangely with the soft lilting cadences of Turkish men. The tempo is slower than elsewhere. But if the atmosphere is Turkish it possesses little oriental glamour. The tiny minority of Bulgarian-speaking Pomaks, a swarthy taciturn people – the Bulgarian frontier lies only fourteen miles to the north – makes little impact. In Hephaestus Street, appropriately lined with coppersmiths' shops, the Mosque of *Yeni Djami*, its wide dome crowned by a gold crescent, is surrounded by a grove of seedy-looking cypresses. Elderly Turks in baggy black breeches pace up and down the entrance court, exchanging agricultural gossip; others, removing sweat-soaked shoes, pad across striped *kilims* to kneel in worship before the *mihrab*. The Mosque of *Eski Djami* in Chrysanthos Square is less picturesque: box-shaped, with yellow walls pierced by white-arched window frames. The minaret is striking and, like all minarets, beautiful in itself, with two balconies carved with elaborate fret-work. For the traveller coming from Turkey, however, neither mosque is really worth bothering about.

The Komotini–Alexandroupoli road is remarkable only for a Roman bridge crossing the Filiouri stream, followed by the almost wholly Turkish-speaking village of **Sapes**, where there is a curious minaret, belly-shaped in the centre. The Rodopi chain recedes to the north, towards the western spurs of Mount Haemus, among whose uninviting fastnesses the Thracian Dionysus had a sanctuary. After climbing scrub-covered hills the road descends through olive groves – a rare sight in north-eastern Greece – to a flat, unbroken coastline and the town of **Alexandroupoli** which has little to offer but some wide streets and a claustrophobic provincial air. It is, however, a useful base for travellers bound for the Evros valley and has a small port with a ferry service to Samothraki.

One continues along the course of the Via Egnatia. Fifteen kilometres east of Alexandroupoli a hill to the north, said to be an extinct volcano, marks the site of **Trajanopolis**, an important station founded by the Emperor Trajan. The scattered masonry on the northern bank of the River Tsai is Roman, incorporated into later Byzantine defence works. All this country was once peppered with Roman forts and strategic points guarding the vital highway.

Seven kilometres beyond Trajanopolis a signpost points the way to **Doriscus**, where there are no ruins, but where Xerxes built a fortress and stopped to count the troops of his mammoth army. The grand total, says Herodotus, probably exaggerating, 'turned out to be 1,700,000'. The counting, he continues,

> was done by first packing ten thousand men as close together as they could stand and drawing a circle round them on the ground; they were then dismissed and a fence was constructed round the circle; finally other troops were marched into the area thus enclosed and dismissed in their turn, until the whole army had been counted.

Beyond the fork to Doriscus the road veers north, up the Evros basin, with the mountains of Turkish Thrace rising in the east. The country around here enjoyed considerable prosperity, with a corresponding increase in population, for the Comnene emperors rightly considered it a vital area, guarding the approaches to Constantinople from the West. It is worth stopping at **Feres**, a dusty village, which is entered across a ruined aqueduct with a Gothic arch. The village is centred around the twelfth-century Byzantine **Church of the Koimesis**, most of the exterior of which is now unfortunately covered with puce-coloured wash. Its proportions are sturdy and harmonious, with five domes, a spacious apse and three recessed blind arches reinforced by four buttresses. Traces of tile decoration, both in the apse and on the small south-east dome, as well as a plaque with an effigy of an heraldic eagle on the wall below the south-east dome, indicate that the church was no mere provincial house of worship. In the interior there are vestiges of frescoes which are obviously not the work of a provincial iconographer.

Past Feres the road to Didimotiho, and the north-eastern border with Turkey, leaves the Istanbul highway, which follows the Via Egnatia, and passes through featureless country associated only with the march of countless conquerors. The Persian army, composed of small, dark-skinned men wearing soft felt caps, embroidered tunics and coats of mail, and armed with spears, cane arrows and wicker shields, tramped past here in 480 BC.

Soon the wide stream of the Evros appears, winding between fields and orchards: a frontier made by geography it would seem, to end the ancient feud between Greek and Turk. The road passes through Soufli, centre of the silkworm trade; a green hill overlooking mulberry orchards, often flooded by the fast-flowing river. The banks are fringed with reeds which the inhabitants cut into strips in order to make brooms. Among its sandbanks gold was once found, says Pliny, and nearly two thousand years later a French nineteenth-century traveller saw men searching the sands for the grains of gold that had been washed down from the river's Bulgarian sources.

At last, out of the flat watery expanse rises the circular hill of **Didimotiho**, crowned by the ruins of its medieval castle and surrounded on almost all sides by tributaries of the Evros. This is the end – ultimate objective of the traveller in north-east Greece. Beyond lies Turkey. The climb up the hill is steep, short and rewarding. It is best to start at the little Church of *Agia Marina* on the west side, where crumbling bastions covered with lichen overlook the tree-lined banks of numerous streams. Passing through an arched gateway you wind up the slope, pitted with caves in which dwell ragged, dark-skinned gypsies, surrounded by barking watchdogs, while crows squawk overhead. There are well-preserved fragments of defensive walls of Roman, Byzantine and Turkish masonry. The grassy summit is littered with fragments of unidentifiable masonry. The view embraces patchwork fields and fruit orchards – Greek and Turkish – with the streams of the Evros meandering in loops in all directions. There is a feeling of water everywhere. On a hill to the north-east, across one of the tributaries, khaki-clad figures can be seen bustling about parade grounds, barracks and other military installations.

Little is left of the town – a mere frontier-post inhabited by a dwindling population of Greeks and Turks. Beside Demarcheion Square there is a block-like mosque with a tall minaret and a striking view of the castle hill with its ruined towers and walls which mount the slope in oblique parallel lines. In Katsandonis Street there is a Turkish timber-framed house with a perfectly preserved exterior – a fine example of Turkish domestic architecture. After that there is nothing left to do but turn one's back on the east.

CHAPTER 20

The Approach to the Peloponnese: Megaris, the Isthmus and Corinthia

Megara – The Scironian Cliffs – The Canal – Isthmia
– The Heraeion of Perachora – Corinth –
Acro-Corinth – Sicyon – The Stymphalian Lake –
Nemea.

The journey from Athens to Corinth, including deviations to Isthmia and Perachora and the ascent of Acro-Corinth, is easily achieved in one day. The excursion to Sicyon, Stymphalia and Nemea requires another half-day.

From Eleusis the coastal highway continues in a westerly direction, with backward views of the landlocked Bay of Salamis, crowded with laid-up ships. The road then skirts **Megara**, its undistinguished modernity spreading across the plain.

Every spring the Megarian Games were held here. A feature of the Games was the kissing contest between youths, at whose conclusion, says Theocritus, 'whoso sweetliest presses lip upon lip, returns laden with garlands to his mother'. Modern Megarian festivities are of a more conventional nature.

Beyond Megara the old road to Corinth is more interesting than the toll road because it keeps closer to the sea. This coast is haunted by the myths of Theseus and his journey from Troezen to Athens, in the course of which he rid the countryside of several disagreeable characters. The corniche, known as the *Kakia Skala* (The Evil Stairway), is hewn out of the side of the lofty Scironian cliffs and overhangs coves of crystal-clear green water. Beyond the cliffs, pine trees – a particularly vivid shade of emerald green – fringe a long

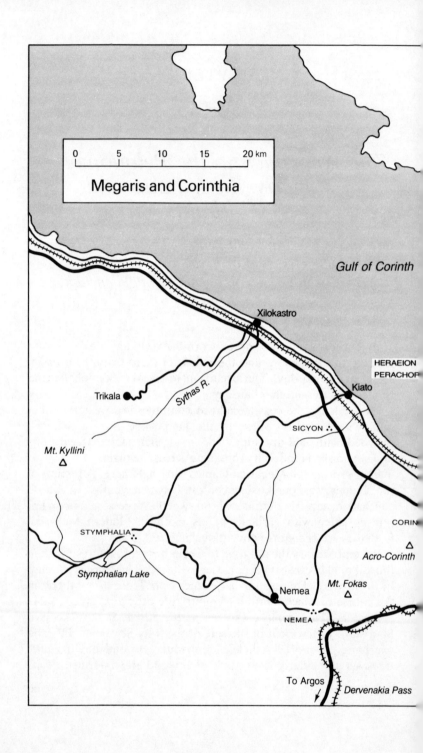

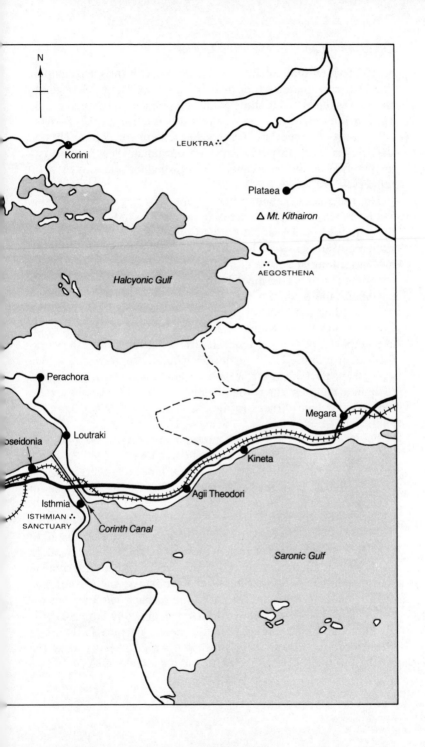

beach of white shingle called Kineta, dotted with villas and camping sites. The currents are strong in this part of the Gulf, which begins to contract as the opposite shore of the Peloponnese draws nearer, and even at the height of summer the sea is relatively cold. Past the village of Agioi Theodoroi (the ancient Krommyon, where Theseus slew Phaea, the Grey Sow who fed on human flesh), there is a terrible blot on the landscape: the sprawling installations of an oil refinery.

The toll road is rejoined just before the bridge over the canal where there is a branch road to Loutraki. The sandy alluvial soil of the Isthmus lies ahead, cut by the **Corinth Canal**, a dead straight ribbon of water between high banks of sand and rock. Three and a half miles long and little more than 100 feet wide, the canal was completed in the late nineteenth century by French and Greek engineers, the project having first been contemplated more than two and a half thousand years before: first by Periander, Tyrant of Corinth; later by the Roman Emperors. In 67 AD Nero went so far as to import thousands of Judaean prisoners to undertake the work, the Emperor himself hacking the first handful of earth with a golden axe. The project, however, was abandoned when he was summoned to Gaul to suppress the revolt of Julius Vindex. The canal shortens the journey from Piraeus to the Adriatic by nearly two hundred nautical miles.

The northward road passes through Loutraki, a popular spa, before climbing inland to the town of Perachora. To the west of the town a long promontory of bluish-grey limestone with a jagged ridge projects into the gulf, terminating in the **Heraeion of Perachora**, a sanctuary of the goddess Hera, the earliest records of which date back to the Geometric period. Before reaching the tip of the headland, one passes a tree-fringed lagoon. After turning right at a small chapel traces of ancient masonry begin to appear, and, to the left of the road, there is an Archaic cistern with a subterranean stairway leading down to water level. Climbing down the south side of the headland from the car park, one reaches another cistern – Hellenistic this time – above which are the foundations of the eighth-century BC Temple of Hera Limenia. Further on there is a fifth-century BC *stoa* and a classical altar with *triglyphs* and, to the north of it, the wall of a Geometric apsidal temple of Hera Acraia.

West of the latter there is a little paved esplanade and the foundations of an Archaic temple, also dedicated to Hera.

It is a remote place: a land's end, crowned by a lighthouse. The little cove at the bottom of the site, the Sacred Harbour, is ideal for deep water bathing. Above rise the steep brush-wood foothills of Yerania with the Halcyonic Gulf to the north. To the south, across the narrow waters of the Corinthian Gulf, the Peloponnesian mountain ranges rise above a fertile coastal belt. When the sea is calm, schools of dolphins follow in the wake of steamers, bounding in and out of the wash; friendliest of animals to men, they were always ready to carry gods and mortals on urgent errands across the ocean.

The first branch road to the left beyond the canal bridge crosses the earthquake-prone Isthmus, covered with thistles and stunted shrubs. The ruins of the **Isthmian Sanctuary**, where the Isthmian Games were held every four years, are close to the eastern entrance of the Canal. Within an enclosure (a few fragments remain on the north side) once lined with statues of famous athletes, are traces of the fifth-century BC Temple of Poseidon. In the stadium on the south side of the Sanctuary, between the temple and the road, is the starting line for races, with the starter's pit and sixteen shallow grooves for cords. These were kept in position by bronze staples and the starter, in his pit, could release the cords simultaneously to start the race with absolute fairness. Nearby are the remains of water conduits and basins. West of the sanctuary there was a theatre, of which only the retaining wall and the foundations of the proscenium remain. The small but well-arranged Museum is worth a visit.

The site shelves down to the apex of the Saronic Gulf, where one can see tugs preparing to pilot ships through the canal. Isthmia had neither the religious significance of Delphi nor the panhellenic spirit of Olympia but during the festival it was the scene of considerable animation, with touts, conjurors and fortune-tellers swarming around the stadium.

South of the Sanctuary are the remains of a fortress built by Justinian in the sixth century as an addition to the Isthmian Wall, itself built by the Spartans in 480 BC. The Wall crossed the Isthmus and the Spartans would have mounted a last-ditch stand here

303

against the Persians if the battle of Salamis had failed to turn the scales against the invaders. In some sections as many as nine courses of fifth-century BC masonry are visible.

From Isthmia a good road skirts the eastern shore of the Argolid as far as Epidavros. The highway itself bypasses Corinth which is reached by another branch road that also leads to the port of Poseidonia. The port is at the western entrance to the canal, where there are traces of the ancient Diolchus, the paved road across which boats were hauled from one sea to the other: a short cut used by Octavian during his pursuit of Antony and Cleopatra after the battle of Actium. Poseidonia is connected with Loutraki by a submersible bridge, the first of its kind in Europe.

Corinth has only stood on its present site since 1858, after the destruction of Old Corinth by a devastating earthquake. Levelled again in 1928, it is an undistinguished modern town. The complex topography – the Isthmus, the two seas, the mainland, the miniature sub-continent – now comes into focus. Corinth is clearly the gateway to the Peloponnese; there is no other land approach. The ruins of **Old Corinth**, one of the most celebrated cities of antiquity, lie to the south, packed into a confined area and superimposed with Roman structures.

The inhabitants of Corinth tended to be mariners. They were the men who founded the colonies of Syracuse and Corcyra in the seventh century BC and who, according to Thucydides, built the first triremes. Their naval enterprise assured the city's commercial pre-eminence, its wealth being increased by the fertility of the coastal plain which extends in a crescent-shaped sweep of vineyards, citrus orchards and olive groves from the base of the 1800-foot-high citadel of Acro-Corinth to the foothills of Sicyon. Wealth promoted luxury, and the Corinthians acquired the reputation of being the most licentious people in Greece. With Aphrodite as patron goddess, the marketplace abounded with prostitutes, often women of refined accomplishments, dedicated to the art of venal love as to a religion, which in fact it was, for they were all priestesses in the temple of Aphrodite. Among the most illustrious was Lais, the modelling of whose bosom was so perfect that painters from all over Greece came to Corinth to reproduce its divine form. Prostitution in Corinth, like pederasty throughout Greece, was not

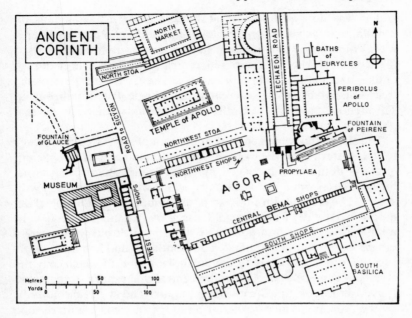

considered a vice, but was an accepted way of life. To abjure either would, for a beautiful girl in Corinth or a handsome youth in any Greek city state, have argued considerable eccentricity.

It was under the vigorous Periander (625–585 BC) that Corinthian trade and navigation began to flourish. Government remained oligarchical, with the well-fed, pleasure-loving merchants showing little interest in the ideals of political democracy. The growth of the democratic Athenian empire aroused their jealousy and consequently Corinth associated herself with Sparta and emerged with considerable benefit from the Peloponnesian War. Eclipse came two and a half centuries later in 146 BC, when the Achaean League, of which Corinth was a member, was foolish enough to challenge the growing might of Rome. The Corinthians went so far as to pour excrement on the heads of the Roman ambassadors from their windows. For this senseless affront they paid with massacre and the sack of their city of Mummius. Corinth literally ceased to exist. The paintings, for which the city was famous, were carried off to Rome

305

and it was not until 46 BC that Julius Caesar made amends by rebuilding the city. When St Paul visited the city a century later it was a flourishing Roman colony; its key position at the crossroads of the Roman world had assured its rebirth. But the Corinthian sky, unlike that of other Greek city states, was never lit with the radiance that emanated from a creative, sophisticated intelligentsia. Throughout history, Corinth remained in virtual intellectual obscurity.

The site of the ruined city lies at the foot of Acro-Corinth, closer to the western than the eastern port. The shambles of the ancient *agora* is dominated by seven massive Doric columns of porous limestone, crowned by flat capitals, which were once covered with stucco. The columns formed part of the **Temple of Apollo**, one of the oldest in Greece, from the golden age of Periander. It was built upon a raised platform and was originally enclosed within a rectangle of monolithic pillars. The southern end of the temple esplanade was bordered by the north-west *stoa*, of which only the stylobate is preserved. Across the central open space of the *agora* (paved in Greek times with large pebbles and with marble slabs by the Romans), once bordered by shops and small temples, one can distinguish a large base with six stone courses in front of the fourth-century BC south *stoa*: the *Bema*, or Roman Governor's tribune. A once-magnificent two-storey building, the *stoa*, whose outer colonnade alone consisted of seventy-one columns (not one survives), was crowded with shops and tavernas, where merchants discussed market prices and local politics.

This was the scene of St Paul's arraignment by the Jewish community, who accused him, in the presence of the Roman governor, of corrupting their faith. At first few Corinthians, Greeks or Jews were impressed by the Apostle's preachings. He was a disturbing element and on one occasion his preaching in the synagogue provoked a riot, in the course of which he was beaten up by Greek hooligans. Nevertheless, he spent eighteen months here, plying his craft of tent-making and preaching the Gospel. He must have been an incongruous figure in this city of the most sophisticated carnal pleasures, picking his way among the affluent merchants and flamboyant prostitutes. In those times of political and spiritual upheaval, the pursuit of his missionary task was often put to the severest test. Yet his sojourn in Corinth was not in vain, for it inspired the two great *Letters* that proved to be among the most profoundly formative influences in the development of the Christian faith.

At the north end of the *agora* there is a ruined Roman gateway, the Lechaeon, once surmounted by two gilded chariots in which Helios and Phaethon, the sun-god and his offspring, were to be seen riding across the heavens. The road which connected Corinth with its port entered the city through this gateway. The outline of the road, paved with limestone slabs in the first century AD, is plainly visible and the paving is well-preserved in parts. It follows an almost straight line, once flanked by shops behind colonnades (a few truncated columns survive), now cutting across fields of thistle and stubble.

To the east of the gateway lies the most attractive extant monument on the site: the **Fountain of Peirene**, a lady who was turned into a spring because of the unquenchable tears she shed for her son, accidentally killed by Artemis. Six rectangular chambers, each faced with an arch during the Roman period, contain basins connected with an underground reservoir fed by two different springs. Long before the Romans came, Pindar had admired the fountain and described Corinth as 'the city of Peirene'. Situated in the centre of the *agora*, the spring was adorned with successive architectural embellishments from the sixth century BC to Byzantine times. In the second century AD Herodes Atticus had the entire front faced with marble. In front of the middle arch stand two columns, one crowned by a Corinthian capital. It is pleasant to sit in the shade of the arches and listen to the water trickling behind the dark chambers. Here the ancient *archons* of Corinth gathered on summer evenings to play draughts and dice. At a later period the gardens of the Turkish governor extended around the fountain.

The **museum**, notable for its wide range of terracotta vases, *kraters*, *amphorae* and other ceramics, lies to the south of the Temple of Apollo. Of the famous Corinthian paintings, only the lively bird and animal designs on the vases remain to remind us that Corinth, despite its lack of intellectual pretensions, was a centre of painters and craftsmen. Up to the sixth century BC large quantities of ceramics were exported to Italy; Corinthian potters, unlike those of Attica, were chiefly interested in the export trade. In spite of mass production, the quality of their products remained high until the middle of the sixth century when the Athenians captured the principal markets. The designs became larger and coarser; there was more lavish use of reddish-purple paint, and rosettes and other floral motifs were employed to fill in an already crowded background. Among the more impressive ceramics in the museum are an eighth-century BC three-legged pitcher with elaborate geometric decoration and stylized deer on the upper band (Case 11); a beautiful *amphora* and *oinoche* (pouring jug) of the seventh century BC, exquisite in shape, supremely elegant in floral and animal design (Case 15); and a late Corinthian *aryballos* (c. 580 BC) depicting a *choragus* leading a dance chorus of black male figures (Case 15). Other exhibits include a mosaic of pebbles (one of the earliest in Greece, c. 400 BC) depicting griffons mauling a horse (vestibule, No. 5); and votive offerings to Asclepius, god of healing, representing the afflicted limbs, breasts, genitals – even a hand with a cancerous growth – successfully treated by the god (west wall of the Asclepion room).

After leaving the museum one can sit in the village square before climbing the great rock of **Acro-Corinth**, which is dominant and aggressive but fits harmoniously into the complex configuration of land and sea. The view from the top is tremendous. In the immediate foreground the fertile strip extends to the wooded hills of Kyllini which rise to barren peaks, metal-coloured in a cloudless sky. The mountains of the Argolid, strangely eroded shapes, roll southwards; to east and west lie the two seas, separated by the Isthmus; to the north, behind the tapering headland of Perachora, extends the placid expanse of the Halcyonic Gulf bounded by Mount Helikon. To the north-west, the hazy massif of Parnassos exercises its eternal fascination.

Although there are remains of Byzantine, Frankish and Turkish fortifications, it is the skill of the Venetian military architects that is most striking: in the watch-towers, the crenellated ramparts and the three imposing gateways connected by ramps. The route followed from the entrance is very steep. You first cross the shallow moat, once spanned by a drawbridge, and pass through the outer gate to the second line of defence. The successive levels of formidable masonry, which seem to grow organically out of the increasingly precipitous incline, permitted the defenders to annihilate all assailants with a devastating plunging fire. After passing through another gate, which is square outside with an arched passage within, paths lead to the two peaks. The steep path to the right leads to the lower, west peak and the ruins of a Frankish dungeon. Following the main path one first passes the shell of a ruined mosque behind which is a postern (scattered all round here are vestiges of former chapels, minarets, barrack-rooms). Climbing up along a trough of ground overgrown with spiky shrubs and long grass, the path winds up to the east peak, once crowned by a temple of Aphrodite, where the goddess of love was worshipped in the most sumptuous manner. Within the ring of fortifications there is not a single habitation, not a single living creature, except the odd sightseer, ants, bees and lizards.

The highway from Corinth to Patras runs inland: it is faster, but less interesting than the old road which runs through flowery villages among orchards and vineyards. As the season advances, pale blue hydrangeas and climbing roses are succeeded by the scarlet of hibiscus and the confetti-pink of oleander; in the late summer, multi-coloured dahlias replace the scorched sunflowers. Bicycles, geese, hens and carts clutter the road. At Kiato, two roads climb up into the hills. The first ends just beyond the village of Vasiliko, at the ruins of **Sicyon**, one of the most beautiful minor ancient sites in the Peloponnese.

The recently restored **museum**, once the site of the Roman baths, contains Corinthian pottery, figurines and Roman mosaics. The hill to the south rises to a triangular tableland on two levels, defended on both sides by shallow precipices. The ancient city extended to the north along the ground which descends to the sea, the existing ruins being those of the Hellenistic town founded by Demetrius Peliorcetes in 293 BC during his attempt to wrest most of Greece from the rival aspirants to the throne of Alexander the Great. He concentrated the city around its citadel and, in his usual extrovert way, gave it the name of Demetrias. In the Greek mind, however, it always remained Sicyon – 'the town of cucumbers'.

It was in the seventh century BC that the salubrious little town, open to all the breezes of the Corinthian Gulf, began to acquire

309

political prominence under the rule of Orthogoras who founded a Sicyonian dynasty which lasted over a hundred years and whose government was praised by Aristotle for its tolerance. But Sicyon's national hero did not emerge until the third century BC when the city was governed by a usurper-tyrant. Aratus, the exiled heir to the throne, stole up on a moonless night with a handful of patriots and, despite the alarm sounded by a pack of howling dogs, scaled the walls. The coup came off and it became Aratus's life-work to strengthen the Achaean League and break the stranglehold of the warring Macedonian Diadochi. He was buried at Sicyon with great pomp after being poisoned by Philip V, the able, if contemptible, Macedonian king. In the first century AD the city was destroyed by a terrible earthquake, and when Wheler visited the site in the seventeenth century he found it inhabited by only 'three families of Turks and about as many Christians'.

From the triangular shelf of ground, green fields descend to the coast; across the Gulf, Parnassos and Helikon provide a dramatic backcloth, with the hump of Acro-Corinth in the east. On the other side of the road, opposite the museum, lies the outline of the Bouleuterion. Following the path up the hill to the south, you reach the gymnasium on a cool, windy site. It was built on two levels surrounded by colonnades: the lower, Ionic; the upper, Doric. Unfortunately only one column remains, but a stone fountain embellishes the southern embankment of the lower gymnasium.

It is a pity that there is not a single statue left to recall the fact that Sicyon was once an important artistic centre, the site of one of the earliest schools of statuary and painting in Greece. Lysippus was born here, and Apelles – most celebrated of Greek painters – came here to acquire a final polish to his style. Pliny says that drawing in outline was invented by a native of Sicyon, which he calls 'the home of painting'. The city was also a centre of fashion, famous for the taste and skill shown by the weavers and cutters of the flowing garments worn by its inhabitants.

Above the gymnasium is the theatre. Scheduled for restoration, the tiers were intersected by as many as sixteen stairways – an unusually large number in relation to the modest size of the auditorium. Apart from its position and its solitude, there is the novelty of approaching the *cavea* through one of the two vaulted passages. The cavity in the proscenium was intended for the appearance of figures from the Underworld. At the top of the hill is the outline of the stadium, overgrown with corn. All over the hillside, broken slabs of limestone are concealed among thistles, mullein and pungently scented shrubs.

The other road from Kiato also leads southward, but climbs much higher, winding through clefts and gulleys filled with thickets of cypresses, towards the windy plateau around the base of Mount Kyllini. By the time the coast is out of sight, a virtual boundary has been crossed. We are no longer in Corinthia, but on the northern fringe of Arcadia. The narrow upland valleys converge on a six-mile-long plain. Savage mountains crowd in on all sides. To the north rises the formidable mass of Kyllini, slate-grey, breathtaking in its cruel desolation. A projecting spur, Mount Stymphalus, rises sheer from the plain and at the southern end below Mount Apelaurum the waters of the **Stymphalian Lake** flow into a subterranean channel. Tall reeds, some fields of maize and a few poplar trees border the shallow lake, which shrinks considerably in summer, and is full of weeds and patches of waterlilies. The waters of the lake, fed by mountain streams, are ice-cold, even at the height of summer. Nothing could be less 'Arcadian' than this forbidding place.

The road skirts the western shore. To the left rises the shell of a Gothic church, a foundation of the Crusaders, with three naves and windows with pointed arches. A little further on to the left are the negligible remains of an ancient acropolis on a little rocky promontory jutting out into the marsh. There are vestiges of a temple of Athena Polias, and to the south-west, traces of foundations of public buildings, often submerged when the water level of the lake rises. Past the lake the road rises into the pine forest to end at a pleasant hotel.

Before Stymphalia a road to the east crosses the saddle of a jagged mountain and descends into hilly vine country with streams, poplars and some cultivation. Under shady plane trees women wash clothes in troughs, to the accompaniment of the furious chirping of cicadas in the long, scorched grass. Opposite modern Nemea a little monastery clings picturesquely to the side of a cliff. The road crosses another hill and enters a narrow vine-clad valley three miles long and less than a mile wide, where the village of Heraklion marks the site of ancient Nemea.

Never a township, **Nemea** was a sanctuary of Zeus where one of the four great panhellenic athletic festivals was held. The grove of cypresses that surrounded the sanctuary has disappeared, but dwarf cypresses grow in profusion on the neighbouring hills. To the north-east, flat-topped Mount Fokas looks as though its summit has been sliced off by a gigantic axe.

The origin of the Nemean Games lies in a melancholy event; ancient Greek athletics, like the games organized by Achilles round the funeral pyre of Patroclus, are often associated with ceremonies intended to speed the passage of souls to Elysium. One day Opheltes, the child of a priest of Zeus, was laid by his mother upon a bed of wild celery in a meadow at Nemea, while she fetched water from the spring for the seven Argive leaders bound for the siege of Thebes. On her return she found the child poisoned by a snake-bite. The Seven then founded the Games to commemorate the child's death. Thereafter judges at the Nemean festival wore black in mourning for Opheltes. The victor's crown was of wild celery.

The grove in which the Games were held was crowded with public buildings. Of these, only the fourth-century BC **Temple of Zeus** has survived. It marks the transitional period between Classical and Hellenistic Doric, and the influence of Scopas, who designed the temple at Tegea is evident. It had twelve limestone columns at the sides and six at either end. Three, of which two support a fragment of architrave, still rise from the stylobate – a pleasing landmark among the vineyards. The columns are unusually slender and their height is thereby apparently increased. To the south-east are the remains of the theatre, the stadium and the hippodrome. The museum contains the usual archaeological miscellany. A hillock to the south is supposed to be the funeral mound raised over the tomb of Opheltes.

The Games, consisting of running in armour, discus-throwing, chariot-racing, throwing the javelin, shooting with the bow, boxing and wrestling, were held every second year. By the sixth century BC the festival had acquired the status of a panhellenic assembly and to win the crown of wild celery was the aim of every Greek athlete.

Five kilometres beyond the sanctuary the road joins the main highway into the Argolid. In this undulating plain, surrounded by deeply eroded foothills, one of the decisive battles of the War of Independence was fought, when the northbound army of Dramali Pasha was ambushed by the Greeks as it emerged from a narrow gorge. The church of St Saviour, visible from the road and surrounded by cypresses on the side of a steep hill, commemorates the victory. A large Turkish army was wiped out by 2000 Greeks, aided by contingents of armed peasants from neighbouring villages. The Greeks captured an immense booty and horses' skeletons littered the highway for years.

From here one can either return to Corinth or enter the narrow pass of Dervenakia (which follows the course of a dried-up torrent, its stony banks bordered with oleanders) to cross into Argolis.

CHAPTER 21

The Argolid: The Homeric Plain

Mycenae: The Lion Gate; The Royal Grave Circle;
The Palace; The Second Grave Circle;
The Treasury of Atreus; The Tomb of Clytemnestra –
The Argive Heraeion –
Argos: The Larissa; The Roman Baths;
The Theatre; The Museum – Tiryns.

The plain, roughly triangular in shape, opens out to the south after
one has negotiated the Pass of Dervenakia between the twin
summits of Mount Tretos. Taking the mountain as the northern
apex, the great triangle stretches down to the east, towards the
citadel of Nafplio squatting above its pellucid bay and, in the west,
to the conical crag of the Larissa which dominates the town of
Argos. There is a warmth and a radiance in the Homeric plain,
fringed by the Gulf of Argolis, that heralds a new climate. The poet
said that horses were pastured there but, today, flocks of sheep have
replaced the mares of Diomedes and in the evening convoys of
trucks roll northward, loaded with fruit and vegetables for the
Athenian market.

A well-marked turning to the left (east) leads from Fihti through
the modern village of Mycenae, over a line of low hills and between
banks of luxuriant oleanders, towards the ancient site, which overlooks the shimmering plain. There is no shade, but breezes sometimes blow across the two peaks above the citadel and there is a
pungent smell of herbs. As the valley begins to narrow, large slabs
of Cyclopean masonry can be seen on the slopes. With one's back to
the plain, the scene acquires a rugged, denuded aspect. The citadel
of **Mycenae** (once a stronghold of immense strategic importance

girded by formidable walls), crowning a rocky eminence above the confluence of two boulder-strewn ravines, commands the upper part of the Argive plain. In antiquity all the roads from the Gulf of Corinth united here and passed under the great natural bastion.

That Mycenae was influenced by the Minoan civilization has become clear since Heinrich Schliemann, the indigo merchant turned archaeologist, excavated the cities of Agamemnon and Priam, and Sir Arthur Evans, brought up in an environment of more conventional scholarship, revealed the sophisticated splendours of the Palace of Minos. After the destruction of Knossos and the eclipse of Minoan supremacy, leadership of the Aegean basin passed into the hands of the Mycenaeans (c. 1400 BC). As sailors and colonists they surpassed the Minoans, whose trade they absorbed and developed, introducing their civilization into islands as far away as Cyprus. At this time a period of great architectural, even artistic, activity seems to have set in. Grim, barbaric edifices of sun-dried bricks were raised on bases of clay-set rubble. Lime plaster, sometimes decorated with frescoed designs or descriptive scenes, covered the floors and walls; the doors were wooden, the windows small, the roofs flat; baths consisted of pottery tubs. The poorer classes dwelt in huts with floors of beaten earth, but it is no exaggeration to say that Mycenaean palaces, and some of the *tholos* tombs of their kings, are the only buildings in Europe before the Hellenic period in which artistic as well as functional ends were aimed at by the architects.

The view of the citadel is magnificently forbidding: a heap of prehistoric masonry that ascends abruptly out of the gorge, surrounded by huge polygonal walls consisting of limestone slabs skilfully fitted together and of an average weight of six tons. The wall reflects the fierce sunlight beating down on the scorched, treeless terrain. Once the nerve-centre of a maritime empire that dominated the Aegean and produced precious objects of the minor arts that have still to be surpassed for excellence of workmanship and elegance of design, no prehistoric tombs have yielded such varied and sumptuous treasure as those of Mycenae. Various fortified cities were scattered about the plain of Argolis, as well as elsewhere further north, but they all had a common culture centred on Mycenae. Under Agamemnon the Mycenaean kingdom, which included Corinth and Sicyon, led a grand alliance of Greek states in the successful war against its commercial rival. Troy. Shortly after, in the eleventh century, the Dorian invasion, from what is now Northern Greece, swept in successive waves across Greece and the great palaces of Mycenae, Argos, Tiryns and Pylos went up in flames. After that the Dark Ages descended on Greece; Mycenae revived for a short period in Hellenistic times, but not as a great power.

The road ends in an esplanade and car-park. In front stands the **Lion Gate**, surmounted by the earliest piece of monumental statuary in Europe: two lionesses sculptured in relief in the triangle above the monolithic lintel. The two heraldic lions (whose heads are missing) are clumsily modelled, their hind legs more like those of an elephant. The detail too is primitive; but there is a grandeur, even a dawning elegance, in the angle of their bodies and shoulders, designed to enable the beasts' features to face those approaching the gate. References in the *Agamemnon* of Aeschylus and the *Electra* of Sophocles suggest that the scenes of both tragedies were set in the vicinity of the Lion Gate.

Set within the Lion Gate, through which men, horses and chariots passed, there was a sentry box – the narrow niche, on the left as one enters, is still visible. Passing through the gate, on the right the **Royal Grave Circle** is marked by a double row of erect stone slabs. The chief interest of this circular graveyard (eighty-five feet in diameter) lies not only in its age (c. 1600–1500 bc) but in the treasure of gold and precious objects that Schliemann discovered here in the summer of 1876 and which is now housed in the National Museum in Athens. Schliemann found six tombs containing sixteen skeletons, judged to be royal personages because of the richness of the treasure interred with them. Gold masks, like the so-called 'Agamemnon death-mask' in the National Museum, covered the faces of the men; gold fillets decorated those of the women. Tombstones, some carved, others plain (two of the latter are *in situ*), marked the graves. When the great citadel wall was built, the Cyclopean blocks were made to curve round the bulge created by the grave circle so as to include it within the royal perimeter. The vast hoard of gold lay under the soil of the hillside for three thousand years, unsuspected by passing brigands, plunderers and conquerors.

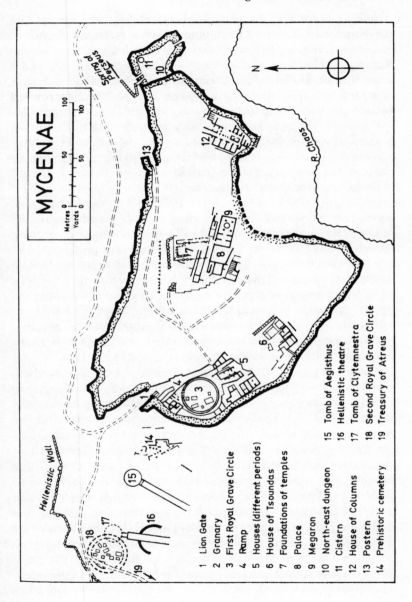

MYCENAE

Metres 0 — 50 — 100
Yards 0 — 50 — 100

N

R. Chaos

Hellenistic Wall

Spring of Perseus

1 Lion Gate
2 Granary
3 First Royal Grave Circle
4 Ramp
5 Houses (different periods)
6 House of Tsoundas
7 Foundations of temples
8 Palace
9 Megaron
10 North-east dungeon
11 Cistern
12 House of Columns
13 Postern
14 Prehistoric cemetery
15 Tomb of Aegisthus
16 Hellenistic theatre
17 Tomb of Clytemnestra
18 Second Royal Grave Circle
19 Treasury of Atreus

South-east of the grave circle, huddled together against the polygonal wall, are the foundations of small houses, believed to have been inhabited by middle class Mycenaeans: the House of the Ramp, the House of the Warrior Vase, the South House; and a minor palace, the House of Tsoundas (named after the archaeologist who discovered it), in the north-east corner of which there was a small court, with a flight of thirteen steps leading down to a corridor and what are presumed to have been storerooms. All that is known of the furnishings of these houses – as, indeed, of all Mycenaean houses – is that low benches were arranged along the walls of the porches and that lamps and charcoal braziers stood in the main hall, in the centre of which there was a hearth.

Returning to the Lion Gate, one follows the course of the original zigzag ramp up which the chariots climbed to the western extremity of the hill crowned by the Palace buildings. It is rough-going, steep and shadeless, the rocky ground overgrown with prickly shrubs. The ramp is narrow and can never have been very imposing. In spite of the gigantic slabs of masonry employed by prehistoric architects, Mycenaean houses and streets were very constricted, with none of the spaciousness associated with Hellenic buildings.

Though the foundations of the **Palace** indicate a complex of rather poky chambers, the royal esplanade commands a dizzy view of the ravine and the lovely patchwork plain below, at the end of which lies the fortified Larissa of Argos, a 900-foot-high conical rock rising sheer out of the plain. The mountains of Arcadia – grim, slashed with tremendous precipices – form a seemingly impenetrable barrier in the west. There is an airy splendour about this impregnable position.

One turns first into the Great Court, which had a cemented floor with painted squares and a dado in the form of a split-rosette frieze running along the base of painted walls. It was approached from the south by a flight of steps, of which one remains. The marks of burning on the floor are presumed to be traces of the great fire that destroyed Mycenae at the time of the Dorian invasion. West of the court is a small throne room, the throne probably having been placed in a sunken part of the floor against the north wall. East of the court one passes through a porch and vestibule into the *megaron*, the largest chamber in the palace, part of which has now fallen into the ravine. Painted designs of circles and other geometric patterns created a blaze of colour on the floor; the walls, judging from fragments in the National Museum, were covered with frescoes depicting warriors, horses and chariots.

The *megaron* was where the court assembled, led by a barbaric monarch, surrounded by his olive-skinned attendants armed with axes and Homer's 'lovely' Argive women in their 'long robes'. Three of the four column-bases surrounding the hearth, which was in the shape of a shallow circular trough, are preserved, as are many door-sills in the chambers.

It is difficult, if not impossible, to identify the maze of small rooms north of the *megaron*. One is believed to have been a bathroom, because its sunken floor reveals signs of red plaster within a raised surround. Some guides like to say it is the bath in which Agamemnon was hacked to pieces.

East of the wind-swept summit one dips down to the so-called 'House of the Columns', near a watchtower overhanging the desolate ravine. There are two interesting points about the foundations of this house: first, the design corresponds with Homeric descriptions of the palace of Odysseus in Ithaca, and second, it possessed a court surrounded by a colonnade aligned with the *megaron* walls – a feature that foreshadowed the houses and *prostyle* temples of the Classical period, with columns at each corner, forward of the side walls.

Following the line of walls, one reaches the **Secret Cistern**, an underground chamber dated to the thirteenth century BC, with a corbelled roof in the form of an inverted V. An initial flight of sixteen steps is followed by a sharp turn and a claustrophobic descent of a further eighty-three steps into the limestone bowels of the citadel. At the bottom, where there is a square stone shaft brimming with water, a feeling of constriction grips the throat. Death is omnipresent at Mycenae; in this fetid chamber it makes an almost palpable impact. The cistern was connected by terracotta conduits with the Spring of Perseus, which lay outside the perimeter of the citadel. The water supply of the fortress was thus assured in times of siege. Back in the open, where nothing seems to disturb the solitude of the bleak slopes of Mount Zara and the surrounding scrub-covered hills, one welcomes the thyme-scented air and the chirping of cicadas.

A westerly course completes the circuit of the citadel after passing the Postern Gate, a small but massive gateway with a double door, carrying an enormous lintel through which Orestes fled after the murder of Clytemnestra. The area between the Postern and the Lion Gate is littered with debris from the short-lived Hellenistic township.

The descent from the Lion Gate to the lower town is honeycombed with foundations of prehistoric dwellings and *tholos* tombs. Immediately across the road from the car-park lies the **Second Royal Grave Circle**, first excavated in 1952, and believed to be considerably older (c. 2000–1600 BC) than the one discovered by Schliemann – in other words about half a millennium before the polygonal wall was built round the citadel. The epithet 'royal' is again inspired by the quantity of precious objects (jewellery, vases, swords and a lovely rock-crystal bowl in the shape of a duck, all now in the National Museum) discovered in the graves. In one, the skeleton of a young woman, a 'Mycenaean princess', was found richly bedecked with gold and silver clasps and necklaces; crystal-headed bronze pins on her shoulders were obviously intended to hold up a garment, the fabric of which had perished. In another grave two male skeletons were buried with their weapons: a lance, a knife and an ivory-pommelled sword, all of bronze. In yet another, a little girl of about ten was adorned with miniature ornaments. Beside the little skeleton lay a baby's rattle of gold.

To the left of the road are the foundations of the House of the Oil Merchant, once a large building containing a store-room with oil-jars ranged in a row against the wall and clay tablets inscribed with Linear B script. Daggers, shields and bronze implements were also dug up. We thus have visual evidence of the weapons used by Homer's heroes, of the ornaments worn by their women and of the layout of the houses in which they dwelt. The archaeologists might be said, therefore, to have performed a notable service to literature, by raising Homer above the level of a mere mythographer with an incomparable talent for story-telling; after visiting Mycenae one returns to the *Iliad* and the *Odyssey* with a sense of increased intimacy.

The **tholos tombs** come next. They are unquestionably the most astonishing monuments of the prehistoric age in Greece. Believed

The Nazim House at Kastoria: wall paintings in the small salon.

The Tower of Prosphori dominates the landscape at Ouranopolis.

Mount Athos: the Protaton. Presentation of the Virgin in the Temple, attributed to Panselinos, early 14th century.

to be an entirely Mycenaean concept, they combined various characteristics of Aegean prehistoric architecture into symbolic representations of man's eternal awe of death. The circular chambers were subterranean, preceded by a *dromos*, or paved way, cut out of the rock. Earth covered the apex of the conical chamber, thus creating the effect of a tumulus. The most impressive is the so-called **Tomb of Agamemnon** or **Treasury of Atreus** (to the right of the descending road), a huge sepulchre dated, by means of pottery fragments, to the fourteenth century BC. The cemented *dromos* is bordered by shaped blocks of dark grey rock set in more or less regular courses. At the end of this 120-foot passage stands the doorway, its sides slanting inwards as they rise, flanked by column bases and covered by triangular stonework which probably contained a sculptured plaque similar to the one above the Lion Gate. The door-sill of reddish rock is perfectly preserved. Passing under the eighteen-foot-long slab of limestone, one enters the dark, empty beehive-shaped tomb, the diameter of which is nearly fifty feet and the height only slightly less. A few bronze nails in the uppermost of the thirty-three courses of stonework indicate the original existence of some form of decoration, probably metal rosettes. To the right is a small rock-hewn chamber, where lay the corpse of the royal personage, encased in gold leaf. However it cannot have been that of Agamemnon, since the building precedes the Trojan Wars by over a century.

Some visitors tend to poke their noses in, sniff the fetid air, think it all looks rather gloomy and return to the *dromos* with a sigh of relief. But it is wise to stay a little longer, to get used to the dark and to run your eye up slowly, course after contracting course, to the towering cone. It is not difficult then to comprehend that this primitive monument must have been designed by an architect who not only knew how to deal with the technicalities of thrusts and stresses, but who was also inspired by creative imagination.

There are eight more tholos tombs, far less well-preserved, scattered about the surrounding countryside. One, the so-called **Tomb of Clytemnestra**, just below the citadel, next to the Second Royal Grave Circle, is interesting insofar as the beehive chamber is taller and slightly narrower with the upper courses ascending more sharply; the design gains thereby in refinement. Beside it is the

321

Tomb of Aegisthus. All these names are, of course, designed purely for classification; they possess no historical significance.

Mycenae is a haunted place, peopled by figures inflated, by legend and literature, into creatures of demonic stature, as sinister as the natural boulders and slabs of Cyclopean masonry raised to protect them, in death, from the hatreds engendered by their own tragic destinies. But the treasure of gold, silver, ivory and alabaster, wrought by the Mycenaeans with such unerring skill and taste, remains a priceless testimony to the degree of civilization achieved by an otherwise cruel and barbaric people.

From Mycenae a road skirts the base of Mount Euboea to the **Heraeion of Argos**. (One can also approach it from Argos itself, passing through Chonika, where there is a restored twelfth-century Church of the *Koimesis*.) The Heraeion is situated on a ledge overlooking the plain, at the western end of which the wall of Arcadian mountains is gashed by a broad, winding gorge that penetrates into the heart of the massif. The worship of Hera, the national deity of the Argives, was centred here. Throughout the Argolid the myths are dominated by the Queen of the Heavens, twin sister of Zeus who was courted by her brother in the form of a cuckoo. They spent their wedding night at Samos and it lasted three hundred years. After this prolonged ecstasy, Zeus, surfeited with his sister's charms, began to look elsewhere for amorous distraction, and his infidelities drove Hera insane with jealousy.

The ruins of the Heraeion are not very impressive, but the prospect is spacious, and the utter loneliness of the site unique in the populated plain. It was, for all its religious significance, a small sanctuary, but nevertheless one to which pilgrims flocked on foot and in chariots along dusty paths, from the various citadels in the plain. A stepped wall leads to the remains of the mid-fifth-century BC south *stoa*, of which the interior colonnade is well-preserved. From this level, a monumental stairway climbs to a higher terrace, across which spreads the stylobate of the Doric Temple of Hera, also fifth-century. Although built of limestone, it had marble decoration, and within the *cella* stood the great statue of the goddess by Polycleitus; made of gold and ivory and depicted in the full panoply of her rank, she carried a pomegranate in one hand, her royal sceptre in the other.

One then climbs to the third terrace, to look at the scanty vestiges of the stylobate of the old seventh-century BC temple and to stand on the deserted ledge where the Achaean leaders swore allegiance to Agamemnon before embarking for Troy. South-west of the terrace are the remains of a Roman bath, with an atrium and mosaic-floored rooms under which there were hollow spaces heated by a furnace. To the south of the baths is a very ruined L-shaped *stoa* of an ancient gymnasium.

Argos itself is a busy market town devoid of distinction, straggling round its picturesque acropolis. However, few Greek towns have such a rich legendary and historical past. Danaus, father of fifty daughters, took refuge here after quarrelling with his brother, Aegyptus, father of fifty lusty sons, who pursued their uncle from Egypt in order to marry their cousins and fulfil an obligation incumbent on all bachelors with unmarried female relations. Girls in ancient Greece were considered a liability and they had to be married off to their closest relations if other suitors were not forthcoming. Danaus, who had a vindictive nature, seized the opportunity presented by the family loyalty shown by his nephews to revenge himself against his brother and the latter's progeny. He consented to the multiple marriage, but secretly instructed his daughters to kill their husbands on the wedding night by stabbing them in the heart with long pins. The girls dutifully obeyed and, as a punishment for their crime, were condemned to pour water eternally into a bottomless well.

At the time of the Trojan Wars, Argos was governed by Diomedes, the famous horse-tamer, and Hera, worshipped as the goddess of fecundity and symbolized as a cow, was revered above all other deities. In the seventh century BC the city reached the height of its power under Pheidon, who defeated the Spartans, and who introduced coinage and a new scale of weights and measures. Though the Argive ascendancy in the Peloponnese was later eclipsed by the rise of Corinth and Sparta, in classical times Argos remained a commercial and artistic centre, situated at an important junction of roads, three miles from the sea.

The modern town spreads across the ancient site, dominated by the **Larissa**, a gaunt, beige pyramid rising out of the surrounding fields and orchards. It takes just under an hour to climb to the castle on the summit, with its double circuit of medieval ramparts studded with ruined towers. It was built by the Byzantines and Franks, with Turkish additions, and proved a more enduring piece of masonry than the Temple of Zeus which once stood above the town. From the castle or even from the whitewashed chapel in a cypress grove less than halfway up, one can view the plain from a new angle. Cornfields spread northward beyond the gravelly, oleander-bordered bed of the Charadrus which flows (when there is any water) into the Inachus. To the east, orchards fringe the coastal strip as far as Nafplio. The lower hill to the east is the *Aspis*, so-called because its shape resembles that of a shield. There are some Bronze Age remains and shaft tombs, and a rectangular terrace on the south-west slope is believed to be the Sanctuary of *Athena Oxyderces* (The Sharp-Sighted).

South of the centre of the town and to the left of the road to Tripolis are some fragmentary remains of the *agora*. A great school of sculpture flourished here in the fifth century BC under Ageladas and ancient writers repeatedly refer to the quantity of statues that embellished the city. It was also a musical centre and Herodotus calls the Argives the best musicians in Greece.

Opposite the *agora* are more important ruins: first the red-brick shell of part of the Roman baths; then the crypt of an apsidal hall containing three sarcophagi, fragments of mosaic floors and marble paving stones. Behind the hall rise the tiers of the theatre, more unusual for its size and its unusually steep *cavea* than its state of preservation. Dated to the late fourth century BC, it had eighty-one tiers and could seat twenty thousand spectators. South of the theatre an aqueduct leads to a first-century AD Roman *odeion*, a small concert hall, of whose *cavea* fourteen tiers survive.

The museum in Vasilissis Sofias Street possesses Proto-Geometric and Geometric vases and Neolithic finds from neighbouring Lerna which include a gruesome female terracotta statuette with sharply pointed breasts, stunted, childish arms and a mouth in the shape of a beak. From these primitive objects one turns to the sumptuous elegance of the large fifth-century AD mosaic floors, depicting hunting scenes, with startlingly life-like portraits, removed from the Roman baths. There is also a head, allegedly of Sophocles, fished up from a nearby stream. Fifth-century BC writers describe the dramatist as one of the most handsome young men of his generation. The head in the Argos museum does little to indicate that he retained his looks in maturity.

East of Argos the low, oblong hump of 'wall-girt' **Tiryns** rises above the alluvial plain, beside the trimly kept garden of a local prison. At first sight unimpressive, it soon makes an impact: for the entire circumference is made up of massive walls, twenty to twenty-five feet thick, the oldest dating from the fourteenth century BC, and composed of huge limestone blocks, grey or reddish in colour, eight feet long and four feet wide. Strabo says the walls were built by the Cyclops, who came from Lycia and were called 'bellyhands' because they were paid in food for their manual labour. Here dwelt Heracles, generally represented in mythology as amiable and chivalrous, though somewhat prone to excesses of lechery and gluttony and occasional bouts of violence.

To view this pile of monstrous stones strung out on three levels it is best to take the path from the ticket office up to the ramp leading to the main east gate. At the ramp turn left to the upper terrace, where the palace was encircled by an inner rampart, until another gate is reached. Judging from its dimensions, it may have resembled the Lion Gate at Mycenae. Cuttings for pivots and jambs, where an enormous bar was drawn back into the wall, are still identifiable. Beyond the gate is a **stone gallery** (thirteenth-century BC) in a remarkable state of preservation and of a singular vaulted construction, with doorways overlooking the orange groves and fields of tobacco and maize. The endless rubbing of sheep against the walls – for centuries the gallery was a sheep-pen – has given the huge stones an extraordinarily smooth, shining patina.

One then turns right to enter the larger of two *propylaia*, the formal entrance to the palace, whose interior was built of sun-dried bricks. Only the foundations of the palace exist. Below them fragmentary remains of a circular building (c. 2000 BC) have been excavated. The *propylaia* led into the great court, at whose southern end there is another covered stone gallery with five doorways. To visit a confusing labyrinth of foundations of small chambers one turns right from the large court, passes through a smaller *propylaia* and enters the *megaron*, preceded by a porch and vestibule. In the centre there was a hearth, surrounded by four wooden columns with stone bases which supported the roof. The floors were stuccoed and painted with designs of sea monsters. Adjoining the *megaron* were the private royal apartments. To the west of the palace, a secret passage, with a well-preserved flight of steps, tunnels through the western rampart to a postern, whence one descends towards the main road.

Tiryns has little to offer in the way of architectural refinements – nothing but the sheer bulk of its masonry. The size of the stones, hewn by men of whom we know next to nothing, haunts the imagination. The architecture was purely military in conception, execution and function. Tiryns was inhabited in the third millennium BC – a thousand years before these stupendous walls were raised. Unlike Mycenae, to which it was probably subject, it had no Homer, Sophocles or Euripides to recount the bloody deeds of its ruling house. No royal tombs have revealed the treasure that astounded the eyes of Schliemann at Mycenae although, like Mycenae, it suffered a violent end and the palace was gutted by fire long before the classical era. Today hotels, petrol stations and the suburbs of Nafplio encroach on the barbaric site.

CHAPTER 22

The Argolid: The Periphery

Nafplio – Tolo – Epidaurus –
The Monastery of Agnoundos –
Kefalari: The Erasinos – Astros –
The Monastery of Loukous – Leonidio.

After the prehistoric nightmare of Tiryns it is a relief to enter
Nafplio, a charming little port sheltering below a rocky headland
and a large natural fortress crowned by a Venetian castle. It is an
obvious centre, with plenty of hotels, from which to visit the sites on
the periphery of the Argive plain and tends to be overcrowded in
summer. There is a hint of Italian architectural distinction in the
town, and though it would be a mistake to expect palazzi, Renaissance order or Baroque extravagance, there are tall, colour-washed
houses with corbelled balconies, and walled gardens filled with
hibiscus and Bougainvillaea, mandarin and rubber trees.

The notable buildings include the seventeenth-century Venetian
fortress, the lower castle and the Cathedral, which was originally
Roman Catholic. There is a small beach which can be reached along
a path, starting at the West Mole, which rounds the rocky promontory surmounted by AcroNafplio. On a fortified islet 500 metres
offshore is Bourdzi, a miniature Chateau d'If, which was built by the
Venetians, embellished with crenellations and a pretty octagonal
tower by the Turks and, more recently, has been used as a hotel.
There is a typically Greek provincial public garden – wispy, with an
equestrian statue of the ubiquitous Kolokotronis – a large main
square, an old upper town with winding stairways and alleys and a
waterfront looking out across the pellucid water of the bay towards

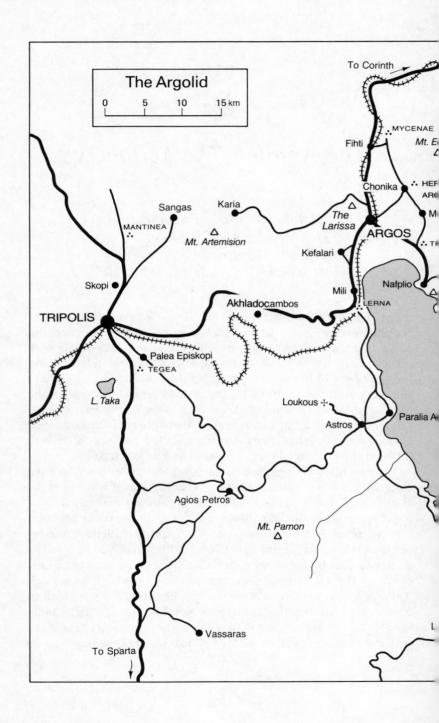

The Argolid

0   5   10   15 km

the Arcadian mountains. The situation is perhaps unrivalled – even in the Peloponnese.

Travellers should not miss the **museum**, housed in the former eighteenth-century Venetian arsenal in Syntagma Square. Here are displayed prehistoric pottery, Mycenaean *stelae*, and, more important, an almost complete and indeed unique suit of Mycenaean armour, as well as the only inscription and some fragments of frescoes from Tiryns, a mould for gold jewellery found at Mycenae, seventh-century BC votive discs, figurines and *amphorae*.

In itself, Nafplio has no ancient history to speak of. The days of affluence and of heroic sieges belong to the Venetian era. It first emerged from obscurity in the thirteenth century as the domain of Leon Sgouros, a venal, violent and blood-thirsty tyrant who went so far as to murder a page for breaking a glass in his presence. On another occasion he invited the Bishop of Corinth, with whom he was on bad terms, to dinner. After feasting the prelate he gouged out his eyes and cast his body over the cliff.

The French Crusaders made Nafplio the capital of a duchy. Later they sold it to Venice and the whole area of the kingdom of the Atridae came under Venetian rule. In the prolonged struggle between Venice and Turkey for possession of the maritime stations of the Peloponnese, Nafplio underwent some great sieges and its inhabitants suffered terrible privations, while the peasants in the surrounding countryside were almost exterminated and had to be replaced by Albanian settlers. The town was finally captured by the Turks in 1715. A bold attack by the Janissaries secured for the besiegers a foothold on the covered way leading to the summit of the rock. The next day the Ottoman fleet opened a devastating bombardment and the Venetians were routed. There were 25,000 casualties and another 1000 Italian soldiers were beheaded, to the accompaniment of wailing fifes and beating drums, outside the Grand Vizier's tent, which was bedecked with Damascus silks and Bokhara rugs and surrounded by fluttering pennons. For the next hundred years the Crescent flew unchallenged on the highest battery of the fortress.

Nafplio was wrested from the Turks early in the War of Independence and from 1829 to 1834 was the official capital of the country. But political machinations and personal rivalries sabotaged all attempts at a proper administration of the liberated areas. Ten years of bitter campaigns against the Turks brought out most of the qualities and the shortcomings of the Greek character: the stubborn bravery and the unquenchable patriotism; the passion for political intrigue and incurable envy of the man at the top. Administrative anarchy and exaggerated reports of burning villages and massacres of civilians by self-styled patriots heightened the tension in the overcrowded little capital and culminated in the assassination of Count Capodistria who had been elected President of Greece by the National Assembly in 1827. In 1832 Greece was declared an independent kingdom and Prince Otho of Bavaria was elected King. In the following year King Otho arrived at Nafplio, the first capital of his tiny, turbulent kingdom. The nineteen-year-old Bavarian boy landed from an English frigate, escorted into the Argolic Gulf by the fleets of the three Protecting Powers, and rode between ranks of English, French and Russian sailors, followed by a train of Bavarian officers in plumed hats and brightly coloured uniforms. Massed bands played martial tunes, which must have rung strangely in the ears of Greek peasants accustomed to *klephtic* ballads.

Sightseeing in Nafplio is limited. The lower fortress is reached through an arched gateway surmounted by a Venetian lion: a welcome reminder of the advantages enjoyed by maritime Greece under the colonial administration of the Serene Republic, at a time when the rest of the country was being reduced to desolation by corrupt and rapacious pashas. The walls now enclose the only luxury hotel in the Peloponnese.

The much higher **Palamidhi**, a gleaming pile of rock towering above the town, is one of the finest fortresses in the Morea. To reach the summit by car one follows 25 Martiou Avenue in an easterly direction. The Church of the *Evanghelistria*, surrounded by cypresses, crowns a rock in the suburb of Pronia. This is where the National Assembly met in 1832 and ratified the election of Prince Otho as King of Greece. The citadel is entered through a gateway consisting of a five-sided fort. Within the enclosure, which is on an incline, five distinct forts are discernible (there were seven originally), all built by the Venetians at the beginning of the eighteenth century. Each fort had its cistern, thus enabling the garrison to withstand long sieges, and the highest battery, dominating the entire defence system, was furnished with shell-proof shelters. At the southern side of the summit there is a sheer drop of over 700 feet to the base of the cliffs, which run eastward in an unbroken line. Westward, across the crescent-shaped bay fringed with mud-flats, the mass of Mount Artemision rises above the Lernean Marsh.

At the western end of the fortress a stairway of 857 steps zigzags down the perpendicular face of the cliff, passing under four arched gateways. It was down this dizzy flight of hairpin bends that the Janissaries poured into the town in pursuit of the routed Venetians in 1715. The stairway leads into the road which winds round the great cliff to the south.

From Nafplio one can visit Merbaka in the plain and its twelfth-century **Church of the Panayia**. Cruciform, with a single dome, its combination of brickwork and faience decoration on the exterior walls creates a charming polychrome effect.

At the beginning of the road to Epidaurus a turning to the right leads to another pretty twelfth-century church, that of *Zoodochos Pighi* (the Source of Life), situated near a spring commonly identified as the Canathus, in which Hera bathed once a year in order to renew her virginity. Remains of an ancient wall and aqueduct add charm to the rustic setting.

Another turning to the right leads to **Tolo**, now a busy holiday resort with many small and medium-sized hotels strung out along a strip of sandy beach. Tolo is still a fishing village and occasionally a caique chugs in and netfuls of slithering silver-grey *maridhes* (the nearest Greek equivalent to whitebait) are unloaded. There are several open-air tavernas, where the freshly caught fish is apt to be expensive. At weekends the village is crowded with Argives anxious to escape the oppressive heat of the plain. At the eastern end of the bay, a little promontory crowned by a prehistoric acropolis has been identified as Asine, mentioned by Homer in the Iliad. East of Asine there is a long stretch of sandy beach but inland the country is flat and featureless.

The road to **Epidaurus** then leaves the plain and continues through citrus groves and farmlands which contrast with the scrub-covered, rocky hills on either side. After the village of Ligourio a turning to the left leads to the **Sanctuary of Asclepius**, which spreads across a narrow plain studded with pine trees and surrounded by

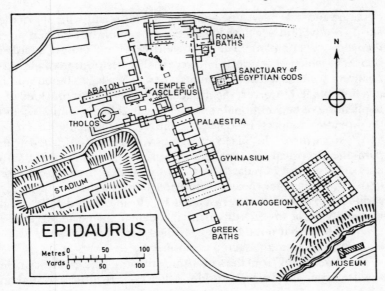

barren grey mountains. The highest, Mount Tithius, dominates the scene and has a forbidding aspect. Asclepius, child of Apollo and Coronis, his semi-divine nature proclaimed by the lightning flashing from his head, was, in infancy, suckled by a goat on the slopes of the mountain. Asclepius studied medicine under Cheiron and then travelled about Greece, healing the sick, devising new remedies and even raising the dead. Zeus was so angry with Asclepius for restoring Hippolytus to life and thus reversing the laws of nature, with which he alone had the right to tamper, that he cast a thunderbolt at him and sent him to dwell in the Underworld. Nevertheless the cult of the god of healing flourished and had its centre at Epidaurus which became famous for the growth of plants with medicinal properties.

The sacred enclosure was called the Alsos, which means grove, and must have been thickly wooded with tall pine trees. A few still cast their shade over the foundations of temples, ancient hostels and dormitories, for Epidaurus was equipped with all the amenities of a spa and invalids flocked to it from the farthest corners of the Hellenic world. Miraculous cures were worked by the ministrations

333

of tame yellow serpents – peculiar to Epidaurus and symbolic of the act of renovation – which licked the patients in their sleep until recovery was complete. The curative rites were a closely guarded secret, to which only priests had access. The restoration of life was apparently effected by the administration of Medusa's blood stored in a holy phial. However, the miraculous cures did not preclude the application of conventional remedies, such as baths, poultices and therapeutic unguents. In some cases the god recommended exercise and a strict diet. The place swarmed with persons afflicted with paralytic, dropsical and renal ailments. Convalescents were able to applaud the most popular athletes of the day on the race-track or find distraction at the theatre. The whole place was fragrant with the resinous pines and was surrounded by shrub-covered hills, from whose slopes the breeze still carries the scent of thyme and sage. It is nice to know that nobody has ever died here, for no deaths were allowed to occur in the sacred enclosure.

The ruins, apart from the astonishing theatre – the greatest single classical ruin in Greece outside Athens – are little more than foundations. However, it is pleasant to wander under the trees, among the marble slabs and limestone bases, to breathe the pure air and yield to the serenity of the place. The outline of the stadium lies on the right of the road, as one drives in from Nafplio. Unlike the course at Delphi, perched on a high ledge, it is hollowed out of a depression, so that one climbs down, not up, to it. On the grassy south embankment there are a few well-preserved tiers, which must once have accommodated querulous patients, exchanging news about their latest symptoms whilst burly wrestlers and swift-footed runners performed spectacular feats on the track. Broken pillars beside the starting point at the eastern end probably formed part of a formal gateway, although the athletes entered the stadium through the passage between the tiers on the north embankment.

Across the road there are the remains of temples, baths, *stoas* and fountains. First come the circular foundations of the *tholos* designed in the mid-fourth century by Polycleitus the Younger: an unimpressive ruin, but once a very holy building and the show-piece of the sanctuary. An idea of the opulent decoration is obtained from the sculpted fragments in the museum. The exterior colonnade of twenty-six Doric columns screened the *cella*, which was paved with a chequer-board of coloured marbles and surrounded by fourteen Corinthian columns. The roof was conical, the stuccoed walls of the *cella* painted with frescoes; the marble gutter was lavishly carved with acanthus-leaf designs and the frieze decorated with large rosettes in the centre of the *metopes*. Originally there were six concentric inner walls and the architectural design was so labyrinthine that in order to approach the centre of the building one had to proceed in serpentine windings round each of the six rings. At the centre was the altar, where sacrifices and offerings were made to Asclepius' yellow snakes which dwelt in a subterranean pit. The curiously sinuous approach was deliberately devised as a symbolic allusion to the movements of the sacred reptiles.

North of the *tholos* are vestiges of a *stoa*, known as the *abaton*, where the supplicants slept and were visited in dreams by the god who diagnosed their ailments and prescribed a treatment. At the east end of the *abaton* was the Temple of Asclepius, the foundations of which are clearly outlined. Built in the second half of the fourth century BC of Corinthian tufa, it was of the Doric order, though somewhat foreshortened, for it had the usual six columns at either end with only eleven instead of twelve side columns. This was the centre of the worship of Asclepius, and his effigy in gold and ivory towered above a pit into which the supplicants descended with offerings. The god was depicted enthroned, touching the head of a snake with one hand, holding a staff in the other. Strabo describes the temple as crowded with the sick and full of votive gifts on which the names of grateful supplicants, and a full description of their treatment, were recorded. A forest of votive monuments surrounded the temple.

South-east of the temple lies the site of the *palaestra* (a court surrounded by chambers), followed by the gymnasium and ruins of Roman buildings. East of the gymnasium is the outline of a large structure, the *katagogeion*, which served as a hostel for visitors. It was built of mud bricks on a stone foundation, and consisted of four equal parts, each with a central court, separated from the adjoining rooms by Doric colonnades. In spite of its size, the *katagogeion* cannot have accommodated all the patients who crowded the sanctuary. More modest hostels were probably scattered about the periphery.

335

Next comes the **museum**. First, there are the inscriptions from the Temple of Asclepius, recording recoveries from diseases ranging from tapeworm to sterility; then statues (some are casts) of Asclepius and Hygeia, goddess of health. These are followed by sculptural pieces from the temple, and reconstructions of sections of it, as well as a fragment of the *tholos* pavement. Next to this is the elaborate Corinthian capital, also from the *tholos*, said to have been carved by Polycleitus the Younger. Finally, there are some lovely architectural fragments from the *tholos*, including part of the circular wall and its deeply coffered ceiling.

South of the museum there is a tourist pavilion and a small motel. In summer it is enchanting to dine under the great pines, the silence of the deserted place broken only by the chirping of a few indefatigable cicadas. From the tourist pavilion one climbs a pine-clad slope to the **theatre**. One can see it from a distance as one approaches the sanctuary, its grey stone tiers, framed by dark green shrubs, on a slope of Mount Cynortium. At close quarters its completeness and the beauty of its proportions are impressive. It was built by Polycleitus the Younger about the middle of the fourth century BC in the hollow of a hillside. The forty-one semi-circular tiers of stone, accommodating up to fourteen thousand spectators, are separated by eleven stairways below and by twenty-one above the wide *diazôma*. They are in an admirable state of preservation. The seats are plain, except for the first two rows and those immediately above and below the *diazôma* whose backs are carved and were reserved for officials. The tiers above the *diazôma* rise more steeply and are completely symmetrical. The acoustics are so perfect that a whisper uttered in the centre of the orchestra, a large circle of white stone, can be heard from the highest tier.

Of the proscenium and *skene* only the foundations exist, upon which a modern construction has been built, which is used as a stage and backcloth for present-day performances. The *skene* consisted of two stories crowned by battlements, adorned with columns and divided by a balcony called a *pluteion* along which the *theologeion*, a platform surrounded by painted clouds intended for the appearance of the gods, would be moved backwards and forwards. From this Olympian perch, divine personages conversed with mortals on the stage or with the chorus in the orchestra. The cast was thus ranged on three levels: gods, protagonists and chorus. Sometimes mortals would be snatched up from the stage by a crane-like contrivance called the *yeranos* and raised to the godly level. From behind the *skene*, movable chambers were rolled out on wheels to indicate a change of scene. Then there were devices such as bladders filled with pebbles which were rolled on copper sheets to simulate thunder and a triangular prism of mirrors to represent lightning. Scenery consisted of painted canvases on wooden frames, placed in front of the *skene*. Tragic actors wore thick-soled leather boots so as to increase their stature; their heads were covered by large masks with wide-open mouths. Comedians, on the other hand, were shod in light-soled buskins. Slaves were distinguished by masks with deformed mouths. Actors were paid by the State and received a high salary. They underwent rigorous training and a strict diet. On the stage their movements were confined by the narrow space, and gestures were probably abrupt and angular. Their lines, it is believed, were delivered in a sing-song stentorian chant which penetrated every cranny of the immense theatre.

On either side of the stage were the *paradoi*, through which the chorus entered the orchestra, whereas actors passed through five doors onto the stage. One of the *paradoi* at Epidaurus has been restored: an elegant Hellenistic structure consisting of a double gateway between pilasters supporting a decorated cornice.

A festival of ancient drama is held in the theatre every summer. The plays are performed in modern Greek except for productions by distinguished visiting companies. Buses for the performance leave from Athens and travel along the west side of the Saronic Gulf. It is worth enquiring whether a ship has been laid on (there is no scheduled service) as the trip by sea is delightful. If possible one arrives with an hour or two to spare to wander among the ruins under the great pines, with the crowds from Athens and the neighbouring towns and villages.

At the play, if you choose a seat on one of the highest tiers, you can lean back against the sun-warmed stone without being jabbed in the back by the feet of some restless neighbour. When the sun sets, a brief twilight hangs over the valley and Mount Tithius assumes a less forbidding aspect. Down below in the orchestra the chorus weave stylized choreographic designs as they invoke the gods and lament the hero's tragic fate. A few cicadas drone on, but never loud enough to prevent a single word uttered on the stage, 193 feet below, from being heard.

If one approaches Epidaurus by the direct route from Corinth the road skirts the Saronic Gulf through dense pine woods before entering a peaceful inland valley of vineyards and orange groves. Below a line of hills stands the small post-Byzantine Church of the *Hodigitria* (The Virgin Indicator of the Way): cruciform with octagonal drum. The descent towards the coast affords glimpses of scrub-covered cliffs rising sheer from deep-water inlets. To the east, Aegina and the islet of Angistri emerge from the sea-haze.

The road swerves inland again; immediately to the right rises the **Monastery of Agnoundos**, surrounded by a defensive wall. The monastery, supposedly founded in the tenth century, flourished in the fourteenth, when it was rebuilt – as it was again during the Turkish occupation. Today it is inhabited by only a handful of nuns and its massive two-storied outer wall is in ruins. On the ground floor were monastic storerooms, the refectory, kitchens and bakery; on the upper, the cells, library and guard-room, from which gun slits project. The small court is planted with flowering shrubs. Above the western entrance to the Church of the *Koimesis* (Dormition of the Virgin), a lion's head, once a gargoyle from a fourth-century BC gutter, flanked by a finely-carved meander pattern, is embedded in the masonry. Local peasants believe the leonine effigy is proof of the monastery's foundation by a Byzantine emperor called Leo. The present church is domed, triapsidal, but not cruciform; a mixture of architectural styles resulting from repeated renovations. The conch of the sanctuary has been dated to the eleventh century. Every inch of the interior walls is frescoed; the paintings, which are entirely derivative, reflecting late Palaeologue influences. Against blue backgrounds, holy figures jostle each other in the familiar cycles of the lives of Christ and the Virgin, and scenes from the Old and New Testaments. According to another local legend, the most venerated icon, that of the Virgin Indicator – a crude piece of post-Byzantine painting – flew from another village in the Argolid and even undertook airborne journeys to the great Monastery of Megaspeleion. Stories of restless icons flitting, generally by night, across the mountains of the Peloponnese once formed part of the stock-in-trade of post-Byzantine folklore and superstition.

Beyond the monastery the village of Nea Epidavros spreads over a crag which rises dramatically out of a rocky gully. Here, in 1822, the National Assembly of Epidaurus was held, which gave modern Greece its first constitution – at least on paper. The rival chieftains, who had risen so boldly against their Turkish masters, were still unable to place national above personal interests, and consequently the constitution proved as ill-starred as any of its successors.

The road then descends through lemon, orange, mulberry and pomegranate orchards to a crescent-shaped bay divided by a spit of land, site of the ancient port of Epidaurus. Traces of polygonal masonry can be identified – with difficulty – and some fragmentary ruins of an early Christian basilica are scattered on the hilltop. At the northern end of the bay are the hotels and houses of Palea Epidavros, set amidst alleys and small squares lined with scarlet hibiscus. Yachts and caiques are moored beside the mole. This ancient little town was situated on a headland, dividing the bay in two. The sea has encroached on the coast and there are thought to be underwater ruins of classical buildings. The maritime strip is surrounded by high mountains; to the south the volcanic mass of the Methana peninsula is very imposing. The drive up to the sanctuary is through a wooded ravine, with streams running through orchards between banks of agnus castus, ivy, laurel and oleander.

Beyond Epidaurus the road continues south-east, climbing to Ano Fanari. This tiny village commands one of the finest views not only in Greece, but in the entire Mediterranean. To the north, over the broken coastline, are the jagged peaks of the volcanic mass of the Methana peninsula, and in the south, the densely green island of Poros, towards which the road descends in hairpin bends.

Five kilometres south of Argos, a side road to the right leads to **Kefalari**, where the waters of the **Erasinos**, after a long underground journey from the Stymphalian Lake, gush out of a rock at the foot of a steep cliff. The smaller of two caves contains a chapel dedicated to the Virgin, painted a garish yellow, with a rock-hewn narthex. Water plants grow in the pool below the cave and the stream divides into willow-lined rivulets which water the fields, uniting again to flow to the sea through the Lernean Marsh. It is a shady place, and the Erasinos is the only Argive stream that is not dry in summer.

Beyond the fork to Kefalari the road continues between the mountains and the sea. The village of Mili is the site of ancient Lerna, where Heracles slew the Hydra, which had a dog-like body, a breath so venomous that one exhalation was enough to destroy life and, according to different myths, anything between ten and ten thousand heads, one of which was immortal. Between the sea and the road, amid the rushes and long grass, a prehistoric site (probably c. 2000 BC) has been excavated by the American School of Classical Studies. It includes the foundations of a two-storied palace called the House of Tiles, because of the large number of roof tiles found here. Above the swampy ground rises Mount Pontinos, crowned by the ruins of a Frankish castle.

Just beyond Mili there is a fork. The main road climbs west into Arcadia. The traveller who opts for the south-bound road passes through the deserted splendour of Kynouria, where the mountains rise sheer from the sea, broken occasionally by narrow strips of fertility. Patches of sea dyed a turbid shade of red suggest the outflow of subterranean streams which pour out the silt and sludge accumulated in the course of their underground meanderings.

The first fertile strip is the Thyreatic Plain, where the road forks. To the left is **Paralia Astros**, situated on a spit of land crowned by the insignificant ruins of a Frankish fortress. On the north side of the headland there are fragments of ancient walls, part of a site that has not been identified.

The right fork leads to Astros, whence a side road climbs to the whitewashed buildings of the **Monastery of Loukous** which spreads across a wooded hill surrounded by cypress thickets. At the left of the entrance to the monastery the ruined arch of a Roman aqueduct, strung with stalactites, spans a brook.

Entering the court of the monastery on an autumn morning I have seen the walls ablaze with morning glory, and well-tended flower-beds filled with salvias, chrysanthemums and multi-coloured dahlias. Slabs of sculpted marble, including a headless statue of Athena, were ranged around the court. Benches were placed in shady corners. Out of the middle of this charming garden rises a sturdy, yet elegant, little twelfth-century Byzantine Church of the *Metamorphosis*, with a tall octagonal drum and three-sided apses. Faience plates are inlaid in the exterior wall and plaques of ancient sculpture have been built into the south wall, at the east end of which there is a fragment of mosaic paving. Two fine Corinthian columns flank the west doorway. The lavish use of materials from ancient pagan edifices is a fairly common feature of rural churches in Greece. It creates an agreeable sense of continuity. Within the church, which is in basilica form, four old marble columns form miniature aisles, and there is a fine decorated pavement with marble slabs arranged in geometric designs of cubes, diamonds and rectangles, with a double-headed eagle in the central medallion. The post-Byzantine frescoes are not outstanding, but some of the icons of the same period on the carved walnut-wood *iconostasis* are worth looking at.

In the garden, nuns in black habits go about their daily chores. The order and serenity of the place make a striking contrast with the picturesque untidiness and slapdash friendliness typical of male monastic establishments. During the War of Independence the monastery provided the rough chieftains with money and shelter, and most of its relics were sold in order to contribute to the war effort.

The road continues south along deserted creeks, shut in by crags and cliffs seamed with bright red mineral deposits. In autumn the hills are covered with heather.

Beyond the little harbour of Tyrou, surrounded by a crescent-shaped expanse of olive trees below great cliffs, a row of windmills stretches along the spine of a hill. Cypress groves increase in number and the coves are fringed with shingle. Soon the mountains withdraw sufficiently to make room for another crescent-shaped enclave, filled with olive and fruit trees, shut in, except on the seaward end, by conical peaks and rugged cliffs of tremendous height: **Leonidio**, one of the most beautiful villages in the Peloponnese. The whitewashed houses, square and low, are splayed out across the mouth of a dramatic gorge which recedes, in a succession of curiously-stepped cliffs of a fantastic flame-like colour, into the heart of the wild Tsakonian country. Streets, alleys and little

341

squares, built on different levels, form a charming architectural pile within the great arena of refulgent cliffs.

The road turns inland past the Monastery of Elona, clinging vertiginously to the cliff, and over the Parnon massif to the Yeraki crossroads, south-east to Monemvasia, south to Gythio and west to Sparta.

The main road into Arcadia from Argos ascends a series of hairpin bends between fierce escarpments just beyond Mili. There are entrancing backward views of the bay of Nafplio and Palamidhi. Bypassing the village of Akhladocambos, terraced on the side of a cup-shaped valley, the road mounts between slate-grey mountains until it reaches the Arcadian plateau, scattered with little oases of poplar and morello cherry trees. One senses a highland climate, barely forty miles from the stifling heat of the Argolid. The road cuts across the plain to Tripolis, the modern capital of Arcadia.

CHAPTER 23

The Arcadian Scene

Tripolis – Mantinea – Orchomenos – Dimitsana –
The Ladon – Megalopolis – Karitaina – Andritsaina –
Bassae: The Temple of Epicurian Apollo – Tegea.

In his famous picture in the Louvre, Poussin depicts a group of shepherds reading an inscription – *Et in Arcadia ego* – on a Roman tomb. In the background there is a leafy landscape with wooded mountains. Pink fleecy clouds sail across the indigo sky. The atmosphere is elegiac. But nothing could be more different from the Arcadian scene of today – or from the one described by ancient Greek writers. 'Leafy' is the last adjective one would associate with Arcadia, though some of the highland valleys are dotted with stunted oaks and the mountain slopes – the colour of gun-metal – with spruce and other conifers.

Arcadia is a scrub-covered massif, dominating the centre of the Peloponnese, from which the sea is seldom visible. In antiquity the inhabitants, reputed to be the most boorish people in Greece, tended flocks of sheep and goats and hunted bears and wild boar. For all their uncouthness, however, they were said to be a musical people, and Hermes, an Arcadian deity born in a cave on Mount Kylleni, made the first pipes from reeds and the first lyre from cow-gut and tortoise-shell on the banks of the Ladon torrent.

Why then has the adjective 'Arcadian' been so long associated with a pastoral landscape traversed by limpid streams, inhabited by rosy-cheeked shepherds and shepherdesses basking in an eternal summer? 'Shepherds' is the operative word. These bare, shut-in valleys were, and still are in some places, the preserve of shepherds – solitary figures, clad in heavy sheepskin cloaks, perched on dizzy

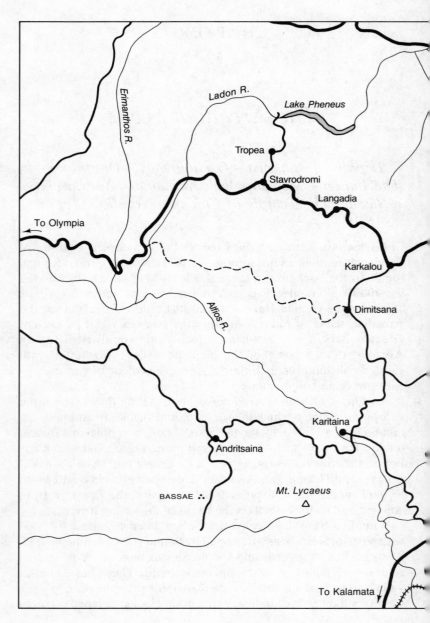

344

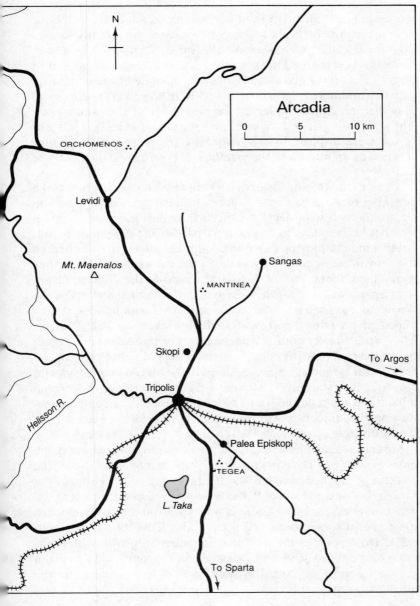

N

Arcadia

| 0 | 5 | 10 km |

ORCHOMENOS ∴

Levidi

Mt. Maenalos
△

Sangas

MANTINEA ∴

Skopi

To Argos

Tripolis

Helisson R.

Palea Episkopi

∴ TEGEA

L. Taka

To Sparta

345

ledges and surrounded by their flocks of mountain-goats scrabbling among the prickly shrubs and jagged boulders. Apparently Roman poets, particularly Virgil, took the word 'shepherds' as a cue, probably because of Pindar's reference to Arcadia as 'a land of flocks'. They imagined a rural landscape inhabited by flock-tenders who had nothing better to do than recline in flowering meadows and play their reed pipes under the dappled shade of elms and planes. The legacy was handed down through the centuries and great works of art were inspired by a wholly false image of Arcadia which reached its apotheosis in the paintings of Poussin and the poetry of Milton.

The local myths and history go a long way back. Pelasgus was the first king of Arcadia and is reputed to have devised shelters and sheepskin coats to protect his subjects from the inclement mountain weather. Later the Arcadians took part in the Trojan war; but, being a mountain people, without ships or sailors, they embarked for Troy in Agamemnon's vessels. In the Peloponnesian War they were allied, under duress, to Sparta, but after the Theban victory over Sparta at Leuctra, they became enthusiastic members of the Arcadian confederacy, the brain-child of Epaminondas, which aimed at breaking Sparta's stranglehold over the Peloponnese. They were equally enthusiastic members of the Achaean League, one of the many abortive Greek attempts at political unity, designed to resist the tyrannical encroachments of the Macedonian Diadochi. No Arcadian state ever became a great power; but the rugged inhabitants seem on the whole to have been on the side of democracy against autocracy, except when under pressure exercised by the formidable Spartans.

Modern Arcadia has, so far, escaped excessive urbanization and industrialization. The chief town, **Tripolis**, first heard of during the Turkish occupation, when it was the residence of the Pasha of the Morea, lies near the site of Pallantium, an ancient Arcadian city, of which nothing remains. There is little to recommend the modern town except some hotels and a large arcaded public square with cafés. However it is the hub of Peloponnesian travel, with roads branching out to Laconia and Messenia in the south, to Olympia in the west and to the Arcadian sites, ancient and medieval, in the north and west.

*   *   *

In the mountainous north the first objective is **Mantinea**, where Spartan militarism repeatedly pitted its strength and near-invincibility against the democratic city states of Greece. The narrow plain, north of Tripolis, is flat and treeless. The sky, except at the height of summer, is often overcast, and drifting clouds are reflected on the dun-grey mountains whose conical peaks surround the elliptical plateau like the rim of a vast crater. At Skopi a line of rocky hills projects into the plain which contracts to about a mile in width. In 418 BC one of the decisive engagements of the Peloponnesian War was fought here, when the Spartans, ten thousand strong, led by King Agis, inflicted a major defeat on the allied armies of Athens, Argos, Elis and Mantinea. The victory was a classic example of the triumph of Spartan discipline and its 'chain of command' system, unknown in other Greek armies, whose generals relied on impassioned rhetoric, exhorting their troops to rush at the enemy in impulsive and sometimes foolhardy charges.

Although the field of Mantinea, in the shadow of its amphitheatre of grey mountains, witnessed the prelude to Spartan supremacy, it was also the setting, eighty years later, of one of the most violent convulsions in the long-drawn-out death agony of Spartan militarism. From this rocky projection, Epaminondas, most brilliant of Theban statesmen and generals, watched the second battle of Mantinea in 362 BC. Only when the irresistible charge of the Theban Sacred Band, clad in shining helmets and armed with burnished shields and spears, had broken the brute mass of Spartan helots did the wounded Epaminondas remove his hand from his breast, which had been pierced by an enemy arrow, and let the blood drain from his body. The loss of this noble man robbed the Thebans of the fruits of victory. The army, horror-struck by his death, remained as though paralysed and allowed the defeated Spartans to stream southward unmolested.

North of Skopi a fork to the right leads to the site of the city of Mantinea, built, contrary to the general rule, on level ground, without an acropolis. The city was surrounded by walls, with ten gates and many watch-towers, of which there is now no visible evidence. The outline of the theatre, however, is easily identified on a low knoll. Two tiers are preserved and some slabs of the proscenium litter the marshy field. The stage was placed at a slightly oblique angle to the orchestra and the *cavea* was greater than the usual semi-circle. All this part of the plain is swampy ground, crossed by unsuspected streams, one of which enabled the Spartan King Agesilaus to crush Mantinea in 385 BC. Raising an embankment across the Ophris, which flowed through the town, he blocked its efflux. The stream overflowed, the low walls made of sun-dried brick collapsed and the town was inundated. The inhabitants were obliged to disperse to neighbouring villages. The reduction of Mantinea into scattered settlements is a typical example of Spartan policy, aimed at breaking up those civilized states on which Hellenism was founded. But with the ascendancy of Thebes and the consequent decline of Spartan power, Mantinea was rebuilt on a plan that excluded the streams from its midst. The problem raised by the constant flooding of this level ground, however, remained unsolved, for in spring the water of the swollen streams was unable to run into the *katavothra*, the subterranean channels with which the Arcadian massif is riddled. Polybius says the Mantineans finally took to cutting trenches through which the waters were directed into the *katavothra* and thence flowed to the coast.

There is a melancholy beauty about Mantinea. In summer the mountains have a forbidding, metallic quality; kestrels fly over the barren slopes and frogs plop in the marshy pools.

Beyond the turning to Mantinea, the main road runs through a wide pass between the arid hills that divide the Mantinean from the Orchomenian plain. At the village of Levidi a road to the right descends into a bowl-shaped valley surrounded by craggy peaks. The village of Kalpaki, at an altitude of 3000 feet on a hillside facing the summit of Mount Maenalos, is the site of the ancient acropolis of **Orchomenos**. From here Orchomenian kings ruled over Arcadia in the earliest times. Beside the chapel of *Agios Ioannis* and a circular threshing-floor there are three well-preserved column bases of a temple of Artemis overlooking the sparsely cultivated plain. A steep climb to the summit, sown with corn, brings one to the fragmentary ruins of a little temple of Athena and some ancient foundations. To the right, the terrace of the Bouleuterion overlooks the valley and the peaks to the east. The hollow of the theatre, its tiers buried in the soil, is discernible. The place has a wintry air: bleak, desolate and grand.

From Levidi the road skirts the northern slopes of Mount Maenalos, passes through fir forests and then forks southwards to the popular alpine resort of Vitina. At Karkalou a branch road leads to **Dimitsana** on a terrace above a deep chasm through which the stream of the Lousios flows in a wide loop. The mountains slope gradually down to the upper valley of the Alfios and the plain of Megalopolis, bounded in the west by Mount Lycaeus and in the south by the Laconian ranges. During the Turkish occupation, Dimitsana was a centre of learning and possessed a school and a famous library. Semi-abandoned today, it is mainly visited for its lovely view. However, antiquarians may search for some very fragmentary remains of Cyclopean and Classical walls. In the gorge below, the Monastery of *Agios Ioannis Prodromos*, originally an imperial Comnene foundation of the twelfth century, is tucked away in a shady ravine.

Partly abandoned villages, inhabited by half a dozen families, a few sheepdogs and some scraggy hens, clinging to the mountainsides like petrified sentinels with nothing left to guard, are a melancholy feature of the Arcadian scene. From Dimitsana a bad road descends into the plain of Megalopolis, past Stemnitsa, where there is a simple but good hotel.

West of Karkalou, the long winding descent to Olympia begins. It is one of the loveliest in the Peloponnese. A bend in the road soon affords an astonishing view of the large village of **Langadia**, its red-roofed houses climbing a steep mountain-side. Here one can stop for lunch at a terrace overlooking the gorge. There are tourist shops, filled with sheepskin rugs, woollen bags, modern imitations of peasant embroideries, striped bedspreads and sheep bells.

Farther down the descent, at Stavrodromi, a turning to the right leads to Tropea, another strikingly situated village; beyond it a rough and boulder-strewn road winds between slopes dyed crimson by manganese deposits. Soon a precipice falls sheer into a deserted valley streaked by the **Ladon**, which flows through a *katavothra* from its source in Lake Pheneus. It is a savage setting: beetling crags tower above the gorge, at the bottom of which lies a pool of pale green, crystal-clear water – the artificial lake formed by a dam.

Beyond Stavrodromi the main road descends into more pastoral country as it follows the course of the Ladon, its banks lush with planes and poplars, the rolling foothills thickly wooded with tall, feathery pines and the gullies bright with gorse and broom in late spring. On these banks, Demeter was found by her brother, Poseidon, who was suddenly seized by an uncontrollable passion to possess her. In order to escape his attentions she changed herself into a mare, whereupon Poseidon changed himself into a stallion and ravished her on the spot. Demeter then bathed in the waters of the Ladon.

Further along the road, a bridge across the Erimanthos, flowing in a swift torrent, marks the boundary between Arcadia and Elis. Green rolling hills enclose the lower valley of the Alfios, as it winds serenely between sand-banks towards Olympia.

Travellers taking the south-western route from Tripolis follow a road which zigzags across a spine of featureless hills separating the eastern plateau from the western Arcadian plain. In a fold of one of these hills a large stone marks the spot where three hundred Resistance fighters were made to dig their own graves before they were shot by the Germans in 1944. Ten of them refused. The Nazi commander was so impressed that he commuted their sentence to life imprisonment.

The descent into the plain, which is traversed by the upper Alfios and studded with copses, hillocks and little oases of vegetation, reveals a new aspect of Arcadia. The altitude is lower and the atmosphere warmer and more humid, the vistas wider, the mountains less austere. The range of Mount Lycaeus, a series of broken ridges running north to south, forms a barrier in the west. In the disastrous earthquake of 1965 the whole mountain is said to have shifted slightly and the villages on its slopes were reduced to heaps of rubble. Featureless modern Megalopolis (whence the main road continues to Kalamata and the Messenian plains in the south) is badly polluted by a lignite-burning power station supplied from open-cast mines along the road. However, the site of the ancient city is worth visiting.

Megalopolis, the 'Great City', founded by Epaminondas during the heyday of Theban supremacy, was the headquarters of the Arcadian Confederacy which aimed to contain Sparta and prevent her from repeating her hitherto all too successful attempts to divide the Peloponnese into small units under her domination. Politically, Epaminondas' idea was a good one, but somehow Megalopolis did not quite come off. The 'Great City', meeting place of the Council of the Ten Thousand (composed of representatives of all the federated states), was 'great' in name only. Laid out on either side of the River Helisson and encircled by a wall five and a half miles in circumference, its size was out of proportion to its population. Polybius, who was a native of the city, says its power quickly declined, and in the late Hellenistic age a comic poet facetiously described the 'great city' as a 'great desert'. When visited by Pausanius it was abandoned and largely in ruins.

Yet the 'youngest city' in Greece possessed the largest **theatre**, capable of accommodating twenty thousand spectators. Hollowed out of a small hill shaded by large pines, its beautifully proportioned *cavea* is turned towards the north and the wide bed of the Helisson, with the earthquake-shattered hills of Mount Lycaeus in the background. To the north-west the undulating plain is dominated by the flat-topped crown of the fortress of Karitaina. Only the front row of seats is more or less intact, with considerable fragments of another six visible. This is one of the few ancient theatres not yet restored for regular summer performances – it could not be enjoyed in the acrid smoke of the nearby power station.

Beyond the proscenium are some bases of the numerous columns of the Thersilium, a great assembly hall seating six thousand people – a kind of ancient prototype of the Palais des Nations in Geneva: equally fleeting, equally ineffectual. The historical stage was now set on infinitely wider dimensions, and the endemic rivalries of the Greek city states, often little more than border quarrels, were destined to pale before the imperial ambitions of Macedonia and Rome. The site of the *agora*, which was built on a magnificent scale, has been identified on the north-west bank of the Helisson.

North-west of Megalopolis rises the formidable pile of **Karitaina**, most splendidly situated of Frankish castles. The deeper one penetrates the Peloponnese, the more one is impressed by this succession of ruined medieval castles. Compared to Venetian military architects, the Franks were amateurs, but the sites on which they raised their strategic redoubts cannot be matched for wild and romantic beauty. The sojourn of the northern knights in this

sun-drenched land of dusty olive groves and vine-clad valleys was
not a long one. Internecine strife and sporadic wars with the
conquered Greeks took their toll. Only two generations after the
Crusaders had overrun the Morea many of the great feudal names
were extinct.

Karitaina is built on twin peaks, dominating the passes leading
into the heart of the Morea. The eastern summit is crowned by the
village; the western, which is higher and has a flat top, by the castle.
Village houses extend across the saddle between the two. A sloping
ledge at the foot of the castle suddenly falls away sheer: hundreds of
feet below, the great streak of the Alfios winds through a narrow
chasm between russet-coloured cliffs. Seen from the other side of
the gorge – from the road to Andritsaina – Karitaina is strikingly
beautiful and perfectly proportioned. On the left of the road up to
the village, a little Church of the *Panayia* (originally of the eleventh
century) clings to the side of a steep declivity beside a pretty
brickwork Frankish belfry. It possesses an elaborate *iconostasis*,
brightly painted with birds and other ornamental patterns. A maze
of increasingly narrow alleys between dilapidated, often uninhabited, houses, some with projecting balconies, ascends towards the
saddle. Huge slabs of masonry which have fallen from the medieval
keep lie smothered in brambles and spurge. The younger generation has packed up and gone to Athens, America or Australia,
though recently the exodus has been stemmed somewhat, as even
mountainous Arcadia benefits from EEC agricultural handouts and
the tourist boom.

North of the saddle, the Byzantine Church of *Agios Nikolaos*
overlooks a cemetery and a grove of cypresses. Cruciform, with four
small domes at the extremities of the arms of the cross, and a larger
one on a squat drum in the centre, its gabled roofs form an agreeable
intersection of planes. The proportions of the interior are strictly
classical and give an impression of loftiness in spite of the church's
relatively small size. The frescoes (probably post-Byzantine) are
too damaged to give one a chance to judge their quality, although
the general effect is of a lovely roseate glow.

The visit to the castle is strenuous for the going is steep. In spring
the path is bordered with bee-orchids and long-stalked, mauvy-pink
Anemone hortensis, with elliptical petals and three bracts well

The Monastery of Simonopetra on Mount Athos, soaring out of dark green
woods a thousand feet above sea level.

Acro-Corinth: amid the remains of previous fortifications, the watch-towers, the three imposing connected gateways and the crenellated ramparts of the Venetian military architects are outstanding.

below the flower. Two-thirds of the way up, a chapel of curious structural design clings to the rock, its west end in the form of a basilica, the east in that of half a Greek cross. The little ruined house beside it is called the house of Kolokotronis, who probably stayed here during the campaign of 1821.

The castle is entered through the barbican. Although it was the seat of one of the great baronies of the Morea, it is disappointing within – very ruined and with little of the splendid military architecture evident in the Venetian fortifications of Acro-Corinth and Nafplio. Founded in the thirteenth century by Hughes de Bruyeres, father of Geoffroy, most famous representative of French chivalry in the Morea, it conveys a greater impression of impregnability than any other medieval castle in Southern Greece, with the exception of Monemvasia. Purely strategic in purpose, its history is uneventful. With the decline of the Frankish ascendancy in the Morea, it was sold to the Greeks in 1320 and became a dependency of one of the monasteries of Mistra. In 1460 it was captured by the Turks. It served a final military purpose in the Second World War, when the German army of occupation, constantly harassed by guerillas, installed fire positions on the summit. From the barbican the path turns left to the main arched gate, which is set in the curtain wall, flanked by a square tower to the north. The gate leads to a vaulted passage into the triangular keep, with a square tower at its apex (north) and a ruined hall at the base (south).

Hundreds of feet below lies a circular threshing-floor, with the foothills of Mount Lycaeus rising abruptly on the other side of the gorge. In the foreground, to the north, the Church of *Agios Nikolaos* hangs precipitously above the chasm. To the south-east the river winds across the undulations of the plain from its source in the distant massif of Taigetos.

Following the road to the west, one crosses a modern bridge beside an old Frankish construction with six arches, of which four remain. A somewhat dotty effect is created by the tiny chapel crowning the middle pier; this is connected by a stone stairway with the bed of the Alfios. The road climbs the foothills of Mount Lycaeus, and the lovely chasm is lost to sight. At the end of the highland stretch, one reaches **Andritsaina**, its houses banked up on the abrupt slope amid gnarled, shady planes, some of whose trunks are so large that they have been hollowed out in order to form reservoirs from which water flows through metal pipes. The library has a large collection of books donated by a native of the village who had literary interests ranging from the ancient writers to master-pieces of nineteenth-century French fiction.

From Andritsaina the main road descends into the lower valley of the Alfios and the coast. Another road climbs up to **Bassae** through a scene of utter desolation: not a dwelling; barely a tree; but in the late spring, wild flowers relieve the austerity of the denuded land-scape. In summer there is only scrub; in the long winter, snow on range upon range of mountains. Several circular stone threshing-floors are the sole evidence that men and animals still inhabit, or once inhabited, these friendless uplands.

Suddenly the road comes to an end, and the columns of the **Temple of Epicurian Apollo**, grey as the stones from which they sprout, raise their fluted shafts, crowned by pieces of architrave, on a ledge at the foot of Mount Kotilion (the whole edifice is now protected from the elements by a huge plastic shelter). It seems extraordinary that a major temple, designed by Ictinus, the leading architect of the fifth century BC, should have been erected on one of the loneliest sites in the Peloponnese, at an altitude of nearly 4000 feet.

Except for the keeper's hut, there is no house, hamlet or village in sight; and yet outside Athens there is no better-preserved temple in Greece. The architectural arrangement is unconventional. It has six columns, front and back, and fifteen, instead of the usual twelve, at either side. The building thus acquires an air of unusual elongation. The *adytum*, the secret chamber from which the public was gener-ally excluded, is not separated from the *cella* by a wall. Since the temple was dedicated to Apollo, the front faces north, towards Delphi, the god's holiest shrine. It would be too much to expect all the subtle curves and refinements of the Parthenon, for Ictinus, no longer working in marble as he did on the Acropolis, was unable to apply these to the hard local lime-stone. Only part of the architrave remains, but thirty-seven Doric columns of the peristyle are still standing. Twenty-three panels of the frieze, depicting battles be-tween Centaurs and Lapiths, Athenians and Amazons, were re-moved to Corfu in the nineteenth century and bought by the British

Government for £15,000. They are now in the British Museum. The *cella* is almost complete, and seven of the ten engaged pillars, with beautiful bases and a smooth grey patina, are well-preserved. They were once crowned with Ionic capitals, which must have added greater variety to the chamber, which also contained the large bronze cult statue of Apollo. At the south end the base of the earliest-known Corinthian column is discernible. The proportions of the temple are best seen from the slope of Mount Kotilion, the rocky hill behind the north entrance. The air is cool and wonderfully bracing, although the sun burns in summer. There is no shade, and the solitude is awe-inspiring; but the cluster of slender columns, worn and rutted by time and weather, still dominates the ring of arid mountain peaks. If ever a place of worship was in harmony with its setting, this was surely it. Like the Acropolis in Athens and the site of Delphi, it makes the most tremendous impact of timelessness.

After Bassae, Western Arcadia contains little of major interest.

From Tripolis a road runs south to Sparta. At the eighth kilometre a road to the left goes to the site of **Tegea**. Once the most powerful city state in Arcadia, Tegea put up a prolonged resistance to Sparta; but in the Peloponnesian War, its position on the Lacedaemonian border obliged its rulers to ally themselves with the hated neighbour. Of the Temple of Athena Alea, burned in 395 BC and rebuilt by Scopas, little remains above the second drum of the columns (town and temple alike were razed to the ground by Alaric). Contemporary writers describe the temple as superior in size and quality to any other in the Peloponnese. The famous cult image of Athena Alea by Scopas was carried off by Augustus after the battle of Actium. Some of the great grey drums, each about four feet high, lie on their sides; others are ranged in rows so that the spacious proportions of the temple are easily perceived. The museum possesses copies of several Scopaic works, including one of the lovely head of the Goddess of Health which is in the National Museum in Athens, some slabs of the architectural decoration of the temple and a fragment of cornice.

The neighbouring village of Palea-Episcopi is the site of medieval Nikli, a well-walled stronghold commanding all the lines of communication across the Morea.

After the fork to Tegea, the main road skirts the marshy, mud-brown waters of Lake Taka, whose southern end, abounding in wild fowl, is bordered by a range of grim-looking hills, followed by a bleak, featureless mountain stretch. Then the slow, winding descent begins. The air loses some of its highland quality; vestiges of vegetation appear in the gullies. Suddenly the road emerges from the hills and a view of immeasurable grandeur opens up. The range of Taigetos, highest of the Peloponnesian mountains and cut by huge crevices, raises its famous five fingers – the Pendodactyla, snow-capped for more than half the year – above the plain of olives. At its foot extends 'Hollow Lacedaemon': a wide and fertile valley traversed by the oleander-bordered stream of the Eurotas. In the middle of it lies the modern town of Sparta.

CHAPTER 24

Sparta

Modern Sparti – The Ancient Site –
The Sanctuary of Artemis Orthia – The Museum –
The Roman Mosaics – Amyclae – Therapne –
The Langada Pass.

The name alone – Sparta – recalls the fear and hatred it once inspired in those Greek city states whose relatively enlightened civilizations were extinguished by the will of this 'master race' who, from their capital city, expanded their control throughout Laconia and much of the rest of the Peloponnese. Yet the landscape has a radiance and a fertility that make an instant appeal to the senses. Homer says that Laconia – or Lacedaemon – was 'full of hollows', and indeed the red earth of the valley, now covered with olive groves, is broken up by escarpments and gullies, thick with ever-greens and aromatic shrubs. Streams flow down from Taigetos through groves of oranges and mulberries into the swift muddy currents of the Eurotas. The river banks are bordered with luxuriant oleanders and the orchards are studded with dwarf palms, from whose branches rope was made in the Bronze Age. Over it all looms Taigetos; the result of some prodigious primeval convulsion, its spurs are rent with chasms and precipices, crowned by a series of jagged summits, on the highest of which horses were sacrificed to the sun. From certain angles the range has a savage, even cruel, aspect; it is not difficult to associate it with the austere militaristic community that dwelt in its shadow.

Laconia is a traveller's paradise. Landscape, mythology, history, primitive sculpture, Byzantine churches, medieval castles – it has

357

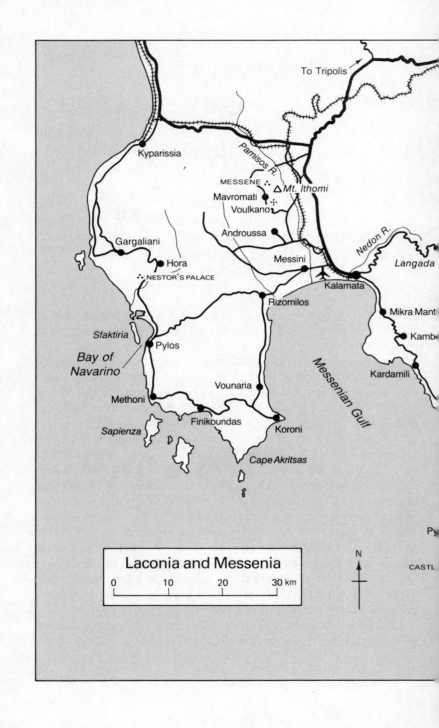

Laconia and Messenia

0   10   20   30 km

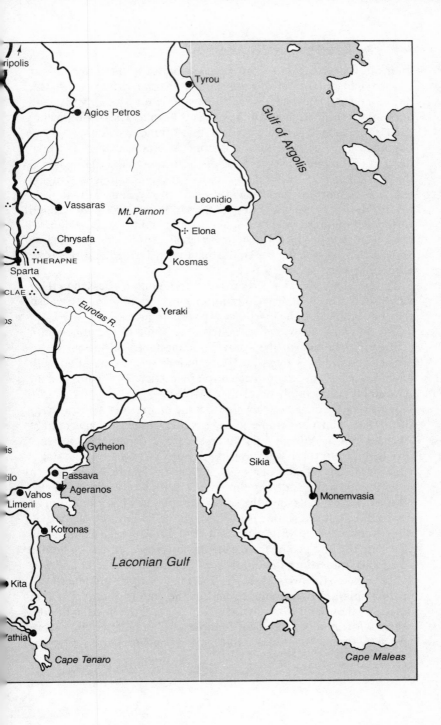

them all. Based on Sparta, the traveller requires a minimum of four days to sightsee comfortably: one day for the sites of ancient Sparta, Amyclae and Therapne; one for Mistra; one for Monemvasia, and another for the churches at Chrysafa and Yeraki. The obvious route runs from north to south, with deviations to the east and west. One begins, in fact, at the end of the story, at a point before the final descent to the Laconian plain, where a turning to the right leads to the battlefield of Sellasia. Here, in 222 BC, the prolonged struggle which the Spartans had waged so stubbornly and courageously against the overwhelming forces of the Macedonian king, now allied to the Peloponnesian states, came to a calamitous end when repeated charges of Macedonian heavy cavalry broke the Spartan line and put their king to flight. For the first time in history a hostile army entered Sparta.

Today, Spartans, who possess a rich soil, emigrate less than their neighbours, the Arcadians. Traditionally right-wing and 'Royalist' they have inherited the love of order of their ancestors.

The modern town, called **Sparti**, was built in the nineteenth century on the site of the sprawling communes of antiquity. Intersecting parallel streets are surrounded by gardens filled with magnolia trees and semi-tropical plants. There are a number of reasonably comfortable hotels.

It is a quarter of an hour's walk from the main street to the ancient site, situated on a low eminence, excavated by the British School of Archaeology at Athens. First to be seen is a rectangular substructure with two or three well-preserved courses of square stone slabs, which is all that remains of a small Hellenistic temple. Next comes a low Roman wall, and, beyond it, the centre of ancient **Sparta**, undefended by walls until the second century BC. The ruins are not impressive, but the setting is bucolic – the hilly ground, shaded by olive trees, covered with vetch and mullein. The relative insignificance of the site, compared with the brilliance of the Athenian Acropolis, underlines the difference of outlook, character and way of life between the two states. The Spartans, having confidence both in their military pre-eminence and in the ring of mountains that defended their land from invaders, did not feel the need to huddle round a fortified citadel. Their temples and public buildings were few and, though scattered amid gardens and orchards, were remarkable neither for beauty of form nor for sculptural embellishments. Thucydides, in a famous passage, was forced to conclude: 'For I suppose, if Lacedaemon were to become desolate and the temples and the foundations of the public buildings were left, that as time went on there would be a strong disposition with posterity to refuse to accept her fame as a true exponent of her power.' Prophetic words. Even at that magical moment when the late afternoon sun turns the snow-capped fingers and peaks of Taigetos to flame, the most romantic of travellers is unlikely to find the verdict of Thucydides exaggerated.

Not only was architectural distinction lacking. Rare among ancient Greeks, the Spartans were indifferent to the arts and literature, music and verse serving only as a means of extolling the martial virtues. Ignorant of international commerce and unmoved by social graces, they were also devoid of any talent for philosophy, rhetoric or dialectics. Conquest, regimentation and observance of the law were deemed worthier goals. Citizens were divided into three classes: Spartans proper, of unmixed Dorian descent, who dwelt in the city and constituted the ruling class; *perioeci*, freedmen, who lived in neighbouring townships but were not allowed any share in government; and *helots*, who were bound in serfdom to the soil, performed military service and farmed the king's estates. The spirit of heredity was ingrained, and it applied, says Herodotus, to all professions – even cooks, flute-players and town-criers. A man with a fine, loud voice, eager to prove his talent as a herald, could not do so unless his father had been one before him. At the summit of the oligarchical chain were the two kings, that curious dual monarchy, peculiar to Sparta, which, as Herodotus relates, had its origins in the birth of male twins to the reigning monarch – an event that placed the Spartans in a dilemma and even perplexed the Delphic oracle. As there was no way of telling which was the elder, both sons ascended the throne and the dual monarchy became a permanent institution. The system prevented either monarch from gaining preponderant power. The kings led the army into battle so that, in the eyes of the people, they were more closely identified with conquest than with government. Administration and policy-making were in the hands of a body of *ephors* (literally 'overseers') who were elected annually and protected the people from royal abuse.

This election, democratic in essence, is paradoxical in an otherwise wholly dictatorial system. The *ephors* wielded immense power and had the authority to recall a monarch from the wars; even to try him and punish him if his conduct of a campaign was questionable. Behind the *ephors* lurked the Crypteia, an unsavoury secret service, as all-pervading as any modern totalitarian institution of its kind. Its agents consisted largely of young thugs, fully armed, who roamed the countryside terrorizing insubordinate *helots*.

The position of women was curiously anomalous. Spartan maidens did not lead as joyless or secluded an existence as their sisters in other Greek states. Clad in short tunics and those famous slit skirts that scandalized the rest of Greece, they underwent as rigorous a physical training as the youths, taking part in foot races, wrestling and boxing matches. In order to toughen the women, Lycurgus ordered them to go naked in processions and, Plutarch adds, to 'dance too, in that condition, at certain solemn feasts, while the young men stood around, seeing and hearing them'. These exhibitions were intended as incitements to matrimony, i.e. procreation, sole Spartan object of union between men and women. At the same time homosexuality between men was not only condoned but encouraged, particularly in the army, where high-ranking pederasts trained their protégés in the science of war and the principles of Spartan discipline. Bachelors, however, were so heartily despised for failing to produce male children that they were disenfranchised and obliged to march naked round the market place on the coldest winter day as a mark of their disgrace. Married men only approached their wives at night and, after spending an hour with them in total darkness and silence, returned to the men's quarters. Often a man did not see his wife's face by daylight until after the birth of their first child. From the age of seven all healthy male children led a barrack-like life. If they showed any physical disability they were left to die on Mount Taigetos. A mother's final exhortation to her son going to the wars was a blunt command to return alive if victorious, dead if defeated. Everything – education, diet, love and recreation – was geared to the single aim of military efficiency.

That the ideals of regimentation and militarism alone should have sustained a whole people and made them a great power which dominated the civilized Hellenic world for nearly five hundred years remains a tribute to their staying-power, selflessness – and stupidity. To realize how such a 'civilization' was possible, one has only to glance at the map. With the Arcadian massif to the north and the sprawling bulk of Parnon in the east, the sea (with its paucity of anchorages) in the south, and the impassable barrier of Taigetos in the west, the 'iron curtain' was complete. There was hardly a chink through which the new currents of thought galvanizing the rest of Greece could penetrate. Moreover, all the records indicate that Sparta's attitude to her victims was one of arrogance and high-handedness. She was, in fact, thoroughly hated by everyone.

Silence now reigns over the exiguous ruins of the 'hated' city. Beyond a late Roman wall there is evidence of some stone-built 'ovens' or 'bakeries', also Roman. To the west, overgrown with thistles and wild olive, is the *cavea* of the Hellenistic theatre which was among the largest in Greece. A few tiers are preserved. The building was apparently reserved for public assemblies, dramatic representations being prohibited on the grounds that they were effete. Nearby was a spacious *agora*, of which nothing remains. Above the theatre is a thicket of eucalyptus and pine trees and some fragmentary foundations of the most famous building in Sparta, the **Temple of Athena Chalkioikos** (The Brazen House of Athena), so-called because its walls were entirely covered with bronze shields depicting the exploits of the Dioscuri and the Labours of Heracles. It stood in a sacred enclosure surrounded by colonnades, with the tomb of the Homeric king, Tyndareus, at the southern end. It was outside the Brazen House that Lycurgus, fleeing one day from his enemies, was attacked by a hot-headed youth, who blinded him in one eye. He took the disfigurement very philosophically and promptly ordered a temple of Ophthalmitis to be raised within the enclosure to commemorate the event.

At the eastern end of the plateau is the outline, with column bases and traces of an apse, of the tenth-century basilica of St Nicon Metanoitis ('The Repenter'), a nomadic missionary. Across the Evrotas the undulating red ground ascends gradually towards the foothills of Parnon, which lies further from Sparta than Taigetos, giving a feeling of spaciousness which is absent in the west, where the immense range rises like a wall. A path to the east leads around a hummock to the **Sanctuary of Artemis Orthia** ('The Upright') on the bank of the river, among the reeds and croaking frogs. This was the religious centre of the sprawling city, where ferocious 'coming of age' rites were performed, including the flagellation ordeal, in which boys were whipped on an altar in front of the temple until their flesh was torn to bleeding ribbons. Those who endured the ordeal without crying out were awarded the title of altar-winner and the prize of a sickle blade. The excavations have revealed a series of substructures of altars one below the other, dating from the eighth century BC to the third AD, the earlier ones consisting of unworked stones and rough slabs. The walls were of unbaked bricks. The site has little to offer, except gruesome memories, the sound of running water and the sight of farm workers tending fruit trees.

The **museum** in Lycourgou Street should not be missed. The exhibits, found mostly around the acropolis and sanctuary of Artemis, are the only existing relics of creative art in ancient Sparta. Laconian Archaic sculpture is crude but arresting. The best fragments – more vigorous than elegant, symbolic than idealistic – belong to the sixth and fifth centuries BC. After that the curtain comes down and all art withers and dies.

The entrance hall contains pedestals of statues of victors in the flogging ordeal. Some are inscribed with the names of youths trained to bear the most atrocious physical pain in the service of a puritanical goddess.

Taking the right wing first, one enters Room 1, the hall of the Chthonian deities. Two sides of a **pyramidal stele** (c. 600 BC) are carved with snakes, symbols of the Dioscuri, Helen's twin brothers, which appear repeatedly in Laconian art. On the third side we see a helmeted Agamemnon beseeching Clytemnestra, the Spartan princess, to marry him. Both figures are very squat. Clytemnestra's hair hangs in tight curls down to her shoulders and she holds the mysterious sickle in her left hand. An early fifth-century *stele*, in the very flat relief typical of Laconian sculpture, depicts an unknown bearded man in profile, seated on a throne, the legs of which terminate in lions' feet. The elegant throne, the self-assured pose of the seated figure and the details of a dog and horse combine to produce a minor masterpiece. An earlier sixth-century *stele* in the same flat relief represents a seated man and woman. The man's face is missing, but the woman's, with large almond-shaped eyes and a firm chin, has an Egyptian impassivity.

Further on are *stelae* of the Dioscuri, the most ubiquitous characters in Spartan mythology. **Stele No. 575** (early sixth-century BC) depicts the immortal twins armed with spears, facing each other on either side of two large *amphorae* with slender necks. Above them, two snakes flank the egg of Leda, from which their lovely sister was hatched. Executed in grey marble in the shallowest possible relief, crude and primitive in technique, it nevertheless possesses remarkable symmetry and formality. Two other *stelae* are worth looking at: one of Pentelic marble representing the brothers frontally, their spears resting on their horses' manes; and a smaller one of red Taigetos marble, in which they are mounted, facing each other.

In Room 3 we move into a more classical atmosphere. An unusual and very fine capital from the throne of Apollo at Amyclae is a good example of the polished workmanship of Ionian sculpture of the late sixth century BC with its blending of Doric vigour and Ionic grace. No. 468 is a fifth-century *stele* of the Attic school, of Artemis pouring a libation into a vase extended by Apollo, who holds a lyre. The richness of the drapery, the flowing line and graceful design seem extraordinarily effortless after the harsh austerity of the stylized Laconian reliefs. The same room contains a bust of a **helmeted warrior** in Parian marble, found on the site of the Brazen House and immediately called 'Leonidas' by the workmen on the dig. Although an early fifth-century work, it was probably executed some years after the death of the hero of Thermopylae. The warrior is depicted at the age of maturity, the half-smiling mouth is full-lipped, the neck short and thickset. It is obviously the work of an accomplished artist. More beautiful is the headless **torso of an athlete** (No. 94), without legs or forearms, sometimes ascribed to Polycleitus. In its economy and perfection of modelling, with the torso growing so beautifully out of the slender waist, it recalls an earlier and greater masterpiece: the Kritios Boy in the Acropolis Museum. The left wing of the museum is less interesting. Room 4 possesses a collection of tiny metal figures in very flat relief of warriors, animals and winged creatures. In Room 5 there are torsos of headless youths, mostly less than life-size – eternal glorification of the self-centred Spartan male.

Two fine mosaic pavements, which once adorned the floors of a sumptuous Roman villa, have also been preserved. Idolatry and superstition have been replaced by an intense pleasure in colour and sensuousness. Thousands of little painted pebbles form compositions of set-piece mythological scenes. They are evocative of wealth and a patrician way of life – Roman, spacious, luxurious. Life in Roman Sparta was uneventful and probably very agreeable, for the conquest of Flaminius had banished all thoughts of further military aggression from the inhabitants.

The first mosaic tells the story of **Europa and the Bull**, in which the pretty daughter of the King of Tyre is borne away on the back of Zeus, transformed into a bull maddened with lust. The second mosaic represents **Orpheus playing to the animals**. The figure with the lyre is conventional and the poet-musician's features lack the spirited expression of the flirtatious Europa. There is a third mosaic of inferior quality, of Achilles dressed as a girl among the daughters of Lycomedes. Sarcophagi, broken columns and capitals overflow into the museum garden.

One tends to leave the museum with mixed feelings: admiration for the vigour of execution of the totem-like *stelae*; nostalgia for the purity and perfection of Attic sculpture, and a sense of relief that a tiny chink of light has illumined the strange sullen character of Xenophon's 'master race'. The Spartans may have been militaristic bullies, but they were not unmoved by the desire to create an aesthetic image, crude but sincere, of their religious aspirations. In the final analysis, however, Laconian sculpture is a blind alley. Like Sparta's citizens, it was incapable of evolution.

Just south of Sparta, along the highway to Gytheion, a road to the left runs through orange groves to a hillock with a chapel of Agia Kyriaki. This is the site of flowery **Amyclae**, where, in pre-Hellenic times, the cult of Apollo was practised. Later Amyclae was linked with Sparta by a sacred way, and the Hyacinthia, a national festival with melancholy associations, was celebrated there at the height of summer, a season of torrid heat and wilting flowers. The festival was in commemoration of one of the god's ill-starred love affairs: practising discus-throwing at Amyclae one day, Apollo inadvertently killed his favourite, Hyacinthus, when Zephyrus, the jealous West Wind, who was also enamoured of the youth, deliberately blew Apollo's discus in the wrong direction so that it struck Hyacinthus on the head. The flower that grew from the soil watered by his blood was the first hyacinth, emblem of death. Now, in early spring, purplish-blue grape-hyacinths grow in clusters among the asphodel at Amyclae. A colossal Archaic statue of Apollo, seated on an ornate throne, the foundations of which lie under the present chapel, was famous throughout Greece. All that remains now is a Roman inscription, part of a votive gift offered by the Emperor Tiberius in memory of Hyacinthus, and a semi-circle of supporting wall running in an arc round the north-eastern side of the hill.

Therapne, probably of equal antiquity, is even more evocative in its commanding position. At the beginning of the road to Yeraki, a track to the left mounts an escarpment covered with tall grass, brushwood and fruit trees, passes a giant eucalyptus, and then climbs between hedgerows of gorse and broom interlaced with honeysuckle. The so-called **Menelaeum** is perched on a precipitous bluff above the orange groves bordering the gravelly bed of the Eurotas. Ruined masonry from the shrine of Menelaus and Helen stands on three platforms, crowning the hill, from which there is a magnificent view. Extending over the two lower terraces are Mycenaean remains, dating back to the fifteenth century BC, which were excavated by the British School of Architecture in 1910 and 1973. The palace, similar (although smaller) than the Palace of Nestor at Pylos, was destroyed by fire in 1200 BC. To the north extends the upper valley of the river, powdery blue in the afternoon sun, its main stream of ice-cold water winding down from the saddle between Taigetos and the Arcadian massif where it has its source. In the east roll the bleak Tsakonian hills, seamed with shallow ravines. The stylobate of the Menelaeum is a stepped rectangular structure, with three courses of enormous stone blocks. Tradition – confirmed by Pausanius – holds that it is the site of a temple of Menelaus which contained both his and Helen's tombs. Suppliants used to flock here: the men to implore Menelaus to grant them victory in battle, the women to beseech Helen to endow them with beauty.

Close by lay the Phoebaeum (the site has not been identified), which contained a temple of the Dioscuri. Sacrifices were held here before the ceremonial fights designed by Lycurgus to harden the young men of Sparta. The nocturnal ceremony involved all-in wrestling fights between youths, with the contestants kicking, biting and gouging each other's eyes out. When the ceremony was over, the winners hurled the battered bodies of their opponents into the river. There were no half-measures in Lycurgus' toughening programme.

West of Sparta, the village of Tripi overhangs the plain on a buttress of Taigetos. Onto one of these spiky rocks the Spartans used to hurl criminals and political prisoners. The only survivor was Aristomenes, the Messenian national hero, who had a miraculous escape. His fall was broken by a projecting ledge and he reached the bottom alive, and clinging to the tail of a fox, found his way out of the gloomy canyon and rejoined the Messenian patriots.

The **Langada Pass**, which crosses the spine of Taigetos and descends towards Kalamata through the most splendid mountain scenery in the Peloponnese, starts at Tripi. Beyond the village the road winds above a torrent between vertical cliffs. In antiquity, Pausanias says all this country was 'well-stocked' with deer, boar and wild goats – the black mountain-goat is still here, hopping from one dizzily perched ledge to another. Passing through a tunnel of rock, the road weaves round towering bluffs and along narrow platforms blasted out of the limestone. Landslides and avalanches are common. After reaching the conifer belt and crossing the frontier between Laconia and Messenia, the road enters a densely wooded valley, bowl-shaped, majestic in its proportions. The ground is covered with thick bracken, and the air, even at the height of summer, is cool and bracing. On one occasion I remember that storm-clouds suddenly blotted out the peaks, the rain pelted down and the thunder ricocheted across the crater-shaped arena which is the heart of the Taigetos range. Equally suddenly it was all over. The brick roofs of two hamlets flashed like garnets; a pale rainbow in the west formed a tenuous arc from one pinnacled summit to another and the chestnut forests turned gold as shafts of sunlight pierced the scudding clouds.

The road then funnels into another narrow gorge and the descent begins, winding interminably between imprisoning heights. Slowly the walls of rock yawn open, the horizon widens and there are glimpses of green lowlands and a distant range of mountains crowned by a perfect 'Japanese' peak. The descent becomes more

abrupt; hundreds of feet below, the town of Kalamata, dominated
by the ruins of William de Villehardouin's castle, sprawls across the
edge of the shimmering plain.

CHAPTER 25

Medieval Cities

Mistra: The Metropolis; The Aphendiko;
The Palace of the Despots; The Castle;
The Pantanassa; The Peribleptos – Chrysafa –
Yeraki – Monemvasia: 'The Violet Rock';
The Fortress; The Church of Agia Sofia.

In the thirteenth century William de Villehardouin, most sympathetic and philhellenic of Frankish Princes of Achaea, built a strong fortress called **Mistra** on a spur of Mount Taigetos. Although not his capital, it was William's favourite residence, from which he could dominate the Slav settlers in the valley of the Eurotas and the tribesmen of the Taigetos range. (After the Slav invasions of the seventh century the Laconians had fled either south to the Mani or into the mountains and Slav blood is assumed to run in the veins of most present-day Spartans.) Looking down from the summit of the keep onto these fertile domains enclosed by ranges of purple mountains, one understands why he felt so deeply about it and was heart-broken when, after his capture at the battle of Pelagonia by the forces of a renascent Byzantium, he was obliged to surrender Mistra as part of his ransom. The hill-town's brief but glorious history began at that moment. Today, unlike any other Byzantine site, it is an entire medieval walled city, where the main churches have been expertly restored and where steep, narrow stairways climb between ruined chapels and roofless houses.

After William de Villehardouin's cession of the castle to the Emperor Michael VIII, Mistra increased in importance as a haven of Byzantine civilization in a rapidly dwindling empire. High-ranking officers came from Constantinople to command its garrison and, by the early fourteenth century, eminent architects were building lavishly decorated churches. In 1348 the Emperor John VI appointed his son Manuel Cantacuzenus, as governor of Mistra, with the title of Despot. During the thirty years of his Despotate, Manuel not only improved the living conditions of the Laconian population but also encouraged church-building, created facilities for scholars, engaged book-illuminators to copy valuable manuscripts and promoted the collection and study of books. By the first half of the fifteenth century the city was a recognized seat of learning, frequented by scholars, sophists and courtiers. The analogy with an Italian city of the Renaissance is not too far-fetched. Politically, too, as the Turks drew the ring tighter round Constantinople, Mistra grew in importance. Moreover, never, in its short heyday of fame, was Mistra's history debased by the catalogue of political crime and assassination which punctuated that of Constantinople with such depressing regularity. In 1449, when the end was near, Constantine XI Dragases, last and most heroic of Byzantine emperors, was crowned at Mistra. It was the final coronation and the first at which the Patriarch of Constantinople did not officiate. Constantine then sailed in a Catalan vessel to his doomed capital. It was all over by 1459 – six years after the fall of Constantinople. Under Turkish rule the town continued to be inhabited, and, at one time, local pashas resided in the Palace of the Despots. They do not, however, appear to have turned any of the arcaded churches or princely mansions into harems or *hammams*.

Mistra was a brief flowering of the best qualities of Byzantine civilization, a last refuge of sanity and scholarship in a dying world. Today its fame rests mainly on its church frescoes, some of which are among the finest examples of late Byzantine painting. The Mistra frescoes are claimed by enthusiastic connoisseurs to be the purest reflection of the Hellenistic tradition continued in terms of Christian art (with additions of eastern mysticism and Oriental splendour), and to have influenced Giotto directly. Greek iconographers had certainly begun to emigrate to Italy by the fourteenth century, and Giotto may well have been influenced by Byzantine models; but he never saw the Mistra frescoes, which were executed between 1330 and 1430 – that is to say, in the century following his death. The frescoes possess undeniable evidence of Western influence, and it was probably a case of two-way traffic, as Byzantine scholars were visiting Italy in increasing numbers and, on returning to Constantinople and Mistra, they passed on the lessons that they had learnt in the West to local artists and architects.

At its worst, Byzantine (or Palaeologue) painting is illustrative and fussy; at its best, as in Mistra, it reveals the development of the twelfth-century desire to introduce a more naturalistic element into the representation of the Divine. Poses, gestures and attitudes are more relaxed, the manipulation of colours fresher and more subtle, attention to detail greater and the treatment of crowd scenes more dramatic. But what Palaeologue painting gains in richness and variety, it loses in economy and sturdiness. The new trends, for all their exhilarating effect, sap the monumental vigour which is the glory of the mosaics of Daphni and Hosios Loukas. After Mistra, true Byzantine painting – whose theme had lasted a thousand years – died. Post-Byzantine art continued the tradition in other parts of the country, notably on Mount Athos, in Crete and the Ionian islands; but it is always a requiem – splendid, solemn and rather redundant.

The road from Sparta goes as far as the upper gate of the city from where a path leads to the Frankish castle. However the usual entrance is by the restored gate into the lower city, which is a warren of dereliction, with the empty shells of churches, houses and shops. A steep north-bound path leads to the **Metropolis**, dedicated to St Demetrius and first in rank, though not in artistic quality, among the churches of Mistra. A three-aisled basilica, it is surmounted by a later cruciform upper storey with a gallery and five cupolas. This architectural plan – a mixture of the Roman-inspired basilica and the Greek Cross plan – is repeated again and again at Mistra and it causes the churches, although small, to seem overcrowded and complex. The upper register, the Greek Cross, creates an air of loftiness within, which is absent from the outside. Here the celestial hierarchy is depicted in frescoes set out in strict conformity with the liturgical canons, and is crowned by the central cupola where Christ reigns over the world. The lower register consists of aisles, side chapels, porches, arches and screens, all possessing a symbolic significance. These break up the main body of the church into

372

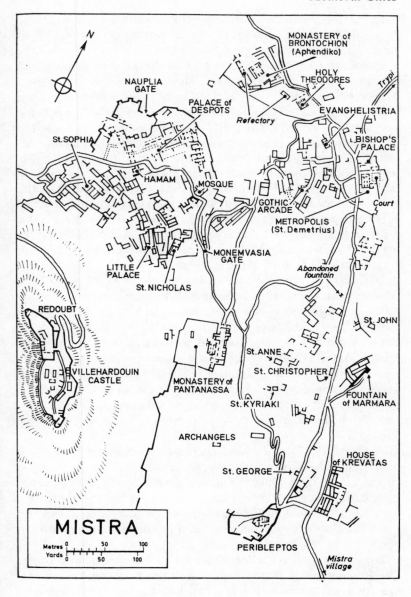

N

MONASTERY of
BRONTOCHION
(Aphendiko)

HOLY
THEODORES

NAUPLIA
GATE

PALACE of
DESPOTS

Trypi

EVANGHELISTRIA

Refectory

St.SOPHIA

BISHOP'S
PALACE

HAMAM

MOSQUE

Court

GOTHIC
ARCADE

METROPOLIS
(St. Demetrius)

LITTLE
PALACE

MONEMVASIA
GATE

*Abandoned
fountain*

St. NICHOLAS

St. JOHN

REDOUBT

VILLEHARDOUIN
CASTLE

St. ANNE

St. CHRISTOPHER

MONASTERY of
PANTANASSA

FOUNTAIN
of MARMARA

St. KYRIAKI

ARCHANGELS

HOUSE
of KREVATAS

St. GEORGE

MISTRA

Metres 0   50   100
Yards 0   50   100

PERIBLEPTOS

*Mistra
village*

different compartments and heighten the impression of complexity. This is deliberate, for Byzantine church-builders sought thereby to create a sense of mystery and religious awe.

The *Metropolis* was built in the early fourteenth century and restored in the fifteenth. The damaged frescoes are rather stereotyped in style but recent cleaning has disclosed the brilliance of the colours, as well as fresh details formerly overlaid by inferior works of later periods. The Last Judgement in the narthex is full of the usual horrors, including naked figures around which snakes are coiled. The marble columns, on either side of the central aisle, support capitals looted from the debris of ancient Sparta. A marble slab, carved with the Byzantine double-headed eagle, indicates the spot where the last emperor stood during his coronation. The small adjacent episcopal palace houses a museum of local finds. The courtyard, surrounded by arcades, is a lovely, quiet place overlooking the plain, with the billowing foothills of Parnon forming a bluish barrier, full of shadows, in the east.

The next two churches, dependencies of the Monastery of the Brontochion, are small. The **Evanghelistria**'s high apse and octagonal drum with four windows alternating with arched niches overlook the outbuildings of the *Metropolis*. In the simplicity of its single dome and inclined roofs, it seems almost out of place at Mistra. **Agioi Theodoroi**, the oldest church in Mistra (late thirteenth-century), is conspicuous for its large squat dome, perched, like a vast tea-cosy, above a confusion of planes created by three roof-levels and a triple three-sided apse with elaborate brickwork decoration around multiple arched windows. The frescoes are very damaged.

To the north of *Agioi Theodoroi* is the rather showy **Aphendiko**, dedicated to the Virgin *Hodigitria*: a mass of rounded forms, almost concentric in effect. Once the main church of the *Brontochion*, the *Aphendiko* is a sumptuous affair, with tall supporting buttresses, toy cupolas, barrel vaults, billowing apses, a succession of inclined roofs and a little loggia composed of three slender columns on the north side.

The interior plan is similar to that of the *Metropolis*, but grander. The frescoes are of better quality, with the accent on movement, narration and dramatic incident. In the narthex, generally reserved for miracles, the Woman of Samaria stands between figures grouped on either side of the well where she is drawing water. The figures are relaxed and naturalistic, the drapery of their garments subtly shaded. In the north chapel of the narthex, nine martyrs of varying ages, their expressions devoid of the usual rigid tension, screen a host of other martyrs, whose haloes recede into an opaque haze. The chapel contains the tombs of the Despot Theodore II Paleologus and the Abbot Pachomius, founder of the church. The Abbot is portrayed in a fresco as a small and humble monk offering his foundation to an upright Virgin. The walls of the sombre south chapel, the so-called 'Chamber of the Chrysobulls', are lined with copies of the imperial charters listing the monastery's assets, which included entire villages and great tracts of the Peloponnese.

In the main nave a beautiful, ancient capital crowns the first column of the south colonnade. A portrait of the **Prophet Melchizedek** in a diminutive south cupola is framed within rolled leaves. It is a venerable head, with an expression of fierce intensity, the flesh standing out ivory-smooth against green and brown shading. He holds a golden scroll, and the drapery of his garment is the colour of faded rose. A new and subtle use of colour is apparent in this portrait. One of the objects in using a wider range of colours was to heighten the human quality of the faces, and the head of Melchizedek is a landmark in this process.

In the centre of the Greek Cross, Christ reigns in glory, worshipped by apostles with conventional expressions of awe. Below the celestial plane, figures of saints and prophets in garments of brown and old gold are scattered across vaults and outer aisles.

Leaving the lower town, you now take the steep path which winds up through the double-arched Monemvasia Gate to the aristocratic quarter, where the Despot dwelt. The size alone of the **Palace of the Despots** is proof of the splendour and solemnity with which the first Despot, Manuel Cantacuzenus, the Emperor's son, surrounded himself. The palace faces north-east, towards the valley through which the Eurotas flows between ranges of foothills. The great shell of the building occupies a wide ledge of the mountain-side. A mass of ruined chambers dating from the mid-thirteenth century to the late fourteenth are ranged along the east wing of the L-shaped court, where the remains of a little Turkish mosque strike a somewhat incongruous note in a setting which could not be less Oriental. Here were held large public gatherings, attended by the social and intellectual élite of Mistra.

The west wing of the palace is more impressive, with its superimposed stories: first a vaulted ground floor which is now half-buried, then a low-ceilinged first floor with eight chambers which do not intercommunicate, and finally a long, rectangular top storey consisting of a throne-room with shallow apses in the walls and stone seats for dignitaries under arched windows; higher still are successive rows of square and round windows through which diagonal shafts of light fell upon the assembled court. On the north façade of the east wing, a narrow projecting balcony, supported by six great arches, overlooks the flanks of Taigetos. It is rare in Greece to find such a finely preserved piece of lay architecture.

South of the palace, near the small Church of *Agios Nikolaos*, is the shell of a large mansion known as the *Palataki* (the Little Palace), residence of one of the leading local families, once full of arcades, balconies and interior stairways. The tower on the south side is rich in brickwork decoration. Even in its present jumble of tottering masonry, the *Palataki* succeeds in conveying the impression of a great town residence, where the good life was led and where rich men and women dwelt in cultivated ease, waited on by well-trained attendants.

West of the *Palataki*, the attractive little Church of *Agia Sofia* crowns a ledge below the castle. It was a palace chapel built in the mid-fourteenth century by the Despot Manuel, whose coat-of-arms is carved on a marble slab. The entrance is through an unusually large domed narthex and the historiated pavement is the most lavish in Mistra. The architectural arrangement is the usual maze of naves, chapels and galleries; the frescoes are negligible. The charming belfry above the north gallery was transformed into a minaret during the Turkish occupation.

A steep twisting path leads up to the keep of the **Castle** built by William de Villehardouin in the mid-thirteenth century. Born in Greece, he loved the country and governed it better than any other Frankish prince. But his education, outlook and way of life were French. At Mistra, where he established a school of chivalry famous throughout Europe, he was protected by a bodyguard of a thousand horsemen, who must have offered an alien spectacle to the inhabitants of the plain when they rode out with the Prince to visit some neighbouring vassal, their lances crowned with pennons fluttering above the dusty olive branches.

The outer gate is on the north-west side. A vaulted passage leads through the curtain wall into the outer bailey. The path ascends again to the inner bailey. To the left is a vaulted cistern; used in times of siege, it still contains a pool of slimy water. Beyond it a round tower commands an immense prospect of the plain. Higher up still extends the rubble of the irregular, oval keep. Its rounded bastions are all Frankish, with a few Byzantine and Turkish additions. On the wind-swept summit wild flowers grow between stone slabs, eroded into strange pock-marked forms. On the western side the rock falls away sheer into a deep and wild ravine.

From the Monemvasia Gate, another path slants to the south towards a narrow ledge where the **Monastery of the Pantanassa**, with its pretty bell-tower, is flanked by cypresses. The Pantanassa is the most homely place in Mistra and it is still inhabited – by nuns. Films, coloured slides, post-cards and pocket guidebooks are on sale in the guest house. The courtyard is full of flowers.

The *Pantanassa* may be small, but there is a great deal to see. An hour is well spent. Take the exterior first. Founded in 1428 by the Despot's first minister, the church is architecturally a replica of the *Aphendiko*, but on a smaller scale, with very high apses decorated with arched windows. The two apsidal stories are separated by a frieze in the form of a garland, painted blue and red. Within the built-in arches there are more blind arches – a central one flanked by two broken ones. Even the belfry at the extremity of the east façade has arched porticoes on its two upper stories and is crowned by an elliptical dome. The whole thing is a riot of warm, red-brick curves.

Passing through a doorway ornamented with Cufic designs, one enters the usual Mistra-type basilica with a cruciform upper storey. The six marble columns which divide the aisles are crowned by capitals with floral designs, combining the Ionic and Corinthian orders. The light is dim and the space confined – the anonymous master of the *Pantanassa* must have had an agonizing task trying to condense the whole of Heaven and Earth into this maze of little cupolas, shallow pendentives and slender barrel vaults. The most important compositions are high up on the cruciform level and it is not always easy to view them from a satisfactory angle.

The frescoes are roughly contemporary with the foundation of the Monastery. In the variety and treatment of costumes, drapery and facial expression, in the lavish architectural backgrounds and, above all, in the startling range of colour, the artists of these crowded compositions seem to have turned their backs on the majesty severity of the eleventh and twelfth centuries. The perspective is still halting, the drawing often awkward, the inspiration liturgical, but the artists of the Cretan school who worked here were clearly trying to achieve a new liveliness and animation. In so doing they were, in a sense, precursors of the religious art destined to flourish on Mount Athos, in Serbia and in Russia during the sixteenth century. If the frescoes of the *Pantanassa* are the swan-song of Byzantine fresco-work, they are also an important stage in the evolution of religious painting in Eastern Europe.

The greatest compositions are those from the *Dodecaorton*. Take the **Ascension** first, in the arch above the altar. Two groups of apostles, centred round the figures of the Virgin and Archangel respectively, gaze upwards in awe. The Archangel, one of the most idealized portraits in Byzantine painting, might also be a forerunner of the celestial beings that swirl across the roof of the Sistine Chapel.

The acknowledged masterpiece is the **Raising of Lazarus**, in the vault overlooking the nave on the left of the altar. The scene is dominated by the tragic corpse, flanked by a weeping figure at once moving and naturalistic, and by a man vigorously unwinding the opaque and mouldering shroud. Within the limits imposed on him by tradition and convention, the artist has succeeded in conveying the dramatic anticipation inherent in the situation. The **Entry into Jerusalem**, on a curved vault above the nave, is another favourite. Although the composition loses in quality from excessive over-crowding, the range of its hues is incomparable. Amid a riot of colour, Christ rides into the city on a snow-white donkey, while the children play along the path before him and the elders of the city advance to meet him.

The very damaged **Nativity** in the south transept recalls in its detail more than one Giottoesque representation of the same scene: the crib, the animals, the dashing yet stylized horses on which the

Magi, in green and yellow cloaks, are mounted. As a composition, it is more quaint than moving; but the figure pouring water from the pitcher is very compelling. In the **Annunciation**, against an opulent, palatial background broken by porphyry columns, the angel, whose face is damaged beyond repair, is borne on outstretched wings painted in metallic greens and yellows tinged with a softening grey. The marble floor is deep pink, and at the angel's feet a striped quail drinks from a pool fed by a pineapple-shaped fountain. In a little north-west cupola there is a particularly impressive head of a bishop: a dark mass painted entirely in green and purple, with light provided (in the Byzantine manner) by a series of white brush-strokes, which follow the wrinkles of the brow and the matted strands of the beard.

From the *Pantanassa* the path zigzags down the hill. This must have been a populous residential quarter; now scattered with the ruins of private houses, it includes that of John Frangopoulos, the founder of the *Pantanassa*, which has a balcony supported by arches, a vaulted basement and a water cistern.

At the end of the incline, the small, early fourteenth-century **Church of the Peribleptos** (The Resplendent One), shelters in a pine-wood. It is a plain, cruciform edifice with architectural adaptations necessitated by the sharp declivity of the ground. Like the *Pantanassa*, it once formed part of a monastic establishment. There is none of the prettiness of the *Pantanassa*, and more Byzantine austerity. The apses are not arched and they have no brick-work decoration. The frescoes are the work of two artists and those of the inferior one are easily distinguished by their oleograph-like quality; but the good frescoes are very good indeed, the most important in Mistra. They radiate sobriety and dignity in the best traditions of Constantinopolitan taste. At the *Pantanassa* the artist's *joie de vivre* and his desire to express the beauty of the physical world are uppermost; at the *Peribleptos* his predecessor blurred his colour tones, making his transitions less clearly defined, thus achieving a greater idealism. The artist's predilection for a luminous dark blue sets the tone immediately – a cool, solemn grandeur. The best-preserved frescoes are in the aisles and apses. In the sanctuary apse a tight-lipped, shrewish Virgin *Orans* stands between two archangels with tender expressions, while the apostles in bold, contorted attitudes gaze up at the wonder of the **Ascension**, and four angels in flowing drapery support the portrait of Christ. In the central apse the Virgin, in a more tender mood, sits enthroned holding the Child, painted in gold, flanked again by archangels. In the north apse, unfortunately very badly lit, unfolds the superb **Divine Liturgy**, a masterpiece of hieraticism, in which russet-haired angels with green wings, clad in long white dalmatics, carry the bread and wine for the Eucharist against a background of intense dark blue. In spite of the solemnity of the procession, the attitudes of the angels are natural and relaxed. Equally impressive is the figure of St John Chrysostom with a gentle, sensitive expression, wearing ceremonial vestments and unfolding a scroll.

Next come the scenes from the *Dodecaorton*: the **Transfiguration** in the west nave with its red-headed Christ in a white robe with orange tints; the **Crucifixion** in the south transept with its variety of costumes; the tragic Virgin in the **Descent from the Cross**, which betrays Siennese influences; the Virgin again, this time a reclining figure, in the **Nativity** (south transept), brooding and sullen, as though stunned by the momentous event that has just befallen her, watched by angels with expressions of wonderment. The *Periblep-tos* frescoes remain among the great masterpieces of Byzantine art. Thereafter a feeling of elegance and elaboration, so pronounced at the *Pantanassa*, increases; but in the process the inspiration becomes blurred.

Descending from the *Peribleptos* to the main road, one passes the ruined mansion of Krevatas, a local dignitary of the eighteenth century; Mistra, or at least the lower city, was thus still inhabited by people of consequence only two centuries ago. Below it, as the hill slopes more gently into the plain, extended the Turkish quarter of Mufteika where Ottoman officials dwelt. It is only a few minutes' walk from here to the hotel in the village.

After Mistra the churches at Chrysafa and Yeraki are an anticlimax. But the setting, among the scrub-covered hills of Parnon, presents a new aspect of Laconia, more rugged and remote. The churches, sturdy country chapels, with their interior walls covered with frescoes painted by peasant iconographers, seem to sprout out of the stones of the Parnon country. Like Taigetos, Parnon is a range rather than a mountain. The two ranges run parallel to each other but Parnon, unlike Taigetos, is composed of detached, amorphous masses. Stony, covered in brushwood and sparsely populated, much of it is dotted with wild almond trees twisted into contorted shapes by the north wind that blows across the plateau in winter.

A road on the east bank of the Eurotas mounts slowly between escarpments of red Laconian earth to the village of **Chrysafa**. It is essential to have a guide (ask for one at the café in the main square) who will know where to find the keys of the churches. The straggling village and the fields below it are dotted with churches dating from the fourteenth century onwards; in late medieval times Chrysafa must have been a prosperous community. The four main churches are typical of Laconian provincial art in the late Byzantine period. The first two are in the village itself: *Agios Demetrios*, cruciform, with a seventeenth-century narthex, its charred walls creating a sombre effect, possessing a good post-Byzantine icon of Christ *Elkomenos* (Christ being dragged); and the fourteenth-century *Koimesis*, smaller and less elegant than *Agios Demetrios*, with a hideous new *iconostasis* and some frescoes in a fair state of preservation in the north transept. The most important outlying churches – half an hour's walk across the undulating upland – are *Agios Ioannis Prodromos*, where there is a fine Transfiguration, with Christ clad in dull yellow garments ascending to Heaven in a pink cloud, and the *Chrysafiotissa* which was once a small monastery.

The road to Yeraki crosses the rugged, high-lying plateau of Tsakonia. Taigetos recedes, and the whole splendour of the range, as it tapers southward into the final extremity, the Mani, is seen in proper perspective – a great bluish, snow-capped spine severing the Southern Peloponnese. In front, the folds of Parnon run in irregular seams towards the Laconian Gulf. Between Sparta and Yeraki there is hardly a village worthy of the name. The few inhabitants are called Tsakonians, a race of which little is known, probably Slav in origin, wild and independent, some still speaking a dialect of their own.

Yeraki lies at the foot of a bare hill, near the site of ancient Geronthrae, a Spartan township, where an annual festival was held in honour of the god of war. Its Frankish castle formed part of the string of fortresses running in a rough horseshoe (west–north–east) that protected the fertile Laconian valley. Yeraki in Greek means falcon: a legacy of the days when French knights, hawks perched on their gloved hands, cantered across the bleak countryside to hunt woodcock and pigeon. As at Chrysafa it is essential to have a guide, for the churches are scattered among almond orchards around the village. When the castle passed from the Franks to the Byzantines after the battle of Pelagonia, it obviously remained a strategic stronghold; a small town grew up around it and a number of churches were built. Unlike Mistra, however, Yeraki was no cosmopolitan centre, no seat of learning. The churches are very small, their architecture and faded wall-paintings wholly provincial. First is *Agios Ioannis Chrysostomos*, a barrel-vaulted church with a single nave and apse. The south exterior has some haphazardly arranged decoration – bricks mixed with inland stone slabs – which creates a quaint but not unattractive effect. More slabs round the main doorway form an impressive frame for this modest entrance to an even more modest interior. The exterior walls of *Agios Sostis* (The Saviour) are decorated with the same inlaid slabs. In the fields below the village lies *Agioi Theodoroi* – its walls again inlaid with inscribed plaques – and *Agios Nikolaos*, now inhabited by bats, with faint traces of painting (probably rather good late thirteenth-century work).

Returning to the village along paths between stone walls there is the *Evanghelistria*, a little cruciform church in a cypress grove. Although the cylindrical drum is disproportionately tall, it is balanced by still taller cypresses. Some of the frescoes are in a fair state of preservation: a Pantocrator with glowing eyes in the cupola; a Transfiguration in the barrel vault above the sanctuary.

From the *Evanghelistria* it is at least an hour's climb up the steep hill, covered with prickly holm-oaks, to the castle, one of the hundred and twenty-two that once crowned the strategic heights of the Morea. A whole side of the hill is scattered with the remains of Byzantine buildings, but, unlike those at Mistra, these were never the dwellings of an aristocracy, either of class or of wealth, and anyway they are utterly ruined. The castle ramparts are also poorly preserved, except on the south side. The thyme-scented keep is entered from the south-west through an arch. At the north end of the enceinte is a postern. More interesting is the Church of *Agios Georgios*, near the main gateway. Frankish in origin – one of the few that remain in Greece – it bears a coat-of-arms, in the form of a shield decorated with chequers, over the arched entrance. Within the church there is a little stone shrine framing a modern icon, with two knotted columns supporting a Gothic arch carved with stars, fleur-de-lys and a coat-of-arms. Nothing could seem more incongruous than this crude piece of Gothic sculpture in the ruined chapel overlooking the sun-scorched Tsakonian wilderness.

The road from Sparta to Monemvasia runs first through flat, then undulating, country. It crosses the rush-bordered Eurotas and the plain of Sikia, covered with dense orchards of fig trees; climbs a range of lonely hills and then descends abruptly to the barren east coast of Laconia, with the rock of **Monemvasia** squatting elephantine at the southern extremity of a crescent-shaped bay (where Pausanias found the prettiest coloured pebbles he had ever seen).

The first, the inevitable, association is with the butt of Malmsey wine (the produce of vines around Monemvasia) in which the Duke of Clarence was drowned in 1478. However today there is no sign of the grapes from which the most highly prized wine in medieval Europe was pressed. When, in 1540, the Venetians surrendered the keys of Monemvasia, the last Christian fortress to hold out against the Turks, they removed not only their garrison and artillery, but also many of the inhabitants who wished to settle in other Venetian colonies: in Crete, Santorini, Corfu and Dalmatia. As they left, the Monemvasians tore up the vines, which they replanted in their new homes. A sweet amber-coloured wine, now produced on the volcanic island of Santorini, is said to be the nearest thing to medieval Malmsey.

The situation is remarkable, with the walled town lying at the foot of a formidable reddish-coloured rock, which turns violet in the afternoon sun. It is joined to the mainland by a narrow causeway – *i moni emvasis* ('the only entrance'): hence its name, Monemvasia. Lying on the main trade route between Italy and the Levant, its strategic value was once considerable. Wisely governed, under Comnene rule in the eleventh and twelfth centuries, the inhabitants enjoyed liberties and privileges unknown elsewhere in Greece, and

383

were renowned for their sense of civic responsibility. Its trading vessels ranged all over the Eastern Mediterranean and its sailors were among the most experienced in the imperial fleet.

As the Frankish conquest swept over Greece, Monemvasia was a formidable obstacle in the way of William de Villehardouin's domination of the Morea. The siege lasted three years and the garrison was reduced to a diet of cats and mice. To effect the final reduction, William had to invoke the aid of the Dukes of Athens and Naxos, the Baron of Euboea and Count Orsini of Cephalonia, as well as the Venetian fleet – an impressive force. But the French did not stay long. Eleven years after Monemvasia's capture, William suffered his humiliating defeat at Pelagonia and was forced to cede it as part of his ransom to the Byzantine emperor.

Once under Byzantine rule, Monemvasia became an important bishopric and a flourishing commercial centre. The Emperor Michael VIII was so impressed that he granted the merchants fiscal exemptions and the great squat rock, with its impregnable fortress, now towered above a port filled with vessels flying the flags of Byzantium, Venice, Genoa and Amalfi.

After the fall of Constantinople, when Sultan Mehmet II was overrunning the Morea, his greatest ambition was to reduce the 'violet rock' as the Turks called Monemvasia; yet even he, brilliant tactician that he was, refrained from attacking it, having a profound respect for the tradition of courage and endurance established by its inhabitants. While he was hesitating, the Monemvasians sought the protection of the Pope, whose local representative was a Catalan corsair. They soon grew resentful, however, of Pius II's attempts to extend his spiritual sway over this stronghold of Orthodoxy, turned out the papal agents, including the Spanish corsair, and placed their fate in the hands of a less bigoted Catholic power, the Serene Republic. The Venetians ruled wisely and tolerantly. Affluence and the special privileges enjoyed by the merchants under Byzantine rule returned. But most of the vineyards on the mainland slopes were now in Turkish-held territory and little Malmsey wine found its way to the dining tables of Western Europe. The rock, isolated, remained a bastion of Christianity on a Moslem shore. By 1540, with Ottoman power reaching its zenith, Venice was no longer able to supply and maintain her maritime forces, and Monemvasia, like

Mycenae: the Lion Gate, surmounted by the oldest piece of monumental statuary in Europe.

Mycenae: the 1st Royal Grave Circle, site of Schliemann's famous discovery in 1876 of six tombs containing sixteen skeletons and much rich treasure, including the so-called Mask of Agamemnon.

Tiryns: legendary home of Heracles. The secret passage leading to the Postern Gate.

Nafplio: the Venetian Palamidhi Fortress.

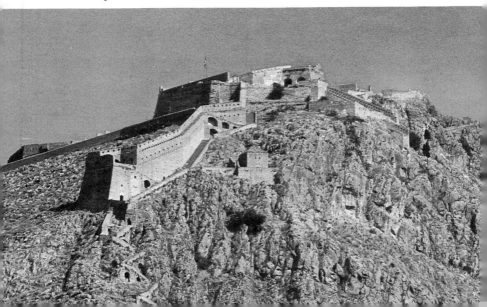

Nafplio, surrendered to the army of Suleiman the Magnificent. The loss of the two fortresses marked the end of Venetian colonial influence in mainland Greece, and the banner of the Lion of St Mark disappeared from the mainland. There was a respite in 1690–1715, when, following Morosini's expedition, the Venetians recaptured Monemvasia, to the joy of the inhabitants. But in 1715 the Turks returned and the curtain came down on Monemvasia. The buildings fell into ruin, the inhabitants lapsed into illiteracy, the birth-rate dropped and commerce languished. When the War of Independence broke out in 1821, Monemvasia was the first fortress in the Morea to be liberated by the Greeks.

The remains of the once-flourishing port are strung out along a narrow ledge between the 'violet rock' and the sea. A modern village with several hotels has grown up on the mainland, where the vineyards once extended. Across the causeway, under the perpendicular cliff, the old town faces seaward and is approached through a vaulted passage forming part of a triangular bastion. To the left of the passage a stairway leads up to the parapet. Two parallel walls run down to the sea, thus enclosing the town from the west and east. The rectangle is completed by the vertical cliff to the north and by a sea-wall along which one can stroll, to the south. Within the walled enclosure there is no wheeled traffic. In summer, boats and hydrofoils from Piraeus call regularly at the port.

A narrow alley, which is the main street, ends in a little esplanade. A Turkish cannon points out to sea. To the south, the last spurs of Parnon run into Cape Maleas, whose wild and rocky coast was the terror of ancient sailors. On the east side of the esplanade is the seventeenth-century Church of Christ *Elkomenos*, restored and whitewashed, built on the site of a more ancient foundation. The church was once the home of a famous icon of 'Christ being dragged', which was considered so holy and so beautiful that Emperor Isaac II Angelus removed it to Constantinople; today the church's only artistic treasure is a fine icon of the Crucifixion. Two pilasters with Corinthian-style capitals frame the main doorway and, above the lintel, there is a cornice with a decorative design in which two peacocks, facing outwards, perform an awkward but animated dance. Above the *Elkomenos* is the more severe pile of the fourteenth-century Church of the *Myrtiotissa*, with its shapely dome. The interior is as bare as the exterior, whose stonework presents a greyish chocolate-coloured surface – very forbidding after the extravagance of Mistra.

Several of the narrow three-storied houses have been restored by foreigners who have brought new life into the dereliction. Low battlements overhang the sea. At the eastern extremity there is another esplanade, larger than the first, with two austere churches: *Agios Nikolaos* is structurally almost identical to the *Myrtiotissa*, mud-grey in colour, and with the same sturdy architectural lines. The *Chrysafiotissa* (The Virgin of Chrysafa) is more modern (early seventeenth-century), ugly and whitewashed, with a huge tea-cosy dome; but in the minds of Laconian peasants, to whom the dividing line between religion, superstition and folklore is often tenuous, this church holds a special place, for it contains a chapel in which the famous flying icon of Chrysafa was found. The Virgin herself indicated the spot – a water-well, which still exists – in a dream to an old woman. The icon, it was said, had flown of its own volition from Chrysafa to Monemvasia at the Virgin's command. The inhabitants of Chrysafa had doubts, however, about the mechanics of the miraculous flight. Suspecting foul play, they came to Monemvasia on some specious pretext and stole back the icon. Again it flew, like a homing pigeon, across the Tsakonian mountains to its new abode. In the end the people of Chrysafa accepted a substitute icon presented by the triumphant Monemvasians, who kept the disputed one. The holy image's nocturnal flights ceased forthwith.

At this point the south rampart is well-preserved and it is possible to walk along the entire length of the sea-wall, which is slit with gun embrasures. Equally well-preserved is the long, descending line of the east wall (from the cliff face to the sea). Beyond it there is nothing but rocks, waves and a lighthouse, with the crenellated fortress towering a thousand feet above.

The **fortress** or upper town is approached by a path zigzagging up the cliff, passing under a low arch, with a sentry post commanding a lofty view of the domed churches and roofless houses below. At intervals the parapet is cut with arrow slits, but it is difficult to imagine how an invader could have contemplated scaling the perpendicular rock. One passes through a second archway to enter the upper town. Above the main arch is a plaque inscribed with the words 'Christ reigns here'. The iron-plated doors are studded with nails, and prison cells line one side of the vaulted passage. Emerging into the open, you face a slope covered with the debris of barracks, posterns, cisterns and guardrooms. A crenellated wall encircles the summit, except on the north side where the cliff is sheer. The bastions and a square fort are Byzantine structures. The shell of one house bears a Venetian coat-of-arms, and the Lion of St Mark is carved on a well-head. The rest of the fortifications, choked in thistles, spurge and thyme, are Turkish. In summer the scent of scorched herbs is overpowering. A wild fig tree points the way to the **Church of Agia Sofia** on a last crowning terrace. Founded at the end of the thirteenth century by the Emperor Andronicus II, an untiring patron of religious art, it was built on the same plan as the church at Daphni – lofty in conception, cruciform in plan, majestic in its proportions. Above the entrance, a marble slab depicts two lambs and two doves. The interior is very bare: some fragmentary frescoes in the pendentives and narthex; a better preserved Christ holding an open Book of Gospels above the main apse; a cornice with carvings along the divisions separating the narthex and nave. In its adornment *Agia Sofia* is negligible, in its proportions it is in the best traditions of Byzantine architecture.

To the north, the crescent-shaped bay, with its mile-long strand of sand, is dominated by the heights on which the Argives founded the colony of Epidaurus Limera. Immediately below, the cliff is fringed with black spiky rocks flecked with the spray of breaking waves.

Monemvasia has an excellent anchorage for yachts. The mainland beach is superb. There is nothing to prevent the abandoned towers, open to the stars, from being transformed into cosy little bars, their Venetian stone-work festooned with fishing-nets and strung with conches. One can see it all happening.

CHAPTER 26

The Mani

Gytheion – Cranae – Passava – Areopolis –
The Evil Mountains – Pyrgos Dirou –
The Niclian Country – Kita – Yerolimena –
Cape Tenaro – Itilo – Kelefa –
Nomitsis: the Byzantine Chapels –
Platsa: the Church of Agios Nikolaos – Kardamili.

The Mani offers no antiquities and little mythology. Pausanias scrabbled among some ruined shrines, but they failed to arouse his enthusiasm. The peninsula, the southernmost point of mainland Europe after Spanish Tarifa, projects like a misshapen fang, flanked by two others, into the Eastern Mediterranean. Its history is that of a small, but important, section of the Greek people, descendants of the ancient Spartans with a strong mixture of Slav blood. Fiercely independent, their warlike virtues inspired sufficient dread in the Sultan's armies to persuade the Sublime Porte that their passion for fratricidal strife was quite sufficient to subdue them and that costly operations were not necessary. For centuries the treeless plateaux and boulder-strewn ravines echoed to the crack of pistol shots fired by feuding families. Swathed in bandoliers and armed with *yataghans*, axes and muskets, they rode out of their towers – all houses worthy of the name possessed their protective towers: tall, rectangular obelisks of grey stone – not to till the fields or tend the vines but to kill their neighbours in the next village. The great Maniot families lived by the rule of blood and iron. In the eighteenth century they were granted official autonomy, thus securing a privileged status in the Ottoman Empire. The Mani may not be the mainstream of Greek history, but for anyone anxious to open a little chink into the fascinating enigma of the Greek character, it is immensely rewarding.

For the lover of landscape the Mani is one of the most exciting experiences in Greece. Starting from Sparta in the morning, one can drive to the southernmost tip of the mainland across the central spine and back along the spectacular west coast, reaching Kalamata in the evening.

The Mani begins at **Gytheion**, once the naval base of Sparta, terraced on a hill overlooking the bay. The houses on the waterfront are colour-washed cream, pink and lemon-yellow. To the south of the once busy harbour a causeway joins the waterfront to a flattish islet, now called Marathonisi (Fennel Island), planted with pine trees and crowned by a chapel built on the foundations of an ancient temple. It is not in the least striking, yet this is Homer's **Cranae**, where Helen and Paris spent the first night of their journey from Sparta to Troy. Everything else about Gytheion pales before the thought of that delirious night under the stars at Cranae.

Geographically, the Mani divides into two distinct regions: the Outer Mani, its deep, fertile gullies overhung by precipitous crags, running east to west from Gytheion to Kardamili and from the Bay of Ageranos to that of Itilo; and the Inner Mani, its southern extension, which, right down to the tip of Cape Tenaro (also known as Cape Matapan), is a scorched land of rocky plateaux, shaded only by ferocious, barren slopes – bold, angular and in the grand style.

From Gytheion the road winds inland through vineyards, olive groves and fields of maize bordered by aloes and cypresses. The sea disappears behind a screen of hills. The spine of Taigetos draws nearer and the road enters a canyon of reddish rock with vestiges of crenellations lining the east ridge. At the exit from the canyon the scene comes properly into focus: the crenellated ridge forms part of a hill, fringed by vineyards and crowned by the remains of the Frankish castle of **Passava** (so-called from the French war-cry '*passe avant*'). The castle, stronghold of Jean de Neuilly, hereditary marshal of the principality of Achaea, commanded the Laconian Gulf in the east and the passes across Taigetos in the west. It takes half an hour to climb up to the ruins through dense bushes of arbutus and brushwood. The centre of the enceinte is empty, except for the roofless shell of a chapel choked with prickly shrubs. But there is a spectacular walk along the west battlements, with narrow slits in alternate embrasures, overlooking the chasm which the fortress was intended to defend against unruly Maniots.

In the mid-fourteenth century Passava fell to the Byzantines; then to the Turks and the Venetians. The latter abandoned the castle, believing they could guard the passes equally well from Gytheion. Passava is one of the few strictly historical sites in the Mani. Seen in the afternoon light, with the woods and vineyards reflecting a lambent serenity, it is an idyllic place. Ahead lies little that can be so described.

The road now follows a narrow valley. In summer feathery branches of agnus castus, flecked with pale blue blooms, straggle among bright pink oleanders along the banks of dried-up torrent beds, where the heat seems to be trapped in an almost palpable stillness. The valley alternately widens and narrows. Beyond the village of Vahos the aridity becomes more pronounced. The saddle has been crossed. The Messenian Gulf opens up in the west. A chain of slate-grey mountains – angular, geometric and desiccated – extends southward. The road dips and bends between low stone walls, enclosing plots of red earth from which stunted trees sprout in twisted, dwarf-like shapes, until it reaches the village of **Areopolis** spreading across a wide ledge.

Originally called Tsimova, it was renamed Areopolis (the city of Ares, the god of war) in the early nineteenth century by the head of the most bellicose clan in the Mani, the Mavromichalis (the 'Black Michaels'), later destined to provide Greek cabinets with eminent ministers. The Mavromichalis and their exploits have passed into Greek folklore. The men, armed to the teeth with scimitars, *yataghans* and embossed carbines, were said to possess a virile, god-like beauty with bushy eyebrows and huge black moustaches. One of them, Petrobey, brought the greatest lustre to the name of Black Michael: in the national interest he managed to effect a truce between the warring clans and, when the War of Independence broke out, led three thousand Maniots to enforce the surrender of the Turkish camp at Kalamata. During the war he fought in forty-nine battles and was regarded as a reincarnation of Ares.

However, when the peace came he succumbed to the heady delights of political intrigue, fell out with Capodistria, whose rank of head of state he coveted, and was thrown into prison. For this intolerable insult to Maniot honour his nephews assassinated Capodistria at Nafplio and the entire population of the Mani rose in revolt against the first government of the new Greek state.

The thing that strikes one about Areopolis is its lazy, sun-drenched air. With the removal of the Mavromichalis to luxurious Athenian penthouses, the spirit of Ares no longer haunts their little capital. The alleys are empty and a hush has fallen on the place. The hoarse shouts, the orders and the blasphemies, the neighing of prancing horses and the shots fired in the air now echo only in the imagination. The Mani is no longer all that different from the rest of the Peloponnese.

The centre of Areopolis is a minute square distinguished by the **Church of the Taxiarchoi** (The Archangels), a domed, single-nave basilica with a tall, tapering belfry of dazzling white and an exterior decoration which is a masterpiece of folklore fantasy. The general effect of whiteness is heightened too by the lime-washed trunks of acacia trees on the raised platform of the church. The decoration of the apse starts with a course of pink rosettes from which rise five pilasters, their capitals joined by arches in shallow relief. Above these runs a fairy-tale frieze of seraphim and grinning, beady-eyed suns with rays like hedgehog prickles. The signs of the zodiac are represented by prancing animals.

The colour scheme of the bas-relief above the main doorway is yellow, black and green: in the centre a shield rests on the breast of a Byzantine double-headed eagle, with rich plumage and outstretched claws, flanked by two lions rampant; below the eagle, a scroll between two large rosettes bears the date 1798 and above the bird, two sun-disks stare with enormous round eyes; on either side stand the Archangels, one holding a sword, the other a cross. The frieze of rosettes is crowned by a sphinx-like face emerging from a crescent moon; on either side, two perky birds with staring faces are almost Archaic in their tense immobility of expression. Peasant art, applied to church architecture, is sometimes monotonous, even boring. Not so at Areopolis. The mind that conceived the exterior church decoration had a sense of both humour and fantasy. The whole composition is an extraordinary example of crude vigour, imagination and expressive force. But what does it all mean?

No less striking is the bas-relief above the south doorway. Again we have the Archangels with the military saints, George and Theodore on either side. Above the frieze of rosettes the Dove and Hand of God are framed within more rosettes. Throughout, the emphasis is on the warlike character of the Archangels, patrons of the main church of a town which was an arsenal dedicated to the god of war. The interior of the church is without special interest.

A few minutes' walk from the Church of the Archangels lies the more conventional Church of *Agios Ioannis Prodromos*. The interior walls of this minute, barrel-vaulted, single-chamber chapel are covered with monkish, peasant-art frescoes. The figures have enormous faces with bulging eyes, out of all proportion to their puny bodies. There is no lack of animation in the scenes of miracles and martyrdoms (for instance, St Peter being crucified upside down) and a charming effect is created by the decorative stars and rosettes on the dark blue robes of a rather plebeian-looking Christ on the *iconostasis*.

South of Areopolis the Inner Mani begins. The last formidable spurs of Taigetos plunge through a series of wild ravines into the sea. These are the **Kakovounia (The Evil Mountains)** – dramatic in their forms and stark in their aridity, their pyramidal peaks, sudden vertical declivities and huge sheets of limestone belonging to a nightmare world. In the middle of the day their colour is that of molten lead; in the afternoon they turn beige, in the evening mauve. The Evil Mountains are well-named.

At the village of **Pyrgos Dirou** the tiny Basilica of *Agios Ioannis* is dated to the early twelfth century, a period associated with the widespread adoption of the domed church. Nearby is *Agios Petros*, of an earlier date. Maniot church-builders, though working far from the centres of culture, were quick at picking up the latest trends. In the wasteland between Pyrgos Dirou and Yerolimena there are a number of Byzantine chapels, dating from the eleventh to the thirteenth century, decorated with the exterior brickwork revetments that had, by then, come into fashion. Of interest to the Byzantine specialist rather than to the average traveller, these chapels emphasize the power exercised by the Church over the remotest regions of the Empire. They also indicate that the country must have been relatively thickly populated before the great vendettas of the Turkish occupation.

A winding descent leads to the Bay of Dirou, once a port, where the beach is strewn with large pebbles and the cliffs are honeycombed with small caves. In summer trippers queue to visit the more spectacular of the two large caves discovered in 1958. So far three kilometres have been lit and opened up to boats. Narrow in parts, the cave occasionally widens out and there are large expanses of water which is fresh on the surface but salty at the bottom. The stalactites vary in colour, and there are some striking ones seamed with red Taigetos subsoil. The second cave, which contains spacious chambers and galleries above water level, is still closed to the public. Anthropologists are researching palaeolithic paintings, stone implements and the remains of a primitive pottery workshop.

The Bay of Dirou is a dead end. One has to return to the village of Pyrgos Dirou, where one has one's first glimpse of a tower-house. From here the towers become more frequent. This is the **country of the Niclians**, a hybrid Franco-Greek people with Slav blood, who fled southward from Arcadia after the defeat of Frankish arms at Nicli in the thirteenth century. They populated the villages of the barren plateau between the Evil Mountains and the sea and soon acquired the reputation of being the fiercest and most warlike community in the Mani. The derelict region in which they settled became the heart of the Inner Mani, epitome of every association that the word 'Mani' conjures up – vendettas, killings, death-laments. During the period of the vendettas the ritual wail of the death-lament – the haunting dirge often sung to the accompaniment of a lute or clarinet – would echo from one warring village to another. As time passed, the Niclians developed into a powerful aristocracy. They possessed arms, owned land and towers, and were skilled in the arts of piracy and pillage. Their tower-houses dominated the villages, their minions – subservient families of non-Niclian stock – inhabiting the lower levels.

To the west extends the Bay of Tigani where the villagers come to gather salt. The long southern arm ends in a rocky hump, the site of the castle of Maina, which, with Mistra and Monemvasia, composed the strategic triangle guarding the Southern Morea. The shadeless plateau at the foot of the Evil Mountains has an infernal quality. Boulders are strewn across walled-in fields in frantic confusion. There are still some stunted olive trees, and occasionally a couple of needle-like cypresses flanking a crumbling tower. The hill tops are crowned with piles of rubble. One is struck by what must once have been the density of the population. Sometimes less than a mile separated one warring village from another.

If the Niclian country was the heart of the Inner Mani, the village of **Kita** was the brain-centre. Today Kita is a shattered monument to this shut-in, self-contained community, whose habits and pursuits had the primitive quality of the granite on which their embattled dwellings stood. It is a maze of ruined towers, their surfaces broken by no visible doorway, portcullis or window below the top storey – thus creating an illusion of exaggerated height. The roofs are flat, with occasional gun-slits. Niclian wars were generally provoked by some infringement of property or quail-shooting rights (in late summer the surrounding country abounds in these migratory birds). To trespass on one's neighbour's property meant war, formally declared by a family council and proclaimed throughout the village by a herald and the ringing of church bells. Victory was only complete when the enemy's tower was captured and destroyed. Running battles were a routine occupation and Maniot children grew up to the accompaniment of day-long fusillades. The Niclian wars only came to an end after the War of Independence, when the inhabitants of Kita and neighbouring villages were despatched to quell disorders in other parts of the Morea.

In summer the sun burns down with a North African intensity and the heat is thrown back in refractory waves from the scorched boulders. Kita is now largely deserted and in the walled lanes goats munch dried-up weeds. The jagged wilderness of grey rock is only relieved by the dust-coated branches of the occasional withered almond tree trailing over a wall. It was thus the ideal setting for *The Girl from the Mani* filmed in 1985 with the participation of all the villagers.

Twenty minutes' walk from Kita is the twelfth-century Church of *Agios Georgios*: cruciform and three-naved. The exterior of the three-sided apse has some brickwork decoration, and a step-pattern frieze – an obvious importation from the north – surrounds the little edifice. The wall-paintings of the interior are hopelessly damaged, but the acanthus-leaf capitals are in the best tradition.

To the west, two miles away, lies Nomia in a shallow trough chequered with labyrinthine stone walls bordered by prickly pear trees, its towers ranged like ninepins across a ridge behind the village.

After Kita the road descends from the plateau to **Yerolimena**, a handful of whitewashed houses strung out round a semi-circular harbour. The bay is small and to the west a rocky bluff, Cape Grosso, terraced into strips by low, parallel walls, juts out into the sea. For centuries Yerolimena, the most southerly inhabited part of the Greek mainland, was a notorious pirates' lair and its inhabitants, like those of other maritime villages of the Mani, had a bad reputation. A French traveller describes priests and children joining gleefully in shipwrecking forays. Today the fishermen and their families are friendly, peaceable people. The harbour, with caiques rocking in the swell, is littered with coils of twine with which the men and boys make nets. There is a feeling of relaxation after the tension and ferocity of the plateau with its clusters of grey obelisks. Yachts and sailing boats now bump against the side of the mole where once, to the accompaniment of beating drums and blood-curdling yells, the corsairs used to moor their galleys when they returned from their buccaneering expeditions.

The road continues south-east to Vathia where several of the characteristic tower-houses have been restored and are to let. They overlook the sea and the last of Taigetos' terrible spurs: the convulsion which is **Cape Tenaro**, one of the several gates of Hell, through which Heracles descended into the Underworld and seized the three-headed dog Cerberus by the throat. Protected by his lion pelt from the furious lashings of the hound's barbed tail, he brought it back to the light of day.

The sea is generally rough near the Cape, whose only historic association is of more recent date, for it was in these waters that the Battle of Cape Matapan was fought between the British and Italian fleets in the Second World War.

The return to Areopolis can be made along the lonely east coast by way of Kotronas. Beyond Areopolis the road winds along the shore of the Messenian Gulf, climbs and descends in hairpin bends, crosses whale-back humps, and skirts pebbly bays bordered with rushes and agnus castus. The first of these is the Bay of Itilo. At the southern end a few dilapidated houses mark the site of Limeni, where the Mavromichalis dwelt in state and Petrobey entertained foreign travellers in oriental style. The little anchorage is protected by a headland rising sheer from the sea, like a huge curtain of grey stone.

In 1770 a Russian expedition under Feodor Orloff, ordered by Catherine the Great to liberate the Greeks, landed in the Bay of Itilo. The Maniots received the Russians with open arms. But the first tumultuous acclamations had barely subsided when distrust of the liberators' intentions began to poison relations. First, the expeditionary force was too small to be effective. Secondly, the Greeks were expected to become loyal citizens of the Empress. It was soon manifest that the expedition was no more than a diversion, though led by a sincere philhellene, in the course of Russia's long struggle with the Ottoman Empire. At first, the Turkish first line of defence was overrun, but as the shock wore off, the Turks threw into battle increasing numbers of Albanian troops, who behaved with their usual atrocious brutality. Invaders and native patriots alike were thrown back and the Russian fleet sailed ignominiously out of the Bay of Itilo, not to reappear in Greek waters for over half a century. For the Greeks the 'diversion' brought nothing but disillusionment and cruel reprisals.

The coastal strip is fringed with olive trees; beyond the anchorage of Nea Itilo the road climbs up to the prosperous village of **Itilo**, its castellated houses overlooking the calm, unruffled bay. The contrast between Itilo and Kita is striking. Here are pergolas of climbing roses and gardens filled with hibiscus and pomegranate trees. Canna lilies grow in pots on the balconies. Domed chapels nestle amid terraced groves of cypresses. Women wearing enormous umbrella-like straw hats (a feature of the Mani) wander along serpentine paths between low walls. Itilo was once the most important place in the Mani, the centre of a slave market, crowded with corsairs from North Africa, not to mention local pirates from the Inner Mani. In 1675 one of the leading families, the Stephanopouloi, crippled by Turkish exactions, invoked the aid of the Republic of Genoa. The Genoese duly came and removed nearly a thousand members of the clan to Corsica. There they remained, proudly speaking Greek, preserving Maniot customs. One of their descendants, the Duchess d'Abrantès, wife of Napoleon's marshal, Junot, declared that Napoleon himself was of Maniot origin – Buonaparte, being a literal translation of the Greek name Calomeris ('the good part').

South-east of Itilo, across the ravine, a series of escarpments rise to a natural platform surrounded by a low wall: the vast enceinte of the Turkish fort of **Kelefa**. This boulder-strewn enclosure, treeless and beige-coloured, represents the limit of Turkish penetration into the Mani. From its commanding position, the inhabitants of Itilo could be carefully watched and the exaction of tribute backed up by force, with guns trained on the bay and its good anchorage. It also served as a defensive bastion against violent eruptions of Niclians from the south.

After Itilo the landscape is much less fierce, and cows graze in green fields shelving down to the sea. Just before **Nomitsis**, the road runs through a little group of minuscule churches. They are of the Middle Byzantine period, charming in their bucolic setting. To the right of the road is the Church of *Agioi Anarghyroi* with a little squat dome. The *iconostasis* is built into the main structure and on the left there is a well-preserved fresco of the two philanthropic doctors – St Cosmas and St Damian – to whom the church is dedicated. *Agios Sostis*, also on the right, contains vestiges of frescoes and four marble columns. To the left of the road is the Folklore Museum of the Mani and, where the orchards dip down towards the sea, the tiny domed *Hyperpanti* (Presentation at the Temple).

From Nomitsis it is only a short distance to **Platsa** where the sturdy Byzantine **Church of Agios Nikolaos Cambinari** stands on a plateau to the south of the village. The church, which is a tenth-century foundation, has no narthex and is awkwardly crowned by a dome and bell-cote of a much later date. From an inscription in the nave we learn that the church was renovated in the fourteenth century by Constantine Spanis, the military governor of a tribe of mountaineers of Slav origin dwelling on Mount Taigetos. However there is nothing 'provincial' about the painted decoration of the interior. Spanis must have commissioned artists from neighbouring Mistra to carry out his ambitious scheme. It is astonishing to find frescoes of such an evolved style in a humble church in one of the remotest parts of the country. Look first at the *Deisis* in the apse of the sanctuary: a great stocky Christ seated on a heavy throne, flanked by the Virgin and St John the Baptist. Among the frescoes in the nave I would pick out the Baptism, full of picturesque detail, the Transfiguration and the Ascension. These are certainly not frescoes by some local Maniot peasant-artist.

The south aisle contains the best preserved frescoes: the cycle of scenes from the life of St Nicholas. The style is quite different from that in the nave; less solemn, more illustrative with astonishingly lively colours.

Beyond Nomitsis the road winds through olive groves separated by cypress alleys, scales brush-covered hills and descends into coves which are popular with campers. It is Mediterranean country *par excellence*. The show-place is **Kardamili**, where a dramatic gorge opens out into a wide, gravelly river-bed. In the little port there is a rocky islet, on which Neoptolemus is supposed to have landed on his way to the court of Menelaus to woo Hermione. Further south another islet is referred to in Spartan mythology as the birthplace of the Dioscuri. A bridge spans the river-bed, and the upper village ascends through orchards towards a wooded hill crowned by the remains of a Venetian castle. An eighteenth-century church with a tall, pointed campanile adds an Italianate touch. To the east the valley contracts into a rugged defile of Taigetos with the familiar jagged peaks towering above a belt of black spruce.

After Kardamili the scenery remains grand and wooded, with thickets of cypress concealed in gullies of red Taigetos rock; but the spirit of the Mani – its towers, vendettas and lunar wastelands – recedes. The village of Kambos is dominated by a conical hill, littered with fragments of the seventeenth-century Turkish fort of Zarnata. The coastline is very steep as the road descends to Mikra Mantinea and Kalamata. Sometimes a tower, shorter and squatter than the grim obelisks of the Inner Mani, is silhouetted against the skyline.

CHAPTER 27

Messenia

*Kalamata – Mount Ithomi – Messene – Koroni –
Pylos – The Bay of Navarino – Neocastro – Sfaktiria
– Coryphasium – Palaeocastro – Methoni –
The Palace of Nestor – Kyparissia.*

The numerous sites scattered around the Messenian plain cover the whole range of Greek history. There is a great deal to see and there are admirable beaches everywhere. However, the general configuration does not help and a circular tour is impossible. Kalamata, which is now recovering from the disastrous earthquake of 1986, and Pylos have good hotels. The following itinerary would take in all the important sites:

First day — Kalamata – Messene – Mount Ithomi – Koroni.
Second day – Pylos (Museum, Neocastro) – Methoni.
Third day — Tour of Sfaktiria (by boat) – Coryphasium – Palaeocastro.
Fourth day – Palace of Nestor – Kyparissia – Olympia (in Elis).

The first night could be spent at Koroni, the second and third at Pylos, the fourth at Olympia. Hurried travellers may confine themselves to visiting Koroni and Methoni and the prehistoric Palace of Nestor.

In a clockwise tour of the Peloponnese, one would reach Kalamata from the Mani but it can also be approached from Sparta over the Langada Pass. The direct route from Athens is through Tripolis: after passing through Megalopolis the road crosses the upper course of the Alfios and descends in hairpin bends into the Messenian lowlands, a shimmering canopy of olive trees, streaked with cypresses. Vineyards are hedged round with spiky cactuses and waving banana trees. Palm-trees shade whitewashed farmhouses. The groves are succeeded by cotton and wheat fields and orchards of mulberries. In winter there is the fluff of mimosa, in summer the blaze of sunflowers. North to south flows the stream of the Pamisos, in whose curative waters ailing children were brought to bathe in antiquity. In summer the sun burns so fiercely on this dazzling expanse of fertility that it acquires an almost tropical quality.

Kalamata was very badly damaged in the earthquake. It is linked by bus, rail and air with Athens, and is famous for its long purple olives, its olive oil – the best in Greece – and the *kalamatianos*, a national dance performed in chain formation by men and women, the leader waving a handkerchief and, at intervals, executing great turning leaps in the air.

A straight road joins the town, which lies at the foot of a spur of Taigetos, to its port. There is a good beach with hotels, fish restaurants and a fine view of the Mani. Near the post-Byzantine Church of Agioi Apostoli, striking for its exterior brickwork decoration, is the badly damaged museum in a former private residence which has been closed since the earthquake. The collection includes ancient fragments from nearby sites and it is hoped that the museum will reopen in other premises in 1989 or 1990.

Flowing through the town is the stream of the Nedon, which issues from a gorge of Taigetos and continues round two sides of a fortified hill: this is the Villehardouin castle. Kalamata was the hereditary fief of the Villehardouins for a hundred years, but after them the castle was bandied about between Burgundian dukes and Florentine bankers until 1387 when it was acquired by Marie de Bourbon, titular Empress of Constantinople. Marie had a mania for collecting baronies on behalf of her son, the Prince of Galilee; at one time she was mistress of sixteen castles in the Principality of Achaea alone. (Throughout the Frankish chronicles of Greece, the figures of proud, strong-minded women stand out, ancestors of future crowned heads of Europe and quite as ambitious and power-hungry as any of the grasping barons.) In the fifteenth century, the Venetians, trying to hold up the Ottoman invasion, set fire to the castle rather than let it fall intact into Turkish hands.

Little is left of the vaulted chambers in which Villehardouin and Anjou, Savoy and Bourbon hatched plots, drew up marriage settlements and drafted acts of restitution. Two oval enclosures can be discerned, the inner one on a higher level. The outer gate, overgrown with moss, was the best preserved: a square tower with an arched entrance, but the earthquake brought down much of what was left. Below the very ruined keep is the ancient theatre.

Leaving Kalamata the road to the west runs along the seaward end of the plain – once a malarial marsh, now a chequer-board of farm lands – and crosses the Pamisos, up which, says Pausanius, deep-water fish used to swim '. . . especially in the spring, as they do up the Rhine and the Meander'. From the town of Messini (not to be confused with ancient Messene) a road winds up into the hills, skirting the walls and ruined towers of the Frankish castle of Androussa, to Mavromati, a village among mulberry trees, and continues right to the entrance of the fortifications of Messene on a slope of Mount Ithomi.

There are three things to do at Mavromati: climb to the summit of Mount Ithomi, walk along the line of fourth-century BC fortifications and visit the ruins of ancient Messene. First, the ascent of **Mount Ithomi**. There are no ruins, but it is, in a sense, a pilgrimage. The mountain, its flat top rising like a lofty watchtower above the Macaria, was a vital stronghold in the long and tragic wars waged by the Messenians in the defence of their country against the Spartans. The First Messenian War (eighth century BC) was provoked by the Spartans who introduced a group of armed youths dressed as girls into a chamber where some eminent Messenian men were resting. Ostensibly provided for the pleasure of the Messenians, the Spartan 'maidens' promptly whipped out daggers and swords. In the ensuing scuffle, however, the 'maidens' were killed and Sparta was provided with a pretext to conquer the fertile lands of Messenia by force.

Although the Messenians performed prodigious deeds of valour, exhaustion and pestilence drove them to abandon their unfortified towns and settle on Mount Ithomi. Moreover, the portents had been consistently unfavourable. When their king was about to sacrifice to Zeus, the sacrificial rams broke loose and dashed their horns against the altar with such violence that they were instantly killed. At night dogs howled around the stronghold and fled to the

401

Spartan camp. A shield fell from the statue of Artemis and the Delphic oracle predicted a harsh fate for 'the dwellers in the circle of the dancing-ground'. After the suicide of their king the last defenders surrendered.

In the seventh century, however, the oppressed Messenians revolted, thus provoking the Second Messenian War. This was celebrated for the exploits of Aristomenes, an intrepid leader who carried out daring raids into Spartan territory, even penetrating the Brazen House of Athena, where he left a shield inscribed with the words 'The Gift of Aristomenes to the Goddess'. In the Second War the Messenians chose Mount Eira, north of Ithomi, as their stronghold and it fell only when the Spartans, well informed by spies, scaled the walls during a torrential rainstorm and surprised the defenders. The country was reduced to serfdom and a large number of Messenians emigrated to Sicily, where they founded Messina. A final revolt broke out in 464 BC (the Third Messenian War) and Ithomi was again the last stronghold to surrender.

On the summit (2600 ft) nothing is left of the sanctuary of Zeus or of the citadel which held out so courageously and for so long; now there are only tortoises and lizards. The zigzag path, bordered by vetch and spiky thistles, is steep, but not as painful as Homer implies when he calls it 'ladder-like'. The view is prodigious, with the Arcadian highlands rising abruptly to the north, Taigetos, gashed by the Langada Pass, tapering off eastward into the Mani and a chain of low mountains, crowned by one higher peak, separating the plain from the Bay of Navarino in the west. The Messenians claim that Zeus was born beside a spring below the summit, where he was nursed by two nymphs, Ithome and Neda. On the eastern slope of the mountain, below the saddle between Mount Ithomi and Mount Eva and among cypress and oak trees, the monastery buildings of Voulkano form a quadrangle round a church; but, apart from its airy position, the monastery has little to offer.

The **fourth-century BC fortifications**, the best preserved and the most extensive in Greece, once guarded the city of Messene from Spartan, and later Macedonian, aggression. Like Megalopolis, Messene was built after the defeat of Sparta at Leuctra, for protection against a possible Spartan recovery. Epaminondas' choice of this well-defended site was deeply resented by the Spartans, who, alone among the Greek states, abstained from guaranteeing the autonomy of the city.

A six-mile circumference of walls, broken at intervals by watch-towers, can still be traced almost in its entirety, straggling across the scrub-land around Mount Ithomi. The enceinte is best preserved in the north, where the road from Mavromati ends at the **Arcadian Gate**, a round court with niches for statues and double gates facing each other. Nine courses of stone-work are preserved, the blocks expertly cut so that each course diminishes in height as the masonry rises. The gateway's massive lintel is propped against the inner wall of the court. A considerable garrison was probably stationed here, and the towers must have commanded such a wide prospect of the hilly countryside that any hostile army approaching from the north would quickly have been spotted by sentinels. One can stroll in either direction along the sentry-walk. To the east, the chain of redoubts climbs the slope of Ithomi; to the south, the fortified line vanishes into a more domesticated landscape. Clusters of cyclamen sprout from crannies in walls which once enclosed a vast area of cornfields intended to save the Messenians, when besieged, from starvation. The superb finish of the stone courses, built entirely of ashlar, makes the rough masonry of Crusader castles, constructed a thousand years later, look very shoddy. The fortifications under-went their severest test when the Messenians withstood a massive siege by a Macedonian army under the young Demetrius, son of Philip V, whose phalanx was so fiercely bombarded with boulders – and tiles hurled by female warriors – that it was almost entirely wiped out.

Halfway back to the village, a path to the right plunges down to the site of ancient **Messene**, lying in a conch-shaped fold of the mountain. Epaminondas attended the foundation ceremony of the city and offered the first sacrifices, mindful of a Boeotian oracle predicting that: 'The bright bloom of Sparta shall perish and Messene shall be inhabited for all time.' Less pretentious than Megalopolis, Messene seems to have been more durable. Leading architects of the day were commissioned to design the monuments, and statues by Damophon, the only Messenian artist of note, who repaired Phidias' great statue of Zeus at Olympia, adorned the temples and courts. The memorial to Aristomenes, the national hero, was one of the principal sights. The ruins are not extensive. On the right, at the bottom of the shell-like depression, are the ruins of four chambers with truncated columns, which probably formed part of the *agora*; on the left, two columns flank a stairway; east of it is the well-preserved **Council Chamber**, in the form of a little theatre – an extremely elegant ruin: at least ten tiers of grey limestone are intact and the floor of the orchestra is composed of red, white and blue paving-stones. Adjoining it to the south are the foundations of two buildings, one in the shape of a large square hall, with a stone settee running round the four walls. To the west of the *agora* extends the rubble of what is thought to have been a temple dedicated to all the gods. A few slabs from the tiers of the stadium lie among the olive groves to the south.

From modern Messini the road follows a south-west course as far as Rizomilos, a well-watered village, where there is a fork. The turning to the left (south) leads to the third prong of the Peloponnese which has an essentially mellow character, with none of the ferocity of the Mani or the ruggedness of Cape Maleas. At Vounaria, large oil and wine jars are still made by methods handed down from antiquity. In medieval times these were filled with oil and loaded onto Venetian merchantmen bound for the Levant. Farther south the town of **Koroni** climbs up the side of a headland crowned by one of the finest Venetian castles in the country. Below the bastions, where galleys used to anchor, fishing caiques chug across the pellucid water.

Koroni and Methoni, with their twin castles, were the first Venetian colonies on the Greek mainland. A provisioning station for merchantmen, Koroni was celebrated for the export of cochineal and olive oil. With their usual religious tolerance, the Venetians allowed Greek bishops complete spiritual authority over their Orthodox flock, and prosperity grew as increasingly large numbers of pilgrims broke their journey to the Holy Land at one or other of the two stations. The Venetians fraternized with the natives and were only insistent upon one thing: they forbade their troops to grow beards, which the Greeks, like good Byzantines, favoured. In 1500 Koroni fell to the Turkish army and the Sultan made a spectacular entry into the port, to the accompaniment of thunderous drum-beats and wailing fifes. During the reign of Suleiman II the Magnificent, the Genoese admiral, Andrea Doria, temporarily wrested Koroni from the Turks; but he was unable to hold it and the inhabitants, who had received him with open arms, suffered appalling reprisals when he sailed away.

Koroni's waterfront is pleasant and the houses on the cliff-side are painted in bright colours. Massive walls and bastions defend the eastern projection of the headland. The **Castle** is in the shape of a quadrangle divided, by a north–south wall, into two separate enclosures of unequal size. One approaches the main entrance (north) from a cobbled, ramp-like street. The gate, a beautifully shaped Gothic arch framing an entrancing prospect of the port and the mountains beyond, forms part of a tower-like structure leading into a vaulted passage. It is one of the most impressive castle gates in Greece and leads to a plateau dotted with tiny houses set among almond trees; there are some small churches, of which the most important is the Convent of *Agios Ioannis* at the right of the Gothic gateway, which is inhabited by nuns. It has black-painted gates, five domes on slender but awkward-looking cylindrical drums and a crypt. There is also a cemetery. The whole plateau is surrounded by crumbling Venetian masonry. To the east of the entrance, two large round bastions, one higher than the other, rise perpendicularly from the rock-fringed shore; a soaring expanse of smooth, perfect stone-work, like a natural cliff which turns gold in the afternoon light, the bastions are most impressive when seen from the harbour. Beyond the bastions there are sixteenth-century Turkish fortifications. The bastion at the south-east end has a domed roof supported by embrasures with a gun-platform reached by a spiral stairway. On all sides, except the west, the vista is one of open sea. At right angles to the south curtain wall stretches a long sandy beach. A modern stairway descends from the plateau to a shaded terrace with a church and a small museum which contains little of interest.

A secondary but very scenic road links Koroni with Methoni, crossing the olive groves of Cape Akritas and touching the sea at the fishing hamlet of Finikoundas. The main road continues westward from Rizomilos to Pylos, affording splendid backward views of the Messenian gulf and plains, with Taigetos vanishing southward into the haze of the Evil Mountains. The road descends towards the west coast and the Ionian Sea where there is a new, much softer, climate.

Companion Guide to Mainland Greece

Below lies the landlocked **Bay of Navarino**, with the cream-coloured houses of **Pylos** at its southern end. To understand all that has happened here it is essential to grasp the configuration of land and sea, which is very complex, with the semi-circular bay (three miles long and two miles wide), the island of Sfaktiria enclosing it like a huge reef from one mainland promontory to another, the two channels, the islets, the reed-fringed lagoon and the elegant peak above the town.

The Bay is, of course, best known for the battle of 1827; but the port, the island and the two castles have a much earlier history. The medieval town grew up round the castle hill at the southern end of the Bay and was originally called Avarino, after the tribes of Avars who overran the country in the sixth century. With the Greek passion for reviving classical names, it has become Pylos, although the ancient city of the same name lies further north.

Here, in the fourteenth century, Marie de Bourbon took refuge from her rival in castle-collecting, the Venetian Carlo Zeno, who was Canon of Patras but had more taste for soldiering than for theology. Later, in the tragic twilight years of Byzantium, when the Emperor John VIII travelled to Florence in a vain attempt to enlist Western aid against the Turks, it was from Navarino, then a flourishing maritime station, that he sailed in one of the Doge's vessels. During the War of Independence Greek patriots seized Navarino, but when Ibrahim Pasha, the scourge of the Morea, laid siege to the castle in 1825, it was found that the untrained Greek irregulars were no match for the better-equipped Turkish army.

In the arcaded square there is a monument to the three Allied admirals who were victorious in the battle of 1827 and it is pleasant to sit here in an open-air café and pore over maps and try to work out the movements of the fleets on that day. It seems incredible that four major fleets should not only have been able to penetrate this landlocked body of water, but also to have engaged in actual combat. In a sense, the battle was a mistake. In 1827 the Greek effort against the Turks was waning; six years after it had begun, the crusade for liberation had degenerated into a squalid civil war between self-styled generals. On the international level, Russia alone championed Greek independence. Austria and Prussia were openly inimical to Greek aspirations, and England and France,

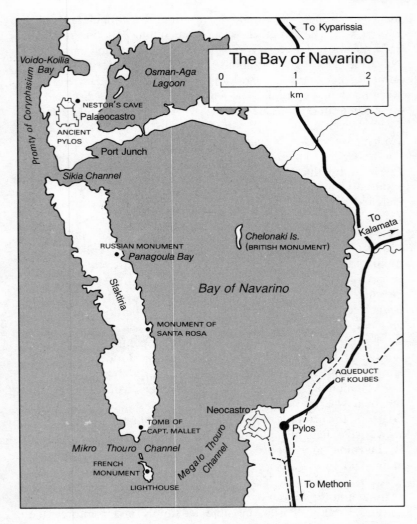

while sympathizing with the Greeks, had no wish to be engaged in a war with the Turks.

The brief of Admiral Codrington, Commander-in-Chief of the Allied fleets of Britain, France and Russia, was to avoid a war with the Turks but to ensure that they did not commit any more atrocities, like the wholesale deportation of the inhabitants of the Morea, which had so shocked European public opinion. In October 1827 the entire Turco-Egyptian fleet was concentrated in the Bay of Navarino. Fearing it was about to break out in order to perpetrate some further enormity, Codrington sailed into the Bay to stage a warning demonstration. The Turco-Egyptian fleet, disposed in a wide semi-circle, consisted of eighty-two ships, the Allied of only twenty-seven, although they had more battleships than the Turks. Codrington, on his flagship *Asia*, was the first to pass between the southern tip of Sfaktiria and the Turkish castle. His squadron was followed by the French, and the Russians came last. Twenty thousand Turkish troops encamped on the slope below the castle watched breathlessly as ship after ship nosed its way through the narrow channel. It was just past noon. The first shot was fired by the Turks – probably in panic, certainly without their commanders' orders. *Dartmouth* and *Sirène*, the French flagship, replied. In a few minutes the action was general. The vessels were stationary – for there was no room to manoeuvre – and the range point-blank. Skilfully avoiding the Turkish flag-ships, Codrington and the French concentrated their fire on the enemy's battleships, while the Russian squadron destroyed the rest of the enemy's frigates and sloops. The conflagration must have been appalling; by the evening the whole Bay seemed to be ablaze, as one Ottoman ship after another exploded, sending myriads of sparks flying through the smoke-laden sky. The rocks of Sfaktiria reflected the fiery lights and the heat was intolerable. Wreckage of masts, poops and yards floated in the lurid sea, with Turkish sailors clinging to them. Allied crews had to fight all night to prevent their own vessels catching fire. By morning only twenty-nine of the eighty-two enemy ships remained afloat.

After Navarino the Turks lost the command of the sea. Never again would the Sultan or his Egyptian vassal, the hideous, pock-marked Ibrahim Pasha, be able to supply and reinforce their mainland troops. Greek independence had virtually been gained, but no Greek fought in the battle. It was won by British, French and Russian sailors in a remarkable demonstration of international co-operation. Navarino, the last major engagement to be fought before the steamship revolutionized naval warfare, was one of the

decisive battles of the nineteenth century. By making Greek independence possible, it altered the map of Eastern Europe and
ushered in the long period of sickness from which the Ottoman
Empire was ultimately to perish. It is also ironical that, exactly
twenty-two years after Trafalgar, British and French admirals
should have been able to operate in such perfect accord and with so
successful an outcome.

It is a few minutes' walk from Pylos to **Neocastro**, the restored
sixteenth-century Turkish castle which guards the entrance to the
Bay, where a museum of Underwater Archaeology is planned. The
hexagonal fortress with bastions on each corner is entered through
the west gate. From the wall-walk, which overlooks barrel-vaulted
prison cells, a curtain wall supported by recessed arches descends
towards the shore where two quadrangular bastions command the
channel. A post-Byzantine church, *Agia Sotira*, lies within the
enclosure, where the Turkish population dwelt in pestilential conditions before the capture of the fortress in 1821 by Greek peasant
patriots. Frantzes, a Greek cleric, has left a lurid eye-witness
account of the fearful blood-bath which followed the fall of the
castle: of Turkish women, their flesh hanging in ribbons from
sabre-cuts, felled as they ran dementedly towards the sea; of babies
torn from their screaming mothers' arms and hurled against walls
bespattered with human brains; of children thrown into the sea
where they were left to drown; of piles of hacked corpses littering
the blood-soaked shore. Six years later, after the Battle of Navarino, the French garrison, commanded by General Maison, demolished all the squalid Turkish hovels and built the modern town
below the castle. Now thyme-scented scrubland has replaced the
putrefying slum.

Motorboats, in which you can make a round trip of the Bay – a
more than worthwhile experience – are moored alongside the jetty
at Pylos. It is wise to start early if you want to see the hulks of the
Turkish vessels lying at the bottom of the sea, before the water is
ruffled by mid-morning breezes. The minimum time for the trip is a
long half-day. The boat bears south-west towards the islet on either
side of which Codrington's squadrons entered the Bay. A rock-
hewn stairway leads to the summit of the island, which is crowned by
a lighthouse and a monument to the French sailors who fell in the

Battle. The channel is dotted with curious flat-topped rocks, one of which is pierced by a natural arch through which the water swirls into the strait. You then chug northward under the lee of the rugged coast of **Sfaktiria**, an uninhabited island three miles long and little more than half a mile wide. Cliffs speckled with evergreens rise sheer from the water, seeming to form an immense breakwater protecting the Bay. The boat pulls in at the little cove of **Panagoula**, where the fiercest fighting took place and the wrecks of the Ottoman vessels sunk by the Russians can be seen through the translucent water. It is the only anchorage on the island. There is a white chapel and a cypress-shaded memorial to the Russian dead, which has been refurbished by the Soviet Embassy in Athens.

Panagoula was also the site of the Spartan defeat in the seventh year of the Peloponnesian War (425 BC). The Athenians, with great audacity, had entrenched themselves in enemy territory on the mainland at Coryphasium, guarding the northern entrance to the Bay. The Spartans countered by landing on Sfaktiria. However, the Athenian triremes, entering the Bay through both channels, inflicted a severe defeat on the Spartan fleet and the garrison on Sfaktiria was cut off. The Spartan *ephors* sent envoys to Athens to sue for peace, but the Athenians refused to parley. Quick to react to adversity, the Spartans made every effort to break the blockade. 'Divers,' says Thucydides, 'swam in underwater, dragging skins filled with poppy-seeds mixed with honey and bruised linseed.'

As winter approached, the Athenians, controlling all sea communications, decided to risk an all-out assault. The attack seems to have taken the Spartans by surprise and they retreated up the cliff, where they were taken in the rear by another enemy detachment. A brief parley was followed by total surrender. The Athenians triumphantly carried off their prisoners, the *corps d'élite* of the Spartan army, to Athens. The siege had lasted seventy-two days. The blow to Spartan prestige was enormous and the victorious Athenians became even more intractable. So the long and tragic war went on.

The line of cliffs, their bases eroded into caves and fissures by the endless lapping of waves, continues northwards; then suddenly Sfaktiria ends in a soaring hump. The Sikia channel between the tip of the island and the mainland promontory of **Coryphasium** is only a hundred yards wide and too shallow to allow passage for vessels other than caiques. The width and depth of the channel must have altered since the time of Thucydides, who speaks of several triremes sailing abreast through it. Vestiges of a fourth-century BC mole are visible beside the landing stage at Coryphasium, site of the Athenian camp and probably of the classical city of Messenian Pylos. Otherwise there are no traces of the 'fortress situated on the sea' mentioned by Strabo, who suggests that it was founded by the inhabitants of Nestor's Pylos when they fled southward from their burning citadel at the time of the Dorian invasion. In the Middle Ages the harbour was used by the Franks and was known as Port Junch.

A sandy, reed-fringed beach borders the shallow sea and from here it is a good half-hour's climb to the castle of **Palaeocastro** on the summit of the hill. Outgrowths of rock thrust jagged edges through a mist of blue-grey thistles. Lizards and snakes keep up a continuous rustling in the brushwood. The castle was built on this imposing site by Nicholas de St Omer, a thirteenth-century baron of Flemish origin who married into wealth and, though renowned for his arrogance, was respected for his expenditure on the construction and preservation of fortifications. The quadrangular castle spreads across the crest. To the right of the arched entrance a passage leads into the enceinte. There are round bastions at either end of the south wall, and the battlements and part of the wall-walk are well preserved. The redoubt at the north end of the plateau, identified by the remains of four towers, may be the site of the classical acropolis. The ruins of the inner enceinte are Frankish; those of the outer, Venetian or Turkish. St Omer's castle went through all the usual vicissitudes and, after the decline of Frankish power, was occupied successively by Venetians, Turks, Morosini and Turks again. There is probably no wall-walk in the Morea along which it is so fascinating to stroll: looking round clockwise, starting from the east, you see first the rush-bordered Lagoon of Osman-Aga, then the crescent-shaped Bay of Navarino sweeping southward towards modern Pylos; Port Junch is at the foot of the south-west slope, with the cliffs of Sfaktiria behind it; westward lies the expanse of the Ionian Sea, with the almost circular Bay of Voido-Koilia biting deep into the north coast. To complete the circle, hazy green hills ascend towards the north-east, with Mount Aigaleon vanishing behind them into the horizon.

On the northern slope of the hill, concealed among rocks and brushwood, is the entrance to Nestor's Cave (the descent from the keep is frighteningly steep). Pausanias calls it 'the stables of the oxen of Neleus and Nestor'. According to another myth, the cave served as a cow-shed for the oxen stolen by the infant Hermes from his half-brother Apollo.

On the return journey to Pylos, the motorboat skirts the island of Chelonaki ('Little Tortoise') in the middle of the Bay. It was around here that Codrington's squadron destroyed some of the Turkish ships, and a low flat rock bears an unassuming monument to the British sailors who fell at Navarino.

South of Pylos, lies **Methoni**, or Modon, where a semi-circular beach of fine sand fringes the battlements of the Venetian fortress, which sprawls across a land's end facing the island of Sapienza. The beach is bordered with small hotels and tavernas.

Methoni's origins are more ancient than those of Koroni. It was one of the seven cities offered by Agamemnon as a bribe to induce Achilles to stop sulking and resume the fight against the Trojans. In the Roman era it was strongly fortified by Antony, who placed his ally, King Bogus of Mauretania, in command of the garrison. In the Middle Ages it was a nest of corsairs who preyed on merchantmen returning from the east. After the Latin sack of Constantinople, Geoffroy de Villehardouin, hurrying to secure his share of the spoils, was carried, he writes, 'by wind and chance . . . to the port of Modon'. The future Villehardouin supremacy in the Morea stems from this fortuitous visit, for, whilst waiting at Methoni for the storm to abate, he realized with what ease a relatively small number of knights would be able to overcome the ill-equipped Greeks and, with his compatriot, William de Champlitte, he did indeed later conquer the Morea. A few years later, however, the French sold Methoni to Dandolo, the blind Doge, and it became the first Venetian station on the Greek mainland. Noted for its wine and its cochineal, the port of Methoni was filled with the vessels of so many nations that one historian calls it 'the Port Said of Frankish Greece'. On the landward side, the citadel was surrounded by orange groves and there was a busy market where the peasants sold pigs to the

Venetians. Another fifteenth-century pilgrim says that all the bacon sold in Venice came from Methoni, where sausages were also made.

The **Castle**, at the western end of the beach, possesses some of the finest Venetian military architecture in Southern Greece. A bridge, supported by a succession of arches, built by the French after Navarino, spans a wide moat which crosses the promontory from sea to sea. Walls and bastions are well-preserved and their un-broken line gives an air of formidable impregnability to the land approach. The arched entrance, flanked by two bastions, is suc-ceeded by a second and a third gateway. Entering the huge enclo-sure, one is faced with a squat, granite pillar crowned by a carved capital, known as the Morosini capital. In the seventeenth-century Turco-Venetian War, Francesco Morosini was the commander of the besieging army. Whilst he was inspecting an advanced position, and accompanied by a retinue of ostentatiously-dressed Venetian dignitaries, the Turks spotted him and opened fire. The noblemen ran in all directions; only Morosini stood immobile, unflinching, the embodiment of Venetian *bella figura*. His behaviour greatly im-pressed the Turks who subsequently surrendered.

The entire enclosure, surrounded by a parapet and dotted with ruined towers, was once a congested urban quarter, first Venetian, then Turkish. The only surviving edifice is a little domed *hammam*. The east walls, with Venetian and Turkish gun emplacements, overhang the beach. The west side, facing the open sea, is the oldest part of the castle – perhaps thirteenth-century – its ruined ramparts overlooking savage rocks against which the waves break with showers of spray. The paths are choked with thistles and it is wise to stick to the wall-walks, although these are often on different levels and involve a great deal of scrambling up and down. On this plateau a Venetian garrison of seven thousand defenders endured a terrible siege by a hundred thousand Turks under Sultan Bayazit II who, throughout the sweltering August of 1500, pounded the garrison with five hundred cannon. When the Janissaries finally scaled the walls, the buildings were set on fire, the Latin bishop was immolated whilst praying with his flock and every male over twelve was decapitated. In Venice the fall of Methoni was regarded as a national disaster.

At the southern end of the enclosure rise the ruins of the Sea

Gate, flanked by two towers, which leads to a landing-stage protected by a parapet with battlements. A causeway connects the Sea Gate – the tip of the headland – with a **Turkish fort** on a rocky shoal. It is the most picturesque ruin at Methoni: an octagonal tower in two sections, the higher one smaller and domed, and surrounded by a crenellated parapet. On this shoal the Venetian garrison made its last heroic stand against Bayazit's Janissaries.

Littered with the ruins of artillery bastions, look-out posts and ravelins, Methoni is one of the most evocative Venetian sites in Greece. The Lion of St Mark smirks down from pointed arches and the escutcheons of famous Venetian families crown blocked-up gateways. However, neither art nor literature flourished here.

Methoni is one of the southernmost tips of the Greek mainland. The traveller now turns northward – through Pylos. All the way up the west coast the country has a mellow, domesticated quality, but the softness never degenerates into formlessness for the chain of Mount Aigaleon also runs northward in a line of rocky saddlebacks. North of Pylos the road skirts the bay and winds up into a region of wooded hills and lush ravines. Eighteen kilometres from modern Pylos a signpost indicates the site of the so-called **Palace of Nestor** and the Mycenaean city of Pylos which extended across a wide ledge, against a background of rugged hills.

Ancient writers do not agree about the locality of Nestor's capital. Some imply that it was in Elis, others in Messenia. Homer is rather contradictory: in the *Iliad* he says that the palace crowns a 'steep hill overlooking the Alfios, on the borders of sandy Pylos' (at no point does the Alfios flow through Messenian territory; it winds through Elis, well to the north), and in the *Odyssey* he says that Telemachus found the inhabitants of Pylos 'on the foreshore' (this palace is situated well inland). However when Telemachus mounted his chariot and drove through 'the echoing porch', the horses 'glad to be loosed, flew down from the steep crag of the citadel of Pylos out onto the plain'. Here the relationship between citadel and plain fits the present site, although 'crag' is an overstatement.

The excavations conducted by Professor Blegen, at the head of a Greek-American team, have cast fresh light on Homeric topography. This palace (1300–1200 BC) is, in size and arrangement, comparable to that of Mycenae and must therefore have been the residence of a great king. As Professor Blegen says: 'The only royal dynasty strong enough and rich enough, in the thirteenth century BC in western Messenia, to build and maintain such a palace was that of the Neleids.' Nestor was the son of Neleus, founder of the dynasty, and his contribution in ships to the Greek expedition against Troy was second only to that of Agamemnon.

Where all ancient writers and poets are in agreement is on the bucolic character of the land over which Nestor ruled. Homer says it was rich in sheep and horses and Strabo mentions herds of sheep browsing in olive groves and describes the cattle raids carried out by Nestor. The poets also agree on the character of the king: although a confirmed cattle-thief, he was also apparently wise, just, cautious, a generous host – and a bore without much sense of humour. More fortunate than Agamemnon or Odysseus, he returned from Troy to enjoy a happy old age in the bosom of his family.

It is fascinating to form an idea of how this man and his court lived, over three thousand years ago. There is, admittedly, none of the drama of the citadel at Mycenae, in spite of architectural features in common and the fact that both palaces were gutted by fire at the time of the Dorian conquest. There are no encircling Cyclopean walls, no gateways supporting huge lintels, no circular royal graveyards. This, as far as we know, was not a blood-drenched palace. Nothing standing is more than waist-high, but, being built on a level hill-top without the declivities of ground that add such complexity to the layout of Mycenae, its architectural disposition and domestic arrangements are more quickly grasped than those of Agamemnon's palace. The metal roof does not improve the general effect, but it does protect the prehistoric foundations and walls of clay from drenching rain and scorching sun.

The main building was the royal residence, with apartments of state, storerooms and wine magazines grouped round it. The king and his household lived well in the residential part of the palace, which was two-storied, with flat roofs on different levels. In the centre of the outer and inner porticoes are two stone bases which supported fluted wooden columns; to the left of the first doorway there are two small chambers believed to have been the tax-collector's offices, in which the palace accounts, recorded on tablets, were kept. To the right of the portico, a stairway (three steps are preserved) mounted to a tower thought to have been a look-out post; from here sentinels commanded a view of the rolling, wooded hills.

The portico led into an interior court open to the sky; to the left were waiting-rooms with benches, where visitors sat and were offered wine by servants. In the 1939 excavations a large quantity of clay tablets, inscribed with the signs of a hitherto-undeciphered language, were found in the palace. More were excavated in 1952. At this point, Michael Ventris, an architect, began the decipherment of the script which had until then baffled scholars and which, it was thought, might even be unrelated to any known Greek dialect. Ventris soon recognized an interrelationship of phonetic values that corresponded with the Archaic declensions used by Homer. The grammatical structure of the language gradually emerged, and the script, known as Linear B, used by the Minoans and Mycenaeans of the Bronze Age, was revealed to be a form of Archaic Greek. The only disappointment was that the Pylos tablets were inscribed with nothing more important than household inventories and accounts.

A long, narrow chamber at the right of the interior court contains, against the south-east wall, a painted terracotta bath-tub set on a clay base. Vessels found nearby were probably used for pouring water into the tub. To the south-east of the bathroom lies the so-called Queen's Hall, with a hearth in the centre and walls, judging from the fragments remaining, once decorated with stucco and frescoes of griffons and wild beasts. The Hall and bathroom are believed to have been gutted by the flames from burning oil which fell from jars stored on the upper floor when the great fire swept the palace. Another chamber, separated from the Queen's Hall by a corridor to the south-west, is thought to have been a lavatory, for there are indications that water could be flushed through an aperture in a stone slab at the east corner and thence flow into a subterranean drain.

It is now best to return to the court and proceed through another portico into what must have been a brightly-frescoed vestibule. From here a stairway to the right, of which eight steps are preserved, led to an upper storey where the royal ladies probably dwelt. The vestibule leads directly into the large Throne Room, a hall of

Epidaurus: the Theatre, built by Polycleitus the Younger (mid fourth century BC). The acoustics are so perfect that a whisper uttered in the centre of the orchestra can be heard from the highest tier.

Mistra: unlike any other Byzantine site, this is an entire medieval city, its ruined buildings and restored churches enclosed within outer walls.

The port of Gythion.

The Turkish fort at Methoni.

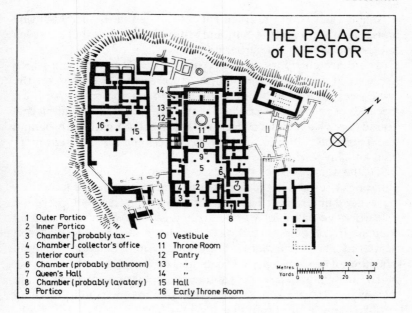

THE PALACE
of NESTOR

1 Outer Portico
2 Inner Portico
3 Chamber ⎤ probably tax-
4 Chamber ⎦ collector's office
5 Interior court
6 Chamber (probably bathroom)
7 Queen's Hall
8 Chamber (probably lavatory)
9 Portico

10 Vestibule
11 Throne Room
12 Pantry
13 "
14 "
15 Hall
16 Early Throne Room

state and the most sumptuous apartment in the palace. In the centre is the great ceremonial hearth of clay, once surrounded by four wooden columns supporting a broad gallery. Impressions of the columns' shallow flutes can be discerned on the floor. The smoke from the hearth, which was the holiest place in the palace, is believed to have escaped through a terracotta chimney in the roof. The wooden throne, decorated with ivory and other inlays, was placed against the right wall. The shallow depression, probably a basin, to the right of the seated king, may have enabled Neleus, Nestor and their royal descendants to pour out libations without descending from the throne.

The grooves in the wall of the Throne Room were intended to receive the ends of beams, which Professor Blegen thinks may have been left exposed. The whole room was bright with dazzling decoration: frescoes of leopards, lions and other wild beasts covered the walls; linear designs within squares covered the floor. The colours used were red, blue, yellow, black and white and all of the gaudiest.

It seems clear from the fragments assembled in the neighbouring museum at Hora and the National Museum in Athens that the scene must have been one of barbaric splendour.

There are corridors on either side of the Throne Room which separate it from a maze of little storerooms. The ones on the south-west side are believed to have been the main pantries, because of the mass of crushed pottery (over six thousand pieces) found here. Tablets stacked in two large storerooms directly behind the Throne Room bore inscriptions describing the different qualities and flavours of olive oil.

To the south-west of the palace a complex of more devastated buildings rises above the sloping olive grove, where the lower city descended in terraces. The walls of a large entrance hall, preceded by two stone bases for wooden columns, were decorated with an elegant frieze of pink griffons, fragments of which were found scattered about the floor. The hall led into a large reception chamber of an earlier period than the Throne Room.

To the right of the palace is another complex of storerooms where raw materials were kept. Tablets referring to repairs in leather and bronze materials indicate that this may have been the main workshop of the city. To the north are wine magazines, where many cracked and broken jars of different sizes still stand as they were found.

Tholos tombs, possibly burial places of kings, have been excavated in the vicinity. The most important is in an olive grove about a hundred yards north-east of the palace. Its contents included gold, jewellery, amethysts, amber necklaces, rings, votive offerings, effigies of little owls and a royal seal on which the image of a winged griffon was stamped. The other tombs lie south of the palace hill.

Beyond the palace, past Hora, where the museum possesses fragments of pottery, frescoes and stucco flooring from the palace, the road continues northward between the sea and the range of Mount Aigaleon, whose rocky fingers thrust upwards in a succession of strange nodular peaks. At **Kyparissia**, founded by Epaminondas in the fourth century BC at the same time as Messene and Megalopolis, and later to become a flourishing Byzantine port, one can drive up to the upper town, Ano-Kyparissia: a maze of rock-hewn stairways and village houses, with the ruins of a medieval castle, built on the site of a Hellenic tower so ancient that it was supposed to have been raised by the giants when they were at war with the gods.

North of Kyparissia a road turns inland to connect with the Tripolis–Kalamata highway. After crossing the densely olive-clad Triphylian plain, the main coastal road to the north enters the territory of Elis.

CHAPTER 28

Olympia

The Altis – The Gymnasium and Palaestra –
The Leonidaion – The Bouleuterion –
The Temple of Zeus – The Heraeion –
The Treasury of Sicyon – The Krypte – The Stadium –
The Museum.

Olympia lies in Elis, which Homer calls 'goodly' – not without reason. When the treacherous Oxylus, an outlawed Calydonian prince, led the Dorian invaders across the Peloponnese in search of rich pasture lands, he deliberately conducted them through the rugged Arcadian defiles so that they should not observe the fertility of Elis, which he coveted for himself. Apparently pleased with his services, the Dorians made him king of the country that he had not shown them. According to a local legend, it was Oxylus who subsequently founded the Olympic Games.

The lower valley of the Alfios, which flows past Olympia and irrigates the ancient country of Pisatis, is one of the most gracious landscapes in Greece: pine-clad hills overlook gullies filled with ilex and arbutus; the hills are covered with wild flowers in spring and the walls of village houses are bright with flowering creepers; streams bordered by oleanders and agnus castus wind through humid, hidden valleys. In antiquity, however, the lagoons were infested with mosquitoes and the inhabitants had to appeal to Zeus and Heracles, two very Elean deities, to rid them of these pests.

Olympia can be approached either direct from Athens via Corinth and Patras, or from Tripolis, or from the south – the route normally taken by travellers making a circular tour of the Peloponnese.

From Messenia the northbound road crosses the Triphylian plain before reaching the Arcadian foothills. Below Mount Minthi lies the pine-fringed lagoon of Kaiafa with a spa situated on a wooded island. The road ascends gently through pine trees, which grow larger and more luxuriant, and about four kilometres beyond Kaiafa a track leads to the fine fourth-century BC walls of Samikon. This fortress commanded one of the passes into Arcadia and was built by the Eleans as a bulwark against Spartan aggression. The highway skirts another lagoon, north of which a road to the right climbs to Andritsaina and Bassae. Along the coast stretch miles of sandy beaches, with no coves and few harbours. After crossing the Alfios the road enters a flat alluvial plain, and at Pyrgos, notorious for earthquakes, you turn off to the east into an undulating wood-land country. The landscape has retained its idyllic beauty but modern Olympia is, however, a sad anti-climax. The better hotels are well situated, but the cheaper establishments and restaurants, as well as the gaudy tourist shops, give the main street an unpleasantly commercial atmosphere. There is now a Museum of the Olympic Games, just off the main street, which contains historical informa-tion about the modern Games.

After Athens and Delphi this is the most important classical site in the country. In one day it is possible to visit the Altis (the sacred enclosure) and the museum in relative leisure. However it requires a rather longer stay to experience that charmed moment when the astonishing harmony between the ruins and their setting suddenly comes into focus and the historical associations can be revived in the perspective of landscape and topography.

Every fourth year during the period of the full moon following the summer solstice, for century after century, men flocked to the sanctuary to praise the benefits of peace and to watch Greek youth display its prowess in the stadium. Primarily, the festival was an occasion for athletic contests and the winning of the cherished olive crown – considered the greatest honour to which a young man could aspire. The sanctuary, scene of the most dazzling assembly of celebrities in the ancient world, was sacred to Zeus. Mythographers say the first games were instituted by Heracles and that Apollo vanquished his half-brothers, Hermes and Ares, in a foot-race and a boxing match. The first recorded festival was in the year 776 BC and

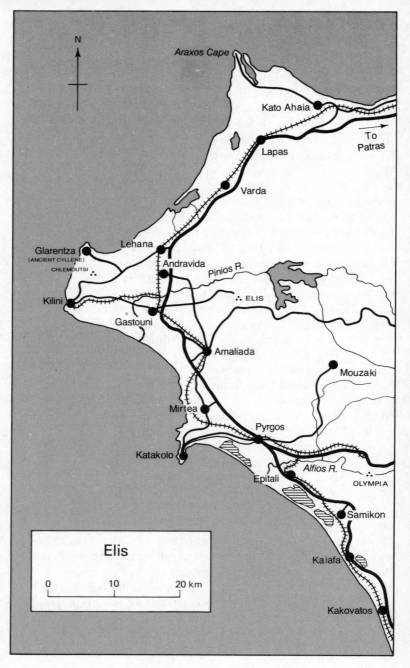

N

Araxos Cape

Kato Ahaia

To Patras

Lapas

Varda

Lehana

Glarentza
(ANCIENT CYLLENE)
CHLEMOUTSI

Andravida

Pinios R.

∴ ELIS

Kilini

Gastouni

Amaliada

Mouzaki

Mirtea

Pyrgos

Katakolo

Alfios R.

Epitali

∴ OLYMPIA

Samikon

Kaiafa

Kakovatos

Elis

```
0          10          20 km
```

henceforward Greek chronology is based on Olympiads, the periods of four years between festivals. The Games began as a series of foot-races, to which more elaborate events were added. It was organized by a confederacy of Western Greek states and gradually acquired panhellenic proportions under the aegis of the Eleans. Throughout the country heralds would announce a Sacred Truce between all warring states for the period of the celebrations. (On one occasion, Elis, a comparatively weak state, had the audacity to impose a fine on Sparta, the mightiest power in Greece, for violating the truce.) Thus peace became the symbol and keynote of the Games, and Hellenic unity, if only for a few days every four years, a reality.

The actual rules were never, according to Aristotle, codified; athletes knew them by tradition and instinct. The sacred element attached to the athletics was illustrated by the sacrifices preceding the events and the quantity of altars raised in the precinct. The Olympian festival soon became a paean of worship to the father of the gods, every athlete offering a solemn sacrifice to Olympian Zeus, Lord of the Lightning, before entering a competition.

The sanctuary was not only the haunt of priests and sports fans, but the resort of men of fashion and eminent politicians. The latter went to the Games as diplomats go to cocktail parties, hoping to make new contacts and pick up useful information. Discreet discussions, held in the shady recesses of the Echo Colonnade, paved the way for new alliances, new alignments, new betrayals.

The place swarmed with temperamental athletes, surrounded by their trainers, admirers and publicity agents; and a vast fly-infested encampment, teeming with beggars and pedlars, spread across the neighbouring fields and vineyards. Roofed accommodation was reserved for athletes, while the crowds slept under canvas or in the open. At night, after the victorious athletes had marched in procession in the light of the full moon, chanting praises of Zeus the All-Seeing, the great concourse was transformed into a vast sexual playground: although women were not allowed to attend the Games, they could – and did – approach the periphery of the sanctuary.

During Roman times Olympia did not decline in importance, but the ideal was tarnished, the standards lowered. Hadrian, as might be expected, did much for the embellishment of the sanctuary, but in 392 Theodosius the Great, anxious to extirpate every trace of paganism in the empire generally, decreed a series of proscriptions which temporarily banished all light and gaiety from the civilized world. Thus the Olympic Games came to an end. With them perished a great Hellenic ideal.

The main street of the village descends to the bridge – a gift from Kaiser Wilhelm II, who financed the excavations – across the Kladeos, just before its confluence with the Alfios. The prospect is one of immense serenity, the Alfios flowing through the wide valley with rolling, wooded country on either side. Across the bridge is the entrance to the **Altis**. At first it is difficult to associate all this rubble of grey limestone with the brilliant panhellenic sanctuary where sport was born and statesmen and philosophers assembled to preach political unity. The setting however, is idyllic, with olive trees now replacing the dark pines planted by the nineteenth-century German archaeologists. In spring the paths between the ruins are bordered with irises and gladioli and the furry, scalloped leaves of golden henbane peep out of cracks in broken slabs of masonry; in summer the bitter-sweet fragrance of agnus castus is overpowering; in autumn the air is balmy with the scent of resin from the pines on the hill of Kronos, whose slopes are covered with deep pink cyclamen. Gradually the spaciousness of the grove and the sheer volume of the rubble – the huge drums, the imposing stylobate of the Temple of Zeus, the ample proportions of the administrative buildings where the athletes trained, ate and slept – begin to make an impact. One is conscious of a sense of grandeur, of immeasurable peace.

The devastation is not wholly the work of Alaric. The Alfios is a capricious river: constantly changing its course and flooding its banks, it has buried many monuments under the porous soil. Earthquakes, to which Elis is very prone, have also taken their toll. It required the patient work of the team of German archaeologists to bring the foundations to light and reveal the ground-plan of the various edifices, which grew up without any architectural or chrono-logical relation to each other. Visitors can choose their own course. One of the most practical is to follow a more or less straight line from the gymnasium to the Bouleuterion (strictly speaking these two buildings lay outside the enclosure wall of the Altis), turn north

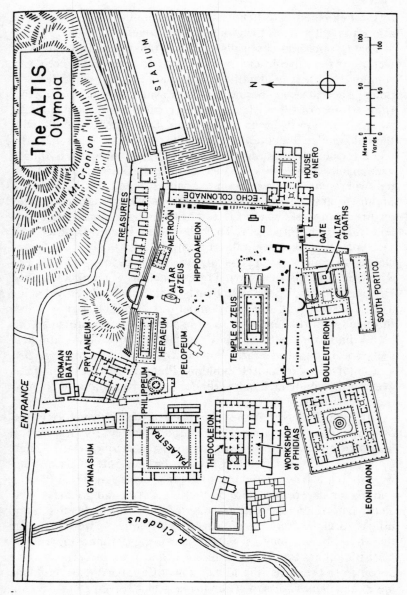

425

to the Pelopeion and then east to the stadium. With minor deviations to right and left the ground is then covered.

The **Gymnasium**, its walls once inscribed with the names of victors of the olive branch, was famous for the excellence of its running tracks. It is identified by a double row of truncated columns. The **Palaestra**, beside the Gymnasium, is a more attractive ruin: a forest of short, slender Doric columns with plain capitals; two pine trees grow in the central court. Seen from the south, with the colonnade silhouetted against a line of cypress-clad hills, the scene is one of extraordinary harmony. The building was square with chambers opening onto the colonnaded courts: a club room; a hall where *ephebes* were anointed with oil; tanks for bathers and drying rooms. There were also *exedrae* where retired athletes lectured, and seats where spectators sat and gossiped while wrestlers trained and practised. The athletes considered themselves a race apart and were generally very conceited; usually of the upper classes, though working-class boys with a talent for sport were not debarred from participating. Professionalism was unknown until Hellenistic times, when the festival became a spectacle provided for a noisy rabble by highly-paid competitors. The Palaestra was also thronged with trainers, who lived in a special enclosure and were highly important people. They were fussy about their athletes' diets, forbidding them starch, but not cheese, and encouraging fish as a suitable diet for muscle-building. Plutarch says they would not even let the young men talk at dinner lest conversation should give them a headache.

After the Palaestra comes the **Theocoleion**, of which only the outline is now traceable. Built around two courts, it was the headquarters of the priests in charge of the sacrificial rites. Then comes the shell of an early Christian basilica, site of an ancient workshop much venerated by the Eleans because the great Phidias and his pupils worked there on the huge ivory and gold statue of Zeus. During the excavations some of the clay moulds that were used to form the draperies of the god's gold *himation* were found on the site. Fluted columns with foliate designs frame the ruined Christian altar. South of the basilica, and near the processional entrance to the Altis, the foundations of a large square building have been identified as the **Leonidaion**, which served as a hostel for high-ranking officials and later for Roman governors. The chambers were ranged round a court with ponds and flower-beds, and there was an exterior colonnade consisting of one hundred and thirty-eight columns. Most of their bases, now crowned with Ionic capitals, survive on the north and east sides. From this shaded *stoa*, visitors obtained a close-up view of the procession of priests and athletes with which the festival opened. A shallow moat surrounds a circular area in the centre of the court. Large rectangular and smaller square chambers (probably bedrooms) are outlined on the west and south sides. In spring wild larkspur grows among the debris in the former flower-beds.

East of the Leonidaion, across a waste of Greek and Roman foundations, two apsidal halls, joined later by a Hellenistic edifice, formed part of the **Bouleuterion**, where the officials responsible for the administration of the festival assembled. The committee room contained a statue of Zeus, the Oath-God, holding a thunderbolt in each hand. These deadly missiles were intended to strike terror into the hearts of athletes, who swore on pieces of boar's flesh to observe the rules. All that remains of the fourth-century BC South Portico – probably a market place – is a row of column bases crowned with Corinthian columns.

To the north-east a ramp ascends to the stylobate of the **Temple of Zeus**, at once the heart of the sanctuary and its holiest edifice. Between them, Alaric, the Alfios and earthquakes have left nothing standing above the level of the lowest drum, but the huge platform, with formidable column bases on the north colonnade, still dominates the grove in a most majestic way. It was built of local shell-conglomerate by Libon, an Elean architect, in the mid-fifth century BC and the fluted Doric columns, six at each end, thirteen on either side, were equal in height to those of the Parthenon but considerably thicker. The superb sculptures of the *metopes* and pediments are, happily, in the museum, few having found their way to foreign collections; hidden from sight for hundreds of years under a protective layer of loam and clay mixed with pine needles, the marbles were at least preserved from the attentions of Western antiquary plunderers. The general impression made by the temple is thought to have been massive yet uninspiring – probably not unlike the Theseum in Athens – but as a ruin it could not be more

427

imposing. All round the high stylobate lie gigantic drums: some neatly sliced in rows, others a mass of contorted rubble as though blown sky-high by some demonic force before crashing down in a pile of shattered masonry.

The mass of the exterior colonnade was only a foretaste of what awaited the spectator in the *cella*, which was entered through massive bronze doors. Here the base of Phidias's Zeus, most celebrated of ancient statues, occupied a third of the nave. Thanks to Pausanias we have a minute description of this mammoth effigy, which stood forty feet high and must have looked like some fifth-century BC version of the Albert Memorial. The god was depicted seated on a throne, his head – almost touching the ceiling – crowned with a garland of olive branches. In his right hand he held an effigy of Niké, in his left an ornamented sceptre surmounted by an eagle. The flesh was of ivory, the drapery of gold, worked with designs of animals and lilies. The finished product, of the greatest sculptor of his age, probably owed much to the popular notion of God as a kind of implacable Nemesis: Zeus' thunderbolts and Poseidon's trident are instruments intended to strike terror into men's hearts. In Byzantine times the Daphni Pantocrator scowled threateningly down at the faithful from his celestial cupola. The continuity is obvious.

Screens, intended to keep curious spectators at a respectful distance, were decorated with panels painted by Panaenus, Phidias' nephew. In front of the statue the floor was paved with black tiles within a circular marble rim intended for the retention of olive oil which, says Pausanias, was 'beneficial to the image', and prevented the statue 'from being harmed by the marshiness of the Altis'. One day Caligula decided to take the head of the statue to Rome and substitute his own effigy. However each time the imperial executioners approached the statue with the intention of decapitating it, the image roared with laughter and frightened them away. In the fifth century the statue was removed *in toto* by the Emperor Theodosius II to Constantinople, where it perished in a fire.

Around the temple extended a forest of votive statues known as *Zanes*, mostly of Zeus, but also of distinguished athletes. Paeonius' great Niké, now in the museum, stood near the east façade of the temple. Pliny estimates the number of statues at three thousand, many of which were removed to Rome and Constantinople.

There were also over fifty altars scattered about the Altis, including one to Zeus – a huge mound of ashes piled up with innumerable sacrifices. Around the statues and altars well-known actors declaimed to groups of theatrical students, and great public figures were surrounded by admirers: Themistocles, at the height of his fame; Herodotus, followed by the boy Thucydides who burst into tears from emotion when listening to a public reading of the *Histories*; the ranting, boastful Sophists.

North-west of the temple is a grassy mound surrounded by stone slabs: the only surviving trace of the pentagonal enclosure of Pelops, Poseidon's cup-bearer, who gave his name to the peninsula and to whom the Eleans annually sacrificed a black ram on a fire piled with white poplar-wood. To the west of the Pelopeion lies the stylobate of the **Phillippeion**, a circular edifice with an external colonnade and Corinthian half-columns engaged in the inner wall of the *cella*. Commissioned by Philip of Macedon after his victory over the united Greeks at Chaeroneia and later adorned with statues of the Macedonian dynasty, it was from here that Nicanor proclaimed Alexander the Great's divinity in 324 BC. The beams of its bronze roof were held together by a boss in the form of a carved poppy. All that now remain are the inner and outer circular walls, up to knee level, two courses of stepped wall and a ring of column bases.

To the east of the shattered Prytaneion, where the magistrates resided, and the Phillippeion, extends the impressive stylobate of the seventh-century BC **Heraeion** (sufficiently well preserved for the outline of the *cella* to emerge clearly). It is the oldest extant temple in the country, Doric and peripteral, and was an enlargement of an older temple originally built of limestone and sun-dried bricks, with wooden columns and a tiled roof. Dedicated to the worship of the Queen of the Heavens, it ranked second to the shrine of Zeus in religious importance and contained the ivory and gold table, carved by a pupil of Phidias, on which rested the victors' olive crowns. Squat and bulky, but with all the dignified self-assurance of Archaic art, the Heraeion, although the most ancient, is the best-preserved building at Olympia. The stone-work of the truncated columns of the north colonnade has acquired a light, almost honey-coloured

429

hue and in spring the shady paths around the stylobate are dotted with cistus – pink, white and mauve. Two short columns, complete with flat Archaic capitals, rise intact at the west end of the stylobate. An elongated base, which once supported a statue of Hera enthroned with a helmeted Zeus beside her, is still visible. Pausanias found the statues 'crude works of art', but he admired the Hermes of Praxiteles which was found lying across the floor of the *cella* at the time of the excavations.

On a bank to the east rises the second-century **Exedra of Herodes Atticus** (or Nymphaeion), with two unbroken fluted columns and a circular basin, its cornice decorated with lions' heads. The little semi-circular enclosure is followed by a row of ruined treasuries belonging to the principal states, ranged along a narrow ledge supported by a stepped base. The first of these, the **Treasury of Sicyon**, is the best preserved (indeed better than its more famous namesake at Delphi) and is easily identified by a single short Doric column, with a complete capital, raised on a stone parapet. Opposite the ledge are three courses of the stone wall of the **Metroön**, a little Doric temple dedicated to the Mother of the Gods. Fragments of broken columns lie lop-sided among the pine needles and volutes of Ionic capitals are framed in straggling weeds.

Beyond the treasuries is the tunnel of the **Krypte**, 'The Hidden Entrance', a vaulted passage of Roman construction leading to the Stadium. Beside it stood two of the numerous *Zanes* which dotted the Altis. The cost of these statues was defrayed from fines imposed on athletes who broke the rules. There is no evidence of large-scale cheating at Olympia, but after the Hellenistic period, when professionalism vitiated the religious nature of the festival, bribery was not unknown. The two *Zanes*, strategically placed at the entrance to the stadium, were probably meant to serve as a warning. From the Krypte, the Echo Colonnade, one of the finest in Greece, ran along the east wall of the Altis. It is now unfortunately completely destroyed. Built in the mid-fourth century BC and famous for its sevenfold echo, it was designed to offer shade to spectators waiting to enter the stadium. Here, during Roman times, were held the musical competitions, in which Nero, with his passion for singing, frequently participated.

At the southern extremity of the one-time colonnade there is another group of foundations and ruins which are believed to have been the residence of the judges and umpires. To the east, where the main stream of the Alfios used to flow below the Altis, stands the villa where Nero dwelt during the summer of AD 67, when, hoping to impress his Greek subjects with his magnanimity, he declared all northern Peloponnesians free men. However the expense involved in surrounding the licentious emperor with the trappings due to a divine personage caused prices to rise astronomically, and the Greeks had to pay dearly for the imperial condescension.

One returns to the Krypte, through which athletes entered the **Stadium**. Ahead extends a rectangular race-track between grassy embankments. Unlike other Greek stadia it never possessed marble, stone or even wooden seats; the spectators, some forty thousand, sat or stood on the ground, which was probably covered with dry grass at the time of the festival. The simplest, most unadorned Greek stadium, it nevertheless ranked first. Assured of attracting the largest assembly, the Hellenodicae preferred to spend money on the architectural and sculptural embellishments of the sanctuary. Strabo says the stadium was situated in an olive grove, and this is now being replanted. The surroundings – the exquisite contours of the wooded hills, the streams flowing through the valley – cannot have altered much.

An initial feeling of anti-climax at the absence of any major visible ruin soon wears off. The length of the track, from start to finish, is 630 feet. At the west and east ends respectively are the *aphesis* and the *terma*, the starting line and the finishing post, consisting of narrow rectangular slabs, with grooves for the toes of the athletes in the slabs of the *aphesis*. The water conduits are preserved and halfway along the south embankment are the vestiges of a tribune for the judges; opposite, on the north embankment, are the remains of an altar of white marble, over which presided a priestess of Demeter, the only woman permitted to enter the arena.

Here then, at the height of the summer, athletes assembled from all over the Greek and Roman worlds to take part in an unchanging programme of events which lasted for a thousand years and whose ideals were handed down to posterity, like an unwritten Magna Carta of sport. The festival lasted five days, beginning with a procession and sacrificial rites and ending with feasts. The track

431

accommodated twenty runners and Lucian speaks of sprinters running in deep, fine sand. All athletes were naked after an incident, it is said, in 720 BC when a sprinter's shorts accidentally slipped off during a race, whereupon the Hellenodicae decided that even the skimpiest garment hindered the athletes' movements and forbade the wearing of any clothing whatsoever. To the Greeks there was nothing immodest in nakedness, and the worship of the human body was strongly ingrained in their aesthetic traditions. It is unlikely that the presence of naked athletes in the Olympic stadium was the cause of the exclusion of women from the Games. In Greek society women held a subservient position; they stayed at home and did not aspire to the pleasures and entertainments provided for men. At Olympia, women who tried to enter the stadium were cast off the neighbouring Typaean rock. One woman, however, succeeded in slipping through the Krypte. Disguised as a trainer, she accompanied her son, a competitor, to the Games; but she was found out and consequently all trainers were also obliged to enter the Stadium naked.

The foot races began at dawn, so that the runners could benefit from the cool air of early morning. Other events were held in the middle of the day. Wrestling and boxing matches (boxers wore thongs bound round their hands instead of gloves) were followed by the pentathlon, introduced in 708 BC, a composite event – long jump, discus-throwing, javelin-throwing, foot race and wrestling match. Finally, most popular of all, came the *pancration*, a form of all-in wrestling, with boxing thrown in to make it an even more severe test of physical endurance. In the blinding August sunshine, the audience excitedly followed the punching, kicking and throttling, as the tanned muscular bodies, powdered with fine sand, grappled amid the clouds of dust raised by their straining feet.

Victorious athletes, clad in purple garments, returned to their native cities at the head of enormous processions – in one case, three hundred chariots drawn by white horses – and laid their olive crowns on temple altars. Sometimes the city walls were torn down to make the victor's entrance more spectacular. Poets and writers of all ages (with the exceptions of Plato and Euripedes, who doubted the wisdom of such extravagant hero-worship) never ceased to laud the athletes. Cicero claims that no victorious general entering Rome was ever received with such manifestations of homage.

After the stadium there are no more ruins. No vestige remains of the theatre mentioned by Xenophon, who lived in retirement in neighbouring Scillus where he owned a large estate with woods, orchards and grazing-grounds, and spent his time hunting, riding and writing his reminiscences. Near the entrance to the Altis a path winds up the slope of the Cronion, a conical hill thickly wooded with the tallest, most luxuriant pine trees in Greece. The scent of resin is intoxicating. The summit, where sacrifices were held at the spring equinox in honour of Cronus, father of Zeus, overlooks the Altis and the stadium. From there, on summer evenings, you may see village boys running races in the stadium. Beyond it, where the hippodrome is supposed to lie under ages-old layers of silt, the streams of the Alfios wind between sandbanks. The heat-haze extends across the vista of vineyards and corn-fields, though a breeze sometimes blows through the branches of the pines.

The new, earthquake-proof **Museum** opposite the Altis contains all the most important statuary, the old neo-classical building now being used as a store. It possesses one of the finest collections of ancient sculpture (Archaic to Roman) in the country. The exhibits are arranged chronologically in eight rooms surrounding a central hall, where the remains of the **pediments and metopes of the Temple of Zeus** are ranged majestically along the walls: huge figures, some headless or limbless, monumental in simplicity of conception and execution. It is that exciting transitional period when Archaic rigidity and tension have relaxed and the liberating breath of classical art begins to galvanize the static figures, rendering them mobile and articulate, without depriving them of the poise and grandeur of the earlier models.

On either side of the entrance are four *metopes*, depicting the Labours of Heracles. Left to right: Heracles bringing the Stymphalian Birds to Athena – it is a relief to find her in a relaxed mood and without her ungainly helmet; Heracles, his head resting on his right hand, reflecting for a moment in the midst of his fight with the Nemean Lion; Heracles, a lithe, vigorous figure cleansing the Augean Stables, assisted by Athena (who has lost her chin and has consequently acquired a rather fatuous expression); and Heracles dragging the dog Cerberus, its jaws open ready to snap, from the Underworld. There are two more *metopes* at this end of the hall: Heracles capturing the Bull of Knossos and Heracles supporting the heavens – the acknowledged masterpiece – with the aid of Athena, while Atlas brings him the Golden Apples of the Hesperides, fruits of the Tree of Life. The vertical symmetry of the composition – the strictly linear folds of Athena's garment and the erect postures of the male figures – is broken only by the horizontal projection of Heracles' forearms. The head of Heracles is identical throughout the series – an indication that the *metopes* were executed by a single artist.

Huge fragments of the temple pediments are ranged along the east and west walls; slightly later in date than the *metopes*, they are executed in the finest Parian marble by an anonymous Elean sculptor. The east pediment depicts the last-minute preparations for the fateful chariot race between Oenomaus, the Pisatan king, and Pelops, suitor to the king's daughter, Hippodameia. The king's assent to their union is dependent upon his own defeat in the chariot race, a matter in fact already settled by the infatuated Hippodameia in collusion with Pelops: she has bribed her father's charioteers to remove the nails from the hubs of the royal chariot wheels. The race is run, the accident occurs according to plan and the king meets his death. In the centre of the composition is a colossal headless Zeus, umpire of the race, holding a thunderbolt, flanked by the two contestants. All the figures, whether erect, crouching or reclining, seem to be filled with an awareness of impending disaster, which heightens the unity and dramatic quality of the composition.

The west pediment, a group of twenty-one statues, is even more exciting. Here the feeling of expectancy is replaced by the confusion of battle. It depicts the climax of the struggle between the Centaurs and the Lapiths at the wedding of Pirithoos and the Lapith Deidameia, celebrated in a cave on Mount Pelion in Thessaly. The Centaurs, guests at the wedding, became so inflamed with wine and desire that they sought to rape the Lapith women, until the Lapith men, led by Theseus, came to the rescue. Stylistically, the west pediment is more evolved than the east. In both, however, the respective moods, tension and conflict, are conveyed by a surprising economy of line. Over it all broods the figure of Apollo. For sheer style – the curve of the neck, the powerful but graceful modelling of the arms, the expression on the imperious mouth with the full, slightly parted lips – there is no finer statue in early classical sculpture. The personification of order and spirit over lust and chaos, austere yet serene, the perfect combination of god and man, he dominates the conflict. The figures of the combatants flanking him are no less striking. Among the finest are the beautiful Lapith bride, very unwillingly submitting to the violent attentions of the Centaur leader; an enraged Centaur preparing to kick a Lapith woman whose nails are dug deep into his cheek, and a Lapith youth strangling a Centaur who bites his arm viciously.

While admiration for the east pediment is universal, this astonishing assembly of primitive creatures depicted in a frenzy of unbridled passion is not without certain blemishes. The modelling of some of the figures is rough, there is an awkward disproportion between the human and equine parts of the Centaurs' bodies and the drapery of the Lapith women's *chitons* is heavy and tubular. Although the pediment was meant to be viewed from fifty feet below, no Athenian sculptor of the fifth century would have tolerated such imperfections.

Paeonius' **Niké** offers a contrast and an antidote as she floats down to earth from Olympus in an ecstasy of sheer movement, her wings (now gone) outstretched, her gossamer garments, fastened to her right shoulder with a clasp, clinging to her rounded form as they are blown back by the wind. The statue, raised during the Peloponnesian War to commemorate the abortive Peace of Nicias, stood on a pillar in front of the eastern entrance to the Temple of Zeus.

Among the most important items in the surrounding rooms is the **head of Hera** in the room devoted to the Archaic period. The late sixth-century BC effigy was probably part of the cult statue in the Heraeion. The Queen of the Heavens has an air of authority and majesty and the half-smiling, autocratic mouth gives remarkable distinction to the broad, flat face under the stylized head-dress.

In a room to himself, the famous **Hermes** – supposedly one of the few extant statues of Praxiteles, the most distinguished sculptor of the late Attic school – stands proudly alone on his pedestal against a sky-blue apsidal background. Chiselled out of Parian marble, which has acquired an astonishingly white patina, the Messenger of the

Gods carries his baby brother, Dionysus, in one arm. The infant god of wine, who has a very knowing look, stretches out a hand to grasp what is believed to have been a bunch of grapes, teasingly held at a distance by his elder brother. The modelling of the god's figure is masterly: neck, diaphragm, buttocks, thighs and calves forming a unity of separate but interrelated volumes. The god is leaning on a tree-trunk, draped with his cloak, which forms an integral part of the composition. His expression is calm and aloof; some critics have described it as 'icy' and the small mouth does almost look mean. The statue is perhaps rather self-consciously graceful, the skilfully arranged locks suggestive of curling-tongs, but the work is an outstanding example of the consummate technique of the late fourth century BC, of that smooth perfectionism which produced a series of polished masterpieces whose insipidity often matched their spiritual emptiness. In the fourth century BC the sculptural scene was dominated by Scopas and Praxiteles. Temperamentally Scopas was attracted by the harsher, more violent aspects of beauty, Praxiteles by the gentler, tenderer sentiments that it inspired. Modern scholars believe that if the Hermes at Olympia, the one described by Pausanias as standing at the west end of the Heraeion, is not the original, it must at least be a masterly copy by a Graeco-Roman sculptor of a work by Praxiteles.

CHAPTER 29

Frankish Elis
and the Achaean Coast

Andravida – The Kilini Headland – Chlemoutsi –
Glarentza – Patras – Rion – Egio –
The Vouraikos Gorge – Megaspileon – Kalavrita –
Xilokastro.

Although there is now a new highway from Olympia to Patras and
Corinth it is more interesting to use the old road, which follows the
coast, from Patras to Corinth. Most of the main sites, which lie
along the road or just off it, can be seen in one day; the deviation to
Megaspileon and Kalavrita will, however, entail spending the night
at either place. The most important sites are Chlemoutsi and the
monastery of Megaspileon; the visit to Glarentza can be omitted by
the hurried traveller. The highlight of the journey is the lovely
Achaean coast: steep, wooded and washed by the inland sea of the
Corinthian Gulf.

North-west of Pyrgos the road enters a flat plain. The mountains
recede in the east and the prospect is less shut-in than elsewhere in
the Peloponnese. The landscape, which is treeless, is richly agricultural and, it has been said, recalls Champagne and Flanders;
perhaps that is why the French knights felt so strongly about it.
From Gastouni, the Frankish Gastogne, a branch road to the east
leads to the site of the ancient city of Elis, where Heracles cleansed
the stables of King Augeias by diverting the course of the Pinios
into the royal yards. The ruins, mostly Roman, are still being
excavated.

Just off the highway to the north of Gastouni is **Andravida**, the

437

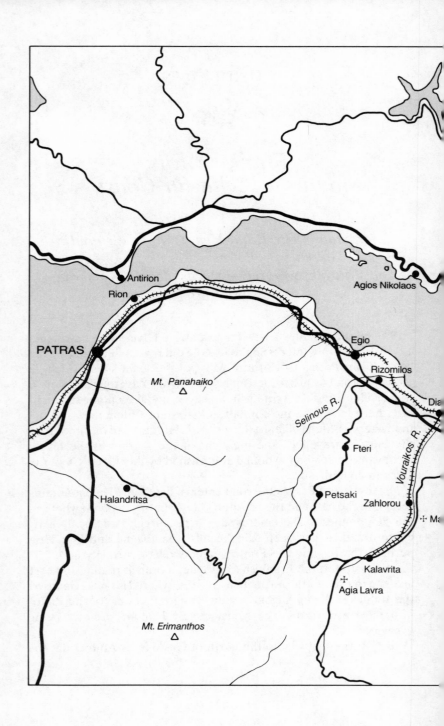

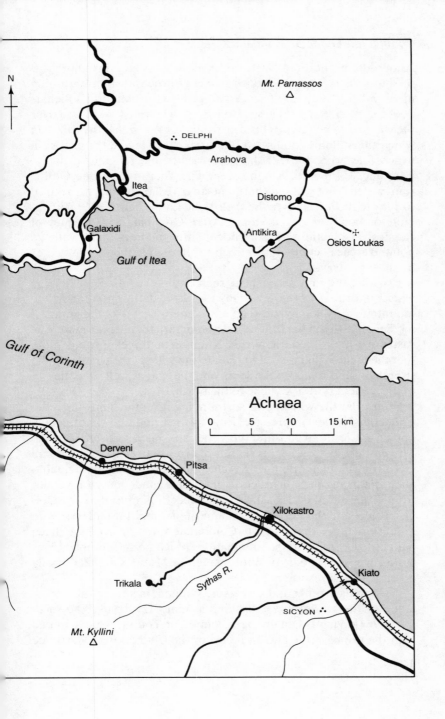

N

Mt. Parnassos
△

∴ DELPHI

Arahova

Itea

Distomo

Galaxidi

Antikira

Osios Loukas

Gulf of Itea

Gulf of Corinth

Achaea

| 0 | 5 | 10 | 15 km |

Derveni

Pitsa

Xilokastro

Kiato

Trikala

Sythas R.

SICYON ∴

Mt. Kyllini
△

Andreville of the Franks. It is difficult to associate this unprepossessing village, once a Turkish market town, with the flourishing medieval city and seat of successive princes – Chamlitte, Villehardouin, Anjou, Savoy, Valois, Bourbon – who ruled from here over the whole principality. Its historical buildings are gone: the palace in which the Villehardouins dwelt in princely state and the chapel in which they were buried; the hostelries of the religious orders – Teutonic, Carmelite, Knights Templar. There is just one Gothic ruin, which is not without charm: north of the main square, the third turning to the left leads to the shell of the Latin Church of St Sophia, built of honey-coloured stone. After Olympia, with its glut of classical associations, this diffident little medieval relic with its pointed arches – choir, apse and rib-vaulted side chapels – fascinates by sheer contrast.

Crossing the railway line, the road enters the village of Lehena where a turning to the left leads to a low, flat-topped sandstone mountain, crowned by the keep of Chlemoutsi, one of the grandest medieval castles in the Morea and a landmark for miles around. The castle overlooks the little port of Kilini. (The traveller should note that the name Kilini is used to refer to the village, the headland, the stretch of sand-dunes to the south and the spa, as well as to the site of the ancient port of Cyllene to the north.)

Seen from the wheatfields surrounding it on the landward side, **Chlemoutsi** is most impressive. Built by the Franks, it was originally known as Clermont and later the Venetians called it Castel Tornese. The castle's history begins with a quarrel between the Pope and Geoffroy II Villehardouin, an Achaean prince who had no qualms about financing the construction of his new citadel out of revenues from sequestered ecclesiastical fiefs. Geoffroy refused to abandon his project and the Pope excommunicated him. More interested in military defence than in Holy Communion, the Prince of Achaea paid little attention to the fulminations of Rome and completed his castle, whose strategic position made the Morea safe against any possible Greek resurgence.

Geoffroy's brother and successor, William, increased the importance of the castle by establishing a mint. The coins, known as *tournois* (having originally been minted at Tours), were stamped with the prince's title and an image of the Church of St Martin de

Tours. From these *tournois* the castle afterwards acquired the Italianized name of Tornese. Here Marguerite, William's daughter and heir, was caught up in a web of intrigue spun by false claimants. A typically strong-minded Frankish princess, she refused to surrender her hereditary rights and, seeking support from a foreign power, arranged a marriage between her fourteen-year-old daughter and the Infante Ferdinand of Majorca. The Burgundian barons, fearing that the principality might pass into Spanish hands, seized Marguerite and cast her into a dungeon of the castle, where she died, the last of the Villehardouins, proud and courageous to the end, in 1315.

In the fifteenth century, Constantine Dragases, soon to become the last Byzantine Emperor, resided here whilst conducting a brilliant campaign against the Italian buccaneer-overlords of the Morea. Finally, some four hundred years later in 1825, when Ibrahim's Egyptian army swept across the Morea leaving nothing but an uninhabited wasteland in its wake, the castle was blown up.

You drive through the village of Kilini in order to reach the castle entrance. Most of the ruins date from the original thirteenth-century construction. The great outer curtain wall, its original height defined by crenellations, sweeps majestically round the north, north-west and west sides, enclosing a hexagonal court with a bailey. The outer gate at the north-west angle of the wall penetrates a mass of masonry nearly fifty feet high. Two domed archways lead into an open space, followed by a vaulted passage and an enclosure with the remains of houses. The inner gate of the keep is at the north angle of the hexagon, flanked to the right by a round tower. A vaulted passage opens into the north gallery – the best preserved of six halls strung around the keep like a chaplet. Now empty except for nesting swallows, its barrel-vaulted roof partly open to the sky, the north gallery still has seven arched windows on the south side. Although the other five galleries are not so well preserved, they contain traces of fireplaces, which must have required enormous logs to heat the lofty stone halls when winter gales blew across the Ionian Sea. From all the galleries doors opened onto balconies, supported by arches, commanding wide prospects of the dunes and surf-fringed beaches of the Zakinthos channel. In this enceinte of spacious galleries, the Villehardouins often took up their official residence.

It is an hour's walk across the fields fringing the coast to the site of

441

Glarentza, once the busiest medieval port in the Morea. The country is flat or faintly rolling, green but never wooded. White-crested waves break on a shoreline alternately rocky or sandy and seaweed-covered. Gulls squawk overhead. Here, too, was the ancient port of Cyllene, with its sanctuaries of Aphrodite and Asclepius, and, Pausanias says, 'a statue of Hermes that the people there worship so devoutly which is just an erect penis on a pedestal'. North across the sea, loom island shapes: mountainous Kefalonia and Homeric Ithaca; to the west, the low outline of Zakinthos (Zante), crowned by its pyramidal peak.

Glarentza has no history before the Fourth Crusade and none after its destruction in the fifteenth century. The only traces now left of its medieval architecture are some fragments of moles and ramparts scattered about the shingly beach. Tufts of arbutus and heather cover the sandstone undulations of the deserted site, once so thriving a trading centre that the Glarentza branch of the Florentine banking firm of Acciajuoli equalled that of London in importance. The harbour, with its artificial defences, was full of Italian trading galleys and amongst its buildings was a great Franciscan monastery.

The few blocks of heavy masonry still to be seen are the substructures of edifices dating back to the ancient Hellenic Cyllene. There is nothing else. For the city's total destruction – more complete than any caused by Goths or earthquakes – Constantine Dragases was responsible. Afraid that Glarentza might fall into the hands of those who would use it as a strategic base for a Latin re-conquest of the Morea, he ordered it to be razed to the ground. Its banks, trading houses, shops and churches were flattened: its bankers, merchants and seamen sent into exile. The Byzantine destruction of Glarentza – ironically enough on the eve of the Turkish conquest – marks the end of the Latin period, that strange elusive interlude in the history of Greece when its sunny plains and rocky defiles became the hunting-ground of successive generations of uncouth Western adventurers. Of the Latin colonizers of Greece, only the Venetians now remained in their maritime strongholds.

Beyond Glarentza there is nothing but the flat, dreary outline of Cape Araxos, an important Greek Air Force base. One walks back to Chlemoutsi and rejoins the highway at Lehena. To the north-west an extensive area of vineyards, producing some of the best wines in the country, is succeeded by orchards of orange, lemon and other citrus fruit.

Patras, a town of almost two hundred thousand inhabitants and terminus of the car ferries from Italy, has a number of arcaded streets and an air of having known better days. The town only seems to liven up during Carnival, when spectacular processions are staged and masqueraders and decorated floats are pelted with flowers and confetti. Its position, however, is impressive, the town being strung out, immediately above the harbour, along a spur of Mount Panahaiko; higher up are wooded foothills with curiously convulsed shapes.

Patras played no important part in ancient history and was devastated during the wars between Rome and the Achaean League, after which it was re-populated by order of Augustus.

After Augustus, Patras' most distinguished visitor was St Andrew (its patron saint) who converted the Roman governor and, it is believed, suffered his martyrdom here, when he was crucified on an X-shaped cross of olive wood. The relics of no other saint have undergone so wide a dispersal: some went to Amalfi; a tooth, a knee-bone and three fingers went to St Andrews in Scotland, and the head, after being bandied back and forth between Patras and Constantinople, was carried by the Despot of the Morea, fleeing from the advancing Turks, to Rome, where the Pope organized a great ceremony for its reception on the Mulvian Bridge. Pope Paul VI returned the head to Patras and it has come to rest – let us hope, permanently – in the large new cathedral. In spite of the far-flung dispersal of his mortal remains, the first-called of Christ's disciples did not forget his flock at Patras even after his death; his intervention, relates the chronicles, saved the town from being sacked by the Sclavonians in the ninth century, when, in the form of a shining apparition, he personally hurled the invaders back from the battlements. After the Frankish conquest in the thirteenth century Patras became a strategically important barony, guarding the Corinthian Gulf from invasion from the west.

Patras re-enters the limelight in 1821 when it was a hot-bed of Greek patriots. Whether the initial call to arms against the Turks, which led to the outbreak of the War of Independence, was made at

Patras or Kalavrita remains debatable. Makriyannis, one of the
most colourful leaders of the insurrection – a brave and honest
soldier, though foul-mouthed – has left, in his picaresque memoirs,
a vivid account of the first days of the war in Patras. Pursued by
Turkish agents, he sought refuge in the Russian Consul's house
(where, incidentally, he was upbraided for his insanitary personal
habits). Venturing out later he witnessed the fighting, which was
very fierce, with the Turks holding the castle while the Greeks drew
up their ranks along the shore.

In Sotiriadou Street there is the unimportant though charming
ruin of the partly restored Roman odeion, with red brick walls, white
marble tiers and fragments of mosaic pavement. One must climb
nearly a hundred steps to reach the summit of the acropolis, scene of
the savage annual festival of Artemis Laphria. The method of
sacrifice to the goddess of the chase was unusual: the festival opened
with a procession in honour of the goddess winding up the hill, with
the officiating maiden-priestesses riding in a chariot drawn by deer.
Logs of fresh wood were then placed in a circle round the altar. The
next day the logs were ignited and the worshippers cast birds, wild
boar, deer and gazelles into the flames, together with the choicest
fruit.

The **Castle**, site of the ancient acropolis, is worth visiting, if only
for the magnificent view of the screen of mountains rising abruptly
from the Locrian shore, with the channel fanning out into the
Corinthian Gulf which cuts deep into a mass of mountain ranges for
another hundred miles to the east; to the west spreads the town and
the fertile Achaean plain. The ruins of the castle are a hotchpotch of
Byzantine, Frankish, Venetian and Turkish work. The approach by
car is from the south side (Papadiamandopoulou Street) and then
through a Frankish arch within a Byzantine structure. On the left
(the south-west angle) rises a well-preserved Turkish octagonal
bastion. The north curtain wall is ninth-century Byzantine – one of
the points from which the Greeks (with the aid of St Andrew) threw
back the Sclavonians. The enclosure is in the form of a triangle, with
the quadrangular keep at the north-east base and a tower at each
corner, reached along a causeway over a shallow moat and then
through a ruined archway on which the effigy of a heraldic lion is
carved. A walk along alleys of oleander, bordered with arbours of

444

honeysuckle and flower-beds shaded by cypress and quince trees, brings one to a round Venetian bastion which marks the apex of the triangle.

Eight kilometres east of Patras a turning off the road to Athens leads to **Rion**, whence a car-ferry sails every twenty minutes to Antirion on the opposite coast. This narrow channel, called 'the little Dardanelles', between the Peloponnese and continental Greece, is one of the most important crossroads of sea and land communication in the country. East and west of the mile-wide waterway extend the two deep gulfs – of Corinth and Patras. Two low circular forts with outworks, built by Sultan Bayazit II on the site of two ancient shrines of Poseidon, face each other across the narrows. Known as the castles of the Morea and of Roumeli, they look oddly toy-like, sprawling across the flat shore. At the end of the War of Independence the castle of the Morea was the last Turkish fortress to hold out – against the French. For, after the Battle of Navarino, the mutual rivalries of Britain and Russia having delayed the pacification of the Morea, the French Government sent an army of fourteen thousand men under General Maison to sweep across the Morea, clearing up pockets of Turkish resistance. Maison was accompanied by a mission of engineers and welfare officers who built roads and cleared up the shambles left by the Turks. The only serious opposition he encountered was at Rion, where the French army delivered the *coup de grâce*.

Beyond Rion wooded coves alternate with reed-fringed strands and bushy promontories, but the beaches of this inland sea are not particularly attractive though there are numerous hotels. Everywhere there are vineyards, for this is currant-producing country – *raisins de Corinthe* – and flowering hedgerows. The mountains to the south are still well inland, but the convulsed nature of the earthquake-rent forms is already apparent.

Egio, built on three levels, is backed by terraced cliffs. Cafés, shaded by plane trees, spread across a square overlooking the railway station and harbour, whence a car-ferry sails for Agios Nikolaos on the north shore of the Corinthian Gulf. Gone is every trace of the sanctuary of Eileithyia, goddess of childbirth, and of the headquarters of the Achaean League, whose federal assembly, one of the few serious attempts to achieve Hellenic unity, met twice a

445

year at Egio to establish a common policy in resisting Macedonian and later Roman aggression.

East of Egio the village of **Rizomilos** is near the site of ancient Helice, an important Achaean city which, as the result of a violent earthquake, sank into the sea one night during the fourth century BC, drowning the entire population. In antiquity the Achaean coast – a mountainous land-mass rising precipitously from the Corinthian Gulf – was, as it still is, a country of earthquakes, which were regarded as manifestations of the anger of the gods. The ever-present menace of earthquakes is always on the surface of Greek consciousness. The inhabitants have had to come to terms with it and a whole lore of superstition has grown up around the manner and place in which 'the Earth-shaker' will strike next. In ancient times earthquakes were said to be preceded by portents: the sun would be screened by a red or black haze, trees would be uprooted by whirlwinds, springs dry up, flames dart across the sky and stars would change their shapes. These would be followed by the roar of winds below the earth's crust – 'the Earth-shaker' working himself up into one of his tantrums. This ominous premonitory rumbling is as familiar to the present inhabitants of Achaea as it was to those of antiquity.

Around Rizomilos the coastal strip is at its widest, but soon the first spurs of the Arcadian limestone mass advance dramatically towards the sea, the chalky soil of their scarred and ravaged precipices sprinkled with pines. South of Diakofto, which lies slightly inland, a huge wooded cleft cuts the mountain wall in two. This is the opening of the **Vouraikos Gorge**, so narrow that the road to Megaspileon and Kalavrita climbs indirectly from Trapeza, further to the east. However, an ascent of the beautiful defile may be made by a miniature railway which is partly rack and pinion. The toy carriages sway and clatter as the wheels grind up the narrow track on an alarmingly steep gradient between walls of rock, then descend into little verdant glens, where pools of ice-green water surrounded by large, smooth boulders are shaded by stunted plane trees. In autumn the imposing cliffs blaze with the orange, amber and coral of dying leaves. Sheets of maidenhair and other luxuriant ferns fringe the turbulent stream and bright pink cyclamen grow beside the rail-track. There are no dwellings and the sun only lights up the chasm with the briefest of shafts at noon.

As the altitude increases, the gorge widens out and the train stops at Zahlorou, a mountain hamlet, which is the station for **Megaspileon**. It takes half an hour to walk to the monastery along a path which mounts the scrub-covered hillside above a mountain valley traversed by the Vouraikos River. Along this path once came two Early Christian fathers from Jerusalem; the Virgin had appeared in a vision and ordered them to travel to Achaea, where they would find her image in a cave in a mountain recess. When they reached the Achaean coast, the Virgin appeared before them again and directed their steps up the gorge to the foot of a great cliff, where St Euphrosyne, a shepherdess of royal blood, stood perched on a rock and hailed them. Imperiously striking the ground with her crook, she caused a spring to gush forth and commanded them to proceed to a cave where a dragon had its lair. A sudden flash of lightning caused the monster to drop dead and the pilgrims then found not only the holy icon of the Virgin but also the table upon which St Luke had copied out his Gospel.

The cave subsequently became a place of pilgrimage and a monastery grew up around it – the *Mega Spileon* or Great Cave. The present monastic buildings date only from 1934, fire having destroyed the older edifice and its fine library. They cling strikingly, storey upon storey, to the surface of a vertical cliff whose flat summit is crowned by a cross. In the fissures of the rock the shapes of three crosses are said to be discernible – to devout Orthodox eyes only. In Byzantine times the monastery was one of the most prosperous in Greece and monks fleeing southward after the fall of Constantinople further enriched the library with valuable manuscripts.

The interior of the monastery is worth visiting, if only to stroll along the gallery overlooking the mountain-girt valley with the orchards and kitchen-gardens of the monks terraced on the slope below. The church is dedicated to the *Panayia Chrysospiliotissa* (The Virgin of the Golden Cave) and its most revered object is the icon discovered, with the help of St Euphrosyne, by the two holy fathers, which miraculously has escaped destruction in successive fires. It is a primitive image of wax, attributed to that most prolific of iconographers, St Luke. Amongst the relics that survived the 1934

447

conflagration are St Euphrosyne's skull in a silver reliquary, one of her hands in a silver sheath, a fine twelfth-century cloisonné Gospel book-cover and the skulls of the two military saints – Theodore the Tyro and Theodore Stratelates.

Visitors may spend the night here – accommodation being provided in a guest-house – in return for a gratuity. The air is wonderfully clear and there are beautiful walks along paths bordered by cyclamen in autumn, by primroses and wild violets in spring.

From Zahlorou the railway and a road continue through more open country to **Kalavrita**, which is both a mountain resort on the rugged Helmos range and a national shrine. Streams course through the village and the waters of one, the Alyssos, were supposed to cure men and dogs of rabies. In the thirteenth century the great French family of La Trémouille dwelt in a castle on the table mountain that towers a thousand feet above the village, guarding the Frankish-held coastline of Achaea against incursions by Arcadian mountain-dwellers. The ruins of the castle, known, like the mountain, as Tremola, are hardly worth the climb however.

Above the town, on the north slope of Tremola, stands a large cross commemorating the wholesale massacre of the male population by the Germans in 1943, as a reprisal against local guerilla activity. It was December and freezing; men and boys were led up the snow-covered slope and machine-gunned; the principal buildings were gutted by fire. The hands of the clock on the main church, the *Metropolis*, still stand at the time, 2.34, at which the massacre took place. That is what Kalavrita means to the Greeks.

The **Monastery of Agia Lavra** is situated seven kilometres southwest of the village amongst ilex woods and cypress alleys. Here Germanos, Metropolitan Bishop of Patras, a prelate inspired by the most patriotic of motives, is supposed to have raised the standard of revolt against the Turks beside the large plane tree in front of the main church on 25 March 1821. The monastery, burnt by Ibrahim Pasha in 1826, rebuilt, and burnt again by the Germans in 1943, has, in its post-war transformation, the air of a Western Roman Catholic convent: neat, well-ordered and colonnaded. The adjacent seventeenth-century cross-inscribed Church of the Dormition, more evocative of the Byzantine heritage, escaped both fires; in it was held the service which preceded the start of the revolution. The treasury

Typical tower houses in the Mani from which, for centuries, the fierce
inhabitants of this wild peninsula would ride out to make war on their
neighbours.

Olympia: the Palaestra; once crowded with athletes, trainers and spectators,
it was a combination of gymnasium, social club and lecture hall.

Olympia: from the West Pediment of the Temple of Zeus. At the wedding of King Pirithoos and the Lapith, Deidameia, centaurs, inflamed by wine, try to ravish the Lapith women.

contains sacerdotal vestments worn by local prelates at the historic service and also the banner, unfurled by the martial bishop, representing the Dormition of the Virgin. The hole in the face of the angel in the top left-hand corner was made by a bullet. There are also manuscripts dating from the eleventh to the fourteenth centuries and a hideous Gospel-cover presented by Catherine the Great.

Beyond the monastery one road continues south over a shoulder of Mount Helmos to Tripolis, while two lesser roads lead back to the coast. The shorter route climbs up into the mountains and passes through the bleak village of Fteri, crossing a watershed, before descending through oak forests into the majestic Selinous Gorge, where towering buttresses of rock overhang a winding torrent which runs parallel to the Vouraikos and is of equal natural beauty. The road reaches the coast at Egio.

A more roundabout route crosses a deserted plain ringed round to the south by Erimanthos, a half-moon of craggy mountains pointing skywards in a series of ever-changing forms of naked limestone, their bases thickly wooded with spruce. Beyond Halandritsa, once a Frankish barony forming part of the ring of strongholds encircling the Arcadian plateau, the road descends into the north-eastern corner of the olive-covered plain of Achaea.

Below the slopes of Mount Panahaiko – a relatively featureless mountain, compared with the splendid peaks and crags of Erimanthos – a path to the right leads through fields of pink garlic, blood-red adonis, funnel-shaped arums and Serapias orchids, to the little **Church of the Panayia**. This minor deviation is not recommended for the architectural beauty of the church – it has none – but it is the oldest extant Byzantine church in the Peloponnese, possibly ninth-century. The dilapidated, roofless little chapel lies half-buried in a flowery field and you have to descend steps to enter it. Two marble columns with sculpted capitals, preserved intact, separate each of the tiny aisles.

The rest of the way is through flat agricultural country to Patras. East of Diakofto the coastline is very splendid and the Corinthian Gulf widens to its greatest extent. Across the water towers Parnassos, its bluish summit often wreathed in cloud. Somewhere on the stupendous mountainside is Delphi. The gorge of the Pleistos, below the sanctuary, is just visible in clear weather. On the Peloponnesian shore the Achaean mountains approach so close to the sea that there is nothing but the narrowest coastal strip left, along which the old road (the new highway is a little further inland) and railway wind below pine forests. Along this road once came the first Crusaders, Champlitte and Villehardouin, from Corinth to Patras to found the Principality of Achaea, which was to include the whole of the Morea and was to last over two hundred years. The chalky surface of the crags and escarpments is scarred with ravines and precipices. There are two more great gorges, the Krathis (into which flows the trickle of the Styx) and the Sythas, which opens out fanwise to reveal terraces of whitish soil thick with cypresses. The inlets are bordered with vines, myrtles, orange trees and willows.

Xilokastro, a popular beach resort, was probably the port of ancient Pellene, one of the twelve Achaean cities, which was said to have been founded by a giant. The shingly beach is bordered by dark umbrella pines. A branch road climbs to Trikala on the slopes of Mount Ziria, the Peloponnese's main skiing centre.

One is soon at Kiato, below the terraced plateau of Sicyon, with the familiar hump of Acro-Corinth, key to all the treasures of the Peloponnese, squatting above the vineyards.

CHAPTER 30

The Approaches to the West

(I) Corinth – Rion – Antirion. (II) Galaxidi – The Northern shore of the Gulf of Corinth – Nafpactos – Antirion. (III) Delphi – Lidoriki – Nafpactos. (IV) The Pindos spine – Metsovo.

Western Greece is a series of formidable massifs more or less parallel to, and west of, the Pindos spine, fringed by fertile coastal strips and washed by the Ionian Sea and the Gulf of Corinth. Variety in landscape is matched by the immense chronological span of the historical sites: ancient, medieval and Ottoman. There are four main approach roads.

I

The easiest way is from Athens, through Corinth and along the northern shore of the Peloponnese as far as Rion, which is linked by a ferry with Antirion on the mainland coast. This route was described in Chapter Twenty-nine.

II

From Galaxidi the road skirts the northern shore of the Gulf of Corinth. After Galaxidi comes Eratini, spreading across a green maritime strip; from nearby Agios Nikolaos ferries ply across the Gulf to the Peloponnesian port of Egio. The Delphi Beach hotel, gaunt and barrack-like, rises incongruously from a shore of spiky rocks. Fishing hamlets are set among little oases and cypress groves, and low islands are dotted about the crescent-shaped bays. Soon the

451

austere mountains recede, making room for the river Mornos to flow through an alluvial valley into the sea; then they advance again, leaving **Nafpactos** to extend, cramped and ribbon-like, along a reed-fringed coast.

After the Third Messenian War (464–459 BC), in which the Messenians were routed by the formidable Spartans, the Athenians established Messenian settlers at Nafpactos. Filled with hatred for the Spartans, who were also the Athenians' chief rivals in the struggle for leadership of the Greek world, the Messenians gladly manned this strategic naval station which commanded the approach through the narrows into the Gulf of Corinth from the west. It was in these confined waters that Phormio, the Athenian admiral, engaged the entire Peloponnesian fleet in 429 BC. Commanding twenty swift triremes, he boldly encircled the larger enemy fleet, constricting it, so that many Peloponnesian vessels fell foul of each other. Then he attacked, forcing the enemy to retire; but they were unwilling to admit defeat and at one point succeeded in driving the Athenians so close inshore that Phormio was forced to deploy his vessels in a dangerously attenuated line. However, handling his small, fast squadron with dash and discipline, he broke through the more cumbersome Peloponnesian triremes and routed them. There was no second round. Timocrates, the disgraced Lacedaemonian admiral, threw himself overboard and was drowned in the harbour of Nafpactos.

In medieval times Nafpactos was ruled by the Venetians, who built the great castle, made it 'the strongest bulwark of the Christian people', and stayed for nearly a hundred years. A Christian island in a Turkish sea, the wall-girt city, then called Lepanto, suffered violent siege, with Turkish cannon-balls raining down for weeks on end. It fell in 1499: the last Venetian stronghold on the Greek mainland. Its loss was such a blow to Venetian pride that Grimani, the surrendering admiral, was lampooned in Venice as 'Antonio Grimani, the ruin of the Christians'.

The little Venetian port, with its painted caiques, is oval in shape and is defended by two towers at either extremity of the break-water – a perfect stage-set. From here the Turkish Fleet of Sultan Selim the Sot (who preferred women and wine to battle) set sail one October morning in 1571 to engage the combined Papal,

Spanish and Venetian squadrons, consisting of two hundred galleys and commanded by Don John of Austria. Within hours the Turkish defeat was total: over a hundred galleys and thousands of men were lost. Christendom, it was proclaimed, was saved; the invincibility of Ottoman power proven a myth. However the battle of Lepanto was not decisive. The allies fell out among themselves and Venice made a separate peace with the Sultan. Turkish dockyards, working overtime, made good the losses and by the seventeenth century the Crescent once more fluttered unchallenged throughout the Eastern Mediterranean.

A steep cone-shaped hill, girdled with a triple line of walls, overlooks the port. A road, passing below the line of well-preserved fortifications, winds up to the **Venetian castle**. Passing on foot through a series of arched gateways overlooked by a crenellated bastion, one enters the bailey, now a shady pine-wood. A slippery path, thick with pine needles, mounts to the chapel of *Prophitis Elias*, once the site of a pagan sanctuary. Fragments of watch-towers, built on ancient Hellenic foundations, form belvederes. A wall-walk north of the chapel commands a view of a steep, pine-clad slope falling away into a ravine. The outer line of the defences makes a fine sweep to meet a transverse wall. Further down, another transverse wall runs impressively along the entire width of the enceinte. From here it is easy to perceive the general design of the castle, which is divided into five successive wards on different levels. Below, the little town clings to the side of the hill, with the harbour, guarded by its two diminutive bastions, in the exact centre of the picture. On either side extend sandy, reed-fringed beaches. Across the strait rise the Peloponnesian ranges.

Beyond Nafpactos, the road runs westward along a well-watered coastline. **Antirion**, terminal of the ferry service from Rion, is little more than an agglomeration of port installations, distinguished by a low fort. Known as the Castle of Roumeli, it was built by the Turks on the site of a medieval defensive position and crowned by a lighthouse. The wash from the ferry boats crammed with vehicles streaks the blue channel, which is less than a mile wide. The sea is often choppy, for the wind is funnelled along the channel between high ranges. Eastward extends the Gulf of Corinth; westward the

Peloponnesian and mainland shores fan out and the mass of Kefalonia, with Ithaca in front of it, emerges out of the Ionian Sea. In the south the eroded hills of Mount Panahaiko pile up towards the Peloponnesian heights.

III

A longer, more devious, route from Delphi goes through the mountains and joins the Mornos valley leading down to Nafpactos. From Amfissa the road climbs the bare, elephantine flanks of Mount Giona, providing prodigious views of the ring of mountains enclosing the Sacred Plain. Continuing in a north-west direction – the desolation only relieved by a rash of battery chicken farms – we reach **Lidoriki**. Situated at an altitude of nearly 2000 feet in an unproductive, sparsely populated wilderness, the village was a famous guerilla hide-out in the Second World War. It is pleasant to break the journey for refreshment in the village; the air is crystalline, the inhabitants blond, ruddy and friendly. Thence begins the grand, meandering descent to the coast. The mountain configuration acquires an increasingly intricate character, with canyons, sunless valleys and hollow gorges. An isolated crag is crowned by a white chapel. The road follows the northern shore of the lake formed by the damming up of the Mornos River to ensure the water-supply of Athens. Only a thin trickle now flows beyond the dam among great cliffs and fir-clad slopes.

A road to the right (a minor deviation of seven kilometres leading to Krokili) ascends steeply above the confluence of the Mornos and one of its tributaries. With the increasing altitude, the vistas become more awe-inspiring, especially in autumn when the lower forest belt is ablaze with colour. Beside a plane tree at Kria Vrisi (The Cold Spring) there is a monument raised to the memory of Makriyannis, one of the ablest and most extrovert generals of the War of Independence. Less than one kilometre beyond the monument is the abandoned village of Isvora, where Makriyannis spent his childhood and youth fostering his flamboyant patriotism and hatred of the Turkish oppressor. More striking is the red-roofed village of Krokili (the terminus of the branch road) below a fearsome peak. The terrace of the village church overlooks a narrow, wooded valley, beyond and around which rise successive ranges, capped by nodular peaks and crags.

The main road to the south continues through the Mornos valley; after a final descent through a valley of orchards and vineyards planted with alleys of dwarf cypresses, it approaches the northern shore of the Gulf of Corinth. The road turns westward, crosses a bridge spanning the Mornos and enters Nafpactos.

IV

Finally there is the route, farther north, from Kalambaka. It is perhaps the most spectacular. Scaling the Pindos range at a tremendous altitude, the road leads to Ioanina, capital of Epirus. From the Kalambaka–Grevena fork it ascends in wide loops; below, to the south-east the Pinios winds through a wide wooded valley, with the tusks and obelisks of Meteora forming a grotesque gateway leading into the plain. Ahead, westward, loom range upon range of mountains. Occasionally a village, with ugly corrugated-iron roofed houses, spreads across hillsides of apple and fig orchards. The deeper one penetrates into the massif – into the actual spine of the whole country – the grander the Alpine land-scape becomes, with wooded heights pressing in on all sides. The holm-oak belt is succeeded by the stone pine – a Christmas tree scene, with the watershed dominated by a beetling crag. At the top of the formidable pass – the Katara (The Damned One) – a large hollow arena opens up to the south-west, its rim circled by the road which gradually descends the slopes of fir, box and beech into the heart of the bowl, where the twin villages that make up **Metsovo** (Prosilio and Anilio) cling to the sides of precipitous cliffs. They are so-called because the former faces towards the sun and the latter is supposedly condemned to eternal shade.

Metsovo, reputedly one of the show villages of Greece, is, by the very nature of its position, claustrophobic (the mountain makes walking an exhausting recreation but favours skiing in this rudimentary winter sports resort). It remains the centre for Roumanian-speaking Vlachs who, it has been suggested, may be the descendants of Roman legions stationed in the bleak, but strategic, passes of the Pindos mountains. The village was always populous in spite of its remoteness and under the Turks the inhabitants did not suffer the worst of depredations. A seventeenth-century vizier, fleeing from the Sultan's displeasure, took refuge here. When pardoned, he became Grand Vizier. In recognition for the hospitality offered him by the inhabitants, he granted them special privileges in the form of grazing rights and tax exemptions. The prosperity of the village never diminished, and today it is famed for its wood-carvers, goldsmiths and silversmiths, its trade in tourist souvenirs (bedspreads and fleecy sheepskin rugs) and its excellent smoked cheese.

Narrow cobbled alleys descend between tall houses (the older ones roofed with grey slate) and tourist shops, to a large poplar-shaded square, where in summer the inhabitants mix with the increasing numbers of tourists, as the sun sets over the mountain peaks. On feast days, round dances are performed here: the men, their ruddy faces set in stony expressions, wearing black kilts and black *tsarouchia*, the women in flower-embroidered dresses and black cloaks, with pigtails hanging down their backs from under black kerchiefs. Adjoining the square is the Church of *Agia Paraskevi*, a sixteenth-century foundation in basilica form, with a clock-tower surmounted by a cross. The departing Turks, after their defeat in the First Balkan War (1912), tried to shoot the cross down and carry it off as loot, believing it to be made of gold. The church's main interest lies in its wooden *iconostasis*, dated to c. 1730, in which the Epirot craftsman has carved representations of God and the Expulsion from the Garden of Eden. South-east of the square is a playground, perched dizzily over the bowl-like valley across which the great peak of Peristeri, towering over the whole central mass of the Pindos, casts its shadow.

The **Tositsa House**, which serves as a museum of local popular art – it is signposted – has been restored as a typical grand old Metsovo house. The lay-out is similar to that of the mansions of the Turkish period at Ambelakia, Siatista and Kastoria: armoury and wash-house on the ground floor, bedrooms on the first, reception rooms surrounded by wide, low divans in the form of banquettes on the second. The floors are carpeted with fine, locally-woven *kilims* and the bedroom cupboards are filled with the elegant cloaks worn by the gentlemen and the bridal dresses worn by their ladies.

Another agreeable visit is to the Monastery of *Agios Nikolaos*. A branch road descends into the ravine of the Metsovitikos stream at the bottom of the sombre mountain bowl. To the south, across the cliff-face, spreads Anilio, in its allegedly permanent shade. The short ascent to the monastery is along a path bordered by ferns. Hens peck among dead leaves under an arbour of walnut trees. Pansies, snapdragons and geraniums create a blaze of colour in the monastic courtyard. Here all is serenity. The ring of awesome mountains is out of sight. The church, restored in 1960, is in basilica form. The post-Byzantine frescoes, also restored, cover every inch of wall space: small panels, rather than the usual grand compositions. A band of saints' heads amid vine tendrils round three sides of the interior is attractive, but the carved wooden *iconostasis* must surely be too fussy for even the most enthusiastic admirer of this form of Epirot church decoration. In the narthex, converted into a miniature museum, are displayed icons, the most striking of which is one of St Matthew, a dark figure depicted in the act of composing his Gospel, while an angel in red garments stands beside him.

Glad as one is to have visited Metsovo and penetrated the heart of the lonely central Pindos massif, it is agreeable to be relieved of its claustrophobic atmosphere and to be on the road again. The westbound way into Epirus continues to offer an impressive spectacle. One crosses torrent beds strewn with huge boulders; one ascends and descends slopes of scrub-oak. It is in this deserted country, at the locality called Peristeri, that the Greek Prime Minister, Tsolakoglou, signed an armistice with the Axis forces in April 1941. After spanning a bridge, the road climbs the foothills of the barren limestone barrier of Mount Mitsikeli and descends one of its southern flanks, passing the Monastery of *Panayia Dourahan*. This was founded by an infidel Turkish pasha as a token of gratitude to the Virgin for protecting him during a noctural ride across the frozen lake of Ioanina. A panoramic view then opens up: the opaque lake, its wooded islet, and the mosque crowning the citadel of the city of Ioanina, all surrounded by hazy, beige-coloured hills.

CHAPTER 31

Western Roumeli

Calydon – Messolongi – Pleuron – Oiniadai –
Agrinio – Boucation – Thermon – Stratos.

Beyond Nafpactos and Antirion variety is the keynote. North of the channel separating the Peloponnese from the mainland rise mountain ranges, from whose gorges flow streams, swelling into rivers, which wind across the plains to lagoons. All this country is known as Western Roumeli.

The plains are scattered with rocky knolls and ridges, some of which were once the sites of well-fortified Hellenic cities. Extant walls recall their military importance. Three days (with two nights at Agrinio where there are the best hotels) is the minimum time required to see all the places described in this chapter. The direct route, without deviations, provides the traveller with glimpses of the acropolis of Calydon and the Heroes' Garden at Messolongi. The ramparts of Pleuron can be identified from the highway, which also runs below the walls of Stratos in the Aheloos valley. But the two most rewarding sites, Oiniadai and Thermon, lie well off the main road.

Beyond Antirion the road loops westward round the formidable mass of Mount Klokova, which rises 3000 feet sheer above the sea. After overhanging the sea at a great height, the road winds through a wooded valley filled with Judas trees and crosses the shingly bed of the Evinos, which flows in serpentine loops between steep, shrub-covered banks.

This was always wild country, its mountains scarred with rugged ravines and once inhabited by warlike tribes dwelling in scattered and unprotected settlements, unlike most of the Greeks, who were basically a gregarious people and who were concentrated in fortified

458

cities. The inhabitants of today seem to have inherited few of the characteristics of their turbulent ancestors. A staid, provincial people, they take little part in shaping the destiny of modern Greece.

The road crosses the Evinos and at a point roughly opposite the village of Evinohori, a whitewashed chapel on the slope of a hill marks the site of **Calydon**. The ruins are not impressive, but the prospect is open and gracious. The city spreads across a ledge of rocky hills above a cultivated strip spiked with cypresses and bordered by a lagoon criss-crossed with dykes. On the prodigious hump of Mount Varasova there are still fragments of towers, commanding the complex prospect of land and sea, from which sentinels signalled the approach of hostile vessels. The city was founded, according to legend, by Aetolus and named after his son, Calydon, and was the home of many famous mythological figures: of Oeneus, who received the first vine from Dionysus; of Thoas who went to the Trojan War in a fleet of forty black ships; and of Oxylus, king of Elis, who, some say, founded the Olympic Games.

A path climbs the hillside; a signpost points to the Heroon, the Heroes' Sanctuary. Ancient slabs litter a wispy olive grove, with vestiges of chambers constructed of rectangular blocks (only a course or two survive) grouped around what must have been a peristyle court surrounded by a colonnade. Beside an adjacent wall, steps descend into a vaulted passage leading to a burial chamber (c. 100 BC) directly under the court. On the west hill, beyond a farmhouse overlooking the main road, are the remains of the sanctuary of Artemis Laphria, goddess of the chase, who was worshipped above all other deities at Calydon, a land of huntsmen. The outline of the stylobate of the fourth-century BC temple with *cella*, colonnades and porch, buttressed with the rectangular blocks of an earlier retaining wall, are clearly identifiable. The temple once contained the famous statue of Artemis Laphria, afterwards removed to Patras. Beside it is the site of the sixth-century BC Temple of Apollo: to the unprofessional eye a mass of unidentifiable outlines.

Of the towers and walls that enclosed the city, powerful though never distinguished for its architectural elegance, only shattered plaques are scattered across the wind-blown hillside, where the

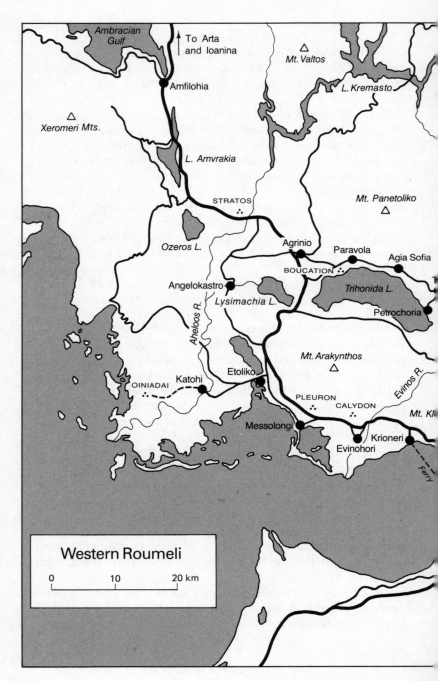

Western Roumeli

0   10   20 km

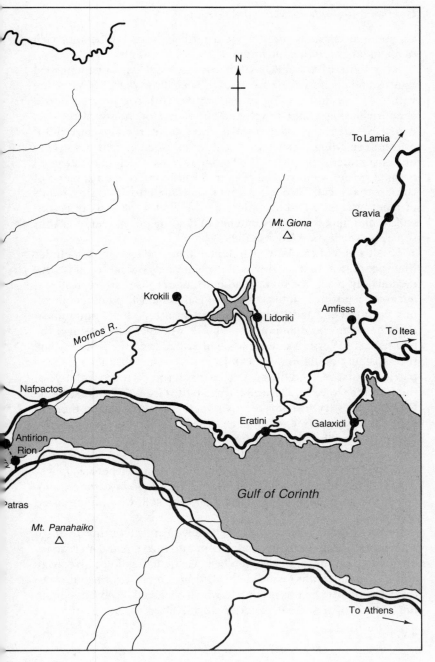

Calydonian sentinels stood on guard, ready to signal the approach of an enemy rounding the hump of Mount Varasova.

It is a short drive from Calydon to **Messolongi**, its undistinguished houses and cheap villas surrounded by shallow water. Flourishing with fisheries and trading in *avgotaraho* (fish-roe pressed into a cylindrical shape and enveloped in a rind of yellow wax – an expensive delicacy), the historic little town remains mosquito-infested, smelling of marsh and salt; rain-lashed in winter, burning hot in summer. At sunset, the lagoon, across which flat-bottomed boats skim between rows of piles, reflects an impressionist blend of colours that recall Turner's, rather than Canaletto's, Venice: bands of amethyst, grey and lavender, speckled with the coils of green, yellow and pink formed by patches of floating oil. A reef of islands separates the lagoon from the sea.

The leaders of the War of Independence, headed by Alexander Mavrocordatos, first President of the National Assembly, chose this melancholy place for their headquarters because, strategically, it occupied a position similar to that of Calydon in antiquity, controlling both the entrance to the Gulf of Corinth and all communications between the mainland and the Peloponnese. It was also the first place in Western Greece to be liberated (and the first in which the Moslem population was exterminated to a man). To it flocked patriots and it seemed the best place for Byron, as representative of the London Committee formed to help the Greeks in their struggle for liberty, to try to unite the rival factions and persuade them to fight the enemy rather than each other. He arrived on 2 January 1824, wearing the scarlet uniform of the Eighth Regiment of Foot and surrounded by kilted Suliot guards. Guns fired salvoes and wailing *klephtic* tunes were played on lutes and clarinets as he was received by the assembled dignitaries the *banditti*-turned-politicians, the gorgeously-robed clerics and the sallow, aquiline-faced aristocrats.

Byron showed unaccustomed patience, endeavouring to instil some notion of constructive patriotism into the vain and mercenary men who paid lip-service to him because he had gold to give away and a title which impressed them. But his greatest contribution to the cause of Greece was his death, which occurred, aptly enough, in the course of a violent thunder-storm, after a ten-day bout of malarial fever. The flamboyance of the end matched the record of the past. Not only Greece and England were moved by the circumstances of his death; all Europe suddenly became conscious of the Greek struggle for liberty. The flow of volunteers from France, Italy and Russia increased. He died, it seemed, and to quote his own words, that 'Greece might still be free'. In the minds of the ordinary Greek people he was – and indeed still is – not only the greatest Englishman who ever lived, but also a symbol of all those qualities that their own leaders sometimes lacked: disinterestedness, reliability allied with eccentricity, authority enveloped in an aura of aristocratic glamour. When his body was taken back to Newstead, the inhabitants of Messolongi pleaded that some part of his body should remain with them. So his intestines were enshrined in four jars and placed in the church of St Spyridon. They have subsequently been lost. The house in which he lived and died is no longer standing.

The Heroes' Garden lies at the north-west end of the town, shaded by dusty pines, palms and eucalyptus trees. The muzzles of old cannon project from gun-slits in the Turkish walls which run along two sides of it. The monuments to the heroes of the war – Byron's occupies the place of honour – are outstandingly ugly, the palm going to that of the Anonymous Philhellenes: a pile of rock and cannon balls crowned by an urn. However it is pleasant to sit on the shady beach. The smells of pine and eucalyptus drive away the saline odours rising from the lagoon.

It was from the landward side that the famous sortie was made. After Byron's death, the siege of Messolongi began in earnest, and a Turkish army under Reshid Pasha surrounded the rampart. The town was defended by a garrison of four thousand Greek soldiers and armed peasants, and a thousand civilians and boatmen. After nearly a year's siege, Ibrahim Pasha brought up his Egyptian army from the Morea and launched flotillas of flat-bottomed boats to attack with musketry and fiery missiles across the lagoon; but every attack was thwarted by the Greeks. The heroism of the defenders was indeed prodigious, but with the Turks in command of the lagoon, it was no longer possible to supply the garrison. So in April 1826 the decision was taken to make a mass sortie through the labyrinth of ditches, dykes and pools surrounding the rampart. As the Greek soldiers sprang forward, writes Finlay, 'neither the

463

yataghan of Reshid's Albanians, nor the bayonet of Ibrahim's Arabs, could arrest their impetuous attack.' However a traitor warned the Turks, and the Greeks found the roads blocked with Turkish cavalry. Hunger, wounds and fever took their toll of the surviving groups which straggled away from Messolongi up the mountain paths. As the Turks entered the shattered town, the few remaining Greeks blew themselves up. Messolongi is justifiably a national shrine.

West of Messolongi a line of ancient walls descends a chain of hills rising abruptly out of the plain. A stony track (to the right) climbs Mount Arakynthos. In order to visit **Pleuron** it is useful to have a local guide to the ruins (who can usually be found at one of the farm-houses on the way). These ruins are known locally as the *Kastro* of *Agia Irinio*. The deviation is worthwhile, the Hellenistic walls being among the finest in Greece. In the prehistoric age the area was ruled by Thestius, father of Althaea, the savage queen of Calydon, but it was deserted by the time of Strabo. A new Hellenistic city rose up in the third century BC, during the wars between the Macedonian kings and the Aetolian League.

The impregnable enceinte, a circuit of about a mile and a half, is a lozenge-shaped quadrilateral, protected to the north by an abrupt spur of Mount Arakynthos, and falling away, east, south and west in rocky declivities. After a steep slope has been climbed, one of several tombs which form a kind of extra-mural necropolis can be seen. Descending through a hole in the ground, one enters a vault consisting of two chambers, one containing a stone bench decorated with a volute. The well-preserved stone wall has a lovely smooth patina. It may have been the tomb of some senior garrison officer, for Hellenistic Pleuron was a military stronghold, ruled by no great kings and claiming no distinguished citizens.

The entry into the enceinte is from the south-west. Huge rectangular blocks of limestone litter the ground, carpeted in autumn with pale pink crocuses. A massive lintel, twelve feet long and three feet wide, is propped against the wall. From here it is best to go roughly northwards across the windswept ledge. First, to the vestigial remains of a theatre, the smallest in Greece, built into the western rampart, where the garrison troops were probably entertained with the farces of Aristophanes and Menander. It had only eight tiers and was entirely unornamented. Next comes a strange sunken structure believed to have been a huge cistern containing the main water supply of this barren, inaccessible place. The pit is approximately 100 feet by 60, its sides overgrown with ivy, and crossed by four parallel walls which may have supported a roof. Each of the oblong chambers formed by these walls is connected with the next by a curious triangular aperture.

To the north, at the apex of the lozenge, extends a deserted ledge, site of the *agora*. The outlines of the foundations are somewhat incomprehensible. The strictly military nature of the citadel, a formidable observation post dominating the plain, may account for the fact that there is not a fragment of a capital, or a column or decorative moulding. A parapet surrounds the north side. Immediately below it, the well-preserved eastern gate, with clearly discernible holes in which the door pivoted, overlooks the bleak slopes of the Zygos range.

Turning south-east in order to complete the circuit, one passes the base of an apsidal edifice and the sunken foundations of a square chamber into which a stairway descends; one then skirts the line of the eastern walls, six foot thick and in a good state of preservation: as impressive an example of third-century BC military architecture as any in the country. Composed of massive stone blocks and crowned at intervals by low, rectangular towers (originally there were over thirty), the line extends unbroken, generally six courses high – sometimes as many as fifteen. Vestiges of steps, by means of which sentinels mounted the *terreplein*, are discernible. In a wide arc running from east to west one can see the cliff of Varasova like a huge beast crouching above the plain, the lagoon of Messolongi intersected with causeways, the fields and cypress alleys of the coastal strip, and a shoal of islets – the Ekhinades, off which the Battle of Lepanto was fought – strung out along the shore where the Aheloos winds through sandbanks to the sea.

After the Messolongi bypass and the Pleuron fork, the road divides briefly, the more scenic western branch passing through the lowlands: a complex of lagoons and salt-pans, with the Zygos chain forming a barrier to the east. A narrow inner lagoon bites deep into the land, spanned by a causeway, with the colour-washed houses of Etoliko reflected in the motionless water.

Companion Guide to Mainland Greece

To visit Oiniadai, one takes the branch road to the west through Etoliko into a domesticated countryside of maize fields and olive groves which form an idyllic landscape. The road passes through Katohi, whose brightly painted houses climb the side of a knoll overlooking the reed-fringed banks of the Aheloos, and enters a reclaimed marshland. Originally Lake Melita, it was connected with the sea by a channel. Now isolated hills, their bases fringed with reeds and luxuriant thistles, rise out of pampas country; all evidence of the lake has vanished. A low, flat-topped hill, locally known as Trikardo, the site of ancient **Oiniadai**, one of the strangest Hellenistic sites in Greece, runs north to south. The debris of polygonal-block walls is discernible through dense thickets. Up to two hours is required to see the main features of the site.

The city acquired considerable fame for its impregnability. An Athenian army, commanded by Pericles, was unable to scale its well-defended sides in 453 BC, and in the Peloponnesian war, in 428 BC, Oiniadai having sided with Sparta, twelve Athenian triremes sailed up the estuary of the Aheloos, but were unable to capture the citadel. In Hellenistic times the hill was encircled with strong new fortifications, and the arsenal and harbour on Lake Melita were joined to the citadel by ramparts. Thus fortified by nature and man, it occupied a strategic position dominating the Acarnanian lowlands; but like other Hellenistic cities of the western littoral, it contributed little to the evolution of Hellenistic civilization.

The whole eminence, obviously once an island, is peppered with fragments of walls (originally a circuit of three miles), with gates, cisterns, posterns, sally-ports and foundations of houses, all buried deep in brushwood and difficult to locate. It is best to begin at the north end, where the contours of the port – once a sinuous creek biting deep into the limestone cliff-side – are discernible, enclosed within parallel ramparts running south to north. A fine polygonal wall and tower overlook the former lake. From here one can climb the hill parallel to the eastern harbour rampart. There are paths, but they are confusing. It is best to keep bearing south-east among the oak trees, whose branches shade a thick undergrowth. The **Theatre**, which is excitingly hidden in a thicket of oak trees, consists of fragments of more than twenty tiers and part of the orchestra. The

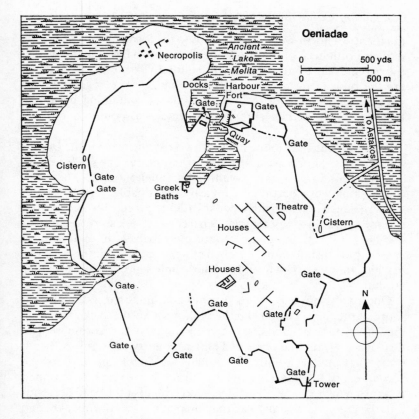

cavea was divided into eleven sections and there were twenty-five rock-hewn seats in the front row for notables. From the highest tier there is a memorable view through a tracery of oak branches. The southern extremity of the hill slopes towards the serpentine estuary of the Aheloos flowing through green fields and shoals of silt. East of the river mouth, a group of hills with craggy crests complete the Poussin-like composition: serene, classical and pastoral. Only the apricot flesh tints of the heroic figures are absent (Oiniadai is a very deserted place). There are few views in Greece which approximate more closely to the French seventeenth-century concept of a classical landscape.

East of the theatre is a large cistern, followed (south-east) by the remains of what could have been an important gateway. From

467

the theatre a north-west descent leads to the former quay, where the narrow bottleneck of the creek opens out into a large inlet in which the triremes once anchored. At the southern extremity of the creek are the ruins of the second-century BC baths: a rectangular edifice with a stone tank and two circular rooms containing basin-like hollows, where bathers stood as hot water was poured over them from cauldrons.

Following the base of the hill northwards, one reaches the **Docks**, situated on the north-west tip of the promontory. The site is unique in Greece. Below a massive wall, tall parallel buttresses, between which ships were berthed, are easily identifiable. Traces of the slipways, once latticed with wood in order to protect the keels of the triremes, are just discernible. There is an uncanny feeling of unreality, of something one cannot quite believe in, about these ancient port installations, barely distinguishable from the rock out of which they were hewn, and with no visible sign of the sea for miles around.

One road from Etoliko to Agrinio continues along the eastern shore of the inner lagoon and then follows a northerly course along the valley of the Aheloos, between the ranges of the Xeromeri (The Dry Places) and the Zygos chain: a country of scrub-covered, sometimes olive-clad, hills. The village of Angelokastro, once the second capital of the Despots of Epirus, is crowned by a ruined Byzantine tower. After crossing a saddle of hills, the road descends into the green bowl of the Acarnanian plains, dotted with lakes and traversed by the streams of the Aheloos, with the jagged spurs of Mount Panetoliko massing up behind Agrinio.

Agrinio, an important market town and centre of the tobacco trade, is linked by a mountain road with Lamia in the east. It is also the starting-point for a visit to Thermon and a tour of Lake Trihonida. Stiflingly hot in summer, the plain of Agrinio is subject to violent earthquakes (the town was completely destroyed in 1887 and subsequently rebuilt). There is a lively public square, lined with hotels, restaurants and the usual provincial confectioners. South and south-east lie the two main Acarnanian lakes: Lysimachia and Trihonida. Distant hills and mountains, blue or gun-metal according to the time of day, form an imposing ring round the well-watered plain.

To visit Thermon you take the road along the north shore of **Trihonida**, the larger and more beautiful of the two lakes, once believed to be unfathomable at its eastern end. Cypress thickets and plantations of pomegranates mount the terraces above the crescent-shaped lake. The route is lined by a succession of prosperous villages; mulberry trees with whitewashed trunks surround open-air wayside cafés. In antiquity all this shore was densely populated. The first place of importance is **Paravola**, where, scattered across a steep hill between the village and the lake, are the ruins of the large, ancient fortress of **Boucation**, of whose history little is known. Hellenistic walls radiate in all directions from the small, oval-shaped summit of the citadel. Climbing the north-west side, one skirts defence works composed of rectangular blocks, twelve courses high. The entrance to the summit is guarded by two round, medieval towers from which sentinels could spot hostile armies debouching from the defiles of Mount Panetoliko. From this platform, studded with wild almond trees and stunted oaks and girdled by fragments of the acropolis wall which follows the irregular configuration of the eminence, one gets a good idea of the fortifications: acropolis walls, inner and outer, with steps leading down to the lower town, also defended by inner and outer defence works. Three fortified salients radiate from a striking semi-circular tower. The north-east side of the terrace, where there are two more very ruined semi-circular towers, is buttressed by a fine wall made from polygonal blocks. A rampart descends in a north-westerly direction to the village school, whence another line of less well-preserved walls run southward in the direction of the lake. The enceinte is nearly a mile in circumference.

Further east, streams cascade through the pretty village of Agia Sofia under arbours of plane trees, the ice-cold water gurgling round huge contorted tree-trunks. On the hillside, amid pines and cypresses, there is the curious barn-shaped Church of *Agios Nikolaos*, built entirely of ancient materials – pilasters, columns, capitals and cornices – plundered from a temple of Aphrodite at Thermon. North of the church the shell of a little Byzantine basilica nestles in the shade of prickly oaks; south of it, a minuscule Turkish mosque raises its shallow dome above the tombstones – one of those numerous examples of the juxtaposition of antiquity, Byzantium and Islam which constantly diversify the Greek landscape. To the north, the spurs of Mount Panetoliko are dotted with fragments of Hellenistic watch-towers and walls which formed a vast crescent-shaped defensive system protecting the prosperous settlements of the lake district.

Just beyond the village of Thermo, is the important site of **Thermon**. Spiritual centre of the Aetolians – to these rough people it was what the Acropolis meant to the Athenians, Delphi and Olympia to all Greeks – its ruins are embedded in marshy ground surrounded by cultivated fields. The spruce-covered sides of the Panetoliko massif, forming a semi-circle round the sanctuary, rise to bare, beautifully proportioned peaks.

In spite of the presence of prehistoric buildings and Archaic temples, we know that the sanctuary did not acquire nationwide renown until the third century BC, when it became the headquarters of the Aetolian League, a loose federation of states which tried to dispute the mastery of Greece with Macedonia. All the treasure of the Aetolians was stored at Thermon. In 218 BC Philip V of Macedon, unwilling to tolerate Aetolian pretensions any longer, set out to punish the League. He sacked Thermon, smashed two thousand statues, and hurried off with much treasure. Twelve years later Philip, infuriated by the Aetolians' provocative alliance with Rome, returned and, according to Polybius, 'once more defaced all the sacred objects that he had spared in his former occupation of the place'. Henceforth Thermon ceased to exist.

A tour of the ruins, which are fragmentary though not unimpressive, follows a roughly straight line north to south within what was a rectangular enclosure once flanked by third-century towers. The barbaric note, associated with the character of the Aetolians, is struck from the outset. Several lop-sided slabs of porous stone, projecting from the soil like a miniature Stonehenge, mark the site of a very early temple. Following the side of the embankment, one reaches the foundations of the Temple of Apollo, originally of the seventh century BC, but later refashioned. This, the holiest shrine of the Aetolians, extended across a stepless stylobate. Its most unusual feature was its length in relation to its width: fifteen columns on each side and only five at each end, as opposed to the Parthenon's seventeen and eight. A row of twelve columns ran along the centre of the *cella*, supporting the roof. There was no front porch at the south end and the wooden entablature was crudely decorated with painted terracotta *metopes*. The massive limestone drums of the north façade give some idea of the heaviness which must have characterized the building. Primitive in conception and execution, it expresses the backwardness of the people whose shrine it was.

Beside the temple are the outlines of two early pre-Hellenic structures known as Megarons A and B, which may have served as palaces. South of the temple's front entrance, a pile of stones indicates the site of the altar, once heaped with the ashes of sacrificial animals, around which pilgrims, priests and savage tribesmen gathered at the Panaetolian celebrations every autumn. Continuing southward, past a square reservoir, one reaches three successive *stoas* which form a long rectangle, now choked with weeds. Landcrabs, on which the local inhabitants fed during the German occupation of 1941–44, crawl among the damp, mossy deposits. Here were situated the shops and stores where Aetolian merchants sold their wares during the annual assemblies. Well-preserved bases of statues extend in a long line, shorn of the stone and marble effigies hacked to pieces by Philip V's soldiers. The brambles grow thicker, the ground more swampy: it is not easy to explore the site. Across the fields, west of the *stoas*, lay the *agora*, in which an annual market was held during the Panaetolian festival.

The **Museum** (a modest building) should not be missed. There is a collection of *acroteria* with heads, gargoyles and grotesque masks, many with their paint still preserved, which were originally placed on the edge of the roof of the Temple of Apollo to screen the tile ends. The execution, though not refined, is robust, and not without a hint of coarse peasant humour. There are also figures and emblems of anatomical features.

At this point, the south-bound traveller may take an exciting, little-used short cut to the coast. Beyond Thermon, just before the village of Petrochoria, the road descends. Superb views terminate in a sun-dazzled haze in the west, where a burnished, metallic surface betrays the position of Lake Lysimachia. A narrow dirt road to the south penetrates a hot, shut-in valley which ultimately gets lost in an Aetolian wilderness, characterized by the absence of all villages and by scrub-covered mountains of no great height crowding round on all sides. The drifting scents of sun-scorched thyme and agnus castus possess an almost medicinal quality. A feeling of claustrophobia is inevitable; and the absence of human beings adds to it. The winding descent affords sudden glimpses, tantalizingly interrupted by the emergence of barren eminences, of the bed of the Evinos: a streak of silver water flowing in a beautiful loop between tree-lined sand-banks. Climbing further down into the river valley, one crosses a bridge and passes through an abandoned hamlet surrounded by groves of dwarf cypresses. One has the feeling that this is not a place in which to tarry. The road then descends through tamer country, affording glimpses of the Peloponnesian ranges, to the Mornos valley and Nafpactos.

The more leisured traveller, anxious to complete a tour of Lake Trihonida and return to Agrinio, ignores the branch to Nafpactos and drives through a string of villages set in a lush countryside of mulberry orchards and olive groves. In the evening old men sit in rustic roadside cafés, playing with their worry-beads as they exchange the latest agricultural gossip. Before striking north to Agrinio, the road fringes the shore of the lake. Through clusters of reeds one catches glimpses of the flat, calm water in which Mount Panetoliko is reflected.

North-west of Agrinio a bridge spans the wide bed of the Aheloos, whose turbid streams, after flowing from their torrent sources in the Pindos, wind swiftly between reed-fringed sandbanks. In antiquity the river, symbolic of all fresh water in Greece, and infinitely perplexing in its innumerable and erratic changes of course, constantly overflowed its banks and flooded the countryside. Strabo says the river was likened to a bull because of the roaring of its waters, and to a serpent because of its endless sinuosities.

A Xenias tourist pavilion on the west bank of the river marks the site of **Stratos**, which is scattered over a low ledge overlooking the Aheloos. Thucydides and Xenophon called it the chief city of Acarnania. Its inhabitants were a tough, disciplined people. In the Peloponnesian War they sided with Athens and when the unruly Ambracians from the north were incited by Sparta to attack Stratos in 429 BC, they were ignominiously routed by the intrepid Acarnanian sling-throwers. In the third century BC neither Philip V of

Macedon, the sacker of Thermon, nor his more temperate successor, Perseus, was able to capture it.

The ruins are scanty. The fifth-century BC river gate (west of the tourist pavilion), which consists of two large, curved slabs covering a postern, leads through the thick walls into a bleak, shadeless plateau, broken up into low eminences. To the north are traces of the *agora*; east lie the negligible remains of the theatre. Continuing northward, one reaches the site of the acropolis. A more satisfying ruin is the fourth-century BC Temple of Zeus at the western extremity. Limestone drums of Doric columns and pieces of architrave are scattered around the foundations. Stratos has little to offer but its walls and a view of the curiously cream-coloured streams of the Aheloos flowing through a bed nearly half a mile wide, along which Strabo says vessels used to sail up from Oiniadai.

The road continues northward through domesticated country where modern agricultural methods are now employed. To the west lies the little lake of Ozeros at the foot of the Xeromeri. Soon another lake, Amvrakia, comes into view, its pale blue waters compressed within a narrow basin fringed with tobacco fields. To the east, the advancing mountains of the Valtos are bare and forbidding. A causeway crosses the lake which tapers off into a slender apex. A short climb between arid hills is followed by a descent towards the Ambracian Gulf, where the houses of Amfilohia are huddled round a narrow inlet.

CHAPTER 32

The Ambracian Gulf

Amfilohia – Vonitsa – Arta –
The Valley of the Arahthos – The 'Red Church' –
Voulgarelli – The Castle of Rogoi – Nikopolis –
Preveza – Actium.

The gulf, entered by a channel no more than half a mile wide, is broken up by bluffs and spits of land, the mirror-like surface of its shallow waters scattered with shoals and reefs. Lagoons, crossed by causeways, fringe the northern shore and many of the creeks are inaccessible to anything but flat-bottomed boats. Two rivers, the Louros and the Arahthos, wind through orange groves, forming wide shingly beds, before pouring their waters, which have risen in the Epirot highlands, into the inland sea. Beautiful mountains rise on three sides: the peaks of ancient Thesprotia to the north; the Valtos spurs of the Pindos to the east, and the abrupt slopes of the Acarnanian Xeromeri to the south. There is a pale, mirage-like quality about the scene which is grandiose yet serene.

A semi-circular tour of the gulf – taking in the medieval fortress of Vonitsa, the thirteenth-century churches of Arta hidden among orange groves, the ruined Byzantine Castle of Rogoi and the extensive Roman ruins of Nikopolis – is easily accomplished in two days. Of Actium little remains but the name and the memory. The obvious place to stay is the Xenias Hotel in Arta. The drive up the valley of the Arahthos to see the 'Red Church', overlooking one of the most spectacular mountain prospects in Western Greece, also starts from Arta.

Amfilohia serves as a curtain-raiser to the new scene: its whitewashed houses with red roofs cling to a steep hillside among

474

mulberry and eucalyptus trees; it has a lively waterfront at the head of a narrow creek. On the hill to the east, vestiges of ancient walls, probably those of Limnaea, are discernible. The port, where it is pleasant to stop for coffee or a drink, was founded by Ali Pasha in the early nineteenth century as a military outpost, when the Albanian tyrant's dominions extended all over Epirus and beyond.

Successive creeks and caves between Amfilohia and Vonitsa afford views of small, flat islands strung out across the motionless gulf. After climbing for a while into the formidable Xeromeri Mountains, the road dips down into a deep inlet, fringed by a little green plain, with the village of **Vonitsa** huddled on the shore, its medieval castle crowning a bluff above the sea.

On the way to the castle there are two picturesque churches. The small Basilica of the Holy Apostles has a wooden *iconostasis*, more Italianate than Byzantine in style and execution, decorated with coloured designs of rosettes and tendrils. The money-box, into which one drops a few drachmas for a candle, is painted with figures of St Peter and St Paul holding a model of the church. In the larger Basilica of St Nicholas (just below the castle) the effigies of two lions with human faces and curling moustaches support the Cross on the summit of the screen.

It takes an hour to visit the castle. Originally a Byzantine fortress guarding the approaches to the inland sea, it passed in 1294 into the hands of Philip of Taranto as part of the extravagant dowry brought to him on his marriage to the beautiful Thamar, daughter of the Despot of Arta. In turn Frankish and Venetian, it was seized in 1362 by Leonardo Tocco of Corfu, whose descendants held it for over a century. In the fifteenth century Carlo Tocco bequeathed Vonitsa to his widow, the Duchess Francesca, a formidable lady of much ability and vigour, and divided the rest of Acarnania among his five bastard sons. Even after the Turkish conquest the fortress remained an Italian outpost in Ottoman territory, but during the War of Independence it fell into ruins. After the establishment of the modern kingdom in 1833, a Greek garrison was stationed in the crumbling keep and the military insurrection which led to the abdication of King Otho and his headstrong queen had its genesis here in 1862. (There are few changes of Greek political regime in which the military does not have the first word.)

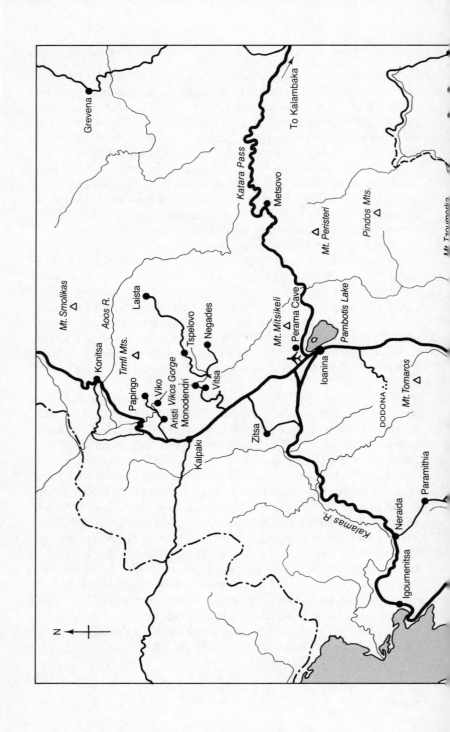

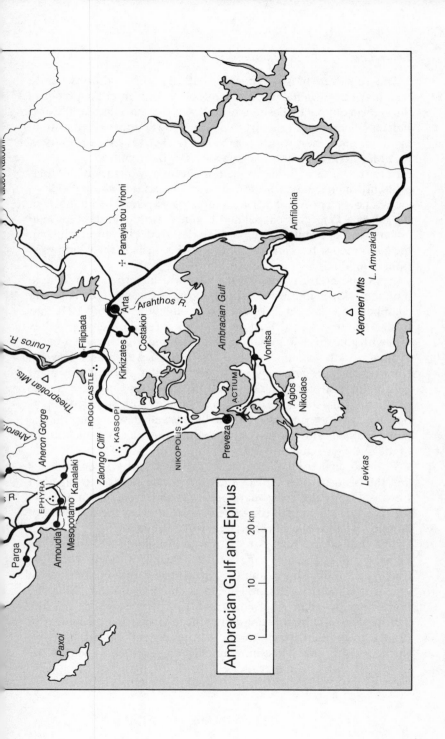

Ambracian Gulf and Epirus

The ruins are mostly Venetian with Turkish additions. Little remains of the original Byzantine masonry. You enter the precincts through an outer gate beside a little pine grove and climb southward (left) along an outer rampart to a ruined tower above the maritime plain. A path then winds northward (right) to a well-preserved bastion and through another gateway. The path continues uphill. A turn to the left brings you to the remains of a two-storied building, probably the residence of the Turkish commander, whose windows look out over a prospect of sea, mountains, islets and headlands. On the left is a long, low chapel and beside it (to the east) steps lead down to a deep, vaulted cistern. All is deserted. Only insects hum in the evergreen shrubs and the wind whistles through the windows of ruined buildings.

At this point, turn right into the keep which is crowned by a large building with a fine doorway. Here were the vaulted halls and chambers to which Philip of Taranto brought the seductive Thamar from Arta, together with all the gold of her fabulous dowry. A low wall with gun-slits and look-out posts surrounds the triangular keep. From it, a path descends westwards to a line of well-preserved walls from which there is a view of a fiord-like inlet, encircled by giant eucalyptus and olive trees whose branches dip into the water. Continuing in a southerly direction alongside a low, ruined parapet, one observes an impressive crenellated wall descending, on the landward side, into a forest of eucalyptus trees. Thence one returns to the outer gate and the village.

From Vonitsa the main road leads to the village of Agios Nikolaos and the bridge which crosses the narrow channel to the island of Levkas. Along the coast there are impressive remains of Turkish fortifications. A branch road to the north ends at the headland of Actium, whence one can cross by ferry to Preveza.

The best course now is to return to Amfilohia and follow the highway along the east coast. Cliffs, thickly wooded with ilex, overhang a rocky shore, and the pastel-shaded gulf is so extensive that it is sometimes difficult to grasp its configuration. Soon the borderline between Acarnania and Epirus is reached: not the Epirus of the mountain redoubt, but the lowland fringe, a country of orange groves that stretch for miles around Arta; indeed, in spring the scent of orange blossom is intoxicating, all-pervasive. On the left side of the road, gullies filled with parallel rows of fruit trees debouch into shallow shingly coves. Alleys of dwarf cypresses form wind-breaks and huge fig trees provide luxuriant shade.

Six kilometres before reaching Arta a lane to the right, bordered by honeysuckle, dog-rose and wild gladioli, leads in less than half a kilometre to the **Church of the Panayia tou Vrioni**, least important of Arta's countryside Byzantine churches; however the deviation is short enough to be worthwhile. The church's exterior walls are decorated with lavish brick inlay, inferior in design and execution to that which distinguishes most of the churches of the plain. But the setting – a cypress grove and cemetery full of rose bushes and flowering Judas trees, their trunks entwined with periwinkle – is charming.

Arta, undistinguished though lively, spreads across a saddleback eminence, with the Arahthos winding in an arc round the northern end of the ellipse. The people are friendly and among the best-looking in Greece; the food is execrable. The **Xenia Hotel** is approached through a medieval gateway. The modern building dominates the castle precincts (now public gardens) which are, however, still encircled by the well-preserved thirteenth-century Byzantine ramparts. A castellated bastion overlooks the plain to the north. No hotel in Greece is more attractively situated: bedroom balconies overlook the streams of the Arahthos estuary where, beyond the sand-banks, groves of orange and lemon trees stretch out in a pastel-coloured haze; clusters and alleys of poplars climb green foothills against the back-drop of the Epirot mountains: grey, lonely, infinitely diversified in their forms. In summer frogs croak on the banks of the streams and the sandflies, which swarm into the damp gardens and orchards, are a pest.

It was in the third century BC that fame and lustre were added to the city by Pyrrhus, the Molossian king. He adorned and fortified the city, made it his capital and fought so staunchly against the Roman Republic that Hannibal considered him the greatest of all generals. In the late second century BC it fell into the hands of the then all-powerful Aetolians. But the star of Greece, whether Macedonian, Aetolian or Spartan, had virtually set, and Ambracia declined in importance. After the battle of Actium, Augustus removed all the inhabitants to Nikopolis.

479

But Arta's renown, as reflected in the visible remains of its remarkable churches, belongs to the Middle Ages. As capital of the Despotate of Epirus, it was, after Thessaloniki, the most important city in Mainland Greece during the thirteenth and fourteenth centuries. The rugged nature of the mountains (through which there are few passes) surrounding the plain and gulf, formed a natural protection against the Crusaders, and in 1204 Michael Angelus Comnenus Ducas lost no time, when the Frankish flood was sweeping Greece, in making Arta the military and political headquarters of his Despotate. He formed a militia of Ambracian natives, hired mercenaries and soon turned to the offensive. Playing one Latin state off against the other, he maintained Byzantine administration within his Despotate, whose boundaries he extended from Ioanina in the north to Nafpactos in the south. While feeble Flemish Counts tottered uneasily on the great golden throne at Constantinople, Michael and his successors created in Western Greece a Byzantine state, with Arta as its capital, which not only became a political reality but rivalled in importance the other more 'legitimate' empire in exile at Nicaea in Asia Minor. In 1215, while campaigning in Northern Epirus, Michael was murdered in his sleep by one of his slaves.

With Michael's successors – his half-brother Theodore and his son Michael II – the Despots of Arta reached the zenith of their dynastic ambitions. Theodore captured the Latin Emperor in an ambush in the mountains of Epirus, and crowned himself Emperor of Byzantium at Thessaloniki in 1222. Michael II, an eccentric character, no less violent than his predecessors, made Arta a brilliant capital, and it was a touch-and-go affair whether an Angelus of Arta or a Liscarid of Nicaea would re-enter Constantinople as Emperor when the ridiculous Latin edifice crumbled and the 'God-Guarded city' was restored to its legitimate Greek masters.

It was, in fact, the Nicaean Emperor who recaptured Constantinople in 1261, though a measure of autonomy was granted to the Despotate: the history of its vigorous defence of the ideal of Hellenism during the half-century of Latin depredation had taken too strong a hold on the minds of the population of mainland Greece to be lightly dismissed. The subsequent Despots, however, were men of less mettlesome character, and by the middle of the

Nafpactos: the old harbour.

Dodona: the Theatre, capable of accommodating eighteen thousand spectators.

Turkish bridge at Konitsa on the Albanian frontier; a single wide arch of the utmost elegance.

Papingo: snowy spring in the Pindos Mountains.

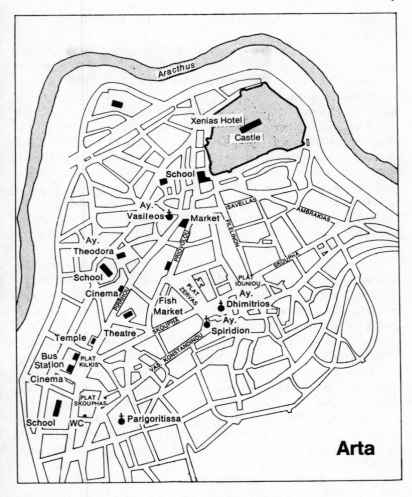

Arta

fourteenth century Arta succumbed to the Serbian flail. But the Serb empire was also a passing phase, and in 1417 Carlo Tocco, Lord of Vonitsa, moved into the citadel. The curtain came down in 1499 with the Turkish conquest. Ali Pasha, the sultan's turbulent viceroy of

Epirus and Albania, was the last notable personage to stay in Arta's ancient fortress.

The number of churches in and around the city bear witness to its one-time importance. Descending from the castle, we come first to the little **Church of St Basil** in Agios Vasileos Street. A rectangular single-nave basilica of the fourteenth century, it is outstanding for its exterior ornamentation, with two courses of inlaid glazed tiles which offer a sharp but pleasing contrast to the brickwork decoration on the north and east sides. In each of the windows there is a single unfluted colonette crowned by an Ionic capital. The church could hardly be smaller – the side apses are positively diminutive – and the interior is now without interest, but this is not peasant architecture and one immediately gets the impression that the Despotate, insulated from the rest of Greece by geopolitics, was, like the far-away empire of Trebizond on the Black Sea, a centre of artistic creativity.

More important is the nearby **Church of St Theodora** in Agia Theodora Square, approached through a gabled arch decorated with brick inlay. The church is dedicated to the pious Theodora, a strait-laced aristocrat, who came from Servia in Western Macedonia as the bride of the despot Michael II Angelus. In spite of her estimable character, Theodora did not enjoy a happily married life. Her husband, infatuated by a notorious courtesan who was also a sorceress and went by the extraordinary name of Lady Gangrene, not only dismissed his wife from the palace but drove her into exile. This saintly woman kept body and soul together by living on the roots of wild plants, occasionally accepting the hospitality of some remote mountain monastery. Eventually, however, Michael had a traumatic vision: Christ appeared to him and denounced him roundly for succumbing to the wiles of Satan's agent, the Lady Gangrene, and threatened to destroy him with fire and thunderbolts. Terrified and conscience-stricken, Michael scoured the country for his victimized wife, found her and restored her to her rightful place in the palace. Thanks to Theodora's merciful intercession, the Lady Gangrene, instead of being strapped to an ass, as ordered by the remorseful Michael, and exposed to the ribaldry of the inhabitants prior to her execution, was allowed to leave Arta unmolested.

The exterior of the church is charming. The building, which is of the fourteenth century, is low, irregular and architecturally eccentric. In spring the garden beside it is a mass of lilac and the snowball blooms of the guelder rose. Two very dark green cypresses of considerable age, one of which serves as a bell-tower, add proportion and perspective to the scene. The west front, through which the narthex, crowned by a small low drum, used to be entered, is decorated with lavish brickwork bands: zig-zag, dog-tooth and herring-bone. The *naos* is well-proportioned, with four old columns disposed in a square and crowned with acanthus leaf Theodosian capitals, plundered from a nearby Early-Christian basilica. The central aisle, higher than the others, is lit by a clerestory. The narthex is distinguished by a marble plaque, believed to be a fragment of Theodora's tomb, sculpted in low relief, depicting the pious lady, who, though crowned and robed as befits a Despot's consort, wears the veil of a nun. The diminutive figure beside her represents her infant son, Nicephorus, who succeeded his father as Despot. Both figures stand under a canopy supported by knotted columns, flanked by two Archangels, while the hand of God points at Theodora.

Next comes the **Church of the Parigoritissa** (The Virgin of Consolation), Arta's most imposing monument, now a museum of Christian antiquities, which stands on a platform above Skoufa Street, overlooking the orange groves beyond the river. Founded at the end of the thirteenth century by the Despot Nicephorus and his wife Anna Palaeologina, it is one of the most important Byzantine churches in Greece. Three-storied, it is in the shape of a tall Greek Cross within a square (the cross is only perceptible in the interior). Drums and cupolas, six in all, seem puny, ill-proportioned affairs without any relation to the barrack-like cube of stone and brick which they crown.

The interior, however, is impressive, if unusual. The sombre, lofty *naos* is an extraordinary structure, height being achieved by a cumbersome architectural disposition which was never repeated, presumably because of its impracticability: at each corner of the central square three superimposed courses of columns support high squinch arches forming an octagon on which the drum rests. The columns of the third and highest course are more slender and decorative in effect than structural in purpose. Each course of vertical columns is supported by horizontal pillars, many of which are cracked by the sheer weight of the structure. The column-courses are capped by a mass of vaults and arches that fail to cohere aesthetically. Admittedly there is no absence of height and spaciousness – even perhaps of grandeur.

Turning from architecture to decoration, one's attention is automatically drawn to the dome crowning the lofty square in which a thirteenth-century **Christ Pantocrator** of colossal dimensions is depicted in mosaic, gorgeously robed and holding an ornamented Book of Gospels. Below are ranged prophets and cherubim in beautiful draperies. Most remarkable is the imposing figure of St Sophronius, boldly modelled, with violent contrasts in the colour scheme, which is unique for a mosaic of this period. Another fragment worth looking at is the rather crude but charming Nativity, full of bucolic serenity, on the topmost north vault. The fourteenth-century frescoes of the apse are hopelessly damaged.

From the gallery, reached by a modern staircase, there is a good close-up view of the amazing architectural intricacies of the Gothic tracery in one of the squinches and also of the fine carving on the north and west arches. One can also examine the beautiful mosaics of the prophets around and below the Pantocrator at approximately eye-level.

Other churches, of considerable interest to Byzantine enthusiasts, are scattered around the countryside and it is enchanting to walk along the flowery lanes. Unfortunately, however, most of the churches lie in different directions, and the smaller ones are not easy to find; it is wiser to drive through the maze of orchards, vineyards and straggling hamlets.

One starts south-west of the *Parigoritissa*. Here the Arahthos, flowing in a series of loops towards the gulf, is spanned by the famous **Turkish Bridge of Arta**, the largest and most striking of all these elegant half-moon structures that bridge the rivers and torrents of Epirus and Albania. This one, built by the Despots on Hellenic foundations and entirely refashioned by the Turks for packhorses, has four graceful crescent-shaped arches of different dimensions through which there are lovely views of the mountain barrier to the north. The fact that the highest point (above the largest arch) is not in the centre of the bridge adds further diversity to the construction. According to a legend, immortalized in Greek folk-song, the thousand Greek masons who built the bridge under the direction of Turkish engineers in the seventeenth century found that the middle pier, at which they would toil all day, was repeatedly swept away in the evening by the waters of the Arahthos. Finally, a little bird perched itself on the middle pier, twittered in a human voice and delivered the sinister message that, until the master-mason's wife was buried in the foundations, the bridge would never be completed. So the unfortunate woman was induced by a ruse to enter the pier, ostensibly to recover her husband's ring which had fallen inside. Stone and rubble were quickly heaped over her, and the masons set to work to strengthen the pier. Since then the bridge has stood intact.

Crossing the modern bridge, from which there is a fine view of the Turkish one, you descend into an olive grove where a tall poplar screens the little Byzantine **Church of Agios Vasileos tis Yefiras** (St Basil at the Bridge), a charming little extravaganza. The cruciform church is minute, crowned by a cylindrical drum which is taller than the main body of the church. The frieze below the cornice and the brickwork decoration on the drum are crude but picturesque. The interior is without interest.

Now take the road to Preveza and then the first turning to the left. A dirt road runs through flat, lush countryside. You pass the hamlets and farmhouses of Costakioi and Plisous under an umbrella of green shade. At each of two successive forks turn to the left, until you come to the **Church of Agios Demetrios Katsouris**, which is surrounded by olive and orange trees, their trunks entwined with ivy. Originally a tenth-century dependency of a Patriarchal monastery, restored under the Despots and finally abandoned in the eighteenth century, St Demetrios has no exterior decoration, but the tall drum, the planes of slanting roofs and the three apses create a pleasing effect. Small, but well-proportioned, this country church has an air of relative loftiness which raises it above the level of a rural chapel. The deserted interior is cross-inscribed. In the middle conch of the sanctuary there is a fine painting of three saints, typical portraits of old men, with serene, expressive faces. Assigned to the twelfth century, this fresco is older than any other in the Arta region and also reflects the relatively high level of artistic creativeness that existed here even before the time of the Despots. In the side conch (right) we see St Basil and St John Chrysostom, and in the apse the Virgin and Child, the former distinguished by an acid and spiteful expression that would do credit to Medea in one of her nastiest moods. The rest of the frescoes, of little interest, are of the seventeenth and eighteenth centuries.

From St Demetrios Katsouris one drives along lanes bordered by mulberry trees and hedgerows of flowering brambles to the hamlet of Kirkizates which is hidden among orange groves and shaded by huge fig trees. A boy from the café will fetch a key from the local priest and conduct you to the thirteenth-century **Church of Agios Nikolaos tis Rodias** (St Nicholas of the Pomegranate Orchard), now standing impressively isolated in the sunken field which has replaced the original orchard. The exterior is distinguished by a tall drum, and brick inlay decoration on the higher courses of the walls. In the *naos* are two squat marble columns without bases, crowned with well-preserved capitals carved with the device of the double-headed eagle. The frescoes, very damaged, are stylistically of the thirteenth century. A panel on the right side of the *iconostasis* contains a fine icon of the Dormition of the Virgin, remarkable for the vividness of its red tints. Though provincial in execution, it is nevertheless elegant and sophisticated.

From here one returns through shady lanes to St Basil of the Bridge and follows the road to the south (right) to the **Monastery of Kato Panayia**. The monastery is set in a garden filled with oleander, pine, olive and orange trees interlaced with creeping vines, which extends across a slope overlooking the Arahthos. An enormous plane tree dips its branches into the water. The cloistered courtyard and domeless church with its cross-roofs, gables, transverse vault and tall belfry (a later addition) creates a complex of subtly graded planes on different levels. The frescoes of the exterior west wall, shaded by a wide projecting gable, which replaced a destroyed narthex, are of no particular merit. To the left of the doorway, however, there is a lively panel of God swirling across the heavens as he creates the world and another in which the Almighty, now crowned, creates man in the garden of Eden. On the right there is another representation of the Creator: this time he is warning Adam and Eve against Evil, while Satan in the form of the Serpent writhes at his feet and angels prepare to expel Adam and Eve from the garden.

The church was founded in the thirteenth century by Michael II Angelus (his monogram is inscribed on the south wall) as a token of penance for his shameful treatment of Theodora. The interior is of little interest, although in some places the overlay of eighteenth-century frescoes has flaked off to reveal earlier paintings. Capitals of different orders crown the unattractive mud-coloured columns in the *naos*.

There remains the **Monastery of Vlachernae**, most important of Arta's outlying churches. A track to the right of the Arta–Ioanina road (north of the bridge) winds through fruit orchards and olive groves between the Epirot foothills to the monastery which was founded at the end of the twelfth century. Originally a basilica, later cross-inscribed and domed, with irregular vaults and three apses of different shapes – one rounded, one three-sided, one five-sided – it creates an architecturally complex effect: varied, asymmetrical but not without harmony. There is much brick inlay decoration in the surrounds of the windows of the central dome and apses, where the different designs that embellish each of the irregular projections provide a decorative ensemble full of fantasy and ingenuity. Sculptural fragments, which originally formed part of a marble screen, decorate the exterior walls and add to the general air of diversity.

In the interior, which is divided into three aisles, part of the floor is covered with boards which the custodian will remove on request to reveal marble paving-stones decorated with stone *tesserae*. The high central octagonal dome, painted with a Christ Pantocrator in a bluish-grey mantle surrounded by prophets and apostles, is flanked by secondary domes above the north and south transepts. In the south nave lies the tomb of Michael II, decorated with crosses, rosettes and stylized foliate bands. Morbidly minded visitors with small hands may slip them through a hole in the east end of the sarcophagus and finger the bones of this violent man, whose lust, ambition and ability combined to make him one of the most colourful personalities of thirteenth-century Greece. In the north nave a second royal tomb is said to contain the remains of his sons, Demetrius and John, who were quietly put away by their younger brother Nicephorus I. I have not succeeded in tracing the subterranean passage that led under the river from the Despot's palace. It is said to have been used constantly by Theodora, when, heavily veiled as a nun, she came to worship at Vlachernae, her favourite church.

The **Church of the Nativity of the Virgin**, commonly known as the '**Red Church**', is the ostensible objective of an expedition along the upper valley of the Arahthos to Voulgarelli. East of Arta the road climbs successive spurs of the Tzoumerka massif. Precipitous grey cliffs have been sliced by erosion and now show the patterns and folds of the rock strata. This is earthquake country. The road climbs and dips, affording entrancing views of the ice-cold Arahthos and the reservoir formed by the building of the Pournari Dam. Houses with slate-grey roofs among orchards of quince and almond are scattered throughout the little green valleys. Ever nearer, more imposing, looms the massif of Tzoumerka, cloud-capped, gashed with forbidding ravines filled with snow, its lower slopes dark with evergreens and scrub. Occasionally a shepherd is seen standing on the summit of a ridge. Invariably he waves. Epirots are among the friendliest of Greeks.

Beyond the hamlet of Palaeo Katouni, which lies in the trough of a valley, the road mounts steeply between groves of almond and Judas trees. Suddenly on the right, a roseate glow emanates from the red-tiled roofs of the 'Red Church': as sophisticated a piece of Byzantine ecclesiastical architecture as one is likely to encounter in a remote highland region. It was founded in 1281 by the *Protostrator* Theodore (the imperial Master of the Horse). Why here in this mountain wilderness? We do not know. A saddleback roof has replaced the broken dome of the cruciform church. The south front is rich in brickwork decoration, a triple band of red lozenges being particularly effective. All the bricks are of a bright red which suffuses the walls with an extraordinary refulgence – especially striking when seen in springtime against a background of pink and white blossom. On the apse, shaded by the plane tree which serves

488

as a bell-tower, more brick inlay outlines the elliptical arches of the windows. The interior, now abandoned, is without interest.

A few kilometres from the 'Red Church' the grey houses of **Voulgarelli** ascend a precipitous mountainside on the fringe of the fir belt, above which towers the sombre summit of Tzoumerka. One can sit at a café halfway up the terraced village and admire the panorama of the Agrapha range extending southwards, with the elegant cone of Timfristos just visible on the horizon. In the last war this mountain redoubt was the headquarters of EDES, the right-wing resistance organization, whose members spent much of their time (as well as much of the gold and arms supplied to them by the British Government) in fighting the Communist-controlled ELAS liberation army instead of the Germans. Today, two unexploded bombs flank the doorway of the main church.

Farther up the mountainside one can join the road to Porta Panayia in Thessaly which follows the route taken by the Despots when they set out from Arta to extend their dominions in Thessaly and Macedonia.

Back in Arta one takes the westerly road around the gulf to Preveza. After crossing the Louros, the road runs west along the fringe of the Ambracian plain. Fifteen kilometres west of Arta an elegant limestone peak rises above the marshy fields on the west bank of the river. It was once crowned by the **Castle of Rogoi**, a stronghold strategically situated between the river and the main route to Arta, built by the Despots to guard their capital against hostile armies advancing from the coast. After 1204 and the Latin sack of Constantinople, Rogoi acquired a curious notoriety: after making off with the remains of St Luke from the imperial capital, a Frankish adventurer sold them to the Duke of Kefalonia who placed them in a shrine at Rogoi, which lay within his domain. After the Turkish conquest, the Evangelist's remains were smuggled to a Danubian fortress.

Remains of strong walls, which sometimes reach a height of twenty-three courses, stand out impressively around the keep. The foundations reveal Hellenic masonry and part of the ancient circuit is discernible to the north-west. It takes no more than ten minutes to climb up to the keep. The towers and crenellated battlements, from whose crannies sprout wild olive trees and thick shoots of dark green ivy, dominate a fine sweep of the Louros river which winds round the base of the hill. On the north side of the keep there is a single-naved chapel, repaired in the seventeenth century, with moderately well-preserved frescoes of the Virgin, the Archangels and the Dormition.

The northern promontory of the Ambracian Gulf now contracts to less than three miles in width: a country of rolling meadows and tall grass, washed to the west by the Ionian Sea, and to the east by a complex network of lagoons. Across the isthmus extend the ruins of **Nikopolis** (the City of Victory), the most extensive Roman site in Greece. Built by Augustus to commemorate the battle of Actium, it was forcibly populated by immigrants from the towns of Ambracia, Acarnania and Aetolia, whose treasures of marble ornaments and statues were removed to adorn his new city. In conception and foundation Nikopolis is Roman; however, it illustrates the continuity of Graeco-Roman civilization, and the prestige attached by Rome to the memory of a decisive battle fought entirely between Romans in the land of Plato and Aristotle. The whole isthmus is studded with remains of walls and foundations of Roman and Early Christian edifices. It is a perplexing site and it can take two or three hours to identify the main ruins, most of which lie a considerable walking distance from each other.

For two centuries it was the chief city of Western Greece. St Paul spent a winter here, and from it he addressed his moving exhortation to Titus. By the fourth century, however, it had declined in importance, and it was left to Julian the Apostate, in one of his transports of pagan fervour, to renovate the city and restore the Actian festival. In the fifth century Alaric and his Goths left little but the debris of broken walls and smashed statues; but in the sixth century, Justinian restored many of the walls, although he diminished the size of the city by reducing their compass.

The **Theatre**, the first monument encountered by the traveller driving from Arta to Preveza, rises against a background of the pale waters of the gulf. The orchestra is overgrown with asphodel, and snakes make sinister rustling sounds among the bushes of wild artichoke that grow between the remains of the stage buildings and the existing tiers of the upper course of the *cavea*. Storks nest in the niches of the upper portico, a semi-circular gallery of arches through which there are views of the meadows sloping down to the lagoon. An ancient geographer says of the lagoon that the fish were so plentiful 'as to be almost disgusting'.

North-west of the theatre lies the outline of the **Stadium**, which, unlike other stadia in Greece, was circular at each end. Here was celebrated the Actia, the quinquennial festival founded by Augustus in commemoration of his victory. Sacred to Apollo, the festival consisted of the usual athletic and musical contests, chariot races and gladiatorial shows, while mock sea-fights re-enacting the Battle of Actium were staged in the bay. North of the stadium, just beyond the hamlet of Smyrtoula, rises the hill on which the future Emperor's army was encamped on the day of the battle. After it was all over he built a temple of Neptune on the spot where his tent had been pitched. All that now remain are scattered fragments of a frieze inscribed with huge letters – part of a description of the battle.

To the west of the stadium, mounds of rubble indicate the site of Roman brick houses; beyond them extend stretches of low Byzantine walls. Opposite the walls, against a background of ferns and long grass descending to the sea, are the ruins of the Early Christian **Basilica of Alcyson** (a local bishop). There is a double aisle, a circular pedestal in the centre and a Hellenistic bas-relief of battle scenes which was later incorporated in the *ambo*.

Beyond the basilica, the sward is littered with more debris of unidentifiable brick buildings. On the landward side of the road, just below the Byzantine walls, we reach the sixth-century **Basilica of St Dometius**, outstanding for its beautiful floor mosaics, masterpieces of elegant design, the work of artists, who, if early Byzantine, were clearly influenced by Roman mosaic work. In one we see two swans floating under fruit-laden pear trees, with an inscription dedicated to Dometius, the Persian monk who was stoned to death for his faith. There are also representations of seagulls and young fishermen spearing tuna. In another, men savagely hunt animals among plane trees.

Further inland from the basilica, and after scrambling over fragments of Byzantine walls, you come to another Roman building, the **Odeion**, built of grey stone on a massive substructure. The *cavea*, almost wholly restored, is one of the most impressive monuments on the site. The position dominates the whole of the tapering peninsula. To the north rise the hills from which Octavian, now confident in victory, watched the rout of Antony's and Cleopatra's fleets.

Northward, beyond the fragments of the Roman aqueduct which probably traversed the whole of the hilly isthmus, the Epirot mountains rise steeply. East and south-east, below the Byzantine walls, a lagoon, where herons wade, is separated from the main bay by a thread of land.

Returning to the main road, one drives south under shady poplars. Remains of small arched buildings, probably sepulchres, are scattered about the meadows. Below the road the lagoon is broken up by reed-bordered creeks, where the water lies motionless. It has become slimily stagnant by the time one reaches the wharves of **Preveza**, a sleepy little port on the tip of the promontory, which has recently made its appearance on the tourist map. There is a saline, fishy smell about the place; but there are some pleasant side-streets bordered with whitewashed houses. Geraniums, hibiscus and Bougainvillea blaze in fragrant courtyards.

The site is that of an ancient city, founded in the third century BC by Pyrrhus. In the Middle Ages it was occupied by Venetians and Turks in turn, until 1797 when it was ceded to France. But Ali Pasha, the Sultan's Albanian satrap, quickly descended upon it and his executioner, a man of formidable stamina, beheaded every member of the French garrison. Their heads were crated and despatched as trophies to the Sultan in Constantinople. There are no ancient monuments in the town: only some outcrops of Venetian walls on the periphery, with the ruined citadel (west of the town) overlooking the Ionian Sea. Among the plane and olive trees, open-air cafés and modest fish tavernas overlook the strait – no more than half a mile wide – which connects the vast three-quarter-moon gulf with the open sea. Empty fishing-boats lie motionless at their moorings in the soporific noontide sun. Caiques and a ferry ply to the opposite point of **Actium**. A few sun-tanned children splash about in a shallow, stagnant inlet. In the background rise the mountains of Acarnania and, westward, the majestic outlines of the island of Levkas.

Scenically, the point of Actium is no more prepossessing than that of Preveza, though it is pleasant to row across the strait in the evening when the waters turn from light blue to mauve and finally to a deep purple-grey. A spit of land, flat and sandy, all but closing the entrance to the inland bay from the sea, the point bears few visible marks of its fame. Slightly to the north are the minimal vestiges of the Temple of Apollo Actios of great antiquity, restored and enlarged by Augustus. On the eminence of Anactorium, overlooking the shore, Augustus built a commemorative temple in the Roman style. Strabo says it dominated a sacred grove and harbour where some of Antony's captured vessels were preserved in boathouses. A kind of naval museum, probably.

But the temptation to ponder on the actual course of the engagement, the third and last Roman conflict fought on Greek territory, is irresistible. On the tactics and strategy displayed by the commanders on 2 September 31 BC, few historians disagree. Antony, whose larger and more cumbersome vessels were crammed bow to stern into the bay of Preveza, is thought to have been encamped, with the élite of his army, on the point of Actium, whereas Octavian's lighter and faster galleys were anchored in an inlet well within the Ambracian Gulf. More impetuous than his rival, Antony decided to risk all – mastery of the empire – in a battle at sea. The attempt proved to be a failure of massive dimensions and the engagement, in which Octavian's smaller vessels possessed greater manoeuvrability in these confined waters, was fought in the Bay of Preveza which serves as a kind of ante-chamber to the Ambracian Gulf. It is said that Cleopatra's unexplained defection with sixty Egyptian galleys, at the crisis of the engagement, turned the scales. Peevish and petulant – as described by Shakespeare thus: 'The ribald-rid nag of Egypt' with 'the breese upon her, like a cow in June' – she hoisted her sail and fled, abandoning her infatuated lover, whose 'lust and sleep and feeding' had sapped 'his honour even till a Lethe'd dullness'. Then 'like a doting mallard, leaving the flight in height,' he flew ignominiously after the purple sails of the royal vessel speeding towards Egypt.

Abandoned by their eccentric, somewhat hysterical, leaders, Antony's captains were pounced upon by Octavian's more manageable galleys which, says Plutarch, sailed 'round and round' and annihilated 'these huge vessels, which their size and their want of men made slow to move and difficult to manage'. Octavian, heretofore imprisoned in the shallow Ambracian trap, was at last able to break out into the open sea. After the naval battle, the land troops were too dispirited to carry on the fight, and Antony's leaderless legions deserted in droves. The last of the great Roman civil wars was over. In this narrow strait between the Ionian Sea and the lagoon-like gulf, skimmed by wild fowl and ringed by mountains, the sickly Octavian won the battle of Actium and became Augustus Caesar.

CHAPTER 33

Epirus

Kassopi – Zalongo – The Aheron – Suli –
Ephyra: The Oracle of the Dead – Parga – Dodona –
Ioanina – Lake Pambotis: The Byzantine Churches –
The Cave of Perama – Zagoria – Konitsa – Zitsa –
Paramithia – Igoumenitsa.

Seamed by narrow valleys funnelling out of forbidding gorges, Epirus is well watered by four rivers. Apart from the Aherousian plain, there are few open stretches. Slate-coloured mountains, bare or wooded, sometimes reaching impressive altitudes, achieve a structural perfection, with peaks, screes and ravines composing an organic architectural whole: highly compressed, though never claustrophobic. In Epirus one has the feeling of sitting on top of the whole of Greece, of being perched on the final crown of this incomparable convulsion of schist, limestone and marble.

In Homeric times, Neoptolemus, the son of Achilles, settled in Epirus with Andromache, the widow of Hector. He was succeeded by his son Molossus, who gave his name to the future kings of the country, a land famous for its dogs, its oxen, and its torrents winding through sunless canyons. The nature of the country gave Achilles' descendants little opportunity to indulge in royal trappings, and the absence of maritime plains retarded, without actually precluding, the process of Hellenic cultural colonization. After the battle of Pydna in 168 BC Aemilius Paulus razed the towns to the ground and condemned the inhabitants to slavery. In medieval times the mountain redoubt remained out of the main current of events, but during the Turkish occupation its inaccessibility made it a stronghold of Hellenism and its chief city, Ioanina, a centre of scholarship. In the

War of Independence its bandoliered brigand-patriots fought ferocious battles in mountain passes of incredible grandeur. During the
Second World War a tiny Greek army and air force checked and
routed a numerically vastly superior Italian expeditionary force
which set out from the Albanian border. Mussolini's illusions were
rudely shattered in the Epirot snowdrifts.

The configuration of the province renders a circular tour imprac-
ticable. Two routes, which include all the main sites, are feasible. (i)
Starting at Preveza, through Kassopi and Zalongo; across the
Aherousian plain, taking in the Aheron gorge, past Parga to
Igoumenitsa. (ii) Starting at Arta, to the classical site of Dodona, on
to Ioanina, the Epirot capital, and north to the Zagori villages and
Konitsa on the Albanian border; back to Ioanina, then to Zitsa, and
down the highway to Igoumenitsa.

The first journey takes two days (one night at Parga); the second
four days and three nights, with Ioanina, where there are plenty of
hotels, as a base. The direct coastal route northwards from Preveza
has little of interest except good beaches.

North of Preveza a country road off the Paramithia road, signposted
Zalongo, climbs the Thesprotian foothills. Towards the end of a
steep climb a signpost points west to a bramble-bordered path
leading to the remains of ancient **Kassopi**. Both in respect of altitude
and the extent of stone debris – there is no marble here – the site is
one of the most striking in Western Greece.

Originally colonized during the Bronze Age, it was the tribal
capital of the Kassopeans, an Epirot people who dwelt in the
country lying between the Ambracian Gulf and the river Aheron.
During the fourth century BC Aphrodite was worshipped here in a
large temple, and her symbols of a dove and serpent, together with
her bust, are found on Cassopean coins.

The first inhabitants raised strong walls on three sides of the
plateau. In Hellenistic times towers were added to an enceinte of
some three kilometres, and the central city plan, laid out in the
traditional geometric style, pivoted on a wide arterial paved way
forming an east–west axis following the line of the great ledge across
which the buildings spread. To the north the city was protected by
tawny-coloured limestone cliffs. Security was thus ensured by

nature, and the situation, one of great dominance, enabled the inhabitants to enjoy a bird's-eye view of sea, gulf, lagoons and promontories.

The ruined city can be traced in its entirety within the fortified enceinte. Most of the walls overlooking the formidable southern declivity have unfortunately been destroyed. Immediately left of the main street in the *agora* area are traces of a long *stoa* consisting of an outer Doric colonnade and an inner one of square columns. Another *stoa* ran north to south (west side of the *agora*); on the east are the remains of an *odeion* with over twenty tiers carved out of the rock, whence politicians harangued the people massed in the quadrilateral market place.

Opposite the north *stoa* is the finest extant ruin: the **prytaneum** or town hall, residence of the city elders and hostel for distinguished visitors. The main walls are of polygonal masonry, and the diagonal interior ones at the four corners of the building constituted a novel feature, probably intended to provide extra support to the upper storey. A large central court was surrounded by Doric colonnades, behind which there were seventeen chambers, in which the town councillors transacted their business. The upper storey, crowned by a roof decorated with *acroteria* carved with lotus flowers and palmettes, stopped short on the south side, thus giving the building the shape of a Greek letter π and enabling the dwellers to enjoy the benefits of the mountain breezes. This well-preserved building, the layout of which is perfectly clear to the naked eye, was destroyed by the Romans in the second century BC when they occupied the whole of Epirus and razed seventy Epirot cities to the ground.

Further evidence of the importance – in this instance not military or strategic – of Hellenistic Kassopi is provided by the ruin of a large third-century BC **theatre**, where ancient drama was taught. Carved out of the cliff-face immediately north-west of the *prytaneum* and reached after a stiff climb, it was capable of accommodating six thousand spectators. The gradient is terrifyingly steep. Two huge rocks lying in the centre of the orchestra remind us of the repeated landslides which have buried the foundations of Kassopi under successive strata of boulders.

At the north-west end of the plateau there is an underground burial chamber. Stone steps lead to a vaulted passage terminating in a square chamber plundered in the early nineteenth century. Ancient graffiti are identifiable on the walls of the passageway which, like those of the chamber, were surfaced with marble dust and sand to give the impression of fine marble panels. Situated within the city walls, the chamber may well have been the funerary sanctuary of some Kassopean military hero. For all its size, and the robust architectural features of its scattered civic buildings, Kassopi remains an enigma. Many large edifices, whose function is unknown, have still to be excavated.

Immediately east of the signpost to Kassopi, the country road dips down to the little eighteenth-century Monastery of *Agios Demetrios*. Above it towers the cliff of **Zalongo**, a national shrine, crowned by a group of modern white figures which commemorate a rather over-romanticized incident during the War of Independence. After the fall of the Suli forts in 1822, a number of Suliots fled southwards and took refuge from the pursuing Turks below this prominent eminence. One day children playing outside the church spied a detachment of Ali Pasha's Albanians approaching from the south-east. The women and children scrambled up the cliff, but the men were ambushed by another Moslem detachment approaching from the north. Caught in cross-fire, they were all killed. About sixty of the women, fearing rape and captivity, reached the summit, whence they hurled themselves, with their children, into the abyss below. It is said that the women performed a slow circular folk-dance on the rocky eminence before falling off one by one, at the end of each revolution, as though in execution of some solemn sacrificial rite. A zig-zag stairway climbs the cliff-face. Halfway up, a little chapel contains the bones of the women whose corpses were found among the boulders. The summit is razor-sharp and one is tempted to wonder whether the dance could ever have taken place in such a confined space. Nevertheless the story remains sacrosanct. To the south undulating grasslands shelve down past Nikopolis to the Ambracian Gulf; to the north roll the Thesprotian mountains, compressed into mysterious billowing forms.

Beyond the fork to Kassopi and Zalongo, the Paramithia road to the north enters a lush wooded valley which contracts into a defile and descends into the Aherousian plain, across which the Aheron flows sluggishly through a series of swamps. Yellow irises border rivulets which criss-cross fields of maize and rice-paddies; buffaloes graze in meadows shaded by poplars, figs and plane trees. In summer the heat is intense. To the north-west the mountain-wall of Suli rises sheer to a height of over 3000 feet: arid, forbidding, with razor-sharp crests sliced by vertical crevices.

The Paramithia road leads to **Gliki**, at the foot of the mountains. The deviation is worthwhile. The streams of the Aheron form meres of sun-dazzled water; cafés spread under immense plane trees.

East of the village a track climbs to the entrance of the **Aheron Gorge**, through which flowed the mythical Styx. Thence a path penetrates the defile of the dead, which is deep, dark and narrow, with a stream of aquamarine water flowing swiftly between banks of ilex. It was in this sinister setting that Charon, squatting on one of those contorted cream-coloured boulders, lay in wait to ferry the souls of the dead across to the world of shades. If the souls, still in the form of corpses, did not have a coin placed behind their ears or laid under their tongues, the avaricious boatman refused to ferry them across to the Asphodel Fields. They were then doomed to wait on the banks of the lugubrious river throughout eternity. Rugged cliffs rise to barren summits dominated by the strange bulbous pinnacle of Kiapha; behind it is a higher peak, and to the south the box-like fort of Kounghi. Rocky bluffs create a zig-zag formation as the defile deepens. No gorge in Greece is more macabre. The silence is total except for the flow of ice-cold water between dipping branches of plane trees. Occasionally one hears the tinkle of a bell hanging from the neck of a black mountain-goat perched on a jagged rock, like some infernal herald pointing the way to Hell. Once the entrance to the gorge is lost sight of, a feeling of constriction, even near-panic, is unavoidable.

Only the deserted forts on the ledges above the path remind us that the gorge was once inhabited by the turbulent people who gave their name to the whole mountain range of **Suli**. The Suliots settled here in the fifteenth century, retaining their Albanian mother tongue and Christian faith. During the early centuries of Ottoman occupation, they enjoyed a measure of autonomy, unconquered by the Sultan's soldiers. They lived by plunder, descending on the farms of Turkish pashas and Greek peasants alike. Towards the end of the eighteenth century their military activities aroused the interest of the Russian Government, and Czarist agents penetrated the Aheron Gorge to encourage and support the Suliots with gold and arms. Ali Pasha's riposte was a full-scale attack in 1792. But the campaign was a failure and most of Ali's soldiers fell to the shots aimed by Suliots posted in hidden crannies overlooking the gorge.

But Ali Pasha could not allow this state of affairs to go on indefinitely. The siege was renewed; it went on for years, the Suliot women fighting in defence of the forts. However as the Turkish ring of pennon-crowned tents tightened round the entrance to the gorge, Suliot stocks of arms and provisions diminished. Eventually, the brigands surrendered, but not until after their leader, the priest Samuel, had blown himself up in the powder magazine of Fort Kounghi. Survivors emigrated to other parts of Greece, but after the outbreak of the War of Independence they returned to their native mountains and once more took up arms against the Turks. The forces of Vrioni, however, were too strong for them and, when offered honourable terms of capitulation in September 1822, they accepted and emigrated to Corfu. Only Markos Botsaris remained in Western Greece to carry on the fight. The legend of Suli, probably over-dramatized, remains engraved in the national consciousness, immortalized in poem, folk-song and history book.

Returning to Kanalaki and the road that crosses the rush-bordered streams of the Aherousian plain, and continuing northward one reaches the village of Kastri, on a hill fortified by nature. Site of ancient Pandosia, founded in the seventh century BC, its enceinte once included twenty-two square towers, and some rough fourth-century BC polygonal walling (east side). The modern village, past which the Aheron flows towards the sea, is green and pleasant.

Five kilometres to the west lies the village of Mesopotamo, where **Ephyra**, site of a celebrated *necromanteion* (oracle of the dead), crowns a rocky knoll above the Kokytos, a tributary of the 'infernal' Aheron. The excavations lie beneath the eighteenth-century Monastery of *Agios Ioannis*. The site, among the most important of its kind in the country, has much in common topographically with the one described by Homer in the eleventh book of the *Odyssey*, in which Odysseus performs the greatest of his feats: the descent into Hell. Archaeologists have indeed demonstrated that Ephyra has a Bronze Age history, and it was here that Neoptolemus settled after the Trojan War and ruled as the first of the Molossian kings.

The ancient Greeks believed that all hollows and fissures in the earth's crust led to the Underworld where dwelt the souls of the dead who uttered prophecies to enquiring mortals bold enough to search them out. At Ephyra pilgrims had to undergo purification rites, as at all oracles. Diet, prayers, ablutions and total silence were among the priority regulations. Sacrifices too. For the dead liked to be propitiated with honey, milk, wine and, above all, the blood of sacrificial animals.

The site is an extremely complex one, and the custodian's assistance is indispensable. Walls of thick polygonal masonry – five massive courses of the east wall are preserved – enclose a labyrinth of corridors roofed with heavy lintels and ancillary chambers, the doors of two of which are well-preserved. In these chambers we may still see the famous jars – once containers of lupin seeds and Egyptian jonquil given to pilgrims in order to produce hallucinations, flatulence and giddiness. The chambers include a bathroom and dormitories. At the end of the maze of corridors, in which the pilgrims submitted to further unusual rites – including the eating of oysters – so that they were worked up into a fit state of psychic hysteria, was the central apartment flanked by three chambers on each side. Here one may still descend through an arched entrance into a gloomy vaulted pit where Hades and Persephone reigned in their infernal 'palace'. Iron wheels and bronze pulley-sheaves, by means of which the shades of the dead were raised in order to gabble their oracles to the open-mouthed pilgrims, lie in the central court. It is worth noting the thickness of the walls which allowed the priests' movements and 'preparations' to be carried out inaudibly. It is the survival of the props, as well as the pleasant, almost pastoral, setting of the oracle, that tend to produce such an impression of ambivalence in the modern visitor. Frankly, there is nothing in the least infernal about the place. How unlike the Gorge of the Aheron.

A short and pleasant diversion may be made along a road bordered by sea lavender and agnus castus which crosses the plain (and the main coastal road) to Amoudia and the mouth of the Aheron, referred to by mythographers as the 'Forest of

Persephone'. The trees that filled the goddess' sacred wood have gone, replaced by a dusty village of shacks; the bay too has been so extensively silted up that it is difficult to believe that this was once the harbour in which an entire Corinthian fleet anchored before attacking the Corcyraean flotillas in one of the early moves of the Peloponnesian War (433 BC).

The main coastal road crosses the northern part of the Aherousian plain. The awful crags of the Suliot mountains no longer dominate the landscape. Turning west off the main road we leave the lowlands of walnut, fig and mulberry orchards and climb above a steep wooded coast of brick-red cliffs, passing a west-bound branch road to the lovely Lihnos beach. Finally the road descends through olive groves to the shore. Here nature and peasant architecture have combined to make the little port of **Parga**, which is in the shape of an amphitheatre, one of the most attractive on the mainland, its paved alleys and stairways mounting steeply between whitewashed houses roofed with slates and courtyards filled with roses, jasmine and orange trees. Tourism has added its contribution: nondescript hotels, caravans, camping sites, a plethora of shoddy tavernas. The crescent-shaped waterfront is animated – in the evenings at the height of summer the animation can be overpowering – resounding with the chug and splutter of caiques, the polyglot chatter of mobs of tourists. Cafés and tourist shops spread across the paving stones, whence one looks out across the harbour, in the centre of which an islet is crowned with a whitewashed chapel, and, further, at the Ionian Sea and the low flat shape of Paxoi. At the northern end of the bay a pine-clad bluff is littered with the ruins of a Venetian castle. Beyond the bluff, another crescent-shaped bay sweeps northwards, fringed by the 'Golden Sands', one of the finest beaches in Greece, with a large hotel. Thence paths mount through terraced orchards and olive groves dotted with whitewashed chapels and farmhouses surrounded by fig trees. The lower levels are the preserve of campers. Overcrowding is now the lot of Parga.

We do not hear much of it before the fourteenth century, when it was included in the domains of the Despots of Arta, and was famous for its sugar plantations. Under Venetian rule, most of its inhabitants were pirates, and the Doge's architects transformed its rocky little fortress into a maritime bulwark against further Turkish expansion. After the Napoleonic Wars, when the Ionian Islands were ceded to Britain, it was supposed to come under Heptanesian administration, but the Sultan persuaded the British to renounce their claim and the little port reverted to Moslem rule. This surrender was considered an act of betrayal by the inhabitants, who dug up the bones of their ancestors as a precaution against desecration and publicly burnt them amid loud lamentations. The majority then took off to Corfu in rowing-boats, hugging their children and little else, for Ali Pasha's cavalry had already descended the steep shady paths, occupied the port and sequestered all Greek belongings. This pusillanimous act of British foreign policy is often recalled in lurid oleographs entitled 'The Exodus to Corfu'.

There is no sightseeing. The Venetian castle is very ruined. On the crest of the ridge between the two scythe-like bays, cafés shaded by plane-trees are enchantingly situated in a whitewashed square. Sea-bathing, underwater fishing, walking in the shade of olive and fruit trees against a screen of rugged mountains constitute the charm of Parga.

Returning eastwards from Parga to the main Igoumenitsa road you climb into the rugged hinterland again. Sea and islands disappear from view; the road crosses a saddleback range and enters the **Valley of Margariti**, scene of much guerilla activity in 1944, which is shaped like an elliptical crater with mountain peaks forming a kind of lunar rim round it. The road then runs northwards down to the sea and follows the coast around a beautiful bay to Igoumenitsa.

Beyond the village of Filipiada the northbound Arta–Ioanina highway forces a way through the slate-grey mountains which form a semicircle round Arta. Ambracian softness is succeeded by Thesprotian ruggedness. Northward winds the narrow claustrophobic valley of the Louros, whose sources lie at a tremendous height at the heart of the Thesprotian massif. Just before reaching the Louros dam – a sheet of pale water surrounded by bare crags – there are vestiges of an ancient water conduit; part of the great aqueduct which supplied Nikopolis with water. Knotted branches of plane trees form an arbour over the stream as the valley contracts. Passing through a tunnel at the narrowest part of the gorge, the road climbs into deserted country where Crown Prince Constantine, in command of an army besieging Ioanina during the First Balkan War, had his headquarters. The site is commemorated by a monument at the khan of Emin Aga. The encircling peaks become higher, more desolate, dominated to the west by the summit of Mount Tomaros. Eight kilometres before reaching Ioanina, a turning to the left leads to Dodona. The road winds up a spur of Tomaros, affording stupendous views of the cruel crevices of the Pindos to the east and the Mitsikeli massif soaring above the lake of Ioanina. A zig-zag ends in an elliptical-shaped valley, with three hamlets straggling across the lower slopes of Tomaros, which is speckled with firs and is crowned with an elegant snow-capped peak. The slopes are scarred with screes and pale russet-coloured crevices down which icy torrents must once have flowed.

In the trough of the hollow, immediately facing the backcloth of Tomaros, are scattered the ruins of **Dodona**, one of the most evocative classical sites in Northern Greece, almost Delphic in its solitude and grandeur. But it is not a smiling scene. 'Wintry Dodona', Homer calls it. The Dodonian oracle, dedicated to Zeus, is the oldest in Greece and was consulted by pilgrims long before Apollo took up his abode at Delphi. It is to Herodotus that we owe the story of the oracle's foundation. Two black doves took flight one day from Thebes in Egypt. One alighted on an oak tree at Dodona and spoke with a human voice, instructing the inhabitants to found an oracle of Zeus; the second flew west to establish another at Ammon. Dodonian Zeus dwelt in a tree-trunk, in the hollow of which stood his statue, and his oracular pronouncements were revealed by the rustling of leaves in the wind. Gods and heroes travelled across the Epirot wilderness to consult the whispering oak leaves.

As Delphi gained international fame and attracted increasing numbers of consultants, Dodona, more inaccessible, declined in importance. Nevertheless poets and writers continued to hold it in high esteem. By the fifth century BC the priests were succeeded by old women who went into transports of ecstasy on the Delphic model. As at Delphi, the oracles were extremely ambiguously worded.

Vestiges of ancient walls stand out prominently, and a few

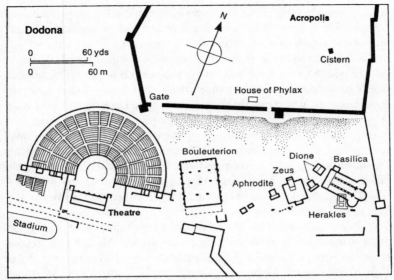

holm-oaks are dotted about the valley. Beyond the outline of the stadium rises the magnificent semicircle of the **Theatre**, built in the reign of Pyrrhus (third century BC) and recently sufficiently restored to constitute one of the major monuments of its kind in the country. There is no ornamentation left – no statues, friezes, pediments or carved seats for notables – only the harmony and simplicity of the concentric tiers of grey stone. The *skene* is a muddle of chambers which are difficult to identify. The west *parados* (side entrance), preceded by a double gate with three fluted Ionic half-columns, leads into the circular orchestra, where the horseshoe-shaped drainage conduit is remarkably well preserved. The large *cavea*, supported (where it is not recessed, like most Greek theatres, into the hill) by a sturdy retaining wall, is intersected by two *diazômai* and ten stairways, leaving nine sections for accommodating eighteen thousand spectators on forty-five tiers. One wonders how so vast an auditorium, concealed in a mountain hollow on the virtual roof of the country, could have ever been filled to capacity.

A gateway behind the theatre leads to the acropolis where extant substructures are mostly of the Hellenistic period. Thence a path descends to the sanctuary. Scattered heaps of stones, among fields where sheep browse, do not compose into an easily comprehensible layout. Three courses of well-fitted rectangular slabs indicate the site of the *Bouleuterion*, where the Epirot confederacy assembled, and a complex of outlines has been identified as the Temple of Zeus, beside which the mantic oak rustled its sacred leaves. The temple was surrounded by tripods supporting cauldrons placed so close together that, when one was struck, the echo reverberated through the others. Here too was a statue of a boy on a tripod holding a bronze whip which, when blown by the wind, hit the cauldron next to it, setting off a metallic twang that vibrated through all the brazen ornaments. Pyrrhus surrounded the sacred enclosure with Ionic colonnades, but in 219 BC the Aetolians, at war with the Macedonians, destroyed the temple as well as the theatre and burnt the sacred grove of oak trees.

The last substructure is that of the small tomb of Dione which retains some evidence of column bases and calcified shafts. To the right, an apse in outline and a marble slab carved with a cross are the only vestiges of a Christian basilica: an indication that Dodona, unlike Delphi, became a Christian sanctuary after the Edict of Theodosius (392).

The short stretch of highway from the Dodona fork to **Ioanina**, capital of Epirus, is without interest. This mountain-girt seat of Ali Pasha, once considered sufficiently important for the British, French and Russian governments to appoint fully accredited Consuls, remains one of the most animated provincial towns in Greece. There is a large choice of hotels. Only the citadel and the esplanade, where the inhabitants stroll in summer, retain an air of nineteenth-century picturesqueness and arouse memories of the semi-oriental city about which Byron enthused. A garrison and university town, most of the public buildings, whether administrative, cultural or military, are painfully plain. From the esplanade the town shelves down to a bluff crowned by Ali Pasha's citadel. A few ruined minarets and domes are outlined against the pale waters of the lake. On the opposite shore Mount Mitsikeli, a bleak wall of grey limestone, rises sheer. To the east the perspectives are more intriguing, and mysterious uninhabited valleys wind steeply into the wilderness of the Pindos.

The city's history is purely medieval. Named after a lakeside monastery of St John the Baptist, it enters the limelight in the late eleventh century, when Bohemond, an uncouth but astute Norman, invaded, made it his winter quarters, strengthened the walls and plundered the surrounding countryside. During the brief Serb domination it was ruled by Thomas Preljubovic who impoverished the inhabitants by creating monopolies so that all their agricultural produce was traded exclusively by his bailiffs. He was murdered by one of his own bodyguard, and his widow, the delightful Maria Angelina, took as her consort a civilized Florentine of the Buondelmonti family. Ioanina settled down to happier days. But in the fifteenth century the Turks came. In 1611 an irresponsible revolt, led by a drunken prelate, hardened the mood of the conquerors. The dead hand of the Turks settled on all Epirus. But the inhabitants were more active than other Greeks in keeping the ideal of Hellenism alive by founding schools: some secret, some open. In no other part of the country was the standard of education so high. The schools of Ioanina and their teachers – historians, geographers, theologians – provided much of the courage, and a little of the learning, that would make the War of Independence a possibility and modern Greece a reality. In the early nineteenth century Ioanina became the capital of Ali Pasha, the cruel, astute and capricious Albanian tyrant who ruled over the pashalik of Southern Albania, which included the whole of Western Greece. Then Ioanina, a miniature metropolis, knew its palmiest days, with its Oriental court, its foreign diplomatic representatives, its prosperous trading-houses visited by merchants, adventurers and travellers from the west.

The focal point of the modern town is the esplanade (Kentriki Square) and the adjoining public gardens, where the fortress palace of Ali's son, Muchtar Pasha, has been partly rebuilt. From the café there is a fine view of the eastern shore of the lake, crowned by snow-capped peaks. On the other side of the gardens is the **Museum**, whose exhibits range from antique finds to a collection of nineteenth-century paintings. The antiquities come from various Epirot sites. There is a fine Roman sarcophagus from Paramithia, carved with a procession of nude male figures and clothed women in Bacchanalian attitudes, their drapery blown back by the wind. There are small lead tablets, inscribed with questions put by

507

consultants of the Dodonian oracle; also prehistoric pottery, weapons from Dodona and two gold icons of St John the Baptist and the Raising of Lazarus.

A few eighteenth-century houses, homes of the grand old families of Ioanina, are scattered about the southern urban slope. From Kentriki Square, Averoff Street descends towards the citadel and the lake between rather bogus antique shops and silversmiths filled with buckles, clasps and boxes inlaid with filigree, for which the craftsmen of Ioanina have long been famous. One passes the plane tree from whose branches Ali Pasha's victims, Christian and Moslem, used to hang until the stench of their decomposing bodies was too much even for the local Janissaries. The Citadel, enclosed within walls of the Turkish period, is a warren of clean, whitewashed cottages and some gaudily painted modern maisonettes; it is crowned by the **Mosque of Aslan Aga**, now the Museum of Popular Art, a medley of icons, weapons and specimens of Epirot Art. The walled-in area can be entered at several points, and arrows indicate the way to the Mosque.

A well-preserved minaret stands beside the seventeenth-century hexagonal mosque, which is entered through a glass exo-narthex supported by six columns. The exhibits, of varying quality, constitute a somewhat eccentric miscellany of different periods. It is like wandering through a rather superior Oriental junk-shop. Exhibits include Epirot costumes and silverware, relics of the War of Independence, Turkish carved wooden chairs with mother-of-pearl inlay, and books by authors ranging from Leake to Proust. The whole strange hotchpotch is crowned by an oleograph of Lady Hamilton.

Following an easterly course from Aslan Aga, you approach the **Fetiye Mosque** through an arched gateway. Its tea-cosy dome and minaret dominate the whole citadel area, from whose fortified parapet the muzzles of old Turkish cannon are still trained across the lake. The plain tomb in front of the mosque is that of Ali himself. The Seraglio, where the old Lion of Ioanina kept his countless wives, was destroyed after his death. Faithfully reconstructed, it now houses cultural exhibits.

At this point it is best to turn back and descend to the café-lined landing stage from which the tree-shaded lakeside road follows the fortifications round the promontory. It takes about ten minutes to cross the green waters of **Lake Pambotis** to the island whose reed-fringed shore is surrounded by eel-traps. Its Byzantine chur- ches can be seen in a single morning or afternoon, but there is no more agreeable way of spending a whole day than roaming along the islet's herb-scented paths and cobbled alleys. One can lunch on eels, frogs, trout or cray-fish at the taverna of Kyra Vasiliki, named after Ali's beautiful Greek concubine who entered his harem at the age of twelve and later used her influence over the ferocious old pasha with such astuteness that she was often able to intercede successfully on behalf of her oppressed compatriots. The taverna and landing-stage are shaded by plane trees.

The sightseer's itinerary, which includes five churches, begins at the jetty. One crosses the fishermen's village, its paved alleys bordered by whitewashed cottages bright with flowering creepers, in order to reach the first church on the west shore. The little **Monastery of Agios Nikolaos of the Philanthropinoi** spreads across a rocky slope where sheep graze among the asphodel. In the court- yard there is a ruined refectory. The church, the most interesting on the island, is a single-nave basilica with a saddleback roof and additional exo-narthexes or side chapels of a later date grouped on three sides, which provide the rustic edifice with architectural unity. It was founded in 1292 by Michael Philanthropinos, who came to Ioanina from Constantinople. Michael was the first abbot, in which office he was succeeded by four members of his family. The frescoes, restored in 1963, were painted in the sixteenth century by the brothers Dikotaris of Thebes. There are no masterpieces, but in spite of the awkward attitudes of the saints, the work is animated. In the south exo-narthex (left of entrance) there are paintings of some of the great figures of antiquity, including Solon, Aristotle and Plutarch. In this side chapel too there is a horrific rendering of the Last Judgement. In an arched niche (left) in the narthex we see the donors, the five abbots of the Philanthropinoi, waiting on St Nicho- las; above him, at the apex of the arch, reigns Christ, with an open Book of Gospels before him. In the north side chapel, believed to be the site of one of the secret schools of Ioanina, the walls are painted with lively scenes of martyrdom: blood spurting from severed heads, truncated limbs lying about in contorted attitudes. On the south wall there is a charming if naive Creation, full of birds and animals and stylized trees.

South of the monastery we come to the **Church of Agios Nikolaos of Dilios**, overlooking a grove of poplars, with rushes full of croaking frogs and the lake beyond. The church, basilica-shaped, with a large narthex and half-cylinder apse with traces of exterior brickwork decoration, dates from the early days of the Despotate. The frescoes are of the mid-sixteenth century, and the artists are believed to have been influenced by the work of Theophanes of Crete who painted more ambitious murals on Mount Athos. The Apocalypse above the narthex door is distinguished by a nice blend of colours; yellows, browns and golds. On the wooden *iconostasis*, said to be the work of the woodcarver responsible for the far more elaborate screen in the Monastery of St Stephen at Meteora, animals browse in a complex foliate setting.

From here one descends to the grove of poplars and follows a shady path in a south-east direction, whence there is an unbroken view across the lake to the mosques, minarets and fortifications of the citadel. The path ends up at the **Church of the Eleousa**. Named after a miraculous icon of the *Panayia Eleousa* (The Virgin of Mercy), it too is dedicated to St Nicholas, patron saint of sailors. The architectural arrangement is similar to that of St Nicholas of Dilios, but on a smaller scale. The uncleaned frescoes are too damaged to merit detailed attention.

The Eleousa is a dead end. Returning, one skirts the swampy shore back to the landing-stage and crosses the village again – but in an easterly direction – as far as the **Church of Agios Panteleimon** which nestles below a cliff shaded by enormous plane trees, over-looking the north-west bay of the lake. A three-aisled basilica of the sixteenth century, it is of little interest except for the architectural oddity of the women's gallery, shaped like the dress circle of a theatre. Beside the church is a ramshackle wooden house, rather pretentiously called the 'Museum of Ali Pasha', scene of the old Lion's dramatic end in 1822. For years Ali's obdurate insubordination had been a growing cause of anxiety in Constantinople. After abortive negotiations with Kurschid, the Sultan's military envoy, Ali retired to his kiosk on the island. There he hoped to gain time in which to manoeuvre Sultan Mahmud II into granting him a pardon before taking up arms again in defence of his quasi-independent little Albanian empire. But Kurschid, suspicious of the old wizard's intentions, sent an armed detachment to spy on his movements. Determined not to submit to intimidation, Ali fired on Kurschid's men from the window. In a moment the peace of the soporific little island was shattered by the crack of musketry. Ali, though wounded in the arm, organized resistance among his bodyguard. The regular troops soon penetrated the ground floor and fired through the frail ceiling. A bullet pierced the old pasha's groin. It was a fatal wound. Resistance collapsed. Ali's head was severed and carried in state to the citadel. Thus ended the long and turbulent reign of the Albanian adventurer, the legend of whose amorous and military exploits had thrilled all Europe. The chamber in which Ali was shot has been furnished in the Turkish style with broad divans ranged against the walls, on which hang nineteenth-century prints illustrating the story of Ali and the War of Independence.

From the museum you pass through a tunnelled passage into a little esplanade overlooking the lake. Here the diminutive sixteenth-century cruciform **Church of Agios Ioannis Prodromos** (St John the Baptist) is picturesquely built into a rocky recess resembling a cave. The architectural arrangement is consequently somewhat eccentric, with the sanctuary facing north, a saddleback transept replacing the usual dome, and two side apses at the east and west ends. The tasteless frescoes are of the eighteenth century.

Four kilometres north-west of Ioanina a hump-like eminence rises out of the plain near the airport, its base pierced by the entrance to the **Cave of Perama**, one of the most remarkable in Greece, accidentally discovered by villagers seeking refuge from Italian bombers in 1940–41. Beyond the recess in which they huddled they caught glimpses of vast caverns and galleries. After the war the speleologists came, electricity was installed, and today guides conduct visitors through a complex of fetid chambers, pools of water and twisting tunnels lined with stalactites and stalagmites. Some of the more fragile stalactites, grouped in organ-pipe formations, produce an audible tintinnabulation when struck.

The journey from Ioanina to the Albanian frontier should include the diversion of **Zagoria**, forty-six villages scattered across upland meadows or perched on crags overlooking the Stygian gorges of the

Zagori massif. Remains of cyclopean walls testify to the antiquity of occupation, but the elegant fifteenth-century stone bridges spanning an abundance of green torrents, are the outstanding features of the Vikos-Aoös National Park which extends to the west of the road. A day's drive from Ioanina gives one time to visit a few of the most strikingly situated villages.

From Ioanina the road to Konitsa near the Albanian frontier skirts the flank of Mitsikeli where a branch road to the east ascends a rocky wasteland speckled with poplars and wild pear trees to the village of **Vitsa**. Its well-preserved grey stone houses, roofed with tiles shaped like lozenges, ellipses and polygons, cling to the mountain-side. Arched windows in the middle of the ground floor enliven the otherwise unrelieved austerity of these grim, rectangular buildings intended to protect their inmates from the elements and to keep wolves and brigands at bay.

The villages are little heard-of before the Turkish occupation, when their inhabitants emerge as Christian communities to whom the Turks granted special privileges. By the eighteenth century they had formed a confederacy, dwelling in a state of semi-independence, exempt from the fiscal extortion that crippled more prosperous communities inhabiting the lowlands. Many villagers, hard-working and ambitious, emigrated to metropolitan centres within the Ottoman Empire and became members of the professional classes. But they always came back to Zagori to bestow wealth and build sturdy houses furnished with fine carpets and furs. After the First World War emigration increased and most of the dwellings now remain firmly shuttered.

Beyond Vitsa the road climbs steeply to **Monodendri**. Architecturally it differs little from Vitsa, for throughout the Zagori massif Epirot stonemasons adopted a uniform plan for dwelling-houses and made use of identical materials. Cobbled mule-tracks are bordered by primitive pavements between stone walls and roofed gates, over which branches of almond trees scatter their blossom in spring. In the paved square is the Church of *Agios Minas* (1630), as typical of the local basilica style as *Agios Athanasios* (1830), both richly decorated with frescoes and elaborate gilt carvings. One of the fine old houses has been converted into an original, if somewhat rustic, guest-house. The outstanding painted church is a few miles east at **Negades**, where the basilica is dedicated to the Holy Trinity, *Agios Georgios* and *Agios Dimitrios*, each with a separate altar at the head of the nave and the two aisles. The vivid frescoes include Aristotle and Plutarch among the saints, while the stream of hell sweeps Judas, bishops and priests, followed by lesser sinners, into the devil's mouth. Surrounded on all sides by cloisters, the church is a fine example of the highly original Epirot architecture, which differs radically from the Byzantine ecclesiastical style.

From the village square of Monodendri a road to the north descends to a shelf of rock, from which one stares down into the immensity of the **Vikos Gorge**, at the point where the Voidomatis and another torrent unite, their confluence forming three mighty chasms. The cliff-walls, absolutely vertical, dotted with evergreens, are carved with crevices and shelves – geology becomes geometry, and the stratification is symmetrical to the point of resembling Hellenic masonry. The hum of thousands of bees echoes up from the boulder-strewn ravines. An abandoned threshing-floor forms a kind of belvedere, and the little refurbished Monastery of *Agia Paraskevi*, built of grey stone with its slate roofs almost indistinguishable from the rock to whose sides it clings, is suspended like an Athonite eyrie above space. To the north the gorge widens out and below the path some horse-chestnut trees are scattered across vertiginous ledges.

Back in Monodendri, one can take the road to the north-east which climbs above the village into an uninhabited lunar landscape of strange rock formations. Groups of boulders, like dolmens, have been weathered into horizontal, parallel and angular folds of great regularity and finish, giving the impression of a forest of man-made structures of varying sizes. The feeling of hallucination provoked by this geological phenomenon is haunting. I recall my relief at seeing a few poppies growing amid the misshapen rocks, and some beehives, although I wondered who ever climbed to this dizzy altitude to tend them. The road passes a point overlooking the Vikos Gorge about midway along its course to the north from Monodendri. From here one looks across the whole massif, which resembles an uneven tableland slashed by multitudinous chasms where bears and lynxes still have their lairs.

Another road, turning off the Vitsa road to the east, crosses the Vikos and ends at the Rongovou Monastery, rebuilt in 1749, near Tsepelovo. A dirt road continues to Skamneli with its Monasteries of *Agia Paraskevi* (1697) and *Agios Nikolaos* (1683). The vegetation becomes lusher round the villages of Laista and Vrissohori, below the snowy peaks of the Timfi.

The Vikos-Aoös National Park is of considerable botanical and zoological interest. Black pine and oak give way to the Rombola tree – a pine peculiar to the Balkans – on the higher peaks. Among the innumerable wild flowers are many varieties of lilies and narcissi. Although there are few bears left, wild boar, cat, goat, birds of prey and wildfowl abound. To the south extend the summits of the Mitsikeli range: strange shapes, like petrified giants caught in the act of executing the most elaborate acrobatics.

Returning to the Ioanina–Konitsa highway one continues north through undulating scrubland. Soon Smolikas, the highest peak of the Pindos, looms majestically in the north-east. On the left of the road a memorial marks the farthest point in Greek territory reached by Mussolini's army in the autumn of 1940. After Kalpaki the main road begins to veer eastward leaving the Albanian foothills behind. At the second fork one can take the road to the east and climb through grassland slopes shaded by holm-oaks, horse-chestnuts and Judas trees. At the top of the pass the colossal cirque of the valley of the Voidomatis is suddenly revealed against a wide crescent-shaped screen of summits shaped like fangs. A dizzy descent in hairpin bends leads to the village of Aristi, architecturally similar to Monodendri, but less abandoned. At the bottom of the bowl a modern arched bridge spans the stream of the Voidomatis where it flows out of the Vikos Gorge. Plane trees line the river banks. The peace and serenity of the scene provide a strange contrast to the immensity of the scale. The road then climbs the east side of the bowl and follows a spine of foothills composed of stratifications of schist resembling regular courses of masonry. To the south the jaws of the Vikos Gorge yawn open: cliffs, screes, crags and dolomites, all peppered with caves and arched recesses, against a background of escarpments disappearing into a tunnel of profound gloom. A bluff is crowned by the village of Viko – like a last human outpost before the gates of Hades.

The road ends at the village of **Papingo**, a sheep village and winter refuge of Sarakatsans (the once-migrant people, with no occupation other than grazing their flocks, whose wooden huts used to be scattered throughout the valleys of upland Greece). Its stone houses with their squat barn-like roofs and cobbled alleys spread among almond trees under castellated cliffs which taper off into six monstrous tusks eroded into shapes as weird as the rock formations of Meteora. The highest peak is called the Camel. There is an inn where one can get fresh eggs and rye bread, and the Church of *Agios Vlasios*, a basilica with a wooden gallery at the west end reserved for the female congregation. Beside the church is a pretty octagonal three-storied campanile – a typical embellishment of Zagori churches.

Back on the main north-easterly road, one should not omit to take a last look at the heights of Papingo which now acquire the semblance of distorted organ-pipes, and at the northern outlet of the macabre Vikos Gorge. The savagery of the scene is equal only to its perfection. We descend into a cultivated plain traversed by the Aoös which rises in the heights of Smolikas. At the point where the river forces its way through the pinnacles and pyramids of rock a **Turkish Bridge** – a single wide arch of the utmost elegance – spans the translucent green stream flowing beneath the sandbanks. Here, on the Albanian frontier, as elsewhere in the Zagori, one has the impression that the deities who presided over the architectural landscape of Greece must have decided to complete their task and put away their rulers, dividers and compasses. They certainly ended with a flourish.

At no distance from the bridge, **Konitsa**, whose inhabitants suffered horribly in battles between the Communists and the Greek national army in 1947–49, spreads across the plain in the shadow of the Albanian foothills. One of Greece's loneliest yet loveliest roads continues north-east between the Smolikas and Gramos massifs to the Neapolis junction in Western Macedonia.

Back in Ioanina one now turns to the west. After twenty kilometres a branch road leads to **Zitsa**. Slate roofs spread among Judas trees across the mountainside. At the inn you may try the local Zitsa wine – much commended throughout Epirus – a sparkling *rosé*, it is sweet and rather sickly. A more rewarding way of spending half an hour is to visit the Monastery of *Profitis Elias*, situated on a windy platform surrounded by oaks and pines. The exterior of the church is barn-like with a slate roof crowned by three shallow domes, hardly perceptible from outside, ranged in a straight line, one above the narthex and two above the *naos*. The frescoes are late post-Byzantine and in no way remarkable. The elaborate *iconostasis* is a good piece of Epirot woodcarving, with gilded floral designs, surmounted by double colonnades, each with seventeen columns terminating in pointed arches. A commemorative plaque informs us that Byron stayed here in October 1809. From the plateau, along which the poet strolled with the monks, there is a wide view of the valley of the Kalamas, one of the four great rivers of Epirus. Byron fell in love with the place. It was the first impact made on him by the Greek landscape.

From the Zitsa fork the highway continues its sinuous descent to the Ionian shore, following the course of the Kalamas above a narrow gorge. Clusters of Judas trees are dotted among pines and ilex, and slate-roofed villages are perched on bluffs below the level of the mountain road. One has an exhilarating feeling of elevation, as one aerial view succeeds another. Emerging from the gorge, the road enters an enormous mountain-girt basin where the right wing of Mussolini's army was decisively defeated in 1940. There are glimpses of Corfu and the sea beyond.

Past the village of Neraida a branch road climbs to the south and descends into the northern part of the Aherousian plain, passing through the valley of the Kokytos. **Paramithia**, a village loud with the din of coppersmiths, sprawls across the lower slope of Mount Korillas which merges into the Suli range. That Paramithia, whose green cultivated valley was always famous for its olives, was an ancient site is confirmed by the discovery of coins and inscriptions and some exiguous Roman remains. In the Venetian era it was known as Castel Donato and there are fragmentary remains of a castle, with Turkish additions, above the village. The road crosses the Aheron south of Gliki and connects with the main network at Kanalaki.

Along the highway beyond Neraida, wayside shells of houses and ugly white monuments commemorate skirmishes between Germans and Greek guerillas during the Second World War. The journey ends at the busy port of **Igoumenitsa**, which has little in common with the rest of Epirus – or indeed Greece. A port of embarkation for Italy, it is distinguished by nothing but its bus terminal and the bustle of arriving and departing ferry-boats and chugging caiques. A string of hotels and tavernas lines the water-front. Islets, like sprawling porpoises, form a garland round the crescent-shaped bay, beyond which flows the Corfu channel. Igoumenitsa has the impersonality of a frontier town. The traveller's main business is with customs, passports and currency regulations. Formalities are a full-time preoccupation, and the mind's eye is already projected westward – towards Italy, beyond the horizon.

Soon, however, memories begin to crystallize: flashes of the tremendous architectural landscape of Zagori; pale reflections of Moslem Ioanina and its lakeside Byzantine chapels; perspectives of the 'wintry' valley of classical Dodona; visions of the infernal Aheron gorge, with the heat-haze hanging over the mythological Aherousian swamp; the Suliot range with its grim forts manned by formidable Amazons – and of all the Hellenic lands that lie beyond, with their marble silhouettes and red-brick domes and medieval bastions; columns, pediments, tombs; *amphorae*, figurines and Attic profiles; icons, frescoes, floor-mosaics; asphodel waving on windswept slopes and dust lying thick in potholed village streets lined with wispy acacias; the inland seas ringed round by mountains with legendary names; the smell of pine resin and burning incense, of scorched herbs and frying mutton-fat; nostalgia for the demise of past genius; affection for an ebullient, contentious people always ready to be won over by a compliment, joke or wink of complicity. The impressions resolve into imperishable, deeply felt experiences. It was Horace who said:

'*As for you,*
Turn over the pages of the Greeks by night and by day.'

For those who have known them at all intimately it is difficult to do otherwise.

517

APPENDICES

1. SOME PRACTICAL SUGGESTIONS

Seasons

January and *February* can be cold and wet, with intervals of brilliant sunshine. A period of cloudless skies and calm seas in early January corresponds to the ancient Halcyon Days – breeding time of the mythological halcyon birds. Brief falls of snow are not uncommon in Attica and Boeotia (the high mountains are snow-covered from November to April). In northern Greece snowfalls and cold spells are of longer duration. Fog is not unknown in Thessaloniki. Almond blossom and the first wild flowers (anemones). Woodcock shooting.

March, unpredictable, as everywhere. Hillsides covered with wild flowers. Mid-March to mid-April is the ideal time for botanists.

April can be showery or idyllic. Good season for travelling, with lengthening days. Dirt roads sometimes impassable after spring rains. Scent of lemon and orange blossom is intoxicating in the orchard country.

May, generally fine and warm. Occasional rain. Flowers in profusion.

June, still a good time for travelling. Not too hot. Sometimes cloudy in the middle of the day.

July–August, very hot. Hordes of tourists. Season of fruits. Crystalline light emphasizes the quality of the landscape. Barren mountains, the colour of gun-metal, turn a glowing purple in the late afternoon. Cooling Etesian winds. Macedonia is sometimes intensely humid. Athens area subject to severe atmospheric pollution.

September, still full summer but not as hot as July–August. Fewer tourists; fewer local trippers. Quail shooting.

519

October, in spite of the first rains, generally lives up to the tradition of a 'golden autumn'. Hillsides covered with cyclamen and autumn crocus.

November, unpredictable. Can be a prolongation of the 'golden autumn' or a foretaste of December. Dirt roads often impassable after autumn rains.

December, inclined to be cloudy; raw, but not very cold, with some fine spells and magnificent winter sunsets.

Museums

Archaeological sites and museums are usually open from 8 or 9 a.m. to 3 p.m. or later on weekdays and Saturdays (though most close on Mondays or Tuesdays); to 2.30 p.m. or later on Sundays and holidays.

However, hours of opening should be checked as they are liable to alter and are certainly not uniform throughout the country (hotel receptionists generally have all the up-to-date information).

All museums and archaeological sites throughout the country are shut on 1 January, 25 March (Independence Day), Good Friday (Orthodox), Easter Sunday (Orthodox) and Christmas Day.

Countryside Churches and Chapels

These, even when of considerable historical or artistic interest, are often locked. The keys are generally kept by the local *pappas* (priest) or *fylax* (custodian). The owner of the main café in the nearest village will send a child to fetch either. The child will also show you the way to the church, return the key to the responsible person and be pleased to receive a tip.

Communications

Olympic Airways provides regular services to various towns in Mainland Greece. Enquiries about bus and train timetables can be made at hotels and travel agencies. Buses are plentiful; even remote mountain villages are connected with the nearest town by a daily service.

Taxis are parked in the main squares of small provincial towns. The price should be fixed in advance.

There are plenty of car-hire agencies in the major towns and tourist resorts. Travel agents and hotels have all the addresses.

The railway network does not cover the whole country. One can go from Athens to Thessaloniki, and thence to Jugoslavia or Turkey (passing through the depths of the Nestos Gorge), but one cannot cross the Pindos spine which runs vertically down the length of mainland Greece. A circuit of the Peloponnese is possible with stops at Corinth, Argos, Tripolis, Kalamata, Olympia, Pyrgos and Patras.

ELPA (the Automobile and Touring Club of Greece) affords free assistance to members of affiliated associations. It issues maps, leaflets on parking, etc. Its offices in Athens are in the Athens Tower, 2 Mesogion, close to Syntagma Square; in Thessaloniki at 228 Vassilissis Olgas. There are also offices in all the major towns. For assistance Tel. 104. For tourist information Tel. 174 (in Athens), 01-7777-452 (from elsewhere).

Travel Agencies

Among the Travel Agents in the centre of Athens are:
AMERICAN EXPRESS, 2 Ermou
WAGONS-LITS/THOMAS COOK, 2 Karageorgi Servias
HELLENIC TOURS, 23–25 Ermou
HERMES EN GRECE, 4 Stadiou
HORIZON, 14 Nikis Street
KOSMOS, 1 Mitropoleos (Syntagma Square)
MANOS, 39 Panepistimiou

in Thessaloniki there are:
DOUKAS (American Express agent), 8 Venizelou
WAGONS-LITS/THOMAS COOK, 15 Komninon

Transliteration of Place Names

On the highways and main roads the motorist will find road signs in Roman as well as Greek lettering. To make the place names internationally comprehensible a phonetic rendering of the Greek pronunciation has been adopted. This often differs considerably from the accepted English spelling, e.g. Athina for Athens. Moreover there is a lack of uniformity, further complicated by the arbitrary use of the subjective and objective forms e.g. Delfi as well as Delfous.

Throughout this book, the most common transliterations to be found on maps and road signs have been used for the majority of place-names. However, where there is a commonly used English form of a place-name this has been used, such as with a few of the larger cities (Athens, Thebes, Patras) and the more important classical sites (Delphi, Epidaurus, Mycenae).

2. HOTELS

There is a wide choice of modern hotels in all towns and tourist resorts. Their most remarkable feature is, on the whole, their lack of distinction. The names of a few hotels are mentioned in the text, largely because of their outstanding positions.

The monthly publication, *Key Travel Guide for Greece and the Middle East* (obtainable from the more central of the kiosks in Athens, the publishers at 6 Kriezotou Street or any travel agent) gives a selective list of hotels, with prices, numbers of rooms and facilities. It also contains similar information regarding service flats and villas.

There are only a handful of luxury hotels outside Athens – of these the Xenia Palace at Nafplio is distinguished by its superb setting within the walls of the citadel. In Athens there are the Grande Bretagne, the Astir, the Caravel, the St George Lycabettus and the hotels belonging to the international chains. Most other hotels are adequate but undistinguished. In minor resorts the small family-run D hotels can usually be recommended. Furnished rooms, with private showers and often cooking facilities, though unlisted, provide an alternative in most villages near the sea.

3. RESTAURANTS, TAVERNAS, CAFÉS

The average Greek has never been a fastidious gastronome and the works of ancient authors contain few references to their repasts. Homeric kings lived on bread, wine, olive oil and roast kid. No elaborate dishes are mentioned by the great dramatists, or by Plato when Socrates and his companions conversed around the dining-table. The same applies to Byzantium: no Byzantine chronicler has left any record of the meals served in the imperial palace or the houses of the Byzantine aristocracy.

The main ingredients in modern Greek cooking are olive oil, tomatoes, onions and garlic. Most dishes are of Eastern (romantics say Byzantine) origin and in private houses, where the quality of the materials is good, the food can be delicious: pilafi, the ubiquitous *mousaka* (minced meat between layers of fried aubergines and onions, a crust of béchamel) and vegetables (tomatoes, peppers, aubergines, marrows) stuffed with rice and herbs or minced meat.

However, the lack of interest in the quality, temperature and presentation of food is not conducive to a demand for a wide range of restaurants. The traveller is likely to be amazed at the paucity of good restaurants in a city the size of Athens. It is the tavernas which provide occasions, often delightful, for dining in a relaxed, informal atmosphere, but the food (at which the Greeks peck in a leisurely fashion and without the Western concept of an ordered sequence of dishes) is seldom memorable – veal, pork or lamb chops, fried potatoes (often soggy), *horiatiki* salad (sliced tomatoes with peppers, olives, onions and slices of goat's milk cheese), sometimes a tepid *mousaka*, and, with luck, among quite a wide range of *mezedes* (starters), the delicious smoky-flavoured *melitzanosalata* (aubergines worked with oil – occasionally with yogurt – into a pulp and flavoured with onions).

Travellers with queasy stomachs had best keep to grilled meat (and fish, when obtainable). Most restaurants (but not tavernas) are indoor, even at the height of summer. Service is slapdash, but waiters are usually friendly – they often lose their heads, but seldom their sense of humour.

Wines are rapidly improving, *Porto Carras* being one of the most reliable. Cheeses are variable; apart from the popular *feta* (white goat's milk cheese), there are several regional *Gruyère (Graviera)* types, which tend to vary in quality according to the season and even the year; *Kasseri* (the Turkish *Kaskeval*); *Manouri* (*Mozarella* type), which is good when fresh (winter and spring) and seasoned with pepper and salt; and *Metsovo* (smoked). The summer fruits (May–September) – strawberries, cherries, plums, yellow peaches, grapes, figs and melons – are excellent, as are citrus fruits and pears in winter. Greek beer is good.

A comprehensive list of restaurants and tavernas would quickly be out of date. A selective list is published in the daily English-language newspaper *Athens News* and the weekly pamphlet *The Week in Athens*, which can be bought at any kiosk in the central area of Athens.

The following are a few restaurants and tavernas which seem to be permanent fixtures in Athens (no restaurant or taverna in the provinces, apart from Thessaloniki, is worth mentioning). It is difficult to think of a single cheap restaurant that can whole-heartedly be recommended.

Restaurants

ATHENAEUM BISTRO, 8 Amerikis. Mainly French and expensive. Slightly cheaper KELLARI downstairs.

CORFU, 6 Kriezotou. Corfiot and semi-international cooking. Centrally situated, but expensive in view of the fare served.

DELFOI, 15 Nikis. Mainly Greek dishes. Excellent and cheap.

DIONYSOS, 43 Roverto Galli (opposite Theatre of Herodes Atticus). Superb view of the Acropolis. International dishes. Expensive.

EDEN, 3 Flessa, Plaka. Vegetarian. Charming and inexpensive.

GB CORNER, 2 Venizelou. Pleasant atmosphere and good service achieved by long tradition. Fine selection of French and Greek dishes. Reasonably priced for what is offered.

L'ABREUVOIR, 51 Xenocratous, Kolonaki. Open-air in summer. French cuisine. Expensive. Good.

STAGEDOOR, 14 Voukourestiou. Central. Greek specialities and seafood. Fairly expensive.

STEAK ROOM, 4 Aeginitou, beyond the Hilton. Meats cooked on charcoal. Medium priced and very good.

YEROFOINIKAS, 10 Pindarou. Restaurant-cum-taverna. Wide selection of Greek and Oriental dishes. Expensive.

ZONAR, 9 Venizelou. Central. International and Greek cooking. Expensive.

Tavernas

KOSTOYANNI, 37 Zaimis. National Museum area. Specialities; Greek *hors d'oeuvres* (well presented); prawn (or crab) salad. Moderate prices. Crowded, unprepossessing, but decent service and good quality Greek cooking. Decent *carafe* wine (a rarity).

PALIA TAVERNA STAMATOPOULOU, 26 Lysiou, Plaka. Lively with music.

PLATANOS, 4 Diogenes (near Tower of the Winds – agreeable setting). Greek cooking. Unpretentious and cheap.

TA TRIA ADELPHIA, 7 Elpidou, Platea Viktorias. Specialities: Greek *hors d'oeuvres* (well presented). Moderate prices.

XINOU, 4 Angelos Yerondas, Plaka. Most Greek dishes (and grills). A good all-round taverna. Guitarists. Relatively moderate prices.

ZVINGOS, 41 Agia Zoni, Kypseli. Specialities: pork, lamb and chicken roasted on the spit. Relatively moderate prices.

The larger tourist tavernas of the Plaka (Athens) – Athens by Night, Mostrou, Palaia Athena – are really nightclubs with a tendency towards 'Greek' floorshows. The food is indifferent and expensive.

The numerous small tavernas with three guitarists are more genuine.

The taverna-type fish restaurants outside Athens are agreeable – particularly at Mikrolimano and Glifada.

The traveller in northern Greece will no doubt observe that the quality of the food is better in Macedonia than elsewhere in the country. The seafood restaurants of Thessaloniki, along Vassileos

Konstantinou Street (the waterfront) and in the Aretsou seaside suburb, are outstanding. The same applies to the taverna Krikelas, Gramou Vitsi Street, also in Thessaloniki (shut in the summer months, May–September).

It is worth noting that all luxury, most first-class and some second-class hotels in Athens, as well as in the provinces, have restaurants.

Cafés (both indoor and open-air) proliferate all over the capital, suburbs and provincial towns. The confectionery element is the most popular with Greeks, who have a very sweet tooth; the range of cream cakes is staggering. The ices are generally good. Many open-air cafés are open until well after midnight.

As in many Mediterranean countries, café life has always played a large role in shaping the people's and the country's destinies. In many of the city-centre cafés of Athens contracts are drafted, debts contracted and settled, dowries discussed, important new contracts made and plots to overthrow the government hatched.

There is no need to list the cafés and coffee bars. They are there for all to see: in the capital at every street corner and in the main squares of all small provincial towns.

4. SHOPS

In central Athens the principal shopping areas are Ermou Street (women's wear and accessories, household goods) and Stadiou Street (shoes, men's clothes). Branches of leading French and Italian fashion houses are to be found in the Kolonaki to Syntagma Square area and in the innumerable boutiques of the luxury hotels.

Antiques and local handicrafts are more likely to interest the traveller. Antique shops of varying quality proliferate in the Plaka, Pandrossos Street – Monastiraki and Kolonaki areas.

Travellers should obtain an export licence from the shopkeeper for any purchase of value (if an antique) which they intend to take out of the country. Failure to do so may result in confiscation and payment of a fine.

International jewellers are represented on their homeground by

Lalaounis and Zolotas, 6 and 10 Venizelou respectively, who sell
original jewellery based on antique and Byzantine designs.

The best selection of handicrafts are found at:

THE NATIONAL FUND, 24 Voukourestiou and 6 Ypatias (near the
Cathedral) (handwoven rugs and carpets with old island and
Byzantine designs; stoles, tablecloths, bags, embroidered slip-
pers, copperware, ceramics).

NATIONAL ORGANIZATION OF HANDICRAFTS, 9 Mitropoleos
Street. Display only, but provides list of approved shops.

Tourist shops, filled with imitation vases, modern icons and
plaster casts of famous statues are centred round the Syntagma
Square area. Here are also displayed *tagharia* (woollen bags) and
tablecloths, etc. woven with peasant designs. Some of the modern
icons (copies of old Byzantine ones) are of a high standard.

There is a brisk trade in furs. The main furriers in Athens are
situated in Filhellinon and Mitropoleos Streets. The leading establishment is SISTOVARIS, 4 Ermou.

The traveller will be impressed by the number of English bookshops, well stocked with standard works and all the latest publications. The main ones are:

AMERICAN BOOK SHOP, 23 Amerikis

CACOULIDES, 39 Venizelou, in the passage

COMPENDIUM, 28 Nikis

ELEFTHEROUDAKIS, 4 Nikis

PANTELIDES, 11 Amerikis

English and foreign newspapers are on sale at about eight o'clock
in the evening at all kiosks in the Syntagma Square and Kolonaki
areas and also in the bookshops of leading hotels.

Shops in the hotels are, as everywhere, more expensive than
outside. It pays to be more adventurous and try a shopping expedition. Villages specializing in regional handicrafts are mentioned in
the text.

5. FEASTS AND HOLIDAYS

1 January. Public holiday. Feast of St Basil, one of the most
distinguished Early-Christian Fathers of the Church. *Vasilopitta*

(St Basil's Cake), a kind of large round brioche, is cut just after midnight in every Greek house; it contains a coin which brings good luck to the finder.

6 January Epiphany. Public holiday. Blessing of the Waters. An official ceremony is held at the Piraeus, attended by high-ranking prelates flanked by acolytes bearing banners, and also by cabinet ministers and representatives of the armed forces. Ships' sirens hoot as the officiating priest throws the Cross into the sea and the waters are blessed. Throughout the country wells and springs are blessed.

At Epiphany the earth is rid of *Callicantzari*, puckish demons with red eyes, monkeys' arms and cloven hooves, who run amok during the twelve days after Christmas and are probably a Christian version of the boisterous and equally grotesque Satyrs and Sileni, who danced attendance on Dionysus. Some of the favourite pranks of the *Callicantzari* include riding piggy-back on frightened mortals, flinging pitch at front doors and dousing fires and polluting food by their own unsavoury methods.

February–March–April

Carnival (the three weeks before Lent). During the three weekends of the period, children in fancy dress roam the streets and gipsies, accompanied by performing monkeys, bang on tambourines (into which pedestrians drop coins) at street corners. In Athens, the tavernas of the Plaka are crowded. Streamers and confetti litter the pavements. The most lively Carnival procession takes place in Patras during the third week-end.

Kathari Deftera ('Clean Monday') – the Monday after the last Sunday of Carnival. A public holiday. So-called because it is the first day of Lent. There is a general exodus into the country and the occasion is one for picnics. Kite-flying begins. In some villages dumb-shows are staged by itinerant mummers. At Thebes there is a lively parody of a peasant wedding, a thinly veiled spring fertility rite, at which the relatives arrive riding donkeys backwards. The bride (a man disguised as a woman) is bedecked with clanging bronze bells round her neck.

Traditional 'Clean Monday' food (meatless and served cold) consists of *phasolia piaz* (beans dressed with vinegar and sprinkled with slivers of onion), *tarama*, (a pinkish purée made of cod's roe and breadcrumbs), *yalantzi dolmadhes* (rice, currants and pine-nuts, flavoured with onion, cooked in olive oil and wrapped up in vine leaves) and *laghana*, flat loaves of unleavened bread.

25 March Independence Day. Public holiday. Anniversary of the day when Bishop Germanos raised the standard of revolt against the Turks at Kalavrita in 1821. Military parades are held in all towns and villages. The Feast of the Annunciation is also celebrated in all churches.

The Easter Cycle. Orthodox Easter, which rarely coincides with that of the Western churches (they are sometimes as much as five weeks apart), generally falls within the second half of April, seldom before, occasionally in early May. The weather can be showery, but the flowers are at their most prolific, the gardens heavy with the scent of lilac, wisteria, Banksian roses and stocks.

Maundy Thursday. Housewives dye the red eggs which will be cracked and eaten on Easter Day. The first egg placed in the dye belongs to the Virgin; it is regarded as a talisman and must not be eaten. The colour red is supposed to have protective powers. Interiors of churches are decorated with black, purple and white shrouds and church bells toll throughout the evening.

Good Friday. A day of complete fast, kept by the overwhelming majority of Greeks. Brown wax candles are sold at street corners. Church bells toll and funeral marches and religious music are broadcast on all radio networks. Cemeteries are crowded with private mourners laying wreaths on graves.

At about nine in the evening (earlier in the villages), the *Epitaphios*, the funeral of Christ, the most moving and beautiful ceremony in the Orthodox calendar, begins. Behind the Cross, the body of Christ, in the form of a gold embroidered pall, smothered with wreaths woven out of scented flowers, is borne under a gilded canopy through the main streets of towns and villages. Priests, ranging from mitred bishops in lavish vestments to black-frocked deacons, shuffle behind it, flanked by acolytes in coloured shifts, carrying banners. Then come the officials (civil and military) followed by a crowd of silent, dark-clothed worshippers, lighted candles cupped in their hands. The procession halts at every street corner where a short prayer is said. By about ten o'clock, when the beflowered bier is borne back to the church and the pall has been kissed by the faithful, many cafés and restaurants, are shut.

Easter Saturday. Nothing could be more striking than the contrast between the solemnity of the *Epitaphios* and the liveliness of the *Anastasis*, the Resurrection service, the greatest feast in the Orthodox Church. Throughout the afternoon funereal drapings are removed from churches and replaced with branches of laurel and myrtle, while sprigs of rosemary are strewn across the floor of the naos. White (no longer brown) candles, decorated with white or blue ribbons (the national colours) are sold at open-air booths.

The service begins in a dim, incense-laden atmosphere. Gradually more lights are turned on until the whole church is brilliantly illuminated. Towards midnight the service is moved out to an open stage in front of the church to enable all to participate in the Resurrection. On the stroke of midnight the priest, in a soaring triumphant tone, chants the words '*Christos Anesti!*' ('Christ is risen!'). The doors of the sanctuary open amid a blaze of light and the bier, only yesterday borne to the grave, is seen to be empty: Christ has risen. Church bells ring, children shout and let off firecrackers in the street. Members of the congregation shake hands or exchange the kiss of Resurrection, murmuring 'Christ is risen!' All personal quarrels are (supposed to be) forgiven and forgotten.

The crowds then disperse homeward-bound, holding their candles – it is a good omen to reach the house with the taper alight – and break their fast with a dish of *mayeiritsa* (a thick soup made of chopped lambs' offal with egg, lemon and rice, seasoned with dill – rich but delicious) and red-dyed hard-boiled eggs.

Easter Sunday. A day of national rejoicing. In Athens, while the Head of State and the Cabinet attend the doxology in the Cathedral, the cannon on Mount Lycabettus fires thunderous salvoes. The paschal lamb is roasted on a spit in gardens and open places and red eggs are cracked by tapping one against the other. Houses are decorated with lilac – *paschalia* – the flower of Easter.

Easter Monday. Public holiday.

Friday after Easter. Feast of the Virgin Mary, who is represented as the *Zoodochos Pighi*, 'The Source of Life'. In villages where the church is dedicated to the Life-Bearing Spring, a procession headed by a priest carrying an icon of the Virgin winds through the streets in the late afternoon, as at Acharnae, twelve kilometres north-west of Athens. The procession is sometimes followed by folk-dancing.

23 April. St George's Day. When the date falls within Holy Week, the feast of St George is moved to a later date. The young Eastern martyr is one of the most popular saints in the Orthodox calendar. Like the equally venerated Demetrius, he represents a Christian reincarnation of the noble ephebe of antiquity.

At Arachova, near Delphi, St George's Day is celebrated with a religious procession and the performance of folk-dances with drums and bagpipes, and athletic contests.

30 April. On the eve of May Day wreaths of flowers – stocks, roses, lilies, pansies – symbolizing the advent of summer, are hung above the front doors of houses, where they remain, brown and withered, until the feast of St John the Baptist.

Athenians flock to the suburbs of Ano-Patissia and Nea Philadelphia, where fireworks crackle and much wine is drunk in tavernas. There is little to eat except hacked pieces of (rather tepid) lamb roasted on open-air spits. The streets are lined with booths where wreaths of flowers are sold and, late at night, the pavements are littered with bruised blooms.

May Day itself may or may not be an official public holiday, according to the party line taken by the government in office.

21 May. Feast of St Constantine and St Helena. The feast's importance derives from the aura of veneration attached to the figures of Constantine the Great, founder of the Byzantine Empire, and his pious mother, Helena.

531

Whit Monday. Public holiday.

June–July. Festival of ancient drama at Epidaurus.

24 June. Feast of St John the Baptist. The summer solstice. Bonfires are lit in villages and Athens suburbs on the eve of St John's Day. The inhabitants cast their May Day wreaths onto the pyre and dance round it, leaping over the embers, thus purifying themselves of their sins. The ashes, which possess protective and divinatory properties, are collected by housewives.

Sea-bathing and the eating of water melon (cheapest and most popular of summer fruits) begin 'officially' on St John's Day, and the proverb runs 'Do not swim before you see water melon peel floating on the sea'.

July to September. Wine festival at Daphni, near Athens. Entrance charge covers unlimited wine-tasting. Rather bogus folk-dances.

17 July. St Marina's Feast. The saint was martyred in Antioch in the third century and her feast ushers in the season of grapes. Peasants flock to the vineyards to cut the first bunches and bear offerings of fruit to the churches.

A fair is held outside the church of Agia Marina in the Theseion quarter of Athens, where the saint is worshipped as protectress against smallpox. She is also the scourge of all insects.

20 July. Feast of the Prophet Elijah, patron saint of thunder, lightning and rain. Worshipped on hilltops crowned with whitewashed chapels where bonfires are sometimes lit (as on Mount Taigetos) and associated with the prophet's ascent to Heaven. As Lord of the Thunder (the thunderclaps being attributed to the rolling of his chariot wheels), he represents a Christian counterpart of Zeus.

15 August. Assumption of the Virgin. Public holiday. After Easter and Christmas the most important religious holiday in the Greek calendar, a symbol of the Orthodox veneration of the Virgin. 1–15 August is a period of fast, which Greeks keep with varying degrees of strictness.

Two great religious pilgrimages are made on this day: to the Aegean islands of Tinos (the Lourdes of Greece) and Paros.

29 August. Anniversary of the beheading of St John the Baptist. The malarial fevers that until fairly recently ravaged many of the plains, especially during the torrid month of August, were supposed to be the manifestations of the shock or spasm suffered by the Baptist when he was beheaded to please Salome (a scene much favoured for reproduction in rustic icons). Fairs *(paneghyria)* are held in villages where the main church is dedicated to St John the Baptist.

14 September. The Exaltation of the Cross. An important Orthodox feast. In churches a priest presents the congregation with sprigs of basil as a token of the herb that sprouted at the foot of the Cross.

26 October. Feast of St Demetrius, one of the most popular saints in the calendar. All churches dedicated to St Demetrius, a gallant young convert martyred by Galerius in a public bath at Thessaloniki, are brilliantly illuminated on the nights of 25 and 26 October.

The weather is usually fine and the last week in October is referred to as 'the summer of St Demetrius' – the Greek Indian summer. The saint's name day is the occasion for the tasting of new wine.

28 October. Public holiday to commemorate the anniversary of the Italian invasion of Greece in 1940. In the course of the invasion a small Greek army routed Mussolini's numerically superior but ill-equipped divisions. Commonly known as 'Ochi' Day, from the simple negative uttered by the Prime Minister, Ioannis Metaxas, when presented with the Fascist ultimatum by the Italian Ambassador.

6 December. St Nicholas' Day. Commonly regarded as the first day of winter. The saint, patron of sailors, is often represented in popular hagiography dressed in clothes covered with brine, seawater dripping from his long white beard, after rescuing sailors from sinking ships in winter storms. His affinity with Poseidon is obvious, but he is more benign, less violent, than the Lord of the Trident. He prefers to pacify tempests rather than to rouse them.

Every Greek ship, from the largest ocean-going liner to the

smallest caique, possesses an icon of the saint covered with votive trinkets in the shape of vessels.

Chapels dedicated to St Nicholas abound in the islands and maritime districts of the mainland.

12 December. Feast of St Spyridon. The embalmed mortal remains of the Cypriot bishop, martyred during Diocletian's reign, and borne overland from Constantinople to Corfu after 1453 in order to escape Ottoman desecration, are now displayed in an ornamental silver coffin in the church of St Spyridon at Corfu. The saint, patron of Corfu, is greatly venerated throughout the country.

The name Spyridon derives from the word *spyri*, a pimple, and, according to popular superstition, the wonder-working properties of the saint's relics act as an antidote against smallpox, rashes and skin diseases.

24 December. Little boys ring doorbells and ask: *'Na ta poúme?'* ('Shall we tell them?'). In other words, should they sing the *kalanda* (the Greek equivalent of Christmas carols) while they beat a miniature hammer on a little metal triangle, in return for a small gratuity.

In Athens the sale of holly, mistletoe, Christmas trees, turkeys and other Christmas fare follows the Western pattern.

25–26 December. Public holidays.

31 December. Singing of *kalanda* as on Christmas Eve. In the evening most Greeks play cards. It is traditional to try one's luck at the gaming-table on the threshold of the New Year.

6. GLOSSARY

Abacus – slab crowning the capital of a column

Acroteria – ornamental effigies or mouldings placed at either end of pediment in ancient Greek architecture

Adytum – inner sanctuary and holiest chamber of a temple where oracles were delivered

Agora – A Greek market place. Equivalent to Roman forum.

Ambo – pulpit in an Orthodox church

Aphesis – starting-post of an ancient Greek race-track

Archon – magistrate in ancient Athens. A notable during the Turkish occupation

Aryballos – ancient flask (swollen in the centre) with a round base, used as a perfume container

Ashlar – masonry of square-hewn stone – often used as facing to a rubble wall

Bouleuterion – senate house

Bouzouki – a large mandolin with a particularly plangent note

Calathus – a basket

Cantharus – a tall, two-handled drinking cup

Cavea – the part of an ancient theatre reserved for spectators

Cella – enclosed inner room of a temple, often containing the cult statue

Cenobite – monk living with others in a community

Chiton – sleeveless tunic, fastened over the shoulder by clasps and round the waist with a girdle, worn by men and women in ancient Greece

Chlamys – oblong outer garment, smaller than the himation and even more ornamented, hung from the neck

Choregic – pertaining to a choregus, administrator and financier of a chorus

Chrysobul – Byzantine imperial charter

Clerestory – the upper part of a church with windows above the aisle roofs

Conch – the concave surface of the vault of an apse

Deisis – representation of Christ between the Virgin and St John the Baptist

Deme – geographical unit for local government purposes in ancient Attica

Diazoma – horizontal passage between the tiers of an ancient theatre which served as a foyer

Dodecaorton – the Twelve Feasts, the principal scenes from the lives of Christ and the Virgin, which (either in mosaic or fresco) decorate the walls of all Byzantine churches

Dormition – the funeral of holy personages, particularly the Virgin (in religious art).

Dromos – a public way, often lined with statues, temples, etc

Entablature – the part of a building above the columns, including the architrave, frieze and cornice

Entasis – a convexity of the shaft of a column: an intentional distortion designed to eliminate the optical illusion whereby a straight column appears thinner at the centre than at the top or bottom

Ephebe – a youth just entering manhood or just enrolled as a citizen in ancient Greece

Ephor – inspector, curator

Epitaphios – flower-decked bier of Christ borne in procession in towns and villages throughout the country on the evening of Good Friday

Eremite – a hermit

Exedra – apsidal (sometimes rectangular-shaped) recess with seats

Ex-voto – votive gift

Firman – an edict or administrative order issued by an Ottoman sultan

Gigantomachia – battle between the gods and giants on the friezes of temples

Glycophilousa – a type of icon of the Virgin and Child (The Sweetly Kissing One) in which the Child is depicted resting his cheek against the Virgin's

Hamman – Turkish bath

Helot – Spartan serf who formed the backbone of the Spartan army

Hetaira – a courtesan in ancient Greece

Himation – cloak of varying texture, colour and embroidered decoration, worn by both men and women in ancient Greece

Hoplite – heavily armed ancient Greek infantryman

Iconostatis – screen adorned with icons separating the sanctuary from the remainder of an Orthodox church

Idiorrythmic – a monastery in which each monk maintains himself independently

Imaret – hospice for pilgrims and travellers in Turkey

Impost – the projecting part at the top of a column

In antis – two porch columns between two prolongations (antae) of the side walls of the cella of a temple

Katavothra – subterranean stream flowing under the hard limestone rock of many Greek mountains

Kelim – a woven carpet

Kellia – retreats of hermits

Kioshk – Turkish palace or pavilion

Kokkineli – slightly resinated rosé wine

Kore – an ancient Greek maiden. Term commonly applied to statues of young women of the Archaic period

Kouros – an ancient Greek youth. Term commonly applied to statues of young men of the Archaic period

Krater – a vessel with a wide mouth in which liquids, chiefly wine and water, were mixed

Lecythos – a slender vessel (derived from the domestic oil-flask) with long spout-like mouth, used at fifth-century BC funerals. The base is sometimes rounded

Linear B – syllabic script used for writing the Greek language from c.1400 to c.1150BC. The form of the Greek Language written in Linear B is usually known as Mycenean Greek.

Liti – a spacious outer narthex in some Orthodox churches

Loukoumi – Turkish delight

Loutrophorus – a tall ancient Greek vessel used to bring water for the bath

Mandorla – almond-shaped aureole surrounding depictions of holy personages in Christian art

Megaron – the great hall of an ancient palace

Metope – one of the square spaces either decorated or plain between triglyphs in a Doric frieze

Metroon – temple of the Mother of the Gods

Mihrab – prayer niche indicating the direction of Mecca in a mosque

Naos – the main chamber, or inner shrine, of a Greek temple, in which the effigy of the deity was kept. Also the main body of a Byzantine cruciform church, entered through the narthex

Narghile – synonym for *hookah*

Narthex – vestibule across the west end of an Orthodox church

Nome – administrative division of ancient Attica

Odeion – concert hall

Oinoche – an ancient jug, with a handle, for pouring

Orans – representation of the Virgin or a saint with arms outstretched in an attitude of prayer

Orchestra – circular space below the lowest tier of an ancient theatre where the chorus chanted and performed dance patterns. A small segment of the orchestra was generally occupied by the narrow stage (see *proscenium*)

Palaestra – an open space for wrestling or athletics in ancient Greece, especially the forecourt of a gymnasium

Pantocrator – The All-Ruler (Christ), of whom there is an effigy in the central cupola of most Byzantine churches

Parados – one of the two side entrances into the orchestra of a Greek theatre used by the chorus only. The *paradoi* often had architectural embellishments

Patera – a broad, shallow dish used for pouring libations at sacrifices

Pendentive – a concave section of vaulting leading from the angle of two walls or arches to the circular base of a dome

Peplos – fifth-century BC dress (ankle length, belted up) worn by women on ceremonial occasions. Often elaborately embroidered

Peribolus – an ancient precinct, or the wall around it

Peristyle – colonnade surrounding a temple or court

Phiale – holy water basin outside a church

Phylax – guard, custodian

Podium – low platform or continuous base carrying a colonnade or building

Pronaos – outer chamber (sometimes a portico) of a temple, in front of the naos

Propylaia – entrance way (generally a monumental gateway) to a sacred enclosure

Proscenium – narrow stage of an ancient theatre on which the protagonists, but not the chorus, performed

Prostyle – colonnaded portico in front of an ancient building

Protome – bust

Quadriga – chariot drawn by four horses

Simandron – oblong wooden board outside an Orthodox monastic church which is tapped to summon monks to prayer

Skene – back wall of an ancient Greek theatre. Sometimes used

loosely to mean the whole stage and its embellishments
Skete – dependency of a monastery
Soffit – the under surface of an arch or beam
Souvlakia – pieces of lamb, veal or pork grilled on a skewer
Squinch – section of vaulting arched across an angle used in
   reducing a square to an octagon
Steatite – soapstone
Stele – upright stone or marble tablet, often sculptured, placed
   above ancient graves
Stoa – a roofed colonnade
Stylobate – continuous base or substructure from which the
   columns of a temple rise
Telesterion – a place of initiation
Terma – finishing post of an ancient Greek race-track
Tholos – a circular building, generally a temple
Tholos tomb – circular mausoleum with a monumental approach
   and a conical beehive roof, covered with earth so as to form a
   tumulus
Thyrsus – a staff borne by Dionysus, tipped with a pine cone or
   sometimes twined with ivy and vine branches
Triglyph – a block of stone or marble carved with three vertical
   bars placed in the entablature of temples of the Doric order
Trireme – ancient Greek galley rowed by three banks of oars
Tsarouchia – Turkish-style red slippers with pompoms
Volute – spiral ornament, especially the distinctive corner feature
   of an Ionic or Corinthian capital
Yataghan – a Turkish sabre with a curved blade, an eared pommel
   and no guard

7. CHRONOLOGICAL TABLE

Neolithic Period (6000–3000 BC)

     Early inhabitants, using stone tools and weapons, lived in
       agricultural communities in Thessaly, Central Greece
       and Crete

Early Helladic Period (3200–1900 BC)

Migration from the East brought the use of metal (copper and bronze) to Greece. Development of the Minoan civilization in Crete. In Greece the Helladic civilization was centred in the N.E. Peloponnese, Attica and Boeotia

Middle Helladic Period (1900–1550 BC)

The Achaeans migrated from Asia Minor and settled throughout Greece. Their civilization, centred in the Peloponnese and Central Greece, was less advanced than that on Crete with its great palaces at Knossos and Phaistos

Late Helladic Period (1550–1100 BC)

c. 1550–1450	Minoan ascendancy
c. 1450–1200	Mycenean ascendancy on the mainland and in Crete. Destruction of Cretan palaces. Building of palaces at Mycenae, Tiryns and Pylos. Use of Linear B script. Destruction of Thebes (*c.* 1250)
c. 1250–1200	Trojan War – the extended, and ultimately successful, Mycenean expedition to capture Troy which, at the entrance to the Hellespont, was the key to Black Sea trade
c. 1200–1050	Decline of the Mycenean civilisation and destruction of palaces

Early Iron Age (1100–700 BC)

c. 1100–750	Dorian invasion from Epirus and Macedonia ended the Mycenean civilization – the cities were destroyed and the 'Dark Ages' descended
c. 750–700	Rise of the Greek city states with Athens dominant in Attica, Thebes in Boeotia and Argos, Corinth and Sparta in the Peloponnese. Greek colonies established in Italy and Sicily
c. 800–700	Fame of Delphic oracle established
776	First panhellenic games held at Olympia

Archaic Period (700–480 BC)

c. 750–700	Homer
c. 600	Byzantium founded by Megarian colonists
c. 680–650	Dominance of Argos under King Pheidon
c. 657	Rulers of Corinth overthrown by Cypselus, first of the tyrants
c. 730–710	First Messenian War – Messenians finally surrendered to the Spartans on Mount Ithomi
c. 635–620	Second Messenian War. Messenians again defeated – this time on Mount Eira – by the Spartans. Many Messenians emigrated to Sicily and founded Messina
c. 594–593	Solon's social reforms in Athens
582	Pythian festival in Delphi transformed into panhellenic celebration
560–510	Tyranny of Peisistratus and his sons in Athens
530–515	Temple of Apollo at Delphi rebuilt by the Alcmonidae, an Athenian family in exile
507	Reforms of Cleisthenes introduced a democratic constitution in Athens
490	Seaborne Persian expedition sent by Darius against Athens as punishment for support of Greek colonies in Asia Minor. Battle of Marathon in which the Persians were routed
480	Second Persian expedition under Xerxes. Athenians defeated by Persian fleet at the Battle of Artemesium. Persian army, advancing overland, overcomes Leonides and the Spartans at Thermopylae and takes Athens; buildings on the Acropolis destroyed. Battle of Salamis at which Athenians, led by Themistocles, regain command of the sea – Xerxes and his fleet return to Persia
479	Battle of Plataea: Persian army under Mardonius defeated by confederate Greek army and forced to return home

Classical Period (480–323 BC)

5th Century	Building of Erechtheion and Theseion in Athens, Temples at Bassae and Sunion and Tholos at Delphi
	Plays of Aeschylus, Sophocles, Euripedes and Aristophanes written
476–460	Growth of Athenian confederacy around the Aegean under the leadership of Cimon abroad and Aristides at home
468–456	Building of Temple of Zeus at Olympia
464–459	Third Messenian War; ends when Messenians surrender to Spartans on Mount Ithomi for the second time
460–430	Athens dominant in the Greek world – the 'Age of Pericles'
447–432	Building of Parthenon and Propylaia on the Acropolis
431	Outbreak of Peloponnesian War – chronicled by Thucydides – between Athens and confederacy of other city states led by Sparta
429–427	Plataea – garrisoned by the Athenians – beseiged and reduced by Peloponnesian army
425	Siege of Sfacteria – Spartans surrender to the Athenians
421	Peace of Nicias temporarily halts hostilities between Athens and Sparta. Dedication of Temple of Niké Apteros in Athens
419	Resumption of hostilities between Athens and Peloponnesians
405	Spartan fleet, commanded by Lysander, destroys the Athenian fleet at Aegospotami in the Hellespont; ends Athenian naval supremacy
404	Athens blockaded and forced to surrender; destruction of the Long Walls. End of Peloponnesian War
403	Thrasybulus overthrows the Thirty Tyrants. Restoration of democracy in Athens

401   March of the Ten Thousand under Xenophon
4th Century   Building of new Temple of Apollo at Olympia,
                    Temple at Tegea and Theatre at Epidaurus
399   Trial and death of Socrates
384   Birth of Aristotle (tutor to Alexander the Great)
                    who settled in Athens in 335 and founded the
                    Lyceum
371   Battle of Leuctra: Thebans, commanded by
                    Epaminondas, drive Spartans out of Central
                    Greece; ascendency of Thebes follows
371–369   Foundation of Megalopolis and Messene
362   Second Battle of Mantinea – Spartans defeated by
                    Boeotians. Death of Epaminondas in battle
359–336   Growth of Macedonian Empire under Philip II
356   Birth of Alexander the Great
338   Battle of Chaeroneia – Philip II defeats the
                    Athenians and Thebans; becomes master of
                    Greece. End of Greek democracy
336   Assassination of Philip II. Accession of Alexander
                    the Great
334   Alexander crosses into Asia to conquer Persian
                    Empire. Macedonian Empire extended from
                    Egypt to India
324   Alexander's divinity proclaimed at Olympia
323   Death of Alexander at Babylon, followed by
                    disintegration of Macedonian Empire outside
                    Greece

Hellenistic Period (323–146 BC)

323   Outbreak of war between the Diadochi (successors to
                    Alexander). Formation of the Aetolian League –
                    guardians of the Sanctuary at Delphi
323–2   Lamian War. Greeks revolt against Macedonian
                    tyranny
307   Demetrius Poliorcetes master of Athens
281   Formation of Achaean League
226   War between Sparta and Achaean League

222	Battle of Sellasia – Sparta defeated by armies of Macedonia and Achaean League
220–217	War between Aetolian League and Achaeans, supported by the Macedonians
215	Second Punic War between Rome and Carthage: Macedonia under Philip V allied to Hannibal, Aetolians and Spartans side with Romans
197	Second Macedonian War: Philip V defeated by Romans. The Consul, Flaminius, declares Rome 'the Protector of Greek Freedom'
168	Third Macedonian War ends with Battle of Pydna. Defeat of Perseus, son of Philip V, by Aemilius Paulus. End of Macedonian Monarchy.
148	Macedonia becomes a Roman province
146	Sack of Corinth by Mummius. Suppression of Achaean League
	Southern Greece added to Roman Empire as dependency of Macedonia

Roman Period (146 BC–330 AD)

88–87	War in Greece between Rome and Mithridates, King of Pontus (Asia Minor)
86	Athens, in alliance with Mithridates, sacked by Sulla.
48	Battle of Pharsalia in Thessaly – Pompey defeated by Julius Caesar
44	Corinth refounded by the Romans; later becomes capital of province of Achaea after separation from Macedonia by Octavian
42	Battle of Philippi – Cassius and Brutus defeated by Mark Antony
31	Battle of Actium – Mark Antony defeated by Octavian
50–53 AD	St Paul's mission to Greece
66–67	Nero visits Greece
125–129	Hadrian visits Greece
132	Completion of Temple of Olympian Zeus at Athens
250	First invasion by Goths

Early Byzantine Period (330–843)

Middle Byzantine Period (843–1261)

	Constantinople and Greek Empire of Nicaea
	Geoffrey de Villehardouin lands at Methone
1204–1261	Expansion of Greek Empire under Lascarid and Palaeologus dynasties to cover much of Northern Greece and western Asia Minor
1205	Othon de la Roche first Latin Duke of Athens. Conquest of the Morea by Geoffrey de Villehardouin and William de Champlitte
1248	Siege of Monemvasia by William de Villehardouin
1259	Battle of Pelagonia. Decisive defeat of Franks by Greek army
1261	Greeks recapture Constantinople. End of Latin Empire of Constantinople – re-establishment of the Byzantine Empire

Late Byzantine Period (1261–1453)

1262	Byzantine Empire recovers Mistra, Maina and Monemvasia from Franks
14th Century	Rise of Ottoman Empire; Byzantine Empire confined to Constantinople, Thessaloniki and Peloponnese
1311	Battle of Cephisus. Frankish Dukes of Athens routed by Grand Company of Catalans
1311–1387	Catalan rule in Athens
1348	Manuel Cantacuzenus first Despot of Mistra
1388	Athens occupied by Florentines
1388–1456	Acciajuoli family (bankers from Florence) were Dukes of Athens
1393–1414	Turkish conquest of Central Greece
1427–1432	Byzantine campaign drives Latins out of the Peloponnese
1453	Fall of Constantinople

Turkish Period (1453–1832)

1459	Fall of Mistra. End of Despotate of Mistra
1499–1500	Venetians surrender maritime stations on Greek mainland to Turks

1685–1687	Venetians, commanded by Morosini, conquer the Peloponnese
1687	Destruction of Parthenon during Venetian siege of Athens
1715	Venetians driven out of Greece by Turks
1801	Lord Elgin receives permission from Turks to remove sculptures from Acropolis
1809–1811	Byron in Athens
1821	Standard of revolt raised against Turks by Bishop Germanos at Kalavrita
1824	Arrival of Byron at Messolongi. Death of Byron
1825	Ibrahim Pasha devastates the Morea
1827	Battle of Navarino. Destruction of Turkish fleet by the British, French and Russians
1828	French army under General Maison liberates the Morea
1832	Protocol of London. Greece declared an independent kingdom
	National Assembly at Nafplio ratifies election of Prince Otho of Bavaria as King of Greece

Modern Greece (1833–)

1833	Arrival of King Otho at Nafplio, capital of new kingdom
1834	Capital transferred to Athens
1875–1881	German archaeologists excavate Olympia
1876	Schliemann excavates Mycenae
1892–1903	Site of Delphi excavated by French School of Archaeology
1896	First revived Olympic Games held in Athens
1900	Sir Arthur Evans excavates Knossos on Crete
1912–1913	First and Second Balkan Wars
1916	Venizelos proclaims provisional government at Thessaloniki
	Greece enters War against Central Powers
1919–1922	Graeco-Turkish campaign in Asia Minor. Expulsion of Greek population from Asia Minor

1924	Establishment of Greek republic
1935	Restoration of Monarchy
1940	Italian invasion of Greece
1941	Landing and evacuation of British Expeditionary Force
1941–1944	German-Italian-Bulgar occupation of Greece
1944–1945	First Communist rebellion
1946–1949	Second Communist rebellion
1967	Establishment of military dictatorship. King Constantine II leaves Greece
1973	Re-establishment of Greek republic
1974	Parliamentary democracy replaces military dictatorship. Referendum goes against restoration of monarchy

8. MOUNT ATHOS

Formalities

Only men, not even 'beardless boys', are allowed to cross the frontier which runs across the neck of the peninsula. A recommendation for a permit of four days is issued to non-orthodox laymen for religious or scientific reasons only if supported by a testimonial from their Consulate, by the Ministry of Foreign Affairs in Athens or the Ministry for Northern Greece in Thessaloniki. Control of passports is effected at the port of Daphni. At Karyes, the capital of the republic, the document issued by the Ministry of Foreign Affairs is exchanged for a residence permit signed and countersigned by the Holy Synod and the Nomarch, the local civil authority. This permit must be presented to the guest-master of every monastery at which the traveller wishes to stay.

Method of Travel

Caiques leave daily from Ouranoupoli and Ierissos. They put in at the landing place of every monastery – and at any skete or hermitage on request. Private caiques can be chartered at Ierissos, Ouranoupoli, Daphni and some of the larger monasteries. From the landing place there is sometimes a steep climb to the monastery. One has to carry one's own baggage so it is essential to travel light.

Accommodation

Monastery gates are shut at sunset, after which it is possible to gain admittance only under exceptional circumstances. It is important to make friends with the guest-master *(archontaris)*, a vital personage, who will accept a gratuity. He allocates beds (often in a dormitory) and regulates hours of meals. Applications to visit the library, treasury and various chapels should be made to the librarian through the guest-master.

Organization

The Julian calendar (thirteen days behind the Gregorian) is kept in all monasteries except Vatopedi. Byzantine time is also kept and the day starts at sunset. In the cenobitic (communal) foundations, travellers share their meals with the monks in the refectory. Lunch is usually at 9 a.m., dinner at 5 p.m. In the idiorrhythmic establishments, where discipline is milder, meals for visitors are served in the guest-house *(archontariki)* at more conventional hours. During fasts (which are frequent) food is likely to consist of boiled vegetables. At other times it can be more varied – and perhaps nastier. Visitors would do well, while travelling light, to take a supply of tinned food, biscuits, cheese, etc. At the Monasteries of Vatopedi and Grand Lavra, biscuits, cigarettes and *loucoumi* (Turkish delight) are sold. There are grocers at Karyes and Daphni.

Itinerary

Foreign tourists are admitted to Mount Athos at the rate of ten a day. The residence permit obtained in Karyes is now valid for only four days but one can go back there to renew it. The journey described in Chapter 17 was an eight-day tour by caique. This would therefore be possible with one renewal of the permit.

A one-day visit is possible from cruise ships.

The Monasteries

There are twenty monasteries, which are listed below arranged in clockwise order, starting from the most northerly. The ten most important are described in Chapter Seventeen; brief details of the remainder are given here.

Chilandari (idiorrhythmic) See page 249.

Esphigmenou (cenobitic)
North coast. Within easy walking distance of Chilandari. Derives its name, 'The Squeezed-together One', from its position at the mouth of a narrow valley. An eleventh-century foundation, destroyed by Crusaders, pirates and fire. Most of the undistinguished buildings are of the eighteenth century. The Church of the *Analypsis* (Ascension), striped red and white, possesses a fragment of the True Cross and an early miniature mosaic of Christ.

Vatopedi (idiorrhythmic). See page 243.

Pantocrator (idiorrhythmic)
East coast. Perched on a high rock above the sea with a fine view of Stavronikita and the Holy Mountain. Founded in the fourteenth century, its fortifications were strengthened in the sixteenth. The dark red church of the Transfiguration (with a whitewashed porch) possesses restored sixteenth-century frescoes and an icon of the Virgin *Yerondissa* (depicted as a nun), from whose eyes oil is said to have flowed when the monastery's supply had run out and a sick priest was in need of a healing unguent.

Stavronikita (idiorrhythmic)
East coast. Situated on a wooded eminence above the rocky shore and crowned by an imposing tower. Superb view of the Holy Mountain. Founded by a tenth-century Byzantine officer. The Church of *Agios Nikolaos* was frescoed in the sixteenth. A panel on the south-east column conceals the icon of St Nicholas-of-the-Oyster, recovered from the sea in the sixteenth century with an oyster embedded in a wound in the Saint's forehead. When the oyster was removed, blood poured from the gash in the wood, made by a fanatical Iconoclast before throwing the image into the sea. The oyster's outline is discernible on the right of the Saint's forehead. At

present the monastery seems to attract relatively young monks with fairly progressive views.

Iviron (idiorrhythmic). See page 257.

Koutloumousiou (cenobitic)
Inland. A short walk from Karyes. Pastoral situation with corn-fields, olive groves and kitchen-gardens. Founded by a thirteenth-century Turkish prince, converted to Christianity, who became an Athonite monk. The Church of the Metamorphosis has sixteenth-century frescoes and a good icon of St Nicholas.

Philotheou (idiorrhythmic)
Inland, overlooking the east coast. Situated among gardens and vineyards. Allegedly founded by the tenth-century hermit Philotheos. Only the eighteenth-century Church of the *Evanghelistria* (Our Lady of Good Tidings) and the refectory escaped the fire of 1871. The church possesses the relics donated by the Emperor Nicephorus III Botaniates (1079–81), who abdicated the throne in order to become a monk. These include an icon of the *Panayia Glycophylousa* (The Sweetly Kissing Virgin) on the north-east column: one of the many attributed to St Luke by monkish super-stition.

Karakallou (cenobitic)
One mile inland overlooking the east coast in the beautiful Provata country: chapels, farmhouses, wells, kitchen-gardens and hazel woods. Founded in the eleventh century, but not, as the monks believe, by Caracalla (whose portrait is included in the church frescoes). The Church of St Peter and St Paul and a fine crenellated tower are of the sixteenth century. The frescoes are of a later period.

Grand Lavra (idiorrhythmic). See page 243.

St Paul (cenobitic). See page 268.

Dionysiou (cenobitic). See page 265.

Gregoriou (cenobitic). See page 270.

Simonopetra (cenobitic)

West coast. Situated a thousand feet above the sea. Most spectacular position in the whole peninsula, otherwise of little interest. Founded by a hermit, Simon, from whose pores flowed myrrh and who was guided by a star to the wild spot where the monastery was subsequently built. It was destroyed by fire in the sixteenth century and again in 1891, the latest rebuilding was paid for with funds raised in Russia; the Church of the Yennesis (Nativity) is late-nineteenth-century. Images of saints and demons are frescoed on the walls of the rock-hewn passages.

Xeropotamou (idiorrhythmic)

Inland. Situated on a plane-tree-shaded plateau above the sea, just off the Daphni–Karyes road. Founded in the tenth century, burnt by pirates and rebuilt c. 1600, the Church of the Forty Martyrs possesses two important artistic objects: (i) the largest piece of the True Cross on Mount Athos, set amid jewels in a silver-gilt reliquary, once the property of the Emperor Romanus I Lecapenus (919–44); (ii) a beautiful twelfth-century steatite *patera* of St Pulcheria, carved with a design of the Virgin surrounded by saints, angels, priests and deacons.

St Panteleimon (cenobitic). See page 271.

Xenophontos (cenobitic). See page 273.

Docheiariou (idiorrhythmic). See page 274.

Kastamonitou (cenobitic).

Inland. Within walking distance of Zographou. Surrounded by gardens, vineyards and myrtles. An eleventh-century foundation, restored in the fourteenth. The Church of *Agios Stephanos*, rebuilt in the nineteenth century of local marble, possesses parts of the True Cross, a wonder-working icon of St Stephen and relics of St Andrew and St Stephen which are said to exude a delicious smell to the sinless.

Zographou (cenobitic)

Inland. Within easy walking distance of Chilandari or an hour's climb from its arsenal on the west coast. A Slav (largely Bulgar) foundation of the tenth century, which rose to prominence in the thirteenth century. Architecturally undistinguished. The Church of *Agios Georghios*, striped red and white, possesses a miraculous, fifteenth-century icon of St George (Italianate in style) which flew of its own accord from Palestine to Mount Athos and was painted by a divine hand – hence the monastery's dedication to the anonymous *Zographos* (painter).

9. SOME BOOKS ON GREECE

This selective bibliography is intended for travellers who want to learn more about the people, their motives, the political forces and artistic achievements that make up the four thousand year old story of Greek ascendancy, decline and regeneration. The list relies heavily on books that can be found fairly easily today in bookshops, though of course there are many other excellent works on Greece available, particularly in public libraries.

History

General

Heurtley, W. A., Darby, H. C., Crawley, C. W., & Woodhouse, C. M., *A Short History of Greece*, Cambridge University Press, 1967. A very useful outline of Greek history up to 1964, with good maps.

Ancient

Burn, A. R., *The Pelican History of Greece*, Penguin Books, 1966. Covers the ground from earliest to Roman times.

Bury, J. B., *A History of Greece* (to the death of Alexander the Great), Macmillan, 1951 edition. Standard work.

Lane Fox, Robin, *Alexander the Great*, Penguin Books, 1986. Thorough study of the life and times of Alexander.

Medieval

Jenkins, R. J. H., *Byzantium: The Imperial Centuries 610–1071*, Weidenfeld and Nicholson, 1966.

Talbot Rice, David, *The Byzantines*, Thames and Hudson, 1962.
Useful introduction for the beginner.
Runciman, Sir Steven, *Mistra*, Thames and Hudson, 1980. History
of the Byzantine capital of the Peloponnese.
Vasiliev, A. A., *History of the Byzantine Empire*, Blackwell,
Oxford, 1952. A definitive general history.

Modern

Campbell, John, and Sherrard, Philip, *Modern Greece*, Ernest
Benn, 1968. A succinct, objective account, covering every
aspect of the Greek character.
Longford, Elizabeth, *Byron's Greece*, Weidenfeld and Nicholson,
1975. An account of Byron's travels in Greece.
St Clair, William, *That Greece Might Still Be Free*, Oxford
University Press, 1972. An elegant account of the War of
Independence.
Woodhouse, C. M., *Capodistria: Founder of Greek Independence*,
Oxford University Press, 1973. The political background to the
War of Independence.

Art and architecture

Ancient

Boardman, John, *Greek Sculpture – The Archaic Period*, Thames
and Hudson, 1978. Comprehensively illustrated.
Coulton, J. J., *Greek Architects at Work: problems of structure and
design*, Paul Elek, London, 1977.
Devambez, P., *Greek Painting*, Weidenfeld and Nicholson, 1962.
A useful introduction.
Lawrence, A. W., *Greek Architecture*, The Pelican History of Art,
Penguin Books, 1957. An invaluable work of reference.
Robertson, C. M., *A History of Greek Art*, 2 vols, Cambridge
University Press, 1975. The definitive work on Greek art.

Medieval

Dalton, O. M., *Byzantine Art and Archaeology*, Clarendon Press,
Oxford, 1911. The standard work in English.

Talbot Rice, David, *Art of the Byzantine Era*, Thames and
Hudson, 1963. Useful for the beginner.

Mythology

Bullfinch, Thomas, *The Myths of Greece and Rome*, Penguin
Books, 1981. This modern edition is fully illustrated. The first
edition was published in 1855.
Graves, Robert, *The Greek Gods*, 2 vols, Penguin Books, 1967.
Exhaustive, discursive, imaginative.

Travel

Curzon, Robert, *Visits to Monasteries in the Levant*, Century,
1983. Modern edition, with introduction by John Julius
Norwich, of classic travel book which includes visits to Mount
Athos and Meteora. Originally published in 1849.
Greenhalg, Peter and Eliopoulos, Edward, *Deep into Mani*, Faber
and Faber, 1985. A journey to the southern tip of Greece.
Lear, Edward, *Journals of a Landscape Painter in Greece and
Albania*, Century, 1988. New edition of classic, with
introduction by Sir Steven Runciman. First published in 1851.
Witty, astute and brilliantly written.
Leigh-Fermor, Patrick, *Mani*, Penguin Books, 1984. Travels in the
Southern Peloponnese.
Leigh-Fermor, Patrick, *Roumeli*, Penguin Books, 1983. Travels in
Northern Greece.
Levi, Peter, *The Hill of Kronos*, Arrow Books, 1983. Travels in
Greece in the 1960s and 1970s.
Lewis, Neville, *Delphi and the Sacred Way*, Michael Haag, 1987.
Fascinating description of the ancient road between Athens and
Delphi.
Pausanias, *Guide to Greece*, Penguin Books, 1971. 2 Volumes.
Translation and commentary by Peter Levi. Comprehensive
guide for ancient tourists, written in the 2nd century AD.

General

Bowra, Sir Maurice, *The Greek Experience*, Weidenfeld and
   Nicholson, 1957. An appreciation of the ancient Greek
   achievement.
Kitto, H. D. F., *The Greeks*, Penguin Books, 1951. Useful account
   of the Hellenic achievement in the social and artistic spheres.

Miscellaneous (special aspects)

Huxley, Anthony and Taylor, William, *Flowers of Greece and the
   Aegean*, Chatto and Windus, 1977.
Schoder, Raymond V., *Ancient Greece from the Air*, Thames and
   Hudson, 1974. Fascinating aerial photographs and explanatory
   plans of more than ninety architectural sites.
Stoneham, Richard, *A Literary Companion to Travel in Greece*,
   Penguin Books, 1984.
Swaddling, Judith, *The Ancient Olympic Games*, British Museum
   Publications, 1980. The origins, events, ceremonies and
   celebrations of the ancient games.
Travlos, John, *Pictorial Dictionary of Ancient Athens*, Thames and
   Hudson, 1970.
Walsh, Frank, *Building the Trireme*, Constable, 1988. Background
   to the re-construction of a trireme in a Greek shipyard with the
   help of the Hellenic Navy.
Ware, Timothy, *The Orthodox Church*, Penguin Books, 1963.
   Useful to the Byzantinist.
Westland, Pamela, *Greek Cooking*, Ward Lock, 1987.

Light literature

Mary Renault, *The King Must Die*, *The Last of the Wine*, *The
   Praise Singer*, *Fire from Heaven* and several others. Romantic
   but authentic novels about life in ancient Greece.

Guide books

Modern guide books to Greece, covering every aspect of contemporary and classical Greek life, are widely available. For detailed information about the geography of the country and its archaeological sites the *Blue Guide* (A & C Black, Fifth Edition 1987) is indispensible to the serious traveller. Less comprehensive but still containing a wealth of practical information – including opening times of museums and archaeological sites – is the *Michelin Tourist Guide to Greece*.

Two pocket guides can also be recommended: *The American Express Pocket Guide to Greece*, edited by Peter Sheldon (Mitchell Beazley) and Collins' *Welcome Guide to Greece*, edited by John and Shirley Harrison – both are packed with details that every tourist needs to know and really can be carried in the average pocket.

The *Phaidon Cultural Guide to Greece*, which is fully illustrated, is a comprehensive guide to the major museums and sites.

In Greece – and at a few specialist bookshops in London – one can buy the English editions of the splendid *Guides* produced by Ekdotike Athenon S.A. and Clio Editions. These *Guides*, written by Greek archaeologists and beautifully illustrated in full colour, cover the National, Acropolis, Delphi and Thessaloniki Museums, as well as Ancient Corinth, Mount Athos, Delphi, Mistra, Olympia, the Acropolis, Mycenae and Epidaurus.

10. MAPS OF GREECE

Good, detailed maps of Greece are not widely available. The following are worth seeking out:

Publisher	Scale	Area Covered	Comments
Daily Telegraph	1:1,000,000	Greece & Islands	Index of place names. Greek & English text.

Companion Guide to Mainland Greece

Freytag & Berndt	1:650,000	Greece & Islands	Greek & English text. Historical map/guide.
Hallwag	1:400,000	Peloponnese & Attica	Very clear.
Roger Lascelles	1:300,000	Mainland Greece	Greek & English text.
Freytag & Berndt	1:300,000	Peloponnese	Greek & English text.
Freytag & Berndt	1:250,000	Athens to Delphi	Greek & English text.
Freytag & Berndt	1:200,000	Halkidiki	Greek & English text.
Freytag & Berndt	1:100,000	Pelion	Greek & English text.

INDEX

Ancient cities and sites are shown thus – *Epidaurus*

559

Companion Guide to Mainland Greece

Battles – cont.
Marathon 71
Nafpactos 452
Navarino 406
Pharsalia 143
Philippi 289
Pidna 176
Plataea 90
Salamis 81
Sellasia 360
Bayazit II, Sultan 445
Beles Mts. 293
Benaki Museum; Athens 50
Bird Sanctuary; Lake Prespa 225
Birthplace of Mehmet Ali; Kavala 286
Birthplace of Mustafa Kemal;
Thessaloniki 197
Black Rock; Meteora 164
Blegen, Professor 415
Bodonitsa Castle 136
Boeobeis Lake 159
Boeotia 85
Bohemond 507
Botheric, Gothic commander of
Thessaloniki 184
Botsaris, Markos, champion of Greek
Independence 139, 500
Boucation 469
Bouleuterion; Athens 44
Bouleuterion; Delphi 122
Bouleuterion; Olympia 427
Bourdzi; Nafplio 327
Bralos 130
Brasidas, Spartan leader 283
Brauron 69
Brazen House of Athena; Sparta 363
British Military Cemetery; Bralos 108
British Military Cemetery; Polikastro
200
Broad Rock; Meteora 165
Bronze Charioteer; Delphi Museum
128
Brutus 289
Bucephalus, Alexander's horse 176
Byron, Lord 17, 462, 516
Byzantine Museum; Athens 52

Cabeiroi Sanctuary; Boeotia 91
Cadmeia; Thebes 87
Cadmus, founder of Thebes 87, 284
Caligula, Emperor 428
Callas, Maria 55
Callerghis, Thessalian painter 208
Callicrates, architect 23
Callirhoe Spring; Athens 49
Calydon 459
Cantacuzenus, John, Emperor 253

Cantacuzenus, Manuel, first Despot of
Mistra 371
Capodistria, Count, President of
Greece 331, 391
Caprus 237
Caryatid Portico; Athens 30
Cassandreia 231
Cassiotis Stream 124
Cassius 289
Castalian Spring; Delphi 125
Castles
Amfissa 108
Androussa 401
Ano-Ipati 138
Argos 323
Bodonitsa 136
Chlemoutsi 440
Coryphasium 411
Didimotiho 298
Kalamata 400
Karitaina 352
Koroni 405
Livadia 101
Maina 393
Methoni 413
Mistra 376
Morea; Rion 445
Nafpactos 453
Passava 389
Patras 444
Platamonas 173
Pylos 409
Rogoi 489
Roumeli; Antirion 453
Seres 279
Vonitsa 475
Yeraki 381
Zarnata 398
Cathedral, Little; Athens 33
Catholicon Church; Vatopedi 253
Cave of Kokkines Petres 230
Cave of Perama 511
Cave of the Wicked Dead; Mount
Athos 263
Cave, Koutouki 70
Caves, Pyrgos Dirou 393
Celetrium 218
Cemetery of the Tumuli; Vergina 208
Chain Tower; Thessaloniki 192
Chaironeia 101
Chapel, Hosios David; Thessaloniki 193
Chapel, Portaitissa; Iviron 257
Chapel, St Euthymius; Thessalonika
190
Chapel, St George; St Paul 268
Charon 499
Cheiron, Centaur 156

562

Companion Guide to Mainland Greece

566